THE
MYSTERIES OF THE GREAT CROSS
OF
HENDAYE

The sphinx protects and controls science. Jean-Julien Champagne's frontispiece for
Le Mystère des cathédrales, 1926.

THE
MYSTERIES OF THE GREAT CROSS
OF
HENDAYE

ALCHEMY AND THE END OF TIME

JAY WEIDNER

AND

VINCENT BRIDGES

Destiny Books
Rochester, Vermont

Destiny Books
One Park Street
Rochester, Vermont 05767
www.InnerTraditions.com

Destiny Books is a division of Inner Traditions International

Originally published in 1999 by Aethyrea Books under the title *Monument to the End of Time: Alchemy, Fulcanelli, and the Great Cross*

LIBRARY OF CONGRESS CATALOGING-IN-PUBLICATION DATA
Weidner, Jay.
    The mysteries of the great cross of Hendaye : alchemy and the end of
        time / by Jay Weidner and Vincent Bridges.
            p. cm.
    Includes bibliographical references and index.
    ISBN 0-89281-084-X
    1. End of the world—Miscellanea. 2. Stone crosses—France—Hendaye—Miscellanea.
        3. Prophecies (Occultism)—France—Hendaye—History—17th century. 4. Fulcanelli,
        pseud. Mystáere des cathâedrales. 5. Alchemy. I. Bridges, Vincent. II. Title.
    BF1999.W435 2003
    001.94—dc21   2003007981

Printed and bound in the United States at Lake Book Manufacturing, Inc.

10 9 8 7 6 5 4 3 2 1

Text design and layout by Virginia Scott Bowman
This book was typeset in Sabon with Schneidler Intials and Avant Garde as the display typefaces

You, who are thirsty, come hither: if, by chance, the fountain fails,
The goddess has, by degrees, prepared the everlasting waters.
TRANSLATION BY FULCANELLI OF AN INSCRIPTION ON THE
STATUE OF MAÎTRE PIERRE, WHICH STOOD ON THE PARVIS OF
NOTRE-DAME-DE-PARIS UNTIL ITS REMOVAL IN 1748

For The Brotherhood of Heliopolis,
the Children of St. Vincent,
and the Knights of the Chateau Marie;
may this Work be a Beacon on the Path.

I would like to thank my teachers—you know who you are—
my parents, George and Ruth Bridges,
and most especially my wife, DARLENE,
without whom none of this would have been possible.
VINCENT

Dedicated to the wisdom of the Great Tradition
and the servants of the Work.

Thanks to Phil Lipson, Jerry Redfern, and John Mullet at the
Seattle Metaphysical Library.

Thanks also goes out to John Major Jenkins, Robert Lawlor,
Janie Noble, Juris Kalnins, and Chris Knab.

A special thanks to my late grandmother
Mary Magdeline Weidner and my wife, partner,
friend, and teacher, Sharron Rose.

JAY

CONTENTS

PART ONE
Fulcanelli and the Secret of Alchemy

PART FOUR
The Mystery of the Cathedrals

APPENDICES

HENDAYE: A MONUMENT TO THE COSMOS

Any earnest inquiry into the reasons for human existence eventually comes up against the two most difficult questions of all, "Who are we?" and "Why are we here?" Despite today's advances in science and technology, these two questions have remained unanswered. Focused as it is on the physical, modern science can show us *how* we got here and it can show us of *what* this world is made, but it cannot satisfactorily answer these fundamental metaphysical questions about the meaning of life.

As a result of this gap in our knowledge, human beings appear to be caught in a delusion, unaware of their vast potential. So where do we go to find answers to life's ultimate questions? Many have sought insight in the texts and teachings of the world's sacred traditions, only to find that many of these ancient traditions are either partially or wholly lost or nearly incomprehensible. These once vital and significant traditions have left behind fragments of knowledge that, at least, seem to point to the solutions, but these answers are often vague, difficult for modern minds to grasp, or else shrouded by the veils of time and cultural changes. Our own Western esoteric alchemical tradition, once guided by a deep and profound understanding of the intimate relationship among human beings, nature, and the cosmos, has been on its last legs for centuries.

Because of the vast changes in culture, language, and perception that have taken place since the Industrial Revolution, any serious study of the past is made much more difficult. The Industrial Revolution caused a serious disruption in Western culture that cannot be overemphasized. The rise of the machine and mechanism changed the way we think, the way we see the past, and the way we view our ancestors. No longer are our ancestors valued for their wisdom or knowledge. As the mechanized Age of Iron enveloped Western civilization, we almost lost our spiritual heritage as well.

From the time of the Inquisition onward, many of our most sacred teachings were rooted out and expunged from the dominant view, creating the continuing drama that we call European history. "Europe's inner demons" is how historian Norman Cohn characterized the spiritual and historical nightmare that has haunted Europe for centuries. The result of the conflict, madness, and destruction that have marked modern European history was the almost complete loss of the mythologies, wisdom, and profound knowledge that sustained the West through the Middle Ages. This loss was the problem that Fulcanelli attempted to correct when he wrote his masterpiece *Le Mystère des cathédrales,* or *Mystery of the Cathedrals,* in 1926. By the beginning of the twentieth century, the secret of alchemy had become lost in the well of time. Replaced by rampant speculation, obscure texts, and many failed attempts to turn lead into gold, the once deeply spiritual science of alchemy was headed for the dustbin of history. With one book by Fulcanelli all of that would change. The twentieth century's entire intellectual and artistic interest in alchemy was reawakened and energized by the appearance of *Le Mystère.* In writing it, Fulcanelli sought nothing less than to resacralize, relegitimize, and reinvigorate the entire Western esoteric tradition. He promised that through an in-depth study of its pages, any sincere and conscientious student would begin to comprehend what is referred to in the lore as "the secret language of the birds," the subtle language of spirit that "teaches the mystery of things and unveils the most hidden truths." From this understanding, a profound inner awakening would begin to take place.

Through a careful and exquisite unveiling, Fulcanelli, himself an adept of this Western lineage of transmission, provides readers with the keys to unlock the doors to the sacred mysteries that lie at the root of the alchemical arts. These mysteries include not only the "science of light and time" but also the path toward communication with living matter itself and with the Divine Intelligence presiding over our galaxy.

In addition to its profound restatement of the Western esoteric tradition, which is significant enough, perhaps the single most important aspect of *Le Mystère* was the single chapter added to the 1957 edition of the book. This chapter, called "The Cyclic Cross of Hendaye," discusses a simple yet mysterious monument located in southwestern France that Fulcanelli dates to the middle of the seventeenth century. The monument's few inelegant symbols reveal that not only was it built by a "master mason," but that its creator possessed a surprising amount of arcane knowledge. It also proved, and Fulcanelli echoes this, that there was, and possibly still is, a group of people, a secret society, if you will, that knows the very secret of time and light, which secret is the basis of all true alchemy. More surprising, Fulcanelli tells us that this secret society was still active as few as three hundred and fifty years ago.

The message of the cross at Hendaye is that time is not a mystery, that the secret of time itself could be understood. Like a river, time has many bends and turns, many tributaries and creeks, but it is possible that time, like a river, can be mapped. And when the map of time is properly understood, the mystery of the future disappears. In addition to this remarkable revelation, the symbols and teachings encoded in the cross at Hendaye offer us a new understanding of the cosmos, especially with regard to the center of the Milky Way Galaxy and its effect on us.

Finally, the cross at Hendaye reveals that its maker understood the great alchemical experiment that occurs at the end of time. The secret alchemical Mercury that rules the primordial essence of life itself is enlivened and invigorated during the time span indicated by the cross. Practical alchemists would know, just by examining the symbols on the cross at Hendaye, when to perform their most secret experiments. As Fulcanelli intimates, this secret experiment is nothing less than the creation of a Golden Age.

History appears to be a long initiation into the mysteries of the universe. As with any initiation, attention to ethical standards, clear communication, and right action are the necessary ingredients for the initiation to take place. When the initiation is over, we shall know who we are and why we are here.

The great return of the alchemical tradition is the road back to a science based on timeless spiritual principles. Alchemy is the science of human development, the art of turning glass into light and lead into gold. But as any true adept will tell you, these are merely metaphors for deep and secret mysteries of the spirit. As we in the West reestablish contact with the primordial source of life and wisdom, we shall shed the veils that conceal the profound nature of ourselves and this planet. With the return of this grand and glorious tradition we shall once again understand who we are and why we are here. The main rule of alchemy, that "only like can become like," will be recognized for what it truly means. As the atoms that make up the flesh and bones of our bodies were once thriving inside the hearts of stars now dead, so will our consciousness one day occupy future stars. Human beings are the stuff of stars endowed with consciousness. We are the seeds of the cosmos. It is our true heritage to take our place in the order of the universe. That is the real promise of alchemy, Fulcanelli, and the Cyclic Cross at Hendaye.

JAY WEIDNER

THE POLITICS OF SECRECY: FULCANELLI AND THE SECRET OF THE END OF TIME

For me, it all started a few years ago when Jay Weidner asked me what I thought of Fulcanelli. Being full of my own opinions and sure of their validity, I gave him the quick rundown on what I knew: "Mysterious twentieth-century alchemist featured in *Morning of the Magicians* and therefore somewhat suspect. Colin Wilson suggests that he is another alchemical con man such as Cagliostro or St. Germain."

Jay laughed and suggested that I read *Mystery of the Cathedrals,* Fulcanelli's first book, and *The Fulcanelli Phenomenon,* by Kenneth R. Johnson. When I did, I realized that the books described one of the most fascinating puzzles of all time. Alchemy was certainly a key part of the mystery. At the heart of this puzzle, however, lay something even stranger—ancient knowledge of the location of the center of our galaxy and from that knowledge a way to estimate the date of a celestial event of eschatalogical magnitude. The sophisticated astronomical culture of the Maya considered this event to be the end and beginning point of time itself. After the fall of the ancient cultures in the Old World, simple knowledge of the event became the secret possession of the initiated elite.

As the mystery unfolded and the puzzle appeared before us, Jay and I were astonished that no others seemed to have seen this. And then we realized that of course they had. We had stumbled on the big secret, the grand MacGuffin of human history. All of humanity's psychodramas seemed to have the secret at their core, even when knowledge of the

1

secret was limited to the initiated few. From this perspective, what we had been taught to regard as history looked a lot like the residue of a millennia-long global conflict over control of the secret and its ramifications. As we researched this story, three main currents or groups emerged. These currents, perhaps better described as collective viewpoints, we defined by their relationship to the secret.

The first group, which we shall call the Priest-Kings, believed it had the right to possess the secret based on ancient traditions and bloodlines. In contrast to this basically Osirian position, and making up the second group, were the nihilistic Sethians, who wanted to possess the secret exclusively and were willing to destroy everything to get it or to keep anyone else from getting it. The ancient myth of Osiris, the rightful king, whose power is usurped by his evil brother, Seth, and then avenged by his son, Horus, echoes this struggle over control of the secret. The myth retains its power even today, as witness the success of Disney's *The Lion King*.

In between these extremes, in some moral and social gray area, are the Opportunists, the group that is willing to own the secret, use the secret, control the secret, or whatever it takes to provide for its own wealth, power, ego gratification, and so on. We have few mythological metaphors for this group because it is recent, developing only in the last two thousand years. All three of these groups are mutually antagonistic, yet interdependent. None of them wants the others to gain complete control, yet none can gain it alone. But most of all, none of them wants to share information with uninitiated outsiders.

Someone in the late seventeenth century, however, built an enigmatic mortuary monument in the quaint Basque coastal town of Hendaye. More than 250 years later, an equally mysterious author, Fulcanelli, would add a new chapter to his thirty-year-old book claiming that the "Cyclic Cross of Hendaye" was the ultimate expression of "chiliasm" (a belief in the Last Judgment as a literal end of time) as well as a description of the Great Work of alchemy. These simple facts point to several interesting conclusions.

Not only have the initiated few survived for centuries, right down into our own time, but apparently some of them wanted to reveal the secret as well. Interesting as these conclusions are, they force us to an even more dramatic one. If one of the initiated gave away the secret in 1957, it could only have been because the secret was in danger of being lost, or, even worse, co-opted and distorted. By 1957, the balance of power had shifted, and the nihilistic Sethians scented final victory in the Cold War breeze.

To understand the importance of Fulcanelli's message, we must remember that by the late 1950s it must have seemed, to those in the know, that something fundamental had changed. The Sethians and the Opportunists had finally learned to cooperate. The Priest-Kings, with their mystical connections, had almost been destroyed. The Sethians were in the process of convincing the Opportunists of the need for mass suicide by way of an atomic war. The secret of the end of time and the possible transformation of the human species were in danger of being lost, forgotten, or changed beyond recognition.

The value of Fulcanelli's revelation can be seen in the amount of misinformation and distortion that obscures any discussion of the person or of his work. Even Johnson's *Fulcanelli Phenomenon,* the only major work on the subject in English, reads like a mass of purposeful confusion, which is epitomized in its penultimate chapter, a bizarre science-fictional analysis of the Cyclic Cross by someone called "Paul Mevryl." From the information presented in this work, we might be forgiven for thinking that, while not quite a con man, Fulcanelli and his disciple Canseliet were perhaps as deluded or delusional as any other alchemist of the past.

And yet, when we read *Mystery of the Cathedrals,* we find no confused charlatan rambling on about imagined esotericisms. We come face-to-face with one of the most penetrating intellects of the twentieth century. The power of this intellect appears, especially in *Cathedrals,* to be driven by an urgent need to communicate the outlines of a great mystery. In delineating this mystery, Fulcanelli tried, by piling up images and allusions, to suggest a vast initiatory process at work in human history. At the core of the book, though, is a question.

The first edition, published in 1926, ended with the question unanswered, although a glimpse of the answer can be seen embedded within the brilliant synthesis of ideas at the heart of *Mystery of the Cathedrals.* By the time of the second edition, 1957, the question had been answered. Fulcanelli decided to reveal the secret of the end of time. When the book was reprinted, he added a new chapter that was more about chiliasm than alchemy and in which he sketched out the ground rules for solving the puzzle of the Cyclic Cross of Hendaye.

Five years later, *Morning of the Magicians,* by Pauwels and Bergier, became an international bestseller. In many ways, this was the start of the New Age movement and the beginning of the process of obscuring Fulcanelli and his work. This occulting would continue in numerous books and articles about enigmatic events and unsolved mysteries by Colin Wilson and others. *The Fulcanelli Phenomenon,* published in 1980, compounded the problem and convinced most readers that any mystery having to do with the cross of Hendaye was simply paranoiac delusion. Perhaps that's what the book was intended to do.

And here matters remained until Jay and I rashly and naively decided to solve the puzzle. Like some esoteric Tar Baby lurking at the astral crossroads waiting for a couple of happy-go-lucky Brer Rabbit–type researchers to come along, the monument's mystery proved irresistible once touched. We were stuck with it—all the way to the briar patch.

The quest took us from Elberton, Georgia (where a mysterious R. C. Christian has built a monument to the end of time), to France, Peru, and Egypt. Along the way, we were aided by so much synchronicity and coincidence that we eventually concluded there was a fourth current or group at work, behind the scenes, that actually wants the secret revealed to as many people as possible. This Free Will party, as we jokingly called it, seemed to be guiding our research and at times manipulating events.

That Jay and I got together at all was the result of complex personal synchronicities that spanned decades and ended with us both, for the most unlikely and absurd reasons, being in Boulder, Colorado, during the fall of 1997. As we started out almost as far apart geographically as it is possible to be and still be in the United States—I live in central North Carolina and Jay lived at that point on the coast of Washington in the Pacific Northwest—Boulder was like meeting halfway.

Deciphering the monument's message turned out to be the easy part. Once we had the message, deciphered in one rush of comprehension on a stormy Halloween night high in the Rockies, our emphasis shifted to finding out what it meant. The monument pointed to a specific time period, the intersection point of several celestial cycles, and we wanted to know exactly why Fulcanelli had described this event as a "double catastrophe" in which the northern hemisphere would be tried by fire—Judgment Day, in other words.

And that's where the real synchronistic fun and games began. Books, necessary volumes that we needed to see but didn't even know existed, began to appear: Once an extremely rare book miraculously turned up after access was denied us, and once, even more synchronistically, a key book was left behind in a smoking lounge at Heathrow Airport for us to find. Beyond the source texts, authorities began to show up—a local Boulder publisher announced a new edition of Fulcanelli's *Dwellings of the Philosophers* and let us read the translation as it proceeded. Dr. Paul LaViolette arrived for a conference and redirected our whole perspective. William Sullivan, John Major Jenkins, Dr. Alberto Villoldo, and Dr. Juan del Prado appeared at crucial moments and added their pieces of the puzzle.

Perhaps the most prominent synchronicity of all centers on the image of the rose-cross ankh. Several years before Jay and I met, I had every rose-cross ankh in the Coptic Museum in Cairo photographed in an attempt to trace the idea in early Christianity. By coincidence, we discovered in Arles and at the Louvre a series of rose-cross ankhs that would have been completely mysterious without the images from the Coptic Museum.

Fulcanelli's use of the word *chiliasm* gave us a clue to their meaning. Chiliasm is a Gnostic conception of the Christian Last Judgment in which a new existence, a new spiritual reality, supersedes our flawed common reality at the end of time. Many scholars, such as Elaine Pagels and Ioan Couliano, consider chiliasm to be the most sophisticated of the many first-century eschatological perspectives. Chiliasm was never declared heretical and survived as a belief in the Coptic Church. The ankh, symbol of eternal life, with the blooming flower at its center, represented the chiliastic ideal of the Second Coming as a renewal of all life.

The Egyptian origin of this concept suggested to us the antiquity of its insight. Following this thread, we found evidence that alchemy, as we have known it historically, is actually a demonstration of the transmutational physics at work in the galactic core, and was apparently know to the ancients. The inner core of alchemy appears in this light as the ability to apply the physics of creation to the task of personal immortality. And with this knowledge, of course, would come the ability to survive the double catastrophe.

If the secret, the grand MacGuffin of human history, is the ability to chart the celestial timing of the eschatological event, then the only serious questions become: "Is it true?" and "Can we survive?"

After compiling and sifting through a huge amount of research, we can definitively answer the first question: Yes, it's true. We are about to receive a cosmic wake-up call from the center of the galaxy.

As for the second question—Will the celestial event bring extinction or enlightenment?—the answer remains open. The existence, however, of a fourth current, the Free Will, share-the-information party, suggests that there is an answer.

Perhaps human evolution, once certain physical parameters, such as the size of the skull versus the width of the mother's hips, are reached, becomes an internal, personal process of initiation. Defining this personal process is a galactic wave of change that brings the opportunity of transformation to those who have reached the required level of internal transmutation. To those who haven't reached this level, perhaps it brings madness and destruction, perhaps even a global catastrophe, in its wake.

Because of the politics of secrecy surrounding the knowledge of this oncoming celestial event, we, as a culture, have been blissfully unaware of its approach. Eschatological speculations long ago became the property of cranks and fringe religions. Science has given the appearance of abdicating its responsibility for interpreting its own findings. And yet, the knowledge, the gnosis, survived the secrecy and persecution and is now on the verge of becoming once again a common cultural perspective.

The fourth current, the Free Will party, might just have won out after all.

VINCENT BRIDGES

PART ONE

Fulcanelli and the Secret of Alchemy

It has long been believed that the Gothic cathedrals were secret textbooks of some hidden knowledge; that behind the gargoyles and the glyphs, the rose windows and the flying buttresses, a mighty secret lay, all but openly displayed.

—WALTER LANG, INTRODUCTION,
LE MYSTÈRE DES CATHÉDRALES

WELCOME TO THE WORLD'S GREATEST MYSTERY. It has everything—clues and ciphers, red herrings, and consciously enigmatic jokes.
There are villains, victims, and heroes littering the plot line, along with
unreadable books, inscrutable monuments, and strange unearthly figures that flit along through the ages as if they had a purchase agreement
on eternity.

At the heart of the great mystery story interwoven through the
whole tapestry of human history lies the Gnostic science of alchemy. In
truth, this ancient science little resembles our modern view of it as a
proto-science practiced by deluded and mercury-crazed visionaries.
Intellects as great and as different as Isaac Newton, Leonardo da Vinci,
and Carl Jung have found important truths within the alchemical tradition and perspective. Newton, in fact, wrote more on alchemy—
although much of it has yet to be published—than he did on any other
subject. Jung spent the last decades of his life unraveling the "Western
yoga" he had glimpsed amid the jumble of alchemical metaphors. There
is something about this strange subject that invites the curious, the
intelligent, and the creative.

Yet the image of the medieval "puffer" foolishly working away at
his furnaces in vain attempts at turning lead into gold remains in our
modern iconography. This view appeals to our sense of scientific smug-
ness, and it allows us to dismiss the tradition itself as a discredited and
archaic hypothesis. But what if the tradition contains a core of truth,
and what if the "puffers" are no more deluded than the modern historians of science who confidently pigeonhole alchemy as a precursor to
chemistry? What if "alchemy" is something far different from what
most of us have ever dreamed?

And what if that core of truth touches upon the deepest and most
important issues of the human condition?

ONE

THE FULCANELLI MYSTERY

THE APOCALYPSE, THE LOST GENERATION, AND THE REDISCOVERY OF ALCHEMY

Nearly one hundred years after the fact, World War I, or "the Great War" to those who lived through it, feels as ancient as all the other wars that came before it. Our only connections with that conflict may be faded sepia-toned images of our ancestors who marched off to fight for reasons vaguely understood, even to them. Demoted in stature by an even greater war, the First World War became merely the prelude to a century of destruction and horror. Reading of the ideals and passions of that long-forgotten era, with its hopes for glory on the battlefield and the romance of nationalism, feels embarrassing to us now. If we think of it at all, we assign the Great War an emotional value somewhere between a massive industrial accident and the migration of lemmings to the sea.

And yet, looking back through history, we find many wars and disasters, plagues and conquests, volcanic eruptions, climatic changes, and mass migrations, but we find nothing quite like the Great War. It was unique. War up to that point had been an extension of politics; now it became just another industrial and mechanized product, taking on a life of its own in the trenches of the Western Front. Four hundred years of European intellectual, moral, and technical superiority created the engines of this industrialized murder, this mass-produced slaughter of the innocents. These technological wonders consumed the very social order that had created them. After four years, the self-proclaimed masters of the universe, Europe's young, the best and the brightest of all the old empires and republics, lay broken and bleeding in the wasteland saved from ultimate extinction only by the interference of the United States and its revolutionary democracy.

Was this cultural suicide, perhaps? An apocalypse by any other name is still an eschatological event; it is the end of the world for the inhabitants of that world. For example, near the end of the Great War, in September 1918, the Turkish Twelfth Army, holding the ridgeline in front of Damascus that included the ancient mound of Meggido, was attacked and destroyed by the combined use of airplanes, tanks, and cavalry. This battle, apparently, and eerily, described in chapter 16 of the Book of Revelation, suggests that Armageddon occurred in 1918.

Not only is the battle described in the biblical text, but it also occurred in the midst of the worst plague since the Black Death of the fourteenth century, the so-called Spanish influenza of 1917–19. Revelation's apocalypse looks much like the history of the twentieth century, leading up to one final millenarian explosion at or just beyond its end. Could this be true? Could the prophetic events of Saint John's Revelation be a description of an ongoing process, a season of destruction that essentially started with the Great War?

When the Great War finally ended, at the eleventh hour of the eleventh day of the eleventh month, the Old World, with its noble and imperial ways, was truly dead. The "victorious" Allies propped up the corpse of old imperial Europe and, using all the tricks of the undertaker's trade, gave it the brief appearance of animation. After the treaty was signed at Versailles, it decomposed soon enough. But while it lasted, through the 1920s and into the 1930s, this zombie summer of fast-fading European superiority galvanized the world.

The epicenter of this fleeting corpse-light renaissance was Paris, the City of Light. During the war this city had been the goal for which millions of men had marched, fought, bled, and died, from the taxicabs of Paris that helped create the Miracle of the Marne until those final days in the late spring of 1918 when the German long-range artillery shells fell in the streets. As it had been for centuries, Paris was a symbol, to both sides in the conflict, of something irrepressible in the human character. After the war, it became a mecca for all those who felt that the world must be changed somehow by the horror and sacrifice of the war, and that this change must mean something, say something, and do something. People came to Paris like insects drawn to the light, having burned their candles all at once in the final auto-da-fé of European civilization. They firmly believed that out of that conflagration would come a better world.

And so they came to Paris to help create that world: mystics, visionaries, painters, poets, artists of all kind, scientists, political thinkers, revolutionaries, all looking for that new world of hope, peace, and freedom that, so they felt, must grow out of "the war to end all wars." Ernest Hemingway's memoir, *A Moveable Feast,* published after his death, gives a vivid account of the era. "If you are lucky enough to have lived in Paris as a young man, then wherever you go for the rest of your life, it stays with you, for Paris is a moveable feast," Hemingway commented.[1]

The conflict of the Great War had made them all equal somehow, the artists and the revolutionaries, the poets and the scientists. They mingled on the boulevards, drank and talked in the cafés and bars and bookstalls, plotted and painted late into the night in small cold-water flats in Montmartre, or danced and drank in the nightclubs and demimonde dives of the Latin Quarter. As if driven by deep-rooted survival guilt, everyone wanted to live fast, fully, and gloriously. Paris, in the postapocalyptic twenties, was the light of the world, the flash point of history. It was also the beginning of the end of time itself.[2]

Out of this all too brief efflorescence emerged artistic, literary, social, political, and scientific concepts that shaped much of the rest of the century. From the surrealism of André Breton, Max Ernst, and Marcel Duchamp to the mathematics of Paul Dirac and the literary pyrotechnics of James Joyce, the idea of "transformation" bubbled just below the surface.[3] It was in 1926, in the thick of this transformative ferment, that an anonymous volume—issued in a luxury edition of three hundred copies by a small Paris publishing firm known mostly for artistic reprints—rocked the Parisian occult underworld. Its title was *Le Mystère des cathédrales* (The Mystery of the Cathedrals).[4] The author, "Fulcanelli," claimed that the great secret of alchemy, the queen of Western occult sciences, was plainly displayed on the walls of Paris's own cathedral, Notre-Dame-de-Paris (see fig. 1.1).

In 1926, alchemy, by our postmodern lights a quaint and discredited Renaissance pseudoscience, was in the process of being reclaimed and reconditioned by two of the most influential movements of the

Figure 1.1. Notre-Dame-de-Paris today. (Photo by Darlene)

century. Surrealism and psychology stumbled onto alchemy at about the same time, and each attached its own notions of its meaning to the ancient science. Carl Jung spent the twenties teasing out a theory of the archetypal unconscious from the symbolic tapestry of alchemical images and studying how these symbols are expressed in the dream state. The poet-philosopher André Breton and the surrealists made an intuitive leap of faith and proclaimed that the alchemical process could be expressed artistically. Breton, in his 1924 *Surrealist Manifesto,* announced that surrealism was nothing but alchemical art.[5]

Fulcanelli's book would have an indirect influence on both of these intellectual movements: indirect, because the book managed a major literary miracle—it became influential while remaining, apparently, completely unknown outside of French occult and alchemical circles. This is perhaps the strangest of all the mysteries surrounding *The Mystery of the Cathedrals.*

One illustration suffices to show the magnitude of the occlusion. Take any art history text on Gothic cathedrals written in the last thirty years and look at what it says about the obscure images found on the walls and entranceways of Notre-Dame. You will find, four times out of five, that alchemy is mentioned as a possible source of these vaguely

Christian images. You will also find, especially if the textbook is in English, that Fulcanelli and *The Mystery of the Cathedrals* are neither mentioned nor given as a source.

We may call this the-dog-that-didn't-bark-in-the-night effect. Like the dog that doesn't make a sound while the house is robbed, Fulcanelli's work has become conspicuous by its absence. On the other hand, the book's widespread influence suggests an importance far beyond the antiquarian idea that the cathedrals were designed as alchemical texts. To understand the silence, we must first understand Fulcanelli.

LE MYSTÈRE DES CATHÉDRALES, ALCHEMY, AND SURREALISM

In the fall of 1925, publisher Jean Schémit received a visit from a small man dressed as a prewar bohemian, with a long Asterix-the-Gaul-style mustache. The man wanted to talk about Gothic architecture, the "green argot" of its sculptural symbols, and how slang was a kind of punning code, which he called the "language of the birds." A few weeks later, Schémit was introduced to the man again, this time as Jean-Julien Champagne, the illustrator of a proposed book by a mysterious alchemist called Fulcanelli. Schémit thought that all three, the visitor, the author, and the illustrator, were the same man. Perhaps they were.

This, such as it is, amounts to our most credible Fulcanelli sighting. As such, it sums up the entire problem posed by the question: Who was Fulcanelli? Beyond this ambiguous encounter, he exists as words on a page and, in some occult circles, as a mythic alchemical immortal with the status, or identity, of a Saint Germain. There were two things that everyone agreed upon concerning Fulcanelli—he was definitely a mind to be reckoned with and he was a true enigma.

What seems to have happened is that a young occultist upstart named Eugène Canseliet offered the publisher the manuscript of *Le Mystère des cathédrales,* after the mysterious visitor had cleared the way. Schémit bought it and Canseliet wrote a preface for the book in which he stated that the author, his "master" Fulcanelli, had departed this realm. He then goes on to thank Jean-Julien Champagne, the man whom Schémit thought was Fulcanelli, for the illustrations.

Champagne, a minor symbolist artist and inventor far into an absinthe-fueled decline, had gathered around him a small entourage including Canseliet. The talk centered on alchemy when they met in the small cafés of Montmartre. Champagne lived nearby, in the rue de Rochechouart, and his sixth-floor room in the crumbling Parisian tenement was often the scene of late-night symposia on all sorts of occult subjects. To his young friends, he must have seemed like a ghost from another age, with his unfashionably long hair, his riddles, and, most of all, his claim to know the secrets of alchemy.

At the time, no one else but Schémit seemed to believe that Jean-Julien Champagne was Canseliet's master, Fulcanelli. His taste for great quantities of Pernod and absinthe indicated a man too dissipated to be as knowledgeable and erudite as the author of *Le Mystère*. Champagne certainly did know a real alchemist, though, whoever Fulcanelli was, and his illustrations show that he indeed had a more than passing familiarity with the alchemical art.

So we are left with the mystery of the missing master alchemist. He is a man who does not seem to exist, yet he is re-created constantly in the imagination of every seeker—a perfect foil for projection. We might even think it was all a joke, some kind of elaborate hoax, except for the material itself. When one turns to *Le Mystère,* one finds a witty intelligence that seems quite sure of the nature and importance of his information. This "Fulcanelli" knows something and is trying to communicate his knowledge; of this there can be no doubt.

Fulcanelli's main strategy, the key to unraveling the mystery, lies in an understanding of what he calls the "phonetic law" of the "spoken cabala," or the "language of the birds." This punning, multilingual wordplay can be used to reveal unusual and, according to Fulcanelli, meaningful associations between ideas. "What unsuspected marvels we should find, if we knew how to dissect words, to strip them of their bark and liberate the spirit, the divine light which is within," Fulcanelli writes. He claims that in our day this is the natural language of the outsiders, the outlaws and heretics at the fringes of society. (See appendix A, "Fulcanelli on the Green Language," for the complete text of this chapter.)[6]

This spoken cabala was also the "green language" of the Freemasons ("All the Initiates expressed themselves in cant," Fulcanelli reminds us) who built the *art gothique* of the cathedrals. "Gothic art is in fact the *art got* or *art cot*—χοτ—*the art of light or of the spirit,*"

Fulcanelli informs us. Ultimately the "art got," or the "art of light," is derived from the language of the birds, which seems to be a sort of Ur-language taught by both Jesus and the ancients.

Fulcanelli also claims that Rabelais's five-volume work *Gargantua and Pantagruel* is "a novel in cant," that is, written in the secret language. Offhandedly, he also mentions Tiresias, the Greek seer who revealed to mortals the secrets of Olympus. Tiresias was taught the language of the birds by Athena, the goddess of wisdom. Just as casually, Fulcanelli notes the similarity between *gothic* and *goetic,* suggesting that Gothic art is a magic art.

From this, we see that Fulcanelli's message, that there is a secret in the cathedrals, and that this secret was placed there by a group of initiates—of which Fulcanelli is obviously one—depends upon an abundance of imagery and association that overpowers the intellect, lulling one into an intuitive state of acceptance. Fulcanelli is undoubtedly brilliant, but we are left wondering if his is the brilliance of revelation or of dissimulation.

The basic premise of the book—that Gothic cathedrals are hermetic books in stone—was an idea that made it into print in the nineteenth century in the work of Victor Hugo. In *The Hunchback of Notre Dame,* Hugo spends a whole chapter (chapter 2 of book 5) on the idea that architecture is the great book of humanity, and that the invention of printing and the proliferation of mundane books spelled the end of the sacred book of architecture. He reports that the Gothic era was the sacred architect's greatest achievement, that the cathedrals were expressions of liberty and the emergence of a new sense of freedom. "This freedom goes to great lengths," Hugo informs us. "Occasionally a portal, a facade, an entire church is presented in a symbolic sense entirely foreign to its creed, and even hostile to the church. In the thirteenth century, Guillaume of Paris, in the fifteenth Nicolas Flamel, both are guilty of these seditious pages."[7] (See fig. 1.2.)

Essentially, *Le Mystère* is an in-depth examination of those "seditious pages" in stone. Fulcanelli elaborates on the symbolism of certain images found on the walls and porches of architect Guillaume of Paris's masterpiece, Notre Dame Cathedral, and its close contemporary, Notre Dame of Amiens. To this he adds images from two houses built in the Gothic style from fifteenth-century Bourges. This guided tour of hermetic symbolism is densely obscure, filled with "green language" puns

Figure 1.2. Symbolic knowledge displayed as ornamentation on the Gothic cathedrals, side panel from Notre-Dame-de-Paris. (Photo by Darlene)

and numerous allusions. To the casual reader, and even the dedicated student, this tangled web of scholarship is daunting.

But even after careful reading, one finds that the "mystery" of the cathedrals is never explained, and that what one assumes to be the basic mystery of alchemy is only glancingly delineated. There are allusions that escape the reader as easily as a mosquito glimpsed out of the corner of one's eye. At moments, a flash of great truth may occur, giving a hint of something profound, and then, like the mosquito, it is gone. Frustrated, the reader starts over, proceeding even more carefully, following the allusions and associations, trying to find and pin down the core of meaning that he senses is there, somewhere.

All this makes *Le Mystère* an almost perfect surrealist text, a modern alchemical version of Lautréamont's *Chants of Maldoror,* the surrealists' favorite nineteenth-century novel. The surrealists also embraced Rabelais and understood this kind of linguistic alchemy in terms of the correspondences and connections between objects or ideas on different levels or scales of being. The classic example of this is Lautréamont's "sudden juxtaposition on a dissecting table of a sewing machine and an umbrella."[8]

And yet, even though Fulcanelli's basic idea—an operational and linguistic alchemy used by sages or hermetic philosophers to transform one's perception of reality—became part of surrealism's intellectual currency, none of the surrealists, with one exception, mentions Fulcanelli or *Mystery of the Cathedrals.* One of surrealism's founding influences, Marcel Duchamp, was deeply interested in all things alchemical and was in Paris in 1926 when Le Mystère was published. Duchamp's work touches on many themes that we shall find in Fulcanelli's work and legend, including a fondness for puns and "green language" usages and a gender-bending sensibility that echoes the androgyny of the alchemical adept. Indeed, Duchamp's alter ego, "Rrose Selavy," and particularly Man Ray's 1920 photos of Duchamp as "Selavy," hint at Canseliet's last encounter with Fulcanelli.[9]

Only Max Ernst, another surrealist influenced by alchemy, makes any allusion to Fulcanelli, and this in his *Beyond Painting,* published in 1936. One of Ernst's early works, *Of This Men Shall Know Nothing,* painted in 1923 (see fig. 1.3), eerily echoes the symbolism on the Hendaye cross, which, as we shall see, did not become part of Fulcanelli's *Le Mystère* until the second edition in 1957. The picture was dedicated to André Breton and painted with the stated intent of defining the myth of our time.

By the late 1940s, the work of the movement's founder, André Breton—in both his book *Arcana 17* and the catalogue for the 1947 surrealist exhibition—appears to be heavily influenced by Fulcanelli. *Surrealism in 1947,* the exhibition catalogue, is full of seemingly Fulcanelli-inspired articles such as "Liberty of Language," by Arpad Merzei. In this article Merzei explains the "occult dialectic through linguistics." Merzei goes on to announce that language is "really an ensemble of symbols. And this conception of language is not far off from that which existed in magical civilizations, because the

Figure 1.3. Max Ernst's *Of This Men Shall Know Nothing,* 1923 (Tate Gallery, London). This intriguing painting echoes the cosmological motif found on the cross at Hendaye.

interchangeability of reality and language . . . is the base and the principal key of all hermetic activity."[10]

André Breton himself contributed a chart to the catalogue for *Surrealism in 1947* showing personalities and their associations with the images of the Tarot cards, a continuation of the ideas that he had laid out in *Arcana 17.* While the Tarot is not an obvious connection to Fulcanelli and *Mystery of the Cathedrals,* as we shall see, Breton's use of the Tarot as a series of alchemical metaphors suggests that he had read Fulcanelli even closer than most. Ten years later, in 1957, Breton wrote *The Art of Magic,* in which he insists that magic is an innate capacity of all humanity that can never be long suppressed or controlled. [11] And with that admission, surrealism takes its place alongside the literary works of Joyce, Lovecraft, and Borges as an important twentieth-century artistic addition to the Western occult tradition.[12]

It would seem that Fulcanelli contributed to that artistic evolution, except that the conspicuous absence of direct reference to him argues against it. Fulcanelli's ideas seem to be present in surrealism from its inception, growing more prominent as the movement matured. Possibly one answer lies in the anonymity of Fulcanelli himself. Since "Fulcanelli" is a pseudonym, the surrealists may have absorbed his ideas from a common source, the real person behind the name. As we shall see, this is an intriguing and possibly significant clue.

Yet, even that idea fails to explain the curious reluctance of anyone, surrealist, art historian, or alchemical scholar, to address the meaning of Fulcanelli's work. Once again, this conspicuous absence is very suggestive. Even the great American occult historian Manly P. Hall fails to mention Fulcanelli. Many scholarly books written since the 1930s about alchemy and its history fail to mention the two known books by Fulcanelli. Why?

The silence suggests a secret. The "mystery" of the cathedrals is the secret of alchemy in the sense that alchemy is an ancient initiatory science. "Fulcanelli" selected his symbolic images carefully to convey that he did indeed know the secret. Much has been made by the few occultists who have looked into Fulcanelli and his work about the difficulty of his writing. Threading a path through Fulcanelli's labyrinth of classical allusions is daunting to all but those who enjoy sampling ancient wisdom for its own sake. Without a key, the text remains, reading after reading, incomprehensible. As in the Sufi story, however, the greatest treasure is hidden in plain sight. Fulcanelli slyly directs us with his comment on *goetic* or magic art: The magic, the secret, is in the art.

As with the surrealists, to the occult savants of Paris in the late 1920s, Fulcanelli's book was almost intoxicating. Here, finally, was the word of a man who knew, the voice of the last true initiate. His student Eugène Canseliet informs us in the preface to the first edition of *Le Mystère* that Fulcanelli had accomplished the Great Work and then disappeared from the world. "For a long time now the author of this book has not been among us," Canseliet wrote, and he was lamented by a group of "unknown brothers who hoped to obtain from him the solution to the mysterious *Verbum dimissum* (missing word)."[13]

Mystification about the true identity of the alchemist obscured the fact that credible people had seen his visiting card, emblazoned with an aristocratic signature. It was possible to encounter people at the Chat Noir nightclub in Paris who claimed to have met Fulcanelli right through World War II.[14] Between 1926 and 1929, his legend grew, fueled by café gossip and a few articles and reviews in obscure Parisian occult journals. Canseliet contributed more information: The Master had indeed accomplished transmutation, Fulcanelli hadn't really disappeared, another book or two was planned, and so on.

By 1929, when Fulcanelli's second book, *Les Demeures philosophales* (Dwellings of the Philosophers),[15] appeared, the world of French occultism was ready for a revelation. What it received, however, was something of a disappointment, an anticlimax. Canseliet, in his preface to this volume, gives away nothing sensational. Nothing is said about the origin of the work or its relationship to *Le Mystère*. The reader is left with the sense that Fulcanelli was still alive and on the scene, with only a few bare hints as to his attainments.

Dwellings of the Philosophers is an uneven work, lacking the thematic coherence and symbolic wordplay displayed in *Le Mystère*, despite the latter's intentional inscrutability. *Dwellings* follows many of the same themes and symbolic threads as *Le Mystère;* in fact, there is little in it that is actually new. What *Dwellings* does, however, is put our understanding of alchemical adeptship in the sixteenth and seventeenth centuries on an entirely different footing. We come to understand that "alchemy" is a deep and rich stream of tradition, but we are left questioning exactly what "alchemy" is. Fulcanelli seems to shift his focus from lab work to astral voyages to an arcane lineage of adepts. The voice that seemed to know so much in *Le Mystère,* although expressed with cryptic imagery and allusions, is here hesitant and unclear. Discussions begin on practical alchemy that do not lead anywhere and the passing references to the key issue of *Le Mystère,* the recognition of a language-like structure behind the alchemical process, only adds to the confusion.

The critical response to *Dwellings of the Philosophers* was lukewarm at best. Interest waned, even when Canseliet revealed the existence of a third volume by Fulcanelli, *Finis Gloria Mundi,* in 1935. By 1937, Fulcanelli was a merely a legend of occult Paris in the twenties, and Canseliet had moved on to writing books on alchemy under his own name. All hope of publishing the last volume faded in the depression and crisis of the late thirties, and disappeared completely as the Nazis occupied France in the spring of 1940. Nothing is known about Canseliet's activities during the war.

After the war, Fulcanelli's legend, and Canseliet's career, profited from an upsurge of interest in all things metaphysical. By the mid-1950s, conditions were right to reprint both *Le Mystère des cathédrales* and *Dwellings of the Philosophers*. Simply by having been the mysterious Fulcanelli's student, Canseliet had become the grand old man of French alchemy and esotericism. But the fifties were not the twenties, and many things had changed. One of those things was the text of *Le Mystère* itself.

A NEW CHAPTER

The Fulcanelli affair would be of interest only to specialists of occult history and abnormal psychology except for the singular mystery of the extra chapter added to the 1957 edition of *Le Mystère*. This second edition included a new chapter entitled "The Cyclic Cross of Hendaye" and a few changes in its illustrations. No mention of these changes appeared in Canseliet's preface to the second edition.

A few detractors, as early as the publication of *Dwellings*, had been suspicious that the whole affair was the work of a group of occult pranksters centered on the bookstore of Pierre Dujols in the Luxembourg district of Paris. The critics have archly suggested that the whole venture was an obscure literary hoax, perhaps designed to give the Brotherhood of Heliopolis, as the group liked to call itself, the cachet of a real tradition.[16] It must be admitted that if that were indeed the case, they failed miserably.

Any motivation for a hoax, in the ordinary sense, seems to be lacking. None of the Brotherhood, such as it was, benefited from or capitalized on the supposed Fulcanelli's teaching, except Eugène Canseliet and possibly Jean-Julien Champagne, who illustrated both volumes. The Brotherhood of Heliopolis seems to have remained small and closed, limited to Champagne and his friends, and faded away after his death in 1932.

The publisher, Jean Schémit, however, assumed that "Fulcanelli" and Champagne were one and the same, and, given his meetings with Champagne and Fulcanelli, his opinion carries some weight. Certainly, if Champagne was not Fulcanelli, he was in fact his agent. Canseliet's role seemed, to Schémit, to be more of an amanuensis or secretary. *Fulcanelli dévoilé,* by Geneviève Dubois, a French examination of the

Fulcanelli legend published in 1993, even concludes that the work was a product of a committee with Pierre Dujols (who died in 1926, the year *Le Mystère* was published) supplying the scholarship, Champagne the operational skills, and Canseliet in charge of assembling the notes.[17]

But even if we agree, for the sake of argument, that Champagne and his friends are our best candidate for Fulcanelli's secret identity, the question remains: Who wrote the extra chapter in the second edition of *Le Mystère?* Champagne was a quarter of a century dead when the second edition appeared. It is unlikely that he was the author, even though internal evidence suggests that it was written at least a decade before his death, as it is unlikely that he was the author of the rest of *Le Mystère.* In the opening paragraph of the Hendaye chapter, Fulcanelli refers to "a new beach, bristling with proud villas," and in the next paragraph comments on the leafy trees surrounding Saint Vincent's church on the town square. Hendaye-Plage, or beach, didn't exist until the early 1920s, and the proud villas appeared in 1923 when the intellectuals and bohemians discovered the town. The trees around the church died in the late 1930s and were cleared away during the war. Therefore, the visit on which the Hendaye chapter is based happened between roughly 1924 and 1938.

With Canseliet's use of everything else by Fulcanelli—or Champagne and Dujols, the "Fulcanelli" group—how are we to account for the absence of reference to Hendaye in Canseliet's works prior to the mid-1950s? If the chapter is the work of Champagne, then Canseliet must have known about it. This is not a trivial question. The Hendaye chapter is perhaps the single most astounding esoteric work in Western history. It offers proof that alchemy is connected to eschatology, or the timing of the end of the world. And it offers the conclusion that a "double catastrophe" is imminent. If Canseliet had known of this, he would surely have used it, or at least mentioned it. Yet the silence is complete and compelling.

So where did the chapter come from? We do have one intriguing clue that serves to compound the mystery. In 1936, Jules Boucher, by Canseliet's recollection a peripheral member of the group but by his own account an integral part, published a two-page spread in the obscure occult revue *Consolation* called "The Cross of Hendaye."[18] Apparently, a painter named Lemoine took some photos of the cross while vacationing near Hendaye and showed them to a friend, the editor of *Consolation,* Maryse Choisy. From there, Jules Boucher, a young

Figure 1.4. Jules Boucher's original article for *Consolation* on the Hendaye cross, 1936.

occult writer, was commissioned to write an "esoteric" article on the cross (fig. 1.4).

Boucher's article is significant more for the differences between his version and that attributed to Fulcanelli than it is for any similarities. Boucher clearly understood enough of the symbolism on the monument to unravel its secret, but he gave no hint of any deeper understanding of the cross. Fulcanelli, however, is direct and clear. He knows specifics and gives clues that can have come only from direct knowledge. There is nothing to suggest that Canseliet copied Boucher's article and fabricated the new Hendaye chapter from it. But there is evidence that Boucher had been exposed, somehow, to the information in that chapter.

The clue lies in Boucher's use of Fulcanelli's translation of the oddly spaced inscription on the front of the cross. Normally arranged, the phrase is the simple *O Crux Ave Spes Unica,* "Hail, O Cross, the Only Hope" of thousands of cemetery monuments. But, as shown in figure 1.5, the final *s* of the Latin *spes,* or "hope," is displaced from the first line so that the inscription reads *O Crux Aves / Pes Unica.* Boucher uses what he perceives to be an additional oddity in spacing to suggest that the inscription should be read phonetically in French as *O Croix Have Espace Unique,* or "O cross, the single pale space."[19] (See fig. 1.5.)

Figure 1.5. Top of the Hendaye cross showing the broken Latin inscription. (Photo by Darlene)

In his Hendaye chapter Fulcanelli phrased it as, "It is written that Life takes refuge in a single space."[20] From this, we can see that Boucher has heard or read Fulcanelli's version and then gone looking for its origin in the Latin phrase. It is unlikely that anyone stumbling on the Hendaye cross without this key piece of linguistic wordplay to guide him would ever consider trying to form French words from a strangely divided Latin phrase. But his derivation is flawed, and yields only a close approximation of Fulcanelli's phrase. As we shall show in chapter 11 when we discuss it in detail, Fulcanelli meant just what he said about how to read this symbolic inscription. It becomes clear that Boucher was consulting a source that seems to be at least partially the text of the new Hendaye chapter.

There is no evidence that Canseliet knew anything about Boucher's article, but considering that Boucher was part of the circle, it is likely that he did. Researchers rediscovered it only long after the second edition of *Le Mystère* was published, and it remains the only contemporary publication on Hendaye's cross. Therefore, Boucher's independent approach to the cross suggests that Fulcanelli was still in contact with some of his students, just not with Canseliet.

So if Canseliet didn't copy Boucher, and the rest of the group "Fulcanelli" was dead when it was published, where did Canseliet get the new chapter? If it had been written in the mid-1920s and not used for some reason, then why the need for secrecy? And was Canseliet in on the secret? Unless we suppose that Boucher received his information from Canseliet, which is unlikely given Canseliet's comments on the peripheral nature of Boucher's involvement in the group, then the mystery of the Hendaye cross was one of Fulcanelli's most closely guarded secrets.

One possible solution is that Canseliet met the real Fulcanelli again and got it straight from the source. Canseliet claims that just such a meeting actually took place, in the Pyrenees in the early 1950s. While Hendaye is never mentioned in Canseliet's account, the story itself is quite spectacular in its strangeness.[21]

To place the tale of Canseliet's last encounter with Fulcanelli in any sort of context, we must cut through the tangled accounts of Canseliet's relationship with "the Master." Born in late 1899, Eugène Canseliet claimed to have met Fulcanelli shortly after the start of the Great War, while still an adolescent. The next year, he claimed to have met Champagne as another of Fulcanelli's students. Later in life, Canseliet declared that he had spent fifteen years with Fulcanelli, implying, since they seem to have met in 1915, that he last saw the Master in 1930.

From the mid-1920s until Champagne's death in 1932, however, Canseliet lived across the hall from Champagne in a cold-water walkup in the Butte-Montmartre district. Therefore Canseliet was the one person most likely to know if Champagne really was Fulcanelli. And to the end, Canseliet denied that Champagne was anything more than the illustrator.

Even though Canseliet had the most to gain by perpetuating the myth of Fulcanelli, it is obvious that there is something more than just self-serving egoism at work in his descriptions of Fulcanelli. If Fulcanelli had really been either Dujols or Champagne, then why would Canseliet continue the hoax long after they were dead? Why change *Le Mystère* at all? Why not admit the whole thing and claim the credit? And yet Canseliet went to his grave declaring that Fulcanelli was a real person, and was certainly not Champagne or Dujols.[22]

The history of alchemy is replete with complex hoaxes and mysterious adepts, and at first glance this appears to be just another of these attempts at mystification. Canseliet certainly had the most to gain from the promotion of Fulcanelli the "Master," and is therefore the least reliable of all the witnesses. And yet his story contains important clues that do point to a possible reality for "Fulcanelli" at the core of the elaborate charade.

Therefore, let us suspend disbelief, take Eugène Canseliet's story at face value, and see if we can find the truth of his relationship with Fulcanelli.

As noted above, Canseliet claimed to have met the group around Fulcanelli just after the war began and seems to have worked directly with them through the war years. Sometime after 1919, Fulcanelli seems to have faded from the scene as a direct presence. At least that is the assumption based on the admittedly conflicting evidence of Canseliet's changing versions of the story. Canseliet later told Robert Amadou that Fulcanelli left Paris for the East in 1922. But the contact with Fulcanelli, whoever he was, left the Brotherhood of Heliopolis—Canseliet, Champagne, and the rest—in possession of several secrets.

These included the secret of physical transmutation, according to some of Canseliet's later accounts. In the mid-1970s, just a few years before his death, he told the American occultist Walter Lang that he and Champagne and another Brother, Gaston Sauvage, performed a transmutation in 1922, in the municipal gasworks laboratory of Sarcelles, with a minute amount of the powder of projection given to him by Fulcanelli.[23] In a conversation with Albert Riedel (Frater Albertus of the Paracelsus Research Society), Canseliet claimed that he performed the transmutation under Fulcanelli's direction.[24] To some, this suggests that Fulcanelli was literally there in the room, demonstrating the correct technique. Actually, Canseliet is saying no more than that he was following Fulcanelli's directions, which could have been written down years before.

Frater Albertus, however, had information from independent sources that Fulcanelli himself had performed a transmutation in Bourges in 1937 in the presence of Ferdinand de Lesseps II and Pierre Curie.[25] This would suggest that our supposition that Boucher had an independent contact with Fulcanelli was correct, and that Fulcanelli was still on the scene in the late 1930s. Unfortunately, Albertus does not supply us with the source of his information. Canseliet claimed to know nothing of the incident. It might be easy to dismiss it as one more occult fabrication, except for the mention of de Lesseps and Curie. Canseliet confirmed that they were among Fulcanelli's large circle of friends. This, as we shall see, is possibly the most significant clue of all.

It is perhaps this early connection with scientists such as Curie that led the OSS and other Allied intelligence agencies to search for Fulcanelli immediately after the Second World War. Canseliet confirms this in his conversation with Frater Albertus, and implies that they are still seeking him.[26] Apparently, then, Fulcanelli, on some level or other, seems have been a real presence right through the end of the war in 1945.

For a man who died or disappeared before 1926, if we are to take Canseliet's first preface to *Le Mystère* at face value, that's a pretty active record. By sifting through Canseliet's statements, however, we can determine a sort of minimal time line. From 1915 to around 1919, Canseliet was in direct contact with Fulcanelli. He visited Canseliet, perhaps to deliver the powder of projection and a stack of manuscripts, at Sarcelles in 1922. Then, Canseliet tells us in his various accounts, he saw him again in 1930 and once more, miraculously, in 1952.

In many ways, this simplified chronology makes the most sense. Fulcanelli was never seen visiting Champagne or Canseliet, because he wasn't in contact with them during the period that they lived next door to each other. He visited Canseliet at Sarcelles and we are never told where the 1930 meeting took place. This literal absence of Fulcanelli explains many of the minor mysteries such as the liberties Canseliet and Champagne took with the project of publishing his work and teachings. Perhaps Canseliet truly meant what he said in the preface to the first edition of *Le Mystère* and never expected to see Fulcanelli again?

What a shock, then, when he returned in 1930, after both books had been published. Perhaps Fulcanelli wasn't pleased by what Canseliet and Champagne had done with his work. This might explain Champagne's sudden decline into apathy and alcoholism, which led to his death two years later. Certainly, Fulcanelli broke off contact with Canseliet, after fifteen years, leaving him to his own devices. Some sort of signal was arranged, however, in case Fulcanelli ever wanted to get back in touch with Canseliet. We know this because, if Canseliet is to be believed, something of the sort apparently happened.

In 1952, after a wait of almost twenty-two years, Canseliet claimed to have met his master one last time. Before his death, Canseliet told the story, in several versions, to a number of friends and researchers.[27] When he received the signal, Canseliet went to a specific city where a car met him and drove him deep into the Pyrenees. Arriving at a large château, Canseliet was greeted by his old master, Fulcanelli, now looking the same age as Canseliet himself—then in his early fifties—even though he would have been around eighty in 1930.[28]

From here on, Canseliet's story becomes vague and dreamlike as shock piled upon shock. Like Parzival's first visit to the Grail Castle, wonders pass in front of Canseliet without his ever asking the question Why? And, like Parzival, Canseliet ends up on the outside, the castle having vanished, wondering just what it was all about.

He was given a room in an upper turret and a *"petit laboratoire"* in which to conduct his experiments. He was so impressed by the small laboratory that he began to wonder what the grand laboratory might be like in comparison. Gradually, as he met the other visitors, it began to dawn on Canseliet that his master's château was a refuge for advanced alchemical adepts. That evening, he saw a group of small children, dressed in sixteenth-century clothes, playing in the courtyard below his window. Canseliet, like Parzival, didn't think to ask any questions. He went to bed and forgot about it.[29]

Days passed, with Canseliet happily puttering around in his laboratory. Fulcanelli stopped by occasionally to see how he was doing, but Canseliet is vague about their discussions. Then one morning Canseliet woke early and went downstairs into the courtyard for a breath of air without doing more than throwing on his clothes. As he stood there with his shirt unbuttoned and his braces hanging loose from trousers, three women entered the courtyard, chattering in happy feminine voices.

Embarrassed, Canseliet froze, hoping that they wouldn't notice him standing in the doorway. As they passed, one of the three turned and looked directly at Canseliet and smiled. Shocked to his core, Canseliet recognized the face of the young woman as that of his master, Fulcanelli.

Canseliet would talk and write about his visit to the castle of the adepts many times before his death, but he saved this gem of pure strangeness for his closest friends. The story appeared in print only after his death, in Kenneth R. Johnson's *The Fulcanelli Phenomenon,* a book about which we shall have much to say later on. The end of the tale is very confused, but Canseliet eventually left the castle. Fulcanelli, however, gave him a word of warning before he left, reported by Canseliet in the 1964 edition of his *Alchimie:* "The time will come, my son, when you will no longer be able to work in alchemy, when it will become necessary for you to search for the rare and blessed land along the frontiers to the south."[30]

And this is as close as we get, from the perspective of Canseliet's mythmaking, to the origin of the Hendaye chapter and its curious mention of a disaster and a place of refuge. But for the reality of that additional chapter, it might be possible to dismiss this story as an old man's fabrication. Whatever really happened, the fact that the second edition of *Le Mystère* contained the new chapter on the Hendaye cross forces us to reexamine the whole problem of Fulcanelli's identity.

After that supposed encounter, however, Fulcanelli seems to have truly vanished. Canseliet never saw him again and neither has anyone else with any degree of certainty. We are left with a trail of obscure clues and semi-mythical events that echo the gender-bending "Rrose Selavy" of Duchamp, the linguistic alchemy proclaimed by Breton and Merzei, and the general "put-on" quality of a surrealist happening.

Could the Hendaye chapter have been meant for inclusion in *Dwellings,* perhaps as a follow-up to the monument on the Marne? Or was it perhaps the only surviving fragment of *Finis Gloria Mundi* not reclaimed by an angry "Fulcanelli" in 1930? If so, why was it kept secret and leaked, as it were, to sources other than Canseliet such as Jules Boucher? Could it be, perhaps, that the Hendaye chapter was withheld because it contained clues to the identity of Fulcanelli, both as an individual and as a group? Would it have given away the whole game to publish it before the mid-1950s?

The solution to that riddle must wait until after we have examined the growth of the Fulcanelli legend.

THE FULCANELLI LEGEND

However we approach the subject of alchemy, we are rewarded with a mystery, until the entire subject becomes an infinite regression of mirrored mysteries. And so, if we are not careful, we end up finding only the face of our own bias. The secret protects itself, even when it is displayed in plain sight.

Fulcanelli serves as an example. The occult savants of Paris wanted to believe in the possibility of physical transmutation, so the suggestion that someone had actually done it grew into an obsession. Fulcanelli was a modern-day Flamel, a renegade chemist who, like the Curies, had stumbled on a way to manipulate the radioactive "light" locked within matter. No matter that not a trace of any speculation concerning atomic energy could be found in *Le Mystère*; all alchemists wrote in code anyway. So the mystery focused on who Fulcanelli was. If his identity could be discovered, then the transmutation could be verified. Unfortunately, no one ever claimed the title and presented his bona fides.

But the idea persisted. There had been a "real" alchemist in the twentieth century. There is even a touch of the surreal to the image: a tall aristocratic elder guiding a group of young acolytes through the transmutational process in a municipal gasworks laboratory. Canseliet, of course, is our source for these images, leaked through the years as a way, perhaps, to carefully perpetuate the myth.[31]

In the same fashion, the idea that "Fulcanelli" was simply a committee "hoax" has also handicapped our understanding of what the work itself has to say. The example of the Hendaye chapter is significant here; because it can't be made to fit neatly into any hypothesis, it is simply ignored. Yet it is key to understanding the deepest secret of alchemy, and perhaps even the key to Fulcanelli's identity.

The appearance of the second edition of *Dwellings of the Philosophers,* in 1959, marked another watershed. The catastrophe theme was openly discussed in the final two chapters, "The Sundial of Holyrood Palace in Edinburgh" and "The Paradox of the Unlimited Progress of Science," as well as in Canseliet's preface to that edition.[32] Within the year, the legend would gain another twist with the publication of the first New Age bestseller, *Le Matin des magiciens,* by Pauwels and Bergier, which would appear in English in 1963 as *The Morning of the Magicians.* The Fulcanelli phenomenon began to exhibit new life, growing in unexpected directions.[33]

Magicians cemented the image of Fulcanelli as the archetypal twentieth-century alchemist, warning of the dangers of atomic energy like the best contemporary "space brothers" and ascended masters. In 1960, this was undoubtedly the view of the occult establishment, whose perspectives Pauwels and Bergier were exploring. Although their work is a mish-mash of ideas, Pauwels and Bergier do manage to ask some of the right questions. In the course of this investigation, we would find ourselves returning again and again to the synchronicities of *Morning of the Magicians.*

The book did serve, however, to introduce the story of Fulcanelli to an English-speaking audience. A decade or so later, this interest would bear fruit in the excellent translation by Mary Sworder of *Le Mystère's* second edition. Soon after the translation was published, the only full-scale work on alchemy and Fulcanelli in English appeared. *The Fulcanelli Phenomenon,* by Kenneth Raynor Johnson, published in England in 1980, raised more questions than it answered.

Johnson's discussion of the history and practice of alchemy and on Fulcanelli and Canseliet is solid and well presented. In some cases, it is our only source for large pieces of the puzzle. The careful reader, however, encounters a fair amount of special pleading, for Johnson, ultimately, is obscuring as much as he is revealing. Nowhere is this more apparent than in the epilogue, an examination of the Hendaye cross written by someone named Paul Mevryl.

In a way, we should be grateful that anyone had the courage to comment on the Hendaye cross in print. Mevryl tackles it head-on in a wild explosion of science fiction and creative cryptography. The skeptical reader may be forgiven for throwing up his hands in disgust and declaring the whole thing a hoax or a hallucination. And, perhaps, that is exactly what the article was intended to accomplish.[34]

Fulcanelli, and alchemy in general, is a subject that inspires obscurantist literature. Most books on alchemy, particularly those written by adepts, are designed to confuse the unwary or naive reader. Only those readers who possess the key to the language can read their real message. But the books written about Fulcanelli, starting with *Morning of the Magicians,* fall into a new category of obscurantism. They seem specifically designed to obscure Fulcanelli, as if he had somehow given away too much.

The next major work to mention Fulcanelli in any depth is also deeply obscure. *Refuge of the Apocalypse,* by Elizabeth Van Buren, begins with a description of the Hendaye cross and Fulcanelli's comments on it. She quotes Fulcanelli's warning to Canseliet, and then jumps to a statement that Fulcanelli told others that the place of refuge was Rennes-le-Château, in the Aude in southern France. From this slender reed, Van Buren builds a complex thesis that involves the bloodline of Jesus, tunnel openings, and landscape zodiacs, all pointing to

Rennes-le-Château as Fulcanelli's "single place of refuge."[35]

This digression into the world of *Holy Blood, Holy Grail,* by Baigent, Lincoln, and Leigh, was strange enough. The next book to dwell on Fulcanelli was not as bizarre, but it raised some curious questions. *Al-Kemi: A Memoir—Hermetic, Occult, Political, and Private Aspects of R. A. Schwaller de Lubicz,* by André VandenBroeck, revealed that Schwaller, an esoteric Egyptologist and author of the monumental *Temple of Man,* had close connections with the Fulcanelli group. VandenBroeck strongly suggests that Schwaller de Lubicz actually was Fulcanelli, or at least the author of *Le Mystère,* and that Champagne stole his work. [36]

At this point, all a researcher can do is to echo poor Alice: "curiouser and curiouser." And, like Alice, somewhere along the line we stepped through the looking glass.

THE CROSS AT HENDAYE

From the mouth of the Nive at Bayonne to the Straits of Bidassoa, the southwest coast of France is known as the Côte d'Argent, in contrast with the Côte d'Azur of the French Riviera. While never as famous as the Riviera, the Côte d'Argent has always been something of a royal playground. The Sun King, Louis XIV, spent his honeymoon on the beach at Saint-Jean-de-Luz, while Biarritz, just a little farther up the coast, was the Victorian royal resort par excellence. During the nineteenth and twentieth centuries, everyone, from the empress Eugènie and Napoleon III to Queen Victoria, Prince Albert, and the Prince of Wales, seemed to show up for the season.

H. G. Wells made the small tuna-fishing town of Saint-Jean-de-Luz famous as a resort for intellectuals. It's not hard to imagine the impeccable Wells and his walrus mustache ensconced on the long white beach, tuna nets strung from poles to dry in the sun while the boats trawl in the far distance, dictating *The Outline of History* to a small army of assistants. Wells, Aldous Huxley, and the smart young London set discovered Saint-Jean-de-Luz in 1920, and by 1923 or so the luxury villas had spread as far down as the new Hendaye-Plage. [37] (See fig.1.6.)

It was a few years after Louis XIV honeymooned there—around 1680, give or take a decade—that someone built an enigmatic mortuary monument in the parish cemetery of Saint Vincent's Church at

Figure 1.6. Hendaye, on the Atlantic coast of southwest France and the border with Spain, lies in the heart of the Basque homeland.

Hendaye. The date of its construction, who or what it was meant to memorialize, even its original location, have all been lost. All that is known about the Cyclic Cross, as Fulcanelli labeled it, is that it was moved from the cemetery to its present location in the southwest corner of the churchyard in 1842, when the church underwent a restoration. Patient conversation with the caretaker yields the further information that the cross was moved to honor the local d'Abbadie family, who paid for the church's restoration.[38]

With this hard-won piece of the puzzle, we come at last to a solid historical figure with connections, in various ways, to many of the themes on the Hendaye cross. The d'Abbadie family originated in the Bearne region of the Pyrenees to the east of Hendaye and was one of the dominant families there up until the Revolution. One branch of the family settled in Dublin and became wealthy in the shipping business. The eldest son, Antoine, born in 1810, would return to Hendaye and the Basque Pyrenees after exploring Ethiopia for the French government and restore the family to its former level of prestige. In 1842, he purchased the arrow-shaped headland between Hendaye and Saint-Jean-de-Luz, paid for the restoration of Saint Vincent's, and moved the cross or had it put together.

In the 1860s, after several more trips to Egypt and Ethiopia, including an attempt at finding the source of the Nile, Antoine d'Abbadie returned to Hendaye and hired the finest architects of the era to build a scaled-down Gothic château. Eugène Emmanuel Viollet-le-Duc, the architect behind the restoration of Notre-Dame-de-Paris and many other Gothic masterpieces, did most of the major design work on the Château d'Abbadie. In the 1870s and 1880s, Antoine was president of the French Academy of Sciences and was a friend and supporter of Ferdinand-Marie de Lesseps in his bid to build the Suez Canal. He left the château at Hendaye to the academy and established an observatory, dedicated to cataloging stars, to carry on his work. The catalog now contains more than 500,000 stars.

Antoine's nephew Michel d'Abbadie and cousin Harry d'Abbadie D'Arrast carried the family tradition into new realms. Michel was a patron of the arts, and a friend of the early surrealists, including Marcel Duchamp and Max Ernst, as well as a close friend and contemporary of Pierre de Lesseps, son of Ferdinand-Marie de Lesseps, the builder of the Suez Canal, and Pierre de Lesseps has been mentioned as a friend of both Champagne and Fulcanelli. Harry's friends were more the film star and literary types. Both Charlie Chaplin and Ernest Hemingway stayed at the Château Etzchau east of Hendaye in the Bearne. Hemingway even mentions Hendaye in *The Sun Also Rises,* which was published in 1926, the same year as *Le Mystère.*[39]

In the end, it boils down to the reality of the cross itself. The family responsible for its erection has many connections, although indirect and circumstantial, with figures at the heart of the Fulcanelli mystery. Could this be the solution to the riddle of why the Hendaye chapter was kept a secret? Would its revelation in the 1920s have pointed too directly at the real "brotherhood" behind the Fulcanelli mystification? Also, the castle in Canseliet's fanciful trip to the Pyrennes sounds like the real Château Etzchau in Saint-Etienne-de-Bagiorry, which has curious connections going back to Gaston of Foix and perhaps even Nicolas Flamel. Could all the subterfuge be hiding, and at the same revealing, for those who can see it, the true source of Hendaye's, and by extension Fulcanelli's, secret wisdom?

The cross sits today in a very small courtyard just to the south of the church. There is a tiny garden with a park bench nearby. Standing about twelve feet tall, the Cyclic Cross of Hendaye looms over the courtyard, a mysterious apparition in the clear Basque sunlight. The monument is brown and discolored from its three-hundred-plus years. The stone is starting to crumble and it is obvious that air pollution—the cross sits a few yards from a busy street on the main square—is speeding its dissolution. The images and the Latin inscription on the cross have no more than a generation left before pollution wipes the images clean and the message disappears forever.

The base of local sandstone sits on a broad but irregular three-step platform and is roughly cubic (fig. 1.7). Measurement reveals that it is a little taller than it is wide. On each face are curious symbols (see fig. 1.8): a strange shieldlike arrangement of A's in the arms of a cross; an eight-rayed starburst; a sun face glaring like some ancient American sun god; and, most curious of all, an old-fashioned man-in-the-moon face with a prominent eye. Rising from the base is a fluted column, with a suggestion of Greek classicism, on top of which stands a very rudely done Greek cross with Latin inscriptions. Above the sun face on the western side is the figure of an X on the top portion of the cross. Below that, on the transverse arm, is the variation on the common inscription noted above, *O Crux Aves / Pes Unica,* "Hail, O Cross, the Only Hope." On the reverse side of the upper cross, above the starburst, is the Christian inscription INRI.

Figure 1.7. The base of the Hendaye cross showing the sun and the shieldlike design with its four A's. (Photo by Darlene)

Figure 1.8. The four sides of the base. The shieldlike design faces south, the star faces east, the sun faces west, and the moon faces north. (Photos by Darlene)

Figure 1.9. The Hendaye cross as it is today. (Photo by Darlene)

Fulcanelli tells us that "whatever its age, the Hendaye cross shows by the decoration of its pedestal that it is the strangest monument of primitive millenarism [sic], the rarest symbolic translation of chiliasm, which I have ever met."[40]

But what does the author mean by "primitive millenarism"? And how are the decorations on the pedestal "the rarest symbolic translation of chiliasm"? What, exactly, is chiliasm?

Fulcanelli provides some guidance by referring to the Fathers of the Church, Origen, Saint Denis of Alexandria, and Saint Jerome, who first accepted and then refuted the chiliast doctrine. Then he tells us that chiliasm "was part of the esoteric tradition of the ancient hermetic philosophy."

Chiliasm was a second-century C.E. Gnostic belief in a literal renewal of the earth after its destruction on the Day of Judgment. This transformed world would be free of sin, a virtual paradise of sensual delights, feasts, and weddings, or so the Gnostic chiliasts preached. Naturally the more orthodox branches of the Church found this threatening, although, as Fulcanelli points out, it was never officially condemned. In the second century, Origen, who is now our main source of information on the chiliasts, refuted the doctrine, and chiliasm slowly faded into the heretical underground.

"Primitive millenarism" is an even more curious phrase. The use of the word *primitive* in this context suggests "prime" or "primeval," definitely pre-Christian. The monument, then, not only is an example of heretical Christian belief, but also somehow describes a primitive, or ancient, view of the end of the world. Fulcanelli underscores his point when he comments that "the unknown workman, who made these images, possessed real and profound knowledge of the universe."

Thus, we are presented with a strange monument that describes both a heretical Christian view of apocalypse and an ancient view of the same, apparently cosmological, event. Also of note, Fulcanelli is implying that this concept is a part of the "esoteric tradition of the ancient hermetic philosophy." In the entire literature of alchemy and its history, no one else has ever openly connected it with eschatology. On first glance, it seems ridiculous. How can the end of the world and the apocalypse be connected in any way with turning lead into gold?

As we dug deeper, we discovered that Fulcanelli had left us an important clue to the big secret at the core of alchemy. We would find that alchemy had always been associated with the idea of time and timing, and that, as Fulcanelli informed us, chiliasm lay at the center of the idea of transforming time itself. We would even discover the simple and literal truth of Fulcanelli's statement that the unknown designer of the cross had real and true knowledge of the universe. From that knowledge, displayed by the Hendaye cross, we would eventually unravel a whole new perspective on alchemy, one that touches on the deepest mysteries of magic, mysticism, and religion, and one that poses the question of extinction or enlightenment for the entire planet.

A LODESTONE OF PURE WEIRDNESS

Although Hendaye has grown into a good-sized resort town, the town square and Saint Vincent's Church look much the same as they did in the 1920s and 1930s, when Fulcanelli and Lemoine the painter came to visit. Wednesday is still market day, and the vendors of fresh fish and vegetables still line the square. The people who pass by on their way to the square barely notice the nondescript cross standing against the wall of the church. Cars park a few feet away, and the everyday bustle of life in a French resort town takes place around it. Occasionally, like Monsieur Lemoine, a tourist stops to take a photograph. The ordinary tourist snaps his shot and then looks for a sign explaining what he has just taken a snap of. Finding no information except more curious images, our tourist shrugs and later labels that slide as "Cross with angry sun face, Hendaye."

Standing before the cross, however, in the bright Basque sunlight on a busy Wednesday market morning, we came face-to-face with the great mystery. Fulcanelli's new chapter in *Le Mystère* was designed to link, uniquely in alchemical literature, chiliasm to the secret of practical alchemy and thereby point directly to the real secret, the nature of time itself.

Like a lodestone of pure weirdness, this juxtaposition of the end of the world with the transmutational process of alchemy attracted us to its mystery. Our involvement began accidentally when one of us picked up a copy of *Le Mystère* at a yard sale. Over a decade later, the code was cracked, and, as the implications emerged, the mystery began to consume our lives. Other than validating the existence of the cross, however, going to Hendaye and researching its history left us with few clues. The cross itself seemed to have almost no history, and other than Fulcanelli and Boucher, it is unremarked upon.

But it does exist. And the symbols on it are just as Fulcanelli described. Could the cross at Hendaye really be a monument to the double catastrophe that will "try the northern hemisphere with fire," as Fulcanelli insists?

That blustery spring morning standing in front of the cross, we decided that it brought into focus five categories of questions that must be answered in order to evaluate its message. These are:

1. Is Fulcanelli telling the truth? Is there any connection, in history or tradition, between alchemy and such Gnostic eschatologies as chiliasm? And if there is a connection, how has it been maintained through the centuries? Is the secret really displayed on the walls of certain Gothic cathedrals?
2. What does Fulcanelli have to say about alchemy and the cross at Hendaye? Does that information shed any light on the connection between alchemy and eschatology?
3. What do the symbolic images and ciphers on the cross mean? How are they "the rarest symbolic translation" of an apocalyptic philosophy? And, most important of all, do they suggest a date?
4. Is there any scientific evidence to support the idea of what Fulcanelli called the "double catastrophe"? And does that evidence also suggest any insight into alchemy?
5. If this catastrophe is cyclical, what happened the last time? Can we find any proof?

Standing in front of the cross at Hendaye that day, we realized the importance of having answers to these questions. We needed information, solid facts, to resolve the mystery. We never suspected that once we had laid bare the meaning of Fulcanelli and the cross, the real work would begin.

As we found answers, both expected and unexpected, to our list of questions, we found that our subject was expanding, also in ways both expected and unexpected. We agreed that we would focus first on the meaning of the Hendaye chapter and of the monument itself. The history of alchemy would have to be included, we thought, but only to support Hendaye's message. We had no intention of attempting to unravel the ultimate mystery of alchemy itself, much less carry out an exhaustive examination of the contents of *Le Mystère des cathédrales* and *Dwellings of the Philosophers*. We simply wanted to know if the things Fulcanelli reported in the Hendaye chapter were true.

Now, after years of intensive research, we can definitively state that not only is the information in "The Cyclic Cross of Hendaye" true but that it also demonstrates a sophisticated knowledge of galactic mechanics, something that Fulcanelli would have been hard-pressed to come by in the 1920s, but even more so the designer of the cross itself, working back in 1680. The implications of this are staggering.

TWO

THE SECRET OF ALCHEMY

THE ALCHEMICAL MEME AND SECRET SOCIETIES

At the heart of the alchemical mystery lies a secret. This is no ordinary secret, however, for it is that which cannot be told, the experience of gnosis. Ultimately, this inexplicable knowing cannot be conferred or taught in any ordinary manner, only incubated and gestated through a mysterious process known as initiation. This initiation can come in a number of ways, usually through someone who already knows, but occasionally it occurs by means of sacred texts and direct insight.

The alchemical gnosis has been transmitted from generation to generation, through thousands of years. We find the same content in experiences of gnosis from the modern *samyama* experiments at Maharishi University to the ancient Egyptians.[1] We find the same content in spontaneous experiences from mystics of all eras. The secret at the core of alchemy is an ineffable experience of the real workings of our local cosmological neighborhood.

So how can one incubate and gestate such an experience? The answer may lie in the word *transmitted*. Modern sociologists have begun to discuss the concept of *memes*, or complex idea groups—such as monotheism and democracy—that appear to have the ability to replicate themselves. Memes seem to have other properties as well, such as an unusual psychic component. The spread of Spiritualism in the nineteenth century is a superb example of a viral-like meme outbreak, and traces of Spiritualism's meme can be found surviving into the New Age nineties, with its dolphin channeling and near-death experiences. Hollywood films such as *The Sixth Sense* are deeply influenced by

41

Spiritualism's perspective on the afterlife, conveying the meme directly and powerfully to millions of moviegoers.

It helps to think of the secret at the core of alchemy as a very special and sophisticated variety of meme. Like a spore or a seed, the meme has a protective shell that is also attractive to appropriate hosts. In the case of the alchemy meme, that shell is the seductive allure of the transmutation of base metal into gold. Even if one absorbs the outer shell of the alchemy meme, however, there is no guarantee that the inner core will blossom and the meme become active. For that to happen, a series of shocks or initiations is required.

The sophistication of the alchemy meme is such that the experience of gnosis at its core can be stimulated only by these shocks. Therefore, to transmit the idea complex of the gnosis meme through time requires a series of encounters between those in whom the meme is active and those who have merely been exposed to it. From this need evolved the idea of priesthoods and then, as religious structures degenerated, mystery schools and secret societies. We can think of these as incubation devices for spiritual memes.

Through the millennia, the undigested seed of the alchemy meme was jumbled together with other spiritual memes, creating a seemingly endless series of hybrid spiritual expressions masquerading as alchemy. From its appearance in first-century Alexandria to its modern expressions, however, the secret at the core of the alchemy meme can be traced by its gnostic ineffableness. The secret protects itself, but in doing so leaves an unmistakable fingerprint. By following these gnostic fingerprints, we can track the progress of the alchemy meme through history.

EGYPT: ISIS AND HORUS

The word *alchemy,* as a name for the substance of the mystery, is both revealing and concealing of the true, initiatory nature of the work. *Al-khem,* Arabic for "the black," refers to the darkness of the unconscious, the most *prima* of all *materia,* and to the "Black Land" of Egypt. Thus, the name reveals the starting point of the process and the place where this science attained its fullest expression. This revelation, however, important as it is, effectively conceals the nature of the transmutation at the heart of the great work.

For three thousand years or more Egypt was the heart of the world. Much of the knowledge that is the underpinning of Western civilization had its origins in Egypt. The lenses of Greek and Judeo-Christian "history" distort our modern, essentially European, view of the ancient world. The Bible gives us an Egypt of powerful pharaohs and pagan magicians, mighty armies, slaves, and invasions of chariots out of the south. Herodotus gives us a travelogue, complete with inventive stories from his guides. To the Hebrews of the Old Testament, Egypt was the evil of the world from which God had saved them. To the Greeks, it was an ancient culture to be pillaged for ideas and information. To understand the origin of alchemy, we must let go of the Hebraic and Greek bias and look clearly at what the remains of the ancient Egyptian culture can tell us.

When we do this, two things immediately jump out at us. First, the ancient Egyptians were the most scientifically advanced culture on the planet until the present day, if we have indeed caught up with them; and second, their science—in fact, their entire culture—seems to be have been revealed rather than developed. The Egyptians claimed that their knowledge was derived from the actions of divine forces in what they called the First Time, or Zep Tepi. A group known as the Heru Shemsu, or the Company of Horus—also called the Company of the Wise, the Companions of Horus, and the Followers of the Widow's Son (fig. 2.1)—passed down a body of knowledge through the ages. Each pharaoh, down to Roman times, was an initiate of the Company of Horus and thus privy to this secret knowledge.

We can think of this secret knowledge as the core of "alchemy" in its broadest sense. But as we look closer at what the Egyptians tell us about their science, we find that it is based on an intimate understanding of astronomy. We also find that it is coded into many of Egypt's

Figure 2.1. The Heru Shemsu, or Company of Horus.

ancient monuments. These monuments, such as the Sphinx and its temple, point to an even more ancient civilization from which the Egyptians recovered their knowledge. In that sense, the knowledge of the Egyptians, of which alchemy is a half-remembered fragment, is the lost science of the last evolutionary epoch. But if this is true, what happened to end this epoch?

In legends and in Plato's dialogues we find a name for this advanced civilization that was destroyed in a great disaster more than 12,000 years ago. The Egyptians told Solon of Athens that the ancient culture was named Atlantis. Little did we know, as we embarked on the search for Fulcanelli and the secret of the Hendaye cross, that the trail would eventually lead us to a place high in the Andes that just might be Plato's Atlantis.

One of the earliest of all alchemical manuscripts is the fragmentary "Isis the Prophetess to Her Son Horus," found in the Codex Marcianus, a medieval collection of Greek texts. This work seems to be a unique blend of Hebrew mysticism and Egyptian mythology that could only have come from Alexandria early in the first century C.E. In this seminal text, the Egyptian goddess Isis tells her son, Horus, that while he was away fighting and defeating the evil one, Seth, she was in Hermopolis studying angelic magic and alchemy. She relates that "after a certain passing of the kairoi and the necessary movement of the heavenly sphere, it happened that one of the angels who dwelt in the first firmament saw me from above."[2] The angel is enflamed by sexual passion for Isis, but he can't answer her questions about alchemy. He bargains on another encounter by offering to bring a higher angel who will tell her everything she wants to know. The first angel shows Isis the magical sign of the higher angel. This sign consists of a bowl of shining water and a moon symbol that resembles the emblem of the moon god Khonsu of Thebes.

At noon the next day, the angel returns with the higher angel, who is called Amnael. This higher angel also finds Isis desirable and is willing to trade information. He reveals the mystery of his sign and then swears her to an oath. In this oath, we find echoes of the great mystery and one of the keys to its explication: "I conjure you in the name of Fire, of Water, of Air, and of the Earth; I conjure you in the name of the Heights of Heaven and the Depths of Earth's Underworld; I conjure you in the name of Hermes and Anubis, the howling of Kerkoros and the

guardian dragon; I conjure you in the name of the boat and its ferryman, Acharontos; and I conjure you in the name of the three necessities
and the whip and the sword."

After this strange oath, Isis is told never to reveal the secret to anyone but her son, Horus, her closest friend. The knowledge will make
them one—as the knowledge has now made Isis and the angel one (fig.
2.2).

And then a curious thing occurs. When the mystery is revealed, it
seems strangely flat, as if something was left unsaid in the answer.
Horus is told by Isis to watch a peasant, who may or may not have been
the mythical boatman Acharontos. He is then given a lecture on "as you
sow, so shall you reap." Horus is told to realize that "this is the whole
creation and the whole process of coming into being, and know that a
man is only able to produce a man, and a lion a lion, and a dog a dog,
and if something happens contrary to nature, then it is a miracle and
cannot continue to exist, because nature enjoys nature and only nature
overcomes nature."[3]

Figure 2.2. Isis the prophetess.

Isis goes on to relate that she will now give Horus the secret of preparing certain "sands." She says: "One must stay with existing nature and the matter one has in hand in order to prepare things. Just as I said before, wheat creates wheat, a man begets a man and thus gold will harvest gold, like produces like. Now I have manifested the mystery to you."[4]

The instruction then passes to hands-on lab work in melting and preparing metals such as quicksilver, copper, lead, and gold. At the end of this lengthy preparation, Isis exclaims: "Now realize the mystery, my son, the drug, the elixir of the widow."[5]

What are we to make of this strange story, with its curiously flat revelations? Possibly our very earliest alchemical text presents us with the same problems and ambiguities that we shall find throughout the entire alchemical corpus. As we unravel alchemy's secret, we shall return to the story of Isis and the angel, the origin of alchemy. But first we need to follow the trail of those who held this information, the latter-day Heru Shemsu, or the Followers of the Widow's Son, Horus.

THE UNDERGROUND STREAM: FROM EGYPT TO THE MIDDLE AGES

According to Manetho, the second-century Egyptian historian, the Heru Shemsu were the predynastic rulers of Egypt. The Builder Texts at the Edfu temple in Egypt call them the Blacksmiths of Edfu. They declare that all human knowledge came from their endeavors. They invented the institution of kingship, and every pharaoh from Menes to the emperor Trajan ruled Egypt in their name. The winged disk was their symbol, and a special ceremony, "the Union of the Disk," was held once a year in every temple in Egypt to symbolize the union of the state with the source of Egyptian civilization.

A multivolume work would be needed to chronicle the record of the Heru Shemsu through three thousand years of Egyptian history. The thread of the Heru Shemsu is clearly interwoven with the basic themes of Egyptian culture and the lost science of alchemy. As the Builder Texts on the forecourt walls at the Edfu temple relate, the Companions or Initiates of Horus were the keepers of the secrets of the Zep Tepi. We can even think of Edfu itself as a kind of time capsule. It was the last major building project of ancient Egypt, finished almost four hundred years after Solon heard the legend of Atlantis, and was purposefully decommissioned and filled with sand in the second century B.C.E.

With the coming of the Roman Empire and then the Christian Church, the old religion and culture of the Heru Shemsu began to melt away. But it did not simply disappear, for it was absorbed into the spiritual fabric of the new, emerging religions, especially Gnosticism, Christianity, and, later, Islam. Christianity in particular was aided in its growth by its similarity to the Isis cult that preceded it. Alexandria, one of Alexander the Great's new cities, epitomized this new Egypt and became the center of learning in the late classical world. Alchemy, in its modern form, seems to have developed in its workshops and academies, as the Isis story from the Codex Marcianus shows us.

The author of "Isis the Prophetess" was probably an Alexandrian Greek who lived somewhere between 50 B.C.E. and 50 C.E. He was familiar with Hebrew and Persian myths concerning angels, and, in the text, he seems to have been trying to communicate something very specific, like a recipe. Undoubtedly, he considered himself one of the Followers of the Widow's Son, the Company of Horus.

In another century or so, parts of this myth would become a Christian metaphor. Jesus would be cast in the role of Horus and Mary in that of Isis. As we shall discover in chapter 3, the Christian version of the myth retained many nuggets of the alchemical tradition, particularly among those groups of Gnostics who insisted on direct mystical experience.

The Gnostic Christians of Egypt were a powerful force in the early Christian movement. It wasn't until the fourth century, when the Church became an organ of the Roman state, that Egyptian Gnostic forms were driven underground. Until then, Gnostic ideas traveled throughout the Roman Empire, reaching as far as southern France and the west coast of England. As Christianity became an organized orthodoxy, these earlier forms were persecuted and Gnostic ideas began to fade away.

This Coptic or Gnostic Christianity of Egypt tried to retain the inner core of the ancient Egyptian wisdom while discarding everything that did not fit a strictly Christian mold. It succeeded enormously well, creating an image of the essence of the mystery of alchemy in the symbol of the rose cross.

In the Old City of Cairo, originally the Roman fortress of Babylon to the southwest of Heliopolis, Coptic Christianity, and its Gnostic roots, survives to this day. Now a part of the sprawling metropolis of greater Cairo, which stretches from the Citadel to the Pyramids of Giza and from Matriyah, site of Heliopolis, to Helwan above Memphis, the Old City is a quaint escape into a medieval garden. Walled on three sides and bounded on the fourth by the vast Christian necropolis, the Old City is an island of piety and mysticism where it is possible to feel that it is the turn of the second century and not the twenty-first.

On the walls of the Coptic Museum in the Old City, one can trace the evolution of the rose cross through the first and second centuries. On one wall, a first-century gravestone from Luxor (fig. 2.3), which contains the combination of a chi-rho emblem and the ankh with the solar boat, sits next to ankh crosses that blossom into roses on the loop of the ankh (such as that shown in fig. 2.4b). By the second century, this had become the accepted rendering of the cross as a mystical symbol. In this we have a connection with the esoteric side of the Coptic tradition that managed to survive the shift to orthodoxy. These rose crosses traveled, along with Gnostic concepts, throughout the Empire.

We find them in fact in southern France, in the crypt of Saint Honoré at Arles, as Fulcanelli reminds us in his discussion of the ankh.[6]

Figure 2.3. The motif of the sacred boat is one that echoes Hendaye's moon face/boat. Note the chi-rho of Constantine's vision and the Saint Andrew's cross on the ship's mast. First-century C.E. gravestone found at Luxor. (Coptic Museum, Cairo)

As the ankh merges over time with the rose cross, the center of the ankh's loop assumes the image of galactic center, a blossoming rose, the Templar cross, the rose as a gnosis gnomon. A series of second-century altar fonts from Luxor, found on another wall of the Coptic Museum, reveals a thread of mystical architecture that unites both the Gothic cathedrals and the enigmatic sixteenth-century credence of the Lallemant mansion in Bourges, which Fulcanelli describes as a "temple in miniature."[7]

Our first font (fig. 2.5), from the early second century, shows a scallop-shell arch supported by two trees, each with twenty-two leaves

B

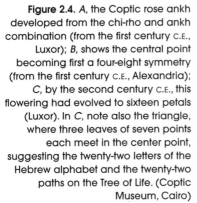

Figure 2.4. *A*, the Coptic rose ankh developed from the chi-rho and ankh combination (from the first century C.E., Luxor); *B*, shows the central point becoming first a four-eight symmetry (from the first century C.E., Alexandria); *C*, by the second century C.E., this flowering had evolved to sixteen petals (Luxor). In *C*, note also the triangle, where three leaves of seven points each meet in the center point, suggesting the twenty-two letters of the Hebrew alphabet and the twenty-two paths on the Tree of Life. (Coptic Museum, Cairo)

C

between, which stands a Coptic ankh with an eight-petaled rose in the loop. The basic simplicity of its symbolism, as we shall see, survived for over twelve hundred years. A late-second-century font (see fig. 2.6) repeats the basic motif and then expands on it to give us an almost complete vocabulary of the mystery.

In the center is our arch and scallop shell now supported by pillars rather than trees. Replacing the rose-cross ankh in the center of the arch is an equal-armed cross with an upside-down alpha and omega in the field beneath the transverse arms. On either side of the arch is an ankh with novel elements added. The loop of each ankh contains a five-petaled rose, while equal-armed crosses stand on the top of the elongated side bars, the bottoms of which end in a five-sided leaf shape. At the top of the ankh's loop is a small triangle, or tetrahedron. Hanging from the outer edge of the arch are two bunches of grapes (See fig. 2.6).

While a complete explication of this altar font would take us too far ahead of our story, let us note some of the symbolic connections. The arch is found on the facades of the Gothic cathedrals, and is mimicked by the credence in the Lallemant mansion that is discussed by Fulcanelli. The five-petaled rose is also found at Lallemant in the

Figure 2.5. This second-century c.e. Coptic altar font, from Luxor, develops the symbolism and numerology from the gravestone shown in fig. 2.4C. Note the twenty-two leaves on each Tree of Life holding the arch. (Coptic Museum, Cairo)

Figure 2.6. A complex symbolic altar font from second-century c.e. Alexandria that suggests much of the imagery and secrets of alchemy. (Coptic Museum, Cairo)

fifteenth-century stained glass above the altar. The *A* of the inverted alpha matches the *A*'s on the Hendaye monument. By the early third century, as shown in the altar font in figure 2.7, the inner mystery has become more abstract and orthodox. Instead of a flowering rose-cross ankh, we now find a cubic cross in the place of our Tree of Life. Soon this image would become the chi-rho of imperial Christianity.

Figure 2.7. Altar font from early-third-century c.e. Luxor with the chi-rho and the inverted alpha and omega. (Coptic Museum, Cairo)

As the Roman Empire fell apart in the fifth and sixth centuries, the various underground groups of Gnostic Christians were left stranded. Even though the Gnostic centers of Alexandria and the East lost touch with the West, the Western Gnostic groups retained the symbol of the rose ankh, and over time this developed into the rose cross, the defining symbol of the underground stream of European esotericism. Fulcanelli's hint about the rose-ankh sarcophagus lid in Saint-Honoré at Arles points us directly to the mid-first-century Christianity of Provence, and indirectly to the origin of the legends surrounding the Holy Grail.

In the seventh century, while Europe was still in the Dark Ages, the breeze from Arabia, the new force of Islam, arrived on the scene. Arab scholars discovered the Greek knowledge that had been long since lost to the West. Jabir, the Arab philosopher of the eighth century, collected the ancient alchemical wisdom into a volume that became the cornerstone of all future alchemical research. The Islamic Sufi alchemists of the tenth and eleventh centuries collaborated with the Jewish kabbalists of Spain and reestablished medicine and philosophy.

Drawing on these sources, Gerbert of Aurillac, who studied in Spain and would eventually become Pope Sylvester II, set in motion a series of events that would result a few centuries later in the Crusades, the persecution of the Cathars, and the Gothic Renaissance. Those books in stone, the facades of the great cathedrals, encapsulate Gnostic eschatology and hermetic philosophy dressed superficially in Christian myth as did the second-century altar fonts of Luxor.

By the time of the Crusades, the Arabs were far ahead of the West. A few of the Christian Crusaders, including Pope Sylvester's Chroniclers, were smart enough to know this and learned all they could from Arab culture. Part of what they learned was the secret knowledge. The Knights Templar, the military arm of the Order of Our Lady of Mount Zion, became by the thirteenth century the main guardians of that knowledge.

When the Templars were destroyed in the early fourteenth century, the secret was fragmented almost beyond repair. By the time the Rosicrucians appeared in the early seventeenth century, alchemy, although still somewhat suspect in the common mind, had been accepted by the new scientific elite. In the next one hundred years, alchemy became chemistry and the secret knowledge became the property of the Rosicrucians, the Freemasons, and the occultists.

THE UNDERGROUND STREAM: FROM THE BLACK DEATH TO FULCANELLI

Dr. W. Wynn Westcott, the medical examiner for the City of London from 1887 to 1898, was a Freemason, an advanced Rosicrucian adept, and one of the founders of the hermetic Order of the Golden Dawn, nineteenth-century England's most notable occult organization. He tells us in an 1890 lecture on alchemy that "it is never taught in so many words. It may dawn on any one of you—the magic event may occur when least expected," thereby demonstrating that he at least understood that there was a gnostic secret at the core of alchemy.[8]

Westcott may be taken as something of an authority. He was steeped in Rosicrucian and Freemasonic ideas, and, in helping to found the Golden Dawn, clearly felt he was part of some larger pattern or process.[9] His "flying roll" lecture is therefore of more than passing interest. It was given early in the organization's history and was presented to the group at large. We can think of it as a preaching-to-the-choir type of exposition of the basic Rosicrucian alchemical tradition.

The lecture opens with the assertion that alchemy means simply "the Higher Chemistry," which treats of "the essential nature of the Elements, metals and minerals." This is a good and direct explanation for the ancient term *alchemy* that avoids the pitfalls of speculative philology, even if it is otherwise unremarkable. The secret protects itself, but it is safe to say that this strange lecture provides an important cluster of clues and impressions with which to understand how the secret survived from the Templars to Fulcanelli.[10]

Westcott quotes from an old French description of the sequence of the alchemical process. "The Sun begins his special form of change in Leo in his own house . . . next Scorpio follows and the Work reaches completion in Sagittarius." To make sure that we understand, Westcott insists at the close of his lecture: "to perform Alchemical processes requires a simultaneous operation on the astral plane with that of the physical. Unless you are Adept enough to act by Will power, as well as by heat and moisture; life forces as well as electricity, there will be no adequate result."[11]

The source for this secret would seem to be the Rosicrucian and Freemasonic movements, which had swirled around Europe since the early seventeenth century. The late-nineteenth-century hermetic Order of the Golden Dawn was a direct descendant of these seventeenth-century secret societies responsible for incubating the alchemical meme.

Beginning in the fourteenth century, the Black Death ravaged Europe every generation or so until the late seventeenth century.[12] As Western Europe strained to deal with these outbreaks, the holders of the secret fragmented even more. At the turn of the fourteenth and fifteenth centuries, rumors circulated of individual alchemists, most notable among them Nicolas Flamel, and thus began an age of mysterious strangers dispensing alchemical wonders and then fading away into the night.

Part of the secret, in those troubled times, went underground into chivalric orders funded and organized by some of the leading families of Europe. The court of King René of Anjou in the mid-fifteenth century became a magnet for the lost fragments of the tradition. King René founded an Order of the Crescent based on the mysterious martyrdom of Saint Maurice and the Theban Legion, which grew into an underground stream of esotericism. The alchemical group in Bourges, as shown by the decorations in the Lallemant mansion, was active during King René's era and made history with the trial of Jacques Coeur, alchemist and royal treasurer accused of treason. This portion of the underground stream influenced the ruling families of Milan and Florence, sparking the Italian Renaissance and inspiring geniuses such as Leonardo da Vinci, Niccolò Machiavelli, and Sandro Botticelli.

Out of these sources, and because of the new freedom found in the collapse of the imperial Church's intellectual stranglehold and the rise of Protestant dissent, emerged an "invisible college" of esoteric thinkers and scientific research. By the turn of the seventeenth century, the times seemed to be ready for a more public emergence of the secret.[13]

In 1614, a publicly printed text appeared of an anonymous manuscript that had been circulating among Europe's intelligentsia for several years. It was called "The Declaration of the Worthy Order of the Rosy Cross." Known by its first two Latin words, *Fama Fraternitatis,* it revealed the purported existence of a brotherhood founded by one Christian Rosenkreuz, who apparently lived in the fourteenth and fifteenth centuries.

In the seventeenth century the word *philosopher* was synonymous with *alchemist*. Here, with a vengeance, was a "new sect of Philosophers." The *Fama Fraternitatis* tells us of the search for occult knowledge by a man called Christian Rosenkreuz. He traveled to the Middle East—Palestine, Syria, Egypt, and North Africa—and Spain before returning to Germany to found his secret brotherhood. One hundred and twenty years after Christian Rosenkreuz's death at the advanced age of 106, one of the brethren discovered his tomb and his uncorrupted body. This was the signal for the Brotherhood to emerge and spread their message, hence the publication of the *Fama Fraternitatis*.

Their message, of course, was nothing less than the dawn of a new Golden Age. The *Fama Fraternitatis* informs us that the Brotherhood possessed the keys to a secret knowledge capable of transforming society and ushering in a new era, one in which "the world shall awake out of her heavy and drowsy sleep, and with an open heart, bare-headed and bare-footed, shall merrily and joyfully meet the new arising Sun."[14] This quote is taken from the next Rosicrucian production, the *Confessio Fraternitatis,* a restatement of the basic themes but with a more direct emphasis on its revolutionary implications. It also goes to the essence of the alchemical mystery.

The Rosicrucians were alchemists, but the *Fama* and the *Confessio* are both highly critical of the "puffer" type of alchemical worker who sits in his lab and actually attempts to get the mineral gold out of boiling lead. The *Fama Fraternitatis* talks of "ungodly and accursed gold-making, whereby under the colour of it many runagates and roguish people do use great villainies, and cozen and abuse the credit which is given them."[15] The *Fama Fraternitatis* implies that the Rosicrucians could make gold but found the higher spiritual alchemy to be more important. Higher spiritual alchemy related to the coming Golden Age and how to prepare for it. That, seemingly, was the intent behind the publications of the first two Rosicrucian documents: to prepare the world for the new era that was dawning.

The third volume, however, was very different. The *Chymical Wedding of Christian Rosenkreuz* appeared in 1616 and is the only Rosicrucian document to be claimed by its author, Johann Valentin Andreae, a Protestant minister from Germany. The *Wedding* is full of occult imagery and surreal metaphors and describes Christian

Rosenkreuz's experiences as he observes a royal wedding.

Like many alchemical works, the *Wedding* is filled with ciphers and green language. No less a mind than Leibniz, who along with Newton invented calculus, solved one of the ciphers. In the *Wedding,* the king announces: "My name contains five and fifty, and yet hath only eight letters." Leibniz correctly unraveled one layer of this mystery by using a simple Latin gematria, where A = 1, B = 2, and so on, to arrive at the answer of ALCHIMIA.

The Chymical Wedding is an initiatory text, much like Fulcanelli's *Le Mystère des cathédrales,* which cannot be understood without the aid of an esoteric gloss. After this strange work, the original Rosicrucians fell silent. It is not known if they did indeed respond to any of the many thinkers, such as Leibniz, who sprang to their defense. We must assume that if they did, the secret was kept, because the movement continued.

Westcott's lecture serves as proof that Rosicrucian ideas retained their continuity through the centuries. This alone is impressive, but it is the continuity of content that strikes us most strongly. We can see continuity of symbolic content even in groups that lost the direct alchemical portion of the secret tradition. Foremost among these are the so-called Freemasons.

Freemasonry started in England in 1717 with the public announcement of the Four Lodges at the Apple Tree Tavern in London. Something like these "lodges" had existed for centuries as guilds. These Freemasons were different because they weren't actually working masons but rather middle-class members of a secret society gone public. They claimed Saint John as their patron as they founded their organization on June 24, Saint John's Day, in 1717. In the next twenty years, lodges were organized publicly all over the British Isles.

The movement spread to the Continent, even as far as Russia, but it took the oration of Chevalier Andrew Michael Ramsay, given at the Paris Grand Lodge on March 21, 1737, to put the new movement into perspective. According to Chevalier Ramsay, the Freemasons came not from the literal medieval guilds of cathedral builders but from the kings and nobles of the Crusades. They were not actual builders, but instead those who had taken vows to restore the Temple in Jerusalem. These "Templars" formed an intimate link with the Knights of Saint John of Jerusalem. The chevalier Ramsay also announced that the order was derived from the mysteries of Isis, Ceres, and Diana, an interesting claim in light of Fulcanelli's comments on Isis and the Black Madonnas of the Gothic cathedrals.

As we shall see in later chapters, Chevalier Ramsay was reflecting a real historical tradition, although dressed up in Jacobin finery and strengthened by rumors of secret masters. The Rosicrucian imitators had popularized the idea of hidden adepts, and the mysterious alchemists of the seventeenth century had given it new credence, but the Freemasons were the first to make it an article of faith.

The idea entered Freemasonry directly with the Strict Observance of Baron von Hund und Alten-Grotkau, who once met a mysterious grand master and was told to wait for further instructions. He waited for the rest of his life, but since the unknown grand master was actually Prince Charles Edward Stuart, the pretender to the throne of England whose cause was crippled forever at the Battle of Culloden Moor, we can understand the lapse. This Strict Observance to an "unknown master," however, would continue to influence Western occultism down to Theosophy and the Golden Dawn.

There is no doubt that some of Freemasonry's traditions and symbols were taken from the Templar tradition. The oration of the good chevalier demonstrates that clearly, but by the mid-eighteenth century the movement had discarded these components and become a political and social organization. The symbolism of the temple and the metaphors of the Masons who built it contained the kernel of the alchemical meme, but it is apparent from the lack of alchemical adepts among the Freemasons that the groups themselves did not have the initiatory shock necessary to activate the meme.

In the nineteenth and early twentieth centuries, the secret began to surface once again as advancing scholarship opened up more of the world and the past. Christianity had lost its appeal and its power, and in its place emerged a sort of primitive psychism—spontaneous and unorthodox psychic activity such as trances, visions, speaking in tongues, and so on—resulting in fundamental Christian sects at one extreme and Spiritualism, communication with spirits and the dead, on the other. By the late nineteenth century, Theosophy had revealed that the mysterious masters were to be found in the romantic East, first in Egypt and then in India.

Fulcanelli changed all of that. One of his main purposes in writing

Le Mystère was to reveal many of the inner secrets of the original underground stream and to recover the history of the entire Western tradition.

The cathedrals of France, especially Notre Dame of Paris, revealed that the tradition was alive and well in the twelfth century when the cathedrals were built. Fulcanelli goes one step further and reveals that the cathedrals are evidence of the full flowering of the Western esoteric tradition in the Middle Ages. This idea, and the proof offered by Fulcanelli, is what really excited the Parisian occultists of the late 1920s.

Fulcanelli revealed to all who could see that once there was a great and glorious tradition in Europe that rivaled the traditions of the East. This tradition understood and practiced the science of light, and this tradition understood how to communicate with the living spirit, or the intelligence, that lives inside matter. In no uncertain terms Fulcanelli reveals that the secret tradition of ancient "Freemasonry" is exactly the same, at its core, as the traditions of the East. Western culture dictated a different style of initiation and communication, however—one that was more active in nature and more scientific in outlook.

In 1926, that secret was about to be lost forever. If it hadn't been for Fulcanelli and his book, it is possible that the true nature of this initiatory tradition would have disappeared in the West, perhaps never to be realized again. The shell of academic studies, and perhaps the isolated alchemist, might preserve the core of the meme like a spore, waiting for a riper moment to sprout again, but the living current would have died away. In many ways, *Le Mystère* is like a message in a bottle from the last adept, dropped on his way out in the hopes that someone might follow behind.

THE THREEFOLD TRANSFORMATION

But what is alchemy? So far we have traced a channel of transmission from the Company of the Widow's Son to the Rosicrucians and Freemasons of the eighteenth and nineteenth centuries. The question then becomes: What were they transmitting?

The "Isis the Prophetess" fragment is in many ways the origin point of alchemy in its modern sense. It is the first text in which mysticism becomes confused with some type of laboratory procedures. In the text, though, it is clear that Isis first imparts a philosophical understanding, and then she conducts a physical operation, supposedly along with Horus, in order to demonstrate the principle and illustrate her mastery of the process of transmutation. We might even think of this as the alchemical method: revelation, demonstration, and transmutation. The key, then, becomes the source of the revelation; where is the information coming from?

In the Isis fragment, the knowledge comes from a higher order of angel, implying that the higher realm from which it comes is at least at a planetary level. The higher angel Amnael who instructs Isis bears the signs of Nut and Khonsu (fig. 2.8) and appears nowhere else in Hebrew angelology. There is a faint resemblance to the name of the angel of Venus, Hanael or Anael, but this line of conjecture quickly comes to a dead end, for if Isis is the morning star, is she learning from herself? It doesn't seem possible.

An easier solution is to take the name as it is, Amn-el, or the angel of Amon. Amon's name means "the hidden one," and Amon-Re is the name of the sun god of Egypt. This meaning makes sense within the

Figure 2.8. Amnael is a complex angelic being combining aspects of the sun, moon, and stars, here the Egyptian Khonsu, Amon, and Nut. (Drawing by Darlene from images on the Karnak Temple at Luxor)

fragment's Egyptian background, and the angel's name provides us with another deity to complete the divine triad of ancient Thebes. Thus, Isis learned the secrets of alchemy from a complex angelic being who combined the aspects of the star (the sky goddess, Nut), the moon (Khonsu), and the sun, Amon-Re. We have already seen this trio on the pedestal of the Hendaye cross.

The Hebrew spelling of Amnael's name gives us a clue to the nature of its composite being. Using Hebrew *gematria,* the letters in the name add up to 123, the number of the three-part name of God, AHH YHVH ELOHIM. As shown in figure 2.9, these three names are also associated with the top three *sefirot* on the Tree of Life—Kether, Chokmah, and Binah. If we break the name into *Amn* and *ael,* we get the numbers 91 and 32. These are both references to the Tree of Life as a whole; 32 is the total number of paths and *sefirot* on the Tree and 91 is the number of the Hebrew word *amen,* AMN, and the word for "tree," AYLN.

The angel Amnael, a composite being, can be seen as the sum of all the knowledge in the revealed tradition. But before the angel will share the secret of alchemy with Isis, it swears her to a great oath. The first part of the oath illustrates the creation of the Cube of Space. As we

Figure 2.9 The three-part name of God corresponds to the top three *sefirot* on the Tree of Life.

shall see, in ancient and occult sources the Cube of Space serves as a matrix for reality by organizing, geometrically, the twenty-two letters of the Hebrew alphabet. And then the great angel says: "I conjure you in the name of Hermes and Anubis, the howling of Kerkoros and the guardian dragon; I conjure you in the name of the boat and its ferryman, Acharontos; and I conjure you in the name of the three necessities and the whip and the sword."[16]

Hermes and Anubis are plain enough. Hermes is Thoth, or Tehuti, the god of science and magic, and Anubis is the jackal-headed god associated with death and funereal rites. These two are also the gods who preside over the act of judgment at the end of the world. The "howling of Kerkoros" suggests the Keres, the dog-faced Furies of Demeter, the Valkyries of Greek myth. *Ker* is "fear" or "malice" and *koros* can be rendered as "cross." This means that the oath is conjured by the "evil cross" and the "guardian dragon." The boat and ferryman are the vehicle and the guide, respectively, and "the three necessities," along with the whip and the sword, suggest Masonic initiations. The whip is one of the royal scepters, the *nekhakha,* which, according to Schwaller du Lubicz in his *Sacred Science,* is an alchemical symbol for the three-part stream of being.[17]

After this oath, or initiation, the great being tells Isis the secret: "Only Nature can overcome Nature." Isis later demonstrates this to Horus by means of a physical process. The transmutation is successful, and she produces "the drug, the elixir of the widow." From this, the pattern of revelation, demonstration, and transmutation, we can determine that the alchemical secret is threefold or, rather, that there are three transformations in one. The inner transmutation, revelation, involves the refining of the cerebrospinal energies and fluids so that more light may be absorbed and transmitted to the DNA. In the Isis fragment this is symbolized by the sexual component. The outer transmutation, the demonstration, is the ability to use those energies to effect transmutations of physical states, including the elements. The third transmutation is that of the quality of time itself, from the darkness of the Iron Age to the splendor of the Golden Age. Remember that Isis could not begin the process until the stars were in the proper place; time and timing are all important. All three transmutations are aspects of the same process, "as above so below," as the Emerald Tablet puts it, and are interconnected by the metaphor of "light."

TRANSFORMATIONS AND TRANSCENDENCE

We are now prepared to see the nature of the transmutation at the core of alchemy. It is not only a transmutation involving a personal or local effect to our environment, but it is also global and universal, involving the nature and quality of time, and the times, in a unique way. Our earliest alchemical text confirms this perspective. A big part of the secret involved time, not just the timing of astrology, but time in the cosmological sense

As the alchemical meme was passed down through the centuries by various secret societies, such as the Company of the Widow's Son, the information fragmented. In this way, some initiates received only the internal and transformational processes without a full understanding of how the parts related to the whole of the ancient science. This lack of a cosmological component meant that what success was attained happened apparently randomly and without any guarantee of repeatability. The most guarded secret was that of time itself and its secret qualities. The secret of all secrets involved an experience of gnosis that included the beginning and end of "time." It is this revelation, this transformative insight, that is demonstrated in the act of transmutation.

Alchemy, the art of transmutation, is based on an understanding of the unified field of matter, energy, and information involving an interlocking series of transformations that demonstrates the identity of these three components of the field. The key to these transformations is the ability to communicate—that is, exchange information—directly with matter. The mechanism of this communication is the phenomenon of photon emission and absorption. Light, particularly coherent light, can cause chemical reactions, and on the organic level it can cause profound effects, such as the process of photosynthesis, where the energy of light is used to build proteins and sugars.

For the last twenty years, various molecular biologists have proposed and experimentally demonstrated that all living cells emit a very weak photon pulse generated by each cell's DNA. This pulse is regular enough to be considered a form of coherent light, and some researchers have speculated that bio-photon activity is a form of language, a medium of communication. Fritz-Albert Popp and Mae-Wan Ho speculated in a 1993 paper that this phenomenon "points to the existence of [an] amplifying mechanism in the organisms receiving the information [and acting on it]. Specifically, the living system itself must also be organized by intrinsic electromagnetic fields, capable of receiving, amplifying and possibly transmitting electromagnetic information in a wide range of frequencies."[18]

This idea is similar to the notion of morphogenetic fields first elucidated by biologist Rupert Sheldrake. According to Sheldrake, biological entities have a memory that forms a field surrounding each entity. This field acts as a blueprint for both the species and the individual's development, and is sensitive to actions at a distance through both space and time. One aspect of alchemy might be the ability to communicate with another entity's morphogenetic field. The alchemists believed that minerals were also living entities and therefore they too had auras, or souls, that act much like morphogenetic fields.

Such transformational communication was achieved in various ways depending on the understanding of the operator. Success in creating the "philosopher's stone" guaranteed success in the whole process. But the "Stone of the Wise" was not the end result of the alchemical process; it was merely a tool, or instrument, required to achieve completion of the process.

The *prima materia* was likewise not just any matter, but matter that had been enlivened enough so that it could retain the charge of memory required to effect transformation. When this *prima materia,* this enlivened matter, is programmed or charged by a communication from the philosopher's stone, it becomes capable of producing a transmutation when activated. This transmutation, on one level, appears to be a geometric rearrangement of the elemental structure of the substance upon which it is acting. The geometrical arrangement that makes a substance lead is transmuted by a morphogenetic communication from the alchemist's philosopher's stone into the geometrical arrangement that makes it gold.

Could the alchemy of cosmological time be a geometrical arrangement of planets and alignments to the fixed stars? The book *Cymatics,* by Hans Jenny, demonstrates the concept of how natural structures can be created and changed by the wave patterns of sound. Jenny placed fine powder on a piece of material that was suspended in front of a stereo speaker. The videotape of the experiments shows that the powder forms itself into different and intricate geometrical shapes based on the volume and pitch of a sound. When Jenny changed the frequencies, the powders magically re-formed themselves into other geometric patterns. Interestingly enough, Jenny found that there is an "in-between" state where the geometrical figure is reduced to chaos before it forms into a new pattern.

But this is only one level of transformation in the alchemical series. There is also the transformation of the alchemist as the body's matter absorbs the energy/information of the transmutation. Absorbing the light given off by a transmutation may have a direct effect on the operator's DNA through the long sequences of nongenetic coding it contains. This so called junk DNA, which constitutes the majority of our genetic code, is divided between introns and extrons. From the research done so far, it appears that the extrons are very good laser pulsers, giving off a weak burst of coherent light several times a second. Introns seem to be reading incoming light, even on the skin, and adjusting indirectly various internal processes, such as the circadian rhythms. Indeed, changes within the operator are necessary to produce both the *prima materia* and the "stone." In other words, both the alchemist and his *prima materia* are altered by the experiment.[19]

These are not the only transmutations involved. There are changes in the fabric of space-time itself as the elemental structure is collapsed and fused into a new geometrical configuration. These changes also affect society and the human condition, promising a new Golden Age. At the heart of the secret is the possibility of planetary transmutation. The final secret of alchemy lies in an approaching moment of planetary crisis that is—perhaps—as Fulcanelli said, the end of the world.

PART TWO

Eschatology and Astronomy

Finally, in the Ave Regina, *the Virgin is properly called the* root (salve radix) *to show that she is the principle and the beginning of all things. "Hail, root by which the Light has shone on the world."*

In this connection, Notre Dame of Paris, the Philosophers' church, is indisputably one of the most perfect specimens and, as Victor Hugo said, "the most satisfying summary of the hermetic science . . ."

—Le Mystère des Cathédrales

THREE

GNOSTIC ESCHATOLOGY

THE GNOSTIC RETURN: ISIS AND MARY THE ALCHEMIST

In what is perhaps our earliest alchemical text, "Isis the Prophetess," we find a glimpse of an ancient science. At the core of this science is something we can recognize as alchemy, which emerged from the intellectual and spiritual ferment of Alexandria in the first three centuries of the modern era.[1] As it developed, it became part of the spiritual tradition of Gnostic, as opposed to orthodox and apostolic, Christianity.

The word *gnostic* comes from the Greek word *gnosis,* which means "knowledge." In a spiritual sense, gnosis implies a direct mystical experience of the divine, and such experiences were the province of many mystery religions. Indeed, early Christianity first appeared as a type of Hebrew mystery school. The Hebrew reputation in the classical world for possessing magical powers helped fuel Christianity's expansion. In Egypt, Christianity was accepted as another form of the old Isis/Horus religious meme that swept through the ancient world two thousand years ago.

As we saw in the "Isis the Prophetess" fragment, Gnostic ideas, alchemy among them, developed contemporaneously with Christianity. The earliest version of the Emerald Tablet, the brief second-century B.C.E. textbook of magic and alchemy (see appendix B), was found buried with its anonymous owner at Thebes, in upper Egypt. It is a fragment of a basically "Gnostic" magical text. Alchemy represents a specific perspective on the ancient creative science, that of the triple transmutation. In its broadest sense, Gnosticism represents the worldview that allows these transformations to occur.

Alchemy texts of all eras show that time and timing are crucially important components in the alchemical process, but they do not openly link alchemy and eschatology, the end of the world. The link is there, provided as subtext, by the Gnostic framework from which the idea of alchemy emerged. Only Fulcanelli revealed the secret: The old Gnostics were alchemists, and the alchemists have always been Gnostics.

At the core of Gnosticism lies a vision of the end of the world. Even before Christianity supplied it with a brand-new mythos, Gnosticism had developed its own unique eschatological flavor. In a sense, like modern Christian fundamentalists, the Gnostics yearned for the end of this world.

Almost every culture has some kind of catastrophe myth. Tracing these myths and stories, one finds similar motifs of cataclysm in such different cultures as Inuit Siberia, Aboriginal Australia, Druid Ireland, and the Shumash tribes in North America. In many traditions, the disaster represents the fall from a Golden Age; in a few, the disaster represents the punishment by God for mankind's evil ways. Gnosticism's peculiar blend of Persian Zoroastrianism, Hebrew eschatology, and Egyptian cosmology with Greek philosophical methods can be seen as an attempt to synthesize all the ancient catastrophe perspectives into an apocalyptic unity.

While keeping in mind that the label "Gnosticism" covers an enormous number of different and often contradictory belief systems, it is possible to sort through its spiritual kaleidoscope and arrive at an overview of a basic Gnostic cosmology at the core of the meme. Gnosticism's main tenets contain both good and evil gods, and its basic approach is radically dualistic. The real force driving Gnostic philosophy was its sophisticated and experiential vision of the end of the world.[2]

According to the Gnostic myth, at the creation of the world the spirit of Light was imprisoned by the powers of Darkness. This light, the essence of God, was trapped in human bodies as separate sparks of light, our souls. Gnostic sects held that the goal of human existence was to travel the path of return, the journey of the individual sparks back to union with the original Light through the process of redemption. According to the Gnostics, this world and its history are the works of the evil Demiurge. This is the false god, or the evil one, who built this world as a trap for souls, or the light.

As each soul is redeemed, it travels back to the source of the divine Light, which slowly, as more and more souls return to it, becomes whole again. Eventually, when all souls have returned, the physical universe, being now completely without Light, will end. Given modern biology's understanding of the light-emitting and information-carrying ability of DNA, and such a system's implication for the kind of holographic reality described by the Gnostics, such an eschatology of light gains a new and more "scientific" meaning. In this sense, we can think of DNA as the small fragments of the hologram, containing the information of the whole but constrained by matter, which it must animate in order to return to the Great Light.

Therefore, this "eschatology of Light" synthesized from Egyptian, Persian, and Hebrew elements can be seen as the framework supporting a variety of Gnostic traditions. These traditions included the new messianic form of Judaism that became Christianity.

Indeed, the Gnostic sects quite naturally believed that they possessed the true meaning of Christ's teachings. Most of them did not believe in a literal Jesus, born of flesh and blood that suffered and died. To the Gnostics, Jesus was a divine messenger or an angelic being disguised as a man. He was sent to reveal the secret knowledge of the path of return, the way out of this world of darkness. In this view, Christ's return will be not physical, but spiritual. The Resurrection becomes a metaphor for the experience of a spiritual triumph over death, and therefore available to everyone.

The Gnostic insistence on a direct experience of salvation, a personal return to the Light, contrasted sharply with the emerging orthodox position that held that only the apostles, to whom Jesus appeared after the Resurrection, could hold and transmit spiritual authority. The Gnostics raised the ante, so to speak, by adopting Mary Magdalene as a kind of super-apostle.

In the Gnostics' view, Mary Magdalene, the sister of Martha and Lazarus, was Jesus' wife. She was also the first witness to the Resurrection. The Gnostics also thought of Mary Magdalene as a source of the secret mysteries. Many of the Gnostic sects held that Mary—mother, wife, and sister of the god-man—was simply Isis, the Queen of Heaven. In *Le Mystère*, Fulcanelli draws our attention to this point when he informs us in no uncertain terms that the Black Madonnas in the crypts of the great Gothic cathedrals are representations of the goddess Isis. This symbol forms the most significant link from Christianity to ancient Egypt.[3]

As with the mysteries of Isis, early Christianity and alchemy were dominated by women. The most important of all the early female alchemists was Cleopatra, author of the classical text *Chrysopeia,* or "Gold Making." In this work, collected with the "Isis the Prophetess" story in the eleventh-century Codex Marcianus, we find the earliest image of the Ouroboros serpent, biting its own tail (fig. 3.1). This symbol of the cosmic cycle is half black and half white and encloses a Greek phrase that says "The sum of all philosophy."

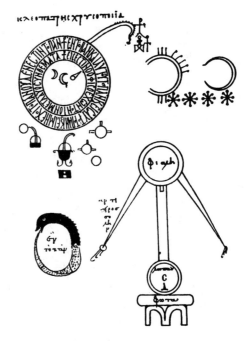

Figure 3.1. Page from the Codex Marcianus showing both the Ouroboros and eight-rayed stars.

Indeed, given what we now know of the importance of DNA in this theology of light, the serpent biting its own tail is a powerful metaphor, a symbolic image of DNA that, according to anthropologist Jeremy Narby, is produced by the "forest television" flow of images coming from the DNA itself.[4] On the same manuscript page in the Codex Marcianus, under a serpentlike crescent moon, we find a line of eight-rayed stars. This image of the star is similar to the Gnostic ogdoad, a grouping of the celestial forces—the ancient Egyptian Neters—in an eightfold pattern.

Reminiscent of both the ogdoad of Hermopolis, city of the god

Thoth, or Tehuti, and the Gnostic systems of Basilides and Valentinus, the eight-rayed star would also become the special symbol of Mary, mother of Jesus. To the Pythagoreans it symbolized the regeneration of the cosmos, being, as Eratosthenes declared, the "double polarity of the elements, producing a stability."[5] The seventeenth-century alchemist Basil Valentine (note the combination of Basilides and Valentinus in his name) claimed that the eight-rayed star symbolized the philosophic mercury and the completion of the first stage of the Great Work.

The New Testament is filled with Marys, which causes considerable confusion. There is Mary, Jesus' mother, and Mary, sister of Martha and Lazarus and first witness to the Resurrection, and Mary Magdalene, the woman at the well, and so on. Some of these Marys may in fact be the same person, as in the case of Mary of Bethany and Mary Magdalene. The Gnostics avoided the confusion by focusing on Mary Magdalene as the wife and closest confidante of Jesus. According to the Gospel of Mary, one of the Nag Hammadi texts discovered in 1947, Jesus taught her secrets that he failed to reveal to his apostles. Interestingly enough, several Gnostic sects, such as the Ophites, held that Mary Magdalene and the noted first-century alchemical author known as Mary the Jewess were one and the same individual (see fig. 3.2).

Whoever she was, Mary the Jewess was an accomplished practical alchemist and the inventor of a series of technical devices still in use today, such as the hot ash box for steady heat, the dung box for prolonged heat, and the double boiler (which the French still call a *bain-marie*). None of her writings has survived, but Zosimos and the other early compilers of alchemical texts quote her with the utmost respect. Zosimos considered her to be Miriam, the sister of Moses. He was, of course, as always, going for the most ancient tradition.[6]

It seems strange at first to think of Mary Magdalene as one of the founders of alchemy. Orthodox Christianity eventually became the only Christianity, obscuring much of the truth about the flowering of competing strains of Christianity in the first century. Behind that efflorescence, however, lay the Gnostic worldview, with its eschatology of light, offering a hope of return to the divine source. It would not be too far from the truth to say that orthodox Christianity was a political development designed to control access to that spiritual reality—in other words, that it was a construct of the Demiurge.

Figure 3.2. Ophite Gnosticism worshipped the snake as a divine principle of change and transformation. In this first-century Ophite gravestone from Alexandria, we see the snake entwined around a very phallic Djed pillar, or World Tree. (Coptic Museum, Cairo)

And yet, the more one studies the Gospels and the early Gnostic alchemical literature, the harder it is to deny that early Christianity was an expression of the same spiritual tradition. Christianity, once understood, becomes a vehicle for an alchemical transmutation that also involves the end of the world. Only in the Gospels, and in other early Christian texts, are the transformational processes of alchemy and eschatology portrayed as part of the same seamless whole.

THE ALCHEMICAL ESCHATOLOGY OF CHRISTIANITY

At the core of Christianity is a cosmological mystery, and our modern view of the end of the world is entangled with this magical mystery at the heart of Christianity. To understand this mystery and its alchemical and apocalyptic importance, we must first look at how the Hebrew culture of Palestine in the first century came to develop its unique perspective on the end of the world.

As their myths demonstrate, many ancient traditions were just as obsessed with the end of the world as were the Hebrews. Flood narratives, such as that of Noah in Genesis, are common to many traditional cultures. The Noah story originally comes from a Mesopotamian tale woven into the Epic of Gilgamesh. But the Old Testament is unique. Instead of treating its story as a chronicle, or a collection of myths, the Old Testament was put together as a way to demonstrate the supernatural intervention of God in the course of human affairs.

The early books of the Old Testament display a kind of pseudo-historical continuity, as if they were intended to make sense together, even if they were written at different times and under different circumstances. By creating the illusion of historicity, the passage of time is given meaning by its fulfillment of God's purpose. This sense of historical spirituality made the Hebrew worldview—and the Christian one that grew from it—highly susceptible to the idea of an end to all things. If there was in fact one specific moment of creation, then it follows that there must be one specific moment of destruction or judgment. By insisting that these metaphors were actual events, instead of mythic patterns within a cosmic cycle, the Old Testament forces the divine into the straitjacket of cause-and-effect history.

This sense of historical unity, however, was itself the product of an apocalyptic event, the fall of Jerusalem to the Babylonians in 587 B.C.E. and the subsequent return of the exiles from captivity a generation later. "The Book of the Law of Moses" was a combination of ancient texts found in the ruins of the Temple and Mesopotamian myths absorbed during the exile. This new version emphasized the power of the Hebrew God to punish or reward His people. The historical nature of God's effort was not lost on the survivors of the exile who heard this version of the "Book of the Law."

In addition to a new sense of God's involvement with the workings of history, the exiled Jews added another element to their emerging religion. Whereas before the exile the Hebrew prophets had been mainly concerned with the social issues of Israel and its relationship to God's plan, after the return the focus shifted to an even greater apocalypse, one of cosmic proportions. The Jews returned from exile with new insights about their history and identity as a people as well as new spiritual perspectives about such things as angels and the existence of a Messiah among them. But the most important of these new ideas was the conviction that the world would end in a great celestial apocalypse.[7]

The Old Testament prophets (the word *prophecy* comes from the Greek and means "ecstatic utterance") appeared around 1000 B.C.E. as a type of monotheistic shaman. The *nevi'im,* or God-speakers, were considered, along with the priests and the sages, to be crucial for the spiritual health of the Hebrew people.[8] There were great numbers of these prophets who performed frenzied rituals of dancing and chanting for large and enthusiastic crowds, not unlike the rituals that once accompanied the state oracle of Tibet; both events ended with a prophetic announcement. Taking their cue from Adam and Eve's banishment from the Garden, as well as the Flood, the prophets soon began to focus on the sinful nature of Israel and God's approaching Day of Wrath.

Amos started the trend around 760 B.C.E., which continued in increasing urgency until the prophecies came true. Jeremiah, the prophet of the Babylonian captivity, around 600 B.C.E., was the first to connect the fate of Israel with the ultimate destiny of the cosmos. He predicted that "the heavens will shudder" with pure horror at God's punishment.[9] For those who experienced the Babylonian captivity, it certainly felt like the end of the world. What had been the essentials of God's favor, a homeland, a temple, and the right of kingship, had all been taken away and destroyed.

Ezekiel, who was a priest of the Temple at the time of the conquest, marks the beginning of a new strain of apocalyptic prophets. Like Jeremiah, he predicted the end of the Israelite nation and the destruction of the Temple. Ezekiel used a variety of symbols—fiery wheels, dry bones, chariots, and multiheaded angels of marvelous countenance—to create a surreal image of apocalyptic transformation. He brings together almost all of the elements used by future prophets to describe the End of the World, and adds a few new ones: a king from the House of David who will rule all mankind; the idea of a purified elect who will survive; and, most important of all, the rebuilding of the great Temple at Jerusalem as God intended it to be. This image of a physical New Jerusalem laid the foundations for the Temple imagery in the Book of Revelation and contributed to the Gnostic idea of chiliasm.

But it was the Second Isaiah,[10] a contemporary-in-exile of Ezekiel's, who created the image of the apocalyptic Messiah from Zoroastrian ideas. It was only during the period of exile that the idea of a redeemer entered Hebrew eschatology. The Messiah, as predicted by Zoroaster (or Zarathustra), will come to wage war on the forces of evil and over-come the darkness. Second Isaiah adds to this vision the coming of a messiah, as Ezekiel said, from the House of David, who will be scourged and rejected. His message will be taken up more by Gentiles than Jews, but in the end the Jews will be proclaimed as God's chosen ones. A new covenant will be declared and a new heaven and a new earth will be created. The wasteland will be fertile once again, and the sun will never set.

It was this image of the Messiah that informed the thinking and actions of Jesus. He seems to have designed his teaching experiences to meet the expectations of Second Isaiah's prophecies. And those around him, who thought he was the Messiah, knew and understood these apocalyptic connotations.

The common beliefs about the end of the world at the time Jesus began his teachings included several key components. The first sign of the end would be the rebellion of Israel, God's people, against the evil forces of Gog, the evil king of Darkness. Gog was identified by all as the Roman Empire. In the one hundred years or so prior to Jesus' birth, several such rebellions had taken place. One, led by Judah Maccabee, had almost succeeded. Every attempt at a revolt, however, only served to tighten Rome's grip.

Following the rebellion would come the Day of the Lord, the Last Judgment, the manifestation of God's wrath on the wicked. Then the nation of Israel would be reunited and all the exiles would return. The dead would be resurrected so that they could experience the final stage, the reign of the Messiah in the new earthly paradise, with, of course, the divinely rebuilt Temple at the center.

In this context, the role of the Messiah was simple. Defeat the evil king of the world, the Demiurge, and usher in the Golden Age. It is difficult to know exactly how Jesus saw himself against these expectations. No one recorded Jesus' teachings during his lifetime. For thirty-five years after his death, his ideas lived on only in the spoken words of missionaries and teachers. Jesus' teachings adapted themselves spontaneously to the expectation of their listeners. Paul, Peter, and the other apostles and Gospel writers adapted the teachings to the communities in which they lived and worked.

To his contemporaries, Jesus appeared to be a miracle-working magus of a sort all too common in troubled Palestine.[11] Outsiders saw

INNER
TRADITIONS

BEAR & CO.

BEAR CUB BOOKS

DESTINY
BOOKS

Park Street
Press

BINDU
BOOKS

HEALING · ARTS · PRESS

Inner Traditions • Bear & Company

P.O. Box 388

Rochester, VT 05767-0388

U.S.A.

Please send us this card to receive our latest catalog.

☐ Check here if you would like to receive our catalog via e-mail.

E-mail address _____

Name _____ Company _____

Address _____ Phone _____

City _____ State _____ Zip _____ Country _____

Please check the following area(s) of interest to you:
☐ Health   ☐ Self-help   ☐ Science/Nature   ☐ Shamanism
☐ Ancient Mysteries ☐ New Age/Spirituality ☐ Ethnobotany   ☐ Martial Arts
☐ Spanish Language ☐ Sexuality/Tantra   ☐ Children   ☐ Teen

Order at 1-800-246-8648 • Fax (802) 767-3726
E-mail: orders@InnerTraditions.com • Web site: www.InnerTraditions.com

him as similar to other great magicians such as Apollonius of Tyana, who also had several Gospel-like biographies written about him. Galilee, Jesus' homeland, had only recently, in the first century B.C.E., converted to Judaism. It still retained a strong flavor of native paganism. Against this background, Jesus' primary significance derived from his ability to work miracles.

In the Gospel of Matthew, the Magi, Zoroastrian astronomers and philosophers, followed a star to Jesus' birthplace in Bethlehem. These Wise Men were prophetlike figures with distinct ethical and eschatological teachings, even if these are not evident to us in the Gospel reference. Jesus became a similar kind of wise-man figure, well known as a type in the ancient world, who taught of the Kingdom of Heaven, attracted followers, and performed feats of magic. The difference between Jesus and, say, Apollonius of Tyana lay in his emphasis on Jewish messianic concepts. Jesus declared himself the "Son of Man," Second Isaiah's title for the redeemer, the suffering and triumphant savior.

But the mystery at the core of his teaching, the secret of Christianity, was the nature and timing of the arrival of the Kingdom of Heaven. There can be no doubt that Jesus left his early followers with the impression that the world would soon end. His death and resurrection symbolized the triumph of the righteous over the evil king of the world, and his return would herald the beginning of the next phase, the Day of Judgment. He even declared that some living at that moment would still be alive when he returned.

If the end was expected at any moment, then there was no need to record Jesus' teachings. After many years, when the return had still not happened, the older members of the community began to record his teachings, and the Gospels came from these early sources. The Gospel of Mark, written around 70 C.E., used a common teaching document, which has come to be known as Q, as the source for the story of Jesus' life. Matthew, the next Gospel to be written down, between 80 C.E. and 100 C.E., used a similar technique and sources, but applied to them a much greater level of understanding of the ancient esoteric tradition.

Matthew gives us the most complete view of Jesus' teachings on the end of the world and the coming Kingdom of Heaven. Matthew was someone who grasped the mystery at the core of Christianity, for it is from him that we hear of Jesus' Egyptian connections, the Star of Bethlehem and the journey of the Wise Men from the East, the

Massacre of the Innocents, the temptation of the Messiah, and many other stories with deep esoteric significance.

The mystery is openly proclaimed in Matthew at the beginning of Jesus' career. Matthew quotes from Second Isaiah: "The people living in darkness have seen a great light, on those living in the land of the shadow of death a light has dawned."[12] To fulfill this prophecy, Matthew tells us, Jesus began to preach: "Repent, for the kingdom of heaven is near."[13]

To see the mystery here a little more clearly, we need to step outside Christianity for a moment and look at another Egyptian magical text, this one from the Paris Papyrus, one of the gems discovered in Egypt by Napoleon's savants. In papyrus IV, lines 475–830, we find a ritual to attain immortality through inhaling light. The aspirant is first told to perform seven days of rituals and then three days of dark retreat. On the morning of the eleventh day, the aspirant is to face the rising sun and perform an invocation: "First source of all sources . . . perfect my body . . . [so] that I may participate again in the immortal beginning . . . that I may be reborn in thought . . . and that the holy spirit may breathe in me."[14]

With this the aspirant inhales the first rays of the rising sun, and then leaves his body behind and rises into the heavens, filled with light. "For I am the Son [of the Sun], I surpass the limits of my souls, I am [the magical symbol for Light]."[15]

In Matthew 5:14 Jesus declares: "You are the light of the world." This echoes the Emerald Tablet in equating successful transformation with the spontaneous emission of light or illumination (see appendix A.) The Lord's Prayer, which appears in Matthew 6: 9–13, also suggests the Emerald Tablet ("on earth as it is in Heaven" and "as above, so below"). When the Kingdom of Heaven is achieved, Jesus declares, heaven and earth, above and below, will be the same. Chapters 24 and 25 provide a blueprint for the coming apocalypse, telling us: "The sun will be darkened, and the moon will not give its light, the stars will fall from the sky." Jesus also tells us that it will be "like in the days of Noah" before the return of the Son of Man, except that no one will know the exact day or hour—no one, that is, except the initiated.

Matthew 24:43–44 suggests that those who follow the Son of Man will indeed be able to calculate the time, and so will be waiting in preparation. When he returns (25:31), he will separate the sheep from the goats, the subtle from the gross, on the basis of their compassion for their fellow men.

In Matthew, we also find the account of Mary Magdalene's witness to the Resurrection, complete with its own light metaphor. "His appearance was like lightning," we are told, and Mary does not at first recognize him.[16] Matthew's account of the Resurrection ends with Christ's ascension in Galilee and his pronouncement of the Great Commission, the last line of which goes to the heart of the mystery: "And surely I am with you always, even to the end of the world."[17]

At the core of Christianity, then, we find a transformation that is alchemical in nature as well as mention of the end of time. The Gnostics embraced a view of Christianity that centered on knowledge of the path of return and ultimate triumph over the evil Demiurge and his prison of matter. The hope they perceived as being offered remains the promise at the heart of Jesus' teachings. As the Gnostics thought, the Messiah opened the way.

And just as quickly, the Demiurge closed it again.

REVELATION, THE ANTICHRIST, AND CHILIASM

Not long after the Gospels were written, an author who identified himself as John, perhaps the same as the apostle John, son of Zebedee, recorded a vision he had had while imprisoned on the island of Patmos, in the Aegean Sea. Eventually, John's apocalyptic vision became the official and orthodox version of the end of the world, mainly because of his identification with the beloved apostle of the Gospel of John. His revelation would become "the Revelation" as the apostolic church closed ranks against the Gnostics and the pagan Romans.

The early Church had many different versions of the apocalypse, just as there were many different Gospels. An entire literature of prophetic apocalypses had developed since the time of Ezekiel and Daniel. Many of these texts, a number of which were among the Dead Sea Scrolls, which are now thought to be the remnants of the Temple's library, have surfaced only in the twentieth century. From these sources, we can see why the early Church, struggling toward some sort of unity, chose John's vision as the authentic image of the end of the world.

Jewish Christianity did not survive the destruction of the Temple at Jerusalem in 70 C.E. The Gospels, all written after this apocalyptic event, reflect a Christianity that had lost its local messianic roots and become instead a universal mystery religion. The three so-called synoptic Gospels, Matthew, Mark, and Luke, were all composed in response to the central question of who had authority within the movement.[18] The answer of the Gospels is clear: Only the apostles and their spiritual descendants could claim legitimate authority in the Church.

Early in the second century we can detect the beginnings of orthodoxy. As the apostolic Gospels spread, an organization developed to look after the people. The priests who performed the ceremonies answered to bishops who were invested with the authority of the apostles. The chain of command was very clear. God had sent Christ, who had called the apostles. To them, He gave the responsibility for His church, and they in turn ordained the leaders of the individual Christian communities.

The mystical aspects of Christianity, however, had spread throughout the Empire, blending with various other currents, such as the essentially pagan beliefs of Gnosticism. This created a vast Christian movement that was far from content with the simple apostolic interpretation of spiritual authority.[19] The Gnostics in particular insisted on a direct experience of Christ that was unmediated by any priest or bishop. This unmediated brand of Christianity was, of course, much more exclusive than the apostolic guarantee of instant salvation conferred by belief and obedience.

Orthodox, apostolic Christianity became a mass movement in the late second century, while Gnostic groups dwindled into closed societies of adepts. Other salvationist religions, such as the Christian look-alike known as Mithraism, competed for adherents and imperial support. By 180, when Irenaeus compiled his authoritative list of books in the New Testament canon, with John's Revelation as its official apocalypse, orthodox Christianity had solidified into a powerful social and political force.[20] For over a century, in the face of periodic persecutions from various emperors, the Church had gained in strength and influence. The extreme persecutions of the early fourth century were a last-ditch attempt to halt the erosion of imperial and pagan authority caused by the growth of Christianity, with its appeal to God's authority as administered by the apostolic bishops.[21]

The Book of Revelation had the authority of the apostle John behind it, as well as a distinctive Gnostic flavor. John was the beloved disciple who sat next to Christ at the Last Supper. In the text, Christ speaks, through John, directly to the seven churches of Asia, lecturing and scolding the Christians while warning them of a coming period of persecution. And then, in a sudden shift of tone, Christ invites John: "Come up here and I will show you what must take place after this."[22] John ascends to the throne of Heaven and sees the seraphim mentioned by Ezekiel. He also sees a lamb, who breaks open the seven seals and reveals the future.

This long, complex, and bizarre vision seems intended to encourage the faithful in their resistance to the pressures of emperor worship. Some of the churches that Christ addresses through John were advocating a policy of compromise with the Roman authorities. The emperor Nero was the "beast" in Revelation.[23] He was a vision of the Demiurge on earth. He was Satan, emperor, and false god all rolled into one. Many of these Christians were willing to compromise with the mad Caesar. This had to be stopped, according to John, because the final showdown between God and Satan was imminent. Satan, in the form of the Roman state, will increase its persecution of believers, but they must stand fast, even in the face of death. They are sealed from any spiritual harm, though their bodies may suffer. They will, in any case, be vindicated when Christ returns to destroy the wicked.

All of Rome is seen in Revelation as the Great Beast; the whore of Babylon and its emperor are the Antichrist. When Christ returns as King of Kings, he will lead the heavenly host in battle against the Beast and the kings of the earth. In John's vision Christ wins and then rules for a millennium. This is the only place in the New Testament where a thousand-year reign of Christ is mentioned. After this, Satan reemerges from his pit and challenges Christ. God sends fire from the sky and Satan, the Beast, and the false prophet all end up roasting in the lake of fire.

This ushers in the final Day of Judgment. After punishing the wicked and resurrecting the saints, God decides to dwell among men and therefore creates a new heaven and a new earth, along with a New Jerusalem. There is no visible Temple in this New Jerusalem and no need of the sun or the moon. The presence of God and Christ provides so much light that it is never dark. From the middle of the new city flow the waters of the river of life. On its bank stands the Tree of Life, which produces fruit continually. The elect will see the face of God and therefore be immortal, reigning "forever and forever."

Clenthius, a Gnostic poet of the early second century, knew of John's Revelation and wove it into his own work, now lost except for disapproving quotes from Origen on chiliasm. Clenthius gained a large following by teaching that the millennium, foretold in John's Revelation, would be a physical earthly paradise where the senses "would be subject to delights and pleasures. . . . There would be a space of 1000 years for celebrating nuptial festivals."[24]

Origen, a second-century Christian apologist, was the first important Christian to discredit the common notion of a physical paradise as the Kingdom of Heaven. He substituted a spiritual and personal kingdom for the literal and collective apocalypse described by John's Revelation. Origen explained that the heavenly feasting prophesied in Revelation, and that so delighted the chiliasts, should be understood as spiritual nourishment from Christ.

But the idea of a physical New Jerusalem of gold and precious stones proved hard to displace. Chiliasm would continue to crop up around the edges of orthodoxy for more than a thousand years. As we shall see, the idea of a physical transformation that accompanies the end of the world would become the inner secret of Western occultism. In alchemy, the process of transformation would be studied in isolation, at least exoterically, from its Gnostic and chiliast origins. Alone among all the alchemical authorities—with the possible exception of Dr. John Dee—Fulcanelli directs us to the connection between alchemy and eschatology.*

The anonymous magician of Thebes, buried with his copy of the Emerald Tablet, was an early-second-century contemporary of the pseudo-Cleopatra and Clenthius. His wisdom papyrus would provide a much needed practical counterpoint to the late-classical alchemical theorists such as Olympiodorus and Stephanus of Alexandria. The seventh-century Stephanus, who dedicated his "Nine Lessons in Chemia" to the Eastern emperor Heraclius, represents the dividing line between the classical period, that of alchemy's emergence, and the new world of Christian orthodoxy. While Christianized Greek hermeticism continued

---

*Dee's Enochian workings combine both alchemical images and apocalyptic content. See Geoffrey James's *The Enochian Magick of Dr. John Dee* (St. Paul, Minn.: Llewellyn, 1998). For a look at Dee's alchemical writings, see Gordon James's *The Secrets of John Dee* (Edmonds, Wash.: Holmes Publishing Group, 1995.)

in the East as a spiritual indulgence for mystical and scholarly monks, the tradition in the West was ruthlessly persecuted.[25] The Church saw it as irrevocably tainted with pagan ideals.

Western Christianity, and even some of the alchemists, believed that investigation into the hidden works of nature was sacrilegious.[26] It smacked of the forbidden fruit of the Tree of Knowledge in the Garden of Eden, and was, after all, part of the illicit arts given to humanity by the fallen angels. Acquiring knowledge, like eating the fruit, allowed man to become more like God. If we are to believe the Emerald Tablet, then alchemy contained the very secret of independent creation.

From this possibility, the later alchemists, from Olympiodorus in the fifth century on down, focused on the symbols of the Tree of Knowledge and the serpent, its guardian and initiator, as clues to the secret of creation. Part of this focus comes from the influence of Gnostic sects such as the Ophites, who worshipped the snake in the garden as the author of wisdom, given to man in order to free him from the domination of the Demiurge Ialdabaoth. Over time, symbols such as the Ouroboros serpent, with its motto of "the sum of all philosophy," would become the most cherished of all in the alchemical tradition.

These symbols, however, certainly did not help the Gnostic sects survive the onslaught of orthodoxy in the fourth and fifth centuries. In fact, they attracted the wrath of the reformers. In the late fourth century, the emperor Theodosius ordered the pagan temples destroyed. The Serapeum in Alexandria and its library of ancient texts were burned. Hypatia, the last great women alchemical philosopher,[27] was able to save some of the library, and for a while esoteric studies continued. Hypatia's murder in 415 put an end to all pagan learning in Egypt. The remaining scholars fled to Athens, where Justinian in 529 finally destroyed them.[28]

As the darkness fell over Europe and the West, a brief hermetic Renaissance occurred in Constantinople. Some of the texts compiled there from the pagan Greeks would eventually make their way to France, purchased by that enigmatic late medieval king, Francis I.[29] Centuries later, a young student of the art, Fulcanelli, would find these manuscripts extremely valuable. From them, we can speculate, he found some of the same symbolic keys—the serpent of wisdom and the idea of a triple transformation—that we have just elucidated.

The fragmentation of the ancient knowledge led to many dead ends and vain quests. The timing of the transformation became more important than the transformation of time.

CONSTANTINE AND THE ORTHODOX APOCALYPSE

Even the chiliasts and other Gnostic Christians agreed with Hippolytus, bishop of Porto, who calculated the history of the world and found that Rome could only be the empire of the Antichrist. He thought that his calculations proved that a century or so was left before the apocalypse. This was heralded as good news. The Christians had so far not been doing too well in their mission of converting the world. They felt they could use a bit more time before the end.[30]

For the first two and a half centuries of Christianity's existence, imperial Rome had been the great enemy, the government of the evil king of the world, the Antichrist. And then, in the second decade of the fourth century, something very strange happened. A would-be king of the world won a battle outside the gates of Rome and attributed his victory to the power of Christ. The battle of Mulvian Bridge made Constantine an emperor, and with him, Christianity became the imperial religion.

This sudden reversal seemed truly miraculous to the Christians themselves.[31] The early years of the fourth century saw the worst Christian persecutions of the Roman era. Even bishops of the Church were forced to renounce their faith.[32] Christianity had begun to disappear in large portions of the eastern empire. In the West, the persecutions had actually served to increase the number of Christians. Constantine used this fact as a political tool. At Mulvian Bridge, his convenient espousal of Christianity was worth a dozen legions, he later remarked to Eusebius, his biographer.[33]

Flavius Valerius Constantinus, or Constantine, was an imperial freebooter in the grand tradition of Julius Caesar and Octavius Augustus. Born the son of one of the four imperial "Caesars" appointed by the last great pagan emperor, Diocletian, Constantine plowed his way through the political intrigue that resulted from Diocletian's abdication in 305. On the afternoon of October 27, 312, Constantine trapped his last opponent, the Christian-hating Maxentius, against the Tiber at Saxa Rubra (Red Rocks) with only one avenue of escape, over Mulvian Bridge.

In effect, this battle decided the fate of both the Empire and

Christianity, which had become inextricably entwined. While position-ing his legions on the afternoon before the battle, Constantine saw a vision of a great flaming cross in the sky with the Greek words *en toutoi nika,* "in this sign, victory." That night, he dreamt that Christ appeared and commanded him to make the flaming cross his battle standard. Constantine awoke and called for his metalsmiths. He told them his dream and ordered them to prepare a new standard, one composed of the first two Greek letters in the name Christ, chi, X, superimposed on a rho, P, as seen in figures 3.3a and 3.3b.

Under this new standard, Constantine's army drove Maxentius's legions into the Tiber, where most of them died. Constantine entered Rome and was proclaimed emperor of the West. Gog, of Gog and Magog, the evil rulers of the world according to Hebrew eschatology, was now at least nominally a Christian.

Soon after his victory, in early 313, Constantine met with the Eastern emperor, Lucinius, and issued an edict confirming the religious toleration proclaimed by one of the earlier "Caesars," or tetrachs, of Diocletian and expanded it to include all religions, even Christianity. This was the end of the great persecutions and the beginning of the meteoric rise in the

Figure 3.3. *A,* The chi-rho symbol Constantine saw in the sky and adopted as his battle standard; *B,* note the similarity to this Coptic altar font from second-century Luxor. (Coptic Museum, Cairo)

fortunes of orthodox Christianity. By 323, Constantine had finally united, by conquest, both halves of the empire. He soon moved the capital to Byzantium, later to become known as Constantinople. Orthodox Christianity had become the official religion of the state.

Constantine, guided by his vision, chose the winning side. It was the Church's insistence on obedience and conformity that appealed to Constantine. He needed a new form of universal religion with which to unify his vast empire, and Christianity filled the bill nicely.

But almost as soon as Constantine embraced orthodoxy, it was threatened by the most challenging heresy in the history of the Church.[34] A pious and ascetic Egyptian priest by the name of Arius startled his bishop with his unorthodox opinions about the nature of Christ. Arius argued that Christ could not be one with the Creator, but was rather the Logos, the first and best of all created beings.[35] Since Christ had lived in time—that is, been born, lived, and died—he could not be coeternal with God. A creation had occurred somewhere, and therefore Christ was not the same substance as his Father. The Holy Spirit, Arius insisted, was even less God than Christ, since it was a creation of Christ's, and therefore twice removed from the substance of God.[36]

Bishop Alexander called a council and excommunicated Arius and his followers. This created such widespread religious turmoil that Constantine himself had to step in and settle it. In a letter to both sides, Constantine declared that the dispute was "trifling and unworthy of such fierce contests."[37] But the Church did not see it that way. To the Church, the matter of consubstantiality versus similarity, a matter of an iota in the Greek words *homoousia* and *homoiousia,* was vital both politically and theologically. If Christ was not seen as God, the whole structure of the orthodox chain of command would crumble. And if anything happened to the unity of the Church, its usefulness to the imperial state would vanish. Settling this issue became a matter of life and death for the new imperial orthodoxy.

Constantine resolved to end the dispute by calling the first ecumenical, or universal, Church Council at Nicaea in 325. Constantine presided in person over the debates and according to Eusebius "moderated the violence of the contending parties."[38] Arius presented his view, but Athanasius, the hired theological gunslinger brought in by Bishop Alexander, made it absolutely clear that if Christ and the Holy Spirit were not considered the same substance as God, then polytheism would triumph. With that, the bishops folded and agreed on a new universal creed that declared the Trinity to be of one essence—that is, of the same substance.

Unity was enforced by banishment and anathema. The imperial church thus embarked on its own pattern of persecution. All books by or about Arius were burned. By imperial decree, concealment of such a book was punishable by death. The Dark Ages had begun.

Constantine, the most nominal of Christians and a good candidate for the Antichrist, became instead the new Christ-model of the imperial church, the Christos Pantocrator, Christ the Ruler of the Universe. The Demiurge had become the Messiah and a thousand and more years of spiritual oppression and persecution lay ahead. The end of the world had become an institution of the Church, both as a doctrine and as an inquisitional practice.

FOUR

THE ANCIENT
ILLUMINATED ASTRONOMY

HEBREW ILLUMINISM

In the divinely rebuilt New Jerusalem, as described in Revelation 21 and 22, the Tree of Life will stand on the banks of the river of the waters of life. This suggests that the new heaven and the new earth, promised to John in the Book of Revelation, would, in fact, be a literal return to the Garden of Paradise. The chiliasts thought so. They saw in this divine re-creation a chance to indulge in the innocent joys of a purified humanity. They quite naturally assumed that, since the re-created paradise had no Tree of the Knowledge of Good and Evil—the original cause of the fall of man into sinfulness—there could be no such thing as sin in the New Jerusalem.

Origen and the other fathers of the early Church disliked this interpretation.[1] But even they could not completely remove the idea of a transformed reality, complete with a transformed body, from the orthodox eschatology. The Gnostic view was that matter could be redeemed, or animated, by an apocalyptic event. The apocalypse, then, was a chance for the sparks of light to return to the Light. This Gnostic concept remained at the heart of the official orthodox apocalypse.[2]

Christianity emerged from the political turmoil of first-century Palestine, which was a truly apocalyptic moment in Jewish history. Christianity did not become a universalist religion until after the "end of the world" for the Jews, which occurred six and half centuries to the day after Nebuchadnezzar's armies destroyed Solomon's Temple when Roman forces under the soon-to-be-emperor Titus sacked and burned the Temple of Herod and drove the Jews from Israel. This was an end of the world far greater than the Babylonian captivity. Cyrus the Great allowed the Jews to return from Babylon after a generation or so. The New Babylon on the Tiber, Rome, never allowed the Jews to return. One thousand eight hundred and seventy-eight years, and many more apocalypses, would pass before a Jewish nation returned to Palestine.

We saw how Christianity slowly became an orthodoxy and then, miraculously, the imperial religion of the hated Romans. By the late sixth century, when the Church was firmly in the driver's seat of the Roman military machine, Judaism was the only tolerated nonorthodox form of religion. This does not mean that the Roman Christians saw the Jews as equals—it was against the law to intermarry and for Jews to own real property such as land—but they were at least accepted as serving one useful function in society, that of scapegoats. Since the Christians could no longer blame the Romans for Christ's death, the blame shifted to the Jews. This created the basic rationalization for one thousand years of Christian persecution. The origin of anti-Semitism lies in the Church's institutionalization of the apocalypse.[3]

After the fall of the Temple in 70 C.E., the largest Jewish communities were centered in Alexandria in Egypt and the old city of Babylon, in Mesopotamia. Judaism was probably saved by the actions of Rabbi Johanen ben Zakkai, who had himself smuggled out of Jerusalem during the siege. A few Jewish communities remained in Palestine, most notably the spiritual community at Safed, near present-day Tel Aviv, on the eastern shore of the Mediterranean. The mystical Jews of Safed would retain their foothold in the Holy Land right down to the twentieth century.

Unlike Christianity, which renounced its mystical origins as heresy, Judaism retained a powerful connection with its mystical roots. Our earliest alchemical text, "Isis the Prophetess to Her Son Horus," points to an Egypto-Hebraic source for its transformational philosophy. Interestingly enough, a Hebrew contemporary of the author of the "Isis the Prophetess" story, Rabbi Nehuniah ben HaKana, revealed to his students the magical technology behind these transformational processes. In the later centuries of the Diaspora, his teachings would form the basis of the traditional Kabbalah.

Compared to the anonymous author of "Isis the Prophetess," Rabbi Nehuniah ben HaKana was a well-known and respected Jewish sage who had studied with Rabbi Johanen ben Zakkai. The few times his name is mentioned in the Talmud leave no doubt about the important position he occupied in the early Talmudic era; his mystical teachings inspired a whole generation of Jewish sages. From the perspective of our inquiry into the origins of alchemy, however, his importance lies in his authorship of the teaching document known as the *Bahir.*

The oldest and most influential of all kabbalistic texts, the *Bahir,* or "Illumination" (from Job 37:21—"And now they do not see light, it is illumination *[bahir]* in the skies,") was also called the "Midrash of Rabbi Nehuniah," to emphasize his authorship.[4] This is unusual, since Rabbi Nehuniah is quoted only once, in the first verse. A Rabbi Amorai, however, perhaps a pseudonym for Rabbi Nehuniah, is cited nine times. The word *amorai* means "speakers" and indicates that he was the spokesman for a committee or group of sages. If this was Rabbi Nehuniah, then he was speaking for the whole tradition as well as his immediate group.

Although the *Bahir* is the primary text of the Kabbalah, it does not use that term. The word *kabbalah,* from the Hebrew root QBL, meaning "received" or "given," came into fashion much later, when the teachings of the first-century mystics were indeed just "received traditions." The sages of the *Bahir* preferred the more ancient term Maaseh Merkabah, literally "Workings of the Chariot."[5] The name connotes an active mystical experience as opposed to a received tradition. The *Bahir* combines the ideas of the work of creation, the animating of matter, with the radical concept of a celestial projection as a way to return to the divine source. By juxtaposing these ideas, the *Bahir* brings us closer to the secret at the heart of alchemy.

THE TELI, THE CYCLE, AND THE HEART: SERPENTS IN THE SKY

The key concept at the heart of Kabbalah is the Tree of Life, the Etz Chaim, which is described in kabbalistic creation texts such as the *Sefer Yetzirah.* As shown in figure 4.1, the Tree of Life is a diagram that pictures reality as the intersection of four great realms or levels of abstraction.

A geometric pattern emerges from the intersecting lines of the Tree like a moiré pattern in a holographic projection. Figure 4.2 shows

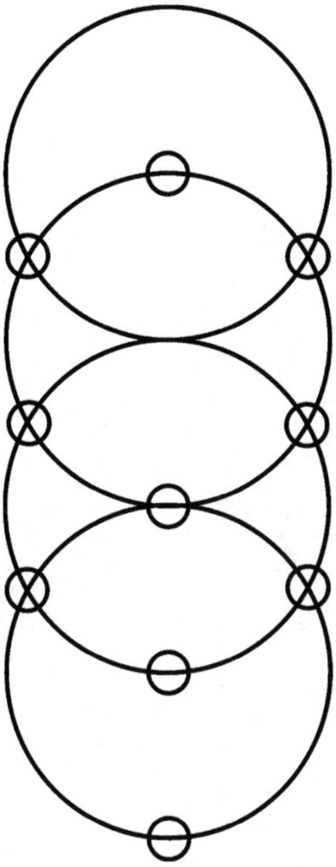

Figure 4.1. The Tree of Life formed from the overlapping of four circles or spheres of abstraction.

twenty-two paths, processes, or states of becoming connecting ten localities, spheres, or *sefirot*. The entire diagram was thought to describe the nature of creation, God's artistic technique, if you will. But its true importance to the sages was its application to the human condition.

As God is supposed to have made man in his image and likeness, so man was thought to contain, in microcosm, the entire Tree of Life. Some medieval Kabbalists used the concepts in the *Sefer Yetzirah* to create an artificial form of life known as the golem, according to the legends about this being from Prague and Warsaw. To Western esotericists, the Tree of Life functioned much like the kundalini diagrams of the Hindu mystics. By mapping the internal power centers, and then projecting outward and aligning them with the forces of nature, the magician sought to reenact the process of creation and so become, with God, a co-creator of the universe.

The *sefirot* and the paths are arranged in a few basic patterns (see fig. 4.3). The top three *sefirot*, Kether, Chokmah, and Binah (Crown,

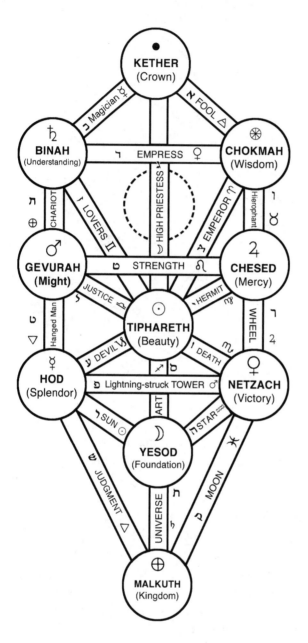

Figure 4.2. The complete Tree of Life, showing the twenty-two paths and the planetary relationships of the *sefirot*. (Drawing by Darlene from the Hermetic Order of the Golden Dawn)

Wisdom, and Understanding), form a triangular motif that is then inverted and projected downward through the pattern. The first inverted triangle, Chesed, Gevurah, and Tiferet (Mercy, Strength, and Beauty), is repeated by the third and last triangle, Netzach, Hod, and

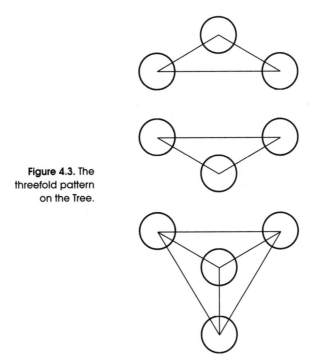

Figure 4.3. The threefold pattern on the Tree.

Yesod (Victory, Splendor, and Foundation). The whole pattern is then resolved by, and enfolded into, the last *sefirah,* Malkuth (Kingdom).

Each of these triangular patterns represents one of the realms or levels of abstraction. The repetition of the pattern also creates three columns or pillars on the Tree, as shown in figure 4.4. From left to right, the three columns are Mercy, Transformation (note that this column connects Kether with Malkuth, heaven to earth), and Severity. These repetitions of three can also be seen as the three persons of the trinity, the law of threes, and the dialectical trio of thesis, antithesis, and synthesis.

The *Bahir* adds that portions of the celestial sphere can be equated with the spheres of each *sefirah,* or globe, on the Tree of Life. In verse 179 of the *Bahir* we learn that our physical world "is like a mustard seed in a ring." In a sphere around the ring are the ten spheres and their animating statements, ten times the phrase "And God said . . ." is used in Genesis, which verse 179 locates in space around a center point, supposedly the mustard seed.[6]

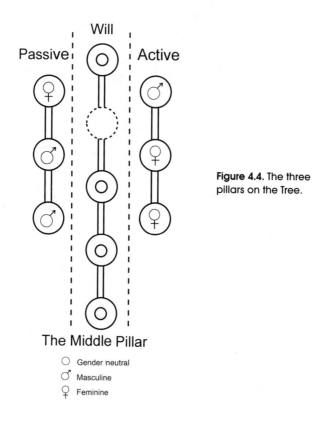

Figure 4.4. The three pillars on the Tree.

We learned that there are Ten Spheres and Ten Sayings. Each sphere has its saying. It is not surrounded by it, but rather, it surrounds it. This [physical] world is like a mustard seed inside a ring. Why? Because of the Spirit that blows upon it, through which it is sustained. If this spirit were to be interrupted for even a moment, the world would be annihilated.[7]

This, of course, suggests the parable of the mustard seed found in Matthew 13:31–33 and Mark 4:30–32: "The kingdom of heaven is like a mustard seed which a man took and planted in his field. Though it was the smallest of seeds, yet when it grows it becomes a tree, so that the birds of the air come and perch in its branches." In Matthew, Jesus goes on to relate the parable of the yeast, a metaphor for the kingdom of heaven as a transformative force that spreads throughout all matter.

Matthew ends the section with another quote from Psalms, explaining why Jesus spoke in parables: "I will open my mouth in parables. I will utter things hidden since the creation of the world."[8]

Verses 63, 95, and 106 of the *Bahir* describe the Tree that grows from this mustard seed in terms of the ancient ideas later written down in the *Sefer Yetzirah* and the *Sefer Zohar,* two books that are part of the Hebrew kabbalistic tradition.[9] We must remember that works such as the *Bahir* were written for the initiated few; if we take them literally, we are sure to misunderstand their meaning.

> 63: The heart [lev] is thirty-two. These are concealed, and with them the world was created. What are these 32? He said: These are the 32 paths. . . .
> 95: The Blessed Holy One has a single Tree and it has twelve diagonal boundaries. . . . They continually spread forever and ever; they are the "arms of the world." . . .
> 106: Rabbi Berachiah sat and expounded: What is the Axis [teli]? This is the likeness that I saw before the Blessed One. . . . What is the Sphere? That is the Womb. What is the heart? It is that regarding which it has been written "unto the heart of heaven." In it are included the 32 mystical paths of wisdom.[10]

These verses from the *Bahir* make the pitfall of literality quite apparent. Attributed to Rabbi Amorai, the spokesman for the *Bahir* tradition as a whole, verse 95 reveals the structure of the Cube of Space and the jewel of the celestial Tree within it. This cubic structure, "the arms of the world," is based on the ancient concepts of the axis, the sphere, and the heart. If we know the secret of their meaning, then this is one of the most straightforward verses in the *Bahir.* Without the key, however, it is merely an incomprehensible string of numbers. The very secret of alchemy lies in the symbolic images of the axis, the sphere, and the heart, which are an ancient, perhaps even pre-catastrophe, astronomical description of the cosmic mill.

The first three verses of the sixth chapter of Rabbi Akiva's *Sefer Yetzirah* supply the key to this astronomical gnosis, although in an oblique fashion. The first verse informs us that as proof of the existence of the Tree of Life, the twelve, the seven, and the three, "He set them in the Teli, the Cycle and the Heart."

These are Three Mothers . . . And seven planets and their hosts, and twelve diagonal boundaries a proof of this true witness in the Universe, Year, Soul and a rule of twelve and seven and three: He set them in the Teli, the cycle and the Heart.[11]

The secret lies in the mysterious word *teli*. It occurs in neither the Torah nor the Talmud, although it is used in the *Bahir*. There is considerable dispute among scholars as to its precise meaning. The only similar word in the Bible is a single reference to some kind of weapon in Genesis.[12] Apparently, from the root of the word *talah,* "to hang," it could have been some kind of bolo, or a weight suspended on a rope for throwing. This reading suggests that the *Bahir* is talking about the celestial axis around which the heavens rotate, a kind of imaginary string from which the celestial globe hangs, as well as a point around which the weight orbits as the bolo is swung.

But what is the string connected to? An ancient midrash, "The Prayers of Rabbi 'In The Beginning,'" tells us that it "hangs [by a thread] from the fin of the Leviathan." This ancient serpent can only be the constellation Draco, the Pole Serpent mentioned in Job 26:13, "By His Spirit the heavens were calmed, His hand pierced the Pole Serpent," and in Second Isaiah 27:1, "On that day [the Day of Judgment] with His great sharp sword, God will visit and overcome the Leviathan, the Pole Serpent, and the Leviathan, the Coiled Serpent, and He will kill the dragon of the sea." It is important to note that three such dragons are mentioned here.

To understand these words, we must look up at the stars. We can all find the Pole Star, Polaris, in the tail of Ursa Minor, the Little Bear. This marks our North Celestial Pole, directly above the North Pole of our planet. There is another pole in the sky, however, and that is the pole of the ecliptic, the path of the sun as it passes through the zodiac. The earth's axis is tilted at 23.5 degrees away from the ecliptic. This tilt causes the celestial pole above our planetary pole to describe a great circle in the sky over long periods of time. For example, in 4500 B.C.E., Thuban, a star in the tail of Draco, marked the North Celestial Pole, which has, over time, shifted to Polaris.

The ecliptic pole, however, does not change, since the path of the sun through the sky never changes. Around this point, which has no star visible to the naked eye to mark it, is the constellation Draco, the

Great Dragon, which spirals through all of the zodiacal signs. The stars appear to hang, *talah,* from it. Draco thereby becomes the Teli (fig. 4.5), which the *Sefer Yetzirah* (6:3) tells us, is over the universe "like a king on his throne."[13] This is perhaps an echo of an ancient form of worship of the God Most High identified with Baal, which predated the arrival of the Hebrews in Palestine. This serpent is also the serpent of the Garden climbing its way up the Tree of the Knowledge of Good and Evil, the brazen serpent used by Moses to heal the plagues in the wilderness, and even Hermes' caduceus staff.

The Gnostic Ophites, who worshipped the serpent in the Garden of Eden for giving us the gift of knowledge that provided an escape from the Demiurge, formulated the image of a snake spiraling around an egg. In simple terms, this is Draco coiled around the ellipse made by the movement of the North Celestial Pole. The Teli here would be the axis of the ecliptic poles through the head and tail of the dragon and the center of the celestial sphere. This is the first dragon, the Pole Serpent.

A

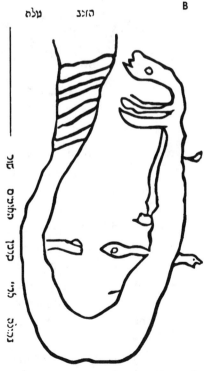

עלה   הזנב   B

אור   ומשם   יצאו   ישראל   במצרים

ראש חמלי דגים דלי גדי קשת עקרב מאזנים

Figure 4.5. *A*, The constellation Draco in early Hebrew star charts; *B*, the Teli appearing as a serpent with gaping mouth. (From the commentary by Rabbi Eleazer Rok of Worms, 1160–1237)

There are, however, two other ways to interpret the dragon-axis of the Teli. Medieval Hebrew astronomers used the term *teli* to denote the inclination of the orbit of a planet from the ecliptic. In the case of the moon, this allows one to track eclipses. Eclipses occur only when the sun and moon arrive at the moon's nodes, or the head and tail of the dragon to the ancient astronomers, at the same time, as shown in figure 4.6. This happens roughly every six months. Solar eclipses were seen as occasions when, metaphorically, the dragon caught and swallowed the sun for a period of time. The concept of ascending and descending nodes as an axis, the head and tail of the dragon, or Teli, was also used with the other planets. The major such *Teli* or axis for the sun is formed by its solstice standstills, which are also the points where the celestial equator crosses the ecliptic in this precessional epoch. This axis can be seen as the second dragon, the Coiled Serpent.

Figure 4.6. The lunar dragon perched between the two circles formed by the orbits of the sun and the moon. (From Agrippa's *De Occulta Philosophia*)

And there is still another way to look at the concept of the Teli. If we think of the Milky Way as the Leviathan because of the way that it snakes across the night sky through the year, then this third Teli, yet another dragon-axis, becomes the galactic axis, running through the ecliptic from Scorpio/Sagittarius to Taurus/Gemini; see fig. 4.7. This is the third and final dragon. Like the ecliptic axis, the galactic axis is constant and unmoving. Between these two pillars, or perpendicular axes, lies the coiled dragon of precession, spinning slowly backward through time, moving one degree of arc every seventy-two years. Knowledge of the backward march of the precession caused by the earth's tilt constituted the great secret of many ancient cultures as different as Greece and the Maya of Mexico.[14]

A Talmudic example makes this even clearer: "The storm wind hangs [talah] between the arms of God like an amulet."[15] The hanging

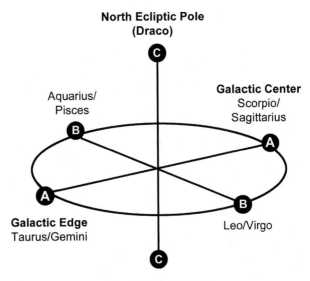

Figure 4.7. The three dragon axes: *A*, the galactic meridian from center to edge; *B*, the moving axis of the precession of the equinoxes/solstices; *C*, the unmoving ecliptic polar axis in Draco.

is, of course, the Teli. The storm wind is the slowly backward-turning spiral of precession and a good metaphor for the mystical experience itself. The prophet Nahum (1:3) declares, "His way is in the whirlwind," and Psalms 50:3 agrees that to experience God is to plunge into the tempest that surrounds Him. The arms of the universe are the unmoving Teli, the ecliptic and galactic axes, from which the initiatory spiral of the equinoxes is suspended like an amulet. It is hard to overestimate the value of the knowledge of one's location in space and in time that these three axes provided. It would also seem as if these axes were creating an address for Earth, the purpose of which remains a mystery.

In verse 106 of the *Bahir* we read that the Teli is nothing but "the likeness before the Blessed Holy One," or the face of God.[16] Verse 96 of the *Bahir* addresses key alchemical symbols, and may in fact be our earliest mention of the philosopher's stone. It begins: "What is the earth from which the heavens were graven [created]? It is the throne of the Blessed Holy One. It is the Precious Stone and the Sea of Wisdom."[17] The verse continues to suggest the spiritual value of the color blue, the traditional color of kingship in ancient cultures, by associating the sea with the sky and the sky with the higher light coming from the Throne of Creation.

From the *Bahir,* we learn that the Tree of Life is actually the "Precious Stone" whose facets are projected onto the celestial sphere and which is part of the continuous flow of the Sea of Wisdom. John's Revelation is a version of this, with the Tree of Life on the banks of the flowing river, deep inside New Jerusalem's Cube of Space. We can also see that all of this weird symbolism actually has a context and a meaning, and is grounded in firm reality.

So what happened to the Tree of Knowledge? Is it banished from the perfected schema? The *Bahir* suggests, in many subtle references, that the Tree of Knowledge forms itself around the axis of the Celestial Pole, whose Teli or dragon-axis would be the backward-spiraling axis of the precession of the equinoxes. The North Celestial Pole, as it circles around the fixed point of the ecliptic pole, first leans in toward the angle of the galactic axis—that is, toward the center of the galaxy (see fig. 4.8). It then moves away from this point in a large precessional cycle. The Fall occurs when the Tree is tilted away from the galactic axis. The Resurrection and Redemption, the arrival of the kingdom of heaven, happens when the Tree tilts toward the galactic axis. The four great ages, then, are the tilting of the pole in toward the center of the galaxy, which translates into the Golden and Silver Ages, and the tilting of the pole away from the center of the galaxy, which brings on the Bronze Age and the current Iron Age.

The mystical experience of the *galgal,* or cycle, of the Tree of Knowledge is the whirlwind, or *sufah* in our Talmudic reference.[18] The *galgal* is also spoken of in the *Bahir* as a womb. This is a cycle of time in which the future is born. All of time happens within the sphere defined by the Teli. The *Bahir* also tells us that the Teli is revealed in the heart of heaven.[19] This is both our own human, personal, spiritual center, the heart of man, and the heart at the center of our own Milky Way galaxy. Together they pulsate in harmonic fractals of the same wave.

THE KAABA, THE EL MOST HIGH, AND THE COVENANT OF ABRAHAM

According to biblical tradition, Abraham learned the great ancient secrets from Shem, the son of Noah, also known as Melchizedek. He was the righteous king of Ur and Salem, which is now thought to be Jerusalem. The most important mysteries of the work of creation con-

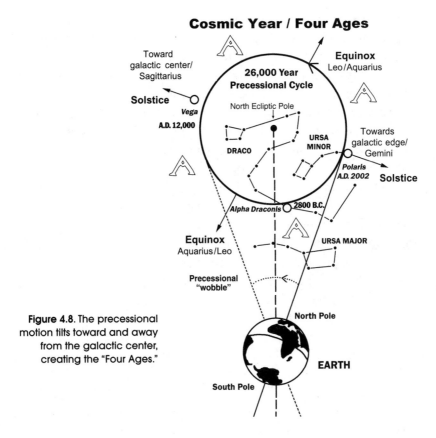

Figure 4.8. The precessional motion tilts toward and away from the galactic center, creating the "Four Ages."

cerned the significance of the letters of the Hebrew alphabet and their relationship to astrology and the mysteries of the calendar, or time itself. Attributing this wisdom to Abraham and Melchizedek places its origin in the eighteenth century B.C.E., the time of the rise of the New Kingdom in Egypt as well as the appearance of Vedic scholars in India.[20]

Abraham was considered to be the greatest magician and astrologer of his age. The Talmud tells us that "all the kings of East and West [Egypt and India] arose early [to wait] at his door."[21] The teachings of the work of creation are one of the primary astrological texts of the ancient world. This teaching incorporates the astrological wisdom Abraham was said to have known "in his heart"—that is, was revealed to him through meditative or magical means.

Forty miles or so inland from Jiddah, in what is now Saudi Arabia, the town of Mecca sits at the juncture of pre-Islamic Arabia's most important trade routes. The mile-long caravans traveling from the spice kingdoms of southern Arabia to the world markets of Mesopotamia turned north and east through the gap in the Hejaz Mountains near Mecca. Cargo from Africa—Abyssinia, now Ethiopia, lies just across the Red Sea—landed at Jiddah and moved inland for distribution at Mecca. The town thrived on trade and travelers. This is significant because, from its founding, the town of Mecca was also an important sacred site and a destination for pilgrims.

The ancient Arabs were pantheists who worshipped the spirit, or genius, of place in a large variety of ways, including pilgrimage and animal—and sometimes human—sacrifice.[22] They personified the sun and the moon, the sky, the stars, and the desert and lived in a world filled with jinns and afreets, or spirits and ghosts. In the vast darkness of the desert, the stars became the backdrop against which the mythological drama of life played itself out. Navigating in the desert, as at sea, required knowledge of the stars and their relationship to time and movement. These factors gave rise to a complex astrological mythology. This astrology was similar, if not exactly the same, to that found in the oldest sections of the *Sefer Yetzirah*.

Abraham, as revealed in the Talmud, was the most famous astrologer of his time. Interestingly enough, even in the eighteenth century B.C.E., Mecca was a junction point in the trade between India and Egypt. According to the tradition within the Quraysh, Muhammad's clan, Abraham and his other son Ishmael, whose name means "God hears," also founded Mecca.

From the *Sefer Yetzirah*, we learn of the Cube of Space (the twelve edges of the cube are formed from the twelve double letters of the Hebrew alphabet, which are attributed to the signs of the zodiac) within which the jewel-like Tree of Life forms. This astrological concept is attributed to Abraham just as the building of the physical cube, the Kaaba of Mecca with its sacred Black Stone, is also claimed as his work. The Kaaba (literally, "cube," and from the same root) is the black stone meteorite that all Muslims attempt to touch at least once in their lifetime. A cube has twelve edges. Each of these edges relates to a different sign in the zodiac. The cube of space in Mecca, here on earth, is a fractal representation of the real Cube of Space.

The pilgrimage to Mecca is one of the five pillars of the Islamic faith. According to Islamic tradition, the Kaaba has been rebuilt ten times, mirroring the number of spheres on the Tree of Life. The Kether, or Crown, cube was said to have been built by the angels in heaven. It is this cube of space that is described in the *Sefer Yetzirah* and the *Bahir.*

Wisdom and Understanding, the second and third cubes, were said by Islamic tradition to have been built by Adam and his youngest son, Seth. The fourth is named Mercy, and Abraham and his son by Hagar, Ishmael, are said to have built it in an after-the-Flood restoration. It is from this point that Mecca dates its founding. Strength and Beauty are the fifth and sixth cubes that were built in Mecca. They are attributed by Arab legends to kings of the Sabean and Himyarite kingdoms. Quasy, the patriarch of the Quraysh, built the seventh cube, Victory. The eighth, Splendor, was completed during Muhammad's lifetime. The ninth and tenth cubes, attributed to the *sefirot* named Foundation and Kingdom, were built within sixty years of his death.

Within the cube is the sacred Black Stone, a piece of purplish red tektite embedded in the wall of the southeastern corner about five feet from the floor—at just the right height for kissing. The Black Stone has been a part of the cube in Mecca since at least the fourth version of the Kaaba attributed to Abraham. Tradition holds that the stone represents the new, post-catastrophe covenant between God and the family of Abraham.

Islamic scholars also point to a verse in Matthew (21:42–43) in support of this tradition. Jesus, during his last week in Jerusalem, often came to the forecourt of Herod's temple to teach. Matthew tells us that as Jesus enters the temple one morning, the chief priests and the elders who demanded by what authority he taught the scriptures accosts him. Jesus asked them a question: Was John baptized by heaven or by men? When the elders cannot answer, Jesus refuses to tell them the source of his authority and then lays into them for spiritual blindness. Even the people on the street, the obvious sinners, could see that John was a man of righteousness, Jesus tells them, but you, the spiritual leaders of the people, still can't decide on the source of John's message.

He continues, making the point even sharper, with the parable of the tenants who wouldn't share the fruits of the harvest with the landlord of the vineyard, but instead killed his servants and his son. Jesus asks the elders what they think would happen when the owner returned. They reply that he would turn the tenants out of the vineyard, of course. Jesus then drove home the point by quoting Psalm 118 (22–23): "The stone the builders rejected has become the head of the corner; the Lord has done this, and it is marvelous in our eyes." To make sure they got it, Jesus said: "Therefore I tell you that the Kingdom of Heaven will be taken from you and given to those who will produce the fruit." It's easy to see how Muslims found in this parable support for their religion. This encounter was very likely the motivating incident that led to Jesus' betrayal and death. From this point on, the Gospels tell us, the Jewish elders plotted a way to arrest him without the people knowing and interfering.

Christian commentators see in this incident the shift from Judaism to Christianity, with Christ as the stone the builders rejected. Jesus is clearly stating that the Jewish elders no longer understood the basis of the religion they professed. To the Muslim, however, who had seen how little spiritual fruit orthodox Christianity produced, this verse suggested another interpretation. The rejected stone was Ishmael, the part of Abraham's progeny rejected by Israel. The stone, the black meteorite, was also rejected, cast out of the sky, or heaven. Since Israel had broken its Abrahamic covenant, the kingdom of heaven reverted to the other heir, Ishmael, who will gather the fruits of the harvest.

The landlord of the vineyard in the parable is, of course, Allah to the Muslim, not Yahweh, or Jehovah, in the Hebraic tradition. In Genesis 14:18, we are told that after a great battle, Abram, as his name was then, worshipped the God Most High with the king of Jerusalem, Melchizedek. As we have seen in the *Bahir*, Melchizedek was thought to be Shem, a son of Noah and a survivor of the catastrophic Flood. He was also Abraham's teacher and collaborator in the work of creation. The titles used in Genesis, "God Most High, Lord of Heaven and creator of the earth," are the same titles used for Baal. They are also the same as the ancient Canaanite name for the Pole Serpent, the Teli, which the *Sefer Yetzirah* tells us is hanging over the "universe . . . like a king on his throne." It is important to understand that all of these mythologies are essentially astronomical. The Teli in Draco is the constellation that rules over all of the signs and therefore the ages and the worlds, the past and the future.

The Islamic creator Allah is simply the Arabic version of this Canaanite El. The name Baal, or Ba-el, is literally translated as "the Space-Filling God." Allah is also called "He who holds the stars in place." This God Most High can only be the constellation of Draco. Not only does Draco fill all the signs of the zodiac, but it also sits atop the Cube of Space very much like a king on his throne.

Before the coming of Islam, at the Kaaba in Mecca the temple of Allah contained altars to his eight wives and daughters. These ancient goddesses are clearly related to the seven planets and the earth. Al-Uzza, the mighty one, was the sun. Al-Manat, the triple-faced goddess, was clearly the moon. The earth goddess, whose name was al-Lat, is actually *talah,* or *teli,* spelled backward. The earth is the mirror of the Teli. Everything that occurs in the heavens will be mirrored down on Earth. Therefore the "Tala" in space becomes al-Lat here on Earth. This serves to clinch our identification of Allah with the Teli, or Pole Serpent.

But there's more—from the ground looking up, the ancient astronomers saw that Draco curved around the still point of the ecliptic pole (fig. 4.9) and that its tail bent backward in the shape of the Arabic letter *laam* (see fig. 4.10). This is perhaps the basis from which the word *El* was derived. Reflected on the earth, however, this *L* of the Teli or Pole Serpent is reversed. If Allah is the God Most High, the *L* in the sky, then his daughter the earth is the reflection of that nature. And so the masculine "El," or "Al," becomes the feminine "al-Lat."

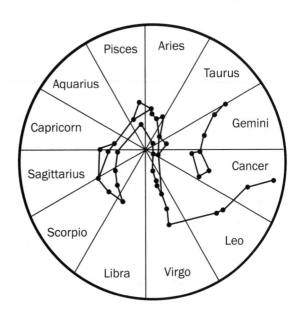

Figure 4.9. A diagram of the constellations Draco and Ursa Minor, according to Ptolemy, shows how the Pole Serpent has stars in all the houses of the zodiac, and how it curves around the ecliptic pole.

Figure 4.10. The Arabic letter *laam*.

The Quraysh, who thought of themselves as descendants of Abraham, worshipped Allah as their chief god. They referred to him as the Lord of the Soil, to whom they must pay a tithe of their crops and herds. This was not quite monotheism—Allah still had his wives—but it paved the way for Muhammad's insistence that Allah was the One and only God. Muhammad, like Abraham, decided that the God Most High was the only god worthy of worship.

The Book of Genesis, chapter 15, tells us that, soon after Abram received the blessing of the God Most High, the Lord visited his word upon him in a vision. He commanded Abram to look up at the stars and count them, if he could. God promises that Abram's descendants will be as numerous as the stars, or possibly will be as the stars. All he has to do is make a covenant with the Lord by performing a peculiar ritual sacrifice. Abram is told to take five animals, split the heifer, the goat, and the ram in half, and leave the two birds whole. The ten resulting sections, the six separated halves and the four unseparated halves, can be attributed to the spheres on the Tree of Life, according to the sages of the *Sefer Yetzirah.*

This arrangement polarized the Tree of Life. The Tree is normally shown aligned along three parallel axes, but, as shown in figure 4.11, it is split in Abraham's sacrifice into two groups of five, like the fingers on each hand (see fig. 4.12). The spheres were then given masculine or feminine qualities. Six are clearly opposite each other, since they occur on the right or left pillar of the Tree, while the remaining four are normally on the middle axis. These four are divided into Kether and Tiferet on the right and Yesod and Malkuth on the left. This also symbolizes Abram's arrangement of offerings, and creates a tension between Binah and Tiferet and Yesod and Tiferet.

Abram made his strange sacrifice of the split animals at sunset and

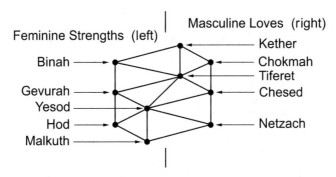

Figure 4.11. The Tree polarized according to masculine and feminine qualities; in this human-scale form, the values of each *sefirot* take a gender specific quality. The interplay of duality is what gives the symbolism of the Tree of Life its diversity and universality.

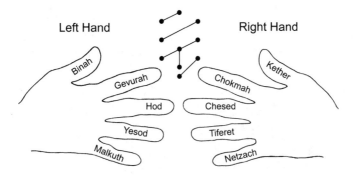

Figure 4.12. The kabbalistic spheres attributed to the fingers.

fell into a deep sleep. We are told that thick and dreadful darkness came over him, and the Lord spoke within it describing the future of Abram's descendants. And then a curious thing happened. Abram had a vision of a smoking firepot with a blazing torch. According to most authorities, this is an ancient symbol of the presence of the God Most High. This torch or pillar went through the gap between Binah and Tiferet and Yesod and Tiferet. This, Genesis tells us, sealed the covenant between Abram and his god.

Later, when Abram was ninety-nine years old, the God Most High made a return appearance to confirm the covenant. This time the Lord changed Abram's name to Abraham, by adding an *h,* or the Hebrew letter *heh,* in the middle. *Heh,* as shown in figure 4.13, is a pictogram of

Figure 4.13. The Hebrew letter *heh* as a pictogram of a window.

a window in ancient Hebrew. The Lord also instituted the rite of circumcision as a physical sign of man's acceptance of the covenant. From this point on, Abraham's descendants were the chosen people of the God Most High.

Much of this makes little sense until we remember that, in the *Bahir*, the twelve edges of the Cube of Space are also the zodiacal paths connecting the spheres on the Tree. The gap or aisle between the sacrifices represents the astrological signs of Sagittarius and Gemini. These signs mark the third dragon-axis, as we noted above, which is the axis of the galaxy itself. The firepot with a blazing torch, symbol of the presence of the God Most High, travels the major axis of the galaxy, from the center out to the edge (fig. 4.14).

Abraham made his covenant, then, with the creative force flowing outward from the galactic core, or third dragon-axis. He called this the God Most High, who is also Muhammad's Allah. Our world is formed from the intersection of the three pillars or axes of the Teli. Abraham's descendants entered the *galgal*, or cycle of time, through the *heh*, or

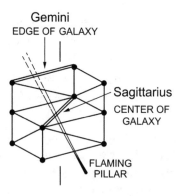

Gemini
EDGE OF GALAXY

Sagittarius
CENTER OF
GALAXY

FLAMING
PILLAR

Figure 4.14. The polarization between the fingers/*sephiot* creates the space through which the "presence" of God, symbolized as a flaming torch or a ball of fire, passed.

window, added to his name by the Lord. *Heh* is assigned to Aquarius, a zodiacal sign at a right angle to the axis of the Galaxy. It also symbolizes the moving axis of the Coiled Serpent, which defines the evolutionary flow of human events and the quality of time. Abraham's descendants would be the chosen people of God as long they remembered the window into the cycle of time that God had given them. This may be the motivation behind Jesus' warning that the Hebrews had lost their true faith—they had forgotten the window into the cycles of time.

The Black Stone was the physical seal of this covenant, a gift from the sky, a token of God's favor. It is interesting to note that the description in Genesis 15:17 of the smoking firepot with a blazing torch coming out of it also suggests the path of a meteor through the sky. The actual placement of the Black Stone within the Kaaba also suggests the northwest–southeast axis of the galaxy as seen in two dimensions. The stone that fell from heaven is a physical piece of evidence for the presence of the God Most High. With this in mind, we can understand the reference in Psalm 118 to the rejected stone that became the head of the corner, and Jesus' denunciation of the Jewish elders for not understanding their own religion.

If Jesus was a student of the *Bahir,* then he would have known the secret of the Teli. From the elders' answer to the question of authority, Jesus knew that they no longer grasped the secret of time. John the Baptist had preached that the kingdom of heaven was near. How could he have known that? This is really what Jesus is asking the priests and elders. They, of course, have no answer, so Jesus refuses to tell them the truth. By asking the right question, we can see that he must have already known the answer.

ISLAM: SANCTUARY OF SACRED SCIENCE

Muhammad, like Abraham and Isis the Prophetess, received his wisdom directly from an angelic messenger. The Koran is the collection of Muhammad's revelations. They were written down within fifty years after his death by his followers, who had memorized the words as they were pronounced. The Koran leaves little doubt about angelic intervention. Like all successful prophets and spiritual leaders, Muhammad gave a voice to the needs and longings of his time.

The Arabs were influenced by the Christians and the Jews who lived among them, and they eagerly awaited their own messenger from God. Muhammad admired the ethical precepts of Christianity and the monotheism of the Jews. He was also conscious of the power of a divinely inspired scripture to mold a religion. Others may have had similar thoughts. From Byzantine sources we hear of several Arab "prophets" who rose to prominence during the late sixth and early seventh centuries. Muhammad's difference, and perhaps the root of his success, lies in his connection through the Kaaba with the mysteries of creation given to Abraham. He could speak with authority because he had rediscovered the window into the cycles of time, and his proof was the Koran, which flowed from above in a torrent of revelation.

Muhammad's revelations began on the night of the twenty-seventh of Ramadan in the year 610 C.E. Muhammad was alone in the great cave at the foot of Mount Hira, a few miles outside of Mecca. He had gone there to pray and meditate, but he was asleep when the angel Gabriel appeared with a curious book and demanded that he read it. Muhammad was illiterate so he protested that he could not read. Then the angel pressed its weight down on him to the point that he thought he was going to smother to death. When the angel released him, Muhammad sat up and found that he could read. On awakening, Muhammad felt that words from the magical book were engraved in his heart. He fled out of the cave, into the early-morning sunlight, and beheld a vision of the angel Gabriel as the cosmic man. In that moment Gabriel declared that Muhammad was indeed the messenger of Allah.

Thereafter, the revelations came thick and fast. Often, when they came, Muhammad would fall to the ground in a convulsion or a swoon. He would become drenched with sweat. Even his camel would become skittish when a spell hit. Muhammad was transformed by these experiences; from a shy and introspective orphan, he became the patriarch of the Arab people.

His cousin and son-in-law, Ali, left us a vivid description of Muhammad a few years after his revelations began. He describes Muhammad as "of middle stature, neither tall nor short. His complexion was rosy white, his eyes black; his hair, thick, brilliant and beautiful, fell to his shoulders. His profuse beard fell to his breast. . . . There was such sweetness in his visage that no one, once in his presence, could leave him. If I hungered, a single look at the Prophet's face dispelled the hunger. Before him, all forgot their grief and pains."[23]

Later, when he was pressed to describe the process of revelation, Muhammad declared that the entire text of the Koran was a book written in heaven. He said the angel Gabriel communicated it to him one piece at a time. Asked how he could remember these divine discourses, Muhammad replied that he repeated each phrase after the angel. The stress from the experience, he said, caused his hair to turn gray.

For a decade, Muhammad preached in Mecca. He made little headway in converting the population, except for his immediate family and the ones that became known as the Companions. The Companions were the true believers, such as Abu Bakr and Omar al-Khattab. For a while Muhammad moved to al-Taif, a center of the goddess al-Uzza, the mighty one worshipped by his mother's clan. From this brief exodus came the so-called Satanic Verses, where the Koran seems to endorse goddess worship. Within a year after this, Muhammad was back in Mecca preaching in front of the Kaaba.

This time, however, he was without protection. The control of the main clan had passed to the mortal enemies of Muhammad's uncle. Islam found itself severely persecuted. But just when things looked bleakest, a miracle happened, or so it seemed to Muhammad. Before he left for the city of al-Taif, Muhammad had preached to a group of pilgrims from the garden city of Yathrib. Afterward it would be forever known as Medina, or The City.

The town of Yathrib had a large Jewish population that responded to Muhammad's teachings. Because of the similarity to their own religion, they accepted his teaching and began to spread the word back home. They were also willing to accept Muhammad as the messenger of a monotheistic Allah who will reign over the earth at the Last Judgment. So Muhammad fled Mecca for Yathrib, which became the City of the Prophet. The year of his departure, or *hejira*, became the starting point for the Islamic calendar.

Eight years later, after much skirmishing and caravan raiding, Muhammad marched back into Mecca as the conquering messenger. He cleaned out the Kaaba, removed the altars to Allah's wives and daughters, but kept the Black Stone and its ritual kiss. He then proclaimed Mecca the Holy City of Islam. For the last two years of his life, Muhammad ruled from Mecca with a gentle hand. As Islam grew, Muhammad sent letters to the capitals of the world announcing his revelation. He received no replies to these letters. Casually he watched the mutual destruction of Byzantium and Persia. There is no indication that Muhammad ever considered spreading the Islamic faith outside of Arabia.

That was not the case, however, with his heirs. Muhammad had appointed no successor. After a brief rivalry, the Muslim leaders elected Abu Bakr, the first Companion, to be caliph, or representative of the faithful. Abu Bakr's faith and steadfastness saw the faith through its first war and rebellion. Khalid ibn al-Walid was the most brilliant and ruthless of the Muslim Arab generals. He went from pacifying Arabia to defeating the Greek emperor Heraclius outside Damascus. With that, Syria became an Arab and Islamic stronghold.

By then Abu Bakr had died and a fellow Companion, Omar al-Khattab, had been chosen caliph. Omar encouraged the Islamic conquest. In 644 Omar was cut down by a Persian slave in the Medina mosque. But by then the Muslim armies ruled Egypt, Palestine, and Persia. The conquests continued under Othman the Unfortunate, until by the time of Ali's caliphate (656–661), the Islamic domains extended from the Atlas Mountains in North Africa to the Black Sea and the mountains of Afghanistan.

Less than thirty years after the death of Muhammad, Islam ruled more of the earth than Rome had at its height. It is hard to imagine how a political, social, and religious shift of this magnitude could have happened. But it did.

Muhammad taught of a stern, yet merciful, God in terms more than faintly reminiscent of the *Bahir* and the *Sefer Yetzirah*. In the Koran, sura 2:255, the famous Throne Verse, we find Allah described in terms remarkably similar to those used to describe the Teli, or Pole Serpent. "His Throne extends over the heavens and the earth . . . He alone is Most High and Supreme."

The Koran is filled with references to the Last Judgment. Only Allah, the Koran tells us, knows the time of the Last Judgment. We are also told that certain signs will prefigure its arrival. Disbelief in God will be widespread, along with moral chaos. There will be tumults in the sky and on the earth. Wars of such magnitude will occur that the wise men will wish themselves dead. The final signal will be three trumpet blasts. At the first, our material universe will be destroyed. The second will "uncreate" all men and angels and spirits, while the third will accomplish the resurrection. Then Allah will arrive to conduct the

Judgment. Only those who can cross the bridge of al-Sirat, which is finer than a hair and sharper than a sword, will be allowed to enter Paradise.

In the Koran, Paradise is described as a perfect garden where all manner of good things to eat and drink are available, including wine that exhilarates while leaving one clearheaded. These eternal feasts are attended by nubile beauties whom neither age nor weariness nor death can mar. The blessed will see the face of Allah and become immortal, "never growing old." Who could resist such an image of Paradise?

The most significant sura in the Koran, from the perspective of the secret at the heart of alchemy, is sura 24 (fig. 4.15). It is named al-Nur, or the Light. In verse 35 of the sura, the secret is revealed with blinding clarity: "Allah is the light of the heavens and the earth. The semblance of His light is that of a niche in which is a lamp, the flame within a glass, the glass a glittering star as it were, lit with the oil of the blessed Tree, neither of the East nor of the West, whose oil appears to light up even though fire touches it not—Light upon Light!"

We shall wait until we have heard from Fulcanelli before we interpret this most significant verse. For now, let us note that this verse is the origin point for Islamic mysticism, illumination, and gnosis. Mansur al-Hallaj, the great Sufi mystic, tells us that the Light is from "a star whose

Figure 4.15. The Light Verse, sura 24:35, in a modern circular motif.

astrological house is in the empyrean." *Empyrean* in this sense refers to the highest of heavens, and this suggests the mid-heaven point of the north ecliptic pole. He also suggests that the light symbolizes the peace of the tranquil heart.

Muhammad apparently gave esoteric teachings on these and other verses of the Koran to his son-in-law Ali, who passed them down to his son and grandson. Ali's caliphate ended in the first great schism of Islam, when the religious and political authorities of the Arabs split away from the family of the prophet. By 680 C.E., most of Muhammad's family had been killed. Only an infant son, Ali's grandson and the great-grandson of the Prophet, survived to carry on the tradition. From this came the split in Islam between Sunni and Shi'ite that exists to this day.

For the first two hundred years or so of Islamic civilization, mysticism took a backseat—except among the Shi'ites, or the "adherents" of the family of the Prophet.[24] The caliphs became ever more corrupt as their power grew. Persecutions of the Shi'as increased. A general feeling developed that Islam had somehow conquered the world and lost its soul.[25] Mansur al-Hallaj, quoted above, symbolized this defiantly mystical spirit. He was burned alive for blasphemy in 923 C.E.

But a new spiritual current emerged from the Islamic underground. Composed of fragments of all the conquered civilizations and religions but held together by the teachings of the Prophet, the mystical tradition that in many cases far predated Islam found a home within it. The new Sufi movement accepted the corruption of the ruling classes and set to work to renovate the human soul. Another branch of Shi'ite Sufis, however, moved from mysticism to covert political action. Their goal was to create a theocracy based on the inner teachings of Muhammad.

The word *sufi*—composed of three Arabic letters, the *sa*, the *wa*, and the *fa*—has many different connotations and derivations. To some, it means *safa*, or "purity." Others see it as *safwe*, or "the selected ones." Other contenders are *saf*, "line" and "row," because the Sufis follow the "straight path" of Muhammad. *Suf*, "wool," is also a good candidate because the Sufis often wore long woolen robes. The Greek word *sophia*, or wisdom, is also a possible candidate. But the inner meaning of *sa-wa-fa* is *sufah*, or "whirlwind."[26] This inner meaning points to the process of spiritual transformation that is at the heart of Sufism. One of the later Sufi orders, the Mevlevis of Turkey, founded by Rumi, made whirling or spinning one of their spiritual disciplines as an outward demonstration of this principle.

Fifty years after the death of al-Hallaj, Sufism blossomed. The eleventh century saw the rise of the first great Sufi teaching orders in the East and the West.[27] As the Sufi movement grew, the more worldly and political branch of the Shi'ites almost succeeded in conquering the Muslim world.

After the first wave of Arab conquest swept over North Africa, its provinces soon became independent kingdoms. By the tenth century, three great Islamic kingdoms ruled in North Africa. They were the Idrisid dynasty in Morocco, the Aghlabid in Libya, and the Tulunid in Egypt. In the first decade of the tenth century, a Shi'ite adventurer, Abu Abdallah, gained a following in Libya and Tunisia by preaching the coming of the Mahdi, the Shi'ite savior or world ruler. Within a few years, Abdallah overthrew the Aghlabid dynasty. To fulfill his claims he invited a descendant of the Prophet, Obeidallah ibn Muhammad, to become king. Since Obeidallah was a descendant of Fatima, Muhammad's daughter, the new dynasty called itself Fatimid.

Under the Fatimids, North Africa regained a wealth and prosperity that it had not seen since the days of Carthage and republican Rome. Trade routes crossed the Sahara to Lake Chad and Timbuktu in central Africa. After the Fatimids conquered Egypt in 969 C.E., the Sudan and Abyssinia were also integrated into the Islamic trading network. Egypt became the commercial link between Europe and Asia. By the early eleventh century, the Fatimid caliph, ruling from Cairo, controlled two thirds of the Muslim world, from Fez in Morocco to Damascus in Syria.

The Fatimid mosques of Cairo provide an important link, both architecturally and spiritually, to the Gothic cathedrals of Europe. The mosque of Ibn Tulun, begun before the Fatimid conquest, combines pointed arches and vaulting with rosette stained-glass windows in stellar and geometrical patterns. This impulse reached its high point with the Al Azhar Mosque.

Jauhar, the converted Christian slave who conquered Egypt for the Fatimids, built the mosque between 970 and 972. The Al Azhar Mosque (*al-azhar* means "the brilliant" or "the illuminated," from the same root as the Hebrew *bahir*, "brilliance" or "illumination") contains the pointed arches and vaulting—supported by 380 pillars of marble, granite, and porphyry—used in the Ibn Tulun Mosque. It is also famous for its stained-glass designs. The reds and blues used in the Al Azhar Mosque were duplicated in the great cathedrals of Europe. But they were never equaled for their depth and purity of color.

In 988, Al Azhar Mosque became the world's first university. The caliph Aziz provided tuition and maintenance for thirty-five scholars. As this school developed, it drew students from all over the Muslim world. It continues to this day with thousands of students and hundreds of teachers. Its influence on the course of history has been profound, especially to medieval Europe.

Al Azhar's most famous scholar was the Muslim scientist known to the West as Alhazen. Mohammed ibn al-Haithan, or Alhazen, was a mathematician and engineer, a sort of Fatimid Leonardo da Vinci. His most important work is a book on optics that anticipates the telescope. Roger Bacon quotes his work extensively, as do Kepler and Leonardo. We can hardly exaggerate the importance of Alhazen for the foundation of modern astronomy.

Attached to the Al Azhar Mosque was the Dar al-Hikmah, or the Hall of Wisdom, where Shi'ite theology was studied alongside medicine and astronomy. Ali ibn Yunus, perhaps the greatest of Muslim astronomers, worked in the observatory of the Hall of Wisdom for seventeen years, compiling the first accurate tables of planetary cycles, measuring the inclination of the ecliptic, and discussing the precession of the equinoxes.[28] These are all astronomical preoccupations suggested by the *Bahir* and the *Sefer Yetzirah,* and provide the key to understanding the great cycles of time.

As the Fatimid dynasty spread, it propped up its power by gathering all of the Shi'ite sects into one grand lodge of Cairo. This vast semi-secret society was held together by complex initiations and hierarchical degrees. Its members were used for political espionage and intrigue. The forms of the order strongly influenced the rituals and organization of the Templars.[29] It is possible that much of Western esotericism and its secret societies originated with the "Illuminated Mosque" and its Hall of Wisdom.

Muhammad's revelation transformed a nomadic and barbarian culture into a world-class civilization. The power of that revelation, as we saw above, came from its ancient roots in the astrological magic of Abraham. With the Kaaba of Mecca as its focus, Islam managed to hold on to its ancient wisdom and even transmit it to the spiritually bankrupt West. The Crusaders, especially the Knights Templar, came look-ing for conquests and kingdoms. They found both, but they also dis-covered the secret mysteries of the alchemy of time. They brought this astronomical alchemical knowledge to Europe.[30] Because of the contact between the Templars and the Islamic scientists, Europe enjoyed an unparalleled spiritual renaissance, the era of the Gothic cathedrals.

PART THREE

The Gothic Renaissance and the Holy Grail

The builders of the Middle Ages had the natural attributes of faith and modesty. The anonymous creators of pure works of art, they built for Truth, for the affirmation of their ideal, for the propagation and the nobility of their science. . . .

The alchemists of the fourteenth century used to meet there once a week on the day of Saturn, either at the main porch, at the Portal of St. Marcel or else at the little Porte-Rouge, all decorated with salamanders.

—LE MYSTÈRE DES CATHÉDRALES

FIVE

THE HERMETIC POPE
AND THE KNIGHTS TEMPLAR

THE ALCHEMICAL TRANSMISSION AND
THE RECOVERY OF THE WEST

Having examined the first thousand years of alchemy's history, it is time to take stock of what we have discovered. The earliest surviving alchemical texts all have pre-Christian Gnostic associations. The Emerald Tablet inclines toward Greco-Egyptian Gnosticism as its source, while the "Isis the Prophetess" story suggests an Egypto-Hebraic origin. The connection point is ancient Egypt.

Zosimos informs us in his *First Book of the Final Reckoning* that alchemy derived from the wisdom of the pre-catastrophe offspring of semidivine beings and humans.[1] As noted in chapter 2, these beings were known in ancient Egypt as the Heru Shemsu, or the Company of Horus, the Followers of the Widow's Son. The "Isis the Prophetess" story is our last text of the ancient wisdom, and in it we can identify the major alchemical themes and preoccupations of the following two thousand years. Alchemy, as "Isis the Prophetess" tells us, is composed of three transformations: an interior transformation, an exterior elemental transformation of matter, and a transformation of time itself.

In the collapse of the ancient world that began with Alexander, this unitary view of alchemy fragmented into several parallel currents. The physical transformative process was seen as separate and became confused with metallurgical and proto-chemical trickery. The internal transformation became the basis for the experiential mysticism, or gnosticism, of Christianity, Judaism, and Islam. The secret of the transformation of time, the advent of the kingdom of heaven, became the inner core of early Christianity. Unfortunately, this vision was co-opted and debased by the Church into an ongoing apocalypse against heretics. In Judaism, the secret of time was intimately intertwined with the work of creation, the ability to animate matter. As we saw in the *Bahir,* Jewish mysticism retained intact a major portion of the secret.

With Islam, the split began to widen even further. The secret of time, contained in the heart of Muhammad's revelation, was retained as a family secret among the descendants of the Prophet. The internal transformative processes became the mystical practices of the Sufis, while the external transformation of the elements became one of the cornerstones of Islamic science, along with medicine, astronomy, and mathematics. Within Islam, threads of all three transformative processes can be found, but it is hard to find anything close to a unitary system.

By the second half of the tenth century, this separation had reached a kind of maximum dispersion. The secrets of the *Bahir* were known only to a few small groups of Jewish mystics. The Islamic mystics were just forming the early Sufi orders, while the Shi'ite owners of the inner secret were trying to conquer the Islamic world. Christianity, of course, had persecuted its alchemists and gnostics out of existence, leaving a shroud of darkness over the entire seven-hundred-year period from the fall of Rome to the Crusades.[2]

Learning in the West sank to a level little above superstition.[3] Such scholars as there were, Pope Gregory the Great (590–604), for instance, dwelt mainly on ecclesiastical matters with an amazing credulity for tales of marvels, miracles, and the possession of human beings by demons. Beyond such writings, there were only confused compilations from fragments of classical authors, variously and often wrongly ascribed. These were the crumbs of ancient wisdom that nourished that dark and arid age.

This sad state of affairs began to change when the Muslim Arabs and Berbers entered Spain from North Africa in the eighth century. Islam, seemingly endowed with an insatiable curiosity for foreign learning and guided by a truly Oriental imagination that was in sharp contrast to the passive intellectualism of the West, revitalized the civilization of the territories it conquered. Europe was saved from this fate by Charlemagne's grandfather, Charles Martel, at the battle of Tours in 732. But Spain became a Muslim stronghold (see fig.5.1).

Figure 5.1. The tenth-century gardens of Cordova in Muslim Spain.

In the centuries that followed the Arab rise to world-power status, its caliphs, sultans, and generals exhibited a great interest in learning and arranged for the literature of the conquered areas to be translated into Arabic. Much of the ancient wisdom was preserved in these Arabic translations. The writings of Aristotle, Archimedes, Apollonius, Euclid, Hippocrates, and Galen were all preserved for later rediscovery in the West by these Arabic collections. It was also through these Arabic sources that knowledge of alchemy was reintroduced to Europe.

We have already mentioned Jabir, an eighth-century collector and interpreter of gnostic alchemical texts, but of even more significance is the treatment given to the hermetic arts in the great tenth-century Arabic encyclopedia, *Kitab-Fihirst.* Several pages are devoted to various hermetic subjects, including mention of the Egyptian Chemes, the pre-catastrophe founder of alchemy, Hermes Trismegistus, Mary the Jewess, Cleopatra, and Stephan of Alexandria. The Arabs, at the close of the tenth century, had created a perspective on alchemy as a physical methodology that would color its subsequent development down to the twentieth century.

Spain served as the transmission point between Islam and Christianity. As the tide of Islamic conquest receded, pockets of Christianity remained on the Spanish peninsula and slowly formed into Christian kingdoms. Along with the religious and political struggles, this close contact provided a convenient means of communication. After the Fatimids conquered North Africa in the tenth century, Arab Spain found itself even more isolated from the centers of Muslim life. The Spanish caliphs of the late tenth and early eleventh centuries were concerned with staying even with or ahead of their Fatimid rivals, particularly in terms of culture and learning. It was from Spain, then, that Europe drew the energy and knowledge needed to reanimate its civilization.[4]

By the early years of the eleventh century, largely as the result of the efforts of one individual, Gerbert of Aurillac, who would become Pope Sylvester II, the intellectual climate in the West had begun to change. Fueled in part by the apocalyptic yearnings centered on the thousand-year anniversary of Christ's death (popularized by Sylvester's student Rodulphus Glaber), the Christian West began to stir itself. The Church of Rome tried a few reforms, driven by the new and growing monastic and Peace of God movements. But most significant of all, waves of pilgrims took the long and dusty road to Jerusalem.

Pilgrimage, journeys of repentance and spiritual seeking, had long been an important part of popular Christianity. But before the middle of the eleventh century, pilgrimages to the Holy Land were rare. Starting around the magical year of 1033 (one thousand years after Christ's death) and continuing in an ever-increasing wave for the next forty years, Jerusalem became the pilgrimage destination of choice. In 1071, the Seljuk Turks conquered Palestine, wrenching the Holy Land from the control of the Egyptian Fatimids, who were sympathetic to the Christian pilgrims. The Turks, however, were not so accommodating. By the early 1080s, pilgrimage to Jerusalem had all but stopped. The few pilgrims who were allowed to visit the Holy City were harassed, robbed, and generally treated as unwanted outsiders.[5]

Most authorities tell us that this was the motivating factor behind the crusading movement that would overtake Europe after Pope Urban II's call in 1095.[6] The pilgrim impulse, however, soon turned into Holy

War. While there is a kernel of truth in this simplification, the real causes of the First Crusade are shrouded by the secrecy of deep political intrigue. From our thousand-year distance, these shadows are almost impenetrable. Like the sudden appearance of a star through the murk of a cloudy midnight, however, certain events and personalities shed some light on the outlines of the Crusades' political intrigues.

The most important of these events was the political conjunction between East and West begun by Pope Sylvester II, the new Holy Roman emperor, Otto III, and the mad caliph al-Hakim one hundred years before the First Crusade was announced. While it is true that the First Crusade was a pilgrim movement with Jerusalem as its focus, it was also much more. It was part of a vast plan conceived and carried out by a group of secret societies for the purpose of creating a world-state in the Holy Land and thereby bring on the chiliast millennium of peace.[7]

THE ALCHEMICAL POPE AND THE CREATION OF THE MILLENNIUM

As the Fatimid influence spread in the tenth and eleventh centuries, some of the esoteric knowledge began to reach Europe through the schools of Muslim Spain, where science and civilization had attained a level unknown elsewhere. The best minds of Europe traveled to Spain to study everything from music to medicine to astronomy. One such student, Gerbert of Aurillac, stands out as particularly notable. It was Gerbert's efforts that almost single-handedly pulled the Christian West out of the Dark Ages.

Gerbert's life is an example of how a poor intellectual prodigy could rise to the very top of early medieval society. He was born around 940 in Auvergne, France, and at an early age entered the nearby monastery of Aurillac. At the abbot's insistence, Gerbert was sent to Spain to study mathematics (see fig. 5.2).

Spain in the mid-960s was at the peak of its civilization. The caliph Hakim II, son of the triumphant Abd-al-Rahman, who forged Muslim Spain into a world power, surpassed every one of his predecessors in the love of literature and the sciences, we are told by the Muslim historian al-Maqrizi.[8] He turned all of Andalusia, Muslim Spain, into a market where the wisdom and learning of the whole ancient and medieval

Figure 5.2. Gerbert of Aurillac, later Pope Sylvester II, the renaissance man of the Dark Ages. (Mural from the Vatican library)

world could be found. It was into this environment that the young prodigy, Gerbert of Aurillac, was immersed, studying at the monastery of Santa Maria de Ripoll (see fig. 5.3).

Gerbert must have done very well indeed, because we find Count Borel of Barcelona introducing him to the pope in 970. Pope John XIII, one of the few popes of the period who seemed sincere and managed to die of old age instead of assassination, was so impressed by Gerbert's erudition that he recommended him to the up-and-coming Otto I, emperor of the Roman West and the Charlemagne of Germany.

After seventy years of internal discord, Otto I, a match for Charlemagne in looks and temperament, became the king of the Franks. At his coronation, Otto surrounded himself with the nobility of the neighboring countries, creating at the very beginning of his reign a sense of transnational importance. No wonder he soon began to see himself as the restorer of the Western Empire.

In the first fifteen years of his reign, Otto strove by any means possible, from war to murder to marriage, to accomplish this goal. In 962,

Figure 5.3. Seventeenth-century engraving of the monastery of Santa Maria de Ripoll, near Barcelona in Catalonian Spain, where Gerbert learned astronomy, mathematics, Greek, and the magic of the Moors. Uncredited figure from James Reston's *The Last Apocalypse* (New York: Doubleday, 1998)

Pope John XII crowned Otto the Holy Roman Emperor of the West. Within a year of his becoming emperor, Otto had marched into Italy and made it a part of the new Holy Roman Empire, which was, of course, a mere appanage of the Frankish crown of Charlemagne. This was the new world power to which the young and scholarly Gerbert was introduced in 970.

For the next thirty-three years, Gerbert would be the spiritual adviser and mentor to all three Ottos, Otto I, his son Otto II, and his grandson Otto III. Gerbert's vast learning and command of all three diplomatic languages of his day, Latin (which he wrote with an elegance not seen since Sidonius in the fifth century),[9] Greek, and Arabic, made him an important player in the diplomatic intrigues of the new imperial court. From the mid-970s to his death in 1003, Gerbert would remain at the center of the changes sweeping through the West.

During the year he served as tutor to the young Otto II, Gerbert also helped Otto I arrange a marriage between the Greek emperor's daughter, Theophano, and his student. This would make their son, the future Otto III, the heir of both halves of the old Roman Empire.

Hard on the heels of the successful conclusion of the marriage negotiations and the wedding, Gerbert was dispatched, at his own request,
to Rheims, the ancient and royal cathedral town of Charlemagne,
where every king of France (from Clovis I in the fifth century to Louis
XVI in the eighteenth) was crowned. Soon after his arrival, he was
appointed head of the cathedral's school by Otto II in appreciation for
his diplomatic efforts. He held this post for a decade, and during that
time he collected manuscripts from around the world and wrote works
on the astrolabe, Arabic astronomy, and geometry.

Gerbert left his post as master of the cathedral school at Rheims in
982. During this period we find him writing letters to various other
cathedral schools promoting the development of libraries and encour-
aging the addition of Greek and mathematics to the curriculum.

Gerbert's opportunity to return to power politics arrived in 987
with the death of the last Carolingian king of France, Louis V. The
unhappy Louis left no heirs, so the choice was between Charles of
Lorraine, Louis' brother and a distant offshoot of the Carolingian line,
and the best candidate from the line of the previous dynasty, the
Merovingian.

This obscure Dark Age dynasty has been made famous by the speculations in *Holy Blood, Holy Grail* that the descendants of Jesus and
Mary Magdalene in fact founded this royal lineage. There is just
enough evidence in support of the contention that the Holy Family, its
relatives, and perhaps even descendants survived in southern France to
make us wonder exactly what their contemporaries made of it all.
While the Merovingians were certainly thought to be peculiar, there is
no contemporary indication that anyone connected the Merovingians
directly to the Holy Family.[10]

Medieval tradition reports that the Merovingians had a supernatural origin. Gregory of Tours, the foremost Frankish historian, tells us
that Merovee, the founder of the dynasty, was the son of two fathers.
The first king of the Franks, Chlodio, was one father. The other was a
strange sea creature, "similar to a Quinotaur," according to Gregory of
Tours, which impregnated his mother while she was out bathing in the
ocean. From this, he was given the name Merovee, "son of the sea."
Merovee can also be translated as "son of the mother" and "son of
Mary."

The latter are strange titles for a barbarian and pagan king. His descendant Clovis I became ruler over a united Gaul and eventually, after much prayer on the part of the hermit monk Saint Remy, was converted to orthodox Christianity. This alliance helped stabilize the Western church. For 250 years, the Merovingian rulers were like priest-kings, strangely above and exempt from the censure of the church they supported. Their "mayors of the palace" handled the actual government. In the end, it was one of these mayors, Charlemagne's great-grandfather, Pepin the Short, who finished off the main line of the Merovingian dynasty.

But other Merovingian lines had survived, most prominently that of Neustria, the Merovingian kingdom that included Rheims and Paris. Descendants of the Merovingian kings had remained in control of the region as its dukes and even as the mayor of Paris. It was almost inevitable that when the Carolingian line died out, the kingship would revert to a descendant of the Merovingian line.

A church council called by Archbishop Adalbero of Rheims and organized by Gerbert of Aurillac decided the issue. Gerbert may in fact have done the research to prove Hugh Capet's claim to Merovingian ancestry. The council found that Hugh Capet's family were indeed descendants of the last king of Neustria, and therefore unanimously elected him the new king of France.

The next year Archbishop Adalbero died and Gerbert rightly believed that he should be his successor as archbishop of Rheims. Hugh Capet, ever the politician, gave the archbishop's post to Arnulf, a bastard son of the Carolingian line. Hugh meant no insult; it was just politics. But it was politics that backfired. Arnulf plotted against Hugh, and in 991 a French church council deposed him and put Gerbert in his place.

For the next four years, Gerbert used his position as archbishop of Rheims to support the growth of the peace movement. He also founded a variety of clerical orders—known collectively as the Chroniclers, or the chronicling orders—and libraries in places far distant from Rheims, including Provence, Aquitaine, Lorraine, and Calabria in northern Italy. During this time, however, the French church was fighting a fierce battle with the current pope, John XV, over whether they had the right to depose Arnulf.

Faced with excommunication over the issue, Gerbert stepped down from the archbishop's post and moved from Rheims to join the young

Otto III's emerging court in Cologne. In 996, Otto III reached his majority and took over the government with Gerbert of Aurillac by his side (fig. 5.4).

When Pope Gregory V died suddenly, in 999, it was inevitable that Gerbert would succeed him. Gerbert had the support of the emperor, on the spot with his troops, as well as that of the abbot of Cluny, the leading force in both the reform movement and the Peace of God movement. Gerbert saw the coincidence of this alignment of forces as the fulfillment of a long-held dream and fully supported his young protégé in his imperial designs. He became Pope Sylvester II, taking the name of Constantine's pope, Sylvester I, to emphasize the similarity between the two emperors.

With the emperor's support, Gerbert, or Pope Sylvester, as we shall now call him, plunged into a whirlwind of far-reaching negotiations. He expanded the reach of the Catholic Church into Eastern Europe, adding the area of Poland, Czechoslovakia, and Hungary by creating archbishoprics and converting kings. Vajk, the Magyar king of Hungary, was baptized as King Stephen, and eventually became a saint. For his baptism, Sylvester sent him a holy crown to symbolize his Christian kingship.

In addition to converting Eastern Europe (perhaps as a bulwark against the press of Asiatic refugees being pushed westward ahead of the early Tibetan/Mongolian invasions), Sylvester was also interested in converting Islam. With that in mind, he made diplomatic contact with the Fatimid caliph al-Hakim in the year 1000. To see the millennial significance that Sylvester and Otto attached to the turn of the year 1000, we need only look at the *Bamberg Apocalypse,* a manuscript of great artistry that took three years to complete. It was presented to Otto III on his way to Rome on the summer solstice of 1000 C.E. In this work, Otto III is presented as the last emperor, the emperor of Armageddon. With this as a context, we can see Otto's global perspective and the vital importance of Fatimid Islam.

The early Fatimid caliphs became fabulously wealthy after conquering Egypt in the latter half of the tenth century. Al-Hakim ibn Aziz, who became caliph in 996, the same year Otto III became emperor, inherited tremendous wealth and power. In the end it was, along with other pressures perhaps, more than he could bear. He went mad, declared himself a god, and died, disappeared, or was assassinated sometime after 1021. But during his reign, far-reaching changes occurred.

Al-Hakim supported the Al Azhar Mosque and its growing university. He founded the Hall of Wisdom (see fig. 5.5), hired Mohammed ibn al-Haitham (Alhazen), the probable inventor of the telescope, and helped Ali ibn Yunus publish his astronomical tables. As much as diplomacy, it was these subjects that Sylvester wanted to discuss. Al-Hakim, a ninth-degree Ismaili initiate,[11] might just have had something to share with the brilliant pope.

In 1001, Sylvester arranged with the Fatimid caliph for a group of clerics and knights from his various chronicling orders to make an expedition to Syria and the Holy Land. Various historians have from time to time pointed to this as the first wave of Crusaders, and just as quickly remarked on their lack of aggressive zeal. Pope Sylvester's Chroniclers, we are told in a twelfth-century papal sermon by John XIX, disappeared without accomplishing anything, except to serve as vassals of the caliph. This implies, of course, that they converted to Islam.

Al-Maqqari, the foremost Muslim historian of the thirteenth century, tells us that al-Hakim greeted the pope's entourage with honor and spent many weeks in Jerusalem discussing with them the virtues of Islam versus Christianity. He was so impressed by their sincerity that the caliph gave them, in September 1002, the use of a Byzantine Greek church on the outskirts of Jerusalem for their chapter house and library.

Figure 5.5. The Hall of Wisdom at Al Azhar Mosque, from an eighteenth-century engraving.

Unfortunately, al-Maqqari doesn't name the entourage or the location of their order, merely that they were there as chroniclers or historians.[12] By the time of the First Crusade, they were established in a Greek basilica on Mount Zion, with the name of The Order of Our Lady of Mount Zion. (See appendix C.)

These were hardly Crusaders. The Muslim authorities do not record that they converted to Islam, but rather that al-Hakim honored them as Christians. They came not to conquer Jerusalem but to do research. We can only speculate on what subjects they researched.

By the time his delegation had established itself in Jerusalem, Sylvester himself had been forced out of Rome by political terrorism. From northern Italy, Sylvester and Otto III struggled with a crumbling political situation. In 1003 they both, within a few months of each other, died under suspicious circumstances. The dream of a united Roman Empire, as some kind of universal world-state, appeared to die with them.

But, in fact, the dream merely went underground for a few generations. To see this, we must look at Sylvester's legacy and his legend.

Combining these perspectives allows us to glimpse the outlines of an ambitious plan and even to note the shuffling of ideas and events behind the official explanations. Sylvester died before the plan began to bear fruit, but the harvest would eventually bring a Christian king of Merovingian descent to the throne of Jerusalem.

The most significant of Sylvester's legacies was the Peace of God movement, which would inspire both the First Crusade and the newly emerging popular heresies, such as those professed by the Cathars and the Bogomils. Church councils and lay preachers spread the idea throughout the West in the century after Sylvester's death, preparing the way for the call to crusade. Both the Peasants' Crusade and its leader, Peter the Hermit, had their origins in the Peace of God movement. Peter the Hermit may, in fact, have had a direct connection with Sylvester's shadowy group of monks and chroniclers.

One of these monks, Richer, of the Order of Saint Remy (the saint who converted Clovis I to Christianity), has left us a portrait of Sylvester's teachings that contains the spark of the legend. Richer tells us, among a list of Gerbert's accomplishments, that he had long studied the hermetic arts. From this remark grew the legend of an alchemist pope.

The most persistent story, first told in the thirteenth century, has Gerbert, while still archbishop of Rheims, constructing a magical bronze "head" that foretells the future. The "head," of course, announces that Gerbert will indeed be pope, which, considering his shaky position as archbishop, was a bold prediction. A similar story of a bronze head would be told about other medieval magicians, including Roger Bacon and Albertus Magnus. It also suggests, in an indirect way, the "head" the Templars were supposed to have worshipped, the mysterious Baphomet.

These similarities are not accidents, but glimpses of the design behind the symbols. Richer, in his *Histories,* gives us the clue. In the sentence after he mentions Gerbert's hermetic accomplishments, we are told that Gerbert had also designed an armillary sphere with which he could determine the location of the sun and the planets in relation to the celestial sphere. Interestingly enough, the earth in this model was round, five hundred years before Columbus.

Later, as pope, Sylvester designed and commissioned a new armillary sphere, a kind of small-scale planetarium, incorporating the information in Ali ibn Yunus's tables. The new sphere showed the plane of the ecliptic, the Milky Way, and the ecliptic and planetary poles (fig. 5.6). It was, in simple terms, a bronze machine for calculating the secret of time, alchemy's third component. In symbolic terms, this sphere of knowledge became the "head" possessed by all famed students of the art in the Middle Ages.

The mysterious name of the Templar's "head," to briefly jump ahead of our story, confirms this assumption. Baphomet, phonetically in Arabic, Aramaic, and Hebrew, is simply *bet'amet,* or "place of truth." The root *ba* or *bet* is the same as the *ba* in Baal, and can signify a house, a place, or the action of filling space. The "place of truth" used as a title could well be meant to signify the space-filling "house" of the Cube of Space in the celestial sphere and the value of its prophetic insight. Over time, the simple phrase became a code word for the secret itself. The Templars did not worship their bronze head; they meditated

Figure 5.6. An eighteenth-century engraving of Pope Sylvester's armillary sphere, the prototype of the Templars' *bet'amet,* or Baphomet.

on it and studied it closely for clues about the secret of time and the timing of their alchemical operations.

Another of Sylvester's chronicling monks, Rodulphus Glaber, jumpstarted the pilgrimage movement with his fanciful account of the millenarian activities surrounding the year 1033, the one thousandth anniversary of Christ's death. While not completely true—we might call it propaganda today—Glaber's tale of cosmic portents and massive pilgrimages to Jerusalem gave voice to the anxieties of its age. A great desire arose in all classes of society to participate in the upcoming millennium, not just wait passively for its arrival. It was this feeling that animated the First Crusade. Conquering Jerusalem brought the millennium one step closer.

The tale of the pope, the emperor, and the caliph remains largely hidden in the fragments strewn through a thousand years of secrecy and internal strife among the holders of various pieces of the secret. Pope Sylvester started a ball rolling that, in a few hundred years, would change beyond recognition the face of European culture. The Crusades opened the East directly to the West, and the hand of Sylvester's design played a part in all of it. Without Sylvester, there might never have been a Crusade. And without Sylvester's Fatimid connections and his chroniclers in Jerusalem, there would certainly never have been an Order of the Knights of the Temple.

The Templars are the point where the political current started by the alchemist pope surfaces into the historical record. The history of the Templars, particularly their mysterious origins and their unaccounted-for wealth, provides for myriad suggestive connections. Without the Templars, there would have been no cathedral-building movement, nor the money to pay for it. From the point of view of our research, without the Templars, there might not have been any such thing as "alchemy" to investigate.

PETER THE HERMIT, THE FIRST CRUSADE, AND THE ROCK OF ZION

Our word *crusade* comes from the Spanish word *cruzada*, meaning "marked with the cross." The Crusaders were indeed marked by the cross in more than just the design emblazoned on their tunics. They were inflamed by a new vision of Christianity, one in which there was work to do—the kind of work the semibarbarian kings of the West understood best, warfare. The First Crusade stands as a kind of human monument to belief in the end of the world.

Sylvester and Otto III had tried to build a new unified world-state from the fragments of the ancient world. They saw this state, which perhaps was meant to include the Fatimids as well, as a bulwark against the rising tide of refugees from eastern Europe and western Asia. In central Europe, these refugees were Kazars, or what would become the Ashkenazi Jews; in Asia Minor, they were known as the Seljuks. These migratory pressures threatened the Byzantine Empire at Constantinople as well the Fatimid control of Palestine. The Western Empire, reviving under Otto III and Sylvester, created the Christian kingdoms of eastern Europe—Poland, Czechoslovakia, and Hungary—as a barrier to further invasions from the East.

United, the three parts of the early medieval world, the two Romes—Constantinople being the second Rome—and the Fatimids, could have resisted not just the pressure of the Turks but also that of the later Mongol invasions. As it happened, however, the Seljuk Turks conquered Palestine in 1071 and threatened the stability of the entire world when they turned on Constantinople. After a disastrous defeat, the Byzantine Empire made a humiliating peace and was left with very little of Asia Minor. The Empire had been saved, but the way to Constantinople was open to the next wave of Turkish invaders.

At this point, a mysterious figure surfaces to begin his career as one of the principle movers and shakers of the First Crusade. In 1088, Peter the Hermit was an unknown monk belonging to one of the clerical or chronicling orders. Curiously, its name has not come down to us, but his appearance on the scene suggests connections at the highest level. That year, Peter the Hermit traveled from Jerusalem to deliver an impassioned plea from Simeon, the patriarch of Jerusalem, to the newly elected pope Urban II (see fig. 5.7). This plea for aid from the West and its offer of reconciliation between the churches would certainly not have been entrusted to a simple itinerant preacher. The patriarch's letter caused years of intense discussion within the Church and set the tone for Urban's papacy.

In early 1095, Alexius I, the Byzantine emperor, sensing weakness in the current Seljuk infighting, sent an envoy to Pope Urban II and the council at Piacenza asking for military aid from the West. Urban II was

Figure 5.7. Peter the Hermit preaching the Crusade. (From a fifteenth-century manuscript illustration, Bridgeman Art Library)

intrigued by the opportunities these entreaties provided, for perhaps the old Sylvestrian scheme of a united world-state could actually be achieved. Urban departed on a six-month tour of northern Italy and southern France collecting support. In August, from Le Puy in southern France, a Church council was called for November at Clermont in Auvergne, not far from the small monastery of Aurillac.

Exactly what Urban had in mind and what he expected from the Clermont council is unclear. He seems to have intended a military expedition, not unlike those he had already sanctioned in Muslim Spain. What he got was something entirely different.

Urban II, born Odo of Chatillon-sur-Marne and a former prior of Cluny, was a man of broad views, an experienced organizer, and a skilled diplomat dedicated to the program of reforms of his predecessor, Gregory VII. Unlike Gregory, whose fiery intensity seemed to leave no one untouched, Urban was supremely human, a medieval pop star of a pope, tall, handsome, socially at ease, and aristocratically distinguished. His overall goal was to reform the Western Church and reunite it with the Eastern Church to create a truly catholic, or universal, Christianity.[13] Toward that end, Alexius I's request for military aid looked like a major breakthrough. Urban was also influenced by the Peace of God movement, which attempted to curtail violence and warfare on certain days of the week and on feast days of the saints, and saw the call to arms against the "accursed race, wholly alienated from God," as he called the Turks in his speech to the crowd at Clermont (see fig. 5.8), as a way to mitigate and channel the violence of the European nobility.

Figure 5.8. Eighteenth-century engraving of the Council of Clermont.

On Tuesday morning, November 27, 1095, thousands had gathered to hear the pope's pronouncement. Itinerant monks and lay preachers had spread the word of the public session for months. When the day arrived, the crowd was far too great for the cathedral, so the meeting was held outdoors, in a field near the eastern gate of the city. After the multitude had gathered, Urban II climbed up on a raised platform and addressed them.

Four contemporary chroniclers reported Urban's words. One of them, Robert the Monk, claimed to have been there and heard the words as Urban spoke them. It is his version that we will paraphrase. He tells us that Urban began by calling on the Franks—"O race of Franks! race beloved and chosen by God!" Robert records—to come to the aid of their brethren in the East. Eastern Christendom had appealed for aid; the Turks were advancing into Christian territory, killing and desecrating as they came. Urban stressed the holiness of Jerusalem and the suffering of the pilgrims who journeyed there. Having painted a somber picture of conditions in the East, Urban made his appeal: Let Western Christendom march to the rescue. Let rich and poor march together and leave off killing each other for the greater good of killing the godless Turks. This was the work of God, Urban declared, and there would be absolution and remission of sins for those who died in this most holy of causes. There must be no delay; let everyone be ready to march by the summer. God will be their guide.[14]

Urban, speaking in French to his fellow Frenchmen, rose to levels of eloquence that the Latin of the chroniclers cannot convey.[15] The enthusiasm, however, was beyond anything that even Urban had expected. A roar of *"Dieu li volt,"* or God wills it, swept through the crowd even before Urban finished his speech. At its conclusion, the bishop of Le Puy fell to his knees, begging permission to join the expedition. Thousands followed his example.

The pope was caught off guard. No plans had yet been made, certainly no arrangements for a mass movement such as erupted over the winter of 1095–96. While Urban reassembled his bishops to make the political arrangements, a group of wandering evangelists began to spread the word. Foremost among them was Peter the Hermit.

The shadowy figure of Peter the Hermit, an enigma even to his contemporaries, haunts the story of the First Crusade. We have seen him in 1088 delivering a message from the patriarch of Jerusalem to Pope Urban. Later, historians would doubt this story because of Peter's humble background and apparent insignificance. And yet there is something about the mysterious rabble-rousing monk that suggests powerful connections and important supporters. Piecing together his career gives us a glimpse of the hidden machinations behind the Crusades.

Peter was born around the middle of the eleventh century in Picardy, possibly near Amiens. Before becoming a monk, Peter was a minor noble who owed his fief to Eustace de Boulogne, father of Godfroi de Bouillon, the future king of Jerusalem. Sometime after 1070, Peter joined a monastery in the Ardennes, where for a few years he served as tutor to the young Godfroi. Sometime after 1080, he departed on a pilgrimage to Jerusalem, where he apparently stayed until his mission to Rome in 1088. Nothing is known of his whereabouts until the winter of 1095, when he began to preach the new crusade at Bourges, in the province of Berry. He apparently did not attend the Church council at Clermont.

Keeping in mind the work of Pope Sylvester II and his various chronicling orders, a pattern emerges from the shadows of Peter's story. Peter joined the only group of monks in the Ardennes, at Orval, near Stenay, a site with rich Merovingian connections, whose patron was Godfroi's aunt and foster mother. This group of monks was part of a mysterious order of chroniclers from Calabria, in northern Italy, who seemed mostly concerned with researching the bloodline of the duke of Lorraine, Godfroi's family.

If these monks were among the chroniclers established by Pope Sylvester, then it is easy to understand the many curious twists in Peter's career, such as his long sojourn in Jerusalem. He could have been transferred to the order's chapter there, the one established outside the city in a basilica given to them by the mad caliph al-Hakim. This makes sense in light of Peter's later diplomatic mission, for only a high-ranking member of a clerical order, founded by the pope himself, would be a fitting enough representative to deliver messages from the patriarch of Jerusalem and the Eastern Church.

Peter's silence between 1088 and 1095 may have been enforced by the dictates of his order. Only after the Church council, and its demonstration of mass approval, was Peter the Hermit given permission to begin his own crusade.

Before the year was out, Peter was in Berry, in central France, preaching his own version of the Holy War, one in which the poor and the pious in Christ would sweep ahead of the nobles and conquer Jerusalem with only God's assistance. Guibert of Nogent, who knew him personally, gives us a glimpse of Peter's authority: "Everything he said or did, it seemed like something half-divine."[16] This unkempt, fiery-tempered monk, who habitually went about barefoot and in filthy rags, was also a spellbinding orator capable of moving masses of people to extremes of emotion. They took the cross by the thousands and followed this Rasputin-like character down the long road to the East.

In January, Peter left Berry and traveled through Orleans and Champagne, gathering crowds whenever he stopped. In Lorraine, he visited his old monastery near Orval and discussed the crusade with his old pupil Godfroi de Bouillon. No record remains of their conversations, but something convinced Godfroi to join the crusade. By spring, as Peter collected his people's army in Cologne, Otto III's old capital, Godfroi took the cross at Amiens. Unlike the other nobles who participated in the First Crusade, Godfroi renounced his fiefs, sold his goods, and moved with his brothers to the Holy Land. Godfroi did not intend to return; perhaps he already saw himself as the chief candidate for king of Jerusalem.

Godfroi wasn't the only noble of ancient lineage taking the cross that summer. The group was officially under the leadership of the bishop of Le Puy, Adhemar, as papal legate, and included Raymond of Toulouse, a veteran of the Spanish wars; Hugh of Vermandois and Robert II of Flanders; and Robert, duke of Normandy, and his brother-in-law, the hapless Stephan, count of Blois. In September of 1096, word reached Urban that the Normans of southern Italy and Sicily were ready to take up the cross. These Normans, led by Bohemund and his nephew Tancred, brought the most experienced and capable soldiers in Europe to the crusading movement. Bohemund's father, Roger of Guiscard, had almost conquered Constantinople itself a few years before, and the Normans scented opportunity in the call to the East.

The long story of the First Crusade, and its People's Crusade prologue, is told in many places. The best of all the histories is still Sir Steven Runciman's multivolume work on the entire crusading era.[17] For our purposes, we shall concentrate on Peter the Hermit and his student Godfroi de Bouillon.

The People's Crusade, after a tortuous journey across central Europe, arrived at the gates of Constantinople in the spring of 1097, a hungry and uncontrollable mob. The emperor shipped them over to the Asian side of the straits, where they rashly attacked a Turkish stronghold and were annihilated. Peter the Hermit wisely stayed in Constantinople and therefore survived. He was still there, and held in some honor, when the next wave of Crusaders arrived.

As the crusading princes gathered in Constantinople, Peter joined them with the remnants of his army. Perhaps because of his old association with Godfroi, by this point the acknowledged leader of the Crusade, Peter was respected as a visionary and councilor to the group. He marched on with them to Antioch, where he played a part in the drama of the Holy Spear, a bizarre intervention of the supernatural involving the discovery of an iron spearhead in the church. After

Antioch, Peter joined with the Tafars, or poor ones, in calling for a speedy advance on Jerusalem.

After the fall of Jerusalem, Peter was one of the secret council, perhaps even its leader, who chose Godfroi as the king of Jerusalem. Godfroi declined the title, preferring instead that of Defender of the Holy Sepulchre, but in 1100 his younger brother, Baldwin, accepted the title readily. During Godfroi's reign, Peter the Hermit was held in such high regard that when the Crusaders pushed on to Ascalon, he was left in charge of Jerusalem. Before Godfroi left Jerusalem, almost his sole official act as king was to reconfirm the charter of an abbey on Mount Zion, south of the city and outside of its walls, and order its immediate fortification.

Peter the Hermit divided his time between the court at Constantinople and the newly rebuilt abbey on Mount Zion, where he is believed to have died, in 1115. The great French historian of the Crusades, René Grousset, commented that Godfroi's throne was founded on the rock of Zion, and that it indicated a royal tradition equal to that of the reigning dynasties of Europe. Grousset, however, does not explain his comment, leaving of us to speculate on its meaning.[18]

Urban's plans for military aid for the Eastern Church were subverted by Peter the Hermit and his followers' insistence on a people's crusade. This popular movement swept control of the expedition out of papal hands and into the hands of military and political leaders. When Adhemar, the papal legate, died at Antioch, a council of such leaders took over. Peter was a part of that council and was perhaps instrumental in electing Godfroi king. The First Crusade changed from a papal expedition to something different, a popular movement with millenarian expectations, and Peter the Hermit was at the heart of that change.

If Peter was indeed a high-ranking member of one of the surviving chronicling orders started by Sylvester II, who were charged with researching the Merovingian bloodline, then his influence becomes understandable. Sylvester's chronicling orders had been working for almost a century to create a new kingdom of Jerusalem, and then, suddenly, the means were at hand. All that was needed was a candidate for king whose bloodline was such that all the kings of Europe could acknowledge him as overlord.

Godfroi may have filled the bill because the Chroniclers believed him to be a descendant of the lost line of Merovingian kings and therefore perhaps a direct descendant of Solomon and the House of David, and perhaps even Jesus himself. That would in fact, if proved, make him the rightful king of Jerusalem, and perhaps of the world. It would at least fulfill a great many apocalyptic expectations and could be seen as the first steps toward the Kingdom of Heaven on earth so beloved of the chiliasts.

The rock of Zion could be Peter (*petros,* or "rock" in Greek) the Hermit of the Order of Zion, to whom both Godfroi and Baldwin directly owed their thrones. This explanation becomes even more plausible if Peter, as the official representative of Zion and the Chroniclers, thus functioned as guarantor of their legitimacy as descendants of the Davidic line. Mount Zion itself seems the most likely candidate for the location of the original order. Al-Hakim donated to Sylvester's Chroniclers a Greek church somewhere outside the walls, but still close enough for access to the city. Mount Zion, which contains the ruins of a fourth-century basilica rebuilt in the early eleventh century, seems the most obvious choice. A group of monks were apparently still there in 1099, and may have played a part in the fall of the city. This "rock of Zion" and its connections in Europe could also be considered the foundation of the dynasty. But, as we shall see, there could in fact be another "rock of Zion" on which the kingdom of Jerusalem was built.

THE SECRET OF THE KNIGHTS OF THE TEMPLE OF SOLOMON

The authors of *Holy Blood, Holy Grail* deserve credit for their discoveries concerning the role played by the Order, or Priory, of Zion in the creation of the Templars. Just as they were right about the unusual and probably Hebraic origins of the Merovingians, they were correct, as far as they went, about the mysterious precursors to the Templars who occupied Mount Zion. While not going back far enough to uncover the pivotal role played by Pope Sylvester II, *Holy Blood, Holy Grail*'s facts about the Order of Our Lady of Zion are suggestive.

By the time the Templars arrived on the scene, in 1118 or 1119, the Order of Zion was already a powerful group with close ties to the kings of Jerusalem. These ties were based, in all probability, on the order's knowledge of the dynasty's true heritage. Therefore, the secret at the heart of the Templars' sudden rise in the medieval world was due to more than just, as *Holy Blood, Holy Grail* suggests, knowledge of Jesus' descendants. Once again something more is involved.

The missing piece appears to be alchemy. The Merovingians, whether or not they were descended from Christ, were indeed practical alchemists and wizard kings. Sylvester II, the hermetic pope, was on the verge of recovering the secret when power politics overwhelmed him.[19] The motivation for the First Crusade, deeply hidden behind religious and political rationalizations, was actually the search for and recovery of the secret, envisioned perhaps as an artifact or relic. A Merovingian king on the throne of Jerusalem was just the first step in bringing about the millennium. Next would come the rebuilding of the Temple, based on the philosopher's stone, the stone the builders rejected.

This was the true mission of the Templars, and *Holy Blood, Holy Grail* is partly correct. The secret did involve the bloodline. The authors of *Holy Blood, Holy Grail* rarely mention alchemy, however, even though several supposed grand masters of Zion are prominent alchemists. Only once in the entire book does alchemy come to the fore-front: in discussing the Templars and their mysterious "head." Whatever the Templars were trying to accomplish, the recovery of a lost secret was the central and critical component of their plans.[20]

By the end of the second decade of the twelfth century, most of the veterans of the First Crusade were dead. Godfroi de Bouillon, exhausted by his labors, died the year after the fall of Jerusalem, in 1100. Peter the Hermit had died in 1115, and Baldwin I, Godfroi's brother, followed him in 1118. Things were changing in Outremer, the land beyond the sea, as the Franks called Palestine. Latin kingdoms, including Jerusalem, had been established from Syria to Gaza, but if they were to remain independent, it was time to look to their collective security.

With this in mind, soon after his coronation, Baldwin II, cousin of Godfroi and Baldwin, legitimized the only standing army in the Holy Land. Not being a truly feudal lord, in the sense that Europe under-stood it, the king of Jerusalem had only his personal retainers and what-ever Crusaders happened to be available with whom to form an army. This left the kingdom of Jerusalem somewhat defenseless, as demon-strated by the Easter massacre of pilgrims by Turkish forces in 1119. As a reaction to this, Baldwin II turned to the only organized military force in the Holy Land, the militia of the Order of Our Lady of Zion, for protection.

That this *milice du Christ* existed before 1119 is shown by the reference to it in a letter from the bishop of Chartres to Hugh, count of Champagne, dated 1114. In the period immediately after the First Crusade's conquest of Jerusalem, the only source of authority in the devastated city came from the remaining religious communities, among them the Order of Mount Zion. We know that Peter the Hermit was left in charge of the city while Godfroi went on to defeat the Egyptians at Ascalon, which, if Peter was a monk of Zion, meant that the order was actually in control. That the existing Order of Mount Zion had some military value is shown by Godfroi's insistence on repairing its fortifications. Someone must have manned those defenses after they were built.

Given the unstable situation in Outremer, Baldwin II made the right choice. He recognized the military arm of the order, put them under the control of the king and the patriarch of Jerusalem, and installed them close at hand, next door to his palace on Temple Mount. The Poor Knights of Christ, as they called themselves, gained another name from Baldwin's gift. They became the Poor Knights of the Temple of Solomon, then Knights of the Temple, or Knights Templar, and, finally, the Templars. Their stated purpose was to protect the pilgrim routes, but their numbers were too few in the beginning to protect more than the area around the Temple ruins. And perhaps that's all they were intended to do.

To understand the Templars and their role in the Holy Land and Europe, we must see them in their proper perspective, that of a military adjunct to a much older organization. The Order of Our Lady of Zion did not create the Templars. The king of Jerusalem created them out of the order's militia for a specific purpose.

The order itself had been reconfirmed and given its new name by Godfroi in 1099. Five years later, a private conclave of nobles and clergy assembled at Troyes, the court of the count of Champagne, to hear a mysterious abbot from Jerusalem and to discuss conditions in the Holy Land. Nothing is known of the subject of that discussion, but whatever it was, the wealthy and powerful Hugh, count of Champagne, decided to depart immediately for Jerusalem. He spent the next four years in the Holy Land, his activities and whereabouts unknown.

The location of the conclave in Troyes is highly significant. Peter the Hermit had stopped there on his winter preaching tour in 1096, and the family of the count of Champagne had been of interest to the Chroniclers because of its connections with the Merovingian dynasty of Burgundy. Indeed, the reported nobles who attended the conclave, Brienne, Joinville, Chaumont, and Montbard, all have connections to the ancient Burgundian royal family. This alone would be enough to make one suspect that the mysterious Jerusalem abbot was from the Order of Zion.

Hugh, count of Champagne, remained in the Holy Land for four years. On his return to Champagne, things began to unfold rapidly. A distant relative, Bernard de Montbard, joined the Cistercian Order. Bernard, in just a few years, would become the principle spiritual leader of Western Christendom. His abbey at Clairvaux, donated by Hugh in 1112, became the center of the medieval spiritual revival, inspiring a wave of religious feeling that resulted in the glories of the Gothic cathedrals. Saint Bernard, as he would come to be known, played a key role in the establishment and the legitimization of the Templars. His uncle André de Montbard was one of the militia of Zion from which the Templars were formed.

Hugh of Champagne himself wanted to return to the Holy Land and join the order's militia. The letter from the bishop of Chartres in 1114 was part of an attempt to dissuade him. Apparently his talents were needed in Champagne, and it was not until 1124 that he officially joined the newly renamed Order of the Temple. By that time, the Templars were solidly established with the support of a now wealthy and powerful Cistercian Order, headed by Bernard. In 1128, the Templars were recognized by the pope, Honorius II, and given a written rule or guide for their order by none other than Bernard himself. The council at which this occurred was held, of course, in Troyes at the court of the count of Champagne.

From these meager facts we are forced to intuit the story. The Order of the Chroniclers on Mount Zion appears to be the shadowy force directing the First Crusade, mostly through the activities and influence of Peter the Hermit. After the Crusaders captured Jerusalem, the order, through Peter, was left in virtual charge of the city and its monuments and churches. As we have seen, Godfroi and Baldwin were beholden to Zion for their thrones, and therefore would have allowed the order free access to anywhere in the city they wanted to explore or excavate.

Sometimes during the five years from the conquest to the conclave in Troyes, the order discovered the secret it had been seeking for over a century.

Zion sent word of this discovery back to Europe, not to Rome or any of the other capitals, but to Troyes. Whatever this discovery was, it so moved Hugh that he left for Jerusalem and spent four years in secret studying it. Immediately after his return in 1108, the wheels of power moved so that one of his adherents, the young Bernard of Montbard, became the head of an orthodox monastic order. When Bernard joined the Cistercians, they were almost bankrupt. Within a decade they were the wealthiest monastic order in Europe, with money to fund the creation of a whole new style of architecture, the Gothic cathedrals.[21]

Therefore, in some way, this discovery of a secret or an artifact led to a flow of unparalleled wealth a few years later. From this discovery and its flow of wealth would come the need for the Templars, whose first and basic activity seemed to be guarding the precinct of Solomon's Temple. But the mere secrets of alchemy alone, even an ancient Solomonic version, would not of themselves produce a flow of wealth. Something else was required. As the later alchemists inform us, nothing can be accomplished in the Great Work without the right *prima materia*. It is possible that what the Order of Zion found, perhaps in the ruins of the Temple of Solomon, was the best *prima materia* possible, a piece of the Black Stone, the meteorite from Mecca.[22] Just possibly, this was the true "rock of Zion" on which the kingdom of Jerusalem was founded.

Some modern authors tracing the Templar connection with alchemy have suggested that the Templars discovered the Ark of the Covenant in the ruins of Solomon's Temple, which perhaps contained a stone from heaven, or meteorite, similar to the Black Stone of Mecca.[23] This, however, seems highly unlikely, given that the Ark disappeared from the temple in the seventh century B.C.E.[24] But a discovery of something like one of the stones contained in the Ark is a somewhat more likely proposition.

The Order of Chroniclers was given the use of Mount Zion by the mad caliph al-Hakim. Al-Hakim's great-grandfather, al-Mansur, was the first and only person since Muhammad known to have close personal contact with the Black Stone. It stayed in his presence for months after it was presented to him and before it was returned to the Kaaba.

Most significant, we cannot be sure how much of the stone was returned.

The Iranian Ismailis, soon to become friends and allies of the Templars, may have kept a piece before it was given to al-Mansur. The Fatimid caliph himself may have decided to keep a piece. That the stone shrank in its absence from the Kaaba is known from Muslim descriptions of the building of the ninth and tenth Kaabas, which tell us that the stone was large and filled the entire space of the southeast corner, protruding so that one did not have to stoop to kiss it. In the current Kaaba, as described by Sir Richard Francis Burton in the nineteenth century, the stone is encased within the wall, leaving only a portion about seven inches long and four inches wide exposed for kissing. Since it was removed from the Kaaba only for those brief years in the mid-tenth century, any carving or splitting of the stone had to have been done at that time.[25]

The madness of al-Hakim can be explained by his possession of his great-grandfather's chunk of the stone. Shi'ite tradition claimed that at the turn of the fourth century after the Hejira, or departure from Mecca, the Mahdi, or savior, would appear and convert the entire world to Islam as a prologue to the Day of Judgment. In 1020, al-Hakim, the foremost Shi'ite leader of his day, announced the arrival of the Mahdi in his own, now divine, person.[26] It was the year 400 A.H. If indeed al-Hakim had a piece of the rock, sign of the holy covenant with Abraham, then it is possible that this knowledge could have unhinged the caliph enough for him to convince himself of his own divinity. Fearing the stone's power, al-Hakim could have hidden it on the Dome of the Rock, perhaps within the ruins of Solomon's Temple, in Jerusalem.

If the stone was in Jerusalem the whole time, why did it take a Crusade for the Order of Zion to gain possession of it? One reason lies in the madness of al-Hakim. As part of his Mahdi-hood, he persecuted the Christians and the Jews, burning their churches and synagogues. Even though he repented of the destruction before his death or disappearance, access to the Dome of the Rock and the Temple Mount itself was restricted to Muslims from that time onward. Once the Seljuk Turks conquered the city, all access to the Holy Sites was restricted. And at that point, Peter, the Hermit of Mount Zion, departed for the West to start the political process that, eleven years later, would bring the order back into control of the Temple and the Dome of the Rock.

Sometime between 1099 and 1104, it is possible that the Order of Zion made at least two discoveries, either together or separately, in Jerusalem. The first was perhaps a text explaining the mechanics of the physics of creation and its application to the process of transmutation. The second might well have been the mad caliph's piece of the Black Stone. Word of this discovery was sent back to France, where, upon receiving the information, Hugh of Champagne and his entourage, possibly including a few Hebrew scholars, departed immediately for Jerusalem.

Between 1104 and 1112, the Order of Zion completed its work and perfected the process of transformation. From 1112 onward, money in great quantities flowed back to France and into the coffers of Bernard's Cistercians. A power base was built on this wealth that forced Baldwin II to legitimize the military wing of the order to protect his throne. The Templars were formed to guard the source of this wealth, the alchemical processes that were perhaps being conducted in the cellars of the great Temple.

While this view of events is admittedly speculative, it does have the value, as we shall see in the next chapter, of addressing some of the key images and motifs found in the Grail legends and the *Bahir,* which emerged in the West at the same place and at the same time. It also answers the many questions that gather around all facets of the Templars' history. And it points up a truly curious fact. Before the Templars, alchemy was a decidedly theoretical science. After the Templars, we find documented tales of actual transmutation. The conclusion is forced upon us that something resembling our speculations must indeed have occurred.

The Templars continued to gain power in Europe at the same time as the Cistercians were beginning their cathedral-building program. Both of these movements were financed from mysterious sources, and both had indirect and hazy connections to the Order of Our Lady of Zion. It is possible to see Saint Bernard and the Cistercians as the spiritual and social parts of a great plan to revitalize Western culture. The Templars were the political and military components of that plan, protecting the secret and its source of wealth. The cathedrals, those vast alchemical monuments in stone, were designed to facilitate the new spiritual change necessary as a prelude to the coming thousand years of peace and prosperity.

The history of the Templars from 1128 until their demise is well documented and too familiar to need much further elaboration. By 1143, the Templars had become the exclusive military arm of the papacy, and remained a powerful force in Outremer even after the fall of Jerusalem to Saladin in 1187. *Holy Blood, Holy Grail* suggests that the Order of Zion split from the Templars at the Cutting of the Elm at Gisors in 1188, and this seems accurate given the further history of both orders. The Order of Zion, after losing its abbey on Mount Zion, seems to have moved to France, with chapters in Orleans, Bourges, Paris, and Troyes.[27]

For a century after the discoveries in the Holy Land, alchemy remained the secret preserve of the initiates within the Church. The Order of Zion and the Templars seem to have had their own alchemical processes and their own individual codes for referring to them. Not until the middle of the thirteenth century did alchemy surface in a direct and unambiguous way.

The greatest scholar of the thirteenth century, Albert the Great of Cologne, or Albertus Magnus, turned to alchemy around 1250 and produced the first original work on the subject since the late fifth century. His treatise *On Alchemy* champions alchemy as a difficult but true art. He does not tell us if he actually made gold, but his directions to the practitioner indicate not only knowledge of the triple nature of alchemy, but also an awareness of the changes in the political winds. He warns the alchemist to choose the right hour for his operations, to be patient and diligent in his prayers and exhortations, to operate by the rules (here Albert gives us the necessary steps: trituration, sublimation, fixation, calcination, solution, distillation, and coagulation, seven in all), and always to avoid contact with princes and rulers.[28]

Albert was also reputed to have had a fortune-telling "head" and seems by contemporary accounts to have been an adept of the Hebraic work of creation. We are told that he had constructed an artificial man, a golem, endowed with the ability to speak but not to reason. The golem's inane chattering so disturbed Albert's pupil, the future saint Thomas of Aquinas, that Albert finally had to destroy it. Another interesting alchemical story, related by William II, count of Holland, has Albert setting a feast in the frozen and snow-covered garden of the monastery, only to have it magically become summer, with birds, butterflies, and blossoming trees, as the diners sat down to their meal.[29]

Intriguing as these suggestions are, it was not the aristocratic Albert the Great who brought alchemy firmly into the mainstream of medieval thought, but rather the humble scholar Arnold of Villanova. Arnold was born in Valencia about the time that Notre-Dame-de-Paris was finished. He gained his initial fame as a physician and could be called the first psychologist, having written a surprisingly modern work on the interpretation of dreams. Although seemingly not a member of any monastic or clerical order, Arnold conducted secret missions for kings, emperors, and popes alike.[30]

In his works, Arnold emphasized the reality of alchemical transformation. To demonstrate this, he performed a transmutation in front of Pope Boniface VIII. It was successful, the first documented account of such a transmutation. A witness, John Andre, the major domo of the Papal Curia, reports that Arnold "submitted the gold sticks he produced to everyone for examination."[31] This is very significant for the simple reason that since the second century, no one, no matter how much he seemed to know about alchemy, had actually done the transmutation in front of witnesses. Arnold's performance in front of Boniface was the turning point in alchemical history. Unfortunately, it was also the beginning of the end for the Templars and, in a lesser way, for the Order of Zion.

One of those observing Arnold's transmutation was the future pope Clement V. Bertrand de Got, the former archbishop of Bordeaux, became the first pope of the so-called French captivity after the strife caused by Boniface VIII's assertion of absolute papal rights. The king of France, asserting a higher spiritual and political authority than the pope, swooped down on Rome and literally captured the Church. Eleven months later, Bertrand, a Frenchman, was finally elected as Clement V. Arnold, unfortunately, had been in the thick of the political infighting.[32]

Philip, the French king, used his power over the pope to recall Boniface's proclamation. And then the king set in motion an idea that had been stirring in his brain since Arnold's demonstration. The king called a general council and proscribed the Templars. Pope Clement V, wanting his piece of the vast Templar wealth, went along with Philip, even though he knew the charges against the Templars were basically groundless. The Templars thus ran afoul of a greedy French king and his puppet of a pope and were persecuted as heretics. Just as the missing link in the Templars' origin appears to be alchemy, so does it appear that their downfall was also caused by alchemy.

The Grail romances provide us with direct connections to the Templars as guardians of the secret, as well as glimpses of the "miraculous stone" at the heart of the mystery and a general tone of transformation and transmutation as a subtext. The sudden emergence of the long secret "illumination" sect, the sages of the *Bahir*, in a public form in the West, supplies us with the missing philosophical and kabbalistic clue needed to see the larger pattern of what might be called astroalchemy, which, as Fulcanelli informs us, was in turn memorialized in the Gothic cathedrals.

During the height of their influence, from 1150 to the fall of Jerusalem in 1187, three different facets of the alchemical secret surfaced in the West and produced a kind of Gothic renaissance. In this emergence, the book and stone of the Templars and the Grail romances became the book in stone of the Gothic cathedrals. Behind this transformation is the theology of Light as expressed in the *Bahir* and made real in the *lux continua* architectural style of the new cathedrals.

By the time Notre-Dame-de-Paris' external decorations—including the magnificent bas-relief rendition of Alchemy itself on the Great Porch—were finished in 1235, the need for subterfuge was thought to have passed. The imperial and orthodox Church of Rome was in ascendancy, with both the Templars and the Order of Zion chastised by the crusade against the Cathars, and struggling to find a new mission. Power politics had also stabilized, somewhat, with the Holy Roman Empire as top dog of the feudal pack. The Middle Ages were reaching for their apogee, while falling, at the same time, far short of the glorious millennial visions of Sylvester II and the pilgrim-warriors of the First Crusade. Little did either the sponsors of these great works or the guilds that created them realize that within a hundred years this renaissance would end in death, betrayal, wars, and natural disasters that would plunge Europe back into a mini-version of the Dark Ages. As Europe recovered from this disaster in the fifteenth and sixteenth centuries, the flowering of the earlier Gothic renaissance was forgotten and diminished.

Without the background these clues provide, understanding Fulcanelli's message in *Le Mystère* is almost impossible. Therefore, before we turn to Fulcanelli himself, let us examine how the light of the

Grail transformed into the continuous light of the great Gothic cathedrals, and in so doing brought the light of alchemy to center stage in world politics and caused the downfall of the Knights of the Temple, which once again forced the alchemical tradition underground.

SIX

GRAIL KNIGHTS, PERFECTI, AND THE ILLUMINATED SAGES OF PROVENCE

THE HERMETIC GRAIL

In the early 1180s, as the shadow of Saladin lengthened over the Holy Land, a nobleman with Merovingian ancestry, Philip d'Alsace, count of Flanders, commissioned the greatest poet of the age, Chrétien de Troyes, to do a French reworking of a strange tale about a poor knight, the son of a widow, who attains the kingship of the Holy Grail. Philip supposedly found the tale in an ancient Celtic chronicle, and wanted Chrétien, the medieval version of a best-selling author, to make it a hit. Chrétien labored over this strange story, sometimes giving its symbolic events a sort of numinous and dreamlike quality and at other times obviously failing to grasp the importance and even the meaning of his source material.[1]

Nonetheless, as Jerusalem fell and the Christian kingdoms of Outremer shrank to a few coastal enclaves, poets in noble courts across Europe took up the story of Chrétien's Grail. Chrétien himself never completed his work, leaving the long poem unfinished at his death. Several poets tried to continue the story, with varying degrees of success. Even more important, other writers took up the theme, as if from a common source, and expanded upon it.

Robert de Boron, writing between 1190 and 1199,[2] Christianized the Grail story. He tells us that the source of his story, in its Christian form, is a great book, the secrets of which have been revealed to him. Robert, unlike Chrétien, is quite sure what the Grail is all about. The Grail is the cup of the Last Supper in which Joseph of Arimathea collected Jesus' blood at the Crucifixion. After the Crucifixion, Joseph's family became the keepers of the Grail. The adventures of the Grail romances involve the members of this family, and in the end the Grail comes to England with Joseph's brother-in-law, Brons the Fisher-King. As in Chrétien's version, Perceval is called "the Son of the Widow Lady," but Robert also describes him as a descendant of Joseph of Arimathea.

We must keep in mind that at this same period, the Order of Our Lady of Zion was in the process of relocating its power base to Europe. Supported by the powerful Cistercians, by 1178, ten years before the schism between the Templars and the older order, Zion was well established in Europe. A papal bull from Alexander III grants the order possession of chapters in Picardy, France, Lombardy, Calabria, Sicily, Spain, and the Holy Lands.[3] After the loss of Jerusalem, the Order cut loose the Templars and embarked on a new program. The Grail romances can be seen as part of this new plan.

The histories collected through two centuries of patient work by Sylvester's chroniclers suddenly appeared as the content of a new kind of popular mythology, one nicely geared to the knightly aspirations of the crusading era. The source, as both Chrétien and Robert de Boron inform us, is a secret book in the possession of certain nobles connected with the Merovingians and the Order of Zion.

Another Grail romance, composed at the same time and from the same sources as Robert's *History of the Grail,* makes this connection even more apparent. The anonymous author of the *Perlesvaus* may have used the same sources as Robert (he agrees with him, for instance, on Perceval's lineage), but his mystical spin on the story puts it in a league by itself.

The author may have been a member of the Order of Zion, which would account for his anonymity. He certainly had a vast command of the Arthurian literature of his day and possibly even access to the order's Merovingian research. Unlike Robert de Boron, who thought the Grail events happened in the first century after Christ's death, the anonymous author of the Perlesvaus clearly dates the events in his story to the late fifth century, the time of both the historical King Arthur and the rise of the Merovingian dynasty.[4]

Another romance, *The Quest for the Holy Grail,* written around the turn of the thirteenth century by a group of Cistercian monks as part of the so-called Vulgate Cycle of Grail romances, gives a precise date for the events it records: 454 years after the death of Jesus on the cross, or 487 C.E., the first flush of the Merovingian dynasty and just a few years before Clovis's conversion by Saint Remy and his pact with the Western Church.[5]

From these details alone, the hand of the Order of Our Lady of Zion and its chronicling predecessors can clearly be discerned in the creation and popularity of the Grail romances. But the *Perlesvaus* goes further by describing the keepers of the Grail's secrets in terms that any contemporary would immediately interpret as referring to the Templars. The castle of the Grail, we are told, houses a conclave of initiates dressed in white robes with red crosses emblazoned on their breasts.

The *Perlesvaus* is full of strange alchemical details that suggest its author's familiarity with the Kabbalah of the *Bahir*. The clearest example of this, and the most cogent to our investigation, is Perlesvaus' voyage to the Isle of Blessed Elders in the closing pages of the romance. In this otherworldly Paradise, Perlesvaus finds a magnificent Tree with a fountain flowing out from it surrounded by twelve golden pillars. This *axis mundi* motif is a junction point between the *Bahir*, which introduced the concept of the Tree of Life to the Kabbalah, and later alchemical symbolism concerned with the timing of alchemical operations. In much of the *Perlesvaus*, alchemy seems to lurk just below the surface, even in the Grail itself. To Perlesvaus, the Grail appeared as a complex and evolving series of five images, the last of which was the Grail cup.

The most significant of all the Grail romances is the *Parzival* of Wolfram von Eschenbach, written between 1200 and 1215.[6] Wolfram minces no words in calling the keepers of the Grail Templars, and then goes to the heart of the mystery by describing the Grail as a miraculous stone. This *"lapsit exillis,"* a green-language pun that suggests the exiled stone of Matthew, as well as the stone that fell from heaven and even the *"lapsit elixir"* of the alchemical philosopher's stone, has miraculous powers, including healing, nourishment, and the ability to communicate its wishes.[7]

Wolfram claimed to have learned his tale from one Guyot, or Kyot, of Provence, who in turn learned it from a recovered manuscript from Toledo, in Muslim Spain. This source, according to Wolfram, is the manuscript of Flegetanis, a heathen astronomer living roughly at the time of the Exodus from Egypt, or about 1,200 years before the birth of Christ. Flegetanis, whose name is simply the Persian phrase "familiar with the stars," claimed to read the "name" of the Grail in the stars and thereby understood the workings of destiny. He also claimed that this astral destiny focused on the family of Christ and his descendants. Guyot augmented this tale with his own Latin research, suggesting that either he was, or had access to, one of Sylvester II's Chroniclers, before he passed it on to Wolfram.

Parzival is a masterpiece of alchemical literature, and as such is worthy of another volume at least the size of this one in order to do it justice.[8] For our purposes, let us simply note that in addition to the direct reference to the Templars and the meteoric stone that fell from heaven, *Parzival* ends by informing us that Lohengrin, the Swan Knight of Lorraine, is the great-grandfather of Godfroi de Bouillon. With *Parzival,* the origins of the First Crusade and its alchemical secrets come full circle as a Grail romance. A mysterious text and an artifact, the miraculous stone, the *"lapsit exillis"* in the hands of a family group of knights that spans both East and West and sounds a lot like the contemporary Templars, should have been a fairly obvious series of references to those in the know at the turn of the thirteenth century. And behind all the legends lurk the Order of Zion and its predecessors, Sylvester's Chroniclers.

After 1210, as the persecution of Cathar heretics in the south of France increased into a crusade, the Grail romances began to fade from favor. The Church never challenged them directly, which is indeed curious, but by the middle of the thirteenth century, their imagery and symbolism had faded from literature and politics, only to be permanently engraved in stone on the porches and naves of the newly constructed Gothic cathedrals. Indeed, one of the magnificent Gothic statues at Chartres Cathedral depicts Melchizedek, the king of Ur and Salem who converted Abraham to monotheism, holding the chalice of the Grail. This symbolic image suggests that a deep understanding of the Grail legend remained, at least among the builders of the church itself.

The flash point where people and events and traditions transformed into the Grail of romance and legend can be found in the south of France, in that favored province of Rome, Provence, where the Holy Family supposedly emigrated from Palestine within a few years of the

Crucifixion. It is here, the home of the mysterious Guyot who wrote the original source tale, where we find Mary Magdalene, holy trophies, and miraculous stones at the core of the earliest community of "Christians" in Europe. And it is here, in Provence, that all the threads of this complex tapestry converge into one single event, the coronation of Frederick I Barbarossa as king of Arles in 1178.

THE GRAIL IN PROVENCE

The Rhône River begins as clay-filled glacial runoff high in the Swiss Alps. It winds its milky way across Switzerland, emptying its alluvial deposits at last into Lake Geneva and becoming, as Byron put it, "the blue rushing of the arrowy Rhône."[9] After curving through the foothills of the western Alps, the Rhône falls into a deep valley and turns south, running along the natural gap between the Cévennes Mountains and the French Alps toward the sea. For over one hundred miles, the river follows the valley, hugging the eastern edge of the Cévennes, until, as the mountains fall away to the east and the west, it gathers its tributaries and fans out in a wide delta across the head of the Gulf of Lion, a small arm of the Mediterranean Sea.

Just before the Rhône splits into its two main channels, a last straggling arm of the Alps, the Alpilles, reaches westward, ending in a jumbled and rocky promontory a few miles from the river. This protective line of hills forms the baseline of another delta, or triangle, with the upper lines created by the confluence of the Durrance and the Rhône. Within this secure and fertile triangle, successive waves of ancient cultures established their communities and towns. Neolithic farmers arrived early in the seventh millennium B.C.E. and dwelt in Arcadian simplicity until Bronze Age trading cultures, such as the Egyptian, Mycenaean, and Phoenician, began to arrive in the second millennium B.C.E. Soon after this contact, Celtic tribes began to filter down the river from their European homeland north of Lake Geneva and conquered or integrated with the local culture to form a unique variety of Gallic Celt (see fig. 6.1).

More than half a millennium before the birth of Christ, Greek traders built a fortress a few miles to the southwest of the old Celtic town, at the point where the Rhône forks. The Romans called it Arelate; in French it's Arles, now known mostly for the visits of artists such as van Gogh and Gauguin. It began, however, as a center of Greek

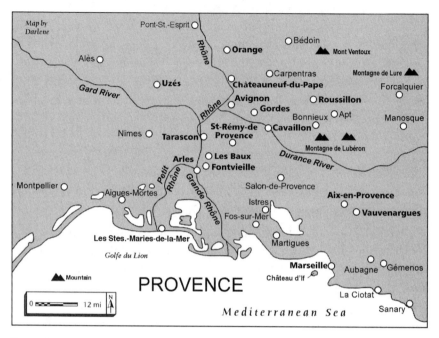

Figure 6.1. Map of Provence.

culture in a barbarian paradise. The two communities mixed and grew into a larger city nestled in the protected delta north of the low range of volcanic hills, the Alpilles, near the present-day town of Saint-Remy-de-Provence.

Michel Nostradamus, the justly famous Seer of Provence, was born at Saint-Remy barely a mile from the arch and monument that is all that remained in the sixteenth century of the ancient Roman city of Glanum Livii, once the most prosperous town in Provence and home, in the first century C.E., to a large community of Diaspora Jews. They are still standing today (see figs. 6.2 and 6.3), stark reminders along the modern road into the Alpilles of the area's ancient past.[10]

While secrets may remain hidden near the lost city of Glanum, at least according to Nostradamus,* other clues to Provence's unusual role in the history of Western esotericism, including its Hebrew and Gnostic Christian roots, are hidden in plain sight. At Arles, which has often

---

*The area around Glanum and Nostradamus's hometown, Saint-Remy-de-Provence, is mentioned in six quatrains, all related to the discovery of a treasure or a "mystery."

Figure 6.2. The mausoleum at Glanum. (Photo by Vincent Bridges)

Figure 6.3. The remains of the "lost" city of Glanum Livii near Saint-Remy-de-Provence. (Photo by Vincent Bridges)

been called the soul of Provence, Greek and Roman relics abound. It is but a brief walk from the lovely Roman arena, equal in elegance if not in scale to Rome's Coliseum, to the town square where a curious Romanesque church with a Gothic facade draws the attention of the serious student of hermeticism in search of the Grail.

On sunny Sunday afternoons in the spring, the tour guides compete with hurdy-gurdy music and the laughter of children as they explain the images on the church front in terms of Hercules' labors. Few tourists ponder why a Christian church in Provence uses the symbolism of ancient Greek myth, why its saint is called Trophime, or Trophy, or even why both Constantine, founder of the imperial Church in the fourth century, and Frederick Barbarossa, the Holy Roman Emperor in the late twelfth century, chose Arles (see fig. 6.4) for their confirmation and coronation.[11]

Attempting to answer these questions takes us deep into the heart of the Grail legends. The coronation of Frederick Barbarossa appears to be the key point of diffusion, the place and time where the Grail myths were inserted into the story of King Arthur. As many other researchers have found, and Robert de Boron openly tells us, the Grail stories have much to do with a bloodline, the descendants of the Holy Family and possibly Jesus himself, hence the "green-languagesque" pun of *sang réal,* "holy blood," out of *san grael,* "holy grail." In the romances, those of the bloodline are depicted as the guardians of the Grail, not the Grail itself. Even though the nature of the object is obscure, it is clearly an object, a relic or artifact of some sort: In Chrétien, it is a wide flat plate, in de Boron it is a chalice that held Jesus' blood; the *Perlesvaus* depicts the Grail as a series of objects, and Wolfram describes a miraculous stone.

Could the trophy of Saint Trophime be the Holy Grail? Could Arles be the home of a sacred relic of such wonder and importance that it became the model for the Holy Grail? And if so, what bloodline, or line of descendants, could be called its guardians?

Farther to the southwest of Arles, where the western branch of the Rhône flows into the Mediterranean, stood an ancient Egyptian port and lighthouse, founded perhaps a thousand years before the Greek traders arrived. Called Re by the Romans, this lighthouse and port marked the turning point in the channel that brought Egyptian merchant ships into the Rhône. Today, the ruins of the Egypto-Roman fortress of Re lie a quarter mile beyond the breakwater off the small

Figure 6.4. Town square and fountain, Arles. (Photo by Darlene)

beach town of Les-Saintes-Maries-de-la-Mer. However, this resort town, far off the beaten path at the end of a region of marshes and tidal flats called the Camargue, holds the key to what happened to the Holy Family after the death and possible resurrection/ascension of Jesus in Palestine.[12]

Hebrew migration to the region around the mouth of the Rhône began with the era of Greek colonization spurred on by Alexander's conquests in the East. The flow increased in the early first century C.E. under the encouragement of the Roman emperor Octavius Augustus. After the destruction of Palestine in 70 C.E., the flow became a torrent, and some of these Hebrew refugees were Christians (see fig. 6.5).[13]

Provençal tradition holds that soon after the Crucifixion, a shipload of Jesus' relatives landed off the old Roman fort of Re, near present-day Les-Saintes-Maries-de-la-Mer. By all accounts, the group included three Marys, covering the interwoven family of Jesus and John the Baptist. One of the three was Mary Magdalene, first witness to the Resurrection and, by Gnostic accounts, Jesus' foremost disciple and wife. Also included were Martha and Lazarus, members of Mary Magdalene's family, a few local Romanized Jews including Maximinius and Sidonius, the blind man from Jericho, and, either welcoming them home or miraculously as part of the ship's company, Sarah the Egyptian. Tradition relates that the group spread out through Provence

Figure 6.5. A ship of Marys. Statue is from l'Église Ste.-Maries-de-le-Mer, unknown date and origin. (Photo by Darlene)

and preached the Good News with such success that by the time of the destruction of the Temple and the Diaspora, barely more than a generation later, Provence was at least partially converted to Christianity.[14]

Two of the Marys, along with Sarah the Egyptian, remained in the seaside village where they landed. When they died, around 50 C.E., Saint Trophime himself came from Arles to administer the last rites. The three were buried near a small oratory, or chapel, they had built in the center of the village. In the ninth century, a new church was built over the oratory and the graves; fortified, it became part of the town walls. When King René d'Anjou, count of Provence, excavated the old church in the 1440s looking for the Holy Grail, he found the holy relics of the two Marys and Sarah and a curious stone buried with them. Called the Saint's Pillar, it was incorporated into a support column when King René built a lofty and imposing church of pinkish stone to house the saints' relics (fig. 6.6). With its parapets, merlons, embrasures, and internal freshwater spring, the church acted as a virtually impregnable fortress designed to protect the town's inhabitants from Moorish pirates and other marauders.[15]

That as late as the fifteenth century someone of the stature of King René d'Anjou should coming looking for the Holy Grail at an obscure seaside church in Provence is evidence in favor of a long-standing tradition connecting Provence, and the region of Arles and Saintes-Maries-de-la-Mer in particular, with a miraculous stone or artifact that came to be identified as the Holy Grail.

Figure 6.6. The fortress church at Saintes-Maries-de-la-Mer, built by King René d'Anjou. (Photo by Vincent Bridges)

Stepping into the cool darkness of the church at Saintes-Maries-de-la-Mer from the bright clear sunlight of Provence is to step back into another age, an age of faith that was at least superficially Christian but actually illuminated, from within as it were, by the antiquity of its goddess worship. Under the chancel, a flight of stairs leads down to the crypt, where King René found the bones of Sarah and the two Marys. Blackened by the candles of myriad pilgrims, most of them Gypsies who come to pray before the statue of Sarah (fig. 6.7), the crypt envelops the visitor with an atmosphere of dark and earthy mystery. If this is Christianity, it's far different from its more orthodox varieties. Here, the feminine is not excluded; it is worshipped in a manner that is far more primitive than early Christianity itself.

This impression is heightened during the Fête of May, when the Gypsy guardians gather to honor Saint Sarah and the two Marys. For several days prior to the festival on May 24 and 25, Gypsies from all over Provence, southern France, and northern Italy pour into Les-Saintes-Maries-de-la-Mer, some still in their colorful horse-drawn caravans. The guardians, those who will carry the relics in the festival, make an all-night vigil at Saint Trophime, then travel in a procession with twelve young girls in white, the virgins of Arles, to the church at Saintes-Maries-de-la-Mer. The three-day festival begins with the guardians taking down the reliquaries of the two Marys from their

Figure 6.7. Sarah of the Gypsies, in the crypt of the church at Saintes-Maries-de-la-Mer. (Photo by Darlene)

chapel above the chancel. The relics are left on display while the statue of Sarah is brought up from the crypt, draped in many rich cloaks, and paraded down to the sea.

The next day it is the two Marys' turn to make the journey. Standing in a small blue boat, piled high with roses and holding an urn full of healing balm, called a *graal* in the local Camargue provençal, the two Marys travel on the shoulders of their four guardians down to the sea, where they landed almost two millennia ago. In this simple ritual can be heard echoes of a goddess tradition going back to Egypt and beyond. After the Marys are returned to their chapel, the dancing and singing goes on late into the night as the crowds prepare for the third day's bullfights, *bandito* runs, and parties in honor of the Gypsy benefactor, Folco de Baroncelli.[16]

These celebrations mark a fountainhead. Like the spring in the church of the two Marys, one of many miraculous springs and wells in Provence, these traditions serve as a source point for the broad esoteric current that King René himself labeled the underground stream of lost Arcadia. And with this knowledge—the mystery hidden in plain sight, known to the Gypsies and the common folk—the true history of that underground stream, the Gnostic Christianity of the West, can be traced through the centuries.

Why should Arles be such an important locality in the history of the Grail? For one thing, there is its ancient history and persistent connections to certain myths and legends. When Hannibal crossed the Rhône a few miles north of present-day Arles in 218 B.C.E., the Gallo-Greek settlement was already a trading post of some note. The earliest versions of the Greek legend of Jason and the Argonauts suggest that they sailed west from Argos, around the heel of Italy and through the Strait of Messina to the mouth of the Rhône. They then traveled up the river, founding the trading center of Theline at the head of the Rhône delta along the way, to the land of the Golden Fleece, located, according to proponents of this theory, around the source of the Rhône at Lake Leman. In this interpretation, the Argonauts' return route was over the Alps by way of the Saint Bernard Pass, and then down the Po River to the Adriatic Sea.[17]

Under the Romans, who called it Arelate, the city retained its commercial status and flourished. Christianity arrived before the middle of the first century, brought, according to legend, by Saint Trophimus, or Trophime. Curiously enough, Saint Trophime dedicated the very first shrine to the Virgin here, even before her death. By the late first century C.E., Arles had become an ecclesiastical center, a position it would retain for the next four centuries, partly on the strength of its legendary cemetery, the Alyschamps.[18]

Perhaps the most famous necropolis of the medieval era, the Alyschamps (from Elisii Campi, or Elysian Fields) owed its fame to Saint Trophime. Built outside the city walls, as were all Roman cemeteries, and along the via Aurelia, the main road to Italy and Rome, the Alyschamps was a perfect location for secret meetings. Saint Trophime soon attracted a following. However, we are not sure exactly who Saint Trophime really was. The Church claims he was the disciple of Saint Paul mentioned in 2 Timothy 4:20.

This seems impossible, given that our Saint Trophime was in Arles at least a decade before the events mentioned in Timothy's letter. He apparently didn't arrive with the Holy Family, although he was close, possibly even related, to the two Marys at Saintes-Maries-de-la-Mer. His devotion to a Mary, possibly the Virgin Mary, but more likely Mary Magdalene, has already been noted. He is reported to have spent years in meditation at his hermitage a little farther outside Arles, beyond the Alyschamps, and in the year before his death or disappearance, probably in 52 C.E., he invoked a blessing on the cemetery. Christ himself was said to have attended the ceremony and left the imprint of his knee on a sarcophagus lid.[19]

In 314 C.E., Constantine came to Arles to swear on this relic before the Church council that the Christian God was his personal protector. He founded a small chapel—Saint Honoré—to house the relic. All of this attention made the Alyschamps famous, and it became so desirable as a final resting place that bodies were shipped from all Europe for burial in its holy grounds. The twelfth-century chronicle of the Pseudo-Turpin informs us that the peers of Charlemagne, Roland, and the other fallen heroes were transported with great difficulty to the Alyschamps.[20]

Arles, therefore, is ground zero for whatever version of Christianity it was that swept the region in those early years. In *Mystery of the Cathedrals*, Fulcanelli also directs us here, to Arles, the Alyschamps, and to the cathedral of Saint Trophime in particular, with several tantalizing references. He points out to us a rose-cross ankh on a sarcophagus lid at Saint Honoré in the Alsycamps and bids us pay close attention to the tympanum on the Great Portal of Saint Trophime (fig. 6.8).[21]

Built in the mid-fifth century by Saint Hilaire and originally dedicated to Saint Stephan, the cathedral was rebuilt in the eleventh century and the Great Portal was finished a century later, in time for the coronation of Frederick I Barbarossa as king of Arles in 1178. Rededicated to Saint Trophime when the relics of his miracle were moved from the Alyscamps in 1152,[22] the cathedral failed to retain the sacred cache of its saint's miraculous status, probably because the Holy Stone, the sarcophagus lid with the knee print, had disappeared. This missing stone, which conferred "knowledge of the Living Christ" to those who beheld it and "certainty of resurrection and eternal life" to those sacred dead who slept in

Figure 6.8. The front of Saint Trophime, Arles. (Photo by Darlene)

its embrace, according to the thirteenth-century *Golden Legends,* might just be the origin point of all the later Holy Grail legends.[23]

Consider that, although Chrétien de Troyes had invented all the other trappings of the Arthurian legends, the Matter of Britain as it was known in the Middle Ages, in his earlier works before 1180 or so, there is no hint that he had any idea of anything remotely resembling the Grail. Then he was supposedly given an ancient manuscript "in the Breton tongue" by Philip of Flanders and asked to render the material into an epic poem, which became *Perceval, or the Story of the Grail.*[24]

So where did Philip of Flanders come by the story? Chrétien doesn't tell us much and, although there have been many suggested sources, we just don't know. However, Wolfram von Eschenbach, author of *Parzival,* a complete version of the story that Chrétien only began, tells us that he had the true story from its source: one Kyot or Guyot of Provence.

This is an important clue, because there was a Guyot de Provins, a troubadour poet. And there is only one place that a young squire soon to be knight such as Wolfram could have met Guyot de Provins: at the coronation of Frederick I Barbarossa as king of Arles in 1178. Guyot de Provins was there, in the company of the Lords of les Baux, a curious clan from the Alpilles north of Arles who claimed descent from Balthazar, one of the three magi. We are less certain that Wolfram was there, but it does seem probable, as it has been determined from the texts of his poems that he entered the service of Frederick I Barbarossa at an early age.[25]

We can be certain, however, that Philip of Flanders and his sister-in-law Marie de Champagne did attend, as they are prominently listed among the assembled nobles in various sources.[26] It is possible that even Chrétien de Troyes was there, as he was at the court of Flanders during these years. Thus, on this one occasion, all of the people involved in the creation and propagation of what would later be the Grail legends crossed paths in Arles. And curiously enough, also in Arles, we find the veneration of a holy stone with miraculous properties.

Perhaps this is more than coincidental, as there are political considerations as well. At the treaty of Vienne (another ancient imperial city up the Rhône) in 1177, Frederick had been forced to acknowledge the authority of Pope Alexander III, effectively ending Frederick's bid to reestablish an empire in the West. Accepting the crown of the ancient imperial province of Arles, with its echoes of Constantine, was for

Frederick I Barbarossa, already Holy Roman Emperor, a kind of lateral move that can be considered a way to establish connections between the two military orders, and through them with an even more ancient, and perhaps more legitimate, form of Christianity. His coronation in the spring of 1178 at the newly finished cathedral of Saint Trophime signaled a shift in focus, one that would lead, a decade later, to Frederick's taking charge of the Third Crusade and his death in the wilds of Armenia.[27]

Behind these political machinations can be glimpsed the string pulling of the Knights of the Temple. Provence had been, since the earliest days of the order, one of its major locations and sources of wealth and support. The Templars held at least twenty-nine major commanderies and over one thousand smaller properties, such as farms and small landholdings, in Provence by the late thirteenth century. In the years before the Third Crusade, as much as half of all Templar revenues that can be accounted for came from Provence. The commandery at Arles was one of the oldest in Europe, having been ceded to the Templars in the 1130s by James I of Aragon.[28]

In addition, Provence was the home of the other major military order, the Knights of Saint John of the Hospital, also known as the Hospitallers in the same way as the Knights of the Temple became the Templars. Founded by papal bull in 1113, fifteen years before the Templars, the Knights of the Hospital were the creation of a single knight, Gerard, whose family name and birthplace are unknown. Like the later Templars, the Hospitallers also held Saint John as their patron. Exactly which Saint John is open to some doubt, but most likely Saint John the Baptist. Their rule, provided by Raymond of Provence in 1130, says nothing about any military role at all. That changed over time, and the Hospitallers were at least the equals of the Templars in battle during the last days of the kingdom of Jerusalem, and their bitter rivals in its politics.[29]

In contrast to the situation in Outremer, both orders of knights, white with red crosses for the Templars and black with white crosses for the Hospitallers, flanked Frederick I Barbarossa at his coronation as king of Arles in 1178. In Provence, this closeness continued even after the fall of Jerusalem, resulting in several calls during the thirteenth century for their unification. The Templars remained a powerful presence in the region; even after the pope and the French king Philip ordered their arrest. In 1311, four years after the arrest, supposedly, of every

Templar in France, nine knights from Provence showed up to defend the order at the Council of Vienne.[30]

They were actually successful. The Church never officially declared the Templars guilty of anything, but King Philip, who was on the scene with a large contingent of troops, carried the day, and the Templars were dissolved as a religious order and then subjected to the secular justice of the French king. The leaders went to the stake, but the regular knights, particularly in Provence, were allowed to join another chivalric order to avoid arrest. In this way, many commanderies of the Templars passed with all hands directly to the Knights of Saint John, soon to become the new Knights of Rhodes, and then finally the still surviving Knights of Malta.

Did the Templars and the Hospitallers use the political ambitions of Holy Roman Emperor Frederick Barbarossa as a way to promote a new spiritual agenda within the framework of a revised Christianity? The Church never challenged the Grail romances perhaps because they were, after all, a hobby of the nobility, with limited influence outside the noble families who copied them and had them read or sung by the court minstrels. But when the spiritual agenda of the Grail romances became the dominant view of both the nobility and the common folk, then the imperial and orthodox Church was forced into action. Just as the Grail legends reached their apotheosis in Wolfram's *Parzival,* the Church launched a new crusade, this time against its fellow Christians in southern France, the Cathars or Perfecti.

THE PERFECTI

The Grail romances tell us of an alchemical secret, transformative even in its most Christian forms, that is held by a family group of initiates or knights of the Temple. The secret, and the genealogy of its guardians, is explicated in an ancient book, which can be read only by those who, like Parzival, understand the language of the birds, the green language of alchemy and astronomy. This is the basic consensus of all the various Grail romances of the period, as we saw above, and may be considered the core of the legend as seen by its contemporary audience.

Like all great and essentially timeless ideas, the Holy Grail is a product of a specific time and place, a specific and exact set of enabling conditions that allowed the emergence of this seminal myth. To understand the impact of the Grail romances, we must look to the times in which the legend emerged, the late twelfth century. These thirty years, from roughly 1185 to 1215, marked, in many ways, the nadir of medieval Christianity. The papal squabbles of the midcentury, along with the general sense of discouragement after the failure of the Second Crusade, created a religious vacuum into which more "heretical" forms of Christianity stepped. The heresies took root so quickly because of the contrast they presented with the Church of Rome. The Cathar priests lived with and cared about their flock. It was common for Roman prelates to spend their whole tenure in absentia, while the lower clergy was often as venal and corrupt as the local landowner.

The decline of the Church had been given an extra push in the 1160s and 1170s by the wide circulation of Abelardian rationalism. Abelard, best remembered today for his romance with his pupil Héloise, had discussed the superstitions of the Church, in the 1120s, with such clearheadedness that two generations later many intellectuals agreed that change was necessary, even essential.

If the Second Crusade had been disappointing, then the fall of Jerusalem in the autumn of 1187 was devastating. It was seen as a sign of God's disfavor. A crusade was proclaimed, joined by such personages as the kings of Germany, France, and England. Frederick Barbarossa died along the way, and even though Richard I of England pursued the crusade with all the force of his fiery personality, Jerusalem remained in the hands of the infidels.[31]

Richard the Lion-Hearted was something of a troubadour himself and gave his own stamp of approval to the new mode of romance. He seemed to embody the Matter of Britain and its chivalric traditions. We can be sure that the new poetry of the Grail accompanied the Crusaders because Richard's nephew and Marie's son, Henry of Champagne, was elected king of Jerusalem. It is tempting to envision the poet Gautier de Danans chanting his continuation of Chrétien's masterwork in the great hall of Acre, with Richard and his queens, his sister Johanna and his wife Berengaria, nodding their approval.

Around 1200, Robert de Boron, following the popularity of the continuations of Chrétien, produced *Joseph of Arimathea,* the prequel to the series that ties it all very neatly into the Holy Family myths. He reveals the themes of a hidden or inner teaching given to Joseph after Christ's Resurrection. These teachings center on the Grail, here called a

chalice, and constitute the heart of the "mysteries." There is a murki-
ness to this version not found in Wolfram's work, for instance, perhaps
as a result of trying to tell the important parts (for those with ears to
hear) and still stay within certain defined limits that would allow the
Roman Church to ignore the tale. Things had changed by 1200. A powerful new pope, Innocent III, had regained the upper hand in his struggles with the Holy Roman Empire and began to turn his attention to
unifying the whole world under his spiritual rule.

And this led directly to the most disgraceful incidents in the history
of the Roman Church. The Fourth Crusade and the Crusade against the
Cathars were waged against fellow Christians. The Fourth Crusade
ended with the sack of Constantinople in 1203. The crusaders, tricked
by those crafty and godless Venetians, fell upon the first city of
Christendom and plundered and sacked with a vengeance, while
Innocent III rejoiced in the "unification of the Church."[32]

The resurgence of a Gnostic heresy in the south of France, however,
threatened to become the majority religion of the region, and Innocent
responded in the manner he knew best: calling out the troops. The
extermination of heretics in the south of France would continue for
almost half a century, long after Innocent III went to his just rewards in
whatever afterlife awaited him.

Why did the Church want to exterminate the Cathars, or the
Perfecti, as they called themselves?

It boiled down to a question of legitimacy. Even the Greek or
Eastern Church, newly sacked by Western crusaders, adhered to a common and recognizably biblical version of Christ. The Cathars, however,
posed a direct threat to the authority of all organized Christianity by
declaring that the Church Fathers had it all wrong. Essentially, the
Cathars were a Gnostic form of the Jewish Messianic tradition that
came perhaps directly from the early Christians in Provence. As such,
their view of Jesus as Christ differed radically from that of the orthodox and apostolic imperial Church, which they saw as a tool of the
demiurge, the Rex Mundi.[33]

The Cathars considered themselves Christians, but they had their
own version of the sacraments as well as a kind of yogic spiritual training and initiation. Jesus for them was a prophetic messiah, not a divine
being, and they utterly rejected the Crucifixion. Women were held in
high regard, were ordained as priestesses, and were even politically

influential in the latter portion of the struggle. The aim of the Perfecti, the inner ranks of the priesthood, was to transcend the cycle of birth and death, to escape from the clutches of the Rex Mundi, and to this end they discouraged marriage, using the energy of sexuality for the purposes of spiritual transformation. Like the Gnostics, they believed in a Great Return, when all the light imprisoned in matter would be released, and there is some evidence that they were chiliasts as well. There is also evidence that the Cathars believed in metempsychosis, or reincarnation.[34]

Just from this brief glimpse of their beliefs it is not hard to see why the Roman Church hated them. Their teachings were deeply antithetical to those of Catholicism; add to that the claim of being the true Christianity expressed by the practical ministry of the local Perfecti, and you have a spiritual force capable of taking on Rome and perhaps winning. It is not surprising that Pope Innocent III, flush from his almost accidental success over Constantinople, should seize upon the murder of a papal legate outside Toulouse in 1208 as a pretext for a full-scale crusade against the civilization of southern France.[35]

Between 1208 and 1244, the fall of the last Cathar stronghold at Montségur (see fig. 6.9), over half a million people went to the stake, or were killed in the series of terrible conflicts, out of a total population of around two million. Whole populations in cities such as Albi, Béziers, Carcassone, Toulouse, and Foix were brutally massacred in the first example in the West of an organized attempt at genocide. Out of this campaign developed the Church's secret police, the Inquisition, which survived with the power to punish heretics until 1835. In the Cathars, the Inquisition found its most implacable opponents. In the fifty-year record of the Inquisition in Languedoc we find only four heretics who recanted their beliefs.[36] Most, like the martyrs of Montségur, marched proudly into the flames and died for their faith. They might well have echoed the saying of the Donatists, persecuted half a millennium before by Saint Augustine: "The true church is the one that is persecuted, not the one that persecutes."[37]

What was the source of such powerful beliefs? Most scholars have, until recently, speculated about other Gnostic-influenced groups, such as the Bogomils, as a source for the Cathars' beliefs. But this has never been convincing, as the Bogomils died out almost a century before anything resembling Catharism appeared in Provence and Languedoc. The

Figure 6.9. Montségur, last stronghold of the Cathars, and the temple of the Grail on the Mount of Salvation. (Photo by Vincent Bridges)

similarities in the broad cosmology of both the Bogomils and the Cathars can be seen as borrowings from the same Gnostic sources, not as direct influences. The Cathars of southern France have distinct qualities, such as the belief in reincarnation, that separate them from other Gnostic survivals. Also, the Bogomils gained influence in Bulgaria as part of a peasant uprising, not by going head-to-head with the official Church in terms of philosophy and spirituality. When the uprising was crushed, in the early tenth century, the original Bogomils faded away.[38]

Remnants of a dualistic heresy similar to and perhaps inspired by the Bogomils survived, however, and by the eleventh century had spread to pockets in northern Italy and southern France. These were "Bogomils" only in the eyes of their orthodox persecutors, as all dualistic, anti-Roman heresies were classed during the era. By the middle of the twelfth century, the change to "Cathar" was under way when Bulgarian bishops arrived from Constantinople to ordain the growing and public heretical movement as true Bogomils. This, of course, would not have been necessary if the Cathars had actually descended from the earlier heretics. From this point on, the movement had a new official name, the Albigensian heresy, named for the largest group of delegates, those from the town of Albi in Languedoc.

So if the Bogomils can be considered a peripheral and parallel influence, then where did the Catharism of Provence and southern France get its sense of spiritual certainty? The local traditions of a kind of primitive Christianity are one obvious source. By perhaps semimiraculous means, two copies of the Catharist outer ritual have survived, one in French and one in Occitan. A prayer from this ritual points us directly to an early form of very Gnostic- and Hebriac-flavored Christianity: "Holy Father, Thou just God of all good souls . . . Grant us to Know what Thou Knowest, to Love what Thou Lovest; for we are not of this world, and this world is not of us, and we fear lest we meet death in this realm of an alien god."[39] This alien god is the Gnostic Demiurge.

This prayer ends with an interesting twist on the source of divinity in the Catharist view: " . . . and God came down from heaven . . . and took ghostly shape in Holy Mary."[40] To the Cathars, Mary was not the physical mother of a physical divine being, but the gateway or portal through which the Gnosis, the unveiling in the original meaning of the Greek *apokalypsis,* entered the world. In this sense, she was Sophia, or the Jewish concept of the Shekhinah.

The twentieth-century French historian of the Inquisition Jean Guiraud proved that even with the most critical and reductionist view of the evidence, the Cathars did indeed possess certain most ancient documents, which were directly inspired by the traditions of the early Church. He concluded that the similarities between the neophyte ritual of the Cathars and the second-century Baptism of the Catechumens were such that they were essentially the same ritual.[41] Except, of course, for the fact that the renunciation of Satan in the Baptism is mirrored in the Cathar rite by a renunciation of the Roman Church. By these lights, it was the Roman Church that was heretical, and the Cathars, with their early and more immediate view of Christianity, were actually the "one true church."

Did the nobles who joined the Templars and listened with such intensity to the Grail romances see them as part of this Gnostic revival? It is likely that they did, because the first and greatest of all the Grail poets, Chrétien de Troyes, was in all probability a Cathar. In his early work, *Erec et Enide,* from 1170, Chrétien expresses the core idea of both the troubadours and the Cathars. "What can I say of her beauty? In truth, she was made to be gazed upon: / For in her one could have seen himself as in a mirror."[42]

For Chrétien, as for all believers in the "court of love," the beauty of the beloved was a mirror of God's beauty. This echoes the Jewish mystical idea of the bride of God, the Shekhinah, which is in fact the "beauty" of God's creation praised in the Song of Songs attributed to Solomon. Among the Shia Sufis, this concept of the Shekhinah became the teaching that "feminine beauty is the theophany par excellence," citing as support of this position the saying of the Prophet: "I have seen my God under the most beautiful of forms." In Hindu Tantra, we find the same idea: "Every naked woman incarnates *prakrti.*" Although from the perspective of their opponents, the orthodox Church of Rome, the Cathars were seen as aesthetics and dualists who found this world irredeemably evil, that is not the perspective found inside the religion itself. What few remnants remain of their liturgy and practices seem to suggest a belief in the perfectibility of matter, not in its ultimate evil. So for the Cathars, as for the troubadours, both of whom valued this meditative contemplation of "beauty" as the ultimate perfection of matter, the beloved served as the middle way between debauchery and aestheticism.[43]

The troubadours of southern France invented a lifestyle and a form of poetry based on the ideals of romantic love at a time, the turn of the twelfth century, when one might expect that the literature of Europe would be focused on the martial zeal of the Crusades. They developed at the same time and in the same location as the Cathars, and their poetry expressed some of the same view of the world. Whereas the Perfecti tended to the people, the troubadours sang almost exclusively for the nobility, who had in most cases strong Cathar leanings themselves. Their influence would be felt in the works of Dante and of Petrarch, who commented that Bertrand de Ventadour's love songs to Eleanor of Aquitaine were almost as good as his own.[44]

The word *troubadour* itself is somewhat puzzling. It seems to come from the provençal *trobar,* "to find" or "to invent," giving the idea of seeking, whether for love, for the Holy Grail, for enlightenment. There is also a possible derivation from the Arabic *tarraba,* "to sing," and some of the lyrical styles used by the troubadours do have Arabic meters and rhyme schemes. The *aubade,* or *albi,* a string of rhymed couplets where the last line always repeats or rhymes, is a form still used by Bedouin minstrels and Arab pop music.[45]

The troubadours called their art the *gaya sciencia,* the "happy science," or even "ecstatic gnosis." Fulcanelli tells us in *Le Mystère* that their art was based on the green language, or the language of the birds,[46] and, indeed, the troubadours took their craft seriously enough to undergo a long period of training. One of the most famous troubadour academies was at the Château Puivert, Castle of the Bold Green (fig. 6.10), where the Court of Miracles, a troubadour conclave and competition, was held. Château Puivert is in the heart of Cathar country, and from the tower of the château one can see Montségur, where the Cathars made their last stand in 1244. Château Puivert, whose seigneur, or lord, Bernard de Congost, was an ardent Cathar, stands as a literal link between the troubadours and the Cathars. When Château Puivert was razed by Simon de Montfort in 1210, Bernard fled for sanctuary to Montségur.[47]

Figure 6.10. The Château Puivert, the Court of Miracles, as it is today. Sacked by Simon de Montfort in 1210, it remained, and still remains, a center of Catharism. Local neo-Cathars use the château for their devotions and pageants to the present day. (Photo by Vincent Bridges)

Perhaps the first of the troubadours was the grandfather of Eleanor of Aquitaine, Guillaume IX, count of Poitou and duke of Aquitaine. He joined the First Crusade but was never considered one of its leaders. His zeal, and respect for the Church's authority, was lacking, and after he returned home in 1100 he became the model of the later troubadours, roaming the countryside singing of love and consorting with all manner of heretics. It is possible that Guillaume of Aquitaine picked up the new verse forms from his contacts with Arabic poetry in Outremer, and they spread by his influence to southern France. The duke led a short but merry life, and when he died in 1137, he left his immense holdings and love for poetry to his granddaughter Eleanor.[48]

In many ways the most remarkable woman of the Middle Ages, Eleanor was outright sovereign of Aquitaine, the richest and fairest province of France, and very young when she was married to the king of France, the saintly Louis VII, who seems never to have known quite what to do with this powerful, beautiful, and headstrong woman. Eleanor started the fashion of the court of love, which flourished throughout Europe and reached its peak at the turn of the thirteenth century. Eleanor's daughter, Marie de Champagne, Chrétien's first patron, inherited her mother's love of provençal troubadours and all the other trappings of the cult of courtly love.[49]

Eleanor and her court accompanied Louis the Young on his expedition to the Holy Land, known as the disastrous and ineffectual Second Crusade. Eleanor returned from crusading and soon embarked on the great royal romance of the period. Henry Plantagenet, Henry II of England, swept her off her feet and married her with the aid of large bribes and good friends in Rome. This left the troubadour Bernard de Ventadour so heartbroken that he penned his most famous poem, the dirge to Eleanor that so moved Petrarch. Their children included two of the most renowned and infamous characters in the long panorama of English history: Richard the Lion-Hearted and King John, the signer of the Magna Carta. With such illustrious siblings as these, it is easy to lose track of a simple princess, no matter what her literary tastes. But Marie de Champagne deserves a better niche in history if only for her encouragement of poetry. She brought to her court the greatest storyteller of the age, Chrétien de Troyes

Not much is known about Chrétien's origins. He was born around 1130 and by 1170 he was famous as the author of a version of Ovid's

Book of Love, now lost, and a version of the Tristan story that has also disappeared. *Erec et Enide* was his first medieval best seller. This poem formally introduces the Matter of Britain, single-handedly created by Geoffrey of Monmouth in 1160, to the cosmopolitan audience at the court of Marie de Champagne, and from there it passed throughout the courts of Europe. *Erec* sets the basic pattern for all Arthurian romances, but though a Catharist perspective is displayed here, and suggested by Chrétien's other early work, the Grail is not yet in evidence.[50]

The shift to the Matter of Britain from classical subjects might be seen as a political consideration related to Eleanor's marriage to Henry II, who was known to be obsessed with Arthurian themes. Chrétien's early but lost work on Tristan is a clue to his Cathar leanings. Friedrich Heer, the great German authority on the culture of the Middle Ages, has suggested that the tale of Tristan and Iseult, particularly in its earliest form from the eleventh century, was a loosely disguised Cathar story. He goes on to speculate that Chrétien's use of themes in that story, such as the contemplation of the beloved as divine, and those in *Erec,* argues strongly for his Cathar affiliation. According to Professor Heer, the glimpses inside the Grail Castle Chrétien gives us are actually bits of the inner traditions of the Perfecti.[51]

If Chrétien, however, was already of the Catharist faith in 1170, why did a mysterious book "in the Breton tongue" given to him after 1178 by his new patron, Philip of Flanders, who appears to have had no Cathar sympathies, produce glimpses of the inner secrets of Catharism? And why was the whole symbolic complex given a Celtic gloss and its location vaguely identified with "Wales" and "Camelot" somewhere in Britain, particularly since everything else points to Provence and southern France?

The link was obscured and overlooked until very recently. The Holy Grail was also the Precious Stone of the Wise from the *Bahir,* and this was hidden because the secret behind the connection is that of alchemy, knowledge more dangerous even than heresy. When we look at all the pieces of the puzzle, however, a meaningful image does appear, one that leads to the Gothic cathedrals and directly to Fulcanelli's message in *Le Mystère.* In fact, the structure and authorship of the *Bahir* suggests a model for understanding just who Fulcanelli really was. As we shall see, the sages of the *Bahir* had many secrets, not the least of which was the Holy Grail.

THE STONE OF THE WISE

In chapter 4, we examined the *Bahir,* or Book of Illumination, at some length. As we saw, the Bahir combined the ideas of the work of creation, the animating of matter, with the radical concept of a celestial projection as a way to return to the divine source. Also in the *Bahir,* we learned that the Tree of Life, seen as an arrangement of the ten *sefirot* into a "tree" for the first time, is actually the "Precious Stone" whose facets are projected onto the celestial sphere. Another series of verses in the *Bahir* supply a mythology of the "Stone" that echoes the hidden mythos behind the Grail legends, ending with the curious statement from Genesis 49:24: "From there is the Shepherd, the Rock of Israel," which, as we noted, sounds an oddly Christian note for a work of Hebraic mysticism.[52]

The source of the ideas in the *Bahir,* such as the ancient astronomy of the Teli, the Cycle, and the Heart, may indeed have been Rabbi Nehuniah and the first-century Jewish Gnostic circle at Emmaus, but the text we have was compiled in Provence between 1150 and its appearance in public manuscript form in 1176, just two years before Frederick's coronation at Arles.[53] Within a decade of its appearance, Chrétien, possibly already a Cathar, had made the Grail legend into a medieval best seller. And just three years after the appearance of the *Bahir,* the Roman Church began its campaign of persecution against the Cathars, resulting in a full-scale crusade in 1208.

If, from this chronology, we can speculate that the publication of the *Bahir* triggered both the Grail romances and the sudden rise to prominence of the Cathars, then we must ask what triggered the public appearance of the *Bahir,* whose secret knowledge was traditionally taught only one-on-one. Answering this question brings us back to the Templars and the secret of alchemy and the end of time. And it suggests just how these ideas came to be immortalized in stone on the facades of the Gothic cathedrals.

The sages of the *Bahir* represent a secret society and a tradition that, according to Gershom Scholem, has its roots in the Hellenistic Gnosticism of first-century Jewish mysticism, and may possibly be connected through the mystic school of Emmaus with the origins of Christianity.[54] The text of the *Bahir* as it emerged in Provence is a collection of sayings and explanations by a series of learned rabbis. Some of these rabbis, such as Rabbi Nehuniah and Rabbi Akiva, are well known from the Talmud, and Rabbi Nehuniah and the school of Emmaus apparently influenced every later kabbalistic tradition. But the *Bahir* goes on to quote rabbis completely unknown elsewhere. There are also fables, teaching stories, and parables that have no parallel anywhere else in Hebrew literature.[55]

The main rabbi quoted is one Amorai, whose name means "speaker." Rabbi Amorai acts as the spokesman for the group, in accordance with the long-standing Hebraic tradition that the head of the group makes the pronouncements and teachings in his name or voice. Curiously enough, this is the same type of pseudonym that we find with Fulcanelli and his circle. Pierre Dujols, a prime suspect for Fulcanelli's real identity, used the name Magaphon, or "voice of the mage," in some of his writing.[56] "Fulcanelli" itself could be this kind of group-spokesman pseudonym for a larger group of sages. Even in the text of the *Bahir,* the identity of the quoted sages is often obscure.

By following those sages we can identify, we can trace a lineage from Nehuniah to the fourth-century sages Rabba and Rabbi Zeira of the Jerusalem school of alchemists and golem makers. An initial draft, called simply Raza Rabba, or "The Great Mystery," was apparently made at this point, and was circulated thereafter in private. As late as Maimonides' commentary on the *Sefer Yetzirah* in the early thirteenth century, thirty years after the appearance of the *Bahir* manuscript, it was completely unknown to the larger Jewish mystical community.[57]

Tradition holds that a small school remained in Ono, a suburb of Jerusalem close to Mount Zion, and in Barcelona in the kingdom of Aragon, now a part of Spain but in the twelfth century part of a cultural grouping that stretched from Barcelona to Provence.[58] The school in Jerusalem disappeared after the conquest of the city by the crusaders in 1099. Ideas from the *Bahir* appear in somewhat truncated form as a part of an eleventh-century Arabic alchemical work. This work, *Mother of the King,* by one Abufalah, refers to a work by King Solomon entitled *HaMaspen,* "The Compass" or lodestar, which suggests that it was an early version of the "Great Mystery" text of the *Bahir.* The anonymous Arabic author, Abufalah, a green-language pun in Arabic for "son of reason," includes some of the *HaMaspen* in the Third Gate of his treatise, but the author clearly doesn't understand it.[59]

Abufalah was an Arabic Jew writing in Jerusalem between the

disappearance of the mad caliph al-Hakim and the fall of the city to the crusaders. His alchemical learning is proudly displayed, but without much in the way of originality. But he does tell us where and how he learned of the mysteries. He studied with one Abu Artush, possibly of the Ono school, who, he informs us, had an ancient book that explained how Solomon learned the secret of alchemy and acquired from the queen of Sheba the precious stone with which he carried out his transmutations. In a somewhat garbled fashion, Abufalah suggests that the Egyptian queen had part of the ancient secret and possibly carried the correct lineage or bloodline, but still needed a mysterious "image of the pictures [of the heavens]" that foretold the future and brought the power of transmutation "out of the vapors" and into reality in order to complete the Great Work. This secret information King Solomon was glad to supply, Abufalah tells us.[60]

Here, in the years before the fall of Jerusalem to the crusaders in 1099, we find a mysterious Arabic Jew writing about alchemy in terms of a precious stone that facilitates the transformation and of a secret text that goes back to Solomon and the foundation of the First Temple. The author lived in Jerusalem and had some connection with the local mystics studying the Raza Rabba, a transitional form of the *Bahir*. This might be as close as we shall come to documenting the secret of alchemy that the Templars apparently discovered in the ruins of the Temple. We would not even suspect the importance of Abufalah's work, which exists in only one manuscript in the British Museum, except for the fact that another provençal mystic in the later *Bahir* tradition, Rabbi Shlomo in the thirteenth century, lifted part of it, uncredited, for his own alchemical text, the *Gates of Heaven*. This curious plagiarism points to an absorption of the concepts within the tradition of the *Bahir* and the loss of a direct contact with the original tradition caused by the fall of Jerusalem, as well as a conscious attempt to cover over the sources of the information.[61]

We can think of this as a clear example of the tendency of those involved in the development of the *Bahir* to obscure and obfuscate their origins, identities, and sources. Like the Freemasons centuries later, our only clue is a series of metaphors involving Solomon and his Temple, including, of course, the very real and problematic Knights of the Temple of Solomon.

The fall of Jerusalem marked the end of the early *Bahir* school in the suburb of Ono. Perhaps their ancient book was one of the secrets that the Templars gathered together in the early years of the twelfth century, along with some kind of "precious stone," either the Black Stone of al-Hakim or even an earlier piece of the stone from the queen of Sheba. It is possible that it was these discoveries that were reported back to Troyes in 1104 and caused such a stir at the court of Champagne. Unraveling these secrets led to a need for the Templars in 1118 and their recognition by the pope in 1128. By 1130, when James I of Aragon gave the Templars their extensive holdings in Provence, Languedoc, and Aragon, it looked as if the Templars were about to become the new power in the land. And for almost two centuries, that's exactly what they were.

At the same time as the Templars rose to power, the 1120s and 1130s, the group of pre-*Bahir* mystics working with the "Great Mystery" text in Spain decided to relocate to Provence. By 1150, a large group of sages had settled in various locations in Provence, including Arles, Aix, and Nimes. Over the next twenty years, their teachings, added on to the basic text of the "Great Mystery," would become the *Bahir* of the published manuscripts. What had been an almost lost secret tradition suddenly blossomed into a vital spiritual current that would spark the future development of both Jewish and Christian mysticism.

This time period, from the 1130s to the 1170s, also marks the rise of the Cathars from a small Gnostic survival to a major spiritual competitor of orthodox Christianity. In 1126, two years before the pope legitimized the Templars, the Cathar heresy had had only one martyr, Peter de Bruys, in the whole of Languedoc. By 1167, just forty years later, the Cathars were extensive enough in the same region to be the majority party at the Council of Toulouse, giving their name, Albigensians, or the believers from Albi, to the entire movement.[62]

Could the sudden rise of the Cathars be related to the combination of the emergence of the sages of the *Bahir* and the Templars, who protected the region from the full power of the Roman Church? The gathering of Jewish sages, mystics, alchemists, and even golemists, devoted to a text that is the only likely source for the discoveries on Temple Mount in Jerusalem, in the European power center of the Templars cannot be considered coincidental. Could the link between the Cathars and the Templars be the Jewish alchemists of the *Bahir*?

Most scholars who note this synchronicity, from Gershom Scholem to Neil Asher Silberman, take their information on the Cathars from the Cathars' opponents and consider that any connection between the traditions is antithetical and in the nature of a response or a reflection. This, however, doesn't explain the admitted connection. Somehow, the traditions are related.

The one Jewish scholar of the *Bahir* who took the trouble to look at what remains of the original Cathar source material, Professor Shulamit Shachar, came to a very different conclusion. Professor Shachar found that the similarities between the Bahirists and the Cathars were far more compelling than the few differences that remained when Christian hysteria was taken into account.[63] While Professor Shachar didn't draw any conclusions, there is one key point that suggests that the Cathars were directly influenced by the *Bahir*.

This point is the aforementioned Shekhinah, called the Divine Presence in the *Bahir* and described as the light that shines even in the darkness. Her beauty is compared to that of a beautiful vessel filled with precious jewels, and her attribute is a kind of cosmic mother-love, the ocean of wisdom. In another verse, the treasure of the Divine Presence is likened to a beautiful pearl, and through a complex series of allusions and green-language punning this is translated as "Bring to life your works in the midst of the pearl that gives rise to the years."[64]

In addition to the Shekhinah connections, the *Bahir* would also seem to be the source of the Cathars' doctrine of reincarnation. In verses 194 and 195 of the *Bahir*, we find reincarnation described in the same terms used by the Cathars, that of vines and viticulture. Verse 196 follows this up with an account of a creation of a golem and a discussion on the Demiurge, and ends with the metaphor of the sacred marriage between the Shekhinah and the Blessed Holy One. It is with a slight shock that we realize that these three verses contain the pearl of great price, the core of the Cathar beliefs.[65]

Immediately before this astonishing sequence of verses, we find a series of equal wonderment. In verses 191 through 193, the *Bahir* sages present us with a version of the Grail myth, one that ties together all the others and just might be the original.

Abraham is the Grail Knight in this version, receiving from Melchizedek, the king of the righteous or consort of the Divine Presence (the Shekhinah), the command to stand watch through time and bring merit and compassion to the world. Abraham plants a tamarisk tree in

Beersheba and announces the sacred word, the name of God, and then institutes the sacraments of bread and water with the words: "Whom do you serve?" These are powerful echoes of the Grail ritual, and verse 193's "Rock of Israel" calls to mind the rock of Zion on which the crusader kingdom of Jerusalem was founded.

This close juxtaposition of the Grail myth, in a possibly original form, with the heart of the Cathars' theosophy in just seven short verses of one mystical text serves as conclusive proof of the close connection among all three traditions. In case more proof is needed, let us look at verse 190, the beginning of this amazing sequence.

Here we find the original of the "Precious Stone of the Wise." When God created Light, it was so intense that life could not develop. God then shaped the extra light into a great stone, into which he engraved the Tree of Life and the world itself, what the *Bahir* calls the Ultimate Future. This stone was passed down through the family of Abraham until, rejected, it passed to the descendants of Jacob and disappeared into Egypt. This, the *Bahir* informs us, is the stone the builders rejected that will become the chief cornerstone of the new Temple. Wolfram is making the same point with his *"lapsit exillis"* pun; the stone is all of these things—the stone of exile, the stone that fell from heaven, the stone of eternal life, and the stone of the heavens, literally a crystallization of the leftover light of creation.

ELIJAH, ESCHATOLOGY, AND THE UNDERGROUND STREAM

The *Bahir*, as we have seen, provides the link among the Cathars, the Grail romances, and the Templars. But the question of why the sages of the *Bahir* decided to go public at just that moment remains unanswered. Given the political situation, we may be sure the step was not taken lightly. There must have been some compelling and overwhelming reason why such a momentous undertaking was attempted. Secrecy was ingrained in the tradition; the work was taught privately and transmitted only from master to student. Suddenly, the secret was out, written down and circulated far beyond the usual small family groups. Why take such a risk?

The answer lies in the message of a mysterious visitor, and provides the link between alchemy and eschatology. Starting around 1150, a series of strange encounters between provençal kabbalists and an enigmatic visitor identified as "Elijah the Prophet" triggered a surge of eschatological speculations. No less a personage than Rabbi Abraham ben David of Posquières, son-in-law of the chief rabbi of Narbonne, received a life-changing visit from Elijah the Prophet. The last recorded such visit was to Rabbi Jacob "the Nazarite" from Lunel around 1170. Rabbi Jacob was a mystic and ascetic with close connections to the Cathars and the local provençal tradition—going back traditionally to Mary Magdalene—of cave-dwelling anchorites.[66]

Elijah's message was simple. Around the year 1216, a new era of revelation would unfold, ushering in the third and last cycle of the age. Forty years of preparation were required to open the new era, so 1176 was chosen as the publication date of the *Bahir,* the work that contained the secrets of transmutation.[67] This key bit of eschatological information can also be seen as the driving force behind the Grail romances and the Cathars. Both seemed to expect a new era, with a new form of Christianity, to dawn in the near future.

But once the secret was out, others began to pick up on Elijah's message. One of the most significant was Joachim of Flores. Joachim was born into the minor nobility in Sicily around the time Abbot Suger began the renovation of Saint Denis in the early 1140s. In the mid-1160s he went on pilgrimage to Jerusalem, where he became converted to a variety of mystical Christianity not too dissimilar to the mysticism of the *Bahir.* After a few years as a hermit on Mount Etna, Joachim returned to Italy, joined the Benedictines, and became a Chronicler at the Order of Zion's influential monastery at Casamari (House of Mary) in Calabria.[68]

Joachim's visions began around 1183, and soon after he was summoned to Rome by Pope Lucius III and encouraged to record his visions and his theories. From this recognition, Joachim became a star, the most authoritative spokesman of his age on the imminent last days. He felt that his knowledge and visions imposed a heavy sense of obligation to spread the news of the impending apocalypse.

Convinced that political events such as the schism in Zion and the encroaching power of the Roman orthodoxy and its struggle with the Holy Roman Empire portended an imminent close of the second age, Joachim retreated to his own mountaintop monastery on Mount Nero, high above the Sila plateau in northern Italy. There he was consulted by the great of his era, including Richard the Lion-Hearted. Joachim told

Richard that the Antichrist had already been born. Given that the date, 1191, was roughly the time when Tamujin began his rise to become the Genghis Khan of the Mongol horde, Joachim may have been right.[69]

His calculation placed the end of the second age at around 1260. By this date, fifty-eight years after Joachim's death in 1202, several apocalypses, such as the fall of Constantinople to the Fourth Crusade, the Crusade against the Cathars, and the conquest of the Middle East by the hordes of Genghis Khan and his sons, had indeed happened. Eighty-seven years after Joachim's target date, the worst apocalypse since Noah's Flood swept the world—the Black Death.

In spite of Joachim's acceptance during his life, after his death the Church condemned his views and his writings. Since that time, Joachim has been treated as both a saint and a heretic, but his views retained their popularity in esoteric circles down to the twenty-first century.

The sages of the *Bahir* published their work, at the urging of the mysterious Elijah, because they saw that the world was descending into a period of darkness. The arrival of the Mongol hordes and the death of many Sufi sages, such as Ibn Al Arabi, combined with the genocide of the Cathar Crusade, confirmed this view.[70] The world was a much darker place in 1260 than it had been in 1160, and by 1360, in the depths of the Black Death, it must have seemed that the apocalypse had indeed arrived.

And what of the sages of the *Bahir* who had thrown in their lot with the Cathars? They had fared only slightly better by their target date of 1216. Thankfully most of the original sages did not live to see the persecutions of the early thirteenth century, the community had been driven underground and out of Provence. The son of Rabbi Abraham, Isaac "the Blind," whom Elijah had visited in the 1160s, led the community in 1215, at the height of the Cathar persecutions, from Provence to Gerona in the Pyrenees northwest of Barcelona. Here, shielded from the Inquisition, the community continued to spread the new mystical doctrine of the Kabbalah across Europe.

In his last, unfinished fragment, the *Titurel,* which was completed a half century later by Albrecht von Scharffenberg,[71] Wolfram tells us that the Grail was taken to a miraculous castle in the Pyrenees, built to serve as home for the Grail, which until then had "no fixed place, but floated invisible in the air." A temple was built to house the Grail atop the solitary Mountain of Salvation. In Albrecht's description it is a combination of the *Bahir's* Precious Stone, the Cube of Space, and the Tree of

Life, a sort of New Jerusalem model of the temple of the cosmos. There are hints here of both the *Bahir* sages' move to Gerona and the Cathars' last stronghold at Montségur, which was constructed at roughly the same time and is less than one hundred miles from Gerona.

After the final destruction of the Cathars, the school at Gerona also faded away. The Grail romances lost their appeal, and cathedral construction eventually ran out of funds and inspiration and ground to a halt. In the fifteenth century, Grail knight René the Good of Anjou, and count of Provence as well, rediscovered part of the tradition and labeled it the Stream of Arcadia. In the sixteenth century this idea of an Arcadian underground stream would appear in the works of Sir Philip Sydney and Shakespeare and in the seventeenth century in painters such as Poussin. Even Samuel Taylor Coleridge, in "Kubla Khan," mentions the mythic river Alph (or Alephus), which goes underground in Asia Minor and was said to surface at Arcadia in Greece, or at the Fountaine de Vaucluse in the Ardèche, according to Petrarch.

The theme continues down to *Le Mystère*. In the discussion on the image from the Great Porch at Notre-Dame-de-Paris labeled "The mysterious Fountain at the foot of the Old Oak," Fulcanelli concludes his overview of the key points of the secret wisdom with a quote from the sacred well at Notre-Dame-de-Limoux, in the heart of the Cathar country of Languedoc only about fifty miles from Montségur.

But there are still some unanswered questions: If the Grail romances derived from Jewish and Catharist sources promoted by the Templars in southern France, why do they appear as part of the Matter of Britain? And even more significant, how did these ideas come to be incorporated into the Gothic cathedrals?

The latter will have to wait until chapter 7, but the former can be answered by referring once again to the chronology of the era. By the mid-1170s, the Cathars had attained both organization and stature from the Council of Toulouse, but had not yet been seriously attacked by the Roman Church. The Templars were at the peak of their influence in both Outremer and Provence, negotiating a deal with Frederick I Barbarossa that would make them independent of even papal authority. In this climate, it is easy to see why the *Bahir* group felt it safe to publish their work.

If we can agree that Chrétien represents an early kind of Cathar troubadour, then the decision had already been made to camouflage

Catharist teachings in a Celtic mode. Catharism seemed to be the correct religion for the court of love at Camelot, and the Matter of Britain, unlike the classical or Carolingian epic cycles, allowed its poets and listeners to approximate reality in a mythical way while relating those myths to everyday events around them. Arthur's court, and Britain, for that matter, was far enough removed that it could serve as a land of the imagination, yet near enough to be familiar.

The archetypal Arthur of Celtic myth, the high king who sailed to the Land of the Dead and retrieved the cauldron of regeneration, was the common property of the entire Celtic West, from Toulouse to Tara. The high king of the Volcae at ancient Toulouse was an "Arthur" figure, as was the fifth-century high king of the Bretons, Rhiotomas, who fought against the Roman Empire. Geoffrey of Monmouth, writing in 1130, made Arthur into a real historical figure, and ensured the Cathars' appreciation by noting that his shield carried the image of the Virgin and setting him up as the foe of Rome. These details recur in Chrétien's early Arthurian work from the mid-1170s.

When the original Grail text of Guyot, possibly the new text of the *Bahir* with some genealogical material added, was revealed to the inner circle at the coronation of Frederick at Arles in 1178, it was simple common sense to continue the cover story by going along with Geoffrey's "Breton" origins for the story. This subterfuge did not save the Cathars. They were proclaimed anathema by the Roman Church the following year, 1179, and soon the persecutions increased.[72] But it did save the core of the alchemical Grail of the *Bahir* by providing an untouchable cover for the stories themselves.

By the time Wolfram finished *Parzival,* the Cathars were being slaughtered by the Church and there was no longer any need for hiding. Wolfram names the guardians as Templars, places the source of the story correctly in Spain, Provence, and the Pyrenees, and gives us, in his Wilhelm, a possible Grail lineage connecting Parzival with the paladins of Charlemagne and the heroes of the First Crusade. He even makes explicit the "stone" metaphor from the *Bahir,* and he insists on an Eastern connection that has been variously seen as Jewish or Islamic, or both.

Wolfram had nothing to hide, and even as the Grail romances faded away, the inner truths and metaphors so courageously revealed by Chrétien and Wolfram coalesced into the imagery on the front of the Gothic cathedrals. The mysterious book and stone so beloved of the

Templars, the Cathars, and the alchemists became public books of stone, open to all who could read their symbolism. As we shall see in chapter 7, the cathedrals of Our Lady designed and built between 1150 and 1260 were the "houses" in which the Divine Presence communed with its beloved souls trapped in matter. The cathedrals were nothing less than an attempt to make a living model of the Stone of the Wise, a new chapel of the Grail and a temple of the cosmos.

SEVEN

TEMPLES OF THE COSMOS, CATHEDRALS OF THE GODDESS

THE HERMETIC CATHEDRALS

And so, at long last, we arrive at the point where Fulcanelli began, the Gothic cathedrals of Europe. In his 1926 *Mystery of the Cathedrals,* Fulcanelli claimed that the Gothic cathedrals were hermetic libraries in stone with the secret of alchemy displayed for all who could understand to read. When our investigation began, this seemed, in its own way, the most incredible of all Fulcanelli's claims. It was easier to believe that someone had stumbled privately onto the real secret behind the alchemical transformation than it was to believe that some secret society, or societies, had encoded this information deliberately into the design and the decorations of the greatest of all Christian monuments.

For the belief that the Gothic cathedrals are alchemical texts in stone to be true, several important preconditions would also have to be true, such as the existence of a secret, or not-so-secret, group with access to the highest levels of the Church, bottomless wealth, connections with the Holy Land and the Muslim world, and knowledge of alchemy. Before we, as researchers, could take Fulcanelli's claims seriously, we needed to validate the existence of such a group. The importance of this point is obvious. If Fulcanelli was merely projecting from his own unconscious the meanings he gives certain images and motifs found in the cathedrals, rather than revealing an ancient alchemical tradition, then *Mystery of the Cathedrals* would be not much more than a work of symbolist fantasy—interesting, and useful to the psychologist perhaps—but of limited value in terms of alchemy.

Yet this is, if anything, Fulcanelli's main point. *Mystery of the Cathedrals* is not the usual alchemical cookbook or *grimoire,* for Fulcanelli implies that he is revealing the mystery of alchemy as it was taught to him, by reference to the hermetic meanings embodied within the cathedrals. *Mystery of the Cathedrals* is therefore a demonstration not just of the alchemical philosophy, but also of how this philosophy animated a lost medieval Golden Age. The key to understanding Fulcanelli's importance, and not just the value of his work, lies in the reality of this lost knowledge and the fact of its emergence as symbols on the walls of these churches.

We began our search with the origin of alchemy and discovered that alchemy, while containing the knowledge of a pre-catastrophe civilization, appeared in its modern form as part of the Gnostic ferment of the first century C.E. This Gnostic worldview, derived from the mystery cults of the ancient world, supplied a theological and mythological framework for the emerging wave of monotheistic mysticism as practiced by traditions such as Christianity and Essene Judaism. This framework also contained the essential ideas of alchemy's triple transformation. The specific magical technology of the triple transformation—inner yogic disciplines, magical ceremonies combined with manipulation of sacred metals, and the secret of time and timing, including the beginning and end of time—developed first within the Gnostic cults, including Christianity, and then dispersed into the intellectual underground of the Dark Ages.

As part of this paradigm, alchemy was influenced by Gnostic eschatological teachings, such as the path of return by the small lights to the One Light. Two thirds of the transmutational secret was persecuted out of orthodox and Western Christianity, while the remaining one third of the secret, that of time itself, was co-opted by its temporal leaders, such as Constantine, Charlemagne, and Otto I. For the Christians, the whole idea of the end of time became confused with the fall of the Roman Empire, and the apocalypse against heretics became an institution of the Church. But the idea of a transformed reality, the chiliast vision of a new heaven and a new earth purged of sin, refused to die.

This chiliast concept of a spiritually animated matter became the keystone of the alchemical process. The illuminated Hebrew mystics of the *Bahir* recorded the techniques for animating matter and related them to the transformational process of galactic alignment. The

Shi'ites, Fatimids, and Ismailis alike believed that Muhammad had received this information and passed on the secret of time and the coming of the Day of Judgment through the family of Ali. The Sufis, of all persuasions, retained the most complete understanding of the internal yogic transformation. Any successful alchemist faced the daunting task of uniting in his own understanding these widely separated fragments in order to complete the Great Work.

We found that by the tenth century, alchemical knowledge had declined to the point that the chiliast secret of animating matter had effectively been lost. The Byzantine Greek compilations of that era are composed of older material, much of it from the first century, such as the "Isis the Prophetess" text. The Islamic current had split into the compilers and philosophers versus the mystical and the political wing. Among the Jews of the Diaspora, knowledge of the *Bahir* was limited to several small family groups in Spain and Jerusalem. The information had been on the verge of vanishing before 1100, and it was hard to see how in a few short decades it could have been revived and then become influential enough to appear on the cathedral walls. But apparently it had.

Working backward from the cathedrals themselves, we found that there were indeed enough mysteries to drive a small army of secret societies through. "Why did western Europe build so many churches in the three hundred years after the year 1000? What need was there, in a Europe with hardly one-fifth of its present population, for temples so vast that they are now rarely filled even on the holiest days? How could an agricultural civilization afford to build such costly edifices, which a wealthy industrialism can barely maintain?" Will Durant asked these questions in his chapter on the Gothic cathedrals in his *History of Civilization* (volume four of *The Age of Faith*).[1]

And who designed them? Who decided on the artwork, laid out the ground plans, and supervised the construction and the decoration? These are mostly unanswered, and now unanswerable, questions. We know the names of these "master masons," but their history and the story of their work have for the most part been lost. But the fact of that work, its skill and symbolic integrity, points to the sophisticated degree of organization, perhaps even on an international level, required to produce such elaborate and long-term projects. Buildings of such complexity and elegance do not happen by accident.

As Durant noted, the year 1000 was a significant one to Western

Christendom. As we began to investigate this significance, we came face-to-face with one of the seminal figures in the transition from the Dark Ages to the Middle Ages, Pope Sylvester II. Though pontiff for only four years (999–1003), as noted above, the hermetic pope proved to be the fulcrum in a complex series of events that resulted in effects as wide-ranging as the Crusades, the Templars, the Peace of God movement and its heretical offshoots, the Grail romances, and, eventually, the cathedral-building movement itself.

As we followed the tangled pattern of Sylvester's career, we found the seeds of our sophisticated international organization in the various chronicling orders established by Sylvester within, and on the edges of, the other monastic orders, the Benedictines, the Cluniacs, and the Cistercians. This fluidity of organization gained a central focus with the establishment of the group of Chroniclers at Jerusalem in 1002. From that point on we can safely speak of an Order of Zion, in Jerusalem, with connections to all three major monastic orders back in Europe.

During the eleventh century, all of these monastic orders began to build in the pre-Gothic style known as Romanesque. Within these monastic communities, groups of specialists developed. These were monks and scholars who knew Greek and mathematics, especially geometry, and were also skilled in building. As these "schools" grew, they were influenced by architecture from many distant places, the Hagia Sophia in Constantinople, the Al Aqsa Mosque, the Dome of the Rock, in Jerusalem, and the mosque of Ibn Tulun in Cairo. It is not hard to think that the Order of Zion, with its Byzantine and Fatimid connections, might have been one source of that influence.

After the First Crusade conquered Jerusalem, the Order of Zion became, as we saw in chapter 5, the "rock" upon which the kingdom of Jerusalem was founded. The order used its connections back in Provence to capitalize on the discovery, around 1102, of the alchemical and cosmological secrets of the "Great Mystery" text and, just possibly, a piece of the stone of the wise, the *lapsit exillis*. A decade later, wealth began flowing back to Europe, mostly to the Cistercians led by Bernard of Clairvaux. By 1130, the Templars had been established, Bernard was the foremost Christian of his day, and Europe was poised on the edge of the cathedral-building mania. Gothic was in the air, but had yet to be given form. For that we have to thank Saint Denis and the abbot Suger.

"BRIGHT IS THE NOBLE WORK . . ."

The Ile-de-France, the heart of the ancient kingdom of the Merovingian Franks, is not a true island, but rather a region surrounded and inter-connected by water, the river system of the Seine, the Oise, the Aisne, the Ourcq, and the Marne. The center of that green and fertile region of deep soil, broad meadows, and dense forests connected by wide, slow-flowing rivers grew out of a chance intersection of roadways and waterways.

For millennia, Paleolithic hunters had camped, without leaving much of a trace beyond a few broken spear points and well-cracked elk thighbones, on an island in the broad bend of the Seine where the north–south hunting trail crossed the river. Eventually, the low rise on the eastern end of the boat-shaped island became a sacred site, and a small community grew up around it. By the third century B.C.E., a group of Gallic Celts who called themselves Parisii had built a small but pros-perous town on the island. They entered history in 53 B.C.E. when Julius Caesar held an assembly in the town, then called Lutetia. The next year, the people of Lutetia joined Vercingetorix in his revolt against Rome.[2]

Labienus, Caesar's lieutenant, crushed them and the island was abandoned for the new Roman city on the left bank, located in what is even now called the Latin Quarter. Roman Lutetia was ravaged in the Germanic invasions of the late third century C.E., and the island once again became a defensive stronghold. By the time the Roman emperor Valentinian visited in 365 C.E., his "dear Lutetia, a small island enclosed within the walls of its ramparts, accessible through two wooden bridges alone," was becoming known as Paris.[3]

Paris became a capital in the late sixth century. Clovis I, Merovingian king of the Franks, founded his realm there and estab-lished the episcopal seat, or cathedra, of the newly dominant Christian Church. His son, Childebert I, built the first pair of cathedrals on the Ile-de-la-Cité, as the island was now called. These two, Saint-Etienne and the first Notre Dame, barely survived successive disasters. Paris would be rebuilt under the Capetian kings, descendants of its mayor, Hugh the Stout—who successfully defended the island against the Vikings in 885–86—but the rebuilding of its cathedrals would await the inspiration of Saint Denis.

The legend of Denis is obscure, and not much is actually known about him. He appears in history in the work of Gregory of Tours, who simply describes his martyrdom by beheading four hundred years after the fact. *The Golden Legend,* an early medieval collection of apocryphal stories, gives us more details. After his beheading, Saint Denis raised himself up and, taking his head in his hands, walked five miles west, his severed head singing psalms the whole way, from Montmartre to the river. The place where he finally collapsed and was buried became a shrine.[4] Figure 7.1 shows a statue of Saint Denis on Notre Dame.

Located a few miles north of the Ile-de-la-Cité, the abbey of Saint-Denis was built around the tomb of the beheaded saint and his venerable relics. Denis, the patron saint of Paris and by extension France itself, had been recognized first by the Merovingians and then by the heirs of Charlemagne. A small Carolingian church replaced the Merovingian shrine, the family chapel of the dynasty, on the site in the mid-ninth century. Hugh Capet and our old friend Gerbert of Aurillac, archbishop of Rheims, founded the abbey itself in the early 990s. As Saint Remy and Rheims became associated with the founding of the first Merovingian

Figure 7.1. Saint Denis holding his head, from the south porch of Notre-Dame-de-Paris. (Photo by Vincent Bridges)

dynasty, Saint Denis and Paris became associated with its Capetian revival.

The future abbot Suger was born in poverty in the village of Saint-Denis. His innate intelligence won him a place in the local monastery school, the Prieuré de l'Estrée, where he became friends with the future king of France Louis VI. The royal family noticed Suger. Philip I encouraged the friendship between his son and the brilliant scholar. In the early 1120s, Suger was sent to Rome several times on diplomatic missions. During his time at the Holy Curia in the early twelfth century, Suger came into contact with all the major intellectual currents of his age, including perhaps what we speculate to be the secret discoveries in the Holy Land.

During the second decade of the twelfth century, Suger served as prime minister of France and was at the center of the struggle between the French state and the Church. Suger naturally sided with his old school chum Louis VI, and his son, Louis VII, against the antipopes of the Holy Roman Empire. He was a man who spent most of his life dealing with the intricacies of medieval power politics, and when he talked, the king of France listened.

In 1123, at the height of his power and influence, Suger became the abbot of Saint-Denis. Perhaps because of his knowledge of the discoveries in Jerusalem and their apparently inexhaustible wealth, Suger pressed for the rebuilding of the old Carolingian church into something that would be the wonder of Europe and the proper venue in which to display the relics of Saint Denis and the regalia of the Capetian kings (see fig. 7.2). Abbot Suger envisioned his church as the center of the new illuminated Christianity that seemed to be overtaking the old politically compromised Roman Church in the early years of the twelfth century.

That Saint-Denis, rather than, say, Rheims, with its much more prominent Merovingian connections, was singled out as the source point for the Gothic transformation depends as much on a misidentification as it does on Abbot Suger's energy and political savvy. As noted above, not much was known of the historical Denis. The abbey library contained a volume of works attributed to him, but these were actually written by the second-century Gnostic philosopher Dionysius the Areopagite, the Saint Denis of Alexandria whom Fulcanelli lists as one of the early proponents of chiliasm. The book, given to one of Charlemagne's sons by the Byzantine emperor Michael the Stammerer,

Figure 7.2. The crypt of Saint Denis, burial site for the early Merovingian kings, from an eighteenth-century engraving.

ended up in the abbey's library perhaps as the result of Pope Sylvester's Chroniclers.[5]

Abbot Suger was greatly influenced by Dionysius's theology of light. Dionysius believed that "every creature, visible or invisible, is a light brought into being by the Father of Lights," and celebrated the Divine Light, God's holy fire, which animated the entire universe.[6] This is similar to the basic Gnostic concept of the path of return. Abbot Suger took this theme to heart. In his three books on the building and consecration of the church, we find no fewer than thirteen separate inscriptions celebrating the holy Light. In one of them, in a verse written to celebrate a gilded bronze gate, Suger tells us: "Bright is the noble work, this work shining nobly / Enlightens the mind so that it may travel through the true lights / To the True Light where Christ is the true door."[7]

From these ideas, Abbot Suger developed his theory of *lux continua,* or continuous light. With these two words, Suger announced the birth of the Gothic style and at the same time pointed to its spiritual roots in the Gnostic illuminism of alchemy. From this point on, the walls of sanctity would be shattered to let in the light. The solemn and stifling darkness of the Romanesque would be replaced by the flow of continuous radiance at the heart of the Gothic.

By 1133, Abbot Suger informs us, he had collected artists and craftsmen "from all lands," including a contingent of Arabic glassmakers. Suger did not invent stained glass; as we saw in chapter 4, the Fatimids had used it in their mosques for over a century. Glassmaking seems to have been a component of the alchemical process. We find it mentioned in the preparations of certain "sands" described in the "Isis the Prophetess" text. The Fatimid scholars and mystics of Cairo used colored glass fashioned in geometrical patterns as a meditation tool, as seen in the remaining stained glass of the Al Azhar Mosque. The good abbot's idea was to use the stained glass to fill the interior of his church with sparkling jewel-like color.

Bright indeed is the noble work. Abbot Suger approached the building of his new church with all the enthusiasm and attention to detail of the alchemist in pursuit of the philosopher's stone. To Abbot Suger, perhaps, his new light-filled church was the true philosopher's stone.

The cathedral (see fig. 7.3) was finished in 1144, and the dedication was attended by a veritable who's who of the mid-twelfth century. Louis VII attended, with his wife Eleanor of Aquitaine (from whom he would soon be divorced), as did most of the bishops of the Western Church and hundreds of knighted nobles. Even Bernard, who was heard to grumble at the expense of gilding a church, attended.

From its beginnings at Saint-Denis, the new style spread first through central France and then all over Europe, from England to Germany, from Portugal to northern Italy. The collection of artists and craftsmen assembled by Abbot Suger developed into schools and guilds that traveled throughout Europe for the next two centuries or so creating a vast collection of Gothic churches and civic buildings. Twelve years after the good abbot's death in 1151, his student the bishop of Paris, Maurice de Sully, and his "master mason," Guillaume de Paris, paid him the compliment of bettering his design.

On an island in the Seine, the new cathedral of Notre-Dame-de-Paris rose slowly into the light-filled sky. Work on the choir and transepts was begun in 1163 and not completed until 1182. By the time the construction of the nave was under way, another change was sweeping through Christendom.

Jerusalem and most of the Holy Land were conquered in 1187 by the forces of the Seljuk sultan Saladin. The West was stunned, and plans began for an immediate crusade, the third according to modern historians. (The Second Crusade had been the unhappy affair undertaken in

Figure 7.3. The cathedral of Saint-Denis, in the suburb of Saint-Denis, just north of Paris. (Photo by Darlene)

1147 by Louis VII, during which Abbot Suger ruled France as regent. Suger, in fact, did do so well with the realm's finances that Louis's disastrous crusade hardly made a dent in the royal coffers.) In the midst of this political upheaval occurred the Cutting of the Elm at Gisors, the schism between the Order of Our Lady of Zion and the Knights of the Temple of Solomon and the start of the persecution of the Cathars. For over a decade, Zion had been building a private power base back in Europe, and after the loss of the abbey on Mount Zion, the entire order relocated, as we saw above, to its various holdings in Paris, Bourges, and Troyes.

This shift began in 1152, the year after Abbot Suger's death, with Louis VII's gift to the order of the large priory at Orleans of Saint-

Samson, another Dark Age saint with Merovingian connections. By 1178, the order was confirmed by the pope in its possession of houses and large tracts of land from the Holy Land to Spain. The Cutting of the Elm at Gisors did more than just split off the Templars from its parent order; it defined the boundary line between the Plantagenets on one side, supported by the Templars, and the Capetians on the other, supported by Zion. This division would eventually produce not just the destruction of the Templars by the French king Philip III and his papal puppet Clement V, but also the catastrophe of the Hundred Years War between France and England.

As the walls of Notre-Dame-de-Paris rose, the foundations of the new illuminated Christendom began to crumble. The loss of Jerusalem, and eventually the rest of Outremer, made the universal nature of the Church questionable. An alternative form of Christianity, whose imagery would appear in the decorations of Chartres, Notre-Dame-de-Paris, and the cathedral at Amiens, attempted an end run around the power of the Roman Church by appealing directly to the nobility's chivalric sense of destiny with the Grail romances and to the common people's unrepentant paganism with an emphasis on Mary as the Mother of God and Queen of Heaven. With the failure of the Third Crusade and the subsequent strife among its leaders, this grand plan began to falter.

The orthodox Roman Church fought back in the so-called Crusades against Christians. First, almost by accident, Constantinople was conquered in 1203 by the Fourth Crusade. This empowered Pope Innocent III to go after the heretics in southern France in 1208. Fifty years later, with southern France and its culture destroyed, the hope of a new kind of Christianity, once so promising, had been lost. The esoteric stream that surfaced briefly to create this Gothic renaissance went underground once again.

THE GOTHIC CATHEDRALS OF OUR LADY

The flowering of the new Gothic architecture and the renewed sense of spirituality that went along with it can be attributed to the conjunction of two powerful intellects, Saint Bernard and Abbot Suger, and a vast source of wealth, technology, and international organization. The only possible sources of such wealth and sophistication were the Order of

Zion and the military orders, the Templars, and, to a lesser degree, the Hospitallers, which the Order of Zion controlled or supported. Evidence to prove the connection between the Templars and the overall construction of the cathedrals is scanty to nonexistent, but what little we do have suggests that the Templars regularly paid for the major decorations on the facades of the cathedrals, while more local sources of financing, including the Cistercians in some cases, paid for the major work on the structural elements of the cathedral building.

This suggests that the Templars were more interested in the images and stories the cathedrals presented to the public than they were in the actual design and construction of the buildings. Yet this is possibly misleading, because as the Templars lost their hold on Outremer in the late 1100s, the master masons and architects who built such Templar masterpieces in Palestine as the Krak de Chevaliers were freed for work in Europe. The sudden twenty-six-year rebuilding of the cathedral at Chartres has been attributed to an influx of workers and masons from Acre and other sites in Outremer. And at Chartres, the Gothic architectural techniques reached their pinnacle. The work on Notre-Dame-de-Paris was changed in mid-project, around 1230, to accommodate these advances in flying buttresses and ogival supports.

While there is no evidence of Templar involvement or financing with Notre-Dame-de-Paris, such involvement is not unlikely. Guillaume de Paris, the master mason who designed the building and most of its exterior decoration, is an enigma without much of a history. Maurice de Sully was a student of Abbot Suger's, and his sudden rise to bishop of Paris in 1160 was certainly accomplished with help from powerful connections. Some of those connections, through Saint Bernard and the Cistercians, did in all likelihood include the Templars. Robert de Sable, first grand master of the Temple after the fall of Jerusalem, was reported to have paid for the decorations on the Portal of Saint Anne around 1195, but the evidence is somewhat contradictory. It is also likely that some Templar masons worked at Notre Dame after the completion of Chartres cathedral in 1220, but again, no direct evidence remains.

What we do have is a pattern of interconnectedness that combines the Capetian and Merovingian royal families and their supporters with the Order of Zion and its fronts and cover organizations, such as the Templars and the Cistercians, and centers on the unparalleled wealth and influence needed to create the Gothic cathedrals. The Templars were not overtly involved in creating the cathedrals of Our Lady; it was the organization behind them, the Order of Our Lady of Mount Zion, and its new power centers in the Church, which was responsible for the explosion of cathedral building that followed Saint-Denis. They of course worked behind the scenes and used prominent spokesmen such as Bernard to push their agenda of reform.

Saint Bernard's family connections to Zion and the Templars—his uncle André de Montbard was a founding member of the Order of Zion's *militia du Christi*—are examined in chapter 5. Bernard was a devoted reformer of the Church who, it seems, wanted to institute a new kind of Christianity that appealed directly to the spirituality of the masses. At the same time that he was proposing the Templars as the model of Christian chivalry, and thereby enlisting the upper classes, he was also preaching a new theology of Mary, the mother of Christ, as the vessel by which divinity reached humanity, and thus reaching the dispossessed mass of people who still believed in the Great Mother Goddess, be she Isis or the Roman Matrona. Needless to say, this is far from biblical, in both tone and authority. The very idea of a goddess, even couched as the Mother of Christ, was slightly blasphemous.

But after the success of Saint-Denis, and under the considerable influence of Bernard's preaching, the new-style cathedrals would all be devoted to Our Lady, the Mother of God and Queen of Heaven. The facades of these cathedrals told the apocryphal details of her life and of those who had interacted with her in wonderfully expressive sculptures that are some of the treasures of the era (see fig. 7.4). There had been churches and even cathedrals dedicated to Our Lady before 1150, but they were few and hardly spectacular or noteworthy. After 1150, and for the next several centuries, it was, in one of a variety of forms, the most popular title for a church or cathedral in Europe. Mary, as an ideal, was the motive force behind the Gothic renaissance.

As we have seen, veneration of Mary began as early as the first century in Provence. Saint Trophime established the first shrine to Mary the Mother of God in Arles around 46 C.E. The full flowering of Marian devotion would take another millennium to develop, until in the twelfth and thirteenth centuries it inspired some of mankind's most amazing artistic triumphs. The brief facts in the Gospels were filled in with rich details in the apocrypha of the early church. Mary is given parents,

Figure 7.4. Shrine to Mary at the eastern end of Notre-Dame-de-Paris. (Photo by Darlene)

Anne and Joachim, to match the Davidic lineage of Matthew, an Immaculate Conception, and her own virgin birth.[8]

Perhaps the most curious of these early stories, and certainly the most significant from the perspective of later developments, is the tale of Mary and the Temple found in the apocryphal Book of James. There we are told that the high priest set Mary on the altar, where she danced as the Shekhinah so that all Israel might love her, and that she remained in the Temple until adulthood "as a dove and she was nourished at the hand of an angel." The angel informed the high priest, one Zacharias, on Mary's fourteenth birthday that it was time for her to wed, and he assembled all the eligible bachelors and widowers in Judea. The angel assured him that an unmistakable sign would allow him to choose the right man.

Among the crowd was Joseph, a young carpenter, and he, in the quaint words of the tale, had his "rod" in his hand along with the oth-

ers. When he presented his "rod" to Zacharias, a dove sprouted from
it with a burst of blinding light and flew up to heaven. This was such
an unmistakable sign, Mary being a dove in the Temple, that Joseph
was immediately chosen. This at first scared him, as well it might, but
eventually he relented and took Mary as his wife, saying: "Behold, I
have taken you from the Temple of the Lord, and now I leave thee in
my house."[9]

This obviously symbolic tale hides a great deal of esoteric information, but it is the next event that truly brings the whole complex of symbolism into focus. After Joseph goes back to work, Mary, echoing her
modern sisters, also goes back to work in the Temple. Since she is no
longer, as the dove of Shekhinah, the intermediary between the Holy of
Holies and the high priest, a veil is now required. Seven holy virgins are
chosen to do the work, and Mary, as the former "goddess," is included
to make eight. Hence, the eight-rayed star became sacred to Mary, who
completed the veil of the Temple—the veil, of course, that is destined to
be torn asunder on the death of her son.

Mary is chosen to dye and spin the thread for the colors red and
purple, the colors of royalty and sacrifice and the alpha and omega of
the visible spectrum of light. As she does so, her old friend the angel of
the Temple returns and tells her what the future holds, including the
birth of the Son of God. She finishes her spinning and shows the cloth
to the high priest who declares on sight of it that Mary will be blessed
as the vessel of illumination to all future generations, the *theotokos.*
This act of spinning connects the Virgin with Artemis/Arachne/Ariadne
and the Greek Fates and the Roman Parcae, as well as with the Gallic-
Celt Parsii, the benefactor goddesses of fate whose temple marked the
lucky island in the Seine where Notre-Dame-de-Paris would rise over a
millennium later.

This apocryphal story has little or nothing to do with Judaism as it
was practiced in the first century in Judea. The wise women of Exodus,
of which one was perhaps traditionally Miriam, Moses' sister, wove the
first temple veil, not a group of virgins in the late first century B.C.E.
And of course, women were never allowed in the sanctuary of the
Temple. If the story has nothing to do with Judaism, then where does it
come from?

The answer is from the Egyptian Gnostic tradition, particularly
such Gnostic texts as the *Kore Kosmica,* or "Virgin of the World," and

other Isis texts in the hermetic works of the era. The Book of James is Gnostic only by subtext, and so it survived to become part of the Catholic apocrypha, but other texts did not fare as well. But even the Book of James goes on to relate Isis to Mary by means of the miracle of the grain during the flight to Egypt. Without realizing it, perhaps, the author of the Book of James has repeated one of the oldest stories of the Egyptian delta concerning Isis, pregnant with Horus, and her pursuit by the usurping king/uncle Seth. In this version of the tale, it is Isis, using the spirit of Osiris inside her, who makes the grain grow to hide her trail.

Fulcanelli informs us directly that the Virgin and Isis are the same symbol. "Formerly the subterranean chambers of the temples served as abodes for the statues of Isis, which at the time of the introduction of Christianity into Gaul, became those *black Virgins,* which the people in our day surround with a quite special veneration. Their symbolism is, moreover, identical . . ."[10] A few pages further on in the same chapter, Fulcanelli casually drops the piece of the puzzle that allows the meaning of the pattern to come into focus:

"It is a curious hermetic analogy that Cybele [just identified with Isis and Mary] was worshipped at Pessinonte in Phrygia in the form of a *black stone,* which was said to have *fallen* from heaven. Phidias represents the goddess seated on a throne between *two lions,* having on her head a mural crown, from which hangs a veil. Sometimes she is represented holding a *key* and seeming *to draw back her veil.* Isis, Ceres and Cybele are three heads under the same veil."[11]

Suddenly, like a clap of thunder on a clear day or a sudden flash of light in a darkened room, much that had been obscure was revealed.

THE STONE THAT FELL FROM HEAVEN, BLACK VIRGINS, AND THE TEMPLE OF THE GRAIL

The Anatolian highlands of central Turkey are as forbidding today as they were for the first wave of Christian crusaders in the summer of 1197. The Sangarius River cuts its way through the cliffs of soft, pink-tinted stone heading northwest for the Sea of Marmara and the ancient port of Nicea, now called Busra. The Sangarius is now the Sakarya, but no matter how the place-names shift in pronunciation, the geography remains the same. The old Byzantine post road and caravan route heads southeast from Nicea along the river, running straight as an arrow until it begins to wind its way up the western edge of the central Anatolian plateau (see fig. 7.5).

A week out of Nicea by caravan was the Byzantine garrison town of Doryleum. Perched on the edge of the plateau at the point where the river heads away from the road, it had clear strategic significance. More important to the locals for the last eight thousand or so years were the hot springs located there. Destroyed in the War for Independence between 1919 and 1922, the Old City, as its Turkish name Eskisehir proclaims, is actually today a small and bustling industrial city. A few miles east of town along the old Byzantine road, however, the site of the crusader battle in 1197 remains virtually untouched.

The old road climbs a steep grade between a cliff face and the drop to the river and then levels off, and the land flattens out toward a curious isolated peak forty miles away on the other side of the river. It is a lovely spot, as isolated now as it was then, and it is easy to see how the Seljuk sultan Kilij Arslan picked this spot for the perfect ambush.

The crusaders had split their forces into two sections. When the vanguard camped at dusk on June 30, 1197, the rear guard was just moving into Doryleum. Before dawn on July 1, the vanguard moved out down the valley toward the ancient road junction, watched by the sultan and his advisers from a small hill known as the Fortress of Falcon. Believing that this was the entire force of crusaders, the sultan sprang his trap.

As the day wore on, the Turkish attacks rolled up in waves to break against the iron line of the crusading knights, inflicting a few casualties but never really threatening to break through. The Turks counted on the heat to broil alive the crusaders in their armor, and as the afternoon lengthened and the knights retreated up the valley, it appeared that the strategy would work. But just as the crusaders in the vanguard were beginning to falter, the consequences of the sultan's error became apparent.

The rear guard poured through the pass and smashed into the Turks in front of the Fortress of the Falcon as another force, under the papal legate the bishop of Puy, swung around the hill and fell on the rear of the Turkish forces. The sultan, knowing a defeat when one was handed to him, fled eastward toward the distant mountains. Most of the Turkish forces were killed or driven into the Sangarius, and the crusaders celebrated a great victory. A few days later they marched southeast by the middle of the three ancient roads and passed over the Taurus Mountains toward their destiny in Jerusalem,[12] never knowing how close they had come to the Temple of the Grail, the original home of Wolfram's lapsit.

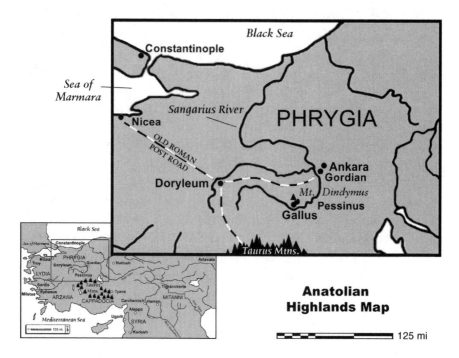

Figure 7.5. The Anatolian highlands of central Asia Minor.

Driving eastward along the modern road to Ankara, which follows the route of the sultan's flight, the stark and solitary mountain dominates the landscape. This is Mount Dindymus, the holy mountain of the ancient Phrygians, sacred to the mysteries of the goddess Cybele, Queen of Heaven and Mother of the Gods. On the southern slopes, a jumble of ancient and modern dwellings tumble down toward the small river Gallus, a tributary of the Sangarius. Farther up, just below the summit, a jumble of stones and walls mark the precinct of the ancient temple, looking in the afternoon sunlight like a ruined and tarnished crown.

This ancient pile of ruins was the sanctuary of the goddess who descended to earth as a stone, a large black and silver-flecked cube of a meteorite. Caves wind from the sanctuary all the way down to the river below, and the actual mysteries were conducted in large corbel-vaulted underground chambers. On Mount Dindymus, little remains of these chambers, but at the Cybele temple in Vienne, France, we can still see the walls of its crypt and its pillars.[13] These massive underground chambers would provide the foundational support, literally and figuratively, for many of the Gothic cathedrals, including Chartres, Notre-Dame-de-Paris, and Amiens, just as the myth of Cybele and her Grail stone would provide the spiritual insight and soaring imagery. And at the heart of the hermetic expression lay the ancient art and science, the threefold transmutation of alchemy.

We've all heard the story. Somewhere far away in Asia Minor there was a king named Midas who wished for the power to turn ordinary objects into gold. The god Dionysus granted his wish, except that everything he touched turned to gold. Since this meant that Midas could not eat or drink, he was soon begging the god for release from his boon. Dionysus sent him to the sacred river and after washing in the water, which sparkled forever after with flecks of gold, the king was cured of the "Midas touch." Here, in brief, is the alchemical archetype itself, the meme in mythic form.[14]

The Midas of Greek legend is undoubtedly mythical, but real kings named Midas or Mitas or Mithras did indeed rule in the Anatolian highlands. While the legend is full of delightful strangeness, as we shall see, the actual history of the region is strange enough.

The Black Sea was a wide forested valley before the Mediterranean spilled over and flooded it in the fourteenth millennium B.C.E., causing the Great Flood myths of Mesopotamia and central Asia. Along its southern edge, the mountains rise slowly to the highland plateau, from which a half dozen rivers tumble down toward the eastern end of the Black Sea. The western end is barren and rocky with only the Sangarius watershed, which empties into the Sea of Marmara. Along the upper reaches of the Sangarius, deep in the mountains and twisted rocks of the high plateau, a sophisticated culture developed around 1800 B.C.E. Called the Hittites, they ruled the region for five hundred years and made their mark on ancient history. They had a hieroglyphic form of writing and were the ancient world's foremost metalsmiths. They worshipped the earth goddess of Old Europe, along with two consorts, the lord of the sky and the lord of the underworld.[15]

Around 1200 B.C.E., the Hittites fell to the roving nomads from central Asia, the Indo-Europeans, who would eventually spread from India to Ireland. Over the next few hundred years these populations mixed and became the Phrygians of the classical era. The Phrygians still worshipped the Mother Goddess, but whether the myth changed with the arrival of the Indo-Europeans or was a remnant of the ancient beliefs is uncertain. What is clear is that the goddess got a new and resonant name: Cybele.

The name is neither Greek nor Hittite, but is a word in the new Semitic languages pushing up from the south. It means "stone of the goddess" and comes from the same roots as Kaaba and al-Lat in Arabic. Indeed, given the similarity of names, and the cubic stone of Mecca with its original goddess worship and meteorite, the Sabeans, ancestors of the Hejaz Arabs, may have been Cybele worshippers. At any rate, as we saw in chapter 4, the idea of a stonelike throne, the Cube of Space upon which the great *L* in the sky of Draco sits, is not too far from Kyb-ele, or stone of the El. It is also the "Precious Stone of the Wise" from the *Bahir.*

The worship of the Mother of the Gods was common to all the ancient traditions of Europe and the Middle East. The cult of Cybele, however, developed into what almost certainly was the first "mystery" school, and as such traveled from Anatolia to Rome and on to Provence. The major temples of the "mystery" of the Mother Stone of the Gods were located on the island of Samothrace, off the coast of Lydia in Asia Minor, at Memphis in Egypt, at Thebes in Greece, and at Nimes in Provence. The oldest and most important center remained at Pessinus on Mount Dindymus, where the cubic stone, the *mystereion* that contained the essence of the goddess, was kept.[16]

Because of the fragmentation caused by time, cultures, and languages, we risk losing the larger pattern if we focus too closely on any one goddess figure or regional mystery teachings. Only by looking at all the versions of the myths and legends can we piece together anything resembling a complete picture.

Cybele was not only mother of the gods, but also mother of humanity. In some versions, as Rhea, she mated with her father, Kronos, and begat the Titans, from whom came both the Olympian gods and mankind. The images that have survived show her on a throne, which resembles the Egyptian glyph for Isis (a throne), flanked by a pair of lions, an echo of the Egyptian goddess Sekhmet. In some images she is shown in a chariot drawn by a pair of lions. In her hands she holds a circular drum or tambourine and a chalice full of the elixir of life. On her head is, usually, a tower or castlelike crown from which hangs a veil.

As Demeter, or as her daughter, Persephone, she descended into the underworld and her return was accomplished with the aid of a clan of Titans, shamans and smiths who dwelt in caves. For their help, Cybele descended to earth as a cubic stone, which she gave into their keeping as the *mysterieon,* or objective focus for the mystery of the cult. As the guardians of the stone, they were called Kabiri, or Kabiroi, the people of the *kaba,* the stone, as well as the *kabirim,* the "mighty ones" in Aramaic and Hebrew. In some myths, these Kabiri are referred to as the children of Aphrodite and Hephaistos, the god of the forge and volcanoes, the latter from the Latin form of his name, Vulcan.[17]

As both Strabo and Herodotus noted, the story of the Kabiri is very close to that of the Egyptian Heru Shemsu, another group of shaman-smiths with ties to pre-catastrophe knowledge and the guardianship, at Heliopolis, of another stone from heaven, the *ben-ben* or phoenix stone of the sun god Re. Indeed, the relationship between Re and his "Eye," the goddess Sekhmet or Hathor, pictured as that of father and daughter, is similar to that of Rhea and Kronos or Cybele and Zeus. Like the *ben-ben* at Heliopolis, the stone of the Mother Goddess was seen as the petrified sperm of the sky god.[18]

The stone remained in the temple of Cybele on Mount Dindymus until the turn of the third century B.C.E. The tale of how the stone that fell from heaven became the stone of exile, to use Wolfram's pun, was one of the grand yarns of the ancient world. In the depths of the Second Punic War, with Hannibal and his elephants rampaging at will on the Italian peninsula, the Roman senate lost faith in its gods. As they were tribal deities from Latinum and Etruscia with Greek glosses, they seemed unhelpful and insignificant in the face of the threat posed by the international power of the Carthaginians. The Roman senate decided to fall back on that "old-time religion," the worship of the Mother of the Gods.[19]

Consultation of the Sibylline Books guided the Romans to seek aid from the same Great Mother known to their reputed ancestors of Trojan fame. The Delphic oracle agreed that it was time for Cybele to come to Rome. The king of Pergamus, under whose control the temple and stone at Pessinus lay, was not so enthusiastic. It took an earthquake and a comet or a brilliant meteor shower to convince him. Accompanied by the Gallae, the priestesses of the shrine, the stone departed by ship for Rome. Miracles occurred along the way, including an interval of divine navigation and an escort of dolphins. The noblest lady of Rome, Claudia Quinta, personally welcomed the entourage of Cybele at Ostia and pulled the ship ashore when it grounded on a sand-bar with her own virtuous strength, an episode considered to be another miraculous sign.[20]

At Rome, the Mother of the Gods was appropriately housed in the temple of Victoria, an echo of the shrine to Nike, victory, on Samothrace, in the 550th year after Rome's semimythical founding. From distant Phrygia came her essence, the silver-and-black meteoric stone from the starry heavens, with a conclave of the Galli, male-born priestesses whose order had served the goddess for millennia. Rome initiated a thirteen-year construction plan to honor Cybele with a worthy temple on the Palatine Hill. From Claudia's own lineage would come many of Rome's greatest, as the fortunes of Hannibal, and Carthage itself, withered like a dying branch.

The temple was called the Matreum, and the worship of the new civic goddess, the Magna Mater or simply Matrona, spread rapidly throughout the Empire, blending along the way all the older forms of the Great Goddess. The stone remained in its domed temple until at least the mid-fourth century, when Julian the Apostate wrote a hymn dedicated to it and the goddess. "Who is then the Mother of the Gods? She is the source of the intellectual and creative gods, who in their turn guide the visible gods: she is both the mother and the spouse of mighty Zeus; She came into being next to and together with the great Creator; She is in control of every form of life, and the Cause of all generation; She easily brings to perfection all things that are made. Without pain She brings to birth . . . She is the Motherless Maiden, enthroned at the very side of Zeus, and in very truth is the Mother of All the Gods. . . ."[21]

Compare this to the anonymous fifth-century hymn to Mary: "And we will write now the praises of Our Lady, and Mother of God, the Virgin Mary. . . . Thou shalt be named the Beloved. . . . Thou art the pure chest of gold in which was laid up the manna, that bread that comes down from heaven, and the Giver of Life to all the world. . . . Thou art the treasure which Joseph purchased, and found therein the precious Pearl. . . . Thou hast become the throne of the King whom the Cherubim do bear. . . . All the kings of the earth shall come to thy light, and the people to thy brightness, O Virgin Mary."[22]

Should we, then, consider the veneration of Mary as the Mother of God to be an extension of the cult of Cybele, the Great Mother? The answer seems to be yes, and Christian tradition appears to agree. After the Crucifixion, Mary was reported to have traveled to Ephesus, in Asia Minor, where she died and was buried. As we know from the Acts of the Apostles, Ephesus was the center of the cult of Artemis, the Roman Diana, as the Great Mother. After preaching against the temple, Saint Paul was accosted by a silversmith who declared: "Great is Diana of the Ephesians." Yet it is in Ephesus that Mary was first officially declared *theotokos,* or Mother of God, in 431 C.E.[23]

As the Church labored on into the Dark Ages, the ancient statutes and shrines of Our Lady were dedicated to the Virgin. The most sacred and venerated of these statues depicted the Mother Goddess as black, echoing the stone itself, and they became the Black Virgins. Their sacred sites and shrines are in the same places: springs and wells, caves on mountaintops, and grottoes of all kinds. The Black Madonna of Lyons is enshrined on a hilltop in a church built from the ruins of the former temple to Cybele, a case of direct transfer still visible to the modern tourist.[24] The crypts of Notre-Dame-de-Paris and Chartres retained their Black Madonnas and shrines to Matrona. The Black Virgin of Chartres, Our Lady Underground, is still there. All of these cave sanctuaries echo the caves, grottoes, and caverns that riddle Mount Dindymus in Phrygia. The original Kabiri were cave-dwelling shaman-smiths, and Fulcanelli instructs us that "[r]eal, but occult, power . . . develops in the darkness."[25]

As we researched the individuals involved in the story of the cathedrals, the Crusades, and the Templars, we discovered that they all, from Gerbert of Aurillac to Saint Bernard, had close connections with, or were directly inspired by, the Black Madonnas. Eventually we realized that tracking the Black Madonna connections was the surest way to follow the current. The Merovingian stories of miraculous Black Madonnas arriving in self-propelled vessels seem to be directly attributable to the Cybele stone's voyage to Rome. Even Peter the Hermit stopped at every major Black Madonna shrine in France as he preached the First Crusade (see fig. 7.6). Clermont, where Urban II announced the First Crusade, has no fewer than five ancient Black Madonnas. The one in the cathedral crypt was originally a Roman statue of Cybele of the Springs, and the cathedral itself was built over the older temple, using, as was common, its underground vaults as the foundation.[26]

Saint Bernard, who brought devotion to the Virgin into the religious mainstream, was inspired by a direct, and miraculously alchemical, encounter with the Virgin herself. As a youth, Bernard would spend

Figure 7.6. Map of France showing (1) Cathar sites; (2) the location of churches dedicated to Notre Dame; (3) the Black Madonna sites mentioned by Fulcanelli; and (4) other Black Madonna sites.

hours in prayer before the Black Madonna of Dijon, another Roman Cybeline statue, this one with enormous breasts and a pregnant stomach. Finally reciting the Ave Maria Stellis, "Hail the Star of Mary," before the Black Madonna one night, the Virgin appeared to him and fed him three drops of her milk. Like the drops from Ceridwen's cauldron that gave the Celtic shaman Taliesin the understanding of the language of the birds and knowledge of all hidden things, these drops of milk transformed the young Bernard into the eloquent saint and reformer who almost single-handedly revitalized the Church.[27]

Fulcanelli, in section 8 of the Paris chapter of *Le Mystère,* gives us a list of ten prominent Black Madonnas, including two of the most famous, Notre-Dame-de-Rocamadour, "the rock beloved of the light," and Notre-Dame-de-Puy, home of Adelmar, papal legate of the First Crusade and home to a Cybele/Mary connection with a sacred stone that dates to the first century C.E. Fulcanelli has much to say about the Black Virgin, and about her miraculous milk, as we shall see in the next chapter, but perhaps the most significant thing Fulcanelli has to impart concerning the Virgin is this: "Obviously what is dealt with here is the *very essence of things . . . the Vase containing the Spirit of things: vas spirituale.*"[28]

If we consider that, like Cybele and her stone, the Grail and the Grail Queen, and the Shekhinah, are identical, then the vessel of Our Lady, which contains the vital spirit, is the mountaintop temple, cave, or grotto. This container acts as a "house" that allows the ethereal spirit to coalesce into the physical form of the goddess. We find this in the *Bahir,* where in verses 4 and 5 we are told that the "house" is built by wisdom and filled with understanding, out of which flows the stream of gnosis. This is the supernal temple, and the *bayit,* or house, of Joseph where the Virgin dwells before giving birth to the Christ. It is formed of the *sefirot* Chokmah, Wisdom, and Binah, Understanding, which in turn creates the non-*sefirah* of Daat, or knowledge. Daat is a void or a vessel in which, when filled by mind, the animating spirit of matter, is the reflection of Kether, the Godhead, which cannot be approached while still in the body. Gnosis, knowledge, or Sophia, the light-filled void of the Buddhists, is as close to the divine as we can come.[29]

Understanding this allows us to grasp the meaning of the ending of Wolfram and Walter von Scharffenberg's *Tituriel.* The Grail, as the essence of the Goddess, must be housed in a vessel or temple before

Sophia, Gnosis, can become tangible enough to communicate her blessings, or the Christ Emmanuel, the christos within us, can be born. The *Tituriel's* vision of the castle of the Grail on the Mountain of Salvation is the esoteric and inner spiritual motive behind the cathedral-building explosion. The Gothic cathedrals, it seems, were designed to house the spirit of the Great Goddess, making them living Grails that heal and transform all who enter their portals.

Everything—the structure, the colored light of the great windows, the images on the facades—was designed to accommodate this sense of wonder and gnosis. In the Gothic cathedrals, with their connection to Cybele, the Great Goddess, and the Black Madonnas, we find all the various threads of the ancient science of alchemy combined into one tangible *mystereion* designed to last through the ages. And the greatest of these Grail cathedrals is Notre-Dame-de-Paris, the cathedral of the philosophers.

THE PHILOSOPHERS' CHURCH

Among the crowd at the consecration of the abbey church of Saint-Denis on June 11, 1144, was a young Parisian student on his way up through the ecclesiastical hierarchy. Our knowledge of Maurice de Sully's early history is sparse. Born in Sully-sur-Loire of humble parents, he apparently studied at the abbey of Fleury and came to Paris around the age of seventeen to study at the university on the Left Bank. Along with most of Paris that day, Maurice would have followed the pilgrim route of Saint Denis's martyrdom, from the place of his torture on the eastern end of the Ile-de-la-Cité to his jail cell near what is now the flower market, and then on to climb Montmartre to the Martyrium on its height. From there it was a pleasant walk down to the abbey. Along the way, some of the pilgrims always discovered that their faith had been answered, that Saint Denis had healed them.

We can imagine the twenty-four-year-old Maurice pushing his way into the new church to catch a glimpse of the Mass of Masses, celebrated by nineteen bishops before the gilded altars. Abbot Suger himself thought that the crowd "believe[d] themselves to behold a chorus celestial rather than terrestrial, a ceremony divine rather than human."[30] It had its effect on the young cleric Maurice. In less than twenty years, Maurice de Sully would rise from obscurity to become the bishop of Paris and a confidant of kings. Along the way, he would plan a new cathedral to replace the aging churches on the Ile-de-la-Cité. The new cathedral, dedicated to Our Lady, would rise over the ruins of the ancient temples to Matrona and the Celtic Mercury, as well as Childebert I's Merovingian cathedrals.[31]

When Clovis I established Paris as the center of the new Frankish Christianity, the Church still honored the traditions of its mystery-school origins by making a distinction between those who had been baptized and those who had not. The unbaptized were asked to leave before the sacrament, and so most early churches had a covered porch where the unbaptized could depart without disturbing the rest of the worshipers. In the fifth century, this practice developed into the habit of building two cathedrals, or seats of episcopal power, one for the unbaptized believers and the other for the elite, the partakers of the sacrament.[32]

And so Childebert I built two cathedrals on the Ile-de-la-Cité. Saint-Etienne was the larger church of the common congregation, while its companion, the smaller church of Our Lady, served the inner core of the baptized elite. Thus, from its very beginnings, Notre-Dame-de-Paris has been the initiates' church. We might even suspect, given the altars found in the crypt in the eighteenth century, that the inner core of the Merovingian church adhered to some very peculiar concepts of Christianity, such as a devotion to a goddess figure similar to Isis. Notre Dame served as a connection point with the very ancient mysteries that Christianity was supposed to supplant.

The Merovingian Notre Dame had been destroyed by the Viking assault of 856. It was quickly rebuilt and served as a rallying point for the successful defense of 885–86. From then on, Saint-Etienne lost its stature and the episcopal seat was firmly established at Notre Dame. Unfortunately, we have no contemporary description of the Carolingian church, and not a stone remains to suggest its appearance. The site was chosen by Maurice de Sully for his new-style cathedral and stripped down to its Roman foundations, the crypts of Matrona, or Cybele.[33]

Planning began in 1160, as soon as Maurice was elected bishop of Paris. The visiting pope Alexander III laid the cornerstone around the spring equinox of 1163. The pope, a refugee in France from the church's first Franco-Italian schism, publicly officiated at the consecration of Saint-Germain-des-Prés, the former church of Saint Vincent and the Holy Cross. A private ceremony was held to lay the cornerstone of the new cathedral, and Bishop Maurice began to build with gusto. The choir was completed and the high altar consecrated in 1182. The patriarch of Jerusalem preached the Third Crusade from the half finished Notre-Dame-de-Paris in 1185. By the time Maurice de Sully died in 1196, the nave was done except for the roof, which was paid for in Maurice's will.[34]

Work began on the western facade around the turn of the thirteenth century, and by 1220 it was finished up to the level of the Gallery of Kings. The flying buttresses were added, influenced by the newly completed cathedral at Chartres, around 1230 as the nave was reconstructed. Chapels were added between the exterior buttresses as the southern tower began to rise above the gallery. It was finished in 1240, and work shifted to the northern tower. The towers reached their present height by 1245 and the first bell, Guillaume, was installed in 1248. As soon as the reconstruction of the nave was completed in 1250, work began on the transept facades. They were finished by 1270. The next twenty years saw chapels and flying buttresses added to the choir and the chancel rebuilt. Except for the interior, major work on Notre-Dame-de-Paris ended soon after the turn of the fourteenth century.

Although construction continued for a century after his death, Maurice de Sully may be considered the guiding intelligence behind the entire project. The western facade was designed and even sculpted long before work began. Some of the sculptures were done in the 1170s, soon after construction on the cathedral started. The transept facades were designed later, but they were inspired by the same mystical vision that inspired Maurice. Although we have evidence of Templar sponsorship only for the Porch of Saint Anne, the Virgin's mother, on the southern tower of the western facade, it seems more than coincidental that all major work on Notre Dame halted, leaving the original design unfinished, just as Philip IV suppressed the Knights Templar.[35]

The 150 years from the consecration of Saint-Denis to the suppression of the Templars defines the main arc of the cathedral-building movement. The impulse faded away in the fourteenth century, leaving cathedrals such as Notre Dame unfinished. The Black Death in the second half of the century seemed to accelerate the decline. The Gothic buildings of the fifteenth century are small churches, such as Saint-Jacques-la-Boucherie, built by Nicolas Flamel, and private homes, such as the Lallemant mansion in Bourges. Clearly, the vision went underground after the disasters of the fourteenth century.

But Notre-Dame-de-Paris remained. A history of France could be written around its rise and fall in the national consciousness. The choir screen was finished just as the Black Death swept over Europe. Paris suffered an eclipse of fortunes, as did all France, during the Hundred Years War. This struggle between Capetian France and Plantagenet England was actually backed and promoted by the opposing sides of the Templar-Zion schism. Notre-Dame-de-Paris saw the funeral of the mad king Charles VI, who in 1422 had repudiated his son in favor of the English. Nine years later, in 1431, the English king Henry VI was crowned king of France in Notre Dame Cathedral.

Unfortunately for Henry, in those nine years Joan of Arc, a vassal of René d'Anjou, had rewritten history. After her example, and the tactical skills of Duke René, lifted the siege of Orleans, Charles VII had been crowned at Rheims. In 1436, he liberated Paris from the English. For the next 346 years, a Te Deum was sung in Notre Dame on the first Friday after Easter to honor the deliverance of the capital from its English occupation. By the time Charles VII died in 1461, nothing remained of Plantagenet France except the port of Calais. His funeral, like his father's, was held in Notre-Dame-de-Paris.

The fifteenth century continued to hold the venerable cathedral in respect, but the winds of change were blowing. It was during the lifetime of Charles VII that the word *gothic* was first applied to the *lux continua* style of Saint-Denis and Notre Dame. The Italian self-proclaimed universal genius, Leon Battista Alberti, misunderstood Abbot Suger's reference to "goth" in its medieval sense of Jewish,[36] and assumed it meant "rustic," from the barbarian Goths who sacked Rome in 410 C.E. From this he dismissed the style, with its exuberance of forms and imagery, as a product of the fantastic tastes of the barbarians. Fulcanelli informs us that this canard has survived the centuries, even though the more exact term might be *ogival* for the style's pointed arches, because it does reflect the inner meaning of the cathedral's truth. The Gothic art of the cathedrals is to Fulcanelli the secret language, the art of light and the art of magic that animate the dead stone of the building into a light-filled revelatory experience.

The idea of the medieval as barbaric, however, was one that was much in tune with the tenor of the Renaissance and its emphasis on classical forms. The sixteenth century saw the old cathedrals as symbols of the Church's power and influence, and as the protest against the Church of Rome grew, the cathedrals, including Notre-Dame-de-Paris, felt the brunt of the assault. It was sacked by the Huguenots in 1548, and it was the site of the beginning of the Saint Bartholomew's Day Massacre, prompted by the marriage of Henry IV and Marguerite of Valois there in 1572.

Religious wars paralyzed France for eighty years. Louis XIII promised in 1638 to rebuild the main altar of Notre Dame if he had an heir to the throne. Later that same year, a Te Deum was sung in the old cathedral marking the birth of the future Louis XIV, the Sun King. Eventually, toward the end of his long reign, Louis would honor his father's request and rebuild the altar. During work on the crypt in 1711, a Gallo-Roman votive pillar was found, and it is from the images on this pillar that we gain a glimpse of the spiritual antiquity of the spot.

This altar stone was the centerpiece of the Roman temple to Matrona that had occupied the space of the earlier temple to the Parcae, or weaving Fates. As such, it can be seen as a symbolic model for the cubic stone of the Great Mother. The images of Zeus, Esus, Hephaistos, and the Great Mother on the pillar suggest the local group of four Kabiri, or alchemical initiators. Hephaistos, or Vulcan, we have already mentioned as the father of the Kabiri, and Zeus is the father/son/lover of the Great Mother. Esus, usually referred to as the Celtic Hercules, is more problematic until we remember that Electra, the Samothracian priestess of the Great Goddess, was the mother of the Argive line, including Perseus and Jason. Esus then becomes the original Grail seeker, the original knight errant in search of the stone of the Goddess.[37]

In general, though, the eighteenth century was not kind to the old cathedral. Renovations damaged much of the original interior. The stained glass was removed from the choir level and the rose windows were remodeled. And then, of course, came the Revolution. The cathedral became the Temple of Reason, and much of its ornamentation was destroyed. The citizens of 1793 toppled the kings of Israel from their gallery and the western facade was severely damaged.

Napoleon restored relations with the Church and crowned himself emperor at Notre Dame in 1804. His son was proclaimed king of Rome in the cathedral at a solemn Te Deum in 1811, as Napoleon planned a vast invasion of Russia. Within a few years, Napoleon would go into exile, twice, and the monarchy would be restored and then overthrown again. The election of Louis-Philippe as king of a constitutional monarchy in 1830 marked an upswing in the fortunes of Notre Dame.

The 1820s and 1830s saw a young Victor Hugo use his romantic sensibilities to shine a light on the medieval exuberance of Notre Dame. Published in 1831 as *Notre-Dame de Paris,* the novel was an immediate hit and launched a craze for Gothic architecture. English readers know it as *The Hunchback of Notre Dame,* after its main character, the bell ringer Quasimodo, but the novel is truly about the cathedral itself. Set in the 1480s, the book captures that transitional moment when traditional forms gave way to the modern, the books of stone to the printed page.

One young Parisian influenced by Hugo's novel was the seventeen-year-old architecture student Eugène Emmanuel Viollet-le-Duc. In the next thirty years his name would become synonymous with restoration. While still in his early twenties, he was appointed to the national commission for the preservation of historic monuments. There was a new feeling emerging, thanks to Hugo's romanticism, about the relics of the past.

The head of the commission, Prosper Mérimée—best known to us as the author of *Carmen*—noticed the young architect and directed his training in the subtleties of medieval engineering. Soon Viollet-le-Duc was handling the commission's difficult projects, sometimes as many as twenty at once. In 1845 he was appointed architect for the restoration of Notre-Dame-de-Paris, and spent the next twenty years on the project. No one could have been better prepared for the task.[38]

The cathedral that we see today, and as described by Fulcanelli, is really Viollet-le-Duc's reconstruction. From the top of the reconstructed *fléchette,* where a statue of Saint Thomas bears the likeness of Viollet-le-Duc, throughout the entire fabric of the cathedral, the touch of its restorer is apparent in everything. The Gothic has been refracted through the lens of romanticism, and, to purists such as Fulcanelli, the result is somewhat pallid. The reconstruction, however, did restore Notre-Dame-de-Paris to its rightful place in the national consciousness.[39]

Joan of Arc's beatification, the first step to sainthood, was celebrated at Notre Dame in 1909. A mass Te Deum was sung for the Armistice of 1918. By the time *Le Mystère des cathédrales* appeared in 1926, Notre-Dame-de-Paris was publicly venerated and privately ignored. The official separation of church and state in 1905 had cast religion in France into an intellectual backwater. Fulcanelli's work drew attention to an aspect of the cathedrals that was in danger of being forgotten. The romantic reworking of the Gothic in Viollet-le-Duc still contained and concealed an important philosophical teaching. Fulcanelli identified it as alchemy.

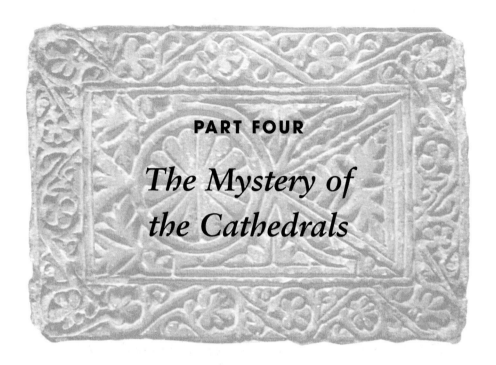

PART FOUR

The Mystery of the Cathedrals

Obviously what is dealt with here is the very essence of things. *Indeed the Litanies tell us that the Virgin is the* Vase containing the Spirit of things: vas spirituale. "On a table, breast high to the Magi," *Ettelia tells us, "were on one side a book or a series of golden pages or plates (the book of Thoth) and on the other side a* vase full of celestial-astral *liquid, consisting of one part of wild honey, one part of terrestrial water and a third part of celestial water. . . . The secret, the mystery was therefore in this vase."...*

It is therefore on the dragon, the sign of mercury, that we should look for the symbol representing the mutation and progression of the Sulphur or of the Elixir. . . .

The Sybil, when asked what a Philosopher was, replied: "it is a man, who knows how to make glass."

—LE MYSTÈRE DES CATHÉDRALES

EIGHT

THE GRAND HERMETIC THEME AND THE TREE OF LIFE

FULCANELLI'S NOTRE-DAME-DE-PARIS

At the very beginning of this journey, we decided to follow Fulcanelli's trail wherever it might lead. A reference to chiliasm in the Hendaye chapter of *Le Mystère des cathédrales* led us to the Gnostic origins of alchemy and its connection to the apocalyptic doctrine of chiliasm. Following the fingerprints of the secret led us into the mystical traditions of all three Abrahamic religions. We saw how these traditions fragmented and went underground, and that a thousand years ago Pope Sylvester II and the Chroniclers of Mount Zion rediscovered them in the West.

These discoveries, which included mathematics and astronomy as well as alchemy, reanimated the West, providing a motive for the Crusades and the great heretical movements. One of these movements was the spread of a gospel of light in the form of the *lux continua*–style of church building initiated by Abbot Suger at Saint-Denis. In ways that are not entirely clear, both the Order of Zion and the Knights Templar were involved in this new cathedral-building movement.

By the time our research brought us to this point, we felt that we had answered most of our main questions: "Is Fulcanelli telling the truth? Is there any connection, in history or tradition, between alchemy and a Gnostic eschatology such as chiliasm? And if there is a connection, how has it been maintained through the centuries? Is the secret really displayed on the walls of certain Gothic cathedrals?"

To answer that last question, we must turn to our hermetic tour guide, Fulcanelli, and the subject of his lessons, the cathedrals themselves. Did the cathedral builders know the secret of the ancient illuminated astronomy, the wisdom of Abraham, and how the alignment of the dragon axis foretold the quality of time? Does this knowledge still appear on the cathedrals? Without that key piece of evidence, we can't be sure that we have the same mystery.

Today, walking across the broad parvis in front of the western facade, armed with a good French guidebook and a copy of *Le Mystère,* one is first struck by how massive the cathedral looks. It is hard to imagine, as we watch the tourist buses come and go, loading and disgorging waves of visitors from around the planet, how the cathedral appeared in its youth. Gustave Doré left us a glimpse of the old congestion on the Ile-de-la-Cité in his illustrations to Rabelais's *Gargantua* (fig. 8.1). The gentle giant looms over the hemmed-in towers of the cathedral and its crowded surroundings like a cloud, and we catch a brief sensation of how it must have felt to stand in the narrow medieval parvis and look up at that massive facade and its soaring towers.

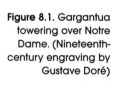

Figure 8.1. Gargantua towering over Notre Dame. (Nineteenth-century engraving by Gustave Doré)

Walking closer, we find that it is possible to stand, at the edge of the new parvis, and see in one eyeful the entire western front (fig. 8.2). The impression it makes from this distance is not so much one of power, but rather of subtlety and refinement. Harmonies leap out at us and we feel the unity of the design. If God is the Supreme Architect, then man could do no less in honor of Him, or Her. With that thought in mind, it is possible, at least slightly, to feel the faith of the cathedral's builders.

Figure 8.2. The front of Notre-Dame-de-Paris from the parvis. (Photo by Darlene)

When we turn to Fulcanelli, we find that his selection of symbolic images focuses our attention almost exclusively on the western facade. The seal of Alchemy (see fig. 8.3), the first image discussed by Fulcanelli in his "Paris" chapter, can be found on the base of the central pillar of the great porch, the Porch of Judgment.

Our guidebook agrees, with a question mark, however, calling it both Philosophy and Theology as well as Alchemy. The other six images around the base are clearly the liberal arts, listed in the guidebook as Arithmetic, Astronomy, Rhetoric, Geometry, Grammar, and Music. Philosophy, whether theological or alchemical, is indeed the overview required to understand the other six.

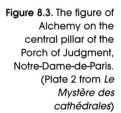

Figure 8.3. The figure of Alchemy on the central pillar of the Porch of Judgment, Notre-Dame-de-Paris. (Plate 2 from *Le Mystère des cathédrales*)

If at this point we can pull our attention away from the Porch of Judgment, then a climb to the towers is in order. On the northeastern corner of the southern tower we find Fulcanelli's second image, the Phyrigian-capped Alchemist (see fig. 8.4). As Fulcanelli suggests, he is watching over his work, and staring intently at one spot deep in the interior of the cathedral. Interestingly enough, both of these sculptures, Alchemy and the Alchemist, are restorations by Viollet-le-Duc. A fascinating photo survives, and may be seen in the Notre Dame Museum, of Eugène Viollet-Le-Duc standing with an enigmatic smile next to the restored Alchemist, who, seen face on, appears to be deeply shocked by what he sees.

Returning to ground level, we find that the rest of Fulcanelli's Notre Dame images can be found on the western porches. The next twenty-two images are on the basement, or lower register, of the central porch, the Porch of Judgment. The guidebook calls them Virtues and Vices, but offers no insight into how these meanings apply to the obscure symbols. To give it credit, the guidebook does mention Fulcanelli and the possibility that these images may have something to do with alchemy, even though it doesn't agree with his theory.

Four images come from the Porch of the Virgin, to the left of the central porch, and the last image from the Porch of Saint Anne, to the right. Fulcanelli uses the central image on the Porch of the Virgin as an example of the planetary metals (fig. 8.5), without mentioning the legend that the scene depicts, the resurrection of Mary. As we contemplate

Figure 8.4. Alchemist from the south tower, Notre-Dame-de-Paris. (Plate 3 from *Le Mystère des cathédrales*)

Figure 8.5. Porch of the Virgin, Notre-Dame-de-Paris. Fulcanelli calls the seven designs on the sarcophagus "the symbols of the seven planetary metals." (Plate 26 in *Le Mystère des cathédrales*)

this inexplicable gap, the light begins to dawn. Fulcanelli is choosing his images to form or reflect a predetermined pattern. He is not concerned with the tales and legends, except as they can be used to demonstrate his point.

His last Notre-Dame-de-Paris image is the perfect example of this selection process. The central pillar of the Porch of Saint Anne contains a sculpture of Saint Marcel (fig. 8.6), the Dark Ages bishop of Paris who defeated a local dragon. Fulcanelli goes on for five pages before he mentions the legend. Along the way he gets in a few shots at restorers

Figure 8.6. Saint Marcel on the middle pillar of the Porch of Saint Anne, Notre-Dame-de-Paris. (Plate 30 from *Le Mystère des cathédrales*)

who add romantic flourishes. Fulcanelli insists, however, that the very key to the mystery of alchemy is contained in the decorative details of the original plinth and its dragon.

In this image, it is the dragon that is important, not the saint who overcame him. Our conviction grows that Fulcanelli is choosing his images carefully to describe a much larger process than just turning lead into gold. Could this image be our evidence of the larger eschatological pattern interwoven with alchemy?

Walking back across the parvis, we turn once more to look at the western facade. There is so much more information in this cathedral, so many more stories. Why did Fulcanelli focus on just those images? He augmented them with images from Amiens and other places, but the heart of the mystery must be here, we feel, bound up with the mystery of Notre Dame itself.

Fulcanelli left us clues, however, and those clues are hidden within *Le Mystère*. The next step is to unravel Fulcanelli's message, the grand hermetic theme behind the alchemical meaning of the cathedrals, by examining the text of *Le Mystère* itself. Fulcanelli structured *Le Mystère* as a series of four—five counting the later Hendaye chapter—interrelated essays, each of which covers similar symbolic territory from different perspectives. The overall result is that of a complex mosaic, whose unity and integrity of design can be seen only when viewed from a distance. Up close, all we see is myriad tiny symbolic pieces, all important and all fitted just so with the ones around them, but the isolated symbol setting limits our perception. We can't see the forest for the trees.

To see the message, we must learn to use our minds in what is for us moderns a very novel and foreign way. Much like those computer-generated 3-D images so popular in the 1990s, in which relaxing the focus of the eyes while allowing "vision" to continue made the hidden image float above the apparently chaotic background, we must relax the focus of our intellect and let the symbols themselves form the hidden message. When we do this, when we internalize the symbols to the point that the hidden message floats above the background noise, we are left with a riddle: How does a Tree become a Stone, and then a Star?

Fulcanelli is telling us, Solve this riddle and you will know the mystery. And like all good puzzle masters, Fulcanelli has included the solution in the riddle itself. But compounding paradox with parable, one can't know the mystery without becoming the riddle. In Fulcanelli's case, the mystery of the cathedrals is the starting point for the personal riddle of his identity.

So, taking Fulcanelli as our hermetic tour guide, let us embark on our quest for the solution to the riddle and the true mystery of the cathedrals.

OUR HERMETIC TOUR GUIDE POSES A CONUNDRUM

"The strongest impression of my early childhood—I was seven years old—an impression of which I still retain a vivid memory, was the emotion aroused in my young heart by the sight of a gothic cathedral." The opening words of the first chapter, which is called "Le Mystère des cathédrales," places us firmly in the personal realm. Fulcanelli, from the very first sentence of the book, strikes us as a real person with a message to communicate. "I was immediately enraptured by it. I was in ecstasy, struck with wonder, unable to tear myself away . . ."[1]

Here is passion, the beginning of a lifelong involvement, an attempt to get to the heart of "the magic of such splendor." It never faded, Fulcanelli tells us: "I have never acquired a defence against a sort of rapture when faced with those beautiful picture books erected in our closes and raising to heaven their pages of sculptured stone."

And so, in his third paragraph, Fulcanelli clearly tells the reader the reason for his work: "In what language, by what means, could I express my admiration? How could I show my gratitude to those silent masterpieces, those masters without words and without voice?" How better indeed than to write a volume explicating, for those who could read the symbolism, the great teachings contained in those "pages of sculptured stone"?

But, of course, as Fulcanelli immediately reminds us, they are not entirely without words or voice. "If those stone books have their sculptured letters—their phrases in bas-relief and their thoughts in pointed arches—nevertheless they speak also through the imperishable spirit which breathes from their pages." This imperishable spirit makes them clearer than their younger brothers, manuscripts and printed books, because "it is simple in expression, naïve and picturesque in interpretation; a sense purged of subtleties, of allusions, of literary ambiguities."

It is this Voice of the Imperishable Spirit, Fulcanelli suggests, that speaks "the gothic of the stones." He links this emotive "language" to the grand theme of music by suggesting that even Gregorian chants can "but add to the emotions which the cathedral itself has already aroused."[2]

At the very beginning of the book, Fulcanelli slyly informs us that he has personally experienced the Voice of that Imperishable Spirit that gives its auditor the ability to understand "the gothic of the stones." He knows, in the ancient sense of gnosis, the secret behind the symbolism. Here in fact we are reminded of Wolfram von Eschenbach's insistence, in *Parzival*, that the mystery of the Grail, the *lapsit exillis*, could be understood only by one who had learned his "ABC's without the aid of Black Magic."[3] Only those who have had the initiatory and illuminatory experience can interpret the language of the mystery.

From this subtle declaration of intent, Fulcanelli moves on to a bold statement on the value of the Gothic cathedral "as a vast concretion of ideas" in which the "religious, secular, philosophical or social thoughts of our ancestors" can be read. He develops this idea by showing how the sacred and the profane mingled in the civic uses of the cathedrals, from guild rituals, to funerals, to commodity markets.

In this shift, we sense a sleight-of-hand taking place under our very eyes. With dizzying suddenness, we have changed our focus from the nature and meaning of language and initiation to the practical details of a laboratory for their explication. The cathedral, we are told, is "an original work of incomparable harmony; but not one, it seems, concerned entirely with religious observance." Fulcanelli assures us that along with "the fervent inspiration, born of a strong faith" there exists "an almost pagan spirit." This allows the cathedrals to express "the thousand and one preoccupations of the great heart of the people" in a way that reveals "the declaration of its conscience, of its will, the reflection of its thought at its most complex, abstract, essential and autocratic."

So far in this first chapter, Fulcanelli sounds a little old-fashioned, a product of Hugo-esque Gothic romanticism from the mid-nineteenth century. To his readers in 1926, this would have sounded quaint, even comfortingly antiquarian. Fulcanelli continues to play on this assumption on the part of his readers, and even references the classic scene in Victor Hugo's *Notre-Dame de Paris,* by shifting his focus to the Feast of Fools.

Here for the first time we encounter Fulcanelli's chief literary device, the use of italicized words and phrases to create a "hidden" metatext that can be read independently of the rest of the words on the page. As an example of this, let's look at just the emphasized words and phrases in the last three paragraphs of section 1 of the "Le Mystère" chapter:

> Feast of Fools . . . disguised Science . . . triumphal chariot of Bacchus . . . Feast of the Donkey . . . Master Aliboron . . . this asinine power, which was worth to the Church the gold of Arabia, the incense and the myrrh of the land of Saba . . . mystifiers of the land of Saba or Caba . . . image-makers . . . Procession of the Fox . . . Feast of the Donkey . . . Flagellation of the Alleluia . . . sabots . . . procession of the Shrovetide Carnival . . . Devilry of Chaumont . . . Infanterie dijonnaise . . . Mad Mother . . . their buttocks . . . Ball Game . . .

If we cannot solve Fulcanelli's first symbolic conundrum, then we haven't much hope of interpreting the rest of the book. Indeed, if we can assume that he is playing fair with us, then an important, perhaps crucial key should lie in this initial group of emphasized words and phrases. So how do we read it?

The first point that jumps out is that Fulcanelli is drawing our attention to two seasonal church festivals that are similar in tone and very pagan in origin. The first, the Feast of Fools, now familiar to millions from the Disney version of *The Hunchback of Notre Dame,* seems to have been a holdover from the Roman Saturnalia. In the Middle Ages it was celebrated as part of the Twelve Nights of Christmas, usually related to the Feast of the Epiphany. As this is the date given in Hugo, we may assume that it is the connection Fulcanelli is drawing for us.[4]

The second, the Feast of the Donkey, is part of the Easter celebration and traditionally marked the spring equinox or the Annunciation of the Virgin, Christ's conception day. Associated, broadly, with the ass that Jesus rode into Jerusalem during his proclamation as a descendant of David, and with the prophetic ass of Balaam who declared that of this lineage, David's, a messiah would come, the Feast of the Donkey, as Fulcanelli suggests, has much more ancient alchemical roots. Fulcanelli's metatext message points to the "image-makers," the "mystifiers of the land of Saba," who are by the implication of their gifts, gold, incense, and myrrh, the Magi.

Fulcanelli then mentions a collection of hermetic holdovers, with "the Gothic church as their theatre," that includes spinning tops, ball games, and other such apparently profane and bawdy activities. He connects them to various Shrovetide or pre-Lenten carnivals, and suggests that these are the last vestiges of the ancient semipagan feasts.

If we read these three paragraphs without focusing on the italicized words, we have a sense that they are meant to inform us of certain pagan traditions connected with the cathedrals, but exactly what these are and what they mean remains elusive. We can read these paragraphs hundreds of times, and be fairly comfortable in our interpretation of their meaning, and yet miss the essential message if we do not look deeply and carefully into the references contained in those emphasized words and phrases. This is what makes *Le Mystère* an initiatory text, a true alchemical document and the "guidebook" to the hermetic quest for the Grail Stone of the Wise, and which marks Fulcanelli as the last great master of the green language.

SOLVING THE CONUNDRUM

How do we unravel Fulcanelli's first conundrum? We start by looking at the significance of the one solid date given us, January 6, the Feast of the Epiphany. To the early Church, the Feast of the Epiphany, which marked the arrival of the Magi, the marriage at Cana, and the baptism of Jesus by John, was much more important than Jesus' nativity. For some sections of the Christian community, such as the Cathars, the Epiphany was the most significant moment in the Church calendar. Some obscure secret seemed to hide behind the juxtaposition of these three events, a secret that threatened to change the very concept of Christianity as taught by the official church.[5]

In this conjunction of symbols, we find a cluster of very revealing clues. There is a sexual component in the marriage at Cana, supposedly the Holy Couple's wedding night, as well as in John the Baptist's acknowledgment of Jesus as his son during the baptism. The visit of the Magi is a symbol of the larger spiritual current and a nod to the original illuminated ones. The Epiphany symbolizes a much older tradition than its Christian gloss, and as such was very disturbing to the Church, which retaliated by shifting the focus to Christ's nativity.

There is no biblical basis for the date of the Nativity, and what

Gospel evidence there is suggests Jesus was born in the late fall, not in midwinter. The early Church had no traditions or celebrations of the Nativity until the third century, and such celebrations didn't become common until the fourth century. It wasn't until the fifth century that the date officially became December 25, which was chosen for reasons of religious politics, not any sense of spiritual or historical correctness. The act of saying a mass in honor of Jesus' birth, hence "Christ's mass," or Christmas, on the birthday of his most powerful pagan rival, Mithras, was plainly and simply an attempt to absorb and redirect the rival cult's followers, in effect saying that Christ is more powerful than Mithras because he supersedes him. It also undercut the importance of the Epiphany, including the Magi as an afterthought to the Nativity instead of as the focus of the story.[6]

But the Feast of the Epiphany remained a popular semipagan festival. In the eleventh and twelfth centuries, the Feast of Fools was revived and swiftly it became a kind of alternative religious expression. The first "guilds," or organized brotherhoods of free tradesmen, developed as sponsors and promoters of the festivities. Within these guilds were many heretical ideas, some of which would surface centuries later as part of Freemasonry. The Church, of course, saw these pageant guilds as little more than secret conclaves of unrepentant pagans and heretics and did its best to restrain them.

The Feast of Fools was connected to the Epiphany through an earlier Feast of the Donkey, or Ass. Held originally between January 14 and January 17, this festival honored the ass Mary rode to Bethlehem, and which stood by at the manger, as well the ass she rode on the flight into Egypt. This ass was also combined with the ass on which Jesus rode into Jerusalem, and with the prophetic ass of Balaam from the Old Testament. In the oldest forms of this pageant, the King of Fools appears as King Balaak, who summons forth the prophetic ass. As the Feast of the Donkey shifted to the pre-Lenten carnival period, the King of the Asses, or the King of Fools, was grafted on the survivals of Saturnalia and settled on the Epiphany. This shift, at the height of the Cathar heresy and the cathedral-building boom, suggests that the influences at work within the Church were no longer completely orthodox.

This festival, or "hermetic fair," signified, in its total reversal of churchly authority, subjecting the "ignorant clergy to the authority of the *disguised Science*," the hidden and "undeniable superiority" of an even more ancient spiritual current. This "gothic" spirituality was symbolized by the King of the Wise Fools, whose coronation on the Feast of the Epiphany, celebrating the tangible evidence of Jesus' Messiahhood, his acclaim by the Magi, his baptism, and his first miracle, made the point of his precedence and authority even clearer. This is the original Great King of the Jews, the one whose line Jesus was merely restoring, Solomon the Wise, builder of the First Temple.

Fulcanelli points us in that direction with his curious mentions of the land of Saba or Caba and its mystifiers and image-makers. The land of Saba is, of course, Arabia and the eastern portion of the Horn of Africa, Eritrea and Ethiopia, home of the Sabeans, ancestors of the Arabs and the original builders of the Kaaba, the holy cube at Mecca, as we saw in chapter 4. The Sabeans were probably worshippers of a mother goddess along the lines of Cybele in Phrygia, whose name may in fact have been adopted from the Sabean original. The Caba of El, Cybele, is certainly the concept behind the sacred stone of Mecca, seen originally as the vulva of the Mother Goddess Allat (or al-Lat), and throne of her son, the El in the sky, or Allah. Saba is also the home of the queen of Sheba, the original perhaps of the Black Madonnas. And it is this reference that Fulcanelli wishes us to see in his curious metatext clues.

Following his thread of clues, we come to a single original source, one that we have discussed in chapter 6, an eleventh-century Arabic alchemical work entitled *Mother of the King*, by one Abufalah, or the "Son of Reason." As noted already, this work entered the later *Bahir* tradition in the thirteenth century through Rabbi Shlomo, who lifted part of it, uncredited, for his own alchemical text, the *Gates of Heaven*. Abufalah's reference to King Solomon's book *HaMaspen*, suggests that it was an early version of the "Great Mystery" text of the *Bahir*. In this work, according to Abufalah, Solomon relates how he learned the secret of alchemy from the queen of Sheba, or Saba.[7]

As if referencing this obscure text, which stands at the juncture point of all the traditions and currents we have been examining, from the *Bahir* to the Cathars, from the Templars to the Grail romances, were not enough, Fulcanelli's metatext clues also direct us to an even more obscure work in the golem tradition that spun off from the *Bahir* and the *Sefer Yetzirah*. His comments on image-makers and mystifiers echo portions of the anonymous twelfth-century work *Sefer ha-Chaim*, or the Book of Life. Written around 1200, contemporaneous with Robert de Boron's Grail romances, this curious work directly connects the golem tradition of animating matter with the main current of Jewish alchemy in the *Bahir*.[8]

In this work, we are told that the secret of animating matter concerns the alignment of the *merkabah,* the triumphant chariot, and the appropriate constellation. Dust is gathered from this alignment and is then used by "all the witches and magicians of Egypt" to animate statues. This was, in fact, we are informed, the method used by Aaron to animate the golden calf while Moses was busy on Mount Sinai, and the technique was still used in India and Arabia, according to the anonymous author. This work is also unique in that it represents an older form of golem making that does not directly relate to the methods described in the *Sefer Yetzirah*. This older form is related, by way of Rabbi Shlomo and the other provençal kabbalists, to the alchemical and eschatological implications of the *Bahir*. The *Sefer ha-Chaim* seems to be the one remaining manuscript in which these connections can be found.

Fulcanelli goes further, however, by emphasizing the word *sabot* as a spinning top, the Hebrew dreidel. This spinning refers to the whirlwind of the mystical experience, and the spinning of the celestial mill as the movement of the sky grinds out time. As we saw in chapter 4, this concept is an important one in the *Bahir*. Fulcanelli's insistence on connecting these metaphors with the Feast of the Epiphany forces us to consider the significance of that moment in time. Is there an astronomical and eschatological clue here as well?

Indeed there is, but we must step back again to see it. Fulcanelli draws our attention to the vernal equinox, the point from which we measure the precessional age. The vernal equinox is now moving from Pisces to Aquarius, as a little more than two thousand years ago it moved from Aries to Pisces. In the medieval text *The Mother of the King,* which Fulcanelli is citing, we are told of a mysterious image that could foretell the future that was required before the Stone of the Wise could be used for transmutation. This "image" could be a blueprint of the precessional process showing the merkabah points, the celestial alignments, from the *Sefer ha-Chaim*. But why the insistence on the Epiphany? Could there be something marked by that date, January 6, that has a significance in the larger pattern of precessional mythology?

In the second and third centuries B.C.E., the vernal equinox fell on the cusp of Aries/Pisces and the winter solstice fell on the cusp of Capricorn/Sagittarius. A thousand years later, due to precession, the winter solstice fell in the middle of Sagittarius. As it is now, another thousand or so years later, it falls on the cusp of Sagittarius/Scorpio. January 6 is fifteen days after the winter solstice, and around 1100 fell on the former winter solstice point, the cusp of Capricorn/Sagittarius. The Feast of the Epiphany is then marking the same precessional era, the "age" noted by the vernal equinox in Aries/Pisces, except that its rise to prominence in the twelfth and thirteenth centuries seemed to be marking more than just the original winter solstice point. We can also see it as a way of counting down to the arrival of the next precessional age, with the vernal equinox on Pisces/Aquarius.

The millennial notions of the era seemed to have been sparked by noting this significant point. When the cusp moved across the Epiphany, as happened in the twelfth century, a crop of new millennial prophecies emerged both in the Jewish kabbalistic groups and in the Christian communities. Both the Elijah the Prophet visits that sparked the publication of the *Bahir,* and the prophecies of Joachim of Flores are connected to this secret event. Joachim, in fact, dated the beginning of the third segment of this zodiacal age to 1260, which is just a little over ten degrees of precession from the next cusp/winter-solstice alignment, which is currently in progress. The sudden and almost desperate boom in cathedral building appears designed to climax at the end and beginning point of Joachim's ages, 1260. Certainly, in the case of the almost incredible twenty-six-year rebuilding of Chartres Cathedral, some prominent but unspoken deadline forced the completion of the work. The cathedrals of Our Lady, perhaps, were intended to house the spirit of the new age, the age of the Holy Spirit according to Joachim of Flores.

Fulcanelli, then, in his very first metatext conundrum, supplies us with all the clues required to solve the mystery of the cathedrals. But to uncover that secret, to find the disguised science hidden in the cathedrals, requires an intellectual quest of the highest order. Fulcanelli plays fair, and gives us at the very beginning all the clues we shall need to interpret the hidden message. But we must do our part of the work, and carefully follow those clues.

SAINT MARCEL'S DRAGON

Fulcanelli's initial riddle supplies us with a vast amount of information, connotations, and connections when we unravel it. However, the dragon-axis component of the Teli as described in the *Bahir* is missing from the riddle. The element of eschatological timing is referenced in the connection to the "image" that foretold the future in Abufalah's tale of Solomon and Sheba, and the hidden impact of the original winter-solstice point crossing the Epiphany is clearly a factor in the sudden rise of cathedral building. But so far, no dragons.

For that we must wait until section 6 of Fulcanelli's "Paris" chapter. This section is devoted entirely to one image, the dragon and plinth of Saint Marcel on the middle pillar of the Porch of Saint Anne (see figure 8.6). Fulcanelli informs us that this statue "describes the shortest practice of our Science and among lessons in stone it therefore deserves pride of place." This short or dry path, in contrast to the longer moist method, is done with *"[o]ne single vessel, one single matter, one single furnace,"* and can be accomplished in days rather than months or years. "The hermetic emblem of this method," Fulcanelli assures us, can be found on the dragon and its pillar.[9]

Considering that Fulcanelli cites no fewer than three other hermeticists on the image of Saint Marcel and the dragon, we might suppose that this is indeed the key alchemical figure on the entire cathedral. This suspicion is heightened by the quote from Grillot de Givry that Fulcanelli uses to launch his discussion: "See . . . sculptured on the right portal of Notre Dame of Paris, the bishop perched above an athenor, where the philosophical mercury, chained in limbo, is being sublimated. It teaches the origin of the sacred fire; and the Chapter of the cathedral, by leaving this door closed all the year in accordance with a secular tradition, shows that this is *not the vulgar way,* but one unknown to the crowd and reserved for the small number of the elite of Wisdom."[10] From this we may safely assume that if there ever was a single agreed-upon image on Notre Dame that did in fact sum up the innermost secret of alchemy, Saint Marcel and the dragon is it.

When Fulcanelli finally turns to a description of the dragon and its markings, after a lengthy digression on the nature of the dry method and a few swipes at restorers who don't understand what they are restoring, we find a very precise depiction of what can only be the dragon axes:

1. A longitudinal band, beginning at the head and following the line of the backbone to the end of the tail.
2. Two similar bands, placed obliquely, one on each wing.
3. Two broader transverse bands round the tail of the dragon, the first at the level of the wings, the other above the head of the king. All these bands are ornamented with full circles, touching at a point on their circumference.[11]

Just to make sure that we have not missed his point, Fulcanelli continues: "As for the meaning, this will be supplied by the circles on the tail bands: the centre is very clearly marked on each one of them. Now, the hermeticists know that the king of the metals is symbolized by the solar sign, that is to say a circumference, with or without a central point. It therefore seems reasonable to me that if the dragon is covered in a profusion of auric symbols—it has them right down to the claws of the right paw—this is because it is capable of transmuting in quantity. . . ."[12]

We can recognize these symbols from the discussion in chapter 4. Fulcanelli notes a line down the spine of the dragon, from head to tail, and this is clearly a *teli* or dragon axis. This image could be representing either or both of the great axes, from the center to edge of the galaxy as well as the ecliptic pole axis from the constellation Draco, the Dragon, to the Lesser Magellanic Cloud. It also symbolizes all the other uses of the head and tail of the dragon, from marking the moments of eclipses to marking the standstill and equal points of the solar cycle.

The lines on the wings represent the backward-moving precessional alignment of the dragon axis, which forms the Cube of Space in conjunction with the other two, more stable axes. On the dragon, these lines are not perpendicular, but are instead set at an oblique angle. Since the original has been lost, we can't measure their angle, but it is just possible that it matched the winter-solstice position, measured from the galactic axis, appropriate for the time it was built, roughly 720 years ago, or ten degrees of precessional arc from a cubic alignment, as is illustrated in figure 8.7.

The two bands of circles on the dragon's tail can be seen as representations of the two opposite-moving cycles, the procession of the solar

2,160 years ago

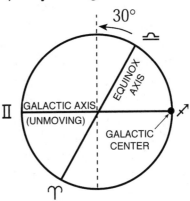

Figure 8.7. This figure illustrates the precession of the equinoxes. The equinox point on the ecliptic moves one degree counterclockwise every seventy-two years, causing the equinox points to move backward through the zodiac one sign every 2,160 years. When the spring or vernal equinox fell on Aries/Pisces in the second century B.C.E., the winter solstice fell on Capricorn/Sagittarius. As we are now entering a new precessional era, the spring equinox and the winter solstices are moving backward toward the cusps of Sagittarius/Scorpio and Pisces/Aquarius. Around 1100 C.E., the actual winter solstice point moved across the January 6 Epiphany date, sparking a wave of millennial fervor.

720 years ago

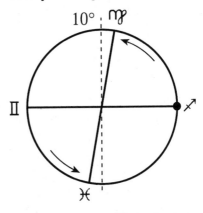

In 2002 A.D.   The equinox axis becomes perpendicular to the galactic axis.

year and the precession of the Great Year. As Fulcanelli tells us, these are in fact solar symbols, noting the solar or zodiacal quality of the months or ages in each cycle. Saint Marcel's dragon is therefore none other than the grand Leviathan of Heaven, the triple dragon axis from which the Cube of Space is formed, displayed as an all-at-once symbol of the entire astronomical and eschatological process underlying alchemy. As it is also a description of the quick or dry path of alchemy, the secret of secrets, then we can see why this image, above all others, is the major initiatory key to the Gothic alchemists, including Fulcanelli.

We can also be sure that Fulcanelli wants us to connect this dragon to the Teli of the *Bahir,* because he also describes the decoration on the plinth in terms of the Tree of Life: "Finally, on each side of the athenor and under the very claws of the dragon are the five unities of the quintessence, comprising the three principles and the two natures, and finally their total in the number ten 'in which everything finishes and comes to an end.' "[13]

The last phrase is an unattributed paraphrase from the *Sefer Yetzirah:* "Their measure is ten which have no end; a depth of beginning and a depth of ending." The *Sefer Yetzirah* continues in the same vein: "Their vision is like the appearance of lightning and their limit has no end."[14] The *Sefer Yetzirah* is describing the ten *sefirot* or emanations of divinity and the twenty-two letters that connect them. These philosophical speculations would be organized in the Bahir into the Etz Chaim, the Tree of Life. Fulcanelli, with his sly paraphrase, directs us toward the real secret of Saint Marcel and the dragon. It is the plinth that holds the mystery.

On the plinth in figure 8.6, we see a central pillar on each face, and four common pillars, one on each corner. Fulcanelli tells us that the athenor is formed from the four elemental qualities. Following the directions from the *Sefer Yetzirah,* to which Fulcanelli has guided us, we can see four overlapping trees on the cubic plinth. We can place the middle pillar of the Tree of Life on the face of the plinth, or on the corner pillar, and still be correct, although the overall design suggests that the corners are the middle pillars of the Tree. In any case, we have the Tree of Life within the Stone of the Wise, which is described in the *Bahir* and was discussed in chapter 4.

Therefore, in this one symbol, Fulcanelli presents us with a capsule summary of the important points of the ancient illuminated astronomy.

Since the Templars were known to have been involved in financing the construction of the Porch of Saint Anne, we might expect that this singular symbol would also reveal something of their secrets. And indeed, the dragon curls around a man's head as it emerges from its athenor, symbolizing the connection between the Templars' Baphomet, the head that symbolized the *bet'amet,* or place of truth, and illuminated astronomy.

We may take this as evidence that the secret of astro-alchemy is truly displayed on the Gothic cathedral of Notre Dame. The image of Bishop Marcel's dragon serves as a thread linking the ancient wisdom of Abraham, Solomon, and the Sabeans with the mystery schools of Alexandria and the medieval secret societies that built the cathedrals. The thread continues down to Fulcanelli, who, knowing the secret, chose his images carefully to fill in the outline of the ancient wisdom.

At first, Fulcanelli's choice of images, out of the many available to him on the facade of Notre Dame and its porches, seems whimsical or even just a chaotic deluge of allusions and interconnections. Only when his pattern of selection is correctly seen as an attempt to present a specific interpretation of the kabbalistic Tree of Life, as suggested by the dragon's plinth, does the apparent chaos resolve into the masterly order of the hermetic grand theme.

This grand theme of ten spheres and twenty-two paths, the Tree of Life, is augmented by Fulcanelli's juxtaposition of symbols from other locations, such as Amiens cathedral and private houses in late-fifteenth-century Bourges. Fulcanelli's system of symbolic juxtaposition reveals, in ways not unlike that of surrealist art, deeper meanings behind the emerging symbolic construct. It is almost as if Fulcanelli, the master of symbolic art, had inadvertently stumbled onto the magic secret of surrealism. Or, more likely, surrealism is merely the latest artistic expression of a hermetic worldview stretching back into the myths of antiquity.

THE WORLD TREE AND ASTRO-ALCHEMY

Our earliest surviving alchemical text, the Egypto-Hebraic "Isis the Prophetess," tells us that Isis received the secrets of alchemy from a composite being, Amnael, whose name is suggestive of the Kabbalistic Tree of Life. But what, exactly, is the Tree of Life?

To the ancient Egyptians, the Tree of Life was symbolized by the Djed pillar, the backbone of Osiris (see fig. 8.8). The Djed began as a power object in the Neolithic cultures of the Nile delta. It symbolized "stability," or rather "divine establishment." The World Tree or World Axis is a common motif in shamanic traditions that stands for the infrastructure of the universe. As this symbolic image/idea of the world pillar as axis of the universe became a word, *djed,* it was associated with similar-sounding words in order to give it a phonetic spelling. *Djed* is also the Egyptian word for "to speak," "to declare," "to say." With emphasis, *Ddd-jed,* it is the sacred word itself, speech deified. Interesting as this is, it is the other roots that really strike a suggestive nerve. *Djedd,* same word with a slightly different emphasis, means "star" or, actually, the culmination or azimuth of the star. This same word, *djedd,* is also a perfectly good Hebrew word *dzeth,* and they both mean "olive tree." The same word, in very similar pronunciation, is found in both Coptic and Arabic. The olive tree is the original Tree of Life, perhaps even the burning bush of Moses (see the light verse, Koran 28:37). The combination of the idea of star and the image of the Tree of Life suggests an interesting cluster of meaning associated with the Djed.

The roots of these Egyptian words form a complex that encompasses the concepts of speech, including divine speech, the culmination or zenith of a star, and an olive tree, the Tree of Life itself. This complex web of words tells us that the ancient Egyptians thought of the Djed as something divinely pronounced, a "word-tree" that links life on earth and the stars.

The Indo-European group of languages has a complex of root words that are similar to that which we have just outlined in Egyptian for the word *djed.* In the reconstructed language known as proto-Indo-European, the World Tree is the oak, *drw.* Just as the olive tree was the Tree of Life in the Mediterranean—because of its ability to supply food and therefore ensure social stability—the oak provided the same benefits for the ancient Indo-Europeans wandering out of the central Asian grasslands into the vast forests of postglacial Europe. The word for "oak" also meant "firm," "strong," "stable," and "enduring" in the Indo-European language groups. Our English words *truth, trust,* and *tree* come from the same root word. *Druid* is also in the *drw family and means "seer of the oak."

In Sanskrit, another Indo-European language, the word for "tree" is *daru,* a derivation of *drw. In the Rigveda, the ancient ceremonial

Figure 8.8. The Egyptian Djed pillar, World Tree and backbone of Osiris. To the ancient Egyptians it was the divinely pronounced Word/World Tree connecting life on Earth with the cosmic drama of the stars.

hymns of the Indo-Aryan conquerors of India, we read that the Tree is the material "from which the gods have fashioned Heaven and earth, the stationary, the undecaying, giving protection to the deities."[15] The Tree is the cosmic pillar around which the entire universe was thought to revolve. This World Tree was often shown in Indian folk art as a great tree crowned with the Pole Star, which is called *dhruva,* another derivative of *drw, and which meant the "firm one" or "fixed one."

To the rational mind, this idea of the Pole Star as an eternal tree strikes us as a kind of nonsense. Yet in an experiment conducted by Dr. Jonathan Shear of Maharishi University in the late 1970s, we find that this tree embodies a strange kind of truth.

The experiment centered on a sutra in part three of Patanjali's *Yoga Sutra* that states that "by performing *samyama* on the Dhruva, the Pole Star, one gains knowledge of the motion of the stars."[16] *Samyama* is a deep state of rapport that allows for an actual transfer of energy or information with whatever one is focusing on, be it an image of a deity or the Pole Star.[17]

In his paper, published in the January 1981 edition of the journal *Metaphilosophy,* Shear reports that he expected his subjects, all skilled meditators, "to perceive the motion of the stars in the context of the heavens as we are accustomed to perceive and think about them." This, however, didn't happen. The meditators were instructed to do the practice that would induce the state of *samyama* while holding their focus on the Pole Star. The expectation was that if they received any insight at all into the workings of the Pole Star, it would be in the form of commonly perceived images and concepts.

However, instead of the usual time-lapse sky wheel familiar to us from *Life* magazine photo spreads, the meditators reported something very different. "The Pole Star is seen [in the meditators' inner vision] at the end of a long rotating shaft of light. Rays of light come out from the shaft like the ribs of an umbrella. The umbrella-like structure on which the stars are embedded is seen as rotating. . . . The whole experience is described as quite spectacular, blissful, colorful and melodious."[18]

The meditators themselves were taken by surprise by this experience. They had no idea that this image of the World Tree was an actual archetype—that is, something that exists outside themselves in the collective unconscious—until they stumbled across it. Shear is emphatic when he states: "[T]he experience is the innocent by-product of the proper practice of the technique." In other words, the practice triggers an experience that is contradictory to the commonsense and educated perspectives of the experiencer.

Here is our archetypal Djed. The Rigveda tells us that "on top of the distant sky there stands / The Word encompassing all." Stability, in the sense of the word *djed,* the backbone of Osiris as the World Tree, becomes the link between earth and the stars. We are stable only as long as we are connected to our stellar source. At the very least, Shear's experiment shows us that a spiritual rapport with the stars can produce information not available to the senses. The image of the World Tree and its umbrella-like spokes is not apparent to the observer. It can be perceived only by entering a state of consciousness where its nature can be experienced.

The ancient seers used techniques such as those in Shear's study to investigate the universe around them.[19] The information they received from these practices became coded into the religious myths, symbols, and structures of the ancient world. This spiritual canon, or structured and geometric organizational hierarchy, is the mathematical equivalent of the green language of the troubadours. "Let none ignorant of geometry enter here" hung over the door of Plato's academy in Athens for good reason.

This ancient canon of number almost disappeared with fall of the ancient world. It survived in fragments and in the quotations of the ancients, until an almost unknown English scholar named William Stirling wrote the first formal explication of it since Vitruvius in ancient Rome. Published anonymously in 1897, his book, entitled *The Canon: An Exposition of the Pagan Mystery Perpetuated in the Cabala as the Rule of All Art,* managed, like Fulcanelli's *Mystery of the Cathedrals,* to become influential in spite of its obscurity. It inspired thinkers as diverse as the psychic archaeologist F. Bligh Bond and the perennial Victorian bad-boy magician Aleister Crowley, who liberally sprinkled his work with swipes from Stirling.

According to Keith Critchlow, a geometric philosopher and student of Buckminster Fuller, "the Canon is based on the objective fact that events and physical changes which are perpetual are never the less completely governed by intrinsic proportions, periodicities and measures." As Critchlow notes, "[I]t is to just such a hidden intrinsic language that the author of this book (Stirling) has dedicated himself."[20]

In his chapter on rhetoric, one of the liberal arts surrounding Alchemy on the base of Notre Dame's middle pillar, Stirling gives us a simple description of the Great Tree of Life: "The process of creation may be expressed by inscribing the cabalistic diagram in the upper hemisphere, so that the apex or crown reaches to the Milky Way, while the tenth step will coincide with earth."[21] Stirling's "cabalistic diagram" is the ten-step pattern of unfoldment known to occultists as the Tree of Life, and according to his explication, it is the basic pattern of the canon itself.

He writes: "The doctrine of the Cabala was reduced to a geometric diagram, in which ten steps were grouped according to a progressive scheme, so that the emanations of the Spirit of the Elohim issues from the first step called the Crown, and after passing through the whole figure is carried through the ninth step, and finally reaches the tenth or last of the series."[22] This cabalistic diagram described by Stirling was first elucidated in the second-century *Sefer Yetzirah.* It depicts reality as the intersection of four different levels of abstraction.

Stirling tells us that "the ideas which the ancients connected . . . and combined into this figure of ten progressive steps, appears to form the basis of all their philosophy, religion, and art, and in it we have the nearest approach to a direct revelation of the traditional science, or Gnosis, which was never communicated except by myths and symbols."[23] From this we can see that the framework, the gnostic pattern, behind the universal language of symbolism, the language of the birds and the green language, is this great Word/World Tree of geometry.

Since Fulcanelli informs us that the *argotique* of the green language is based on a cabalistic pattern of meaning, it should be obvious that this pattern is the Tree of Life of his fellow adepts. That it is not obvious is the result of misdirection, conscious or unconscious, on the part of Fulcanelli's student, Eugène Canseliet.

In the "Preface to the Second Edition" of *Mystery of the Cathedrals,* Canseliet, while displaying his knowledge of the importance of stellar imagery in his master's work, ends with a major piece of misinformation. He states that the justification for the republication of the book lies in the fact "that this book has restored to light the phonetic cabala, whose principles and applications had been completely lost." While this is somewhat true, Canseliet goes on to conclude that after his and Fulcanelli's work, "this mother tongue need never be confused with the Jewish Kabbalah."[24]

He continues by asserting that "the Jewish Kabbalah is full of transpositions, inversions, substitutions and calculations, as arbitrary as they are abstruse." Again this is true for many explications of the kabbalistic mystery, but it does not address the issue of the universality of the Tree of Life itself. Canseliet further muddies the water by suggesting that *cabala* and *Kabbalah* are derived from different roots. *Cabala,* he declares, is derived from the Latin *caballus,* or "horse," while *Kabbalah* is derived from the Hebrew word for tradition. On the surface, this is indeed correct, but Canseliet is skillfully avoiding the deeper meanings of both these words, which leads us ultimately to their common root—*kaba,* the stone.

Fulcanelli never voiced such opinions in the body of the book. In *Mystery of the Cathedrals,* he obliquely refers to the cabala as the "language of the gods" and scorns the "would-be cabalists . . . whether they be Jewish or Christian," and "the would-be experts, whose illusory combinations lead to nothing concrete."[25] He goes on to say: "Let us leave these doctors of the Kabbalah to their ignorance," implying those who claimed to be authorities on the Hebrew Kabbalah. He says nothing against the Kabbalah itself but merely notes that it is misunderstood by almost everyone. By implication, Fulcanelli is also saying that he does understand it properly.

As we saw in chapter 2, "Isis the Prophetess" points to a Tree of Life motif for its source of wisdom. The Hebrew spelling of Amnael's name gives us a clue to its nature. Using Hebrew *gematria,* the letters in the name add up to 123, the number of the three-part name of God, AHH YHVH ELOHIM, associated with the top three *sefirot* on the Tree of Life, Kether, Chokmah, and Binah (see fig. 2.9). As noted already, if we break the name into *Amn* and *ael,* we get the numbers 91 and 32. These are both references to the Tree of Life, 32 being the total number of paths and *sefirot* and 91 being the number of the Hebrew word *amen,* AMN, and the word for "tree," AYLN.

Stirling, in his rediscovery of the ancient canon, concludes that the Tree of Life is the pattern that underlies the secret language of symbolism, which is the language expressed by the liberal arts that accompany Alchemy/Philosophy on the base of the middle pillar of the Porch of Judgment. Fulcanelli himself points to the Tree of Life as the key secret in his description of the dragon's plinth, going so far as to paraphrase the *Sefer Yetzirah.*

Therefore, why should we, on the basis of Canseliet's prejudice, associate anything else with Fulcanelli's kabbalistic image pattern? Fulcanelli also instructs us that language is a reflection of the universal Idea, a clear reference to the Word/World Tree. The kabbalistic origins of the art of light, Fulcanelli reminds us, are but a reflection of the divine light.

Fulcanelli is not only making use of this kabbalistic Tree of Life pattern, but he is a master of its symbolic subtleties as well. As he unfolds his array of images and concepts, we see the guiding matrix of the ancient Word, the *verbum dismissum* or lost word of Western esotericism, revealed as the divine World/Word Tree.

NINE

FULCANELLI'S TREE OF LIFE AND THE MYSTERY OF THE CATHEDRALS

LE MYSTÈRE AS THE TREE OF LIFE

Fulcanelli informs us that the images on the cathedrals speak more clearly than words and books. They are "simple in expression, naïve and picturesque in interpretation; a sense purged of subtleties, of allusions, of literary ambiguities."[1] The Gothic, he implies, is like Gregorian chants, many voices coming together in a single note. This is important guidance for understanding the book as a whole. Fulcanelli combines images or voices all juxtaposed on a single note or theme in such a way that every voice is related to the theme as a whole. As in music, the structure that allows this interrelatedness is based on geometry and mathematics. It is nothing less than the hermetic Grand Theme, the music of the spheres, which is depicted within the Gothic cathedrals.

Fulcanelli introduces the Grand Theme with the arrangement of sections in his first chapter, called "Le Mystère des cathédrales." From its title we may suppose that it was meant to impart an overall viewpoint from which the rest of the book, the details of the pattern, is to be understood. These nine sections can be seen as the lightning flash of creation from the *Sefer Yetzirah,* with each section's images and subjects attributed to one of the sefirot, from Kether, the Crown, to Yesod, the Foundation. The pattern can also be seen as another interesting symbol: the sword in the stone. The first three sections of the book make up the hilt of the subject, and the blade of the sword, whose basic theme, the hermetic wisdom of the Gothic cathedrals, continues through a stone of five interrelated symbols within the cathedrals and on into the foundation "stone" of Notre-Dame-de-Paris

The next three chapters replicate this initial Tree. "Paris," the second chapter of *Le Mystère,* gives us the most complete rendition of the Grand Theme of ten spheres and twenty-two paths, including the Gnostic Path of Return, in the arrangement of the twenty-two images from the basement register of Notre Dame's Porch of Judgment (plates 4–25 in *Le Mystère*). "Amiens," the third chapter, fills in another Tree by giving the reader a deeper understanding of the planetary influences with images from the lower register of the cathedral of Amiens' Porch of Judgment. The fourth chapter, "Bourges," juxtaposes a series of mythological images on the planetary spheres, thus creating a fourth Tree. Therefore, each of the "locations," or *sefirot,* is attributed to multiple images from which a composite meaning of the *sefirot* can be derived. (See appendix D.)

The crowning experience, the personal gnosis in the first chapter, is the starting point of a flash of illumination that Fulcanelli uses to reveal the essential pattern of the alchemical Tree of Life. To the kabbalist, the lightning flash, the creative sequence of the unfolding Light, reveals the underlying structure of reality in the ten *sefirot.* In the same way, Fulcanelli uses his experience of the cathedrals, his gnosis, to reveal the pattern at the heart of the mystery. In the symbolic Kabbalah, this lightning flash becomes the flaming sword, which protects the Garden of Eden from human rehabitation. In Fulcanelli's hands, the image becomes the sword in the stone (see fig. 9.1), the alchemical extraction of knowledge from the Stone of the Wise, which initiates the Golden Age, a new Camelot, here on earth.

The pattern emerges clearly in the first three sections of the first chapter. Following the path of the lightning flash, if section 1 is the point of light, Kether, then section 2 is the light's expansion into the world of space-time, Chokmah. And so in that section, Fulcanelli tells us of the medical school and the Saturday meetings of alchemists at "the little Porte-Rouge," clues to those who knew and made use of the cathedral's secrets. He quotes Victor Hugo to direct us—if we haven't made the connection yet—to his works, particularly his Notre-Dame de Paris. Section 2 concludes with another glimpse of Fulcanelli's motivation.

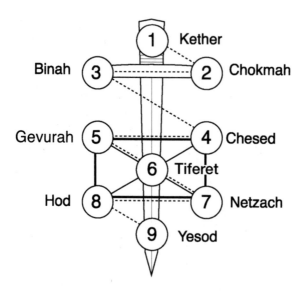

Figure 9.1. The sword-in-the-stone pattern of the *sefirot* on the Tree of Life applied to the nine sections of the first chapter of *Le Mystère des cathédrales.*

"Indeed I shall consider myself satisfied and amply rewarded if I have been able to awaken the curiosity of the reader, to hold the attention of the shrewd observer and to show to lovers of the occult that it is not impossible even now to rediscover the meaning of the secrets hidden under the petrified exterior of this wondrous book of magic."[2]

Section 3 of Fulcanelli's first chapter, whose subject is the secret language, was discussed in chapter 1. As we noted there, this section is the key to understanding Fulcanelli's method, which is appropriate for the *sefirah* Binah, or Understanding. Together with the first two sections, it completes the supernal triad at the top of the Tree of Life. We can also think of the triad as the hilt of a sword, which comprises a pommel, a grip, and a crossguard, and whose blade is the extension of the idea through the stone of symbolism into the reality of Notre Dame, the Philosophers' Church.

To pull the sword from the stone, it is necessary to grip, or grasp, the ideas supplied by the hilt. The first three stages of the lightning flash form a pattern from which the rest of its path unfolds. Fulcanelli combines these ideas with his subject, the cathedrals, in such a way as to compel us to look deeper and more closely at the symbols expressed within those cathedrals. In the remaining sections of chapter 1 of *Le Mystère des cathédrals,* Fulcanelli suggests that the symbolic components of those "books in stone" are fivefold and that they form, within themselves, the Stone of the Wise.

The lightning flash cuts across the abyss as it passes from Binah to Chesed, from Understanding to Mercy. Thus the flash creates its own reflection, and the reflection of the upper three stages in the sequence, as it travels down toward matter. Fulcanelli follows this pattern, and his fourth chapter focuses on the literal symbolism of the cross as the basic plan for all Gothic churches. The shift from theoretical discussions of the language of the birds to the literality of a cathedral's ground plan is sharp enough to suggest the pathless spark of transmission from Binah to Chesed, while the subject of section 4, the cross, directs our attention to life itself.

According to Fulcanelli, all Gothic churches, with rare exceptions, are laid out in the form of a Latin cross, which he tells us "is the alchemical hieroglyph of the crucible," since *crucible* and *cross* are derived from the same Latin root. And here, Fulcanelli begins to play his symbolic shell game: "It is indeed in the crucible that the first matter suffers the Passion, like Christ himself."[3]

Unless we understand the need to connect the cross to the idea of Mercy as conveyed by the fourth *sefirah* or stage in the unfolding sequence, we shall not quite follow Fulcanelli's sudden shifts of tone and meaning. His Christian take is somewhat surprising here until we realize that it is the "mercy" brought by the experience of the cross that he is trying to convey. The Passover lamb roasted on a cross of transformation makes a good literal symbol of God's mercy. But Fulcanelli, of course, is taking the obvious one step further.

"Remember too, my brother alchemists, that the cross bears the imprint of the three nails used to sacrifice the Christ-body," Fulcanelli reminds us, like a carnival barker pointing to the pea. These three nails are the anchor points of the three axes of the Galaxy, the clue to understanding the true ancient nature of the cross. After shuffling with Saint Augustine and the Paschal lamb, Fulcanelli comes to the point:. "The cross is a very ancient symbol, used in all ages, in all religions, by all peoples, and one would be wrong to consider it as a special emblem of Christianity." Here's the pitch: Can you find the pea of truth under all the Christian special pleading?

He gives us a hint. "We say further that the ground plan of the great religious buildings of the Middle Ages, by the addition of a semicircular or elliptical apse joined to the choir [see fig. 9.2], assumes the shape of the Egyptian hieratic sign of the *crux ansata,* the *ankh,* which

Figure 9.2. The Tree of Life and the ankh superimposed on the floor plan of Notre-Dame-de-Paris.

signifies *universal life* hidden in matter." He points to an example of this from the "crypts of St. Honoré at Arles," a sarcophagus lid from the first century that echoes the rose-cross ankhs of the Coptic Museum in Cairo.

To make sure we grasp his point, he adds that the ankh is also the sign of Venus in astrology and of copper in alchemy. Traditionally, as shown in figure 9.3, the ankh sign in the shape of the glyph for Venus is the only form of the cross to contain the complete Tree of Life.

The first six *sefirot*, from Kether to Tiferet, form the loop; Hod and Netzach are the cross arms; and Yesod and Malkuth complete the lower arm. Fulcanelli emphasizes the completeness and ubiquity of this symbol and then begins to shuffle metaphors once more.

The cross metamorphoses into a stone: "It is thus that the ground plan of a Christian building reveals to us the qualities of the first matter, and its preparation by the *sign of the cross*, which points the way for the alchemist to obtain the *First Stone*—the corner stone of the philosophers' Great Work." Fulcanelli raises the stakes by telling us that "[i]t is on this *stone* that Jesus built his church" and by insisting

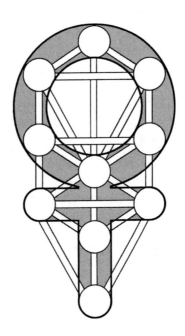

Figure. 9.3. The ankh-shaped symbol of Venus contains the Tree of Life.

that the medieval Freemasons did the same symbolically, giving the undressed, rough stone the image of the devil.

Fulcanelli tells us that once just such a "hieroglyph" could be found within Notre-Dame-de-Paris. This "figure of the devil," called Master Peter of the Corner, was located at the corner of the choir rail, under the rood screen, and this smudged and blackened stone was used by the congregation to snuff their candles. Fulcanelli instructs us that this stone, which "was intended to represent the first matter of the Work, personified under the aspect of *Lucifer (the morning star),* was the symbol of our *corner stone,* the *headstone of the corner.*" He cites a seventeenth-century reference about the stone the builders rejected and then directs us to the very first specific image from Notre Dame mentioned in the book, a bas-relief of Jesus blessing an oddly shaped stone in the arch of an apsidal chapel on the north side of the cathedral.

Somehow the cross, the ankh, became a stone, and not just any stone, but the rejected stone that became the headstone of the corner, the support on which Jesus built his church. And somehow this is "the first matter," "the First Stone," the cornerstone of the alchemical Great Work? Just how does a tree—the ankh contains the entire Tree of Life and the cross is a component of the World Tree—become a stone?

Herein are revealed great mysteries, to echo our occult carnival barker. Fulcanelli has presented us with the first part of a conundrum, the unraveling of which will take us into deep waters indeed.

The answer seems to lie with the ancient myths of the World Tree, at whose feet, in many if not most of the very ancient myths, there can be found a stone or cube that is somehow plugging up the torrent of the deluge. Giorgio de Santillana and Hertha von Dechend uncovered this motif as part of their epic examination of the transmission of precessional information through the medium of mythology in *Hamlet's Mill*.[4] Their scholarship suggests a connection between the Ark, which in Sumerian myth is a perfect cube, and the foundation stone that stops the flood. In another version of the ancient Sumerian Noah/ Utnapishtim myths, there is no ark at all, just a cubic stone with a pillar on top that stretches from earth to heaven and plugs the entrance to the watery abyss.

This idea is also found in Jewish mythology. The Eben Shetiyyaah, the foundation stone uncovered by King David on Mount Zion, was thought to cap the watery abyss beneath the Holy of Holies. The idea of a stone, the white altar of tradition, holding back the flood of chaos and catastrophe survived within Christianity. In addition to Fulcanelli's Master Peter of the Corner, similar images are found in Russian and Germanic prayers, where the fire-blackened stone, Christ's throne and the habitation of the Devil, symbolized the entrance to hell, whose fires are safely contained by its bulk. A German prayer, quoted in *Hamlet's Mill*, seems even more explicit: "In Christ's Garden, there is a well, in the well there is a stone, under the stone lies a golden scorpion."

The first of our five symbolic components, the stone from which the sword of wisdom is extracted, is the cross/stone of space-time itself, the Cube of Space formed from the three axes of the Galaxy. Fulcanelli seems to understand this in a way that is even more comprehensive than that of Santillana and von Dechend's scholarship. And with that deep and ancient understanding, Fulcanelli is pointing us toward the truth about the alchemical and transformative nature of Christianity.

The Tree can also become a stone when the lightning flash from which it is formed strikes the ground. These Zebedee stones, so-called from the sons of thunder, John and James, in the New Testament, are crystallizations of a subtle energy, electricity, lightning, grounded into matter. Along with meteorites, these thunderstones, called fulgurites after the thunderbolts forged by Vulcan, have always been considered sacred, as in the Kaaba of Mecca and the *ben-ben* of Heliopolis.

In many ways, Fulcanelli validates our reading of his pattern with this chapter, so filled with cubes and fours, just as one would expect from the fourth *sefirah*. (Kether, as a zero point, has no dimensions. Chokmah, as two or a line, has one; while Binah, three, a plane surface, has two dimensions. Only with Chesed, four, do we arrive at three dimensions, hence the cube.) The section also points to the overall pattern of the stone or cube formed by the middle five sections of this first chapter, reinforcing our supposition about the sword-and-stone design. Fulcanelli is forcing the reader to look for deeper patterns of meaning within ideas that are themselves almost bottomless. At the end of this section, we may not know exactly what the First Matter of the alchemist truly is, but we do know that it is far more comprehensive, and downright cosmic, than we could otherwise have imagined.

Continuing the lightning flash from one side of the Tree to the other, we jump from Chesed to Gevurah, from Mercy to Strength. Again, the discussion in this fifth section, while it focuses on the labyrinth, circles around the attributions of Gevurah—strength, power, Mars, iron, and so on. On the surface, it seems that the labyrinth has little to do with ideas of strength and power. And yet, as we dig deeper into Fulcanelli's clues, we find that the metaphor is very apt indeed.

Fulcanelli tells us that church labyrinths were placed at the intersection of the nave and the transept, and gives us a list of the remaining church labyrinths. He notes the golden rising-sun motif at the center of the Amiens labyrinth in former days, then turns to Chartres. Here he emphasizes the similarity between what is "called in the common tongue La Lieue (the league)," and "Le Lieu (the place)," leaving open the suggestion of far travel in one place, and moves on to the no-longer-extant illustration of Theseus and the Minotaur that occupied the center of the labyrinth. This, he assures us, is "yet another proof of the infiltration of pagan themes into Christian iconography and consequently of an evident mytho-hermetic meaning."

Fine, says the reader, but what meaning?

Fulcanelli sidesteps this by declaring that the whole issue is moot because "it is not a matter of establishing any connection between these images and those famous constructions of antiquity, the labyrinths of Greece and Rome." Why not?

The theme of the Minotaur fits rather well into the concept of Gevurah, Strength and Power, so outright avoidance isn't the answer. It must be that Fulcanelli wants us to focus on a specific kind of labyrinth, not just the broader myths associated with the concept. It is not just Gevurah, but rather one specific aspect of Gevurah, the thread of strength that leads to the rising sun, to which Fulcanelli draws our attention.

He does this by quoting Berthelot's *Grande Encyclopédie* on "the *Labyrinth of Solomon* . . . a cabalistic figure found at the head of certain alchemical manuscripts and which is part of the magic tradition associated with the name of Solomon." This magic image is none other than the ancient seven-turn maze known to humanity in one form or another for thousands of years and that has come to be called the Cretan labyrinth. Fulcanelli declares that this labyrinth is "emblematic of the whole labour of the Work," and, after a long linguistic digression on the meaning of spiders and Ariadne's thread, openly admits that this form of the labyrinth is a version of the philosopher's stone.

The effect of this rather unexpected explication is stunning, for both its directness and its unusually specific focus. Just what is it about this labyrinth that could lead Fulcanelli to make such a pronouncement?

For one thing, the classical seven-turn labyrinth is mankind's oldest complex symbol. We have specific examples that are more than six thousand years old, and, if we accept that the Greek meander is one form of the classic labyrinth, then examples can be found that are almost ten thousand years old. Perhaps the best single-volume work on the labyrinth, Sig Lonegren's *Labyrinths: Ancient Myths and Modern Uses,*[5] suggests that the original use of all labyrinth forms was as a kind of space-time location tool.

Lonegren bases this assumption on the sacred geometry of the Cretan *labrys,* the double-headed-ax symbol of the Goddess. As shown in figure 9.4, by using this pattern, which depends on determining true north and designing the width of the ax head to match the latitude of one's location, it is possible to lay out a design that is correctly aligned to the local lunar and solar year. Of course, this can be done without the addition of the curving and interconnecting lines, which is what makes the *labrys* a labyrinth.

These interconnecting paths are meant to be walked, to be experienced as that long journey in one place—in other words, as a metaphor

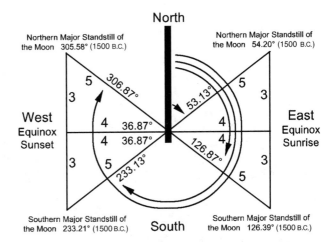

North

Northern Major Standstill of
the Moon 305.58° (1500 B.C.)

Northern Major Standstill of
the Moon 54.20° (1500 B.C.)

Figure 9.4. How the
labrys, here
composed of four
3-4-5 right triangles,
can be used as a
cosmic orientation
device and as the
ground plan for a
seven-turn labyrinth.

West
Equinox
Sunset

East
Equinox
Sunrise

5   306.87°
3
4   36.87°
4   36.87°
3   5   233.13°

5   53.13°
4
4   126.87°
3
5

Southern Major Standstill of
the Moon 233.21° (1500 B.C.)

South

Southern Major Standstill of
the Moon 126.39° (1500 B.C.)

3-4-5 labrys and astronomy at 35° latitude at 1500 B.C.
The ax head becomes wider at more northern latitudes.

for the soul's quest for meaning. The golden dawn at the center of the
Amiens labyrinth is exactly the point. By walking the pattern that orients
you, literally, it is possible to glimpse the rise of the inner sun.

Following the thread of Ariadne into the maze and then returning,
we are reenacting the soul's journey through death and resurrection.
Fulcanelli instructs us that the thread of meaning that navigates the
complex fields of the universal "lodestone," the rising sun behind or
beyond our sun, is the architecture of the Temple of Solomon, an esoteric reference to the planetary six-pointed star found in the center of
the Tree of Life. The philosopher's stone, by implication, is formed of
these seven planetary components, as shown in figure 9.5.

Fulcanelli highlights five of the seven, Jupiter, Mars, the Sun, Venus,
and Mercury, as the stone from which the sword is drawn. Saturn, of
course, is the gnosis expressed collectively by the first three chapters,
the hilt of the sword, while the Moon is represented by the section on
Notre Dame, the sword's point.

Each of these inner five is given, by Fulcanelli, very specific images
related to both the quality of the *sefirot* and the Gothic tradition of the
cathedrals. The cross and cube of Chesed transposed into the headstone
of the corner is obvious when compared to why a labyrinth should represent Gevurah.

Yet sacred geometry is the answer. Each of the planetary qualities,

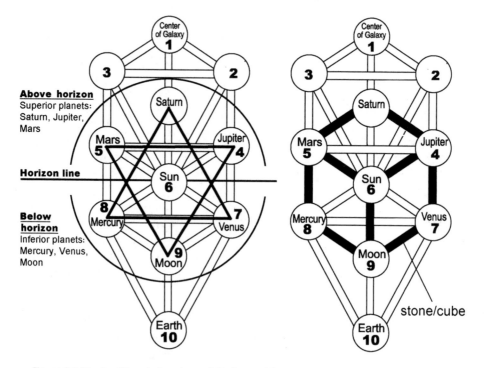

Figure 9.5. The traditional planetary attributions of the *sefirot.*

from Saturn to the Moon, can be given a structural and mathematical form by constructing squares based on their numerical lightning-flash order, so that 3, Binah, is Saturn and forms a three-by-three square (see fig. 9.5). Within this, it is possible to arrange the first nine numbers $(3 \times 3 = 9)$ in a pattern so that each line, horizontal, vertical, and diagonal, adds up to 15.

Magic squares can be formed for each successive number; 4, or Jupiter, is formed of the first sixteen numbers and adds up to 34 in all directions, and so on. There are many different theories about magic squares, all of which are fascinating and insightful to the mystical mathematician as well as to the magician, but Fulcanelli is directing us toward how the magic square constructs the labyrinth.

One of the mathematical theories about magic squares concerns the mirror symmetry of their odd/even patterning. Even-numbered magic squares, Jupiter, the Sun, and Mercury, or 4, 6, and 8, respectively, exhibit hemispherical symmetry where each side is a reflection of the other;

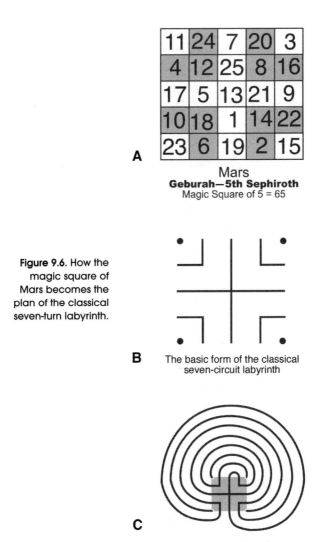

11	24	7	20	3
4	12	25	8	16
17	5	13	21	9
10	18	1	14	22
23	6	19	2	15

A

Mars
Geburah—5th Sephiroth
Magic Square of 5 = 65

Figure 9.6. How the magic square of Mars becomes the plan of the classical seven-turn labyrinth.

B   The basic form of the classical seven-circuit labyrinth

C

whereas the odd squares, Saturn, Mars, Venus, and the Moon, or 3, 5, 7, and 9, respectively, exhibit radial symmetry that is reflected outward from a central point. From this we note that the odd-numbered squares all have central crosses of odd numbers and alternating odd and even numbers in the corners. This pattern of radial symmetry allows us to use the odd-numbered magic squares as templates for the classical labyrinths.

Saturn, which in Fulcanelli is the sum of the first three *sefirot,* is a classical three-circuit labyrinth. Since Jupiter is an even-numbered symmetrical cube, it is Mars, attributed to Gevurah, and the square of Mars that form the exact seven-circuit labyrinth indicated by Fulcanelli (see fig. 9.6c). (To see how this works, take a magic square and lightly color in the even numbers. Then, if you have an odd-numbered magic square, go either to the right or to the left connecting odd numbers to even numbers around the outside of the square. This will form the basic labyrinth pattern.)

Planet	Number	Sefirah	Geometric Pattern
center	1	Kether	0 dimensions: zero point
stars	2	Chokmah	1 dimension: line
Saturn	3	Binah	2 dimensions: plane/3-turn labyrinth
Jupiter	4	Chesed	3 dimensions: tetrahedron/cube
Mars	5	Gevurah	7-turn labyrinth
Sun	6	Tiferet	4th dimension: hypercube
Venus	7	Netzach	11-turn labyrinth
Mercury	8	Hod	hyperoctahedron
Moon	9	Yesod	

Figure 9.7. A table of kabbalistic planetary and numerical relationships.

The magic square of Mars contains the first twenty-five numbers arranged so that every direction adds up to 65. This number is indicative, by means of *gematria,* of both light and Adonai, the Lord, in Hebrew. This suggests that the Mars square is somehow a master pattern of light, which when translated into the classical seven-turn labyrinth becomes the interactive architecture of Solomon's Temple, or, even more exactly, the philosopher's stone.

On the Tree of Life, the path from Gevurah, or Mars, to Tiferet, the Sun, lies through the Sphinx, the sign of Leo, the Hebrew letter *teth,* and the Tarot trump Strength. This turn toward the light, which is the subject of Fulcanelli's next section, follows the thread to the center, the rising sun. But before we move on, we need to look again at Fulcanelli's planetary pattern.

Fulcanelli drops the simplest labyrinth square, that of Saturn, and the most complex and enfolded of the magic-square dimensional patterns, that of the Moon, to focus on Jupiter, a cube; Mars, a seven-turn labyrinth; the Sun, a hypercube; Venus, the eleven-turn labyrinth; and Mercury, a hyperoctahedron (see fig. 9.8). While these hypersymmetry patterns are revealing of an even deeper structural organization, their planetary attributions suggest an actual pattern in the sky, that of a rising sun with Jupiter and Mars above the horizon and Mercury and Venus below.

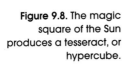

Figure 9.8. The magic square of the Sun produces a tesseract, or hypercube.

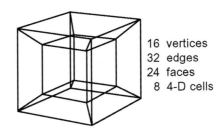

16 vertices
32 edges
24 faces
8 4-D cells

When we see these symbols again, on the Cyclic Cross of Hendaye, we shall find not only the obvious synchronicity of the appropriate alignment of planets, but also the possible meaning of the transformation that they symbolize. We shall also find that the complex geometry of the labyrinth contains the secret of time itself, the ancient technique of celestial projection and orientation symbolized by the eight-rayed star of Isis/Mary. But that is far beyond the level of initiation that Fulcanelli has planned for the reader at this point.

Indeed, at this point, it is enough if the reader grasps the potential importance of the labyrinth and its connections to Mars, the thread of Ariadne leading toward the rising sun of Tiferet, and the sacred geometry of the philosopher's stone. Having made this as clear as we can, let us turn, with Fulcanelli, toward the wondrous light of the rose windows and the *sefirah* of Tiferet, or Splendor.

"All churches," Fulcanelli reminds us, "have their apse turned toward the south-east, their front toward the north-west, while the transepts, forming the arms of the cross, are directed to the north-east and the south-west. That is the invariable orientation, intended in such a fashion that the faithful and profane, entering the church by the west, walk straight to the sanctuary facing the direction in which the sun rises, i.e. the Orient, Palestine, the cradle of Christianity. They leave the shadows and walk towards the light."[6]

In this simple and elegant paragraph, Fulcanelli connects us with the labyrinth he discussed in the previous section, which is oriented according to the same principle, as well as the ancient tradition of temple orientation that extends from the Egyptians to such modern Rosicrucian groups as the hermetic Order of the Golden Dawn. Indeed, a study of the surviving rituals of this late-nineteenth- and early-twentieth-century magical order provides many curious nuggets of the secret tradition. While it is not surprising that a magical order would base its temple space on the orientation of the Gothic cathedrals, what is surprising is that Fulcanelli knows the underlying geometric reasons why both of these "temples" are indeed sacred.

To glimpse this level, it is necessary to return for a moment to our evolving magic-square pattern. We noted that the Sun's square, an even-numbered one, could be considered a hypercube, or fourth-dimensional cube. Its mirror symmetry allows one to fold it through the third dimension and form a cube within a cube of 16 vertices, 32 edges, 24 faces, and 8 four-dimensional cells, as shown in figure 9.8. These numbers, as we shall find in chapter 10, are important to Fulcanelli's explication of the Sun as shown on the Cyclic Cross of Hendaye. A temple based on this hidden geometry would therefore partake of the mystical activity of the sun itself, that of radiating light or illumination.

Fulcanelli then directs our attention to the play of light through the rose windows of the cathedrals, telling us that "the Work unfolds in a circular progression."[7] This progression Fulcanelli associates with the wheel of fire, both physical and psychic. He quotes a seventeenth-century alchemical poem that restates the aphorisms of the Emerald Tablet by advocating the middle way, then declares that "the rose alone represents the action of the fire and its duration," telling us that this "is why the medieval decorators sought in their rose windows to translate the movement of matter, stirred up by the elementary fire"[8] into a temporal organization of light.

This image of the wheel of the year as a wheel of light describes the meaning of Tiferet, which is attributed to the sun, quite well. Fulcanelli emphasizes this by drawing our attention again to the star of Solomon, the philosopher's stone at the heart of the Tree of Life. He directs us to a collection of six-petaled rose windows, ending with "the splendid blue rose of the Sainte-Chapelle,"[9] and then suggests that, "since this sign [the six-pointed star] is of the greatest interest to the alchemist,"[10] it would be wise to examine in detail the star motif. And so, leaving "to the reader the task of making useful comparisons" and "picking out the positive truth,"[11] Fulcanelli turns to the fourth component, the star.

Instead of the clarity and simplicity of the previous section, Fulcanelli builds his seventh section, attributed to Netzach, Victory, out of a series of quotes or descriptions from ancient sources on the Star of Deliverance, our fourth component of the Stone of the Wise. (For the mathematically curious, please note that 7 + 4 = 11, the number of turns in a labyrinth formed from the magic square of Venus, the planet attributed to this *sefirah*.) As Fulcanelli suggested, at the end of the previous section, this star was the one that signaled the Savior's birth, but it is up to the reader to figure out why it has been given this position and attribution.

And so we are presented with the second half of the great conundrum started in section 4. There we saw how a Tree could become a Stone, and now in this section we shall glimpse how that Stone becomes a Star. But the answer to the conundrum is not easy to unravel, even with Fulcanelli's help.

For starters, he gives us thirteen different glimpses of the star motif, as well as one bogus reference of modern origin just to see if we are paying attention. The quotations run from Varro's retelling of the *Aeneid* to Witkowski's description of a stained-glass window in the old church of Saint Jean at Rouen, and seem to suggest a subject much broader than the Star of Bethlehem.

Here are the sources and motifs in the order in which Fulcanelli presents them:

1. Varro: The Star of Venus leads Aeneas to the Land of Grafted Gold, allotted to him by destiny.
2. Gnostic Book of Seth: A people far to the east have a Writing, which tells of the star and the birth of Child, and prescribes the offerings, which should be taken to him at the appropriate time. This prediction was passed from one generation of wise men to the next, who became over time the twelve Magi. Once a generation they gathered in a cave on Mount Victory, where they meditated for three days, waiting on the sign. When it came, it took the form of a small child holding a cross and the instructions to depart for Judea. The rest is in the Bible.
3. Unknown author, apocryphal fragment: Here, the journey lasts thirteen days and the closer the Magi came to Bethlehem the more the star looked like an eagle with a cross above it.

4. Julius Africanus: The scene is a Persian temple built by Cyrus the Great where a star descends to announce the birth of a child, the Beginning and the End, at which all the statues fall down with their faces to the ground as if worshiping the star. The Magi interpret this sign and advise the King to send ambassadors. Bacchus, or Dionysus (of all the gods!), appears and predicts that this new god will drive out the false gods. The Magi depart, and, guided by the star, find Mary and the Child. They have a portrait painted of them, which bears the inscription *"To Jupiter Mithra, to the Sun God, to the Great God, to King Jesus, the Persian Empire makes this dedication."*

5. Saint Ignatius: He tells us that the light of this star outshone all others in the sky and that *"The sun, moon and the stars formed a choir around this star."*

6. Huginus à Barma: This eighteenth-century alchemist who echoes Saint Ignatius by suggesting that the "real earth" of the *prima materia* should be *"well impregnated with the rays of the sun, the moon and the other stars."*

7. Chalcidius: This fourth-century Gnostic who apparently taught Egyptian star magic comments on Ahc, the Egyptian star of bad fortune, then moves onto the Star of Destiny and the Chaldean astronomers.

8. Diodorus of Tarsus: This Greek post-Pythagorean philosopher of the second century who was influenced by Philo and the Hebrew Kabbalists suggests that the star wasn't a real stellar body, but a formation of "urano-diurnal . . . force" that assumed the shape of a star to announce the birth of the Savior.

9. Luke 2:8–14: The angel and the shepherd verses familiar to us from our childhood Christmas stories.

10. Matthew 2:1–2, 7–11: The familiar gifts of the Magi story.

11. Numbers 23:8, 24:17: The famous Star out of Jacob verses from Balaam the prophet of Mesopotamia, land of the Chaldeans.

12. Triptych of the Virgin at Larmor: The central panel showing the Virgin surrounded by the sun, moon, and a nimbus of stars, while holding a large eight-rayed star in her right hand, suggests, as Fulcanelli says, the *stella maris* of the Catholic hymn.

13. Witkowski's description of a lost stained glass at Rouen shows us a stellar conception attended by the planetary deities.

Now, let us do as Fulcanelli directs, and make useful comparisons that will allow us to pick out the positive truth.

1. The Star of Venus tells us that we have the correct *sefirah* and the Land of Grafted Gold suggests exile and lost homeland themes.

2. Mount Victory again points to the correct attribution, while the story of the Magi introduces the number twelve and, by extension, thirteen when the sign is given. From the Last Supper to the Round Table, this pattern will repeat time after time.

3. The apocryphal fragment echoes the thirteen and points to the star as being in the old constellation of Scorpio, symbolized as an eagle with a cross as the stinger of the current scorpion.

4. Dei Helios is really the Great Sun, or the sun behind the sun, which was seen to control the Great Year of the precession, while mention of Dionysus points to the shamanic roots of Christianity as an ecstatic mystery religion. The image of Mary and child is also suggestive of Isis and Horus, whose cult was contemporary to that of Dionysus.

5. In this snippet, Isis is clearly identified as the center of the galaxy, with the sun and moon and stars forming a choir around her.

6. This alchemical quote suggests the closeness in process between that of the center of the galaxy and the very basis of alchemy.

7. Chalcidius suggests that the same Star of Destiny can be either good or bad, as the Egyptians knew.

8. Diodorus seems to be saying that this stellar sign is not quite what we would think of as a star, but some form of periodic subtle energy outburst.

9. Here's the good news behind the Gnostic incarnation of Jesus. Matter can be redeemed by an infusion of divine glory, symbolized by the babe born at the cusp of Leo and Virgo.

10. Our familiar story of the Three Kings of the Orient, the Wise Men of the East whose astronomical observations led them to the birth of the Savior.

11. Balaam's prediction of the Star of Jacob and the scepter out of Israel is very interesting as it is the first messianic prediction in the Old Testament. Balaam of course is not a Hebrew, but a priest or Magi of the god Baal, the God Most High, the old

dragon constellation coiled around the still point of the universe, the north ecliptic pole.

12. The Virgin identified with Mary, Isis, and the star of the sea.
13. A glimpse of a Tantric or alchemical procedure for creating a star child.

Having found our nuggets of "positive truth," what can we make of Fulcanelli's message in this section?

An ancient group of astronomical adepts, the Magi, watched the skies for the sign, which seems to be a new starlike eruption of light in the region of Scorpio's crosslike tail, near or at the center of our galaxy. When the sign comes, the Magi travel to acknowledge the Savior and find Mother Isis/Mary and her child. They acknowledge her as the center of the galaxy and her child as the source of the new light, known in the past only to the Magi and the shamans. This new light is linked to the alchemcial process and the Tantric star-child in particular, while a hint is given that the whole secret can be found in the ancient astronomies of Egypt, Canaan, and Mesopotamia.

The quotations also suggest, by their number, an esoteric thirteen-sign zodiac, one that is oriented toward the center of the galaxy between Scorpio and Sagittarius. This gives us a distinctly different, and quite ancient, view of the universe, echoes of which remain in modern superstitions such as the unlucky Friday, Venus' day, the thirteenth. This chapter is Fulcanelli's clearest example yet of the initiatory quality inherent in his presentation of the material. By forcing the reader to think and sort through the star myths, Fulcanelli is pushing the reader into an altered state of awareness. Suddenly, the universe looks quite different, older and more significant.

And, the careful reader will note, we are far from what is normally considered alchemy. The next section, taking us deeper into the *prima materia*, only reinforces this sense of strangeness. Alchemy, as Fulcanelli reveals it to us, is very far indeed from the vain lab work of the puffers.

"Just as the human soul has its hidden recesses, so the cathedral has its secret passages." Fulcanelli guides us through the *crypt*, a word from the same Greek root as Venus and *copper*, of the cathedrals to the secret hiding place of Isis, the Black Virgin. He quotes the "learned Pierre Dujols" that this Black Virgin is an "astronomical theogany," the Mother of the Gods, the Great Idea, as the stone at Die informs us, and then states that the esoteric meaning of the Black Virgin could not be better defined. *Theogany*, however, is a curious word, suggesting a blend of meaning. A *theogony* (as in Hesiod) is an account of the birth of the gods or a genealogy of the gods, while a *theogamy* is a marriage of the gods, a version of the *hieros gamos*. The original French *theogany* suggests both of these, implying a genealogy of the union of earth and sky. Using this odd word in conjunction with the Die stone and its associations with Cybele and the stone that fell from heaven suggests that both Fulcanelli and Dujols were aware of the tradition we have examined above.

In the mention of Dujols here, we are tempted to see a clever tip of the hat from pseudonym to real person, or from teacher to student, but however we read the personalities, the meaning is clear. The Black Virgin is a symbol of an ancient "astronomical theogany," centered on the mystery of the heavenly stone. In hermetic symbolism, Fulcanelli informs us, this "theogany" is "the *virgin earth,* which the artist must choose as the *subject* of his Great Work." He quotes an unreferenced text on the *"black substance,"* one of the few occasions when Fulcanelli

Figure 9.9. The Black Virgin of Saint Victor's in Marseilles. (Plate 1 in *Le Mystère des cathédrales*)

does something so unscholarly, and then hurries on to a list of the surviving Black Virgins.

Since Ean Begg's masterly opus on the subject covers all of the Black Virgins listed by Fulcanelli, we shall merely refer the reader to his work. Fulcanelli lists seven famous Black Virgins: two at Chartres; one at Puy; one, illustrated, from Saint Victor's in Marseilles (fig. 9.9); one each at Rocamadour and Vichy; and one at Quimper. He then mentions the Black Virgin seen by Camille Flammarion in the crypt of the Observatory, and called Our Lady Underground, in order to round out his eight.

Fulcanelli then shifts to the very ancient statues of Isis mentioned by Witkowski and formerly found at Metz and Lyons. From there, he launches into an examination of the "cult of Isis, the Egyptian Ceres." This he equates, with no more reference than a quote from Herodotus, to the hermetic sciences. He divides the order into four degrees that are suggestive on many levels. Fulcanelli, however, seems to be using insider information here, information whose source, probably because of an oath, he cannot reveal. He wants us to note the egg, "the symbol of the world," and the four degrees of initiation represented by the Sun, Moon, Mercury, and hierophant, and tries in the next paragraph to give us some glimpse of their meaning.

In many, many ways, this is the most important single paragraph in Fulcanelli's entire book. He begins by directing us back to the stone at Die, which labeled Isis as the mother of the gods, whom he identifies with Rhea or Cybele. From there, he takes us to a village church in the Camargue where until 1610 a bas-relief featuring Cybele and with an inscription reading MATRI DEUM could be seen. Then he jumps to Phrygia, where the Goddess was worshipped as a black stone that fell from heaven, echoing the *lapsit exillis* of Wolfram's *Parzival*. He tells us that she was also worshipped seated between two lions, holding a key as if to draw back her veil with it. These images, piled on top of the other images in this chapter and so far in the first chapter, compel us to look at the whole subject of esotericism, hermeticism, Christianity, and religion in general in a wholly unique light, as we have seen in the earlier chapters of this book.

Following the clues he gave us, we have come to a surprising answer. Alchemy, the sword in the stone, and the Tree of Life all have to do with universal or cosmological forces whose origins seem to be in the patterns of the heavens themselves. Fulcanelli is leading us into ever-deeper symbolic waters while very subtly building a solid ground of understanding beneath us. In this first section, he is laying the metaphysical underpinning upon which he will erect, in the rest of the book, his edifice of Gothic understanding. This will become even clearer as we turn to the last section in the chapter, which represents the ninth *sefirah,* Yesod, or Foundation, attributed to the Moon. For Fulcanelli, the foundation of his metaphysical system is the Gothic church, the exemplar of which is the Philosophers' Church, Notre-Dame-de-Paris.

And for those of you waiting for Fulcanelli to make explicit the connection between the Black Virgin and the *sefirah* Hod, or the planet Mercury, you may relax. Fulcanelli cites eight Black Virgins and mentions Mercury in his discussion of the mysteries of Ceres, just to let us know that he hasn't forgotten his pattern, but he never otherwise makes the connection apparent.

However, if we remember that in Egyptian myth, Isis learned magic from Thoth/Hermes, the Egyptian Mercury, then connection becomes the information itself, the secret language of the Magi. As we explore Fulcanelli's evolving pattern on the Tree of Life, we shall see this meaning for Hod become even clearer. In this usage, Fulcanelli will examine the nature of the Philosophic Mercury and its role in the formation of the first matter. But that is still to come, and for now Fulcanelli is content to have us focused on Isis as we turn to the church of Our Lady.

Fulcanelli opens the last section of his first chapter by telling us that "having disposed of these preliminaries," he will now turn to a hermetic examination of one specific cathedral, Notre-Dame-de-Paris. However, he warns us that his task will be difficult, because, unlike the medieval students of the Art, the modern hermeticist must deal with the ravages of both time and vandalism.

This is a complex section, in which the motif is clearly the foundation of the church, in several different meanings of the word, from the eleven-step foundation upon which the church was built to the foundation of its Gothic art in the spirituality of the High Middle Ages. Mixed in with this subtle foundational imagery is Fulcanelli's nod to the whole sword-in-the-stone pattern, along with an examination of two statues that no longer grace the cathedral front.

The first of these stood above the fountain in the parvis of Notre Dame, the street in front of the cathedral. Fulcanelli describes it as "a tall, narrow stone statue, holding a book in one hand and a snake in the other." He quotes the inscription on the now lost statue: *"You, who are thirsty, come hither: if, by chance the fountain fails / The goddess has, by degrees, prepared the everlasting waters."* He also tells us that the common people called it "Monsieur Legris (Mr. Grey)" or "the *Fasting Man of Notre Dame."*

Fulcanelli turns to Amédée de Ponthieu, a nineteenth-century folk-lore scholar, to explain the meaning of this fountain. This is odd, because, as Fulcanelli admits, Amédée is no hermeticist. However, the good folklorist collected the very ancient insights that Fulcanelli needed to convey. He tells us that the statue was called the *Son of Apollo, Phoebigenus,* as well as the *Master Peter,* "meaning *master stone, stone of power."* Amédée lists the various identities proposed for the statue, including "Esculapius, Mercury, or the god Terminus," "Archambaud, Mayor of the Palace" in Merovingian times, Guillaume de Paris, the master mason of Notre Dame, and even Christ and Saint Geneviève, the patron saint of Paris.

Amédée also informs us that the statue was removed when the square was enlarged in 1748. The interesting point is that Fulcanelli does not tell us his source for the inscription on the fountain. Amédée seems not to have mentioned it, since none of his suggestions is a goddesses. So, we are left with the small mystery of how Fulcanelli knew of the inscription. From small mysteries such as this, we shall find that the larger mystery of Fulcanelli himself can be unraveled. However, when that mystery is resolved, we shall find that "Fulcanelli" has left us with even larger questions, even greater mysteries, yet to be answered.

From the statue and the fountain, Fulcanelli turns to another lost figure, that of Saint Christopher, which stood with its back to the first pillar on the right as one entered the nave until its destruction in 1781. He tells us of other *Saint Christophers* removed around the same time, and suggests the ones that remain do so only because they are either a fresco or a part of the wall. He concludes that behind such acts "there must obviously have been powerful motives."

Fulcanelli speculates that this reason could have been related to the statues' hermetic symbolism. He reveals the primitive name of Saint Christopher, Offerus, with its echoes of Orpheus the Gnostic Greek Christ, and then goes on to tell us that this Christopher, *"he who carries Christ"* to the masses, is also "Chrysopher," or *"he who carries gold"* to the hermeticist. And then Fulcanelli adds a few sentences in green-language code that go to the heart of the matter.

"From this one can better understand the extreme importance of the symbol of St. Christopher. It is the hieroglyph of the *solar sulphur* (Jesus), of the *nascent gold,* raised on the mercurial waters and then carried, by the proper energy of this Mercury, to the degree of power possessed by the Elixir."

In these lines, we shall find by the end of our quest that Fulcanelli has not only explained the secret of the alchemical transformation, but also pointed in very direct language at the true meaning and history of Christianity. The key, of course, is the meaning and origin of the Saint Christopher myth. Fulcanelli will return to this topic later in the book, when we see that the Saint Christopher myth is actually part of a much larger, galactic-scale, in fact, cosmological myth. For now, though, Fulcanelli gives us one more spin on the Saint Christopher motif.

He draws our attention to an ancient statue at Rocamadour in Brittany, a Saint Christopher high on the Saint-Michel heights guarding an old chest out of which protrudes a broken sword chained to the rock. He tells us that this is an example of all the ancient sword-in-the-stone myths, validating our design supposition while expanding the concept to include all sorts of rod-and-stone motifs, from Moses to Atalanta the Amazon's javelin. They are all "the same hieroglyph of this hidden matter of the Philosophers, whose nature is indicated by St. Christopher and the result by the iron-bound chest."

Fulcanelli ends the chapter with an attack on the Renaissance, and Francis I in particular, while looking back with longing on the splendor of the Middle Ages. "From the twelfth to the fifteenth century, there was poverty of media, but a wealth of expression; from the sixteenth century onwards, art has shown beauty of form, but mediocrity of invention." He instructs us that Renaissance art exalts the senses and the ego, while in Gothic art "the actual execution remains subordinate to the idea; in Renaissance art, it dominates and obliterates the idea."

And to Fulcanelli, this split is the cause of all the artistic and political chaos that has since been the lot of mankind. In these paragraphs, however, we shall find that there is more than just a romantic theory of art. There is also the germ of a clue to the political upheavals that produced the Renaissance. But that is a subject for later. For now, let us agree with Fulcanelli that the world is indeed impoverished by the loss of such wisdom and skill, such understanding and execution, as was once lavished on the Gothic cathedrals.

THE ALCHEMY OF LIGHT: FULCANELLI'S KABBALAH

The Etz Chaim, the Tree of Life from the *Bahir* and the *Sefer Yetzirah,* can be seen as the prototypical kabbalistic pattern, a sort of symbolic geometry (see fig. 9.10). In *Le Mystère,* Fulcanelli shows us this by his arrangement of chapters and sections and the images within those sections. Fulcanelli gives us four chapters in the first edition: "The Mystery of the Cathedrals," "Paris," "Amiens," and "Bourges." These represent the four worlds, or levels of abstraction, and a Tree of Life, or a part of one, forms in each world.

The first chapter, "The Mystery of the Cathedrals," contains nine internal sections, as we saw above, each of which can be attributed to one of the *sefirot* from Kether to Yesod. This first tree is the kabbalistic Divine World, Atzilut, where the theory of creation is displayed. Interestingly enough, Fulcanelli's thematic breaks in this section, while evolving the *sefirot* in the basic lightning-path order (see figures 9.4 and

The Etz Chaim

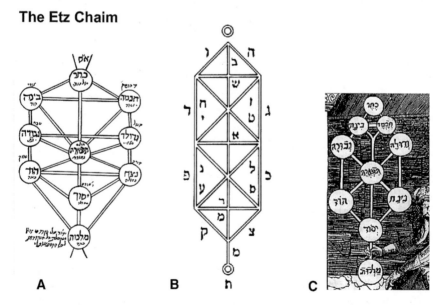

Figure 9.10. Three different versions of the Etz Chaim, the Tree of Life. *A.* from a fifteenth-century manuscript of the *Zohar; B.* from the *Sefer Yetzirah,* nineteenth century; *C.* from a fifteenth-century woodcut.

9.5), divides naturally into a sword-in-the-stone pattern. The first three sections form the hilt, the next five compose the stone, and the continuation of thought from section 1 straight through into section 9 creates the blade of the sword.

The next chapter, "Paris," creates an entire Tree of Life, with the addition of an image from the first chapter, the Black Madonna, in the position of Binah. This arrangement, as we shall see, is a clue to the astronomical nature of this archetypal Tree of Life. On a projected or celestial Tree of Life, the earth's pole is tilted toward Binah—the Dark Mother of the Cosmic Sea in kabbalistic symbology—hence its importance in Fulcanelli's design. He continues the pattern with the Kether image Alchemy from the main porch at Notre Dame and the Chokmah image of the alchemist from the south tower. These three images form the top three *sefirot*, the Supernatural Triad, and then, quite appropriately, Fulcanelli creates a break to represent the abyss of Daat, or gnosis.

He starts over at the bottom, at the foot of the Path of Return, the Serpent's Path back up the Tree. Plates 4 through 25, discussed in the "Paris" chapter of *Le Mystère*, represent the paths on the Tree, the letters of the Hebrew alphabet, and the trumps of the Tarot, and are attributed to the twenty-two individual letter paths that connect the *sefirot* listed above. Their pattern is the classical Path of Return, pictured as a snake winding its way up the Tree (see fig. 9.11). For example, plate 4, called "The mysterious Fountain at the foot of the Old Oak," is attributed to the letter *tau* and the Tarot image The World, linking the pilgrimage and persecution of the Kingdom, Malkuth, with the foundational symbology of Notre-Dame-de-Paris and with heraldry, the Grail legends, and the philosophical dew in the *sefirah* of Yesod. Filling in the rest of the Tree with these symbols reveals the ongoing alchemical process of creation.

With plate 26, the *sefirot* pattern picks up with Daat, the gnosis of the abyss, and proceeds down the Tree to plate 32, an image of the Massacre of the Innocents from Saint-Chapelle, appropriate for Malkuth considering what happened to the Gnostic current in the West. Fulcanelli has here provided us with a very clear and direct image of the entire thirty-two components of the classical Etz Chaim symbology (see fig. 9.12). In terms of worlds, this second level is the archetypal Briah, or the World of Ideas. Fulcanelli demonstrates this by including an almost complete idea Tree at this level. Our inspiration, of course,

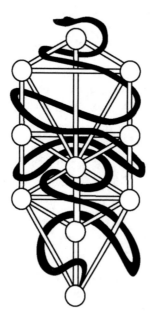

Figure 9.11. The Serpent's Path or Path of Return up the Tree of Life.

Binah or the Black Isis Madonna, comes across from the realm of the Divine.

The next level or world is Yetzirah, the World of Formation or the etheric world. This is the level of the astral or spiritual world so beloved of shamans and mystics of all sorts. Fulcanelli shows great restraint by describing only part of the etheric Tree. He focuses on the seven planetary intelligences and their influence on alchemy. In these seven images, six shown and one mentioned only in the text, Fulcanelli gives us clues to the operational nature of the work. The unshown image is the hidden sun, the mythical sun behind the sun, and the formative images all seem to show how this hidden or Dark Sun affects the planetary intelligences. Since these intelligences are also attributed to the seven metals, there does indeed seem to be a vast operational secret contained in these images.

Once this multiple Tree of Life pattern is built up from the sections of the first chapter and the plates from Notre Dame and Amiens, with a few extra additions from Sainte-Chapelle, Saint Victor, and elsewhere, an understanding of the basic process of astro-alchemy can be gleaned. This is the real secret, and from Fulcanelli's point of view there is no mystery about it. But once this secret is revealed, Fulcanelli goes on to propose a fourth Tree of Life that neatly ties the historical, mythological, and cosmological elements into one coherent framework.

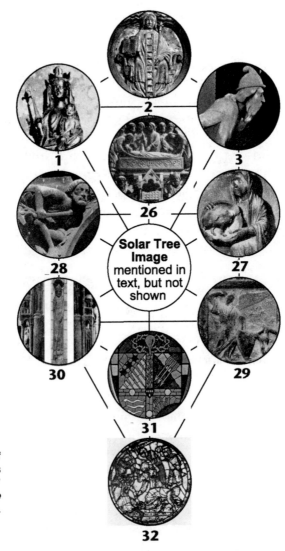

Figure 9.12. The Tree of Life illustrated with plates from Fulcanelli's "Paris" chapter in *Le Mystère des cathédrales.*

DAAT IMAGES

26
Planetary Metals

33
Wheel of Fire

46
The Credence

This fourth Tree of Life pattern represents the world of action, our world of stars and suns and planets. This Tree of Life grows out of Bourges in Berry. Fulcanelli ignores the town's Gothic cathedral, with its stunning apocalyptic stained glass, and concentrates on two contemporaries of Good King René in the mid-fifteenth century, Jacques Coeur and Jean Lallemant, and their respective houses. This is a significant departure; up to this point Fulcanelli has focused exclusively on cathedrals. This departure signals the shift from the theoretical and mystical to the operational. Here we are firmly in the world of action. (See appendix D for a complete outline of Fulcanelli's four Trees.)

Fulcanelli is pointing us toward a moment in the late fifteenth century when the underground stream at last broke the surface of history. He suggests that the mystery of Bourges is the mystery of the esoteric current in the ancient past, the present of the fifteenth century, and the future down to and beyond the twentieth century. The mystery of initiation encompasses a vast reach of time, Fulcanelli insists, but the strands of the tapestry emerged into a pattern at Bourges in the mid-1400s.

Fulcanelli directs our attention toward eight images in the two houses. Two are from Jacques Coeur's house (plates 39 and 40) and six are from Lallemant (plates 41–46). They can be analyzed as two images that establish both individuals as alchemists, the scallop shell and the vessel of the Great Work; three historical and mythological themes, Tristan and Isolde, the Golden Fleece, and Saint Christopher; and three initiatory images from the inner sanctum of Lallemant mansion, the pillars, the ceiling, and the credence of the chapel.

Even this simple pattern reveals groups of threes within threes. The first of the three groups of symbols shows us that Jacques Coeur was a pilgrim, a fellow traveler, but Jean Lallemant was the operating agent with the vessel of the Great Work. The role of grand master, however, is undefined. We are left with the impression that a third personality exists, made conspicuous by his absence. Who was he?

The next of the three groupings reinforces this impression. Here we are met with three narrative images, symbolic stories balanced on that fine line between history and mythology. There is a core of reality to these tales, even when we are aware of their mythological elements. But, on the surface, there is nothing to connect the love story of Tristan and Isolde with the ancient Greek legend of the Golden Fleece, and both seemingly have nothing in common with the Christian legend of Saint Christopher and the very heavy Christ child. And yet Fulcanelli presents the simple but overwhelming evidence from their own houses that these masters of the subtle art, the green language itself, placed the utmost importance on these three myths. What do these three stories have in common?

Of course, the third mystery grows out of the first two: Just what were these initiations designed to reveal?

The answer to that is the ultimate secret, the secret of time itself. In the second edition of *Le Mystère,* Fulcanelli provides the solution by adding a chapter on the Cyclic Cross of Hendaye. The three images that illustrate that new chapter, the plates numbered 47, 48, and 49, added to the eight of Bourges, plates 39 through 46, complete the *sefirot* of the fourth Tree of Life, including Daat, Gnosis or Knowledge. This Tree, as appropriate to the world of action, reveals the cosmological underpinnings of the entire hermetic philosophy of astro-alchemy. The final image in the group, plate 49, the Tympanum of Saint Trophime at Arles, completes the circle, both symbolically and on the ground, returning us once again to the ancient Grail city of the Argonauts.

There is also a threefold pattern reflected in the design of the whole book. The first secret, the Tree of Life itself, is formed from the sword-in-the-stone pattern of the nine sections in chapter 1. They form a framework for the *sefirot,* which is then amplified and deepened by the images from Notre Dame. To this is added the third level, the planetary seals from Amiens cathedral. The next threefold pattern is the mystery of Bourges outlined above. The last grouping of three is the three inter-locking cycles of the Hendaye cross, their symbolic reflection on the cathedral at Arles, and finally the three dragon axes in the sky that form the triple alignment of the galactic Great Cross.

This compounding of threes, $3 \times 3 \times 3$, or 3 cubed, equals 27, presents us with the key number in the precessional cycle, the core of the secret hidden behind the Christianized INRI, whose letters in Hebrew add up to 270 (see chapter 11 for more on the significance of 270). From this brief explication of the mystery at the heart of *The Mystery of the Cathedrals,* it is possible to glimpse the genius and coherence of this very guarded and hermetic masterpiece. The message is the medium, language contains its own gnosis, and initiation truly is, as the Grail legends declare, the ability to ask the correct questions.

As we unravel the triple weave of this hermetic tapestry, we shall discover the answer to all of our questions, and in doing so experience a glimpse of a very different reality. Fulcanelli, whoever he was, wrote as the last initiate: not as the one who puts the light out as he leaves, but as the one who makes sure that the eternal flame is burning brightly in some lost corner of Plato's cave. What we have discovered in the course of this book of our own past, our spiritual heritage, and the hope of human evolution is due to his guidance and insight. Without the help of someone who knew, and could prove it, the mystery might never have been unveiled.

Let us turn now to the master for his summation of the secret that the design contains. Fulcanelli, in the Bourges chapter of *Le Mystère,* called the credence, plate 46, a "temple in miniature." Indeed, when we compare it to the facade of the cathedral of Saint Trophime in Arles, we can see that both pieces of symbolic architecture are built on the same plan. Since Fulcanelli also declares that "this credence itself bears the alchemical imprint, the details of which I have merely tried to describe in this work," we have another opportunity to test our Tree of Life hypothesis.[12]

When we superimpose the Tree of Life on the credence, as shown in figure 9.13, we find that it matches perfectly. The three fiery pome-

Figure 9.13. The enigmatic credence from Lallemant mansion the with the Tree of Life superimposed.

granates of the pediment, which Fulcanelli informs us "confirm the triple action of a single procedure," are the three upper *sefirot*, Kether, Chokmah, and Binah. The capitals of the pillars are Chesed and Gevurah and the feet are Hod and Netzach. The center niche is Tiferet, here displaced upward and focused on the rising-sun/scallop-shell motif above the inscription. The bottom step represents the foundation of Yesod and the greenery below it symbolizes Malkuth. The three pillars of the Tree are clearly delineated. The middle pillar is curiously focused on the rising sun of Tiferet, with another larger, inner sun—"fire above the abyss," as the I Ching puts it—rising above the ledge attributed to Daat. The ornamentation in this space suggests the geometry found on another Daat image given by Fulcanelli, that of the Planetary Metals from Notre-Dame-de-Paris, which is plate 26 (see fig. 8.5).

The facade of the cathedral of Saint Trophime in Arles also matches the pattern (fig. 9.14). Built in the mid-twelfth century as Notre-Dame-de-Paris rose from the ruins of the Carolingian cathedral, Saint Trophime's Tree of Life is rich and complex with interwoven metaphors peculiar to Provence and its early Christians. Saint Trophime actually has

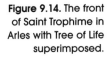

Figure 9.14. The front of Saint Trophime in Arles with Tree of Life superimposed.

two Trees collapsed into one, showing the "portal" grade in which the initiate passes into the Grail Castle. The facade itself contains a Tree, with Daat at the upper arch, inside a larger Tree, which displaces Daat upward and onto a columned window. Clearly, the "portal" is the passage through Daat, the true door of Christ as Abbot Suger described it. The facade of Saint Trophime is indeed a hermetic trophy of great price.

Most Gothic facades are based on this simple, collapsed Tree of Life principle. The two towers of Saint-Denis or Notre-Dame-de-Paris represent the two pillars of the Tree, with the middle pillar beyond Tiferet displaced backward toward the central spire (fig. 9.15). This suggests that when walking into the cathedral, one is navigating the "portal" between the worlds.

We can see this clearly if we think of stretching out the facade over the floor so that the western rose window, the Tiferet *sefirah*, is above the labyrinth on the nave in the center of the cathedral. In addition, the basic shape of the cathedral, as Fulcanelli reminds us, is that of an ankh, the Egyptian symbol of life. As some of Fulcanelli's readers were

Figure 9.15. The Tree of Life superimposed on the facade of Notre-Dame-de-Paris.

aware, the ankh is the only form of cross that contains all the *sefirot* on the Tree of Life without rearranging their pattern.

In this symbolic approach, the cathedral is a way to walk through the portal—the True Light of the Christ's door—and between the worlds. The vertical facade orients the wise to the transition, while the horizontal pattern inside evokes a response whether one is aware of the technique or not. From above, Notre Dame looks like nothing so much as an ankh with a roselike spire blossoming from the central Tiferet junction. This spire, of course, seen from the front is the middle pillar from Tiferet to Kether. These are not accidental metaphors; they show a basic symbolical harmony designed by someone who knew the geometry of the Tree of Life.

Fulcanelli informs us that "this credence itself bears the alchemical imprint, the details of which I have merely tried to describe in this work," and we have found that not only does the credence bear this alchemical imprint of the kabbalistic Tree, but so does the design of the cathedrals themselves. Once the concept is grasped, however, it makes one wonder why anyone of the intelligence of Canseliet and friends would try to deny the kabbalistic connections.

In the original edition of *Le Mystère*, Fulcanelli closed his study of hermetic symbolism "by analyzing a curious and strangely rare specimen," our "temple in miniature," the enigmatic credence. From this we may assume that he intended his remarks to be a summary of the entire work. As usual, however, his approach is somewhat oblique.

After drawing our attention to the Golden Fleece bas-relief, which, he tells us, "could have served as a guide," he jumps to the scallop shells on each pillar of the credence. These he identifies as symbolic of the Philosophic Mercury, while connecting them with the wings and trident of Neptune. He calls our attention to the two dolphins and the three fiery pomegranates. With that, he leaves off describing the other details of the credence and moves on to interpreting the inscription. In that interpretation can be found the essential clues to the nature of astro-alchemy and its secret.

Working backward from Fulcanelli's comment on chiliasm in the Hendaye chapter, we have unraveled a new perspective on alchemy and its relationship with eschatologies such as chiliasm. Can we now confirm our speculations from Fulcanelli's guarded and symbolic words?

Indeed we can. At the very beginning of his discussion of

Lallemant's credence, Fulcanelli insists on the same triple transformation that we found at the heart of the alchemical process. "Thanks to this simple arrangement [the RERE pattern from the Lallemant credence], I can already find a clue in the three repetitions of one and the same technique," Fulcanelli instructs us. "Furthermore, the three fiery pomegranates of the pediment confirm this triple action of a single procedure," he continues, "in order to achieve the three philosophical works, according to the doctrine of Geber."

The reference to Geber, or ibn Jabir, introduces the idea of the three alchemical principles, Salt, Sulfur, and Mercury. Fulcanelli expands this concept to cover the triple transformation of the entire ancient Gnostic science. "The first operation," he tells us, "leads primarily to the Sulphur, a medicine of the first order." We can see this as the inner yogic alchemical process. "The second operation," Fulcanelli states, "completely similar to the first, provides the Elixir, or medicine of the second order, which differs from Sulphur only in quality, not in nature."[13]

This second or outer transformation follows the same pattern as the inner transformation, and is not different in nature. The transmutation of metals is the demonstration of the inner transformation. The quality of the transformation is projected outward onto matter by the nature— "Only Nature can overcome nature," Isis the Prophetess reminds us— of the transformative process itself.

"Finally, the third operation, carried out like the two former ones, produces the Philosophic Stone, the medicine of the third order, which contains all the virtues and perfections of the Sulphur and the Elixir, multiplied in power and extent," Fulcanelli instructs us. The third transformation is the transformation of time itself, and it is, as Fulcanelli points out, carried out like the others. Calling this transformation the Philosophic Stone takes us directly back to the *Bahir*, where the universe is described as the "Precious Stone in the Sea of Wisdom." The transformation of time contains "the virtues and perfections" of the other two transformations, as Fulcanelli insists, and it is definitely greater in power and extent.[14]

Fulcanelli closes the discussion by pointing to another symbol on the ceiling of the strange little room. "If anyone asks, in addition, what this triple operation consists of, whose results I have shown, and how it is carried out, I would refer the investigator to the bas-relief on the ceiling, which shows a pomegranate being roasted in a certain vase."

"Pomegranate" describes the internal alchemy, "roasted" is the action of projecting the transformation, and "vase," as we shall see, is a metaphor for all three transformations at once. This vase is, in fact, nothing less than the Holy Grail itself.[15]

Next, Fulcanelli turns to the clues we used above to unravel the mystery of the inscription. As we saw, his rebus of RERE matches the idea of Light shining in and then light, internally derived, shining out again. He describes this as "a double occult property, exactly equilibrated, from nature (the Light) and from art (the light)." Fulcanelli tells us that he would like to be as clear "about the explanation of the second term RER, but I am not allowed to tear down the veil of mystery concealing it." Fulcanelli tells us that RER contains "a vitally important secret, referring to the vase of the work." He insists that the creation of this Philosopher's Vase is the only way to gain "the slightest success in the Work."[16] Fulcanelli is here constrained by his vow to the secret society from which he learned these important truths. And so we come face-to-face with the proof of the existence of those who know. He strains the boundaries of his oath by making his warnings: "Do not, therefore, undertake anything until you have received the light on this eggshell, which the masters of the Middle Ages called the *secretum secretorum* (secret of secrets)."

"What then is this RER?" Fulcanelli asks rhetorically. He then gives us a lesson in chemical symbology. In arsenic sulfide, he asks, which is the sulfur and which is the arsenic? This alchemical koan provokes in us the realization required to light the inner lamp, the fusion of inner and outer symbolized by the transformation of time.

Fulcanelli gives us more advice. Seek the vessel or vase first, and then the flow of Light will be easily recognized. Pushing the boundary of his oath, Fulcanelli goes on to tell us that according to the Sybil, a philosopher, an alchemist, is "a man who knows how to make glass."[17]

"Therefore make your vase, then your compound; seal it with care, in such a way that no spirit can escape; heat the whole according to the art until it is calcinated. Return the pure part of the powder obtained to your compound, which you will seal up in the same vase. Repeat for the third time and do not give me any thanks." Fulcanelli insists that he is "but a beacon on the great highway of the esoteric Tradition."

With this outburst of what seems to be clarity, Fulcanelli ends his original tour of hermetic symbolism. He expresses his gratitude to the virtually unknown author of these works, Jean Lallemant, who, "following the example of the great Adepts of the Middle Ages, . . . preferred to entrust to stone, rather than to vellum, the undeniable evidence of an immense science, of which he possessed all the secrets." Fulcanelli places Lallemant in the first rank of alchemists, along with Geber, Roger Bacon, and Basil Valentine, and above them in his modesty and sincerity. He also tells us that Lallemant was a Knight of the Round Table, a curious title for an alchemist, until we considered the importance of the Grail Stone.[18]

We began our research on the basis of a remark in the Hendaye chapter, which chapter was not included in the first edition. Without the clue of the connection between alchemy and chiliasm, Fulcanelli's original big finale is impossibly obscure. In the end, we are left hanging, having heard the voice of an initiate whose words remain occult.

We can only guess that Fulcanelli fulfilled his oath to the secret society that taught him. Between the 1920s and the 1950s something happened, and someone was instructed to reveal the secret. The decision being made, Canseliet was apparently dispatched with the final clue, the Cyclic Cross of Hendaye.

So, how does a Tree become a Stone and then a Star?

Simple. The eternal polar axis of our celestial sphere, whose equator is the sun's apparent motion against the stars, or the zodiac, forms the middle pillar of a cosmic Tree of Life. This Tree is also found within our bodies, and when we align these Trees and project them outward on the celestial sphere, we create a jeweled sphere, the Precious Stone of the Wise, in which forms the Cube of Space. The Tree has become a Stone.

The next step, from Stone to Star, requires the transformation of light. Aligned properly, the Precious Stone can tell us the quality of time and the physics of creation. Internalized, this projected alignment leads to bursts of light, flashes of kundalini. If the process is supported by dark retreat and sudden light immersion, then it is possible that the entire body could be transformed. Something similar seems to have happened in the case of Padmasambhava, the Tantric master who brought Buddhism to Tibet in the eighth century.

The Tree of Life unites our universe across vast scales of existence. When we identify with that immensity, we expand as we try to encompass it all. The flash of gnosis is the result, and from that, if we are lucky, comes the science of alchemy. Fulcanelli has given us excellent guidance on the alchemical and initiatory process. He shows us how the initiation worked in the past, and points, as we shall see in chapter 11, toward the mass initiation that may be unavoidable in our future. When Isis, the Great Cosmic Womb of the Galaxy, gives birth to the new Horus Light of transformation, let us hope that we have all solved the riddle of becoming a star.

Omnia quia sunt, lumina sunt. "All that is, is Light."

PART FIVE

Hendaye's Message: The Season of Catastrophe and the Place of Refuge

For it is by fire and in fire that our hemisphere will soon be tried.
And just as, by means of fire, gold is separated from impure metals,
so, Scripture says, the good will be separated from the
wicked on the great Day of Judgment. . . .
The age of iron has no other seal than that of Death.

—LE MYSTÈRE DES CATHÉDRALES

TEN

THE MYSTERY OF THE GREAT CROSS AT HENDAYE

A FORGOTTEN CROSS

It is possible to date Fulcanelli's visit to Hendaye to the early 1920s because of his comment on the "special attraction of a new beach, bristling with proud villas."[1] H. G. Wells, Aldous Huxley, and the smart young London set discovered nearby Saint-Jean-de-Luz in 1920, and by 1926 or so the tourist villas had spread as far south as Hendaye. Today, Hendaye-Plage, Hendaye's beachfront addition, bustles with boutiques, dive shops, and surfboard emporiums, having become a popular stopover for the young, international, backpacking-nomad crowd.

Although Fulcanelli declares, somewhat disingenuously, that "Hendaye has nothing to hold the interest of the tourist, the archaeologist or the artist," the region does have a rather curious history. A young Louis XIV met his bride on an island in the bay below Hendaye, along the boundary between Spain and France. Wellington passed through, making nearby Saint-Jean-de-Luz his base of operation against Toulouse at the close of the Napoleonic Wars. Hitler also paid a visit, during World War II; in 1940 he parked his train car within walking distance of the cross at Hendaye.

The region has other, more esoteric connections as well. Hendaye is in Basque country, and the Basque people's genetic makeup has proved to be unlike any other in Europe. The Basque language is also a mystery. It is one of only five non-Indo-European languages to survive, and it has no links to any other language in Europe. These facts have suggested to some researchers that the Basques are the remnants of a global pre-catastrophe civilization, the lost "Atlanteans" to the more imaginative. The Basques were also well known for their magical practices, and were the focus, in the late sixteenth and early seventeenth centuries, of a major Inquisitional witch hunt.[2]

When Fulcanelli visited in the 1920s, Hendaye was a very small town. He noted its "little houses huddled at the foot of the first spurs of the Pyrenees," and commented on the "rough and rugged landscape" in which "the natural austerity of the wild scene is scarcely relieved by the headland of Fuenterrabia, showing ochre in the crude light, thrusting into the dark greyish-green mirror-calm waters of the gulf."[3]

Keep in mind that, although "The Cyclic Cross at Hendaye," the penultimate chapter of *Mystery of the Cathedrals,* was apparently written in the mid-1920s, it was added to the book only when it was republished in 1957. Hardly anyone in the occult world noticed this addition or commented on it, perhaps because it doesn't fit neatly into any of the preconceived notions of alchemy. The importance of Hendaye is revealed by Fulcanelli's declaration: "Whatever its age, the Hendaye cross shows by the decoration of its pedestal that it is the strangest monument of primitive millenarism [sic], the rarest symbolical translation of chiliasm, which I have ever met."[4]

Because Fulcanelli openly connected alchemy and the apocalypse, the true nature of that very specific gnostic astro-alchemical meme whose fingerprints we have traced through several millennia emerged into public consciousness. This meant that the secret was no longer contained among the elect societies. For the first time since the age of the Gothic cathedrals, the meme had broken out of its incubational structures.

In a way, the cross and its message serve as proof that there are such things as secret societies. Found throughout history, these societies preserve and present the secret of the cross in various ways. The Kabbalah in Judaism, Sufic Islam, esoteric Christianity, Gnosticism, and the hermetic tradition have been the keepers of these ideas. The central message of the three main Western religions, that of an eschatological moment in time, is the secret that also lies at the heart of the cross at Hendaye. The meme, the ability to understand the myth and its metaphors, seems to have survived only through the actions of these secret and insular groups.

The cross at Hendaye stands today at the southwest corner of Saint Vincent's Church, on the busiest street corner in town. No one notices the ordinary-looking monument with its message of catastrophe; perhaps it was intended to be that way. The secret hides in plain sight.

PRECESSIONAL MYTHMAKING AND AN ENIGMATIC ALTAR TO THE GOD OF TIME

In 1901, a career civil servant in the British East India Company and former commissioner of the province of Bengal published what he thought would be a revolutionary work on ancient history and prehistoric star religions. *History and Chronology of the Myth-Making Age,* by James F. Hewitt, "late Commissioner of Chutia Nagpur," as the title page styles it, is one of those grand summations of universal knowledge so beloved by the late Victorians. Hewitt, however, is not your usual colonial civil servant, and his work, unlike his contemporary James Churchward's books on the lost continent of Mu, is actually based on solid linguistic ground, at least for the turn of the twentieth century. His work, with all its flaws, is a connection point for many pieces of the Hendaye puzzle, and it offers us another mysterious stone, one that just might be the original of the Hendaye cross.

Hewitt's expertise in Sanskrit is both the strength and the weakness of his argument. Sanskrit becomes the lens through which Hewitt views every other culture and mythic structure on the planet, and this produces some surprising distortions. Occasionally these funhouse-mirror images are accurate, if somewhat inexplicable. Hewitt is correct on things where he should be dead wrong and totally inaccurate only when he tries to convince us of the universality of his conclusions. But through the verdant and tangled overgrowth of Sanskrit roots and cultural imperialism, the outlines of something truly astonishing can be discerned. *History and Chronology of the Myth-Making Age* is not only an attempt at uncovering the origins of the symbolic green language, spoken, as Fulcanelli reminds us, by all initiates, but it is also a masterful attempt to link that symbolic argot to its source in the astronomy of precession. That Hewitt fails is not surprising; we are impressed, however, by the fact that he made such a valid attempt.

With the first sentence of his preface, Hewitt informs us: "The Myth-making Age, the history of which I have sketched in this book, comprises the whole period from the first dawn of civilization . . . down to the time when the sun entered Taurus at the Vernal Equinox between

4000 and 5000 B.C." He laments the lack of a precise date for this event, and then offers an average, 4500 B.C.E., which is close enough to be quite accurate. He tells us that this was the closing event in the myth-making age, and that after this point, "it ceased to be a universally observed national custom to record history in the form of historical myths, and . . . national history began to pass out of the mythic stage into that of the annalistic chronicles recording the events of the reigns of kings and the deeds of individual heroes, statesmen and law-givers."

Making allowances for Hewitt's anachronistic use of the word *nation*, we can discern something quite profound here. Around 6,000 years ago something did in fact shift. This is recorded in the Egyptian king lists and in Manetho's chronology as the point where the Heru Shemsu, the blacksmiths of Edfu, ruled as transitional figures between the reigns of the living gods and the reigns of kings and pharaohs. It also marked the beginning of the spread of agricultural societies. Hewitt is also correct, for the wrong reasons as usual, that the Indo-European languages spread with the diffusion of agriculture across Europe. Modern linguistic archaeology places the origins of Indo-European languages and organized farming in Anatolia, homeland of Cybele, Mother of the Gods.[5]

Identifying the spread of Indo-European with agriculture helps to explain how non-Indo-European languages, Finno-Ugaric, Hungarian, Estonian, Causasian, and Basque, survived in isolated pockets. These were places where, for whatever reasons, the old hunter-gatherer traditions survived. The Finno-Ugaric speakers still have a large nomadic population, the Laplanders, and the Hungarians were isolated by geography. The other three, Caucasian, Estonian, and Basque, were all fishing or trading communities. Of them all, only Basque has survived into the twenty-first century as a living language, and Basque culture has always been based on the sea.

Hewitt has a curious view of the Basques as a mixture of his southern non-Indo-European agriculturalists and the northern Gotho-Celts, the European Aryan nomads and cattle-driving warrior-kings. From our modern archaeological perspective, we can see how skewed Hewitt's premises are: The Neolithic Basques were not agriculturalists, for instance, and not even four hundred years of Pax Romanitas made much of a dent on their language or culture. And yet, Hewitt's precessional mythology has many points of great interest to our research.

How he came by this mythology is a subject to which we shall return a bit later, but first let's take a look at the broad outline of this mythic pattern.

According to Hewitt, the first myth to develop among the agricultural societies was that of the Measurer of Time, analogous in Egyptian terms to Tehuti, who divided the solar year into two sections of thirty-six weeks of five days each to match the monsoon patterns in the Indus Valley, Hewitt's original home of civilization.[6] (Note that these are precessional numbers as well numbers related to the pentagram.) Hewitt also identifies his "Bird of Life" with the Egyptian *khu*, which he interprets to be a raven. This he identifies as the dark bird of the winds that divides the year by bringing the monsoons.

In this first age, the focus of cosmogony, according to Hewitt, was the Pole Star and the Tree of Life that grew from it. Here he cites the Celtic myths related to the Grail, where "the world's mother-tree was born from the seed brought by the rain-cloud-bird, the offspring of the Cauldron of Life, the creating-waters stored by the Pole Star god as the Holy Grail or Blood of God, and guarded by his raven vice-regent, the god whose name is Bran, in the watch-tower called the Caer Sidi or Turning Tower of the heavens."[7]

Hewitt's next age presents a different cosmogony. Here the world is seen as an egg, laid by the Bird of Life in the Tree, and around which the serpent coils. Hewitt sees this as a new kind of Pole Star/World Tree alignment, and identifies the serpent as the ecliptic zodiac, thus making this alignment that of the north and south poles of the ecliptic. His origins for these concepts are entertaining as usual, including a race of Finnish ogres who worshiped the storm bird and the snake god, but the concept itself is, as we have seen, a crucial part of the ancient astronomy.

His third myth-making age is strictly solar, evolving into the sun god as primeval ass or horse god. The process by which this occurs is too long to summarize, but Hewitt arrives at a series of images and metaphors that deserve quoting here:

> This last god, whose genealogy shows him to be the son or successor of the ass sun-god . . . was born, as I have shown, under the star Spica a Virgo the mother of corn. . . . The birth took place when the sun was in Virgo at the Vernal equinox, that is, between 13,000 and 12,000 B.C. . . . This primeval ass . . . who is said . . .

to traverse the holy road of the divine order, the path of the god of annual time, was the god of the boring *(tri)* people, the bee-inspired race. . . . They . . . were deft artificers, the first workers in metals, who introduced bronze and made the lunar sickle of Kronos . . . and the creating trident of Poseidon. This latter god was nurtured by them with a nymph, the daughter of the ocean Kapheria, the semitic Kabirah, the Arabic Kabar, the mother goddess of the Kabiri and another form of Harmonia, mother of the sons of the smiths of heaven. She was also the black Demeter of Phigalia, the goddess with the horse's head who was violated by Poseidon. . . . We can thus by their genealogy trace their traditional history from between 14,000 and 15,000 B.C. to between 13,000 and 12,000 B.C. These priests were the Kuretes whose religious dances were circular gyrations like those of the heavenly bodies8round the pole.[7]

While Hewitt's methods are decidedly odd, quoting a medieval Grail romance as a motif from around 18,000 B.C.E. might strike some scholars as downright bizarre, and his "facts" are, by anyone's reckoning, inaccurate. We have no evidence for metalworking in Europe 15,000 years ago, for instance. But his symbolic mix of metaphors and mythology strikes us as meaningful, particularly in light of the research we presented in chapter 7. As we ponder these symbolic echoes and synchronistic themes, the conclusion dawns on us that Hewitt is trying to make the evidence, wherever he can find it, match the underlying esoteric understanding that he brings to this work. This underlying theme is absent in his earlier, and slightly more sound, *Ruling Races of Prehistoric Times,* published in 1894 and 1895. Between 1894 and 1900, Hewitt ran into a current of the underground stream of hermetic esotericism, one in which the secret of time, the eschatological secret at the core of alchemy, was sketched out in a specific way that was a blend of Indian sources and Western traditions.

Before we go looking for Hewitt's esoteric sources, we must look at one of Hewitt's few pieces of physical evidence, and from the perspective of our research the most important part of Hewitt's book. During his examination of the Second Age migrations of what he calls the "Turanic-Semitic seafaring races," which, according to Hewitt, were the builders of the megalithic structures from Malta to Scandinavia, he turns to a carved stone found, he supposes, near the megalithic ruins of Carnac, in Brittany.

Carnac, in Hewitt's Sanskrit lens, is an example of the "Hindu ritual of the Soma sacrifice," and therefore the rows of stones "mark in other particulars their descent from Indian year reckoning." To back up this highly unusual, even for the time, contention, Hewitt points to "the Linga stone altar in the collection of M. du Chatellier at Kernuz, near Pont-l'Abbé, Finistere." He declares that it follows the rules of form laid down by "the Hindu religious books," and, as he examined it, he "saw at once" that whoever carved it "must have learnt the theology expressed in the engravings in India."[9] (See fig. 10.1B.)

Hewitt's description is important enough to quote at length.

On the top there was drawn the St. Andrew's cross (X) of the solsticial sun, the sign of the flying year-bird beginning its flight at the winter solstice. On one side was a pattern of interlaced female Su-astikas representing the annual course of the sun, beginning its journey round the heavens by going northward at the winter solstice. On the side next to this was the square of the eight-rayed star representing the union of the St. Andrew's Cross of the solsticial sun with the St. George's Cross of the Equinoctial sun (+).

Hewitt then describes how, according to the ancient Vedic sages, this wheel of life was drawn as the dimensions of a cube marking the "history of the sun year," and that "of the Su or Khu year-bird which explains the meaning and historical importance of the name Su-astika, denoting the yearly course round the eight (ashta) points of the heavens of the sun-bird."

He continues with the third side, on which was "a pattern of four leaves . . . arranged in the form of a St. Andrew's Cross." On the fourth and last side, he informs us, is a St. George's Cross in the form of "a Palasha Tree." Around the top of all four symbols, Hewitt describes "a scroll of female Su-astikas and at the bottom one of the snakes coiled in the form of the cross bar of the male Su-astika." Then Hewitt tells us that the sculpted stone was found by M. du Chatellier "at the end of an avenue marked by two rows of uncut stones."

Hewitt moves on quickly to his point. "It was doubtless to this god of time that the earliest stone-altar or sun-gnomon-stone was erected, and

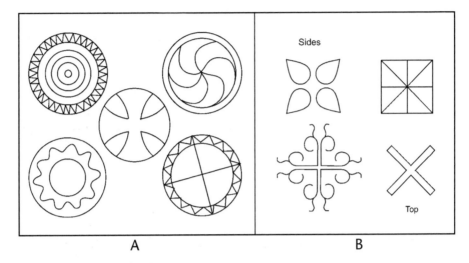

Figure 10.1. Designs from *A*, Basque gravestones, and *B*, from Hewitt's mysterious "linga stone."

similarly the original tree Yupa, the tree-trunk, denoted the god who measured time by the changes . . . of the three seasons. . . . The designs engraved on this stone-altar . . . say as clearly as written words could do, 'This is an altar to the God of Time who sent the sun-bird of the winter solstice to fly its annual course from South to North and North to South 'round the Pole, and to supply the light and the heat which nourishes the mother-tree of life.' "

VISHNUNABHI, THE MOTHER, AND THE HERMETIC BROTHERHOOD OF LUXOR

It is hard to know what to make of Hewitt. From our modern perspective his ideas on languages and migrations strike us as quaint relics of an age when the height of sophistication was a British passport and Britannia ruled the waves of a global empire. In such an age, the pronouncements of an educated Englishman carried a certain weight, and even those he classed as inferior accepted his definitions of culture. It would be more than a generation before Indian scholars would take charge of the study of their own history and languages, and another generation before archaeology caught up to philology and began to supply the missing gaps in the theories of language diffusion and displacement. With that in mind, we can give Hewitt credit for the effort and appreciate his difficulties, while still trying to understand how he arrived at his conclusions.

It is tempting to see Hewitt's four ages as the same as the Hindu *yugas,* although Hewitt never makes the comparison. He clearly sees them as precessionally based, and tries to place them within the accepted framework of the astronomical understanding of his era. He cites Sir Norman Lockyer's 24,400-year length for precession and tries to make his data fit the pattern, even though numerically Hewitt keeps turning up an older pattern based on 72 times 360, for a Great Year of 25,920 years. It is this uncertainty on such a key point that allows us to track Hewitt's esoteric source.

In addition to the precessional plan of his four 6,000-year ages, Hewitt has supplied us with a mythic symbolism that encompasses all three of the great alignments—galactic, ecliptic, and celestial—that we examined in chapter 4. Thus, his mythological symbolism combines in a series of overlapping images the ancient secrets of illuminated astronomy, and therefore, as Hewitt implies, the secret of time itself. Hewitt applies this understanding to the past, but, if his timing of the age of Taurus is accurate—and it is within acceptable limits—then we are now at the turn of another age, and the beginning of a new round of four ages.

That Hewitt does not directly connect his scheme of ages with the four *yugas* is somewhat surprising. He is aware of Manu, whom he calls the lawgiver to the Minyan race, and cites his 24,000-year period for the *yugas,* even comparing this to Lockyer's modern estimate, but he stops short of direct comparison. The reason for this omission is obscure, until we look directly at the numbers Manu gives in his Laws. Adding Hewitt's pattern of ages, we find that they cover only half, or 12,000 years, of the cycle Manu has proposed. Hewitt avoids the contradiction as unimportant to his major thesis, but if we stop to examine it, we find that it points to what is perhaps the deepest secret of all in the ancient illuminated astronomy, the location and significance of the galactic center.

A contemporary of Hewitt's, Swami Sri Yukteswar, was at the forefront of the late-Victorian movement in India to reclaim and update its ancient spiritual heritage. At that time, there were still forest sages, such as Yukteswar's guru Mahavatar Babaji, who practiced the ancient Vedic sciences, and in the face of the imperial raj's inroads on Indian culture a reaction developed in which the ancient wisdom would be vindicated and revived by means of the Western sciences of history, philology, and astronomy. Sri Yukteswar stood at the forefront of this movement, which would eventually see such strange mixtures as Mahatma Gandhi and Annie Besant, and his influence, through his student Paramahansa Yogananda, founder of the Self-Realization Fellowship and author of the classic *Autobiography of a Yogi,* has been profound and far-reaching.

Sri Yukteswar, in his book *The Holy Science,* attempts to address the problem with Manu's dates. His basic idea is that while a complete cycle is 24,000 years, it has two expressions, each 12,000 years long; and following Manu's pattern, both converge on the point where, according to Yukteswar, the sun is at its closest point to "this grand center, the seat of Brahma," and again 12,000 years later at the point where the sun is farthest away from the "seat of Brahma." This grand center is called "Vishnunabhi, which is the seat of the creative power, Brahma, the universal magnetism."[10]

Modern Vedic scholars, such as David Frawley, clearly identify Vishnunabhi with the center of the galaxy. In *Astrology of the Seers,* he comments: "The galactic center is called 'Brahma,' the creative force, or 'Vishnunabhi,' the navel of Vishnu. From this galactic sun emanates the light which determines the life and intelligence on Earth."[11] John Major Jenkins, in his book *Galactic Alignment,* goes even further: "Without mincing words, it is clear that the ancient Vedic skywatchers were aware of the galactic center, and, indeed considered it to be the center and source of creative power in the universe."[12]

Jenkins also remarks: "[T]he critical information encoded in Yukteswar's book—written decades before the Galactic Center was officially discovered in the 1920s—is that the ancient Vedic *yuga* doctrine was calibrated with the periodic alignments of the solstice sun and the galactic center."[13] Frawley agrees, and asserts that all of Vedic astrology "orients the zodiac to the galactic center." The lunar mansions of Vedic astrology also point to the region of the galactic center, six degrees Sagittarius. The thirteen-degree lunar sign that includes the galactic center is called *mulla,* or root, indicating the importance of the center of the galaxy as the source and origin of life and time.[14]

Hewitt is referring to this tradition, although obliquely, with his comments: "This is an altar to the God of Time who sent the sun-bird of the winter solstice to fly its annual course from South to North and North to South 'round the Pole, and to supply the light and the heat which nourishes the mother-tree of life. . . ."[15] The arc of movement toward and away from the galactic center is indicated by the "sun-bird of the winter solstice" who flies from "South to North," or from the point closest to the galactic center to the point farthest away. The pole it is "circling" is the galactic axis, from Vishnunabhi to the edge of the galaxy, and as the Vedic sages suggest, it does bring the Light that nourishes the "mother-tree" of the ecliptic axis. By Hewitt's reckoning, the stone "linga" he describes is a physical summation of his precessional mythology, an object that identifies the mystery of time and evolution as the symbolic union or alignment of all three centers and cosmic dragon axes.

Did Hewitt learn his precessional mythology from such Vedic reconstructionists as Sri Yukteswar or did he intuit it from the original sources? Both of these seem somewhat unlikely. Sri Yukteswar's work, *The Holy Science,* was not available in the West until 1949, and the date of its composition is uncertain. Hewitt may have heard of such teachings, but if he did, he does not mention them as sources. Also, even though his grasp of Sanskrit is quite sound, Hewitt often overlooks important sources and implications. We have seen this in his treatment of Manu, and there are many other examples. We can safely assume, then, that since Hewitt draws on so many non-Vedic sources to support his theme, he did not find his mythology completely within his Indian sources.

So where did it come from? The answer to that question can be found in the work, sixty years after Hewitt's book, of a disciple of another Hindu saint intent on reconstructing ancient Vedic wisdom with a Western spin. Sri Aurobindo spent his early life in England, graduating from Cambridge in 1892 and returning to India the next year as a civil servant. He quickly educated himself in Sanskrit and other modern Indian languages and by 1902 was deeply involved in political activity. In 1910, under legal and political pressure for his outspoken support of *swaraj,* or Indian independence, Aurobindo went into a spiritual retirement and departed Bengal for Pondicherry in French India.

A group developed around Aurobindo, including a young married Frenchwoman by the name of Mirra Alfassa, who rapidly became Sri Aurobindo's spiritual mate. She was simply called the Mother, and was seen by the community as an incarnation of the divine presence. In

1968, eighteen years after Sri Aurobindo's death and only five years before her own death, the Mother began a major series of building projects at Auroville, as the expanding commune at Pondicherry was called. One of these was something called the Matrimandir.

The Mother worked closely with another young Frenchwoman, Patrizia Norelli-Bachelet, on the design and symbolism of the Matrimandir, a shrine intended to symbolize the godhead on earth. As John Major Jenkins points out in *Galactic Alignment,* the Matrimandir, like Hewitt's linga altar stone, is a combination of all three cosmic centers and axial directions in a single symbolic object. Although the completed structure didn't follow the Mother's precise geometrical specifications, and therefore failed in its initiatory intent, the descriptions and conclusions Norelli-Bachelet preserves for us in her works *The Gnostic Circle* and *The New Way* clearly point to the importance of the center of galaxy, and its periodic precessional alignments, for our spiritual evolution.

"We can go so far," Norelli-Bachelet instructs us, "as to know that there is a great Centre to which we in our system are related and which holds the key to the Precession of the Equinoxes. It is this Centre that makes the axis Capricorn and Cancer the Evolutionary Axis of our planet. And through our study we can know that in ourselves, in our very bodies, we can find the exact reproduction of this galaxy which then gives us the revelation of the Supreme Herself." Her "Evolutionary Axis," given as the tropical* signs of Capricorn and Cancer— Sagittarius and Gemini in sidereal terms—is, of course, the galaxy axis from center to edge. Jenkins suggests that Norelli-Bachelet derived this axis from the works of René Guénon, but the chances are that Norelli-Bachelet learned it directly from the Mother, who in fact seems to have learned from the same source as Guénon.[16] And, even more curiously, the Mother and Guénon's sources lead us back, indirectly, to Hewitt.

Mirra Alfassa, the Mother, is in her own right one of the most fascinating figures in twentieth-century occultism. Long before she moved to India and met Sri Aurobindo, Mirra was seeking sources of esoteric wisdom. In 1906, five years after Hewitt published his masterwork,

---

Tropical refers to the zodiac as canonized in the second century B.C.E.; *sidereal* refers to the actual location of the signs as they are at the present.

Mirra found her first master, Max Théon, founder of the hermetic Brotherhood of Luxor. Théon, to whom we shall return later, was by all accounts an amazing individual, and the only spiritual exemplar of the era that earned René Guénon's admiration. The Mother, who was also not lavish in her praise, calls him a man of enormous occult power, knowledge, and perception. But the Mother was even more impressed with his wife, Mary Christine Woodruffe Ware, a renowned psychic before she married Théon. Mrs. Théon, née Woodruffe, was the sister of another Sanskrit scholar, Indian civil servant, and Victorian mystic, "Arthur Avalon," or Sir John Woodruffe.[17]

At the same time, 1907, that Mirra Alfassa was learning occultism from Théon, Woodruffe was writing Hewitt looking for information on Tantric texts in Bengal. Woodruffe and Hewitt apparently became friends, as the anonymous review of Hewitt's last book, *Primitive Traditional History,* in the journal *Nature* was actually written by Woodruffe. Woodruffe's books, published under the pen name Arthur Avalon, began to appear in the early 1910s and continued into the 1920s, and they remain influential in modern mystical circles.

While Woodruffe knew Hewitt and knew Théon, we have no direct evidence that Hewitt knew Théon. Yet the indirect evidence can be found in the expressions of other people such as the Matrimandir of the Mother, who certainly knew Théon, and in the very interesting uncertainty over the precise length of the precessional year we mentioned above. Hewitt is trying to make his evidence for a longer precessional period of 25,920 years fit within a framework of 24,000 years, composed of four 6,000-year ages. And this same confusion recurs in T. H. Burgoyne's *Light of Egypt,* which was derived, somewhat loosely, from the original teachings of the hermetic Brotherhood of Luxor. Although Burgoyne confuses different kinds of years, and even invents a few new kinds, à la Hewitt, he correctly states that the 12,000-year period of the Great Age is actually "the motion of the earth's center (the sun) through space, around a still greater center," echoing both Hewitt and the Mother, and then follows up in another direction by using the larger period of 25,920 years.

THE MYSTERY OF THE STONE ALTAR

While this doesn't conclusively prove that Hewitt's mystical leanings were fueled by contact with the hermetic Brotherhood of Luxor, the connection, as we shall see later, is very suggestive. More problematic, however, is the origin of the mysterious linga altar that Hewitt describes. This is his key piece of physical evidence, and, as we saw above, it is, at least as Hewitt interprets it, a summation of the cosmic axes and centers in the same manner as the Mother's Matrimandir. But as our research on this subject went deeper, a most curious enigma developed.

Pierre du Chatellier, in whose house Hewitt examined this linga stone, was in fact the leading archaeologist of megalithic Britanny, with many published papers to his credit. In 1894, he excavated a Neolithic tumulus, or mound, at the end of a much older row of standing stones, and he found an omphalos-like marker stone. In 1896 he published his results, and in his published monograph we find that the marker was devoid of any carvings at all. Chatellier did not excavate any other tumuli that match Hewitt's description, and nowhere in his monographs does he describe any stone with the carvings mentioned by Hewitt. Indeed, Neolithic stones with any carving similar to those described by Hewitt are so rare as to be nonexistent. At least none has been found to date. Carvings, of the nature Hewitt describes, belong to a much more recent time, perhaps even down to the historical period, not to the Neolithic or megalithic era.

But unless we are prepared to claim that Hewitt simply made it up, he must have seen something at the Château Kernuz. Hewitt was there apparently after 1896, the published date of Chatellier's article, and before 1900, when the book went to the publisher. Could there have been another stone, one not excavated by Pierre du Chatellier, that Hewitt examined and interpreted? And if so, where did it come from?

Following the basic designs Hewitt describes brings us back to Basque country. Marker stones, similar to Hewitt's linga, are common throughout the Basque region, complete with crosses and sun wheels, Hewitt's female swastikas. Could his linga have come from the Basque country? From his comments, Hewitt obviously never connected it with the Basques, even though he considers them to be related to the Neolithic Gothic Celts who he thought had carved the linga stone on a Vedic basis. If he had known the stone's true origin, he would certainly have made much more of it than he did. After his linga example, Hewitt never again mentions the Basques.

In one of those research synchronicities that suddenly connects what were until then widely separated pieces of the puzzle, we came across the solution to this minor mystery and found that it led us back to the heart of *Le Mystère,* the Cyclic Cross of Hendaye. With that solution in hand, we were finally able to answer the question of why, if the Hendaye chapter was written in the mid-1920s, it was not included in *Le Mystère* until the second, 1957 edition. And that solution pointed us even deeper into the mystery of Fulcanelli's identity.

"Leaving the station, a country road, skirting the railway line, leads to the parish church, situated in the middle of the village," Fulcanelli comments in the Hendaye chapter.

> This church, with its bare walls and its massive, squat rectangular tower, stands in a square a few steps above ground level and bordered by leafy trees. It is an ordinary, dull building, which has been renovated and is of no particular interest. However, near the south transept there is a humble stone cross, as simple as it is strange, hiding amidst the greenery of the square. It was formerly in the parish cemetery and it was only in 1842 that it was brought to its present site near the church. At least, that is what was told me by an old Basque man, who had for many years acted as sexton. As for the origin of this cross, it is unknown and I was not able to obtain any information at all about the date of its erection. However, judging by the shape of the base and the column, I would not think that it could be before the end of the seventeenth or beginning of the eighteenth century.[18]

This is all that Fulcanelli tells us concerning the origins of the cross at Hendaye, and it is as misleading as his preceding comment that Hendaye has nothing to interest "the tourist, the archaeologist or the artist." The date of 1842 for the placement of the cross in the churchyard points directly to the local d'Abbadie family, who purchased the headland in that year and paid for the renovations to the church. The current sexton, who may be the grandson or great-grandson of the one to whom Fulcanelli spoke, quite clearly knows that the cross was moved and placed by the d'Abbadie family, so it is hard to believe that Fulcanelli's sexton didn't also have that information. Yet Fulcanelli doesn't mention it.

According to the history of the Château d'Abbadie that was published by the Cape Science Foundation, several carved "Basque head-stones" were discovered at the site of the château during its construction. These remained for years on the grounds, displayed in a small garden, until they were sent to the foremost megalithic archaeologists of the era for study in 1896, two years before Antoine d'Abbadie died.

The archives at the Château d'Abbadie, which is now open to the public as a museum, describe one piece has having a Basque sun wheel, several crosses, and a directional "wind rose." This piece, according to the archives, was sent to Pierre du Chatellier, of the Château Kernuz in Britanny, in late 1896 at the request of M. d'Abbadie. It was never returned, apparently, because there is no further record of it in the archives of the Château d'Abbadie.[19] The "wind rose" is specific enough for us to be sure that this stone, from the headland at Hendaye, was in fact the linga Hewitt was describing. His eight-rayed star in a square is most clearly seen as a kind "wind rose" or compass marker for the four directions and their quarters. As the Basques were sailors, this symbolism seems appropriate, and serves to clinch our identification.

Hewitt's altar stone, his object that sums up the alignment of the three axes and the three centers, originally stood on an isolated plateau overlooking the sea at Hendaye. It is perhaps the original model from which the seventeenth-century craftsman composed the cross at Hendaye. Hewitt's stone, and his oddly derived and very esoteric interpretation of it, serves as a kind of touchstone, one that shows up the true "gold," as we work our way through the different views of the cross.

The d'Abbadie connection presents us with a solid fact, that the d'Abbadie family was responsible for placing the cross in the churchyard, which Fulcanelli is at pains to avoid mentioning. Even with his careful avoidance, the date of 1842 would have led any reader or researcher in 1926 straight to the family. Exactly what revealing the d'Abbadie family's involvement with the Hendaye cross would have disclosed is a subject that will have to wait until after we have examined both our three commentaries on the cross, by Boucher, Fulcanelli, and "Paul Mevryl," and the cross itself. Once we understand the cross's message, then we can return to the mystery of what this connection, and its obscuration, tells us about the real Fulcanelli. But first we must examine the three perspectives on the cross that comprise the Hendaye myth.

ELEVEN

THE MESSAGE OF THE GREAT CROSS AT HENDAYE

TRIANGULATING THE MYTH AND THE MESSAGE

In attempting to decipher the cross at Hendaye's mythic meaning, we can draw on three different but interrelated interpretations or viewpoints. Along with Fulcanelli's chapter on the cross in *Le Mystère*, we have Jules Boucher's 1936 article in *Consolation* and Paul Mevryl's epilogue to *The Fulcanelli Phenomenon*. These perspectives act like lenses, some microscopic, some telescopic, some as distorting as a fun-house mirror, but before we turn to the monument we need to review these viewpoints with care. Even the distortions, we shall find, can offer us valuable information. So let us examine them in chronological order.

Jules Boucher's 1936 article is our first glimpse of the monument to the end of time (see fig. 1.4). According to the article, a M. Lemoine, a painter of "great talent," gave Boucher some vacation photographs of the cross and thereby brought the monument to Boucher's attention. A search of French artists of the period turns up no Lemoines. The name Lemoine, which is simply French for "the monk," is not very common, which leads us to suspect that it is a pseudonym.

Boucher quotes Fulcanelli in the article, but does not connect him directly to Hendaye. He quotes from Fulcanelli's *Dwellings of the Philosophers* about the symbolism of the Saint Andrew's cross, a quote that echoes Hewitt's comments. The article begins with a description of the cross. Boucher lists the points that interest him—the four faces of the base, the Latin inscription, the INRI, and the Saint Andrew's cross above the inscription—and then he plunges immediately into an interpretation of the inscription. As we noted in chapter 1, Boucher's attempt shows some familiarity with Fulcanelli's interpretation and method. Boucher, however, stops short of revealing the complete decipherment, appearing in fact to veer off in an odd direction.

Boucher moves to the symbols on the base, going west, east, north, and south in a zigzag, forming a crossing pattern that closely resembles a Gothic mason's mark (see fig. 11.7 on page 323).[1] He begins with the western face, which he calls the "devouring sun," telling us that its sixteen rays suggest the sixteenth trump of the Tarot, The Blasted Tower, an image of catastrophe. While this suggestion is close to the mark, particularly the idea of using Tarot images for the pedestal symbols, it is also an interesting choice, for if one knew that the image had something to do with a catastrophe, one might simply focus on the catastrophe trump without looking any further. The more obvious Tarot trump would be The Sun.

The star image on the eastern side receives the same treatment. Boucher says that it greets the east and has eight rays and therefore symbolizes trump number eight, Justice. On the north side is the moon image, yet Boucher does not follow his Tarot interpretation and suggest that this is trump number eighteen, The Moon. He merely says it is an obscure Egyptian symbol that hides a secret.

The south side contains an image of the Four Ages according to Boucher, but he does not mention the obvious Tarot analogue, The Last Judgment. He gives the Four Ages Ovid's names, the Ages of Gold, Silver, Bronze, and Iron. He concludes that we are living in the Iron Age, full of "crimes and calamities," but does not offer any predictions of double catastrophes. Indeed, later in the article Boucher says that it is not possible to pinpoint the exact location or time of the catastrophe. But he does predict something dire.[2]

Perhaps that was all the information he was given, and, not having the whole story, was left to fill in the gaps as best he could. The Tarot suggestions alone point to the fact that Boucher's sources, if not Boucher himself, understood the importance of the Tarot in deciphering the monument. The attributions that Boucher gives are somewhat off base, as we shall see, but what he leaves out points to the correct attributions. There are obvious Tarot choices for all four faces, which Boucher seems to avoid at all cost. At best, this is curious, and suggests that we are meant to complete his speculation and look deeper for our Tarot images. It is even possible that Boucher planned it that way, with obvious misdirection and gaps in symbolism.

"The Cyclic Cross at Hendaye" is the penultimate chapter of Fulcanelli's masterpiece (see appendix E for the complete text of the chapter). After wading through thickets of erudition and punning slang in the rest of *Le Mystère*, this chapter feels awash with the bright sunlight of its Basque setting. The description of the monument and its location is seemingly clear and direct. Even the explanation of the monument's apparent meaning is simple and virtually free of the green-language code used throughout the rest of the book. Or so it appears on the surface.

"Whatever its age, the Hendaye cross shows by the decoration of its pedestal that it is the strangest monument of primitive millenarism [sic], the rarest symbolical translation of chiliasm, which I have ever met." Coming from Fulcanelli, this is high praise indeed. He goes on to tell us that "the unknown workman, who made these images, possessed real and profound knowledge of the universe."

Figure 11.1. The Latin inscription on the transverse arm of the cross, which reads "Hail, O Cross, the Only Hope."

Fulcanelli continues with a description of the Latin inscription on the transverse arm of the cross. As shown in figure 11.1, the inscription contains seventeen letters in the following order: OCRUXAVES / PESUNICA. As Fulcanelli notes, this translates quite simply as "Hail, O Cross, the Only Hope," a common Latin mortuary inscription. On the cross, however, the phrase is oddly broken, for the first *S* in the word *spes*, "hope," is found on the first line, and the rest of the word is found on the second, which leaves us with the words *aves* and *pes*. This creates an obvious grammatical error. If *pes*, "foot," is the correct word, then its adjective should agree in gender and be the masculine *unicus*, not the feminine *unica*.

Oddly enough, Fulcanelli does not try to create meaning from this discrepancy. He doesn't indulge in anagrammatic wordplay, only notes that it was done on purpose. As he says, "[S]ince this *apparent* mistake exists, it follows that it must really have been intended." Regarding the meaning of the inscription, he writes, "I had already been enlightened by studying the pedestal and knew in what way and by means of what key the Christian inscription of the monument should be read; but I was anxious to show investigators what help may be obtained in solving hidden matters from plain common sense, logic and reasoning." Then he moves on to interpret the inscription by reading the Latin as if it were French. The result is *"Il est écrit que la vie se réfugie en un seul espace"*—that is, "It is written that life takes refuge in a single space."

It is difficult to take this reading seriously. The transformations of meaning are almost unexplained, except by reference to obscure authors and periodicals, and seem based mostly on a deliberate mistake. Fulcanelli declares: "The letter *S,* which takes on the curving shape of a snake, corresponds to the Greek *khi (X)* [or *chi*] and takes over its esoteric meaning." This is so odd as to be jarring. In no system of esoteric knowledge have we been able to find any such correspondence as Fulcanelli suggests here. Therefore, it must be a specific attribution, an unusual but precise meaning, used to suggest something important that could not be conveyed without bending the rules.

Fulcanelli continues about the meaning of the *S:* "It is the helicoidal track of the sun, having arrived at the zenith of its curve across space, at the time of cyclic catastrophe . . . thanks to the symbolic value of the letter *S,* displaced on purpose, we understand that the inscription must be translated in secret language." Following his French rendering of the Latin mentioned above, he casually suggests that the phrase means "that a country exists, where death cannot reach man at the terrible time of the double cataclysm." What is more, only the elite will be able to find "this promised land."

On very little direct evidence, Fulcanelli is telling us that the cross at Hendaye is a marker stone for some future catastrophe. Fulcanelli continues his survey of the monument, moving to the INRI inscription on the opposite side of the transverse arm of the cross, which he calls the front of the monument. He confuses the order of the images by saying that the INRI corresponds with the "schematic image of the cycle," the four *A*'s in the angles of a cross found on the south side of the pedestal.

This could imply that the INRI and the four *A*'s are on the same side or face of the monument. In fact, this is not the case. The eight-rayed star faces in the same direction as the INRI inscription. Again, Fulcanelli uses a deliberate obscurity to make an important point: "Thus we have two symbolic crosses, both instruments of the same torture. Above is the divine cross, exemplifying the chosen means of expiation; below is the global cross, fixing the pole of the *northern hemisphere* and locating in time the fatal period of this expiation."

And then Fulcanelli adds a very strange image: "God the Father holds in his hand this globe, surmounted by the *fiery sign*. The four great ages—historical representations of the four ages of the world—have their sovereigns shown holding this same attribute. They are Alexander, Augustus, Charlemagne and Louis XIV." He then states that "[i]t is this which explains the inscription INRI, exoterically translated as *Iesus Nazarenus Rex Iudeorum* (Jesus of Nazareth, King of the Jews), but which gives to the cross its secret meaning: *Igne Natura Renovatur Integra* (By fire nature is renewed whole). For it is by fire and in fire that our hemisphere will soon be tried. And just as, by means of fire, gold is separated from impure metals, so, Scripture says, the good will be separated from the wicked on the great Day of Judgment."

Fulcanelli supplies us with a footnoted comment on the four sovereigns: "The first three are emperors, the fourth is only a king, the Sun King, thus indicating the decline of the star and its last radiation. This is dusk, the forerunner of the long cyclic night, full of horror and terror, 'the abomination of desolation.'" His esoteric interpretation of INRI, "by fire nature is renewed whole," goes directly to the issue of chiliasm and a cleansing destruction as a prelude to a re-created and Edenic world. Alchemy, according to Fulcanelli's last sentence above, is the very heart of eschatology. Just as gold is refined, so will our age be refined—by fire.

Next, Fulcanelli takes up the images on the four faces of the pedestal. Fulcanelli changes Boucher's zigzag listing of them to a clockwise list, giving them as sun, moon, star, and "geometric figure." The illustration accompanying the text (plate 48 in *Le Mystère*) shows the same pattern. Fulcanelli ignores the sun, moon, and star and spends the last pages of the chapter elaborating on the fourfold nature of the "geometric figure, which . . . is none other than the diagram used by the initiates to indicate the solar cycle."

It is a simple circle, divided into four sectors by two diameters cutting each other at right angles. The sectors each bear an A, which shows that they stand for the four ages of the world. This is a complete hieroglyph of the universe, composed of the conventional signs for heaven and earth, the spiritual and the temporal, the macrocosm and microcosm, in which major emblems of the redemption (cross) and the world (circle) are found in association.

In medieval times, these four phases of the great cyclic period, whose continuous rotation was expressed in antiquity by means of a circle divided by two perpendicular diameters, were generally represented by the four evangelists or by their symbolic letter, which was the Greek *alpha*, or, more often still, by the four evangelical beasts surrounding Christ, the living human representation of the cross. This is the traditional formula, which one meets frequently on the tympana of Roman porches. Jesus is shown there seated, his left hand resting on a book, his right hand raised in the gesture of benediction, and separated from the four beasts, which attend him, by an ellipse, called the *mystic almond*. These groups, which are generally isolated from other scenes by a garland of clouds, always have their figures placed in the same order, as may be seen in the cathedrals of Chartres (royal portal) and Le Mans (west porch), in the Church of the Templars at Luz (Hautes Pyrénées) and the Church of Civray (Vienne), on the porch of St. Trophime at Arles, etc.[3]

Fulcanelli connects the traditional image of the Four Ages, the cherubic beasts or the evangels, to an ellipse, the *vesica piscis* or the "mystic almond," and the letter *A* or alpha, which suggests that he meant this image to be a direct interpretation of the "geometric figure" of the cross and four *A*'s. The secret nature of this "complete hieroglyph of the universe" can be found in public view, on the facades of the Gothic cathedrals—for example, in figure 11.2.

On Fulcanelli's list, however, every cathedral is connected with the cult of the Black Madonna, or ancient goddess worship. While directing us to the meaning of the Four Ages, Fulcanelli is also inspiring us to look closer, to understand why certain places, such as those he lists, are important and how they are related.

Fulcanelli makes sure that the reader follows his main point. After

Figure 11.2. *A.* The twelfth-century tympanum on the porch of Saint Trophime in Arles showing the "complete hieroglyph of the universe." This image is the concluding plate (no. 49) in *Le Mystère des cathédrales. B.* The geometry of the traditional medieval schematic for representing Christ surrounded by the symbols of the four evangelists is also the design of the New Jerusalem as described in Revelation.

quoting from Saint John regarding the four beasts (Rev. 4:6–7), he then cites Ezekiel's vision of the "four living creatures" (Ezek. 1:4–5, 10–11). His penultimate paragraph takes up the notion of the Four Ages, or *yugas,* in Hindu mythology and notes that "our own age," the Age of Iron, or Kali Yuga, is the time when "human virtue reaches the utmost degree of feebleness and senility," being "the age of misery, misfortune and decrepitude." In this passage, Fulcanelli's comments echo both

Hewitt and Max Théon, of the Hermetic Brotherhood of Luxor. Fulcanelli makes no further predictions other than to note that we are in the Iron Age of the Kali Yuga.

"The *age of iron* has no other seal than that of *Death*. Its hiero-glyph is the skeleton, bearing the attributes of Saturn: the empty hour-glass, symbol of time run out, and the scythe, reproduced in the figure seven, which is the number of transformation, of destruction, of anni-hilation," Fulcanelli instructs us. "The Gospel of this fatal age is the one written under the inspiration of St. Matthew." He follows this obser-vation with a group of Greek words related to the basic *mu-alpha-theta* root of the name Matthew, connecting it to the words for "science," "knowledge," "study," and "to learn." "It is the Gospel according to Science, the last of all but for us the first, because it teaches us that, save for a small number of the elite, we must all perish. For this reason, the angel was made the attribute of St. Matthew, because science, which alone is capable of penetrating the mystery of things, of beings and their destiny, can give man wings to raise him to knowledge of the highest truths and finally to God."

On the surface, Fulcanelli's chapter takes us little further toward our goal of understanding the Hendaye cross than Jules Boucher's 1936 magazine article. Fulcanelli adds the explicit warning of an imminent catastrophe, a season of double catastrophe that will try the northern hemisphere by fire, and the hope of a place where "death cannot reach man at the terrible time of the double catastrophe." He relates the Vedic idea of the four *yugas* to the Western prophetic tradition of Revelation and Ezekiel. By aligning his apocalyptic traditions, Fulcanelli points the reader toward a few important symbolic clues: Saturn and the Gospel of Matthew.

In chapter 3, we saw that Matthew gives us the most complete view of Jesus' teachings on the end of the world and the coming Kingdom of Heaven. Matthew was someone who grasped the mystery at the core of Christianity, for it is from him that we hear of Jesus' Egyptian connec-tions, the Star of Bethlehem and the journey of the Wise Men from the East, the Massacre of the Innocents, the temptation of the Messiah, and many other stories with deep esoteric significance.

Matthew 24:43–44 suggests that those who follow the Son of Man will indeed be able to calculate the time, and so be waiting in prepara-tion. When he returns (25:31), he will separate the sheep from the goats, the subtle from the gross, on the basis of their compassion for their fellow men. In Matthew, we also find the account of Mary Magdalene's witness to the Resurrection, complete with its own light metaphor. "His appearance was like lightning," we are told, and Mary does not at first recognize him.[4] Matthew's account of the Resurrection ends with Christ's Ascension in Galilee and his pronouncement of the Great Commission, the last line of which goes to the heart of the mystery: "And surely I am with you always, even to the end of the world."[5]

Fulcanelli announced that the cross at Hendaye points to the "great Day of Judgment," and that the seal of this moment in time is Death, with the attributes of the planet Saturn. This suggests that Saturn will somehow play a role in marking the end of this fourth age, a very unusual and productive idea, as we shall see a little later.

In *The Fulcanelli Phenomenon,* K. R. Johnson included a chapter on the Hendaye cross by someone called "Paul Mevryl." Entitled "Epilogue in Stone," this commentary on the Hendaye cross raises as many questions as it answers, not the least of which is who is "Paul Mevryl"? In the introductory blurb, we are told that Mevryl "is a retired engineer, has an interest in cryptograms and has studied alchemy, Fulcanelli and other areas of arcane knowledge for many years." In the text, Mevryl assumes a tone that suggests that if he is not Fulcanelli's heir, he is at least his equal. Whoever he is, and he is as anonymous as Fulcanelli, Mevryl is in on the game, and, with this article, became one of its major players.

Following Boucher and Fulcanelli, Mevryl confirms the apocalyptic content of the monument, and then spins off into a science-fiction story about exploding suns and moon-size ark-ships. His explanation of the pedestal images becomes a somewhat murky discussion of planetary exchanges, first interstellar, involving Sirius, which he calls, suggestively, "the Sun behind the Sun," and then within the solar system, involving Venus. This is so strange as to make a reader pause in amazement, if not give up entirely. Alchemy, as a subject, is absent from the article, which focuses solely on eschatology and catastrophe. His goal is simply "to lift a corner of the veil obscuring one vehicle of that teaching." Mevryl suggests that this division between alchemy and its eschatological content "is both interesting to the casual reader and helpful to the student of hermeticism." And indeed, Mevryl's article is very helpful, but only when you know the secret. Otherwise, it obscures more than it reveals.[6]

But Mevryl does know something: "The Cyclic Cross at Hendaye is a statement in stone about The Stone and a record of the fact of success in the Great Work by an unknown man. Simultaneously, it is an observation upon the nature and timing of tremendous world events involving yet another kind of stone." And his first, and perhaps most significant, question is: Why is the cross even at Hendaye? Concerning the alchemist-builder of the monument, Mevryl notes that "[t]here is certainly no other indication that it was the scene of his triumph, except in the possibility that it was so because the monument was originally erected in the local cemetery."

At this point, Mevryl makes one of his leaps, suggesting that the cause might be Hendaye's closeness to the pilgrim route to the shrine of Santiago de Compostela in Spanish Galicia. He mentions Nicolas Flamel in passing and then focuses on the green-language meaning of the Hendaye name itself. He breaks it down into "Hen Day–End Day–Ande" or "Egg–Apocalypse–Mountain," and suggests that this multiple meaning of the word Hendaye was a determining factor in its choice. And he squeezes in another reference to Flamel: "The Egg is the philosophical Egg of alchemy, reminding us of Flamel's 'little poulet.' This place name demonstrates the presence at Hendaye of a double teaching."

Mevryl then smoothly jumps to his other, and perhaps more significant, reason for why the cross is at Hendaye: "Immediately following the Atlantean catastrophe, the pitifully small remnants of that multi-million-strong civilization reached safety along the shorelines of the Atlantic basin." Mevryl continues: "[T]hese are the Basques, survivors of the last cyclic catastrophe to overwhelm mankind and who have had a unique tribute to chiliasm set down on their border. Through this strange device, a memory is preserved from Iron Age to Iron Age—nearly 12,000 years." Mevryl sounds almost as if he were reading from Hewitt, down to the confusion over the length of time from Iron Age to Iron Age.

He continues by using the 12,000-year figure as a one-foot ruler to illustrate that even such a period of time is but a collection of human lives. "The whole span of 12,000 years represents only a series of 192 such lifetimes. Knowledge and teaching transmitted a mere 200 times is hardly inconceivable even to we short-lived creatures." Mevryl brings this back to Hendaye: ". . . and very close to the zero of today, [we find] the erection of the Cyclic Cross at Hendaye. Here then, is a tribute to the long medley of more-than-human endeavour and an indication that there is an unbroken purpose at work in history. It is also a reasonable point upon the time-scale to place a prediction that time is running out and that the Age is about to end."

And then Mevryl makes a very revealing and curious comment: "Yet we have here prediction, not prophecy. Prophecy implies seership—long-sightedness, of being accurately informed about future time, coupled with a measure of certainty often not intended by the prophet himself. The Christian Bible is full of prophetic utterances that are for the most part *warnings* rather than statements of *inexorable fact*."

Just as we are absorbing the implications of Mevryl's distinction between prophecy and prediction, he switches gears and presents us with the biblical "prophecy" found in the thirteenth chapter of Mark's Gospel. He concludes: "Jesus took a penetrating look into and through our own times to the future events symbolised at Hendaye. We can be reasonably sure that they are in our own times, since He put together a number of more or less simultaneous events that could only occur separately in other epochs." But even Jesus didn't know the exact time. Mevryl suggests that any adept could have calculated the rough timing. He points to Nostradamus and the "1999" quatrain, and suggests that Jesus may have known as much as Nostradamus, even if not the exact day and hour.

He then suggests a parallel between an object coming in from deep space and scientists' inability to predict with much accuracy the fall of Skylab to the earth. He concludes: "It is fair to suggest that the precise timing may be beyond computation." In this, Mevryl sees a possible hint of a reprieve from the "inexorable fact" of the coming events.

But instead of being explicit, Mevryl quotes two significant passages from the Koran and then shifts to ancient Egypt and speculations on the "Osirian race . . . God-like men rather than gods." Are they, "perhaps, mentors and directors of terrestrial mankind?" Mevryl questions. From this, he determines that "within the highest levels of prophecy in Holy Writ there remains hope. A hope based upon astronomical realities."

Mevryl then follows this up by suggesting that there is "a protective power" that has allowed mankind time to develop without destructive collisions from outer space. "In that event," he continues, "the chiliasm of Hendaye symbolises not *absolute prophecy* but an *accurate prediction* based directly upon humanity's experience over many Ages of cyclic time. Timings can be calculated; manifestations cannot."

He moves on from this point to his complex interpretation of the separate elements of the cross. While this section is filled with odd clues and equally insightful game playing, it is too extensive to cover in detail here. We shall refer to the important clues and suggestions as we unravel the message of the cross itself, but for now we must get an overview of Mevryl's thesis.

Whoever Mevryl may in fact be, he presents us in these opening pages a handful of basic truths without which it is impossible to go any further with an understanding of the Hendaye cross. We can summarize them as follows:

1. The location of Hendaye is critically important, both to the identity of Fulcanelli and in the symbolic sense of a "double teaching."
2. The monument is a "prediction" of a specific group of astronomical events that happen separately at other times, but are forming an alignment or arrangement at just the time predicted on the monument.
3. This arrangement of astronomical events has been used as the traditional marker point of the Day of Judgment mentioned in the Gospel of Mark.

Armed with these important points, it is time to turn to the cross and its unusual symbols. Do they really say what Boucher, Fulcanelli, and Mevryl claim they do? Can we solve the riddles and mysteries left by our three commentators and unravel the true message of the Hendaye cross?

DECIPHERING THE CODE

The effect of reading Fulcanelli's Hendaye chapter is not unlike that produced by a good conjuring trick, a sort of intellectual now-you-see-it-now-you-don't. You think Fulcanelli has told you a secret, and he has, but you can't quite figure out what or how the secret works. All the clues are there, including instructions, but the picture is still confused.

For example, we are told that the monument marks a future catastrophe, and then we are lectured on the evangelical beasts without being given a way to connect these concepts. Fulcanelli is painting a picture that tells the reader, as clearly as he could, that the world is coming to an end.

The unknown builder of the cross also knew that the world was coming to an end, and both Fulcanelli and the unknown builder suggest that they know the cause of the apocalypse. Fulcanelli even says that he knows where the place of refuge is located for the time of the end of the world.

Armed with the clues from Boucher, Fulcanelli, and Mevryl, it's time to look directly at the monument and let it speak for itself. If it is a marker of some future catastrophe, then exactly how does it tell us this? And, even more important, does it really tell us when?

The monument itself has three basic components: the upper cross, the column or pillar, and the pedestal. The upper cross has three symbolic components, the pillar is its own symbol, and the base has four symbols, for a total of eight symbolic images. We can think of the entire monument as a schematic, or exploded-perspective view, of a single geometrical construct, the Cube of Space of the *Bahir's* Precious Stone of the Wise.

As shown in figure 11.3, the three symbolic components of the upper cross are the INRI inscription, the *X*'s on the top cross, and the

Figure 11.3. The front of the cross at Hendaye.

oddly broken Latin inscription. These symbols offer us three interrelated meaning systems that, when taken together, give us the key to understanding the entire process symbolized by the monument.

The pillar stands as a unifying image that brings together the symbolic content of the cross and the base. The pedestal's four symbols must be taken as a unit, one in which the order and meaning of the symbolic components are in a state of flux, but the nature of the whole is constant. That is, the way the meaning is derived is flexible, but the meaning, as we shall see, remains the same no matter how the sides are read. As shown in figure 11.4, the images on the pedestal, starting in the east and moving counterclockwise, include an eight-rayed starburst

Figure 11.4. The images of the faces of the pedestal.

and an oddly shaped half moon/boat with a prominent eye. Next comes an angry sun face with bulging spiral eyes, dumbbell-shaped mouth, and prominent chin. Sixteen large spikes and sixteen smaller spikes inside a containing outer circle surround the face. The sun circle itself is surrounded by four stars, placed in the corners of the rectangle and tilted so that their diagonal axes cut through the center point of the sun face. The final image is an oval that fills the entire space of the side and contains a cross with four *A*'s in it. The *A*'s are unusual for having a sharply angled crossbar rather than the usual horizontal one.

After taking each symbolic component in turn, we shall proceed to assembling them into an overall pattern of meaning.

The Upper Cross

The INRI inscription on the upper cross places us firmly within the Rosicrucian alchemical tradition. As Fulcanelli tells us, this inscription can be interpreted as one of the key maxims of alchemy: *Igne Natura Renovatur Integra,* or "By fire nature is renewed whole." It is also *Igne Nitrum Raris Invenitum,* or "The shining is rarely found in fire." Perhaps a more accurate way to view these four letters is as the initial letters of the Hebrew names of the elements: *yam,* which is water and the letter *yod* or *I; nur,* which is fire and the letter *nun* or *N; ruach,* which is air and the letter *resh* or *R;* and *yebeshas,* which is earth and the letter *yod* or *I* again. Figure 11.5 shows a complete table of esoteric correspondences.

This quaternity also suggests the Four Ages, one for each of the elements from water to the earth. In the rituals of the Golden Dawn, these Hebrew letters were considered the "key word" and subjected to a sort of gnostic and kabbalistic analysis. After the letters are converted into their Hebrew equivalents of the four elements, they are then given their Yetziratic—that is, their zodiacal and planetary—correspondences: Yod is Virgo; nun is Scorpio; resh is the Sun; and the final yod is Virgo again.[7]

From this a pattern of the sequence of life, death, resurrection or rebirth, and new life can be abstracted. The Golden Dawn then applied Egyptian god-forms to these concepts: Life is Isis; death is Apophis; resurrection is Osiris. From this they derived the name of the Gnostic high god IAO. These vowels had long been associated with a mysticism of

Upper Cross Inscription	**I**	**N**	**R**	**I**
Common interpretation	*Iesus*	*Nazarenus*	*Rex*	*Iudeorum*
Fulcanelli's interpretation	*Igne*	*Natura*	*Renovatur*	*Integra*
Hebrew names of elements	yam (water)	nur (fire)	ruach (air)	yebeshas (earth)
Hebrew letters, their names, and their numerical association	׳ YOD 10	ו NUN 50	ר RESH 200	׳ YOD 10
Zodiacal and planetary attributions	♍ Virgo	♏ Scorpio	☉ Sun	♍ Virgo
Cycle of Life	Life	Death	Rebirth	Life
Golden Dawn Egyptian God-forms	Isis	Apophis	Osiris	Isis
Isis interpretation	*Isis*	*Naturae*	*Regina*	*Ineffabilis*

Figure 11.5. A table of INRI correspondences.

light, as shown by their prominence in the *Bahir*.[8] Note that this arrangement begins and ends with Isis, implying the centrality of the "life" she bestows. We should also keep in mind that another, more Rosicrucian version of INRI can be read as *Isis Naturae Regina Ineffabilis*, or "Isis, the ineffable Queen of Nature."

In Hebrew *gematria*, which assigns each letter a numerical value, yod is 10, nun is 50, and resh is 200, making the number of the word equal to 270. The number 270 is one of the precessional numbers, for multiplied by 8, the number of all the symbols on the monument, the product equals 2,160, the number of solar cycles in one precessional month ($12 \times 2160 = 25,920$ years, or one complete precessional cycle or Great Year).

Therefore, our first symbol tells us of a basic elemental pattern, that of life, death, resurrection, and new life, which is related to the mysteries of light, the "Fire where the shining can be found," and the precessional cycle caused by the earth's tilted axis. The *Bahir* suggests that the tilted axis is the Tree of the Knowledge of Good and Evil, or that which gives each age its quality.

There are two *X*'s on the upper cross, on the opposite side from the INRI inscription. The lower one is the middle *X* of the Latin inscription, so that these two *X*'s are stacked one on top of the other. The first impression is that of the Roman numeral twenty written sideways. Fulcanelli goes to great lengths to call our attention to them without giving the most obvious correspondence, that of trump 20 (or XX) of the Tarot, The Last Judgment. He does tell us that he already knew the meaning of the upper cross from looking at the images on the pedestal, where the Last Judgment is indeed portrayed.

Fulcanelli is not being misleading here, for the snake of the ecliptic, the curving shape the path of the sun makes in its yearly round, is an important piece of the puzzle, even if it is nowhere else attributed to the Greek letter *chi*. As shown in figure 11.6, the pattern formed by the two *X*'s on top of each other is indeed a diagram of the ecliptic snake, with the cross mark of the *X*'s showing the equinoxes.

This symbol tells us that the Last Judgment is the time when the elements, described by the INRI inscription, align in the right way, and *X* marks the spot on the equinoxes.

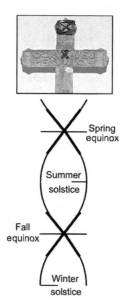

Figure 11.6. The ecliptic snake formed from combining the two *X*'s.

Turning to the Latin inscription, the obvious meaning, "Hail, O Cross, the Only Hope," should not be discarded, for the phrase also refers to the crossing pattern of the equinoxes and the alignment of the ecliptic and the galactic meridian. But the odd split in the middle of the inscription does suggest a riddle. Given Fulcanelli's insistence that the X be read as an S or a snake, it is curious that *spes* backward is *seps,* Latin for "venomous serpent." Reading this word backward in translating the inscription produces "Hail, O Cross, the Only Snake (or Serpent)." Perhaps this is another reference to the ecliptic or to the snakelike motion that the Milky Way makes as the year progresses. The word *pes,* or foot, is clearly shown, although, as Fulcanelli notes, *unica* does not agree with it in gender. If we transpose two letters in *unica,* however, we get *uncia,* meaning "twelfth part," and the phrase can be translated as "Hail, O Cross, the measure of the twelfth part." If we look at the top line of the inscription, we are left with two letters that are not really needed, the O and the S. Putting these together at the beginning of the sentence gives us the Latin word OS, "bone" and also "inmost part" or "essence." The phrase then becomes *Os crux ave pes uncia,* or "The essential cross salutes the measure of the twelfth part." We can also read it as *Os crux ave spes/seps unica,* or "The essence of the cross salutes the only hope/snake."

From all of these options, and without complicated anagrammatic play, we get an immediate complex of meanings. Just from a glance at the inscription, we can tell that the secret concerns an equinox cross, the cross of the ecliptic and the galaxy and a snake that somehow measures the twelfth part, the last inch of Mevryl's 12,000-year ruler. The inscription is telling us that the monument is a way to measure when the snake and the crosses coincide. It also suggests that this knowledge is our only hope.

The Pillar

The pillar is the single symbol that unifies the whole vision. It is simultaneously the World Axis, the spine of the world, the World Tree, and the Tree of Life. It is also the Egyptian Djed column, the backbone of Osiris, which was also thought of as the polar axis of the planet and the galactic meridian.[9] It is the stable axis through the center of the galaxy that anchors the moving axis of the precession of the equinoxes. It also represents the Teli from the *Bahir.* The Egyptians celebrated a realignment of the Djed pillar every 27, 54, and 108 years.[10] These are, of course, numbers involved in the precession of the equinoxes, reduced by a factor of ten. The Djed, then, was also seen as a marker of a particular time, the beginning and end of a long cycle.

The central pillar of the cross at Hendaye, in suggesting that it has a Djed-like function, possibly points to the precessional realignment, of the Egyptian temples and of life itself, with the galactic axis. As the connecting concept between the symbolic meaning of the upper cross and how this meaning is played out in the multileveled cross of the base, the pillar has been conspicuous in its absence. None of our sources bothers to mention it. After all, the monument doesn't need a pillar. Even if the upper cross rested on the base, it could still be seen as above and not change the meaning. Direct mention of the column was not included for a reason, for it symbolizes the Djed-like cosmic alignment the monument is describing. Not even Fulcanelli felt comfortable drawing attention to its symbolic implications.

The Base or Pedestal

Given Fulcanelli's identification of the double *X*'s on the upper cross with one of the images on the base, we can only surmise that the image of the four *A*'s was indeed meant to represent Tarot trump 20, The Last Judgment. There are no clues about what Tarot cards correspond to the star, the moon, and the sun, images that Fulcanelli does not comment on at all. As noted above, he does, however, go on at great length about the fourfold attributes of the Last Judgment, insisting that we pay attention to the four evangelists and their animal forms. Fortunately, all of these symbols relate to the monument as a whole as much or more than they relate to the four *A*'s of the Last Judgment, and they give us an important clue about how to use the monument as a galactic marker.

To understand this, we must first of all locate the monument and its symbols in space. Fulcanelli tells us that the front of the monument is the side with the INRI inscription. This is also the side of the pedestal that has the star, and it faces east. The sun faces west, the moon faces north, and the Last Judgment, the four *A*'s, faces south.

Now let's look at each symbol individually. As figure 11.7 shows, our three sources have each suggested a different pattern for ordering

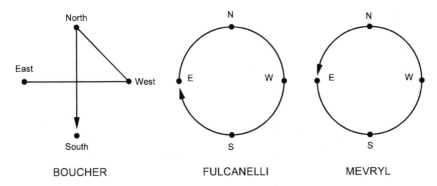

Figure 11.7. Three analysis patterns of the images on the base.

the images on the pedestal. Boucher proposed a zigzag, Fulcanelli a clockwise circle, and Mevryl a counterclockwise circle, and we must be careful not to lose sight of their intrinsic interconnectedness.

Because the star is on the side that faces east, one might tend to think of it as the Morning Star, Venus, but also Sirius. Both of these are intriguing attributions, pointing as they do toward Isis, the Egyptian goddess who was the model for the Christian Mary. Isis was linked to Sirius in Egypt. Her husband, Osiris, was thought to be the constellation Orion, which Sirius follows at a respectful distance. Sirius was also used as a time-keeping star in ancient Egypt. Its rise before the sun, as the Morning Star, marked the annual flooding of the Nile. Venus can also be used as a time-keeping marker, one whose periodicity can be used to track the precessional motion.[11] Neither of these options, however, seems to fit the meaning on the monument. Given the monument's current alignment, we can't help but stand in the west looking east through the rising sun toward the eight-rayed starburst, which suggests some sort of heliacal rising. (To see this we must imagine the base as transparent, as shown in fig. 11.8.)

The problem is that heliacal risings of Venus and Sirius are too common to be used as an indicator of any large period between catastrophes. Following our Tarot trump pattern, the star on the pedestal would be simply The Star, trump 17. Interestingly enough, most Tarot cards of The Star show it as eight-rayed. Its zodiacal attribution is Aquarius, the sign opposite Leo, and its Hebrew letter is *heh*, the window. From this we can speculate that this star is somehow related to the cycles of time, the dragon axis of the Teli, revealed to Abraham.

Figure 11.8. The sun and star panels seen in transparency, making "the sun behind the sun."

At first glance, the sun face is indeed a devouring sun as Boucher tells us. Its design is vaguely Mesoamerican, suggesting Aztec or Incan calendrical sun disks. None of our sources draws any attention to this obvious fact. While the angry sun does suggest a catastrophe motif, the more obvious Tarot image for this face is The Sun, trump 19. This card is attributed to Leo, and the Hebrew letter *resh*, the *R* of the Lallemant mansion's enigmatic credence, is its Hebrew letter. Its simple meaning of "completion of a cycle" points to its basic meaning on the monument. The sun will complete a great cycle, perhaps even the great cycle, the monument implies. The sun face is opposite the eight-rayed star, and, as Boucher suggests, there is a numerical connection between them (see fig. 11.9). The star's rays grow by a geometric progression on the sun face, doubling or crossing from 8 to 16 to 32. Mevryl's idea of the sun behind the sun is suggestive, for it makes the star a symbol of Sirius. We are given no clue concerning the four stars surrounding the sun. Mevryl does have a few ideas on the stars, including the possibility that they are the inner and outer planets.[12]

The Moon is the most curious of the images on the pedestal of the Hendaye cross (see fig. 11.10).

It is clearly the storybook man-in-the-moon face, but with a

Figure 11.9. The sun superimposed on the star.

Figure 11.10. The moon on the pedestal of the monument.

326 Hendaye's Message: The Season of Catastrophe and the Place of Refuge

prominent eye. The image is also echoed on the traditional rendition of the Tarot trump called The Moon. This makes the association to the trump easy, but we are left unsure of its meaning. The Moon, trump 18, is the card of illusion and unconscious forces, and it is attributed to Pisces and the Hebrew letter *qoph*. The Moon is across from the Last Judgment, indicating that it is somehow involved in marking that moment in time. But how? The answer becomes obvious only when we arrange the pedestal's faces into their Tarot equivalents.

Fulcanelli focuses most of his discussion on the final image, the four A's/Last Judgment, because of its undoubted importance. But what exactly is it showing us? Since Fulcanelli is so clear in his insistence that this face is the Last Judgment, we shouldn't hesitate to examine the traditional image for this trump, which is number 20, for clues. In the oldest versions, an angel with a trumpet sporting an equal-armed cross, such as found on the monument face, resurrects three people from their graves. The angel, perhaps Gabriel, is surrounded by a heavenly radiance, and thirteen rays shoot down toward the newly risen dead. From this we can discern that the Last Judgment is not the Day of Wrath, when the wicked are punished, but rather the beginning of the chiliast millennium.

Fulcanelli's discussion, however, seems to jump from obvious references to the Last Judgment, reinforcing our Tarot interpretation of this face, to equally obvious references to the last Tarot trump, number 21, The World, whose Hebrew letter is *tau* and astrological attribution is Saturn. The four archangels are not shown on The Last Judgment trump, but are the principal motif of The World card. Thus, Fulcanelli is telling us that we must include the Tarot trump The World in our interpretation.

Each of the four A's symbolizes an age of the Great Year, and their broken crossbar is used in printer's mark code to signify a millennium (see fig. 11.11). From this, we can see that the A's represent either 4,000 years, taking us back to the time of Abraham, or 12,000 years, Mevryl's asteroid periodicity, if we think of each A as 3,000 years. Both of these dates are suggestive, but, as we shall find, the 12,000-year date, 10,000 B.C.E., is the most interesting.

The Tarot trump The Last Judgment is also associated with the element of fire—hence, the predictions of being tried by divine fire. If we take Fulcanelli's suggestion and place the four fixed signs of the zodiac

Figure 11.11. Samples of sacred *A*'s from early French Gnostic watermarks. To the medieval mind, the V-shaped cross stroke of the capital *A* implied an *M* as in "Ave Millenarium." From Harold Bayley, *The Lost Language of Symbolism*, 2 vols. (New York: Citadel Press, n.d.).

on the four *A*'s, an interesting pattern emerges. The upper pair would be Leo, the Lion, and Scorpio, the Eagle; below that would be Aquarius, the Water Carrier, and Taurus, the Bull, if we match the pattern on the facade of Arles' Saint Trophime Cathedral (see fig. 11.2A). The *X* formed by this arrangement becomes Leo/Aquarius and Scorpio/Taurus. Since this *X* is also our Saint Andrew's cross from the upper part of the monument, we can conclude that the ages are measured from equinox to equinox. The Last Judgment begins when the Great Cross is formed, at the equinox period when Leo/Aquarius forms a right angle with Scorpio/Taurus.

THE MONUMENT SPEAKS: THE SEASON OF THE APOCALYPSE

With all the pieces of the Hendaye puzzle now spread before us, we must make sense of the mystery. Our solution must be self-contained and it must be accurate—that is, capable of interpreting astronomical reality. Only then will the monument's message be clear and unambiguous.

The upper cross tells us that the Last Judgment is timed to the precessional cycle of the equinoxes, and, whether or not there is a place of refuge, this disaster happens when the precessional dragon axis, also the Tree of the Knowledge of Good and Evil, forms a cross or right angle to the Tree of Life, the galactic dragon axis. The pillar, the Djed, reinforces this idea of a precessional alignment with the galactic axis. The base presents a way to refine the timing of this event.

We needed a starting point, however, to begin our calculations. The Hermetic Order of the Golden Dawn, which preserved some key pieces of the puzzle, supplied the hint that if Leo is put on the spring equinox, the zodiac will align properly.[13] If we use the beginning of the Age of Leo, roughly 13,000 years ago, as our starting point, then the monument, once its symbolism is understood, could be made to reveal a date for the beginning of the end of time.

The answer is at once both simple and complex, and it confirms the depth of understanding of the Tree of Life as a cosmological model on the part of Fulcanelli and of the builder of the monument. Starting with the directions, the images on the base, and their Tarot and zodiacal associations we get:

DIRECTION	PEDESTAL IMAGE	TAROT TRUMP	SIGN/ ELEMENT
East	star	The Star	Aquarius
West	sun	The Sun	Leo
North	moon	The Moon	Pisces
South	four A's	The Last Judgment	Fire

On the monument, the star on the east and the moon on the north together suggest that the northeast corner symbolizes the cusp of Aquarius/Pisces. Opposite is the junction of the sun and the element of fire. We can take this as the cusp of Leo/Virgo, since The Sun trump is attributed to Leo. This forms one of our axes. The northwest/southeast line becomes the Scorpio/Sagittarius–Taurus/Gemini galactic axis, from center to edge, so that our simple arrangement of Tarot attributions, shown in figure 11.12, gives us our correct alignment of the Cube of Space.

If we use as our starting point the moment when the spring equinox fell on the cusp of Leo/Virgo, we arrive at a date of March 22, 10,958 B.C.E. Half a precessional cycle later, 12,960 years, brings us to 2002, when Leo/Virgo falls on the fall equinox. The monument also records this 180-degree rotation of symbols around the galactic axis. In 10,958 B.C.E., the sun rose in the east in Leo/Virgo as the moon set in Aquarius/Pisces. The monument reverses this, with the sun in the west

Correspondences of Hendaye Cross
and Tree of Life/Tarot Images

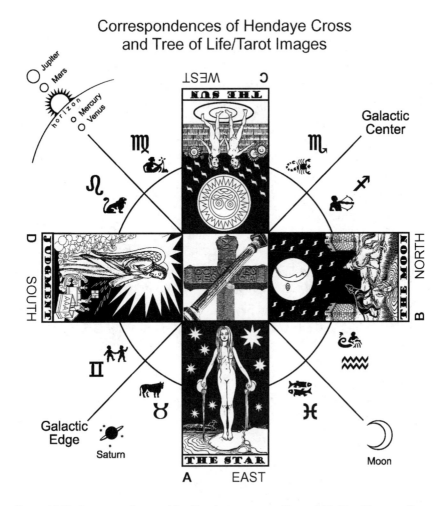

Figure 11.12. Correspondence of the Hendaye cross and Tree of Life/Tarot images. The four Tarot trumps, The Star, The Moon, The Sun, and The Last Judgment, represent the four faces of the Hendaye cross. The edges are aligned to the great cross of the galactic alignment, September 22–23, 2002.

and the moon in the east, to show the flip of precessional midpoints, the Leo/Virgo equinoxes.

If the midpoint of the classically counted Great Year really falls on the fall equinox of 2002, then the monument should point directly to that moment in time. The arrangement of the four evangelists or fixed signs in the pattern of the four *A*'s on the Last Judgment panel supports this alignment, as does the tympanum designs of Arles and Chartres.

But to be truly specific, the monument must give us something that precisely defines that moment in time. On the sun face, it does.

The key, of course, is where to stand. Mevryl's clues suggest that we take Champagne's frontispiece to *Le Mystère* literally and stand between the paws of the Sphinx on the Giza plateau. Thanks to the Voyager 2 computer software, we were able to do this prior to the event and check our conclusions. Dawn on September 23, 2002, local Sphinx time, is also close to the moment of the fall equinox, which brings the whole pattern into synchronization.

On that day the sun rose on the cusp of Leo/Virgo, with the near-full moon setting on the cusp of Aquarius/Pisces. As shown in figure 11.13, in the sky as the sun rose on that day were the three superior planets, Mars and Jupiter close together in Leo and Cancer, respectively, and Saturn on the mid-heaven cusp of Gemini/Taurus; below the horizon were the two inferior planets, Venus and Mercury in Virgo and Libra, respectively. This matches the four stars of the pedestal's sun face, with Mars and Jupiter above the horizon and Mercury and Venus below.

But all three superior planets are visible, for Saturn stands high in the mid-heaven on the cusp of Taurus/Gemini, in opposition to the center of the galaxy. Fulcanelli is aware of this: "The *age of iron* has no other seal than that of *Death*. Its hieroglyph is the skeleton, bearing the

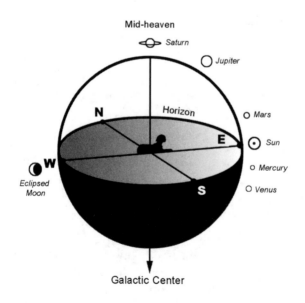

Figure 11.13. Planetary alignment at dawn on the fall equinox, September 22, 2002, with the Sphinx as zero point.

attributes of Saturn: the empty hourglass, symbol of time run out, and the scythe, reproduced in the figure seven, which is the number of transformation, of destruction, of annihilation."[14]

But it is hard to see how this configuration of the planets can be derived from the monument unless we consider the kabbalistic Tree of Life. Even though he insists that the four *A*'s represent the Last Judgment, Fulcanelli associates the panel with the Tarot trump The World. As we noted above, this suggests that we must somehow include The World in our interpretation.

The answer, of course, is Saturn, the planet associated with the trump The World. In our alignment, Taurus/Gemini falls on the southeast corner, the junction between the star, our first symbol, and the four *A*'s, our last. It seems a natural continuation of the pattern to insert our extra trump at this juncture, and when we do, the Tarot image matches the pattern in the sky. Saturn does fall on the galactic edge of Taurus/Gemini on our equinox morning, demonstrating the precision of the monument's timing.

This becomes even clearer when we look at our Tree of Life diagram and note that we have been using the bottom five paths on the Tree (fig. 11.14).

Figure 11.14. The lower paths on the Tree of Life showing the correspondences to the alignments on the Hendaye cross.

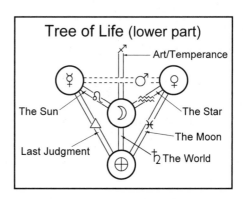

The paths are arranged in the same symmetry as the faces of the monument. The star and the sun paths are connected through the *sefirah* Yesod, as the moon and the Last Judgment are linked through Malkuth, forming the same oppositions as on the monument. The star and the moon, however, are on the same side of the Tree as are the sun and the Last Judgment, creating our main northwest/southeast axis.

This interlocking symmetry mirrors the arrangement on the monument, and both seem to circle the middle pillar of the galactic axis. Indeed, with the addition of The World/Saturn on the galactic edge, the attributions of the middle pillar of the Tree of Life are revealed.

Opposite The World through Yesod as we go up the middle pillar is the path of the Tarot trump called Art or Temperance, associated with the zodiacal sign Sagittarius, marker of the center of the galaxy. Thus, our pattern of alignments is as complete as on the Tree if we add Art for the center of the galaxy in the northwest corner. We are not only marking a moment, but also recapitulating the art of alchemy. The Tarot itself has always contained this insight. The image of Art, or Temperance, from the very earliest decks has been full of alchemical motifs. Some decks have even made the connection explicit by calling the trump Alchemy.[15]

What in the Tarot and on the Tree of Life is a philosophical construct becomes a way to calculate a specific moment in time on the Hendaye monument. In this we are reminded of Fulcanelli's admonition on the short or dry path—"one single vessel, one single matter, one single furnace"—from his discussion on Saint Marcel's dragon. Could it be that the short method, the quick transformation, is linked to the quality of time? Does Hendaye record the precise moment when the "dry work" becomes universal or simply happens spontaneously? Could this be Fulcanelli's double catastrophe?

Once again the Tree of Life and Tarot attributions provide a clue. The trump called The Blasted Tower, attributed to Mars, and whose symbol is a bolt of cosmic lightning striking a castle tower, crosses the path of Art/Alchemy. This image of destruction blocks the path to the center of the galaxy, giving support to the idea of its destructive nature.

The Tarot attributions on the Tree of Life thus tell us the major chiliast secret, that the events at the end of time are also the processes of a universal alchemical transmutation. Art/Alchemy and The Blasted Tower are linked, at right angles on the Tree, in the same way that the Great Cross of the fall equinox in 2002 linked them in the sky, with Mars rising at right angles to the center of the galaxy and Saturn. Could this arrangement be a harbinger of Fulcanelli's "double cataclysm"?

Fulcanelli, in the Hendaye chapter, is very careful in his choice of disaster words. He begins with chiliasm and "millenarism," two quaint, almost antiquarian terms. Then he uses "cyclic catastrophe" and proceeds quickly to "the Beast of the Apocalypse, of the dragon, which on the days of Judgment, spews out fire and brimstone on macrocosmic creation." Soon after, in the same paragraph, Fulcanelli makes his only use of the phrase "double cataclysm," while discussing the single place of refuge. His care could be taken as a sign that he is warning of something more indefinite than Mevryl's rock from outer space.

Fulcanelli also tells us that the INRI of the upper cross "corresponds to the schematic image of the cycle shown on the base." This can either be the four *A*'s or the four images on the base as a whole—the metaphor works for both. The inner meaning of INRI is nature renewed by fire, and its *gematria* points to the precessional cycle, which implies a cyclical disaster by means of celestial fire.

"Thus," Fulcanelli continues, "we have two symbolic crosses, both instruments of the same torture. Above is the divine cross, exemplifying the chosen means of expiation; below is the global cross, fixing the pole of the northern hemisphere and locating the fatal period of this expiation. God the Father holds in his hand this globe, surmounted by this fiery sign."[16] From our work so far, this is easily understood. When the cross in the sky, the galactic alignment made by the first two dragon axes, is completed by the cross on earth, the equinox sunrise on the cusp of Leo/Virgo, then the fiery sign will be seen and the "days of Judgment" will be at hand.

The cross will "fix" the North Pole because, on the equinox, the earth's tilt, which causes the seasons, will be at the balance point, its "fixed" standstill. And this does in fact locate the "fatal period," with September 22, 2002, the equinox of the Great Cross, as the midway point of the period. Fulcanelli insists that our hemisphere will be tried by fire, in the same way that fire is used to separate gold from its impurities. In the rest of the chapter, he gives us no further clues to the disaster he is predicting, except that only the elite will survive.

When we assemble Fulcanelli's clues we find that we are looking for a cyclic catastrophe that is timed to the equinox intersections of the precessional Great Year. It will be a double catastrophe in which the northern hemisphere will be tried or destroyed by fire, seemingly from the mouth of the dragon, or the center of the galaxy. The deepest secret of the mysteries, from Isis to the Tarot trump Art/Alchemy, has been the location of the center of the galaxy.

Even more curious is the fact that Pope Sylvester's Chroniclers, with the blessing of the Fatimid caliph, established the Order of Our Lady of Zion on Mount Zion at the fall equinox of 1002. One thousand years before the Day of Judgment predicted by the ancient illuminated astronomy and rediscovered by the alchemist pope, that same pope founded an order in Jerusalem that would have far-reaching effects on the history of the next millennium. Pope Sylvester was planning on creating the millennium of peace, ending in the chiliast paradise of the New Jerusalem. Like so many other millenarian visionaries before and since, he began with the historical Jerusalem, his influence provoking first pilgrimages and then the Crusades to control the earthly location of the heavenly kingdom.

Pope Sylvester is the link between the lost wisdom of the ancient world and the monotheistic gnosticism that grew out of it and the Gothic age and Italian Renaissance out of which our modern world developed. With Fulcanelli's help, it is possible to see the entire current, going back at least two millennia to Alexandrian Egypt. From "Isis the Prophetess" and the gnosticism of the emerging popular religions, to the family groups of Islam and Judaism and the solitary philosophers of the West, down to Pope Sylvester, the Templars, and the builders of the cathedrals, on through the underground centuries of alchemists and Rosicrucians, to its twentieth-century explication by Fulcanelli, the current retained its coherence.

The cross at Hendaye, a true monument to the end of time, demonstrates how to calculate the traditional date of the Day of Judgment. It points to a very specific date, the fall equinox of 2002, and, by Champagne's implication, a specific place, the paws of the Sphinx on the Giza plateau. Interestingly enough, the Great Pyramid, another mysterious monument at Giza, is thought to contain a prophetic design in its passages and Grand Gallery that ended on September 17, 2001.[17] This is exactly one year and five days before the Hendaye date, which is the time period required to prepare for the transition from pharaoh to a living star in Orion according to the Pyramid texts.[18]

Keeping in mind Jesus' admonition that no one knows the exact day or hour of the Judgment, we might think the monument's exactness to be presumptuous at the least. Fulcanelli, however, gives us another clue with his use of phrases such as "days of Judgment," and "fatal period." The exact date derived from the monument is a marker to an apocalyptic season. The easiest way to identify a time period by one date is to choose the midpoint. This is logical enough, since an equinox itself is a midpoint in so many ways.

If September 22, 2002, is the middle of the season, then how do we identify the beginning and the end, or culmination? If we think of the XX on the upper cross as meaning twenty years, in addition to referring to trump XX and the twentieth century, then we have an acceptable period on either side of our target date. Strangely enough, this brings our monument into line with two vast systems of counting time from opposite ends of the planet, the Mayan calendar and the Tibetan Kalachakra, or Wheel of Time. It also solves the remaining problems of the monument's design.

The Tibetan Kalachakra contains a prophecy indicating that 860 years after its introduction into Tibet, which happened in 1127, the conditions would be fulfilled for a twenty-five-year period that would culminate in the appearance of the Tibetan version of New Jerusalem, the hidden city of Shambhala.[19] Eight hundred sixty years after 1127 is 1987, and twenty-five years after that is 2012. These dates are also significant in various versions of the Mayan calendar.

The Harmonic Convergence, José Arguelles's attempt at a global New Age coming-out party in 1987, was billed as a significant date in the Mayan calendar. While this is debatable in terms of the traditional Mayan calendrical system—a better choice would have been 1992, the beginning of the last *katun,* or twenty-year period—it does mark the significant moment when the eschatological calendars of these widely separated cultures began to synchronize.

September 22, 2002, falls on the midpoint of this last Mayan *katun,* 13 Reed and 20 Ahau, calculated from the summer solstice of 1992 to the winter solstice of 2012. While this is a nice fit, and a confirmation that all of these systems are working from the same ancient traditions, the question is, Can we find this season on the monument at Hendaye?

So far, our interpretation of the base has been more concerned with the corners and their alignments and attributions than with the faces of the base. We have used their Tarot images to calculate the attributions that led us to our target date. We found that date displayed in the Saint Andrew's cross of the upper cross, a symbol for the equinox alignment. The upright square cross, known, as Hewitt informed us, as the cross of Saint George (see fig. 11.15), is also displayed by the opposition of the east/west and north/south faces. The Saint George cross is traditionally

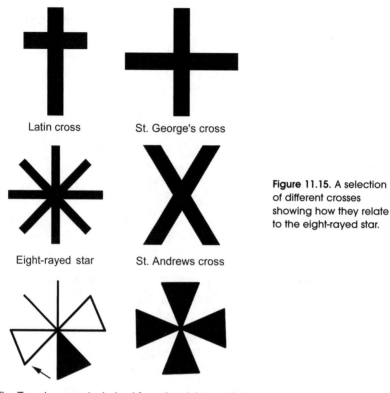

Latin cross

St. George's cross

Figure 11.15. A selection of different crosses showing how they relate to the eight-rayed star.

Eight-rayed star

St. Andrews cross

The Templar cross is derived from the eight-rayed star.

used to mark the solstice alignments. The eight-armed cross, the Templar cross, is the combination of the two. Since our interpretation of the Hendaye cross evolves it into this same eight-sided figure, the unavoidable suggestion is that our equinox cross is the midpoint between two solstice events.

Looking at the monument, we find that the sun and the star are paired, as are the moon and the four A's. Since each member of the pairs is found on opposite sides of the monument, we might think of them as being in opposition. Another way to see it is to think of the base as transparent so that the images are in conjunction. Actually, as we shall see, either way works because what is conjunct on one solstice is in opposition on the other. The problem lies in identifying the star and the four A's.

We must discard both Venus and Sirius as candidates for the star. While a summer solstice alignment is possible with both, neither fits our dates. Such an alignment happens every year with Sirius, too often to be a marker of any singular celestial event, and Venus was behind the sun for the summer solstice of 1992 and will be in front of the sun for the winter solstice of 2012. The star, therefore, cannot be either of these. The sun, however, does relate to the center of the galaxy in the right pattern. It rises in opposition on the summer solstice and in conjunction on the winter solstice during this period, becoming exact on the winter solstice of 2012, the end point of the Mayan calendar.

If we think of Fulcanelli's image of the dragon's mouth, the center of the galaxy, spewing out flame and light, then the star might just relate to an eruption from the galactic center. Coupled with the angry sun face, this might also be a clue to the "double cataclysm." The star-like disturbance from the center of the galaxy might trigger a reaction in our own sun, hence Fulcanelli's insistence on a "double" catastrophe.

If the star is a representation of the center of the galaxy, then what is the meaning of the four A's? Since this image depicts the great cycle of time, it might also stand for the main alignment point of the cycle, the galactic center. In that case, the moon would also be in opposition or conjunction on the solstices. And this was, in fact, the case.

Standing again on Giza between the paws of the Sphinx, we note that on the morning of the summer solstice, June 21, 1992, there was a partial lunar eclipse in Scorpio, in opposition to the rising sun in Taurus/Gemini. This is the starting point of our twenty-year countdown, and matches the moon–four A's alignment on the Hendaye cross, even to the partial eclipse of the moon face.

Even better is the winter solstice, December 21, 2012, when the sun rises in perfect alignment with the center of the galaxy on the cusp of Scorpio/Sagittarius, while the moon sets on the cusp of Taurus/Gemini. On the summer solstice at the beginning of our apocalyptic season, the moon was conjunct the center of the galaxy and the sun was in opposition. On the winter solstice, the end point of the period, the sun will be conjunct the galactic center and the moon will be in opposition. Thus the solstice alignments, as revealed on the Hendaye monument, act as brackets or bookends to our midpoint of September 22, 2002, defining a twenty-year period as the season of apocalypse.

We have now answered our third question from chapter 1: "What do the symbolic images and ciphers on the cross mean? How are they 'the rarest symbolic translation' of an apocalyptic philosophy?" And, most important of all, "Do they suggest a date?" We have unraveled the meaning of the images on the cross and now understand how, in truth, they are the "rarest symbolic translations" of an ancient astronomy. While our answers are somewhat disturbing, they do at least make astronomical sense.

They also raise more questions. How did Pope Sylvester know about the center of the galaxy, and about its millennial anniversary? For that matter, how did the designer of the Hendaye cross or even Fulcanelli know? The galactic core was not officially discovered until 1917, and yet they, as well as the Maya and the Tibetans, clearly knew. Fulcanelli is at his most simple and truthful when he tells us that the unknown sculptor of the monument "possessed real and profound knowledge of the universe."

THE PHILOSOPHER'S STONE AND THE QUALITY OF TIME

After decoding the cross at Hendaye, we found ourselves on the horns of a dilemma. On the one hand, we could be fairly certain that we were reading Fulcanelli and the monument's message correctly. On the other hand, there seemed to be no way its message could be true. The end of the world has been predicted many times before, and since those predictions have failed to come true, why would the prophecy encoded in the Hendaye cross be any different? If the end is coming, it is a self-fulfilling prophecy based on our capacity to destroy ourselves. Cosmology would seem to have little to do with it.

And yet Fulcanelli insists that it does. His suggestion that alchemy and chiliasm are connected led us to the Gnostic concept of the Great Return of the lesser lights to the Light and its origin in the illuminated astronomy of the *Bahir*. According to tradition, this ancient science derived from Abraham's covenant with the God Most High, the El in the sky. As we saw above, Abraham was revered as the greatest astronomer of his age, drawing on the wisdom of Egypt and India.[20]

From the *Bahir*, the Bible, and surviving esoteric fragments from groups such as the Golden Dawn, we can reconstruct the major points of this astronomical perspective. Space was envisioned as a cube within a sphere. The equator of that sphere was the sun's apparent path through the constellations of the zodiac. As shown in figure 11.16, the cube was positioned so that its vertical edges intersect the cusps of

Sagittarius/Scorpio, Gemini/Taurus, Pisces/Aquarius, and Virgo/Leo. Above the cube, in the top portion of the sphere, the constellation of Draco coils about the still point of the north ecliptic pole. This El in the sky was antiquity's High God, with the planets hanging from its coils. The south ecliptic pole of the sphere rests on the brilliance of the Lesser Magellanic Cluster.

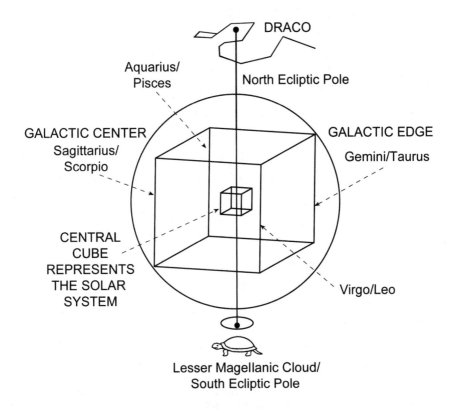

Figure 11.16. The alignment of the Cubes of Space, solar cube inside the large galactic cube. Draco sits enthroned above the Cubes, which rests on the back of the "turtle" of the Lesser Magellanic Cloud.

This eternally unmoving axis was thought to be the middle pillar of a vast Tree of Life in the world of action. Kabbalistic theory suggested, however, that if there was one Tree in a world, there should also be a reflection of all four Trees in the multiverse. The *Bahir* addressed this by implying a projected, jewel-like Tree that covered the surface of the sphere. The center point of the sphere, our sun in the Tiferet position, would then be projected outward onto the edges of the cube to form four interlocking trees, as shown in figure 11.17.

This arrangement also gives us the basis for the Four Ages. The sun's precessional alignment with these projected Tiferet centers is the

Projecting the Tree of Life onto a Sphere

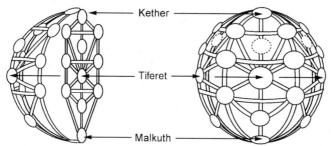

The Kether point of the projected Tree of Life would correspond to the North Pole, Tiferet with the equator, and Malkuth to the South Pole. The spherical Tree is composed of four Trees that share the sefirot of the outer pillars.

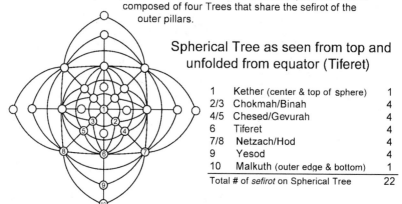

Spherical Tree as seen from top and unfolded from equator (Tiferet)

1	Kether (center & top of sphere)	1
2/3	Chokmah/Binah	4
4/5	Chesed/Gevurah	4
6	Tiferet	4
7/8	Netzach/Hod	4
9	Yesod	4
10	Malkuth (outer edge & bottom)	1
Total # of *sefirot* on Spherical Tree		22

The flattened version of the above is divided at the equator into two views. If the four Tiferet points are the fixed signs and stars of the zodiac and Malkuth is the Greater Magellanic Cluster, it is not difficult to locate other coordinates in space based on the location points of the sefirot.

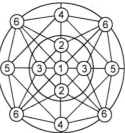

northern hemisphere
(as seen from top)

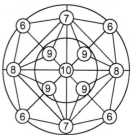

southern hemisphere
(as seen from bottom)

Figure 11.17. Projecting the Tree of Life onto a sphere.

transition point between ages. Each time the equinox or solstice crosses one of these points in the 26,000-year precessional cycle, the earth enters a new age. But our illuminated astronomy also provides us with two more Teli, or dragon axes. These can be seen as the "snake" of the Milky Way and the "snake" of the planetary equator formed by the wobble of the earth's tilt. The snake or dragon of the Milky Way crosses the solar ecliptic in the northwest at Scorpio/Sagittarius and in the southeast at Taurus/Gemini, both Tiferet corners. The equatorial snake of the planet, however, controlled by the precessional wobble, moves its equinox point on the ecliptic one degree counterclockwise approximately every seventy-two years. Thus, those moments when the snakes make right angles or direct conjunctions with each other determine the quality of time for that age.

The event, which gave Abram his insight into the nature of time, which was the window of the letter *heh* needed to spell Abraham, was his covenant with God. At this event, we are told in Genesis, a fiery torch passed through the alignment of sacrifices from the northwest to the southeast, an alignment preserved to this day by the location of the Black Stone in the cube or Kaaba of Mecca. This line from the northwest to the southeast corner is the galactic axis, of course. Abraham's covenant represents a shift from the High God of the El to a new hidden god controlling the temporal quality of the galactic axis and its alignments. This God, unlike the placid and benign El, could become angry and dispense judgment and destruction.

This God promised Abraham that his descendants would become as the stars, but whether in number or quality is uncertain. The chiliast promise also lay at the heart of the hidden God's covenant. Just as He could dispense judgment, so too could He dispense transformation— *Inshallah,* "as God wills it," as a Muslim would say.

Now, let us imagine this astronomical object, this sphered cube or "stone of the wise," from the outside. As in figure 11.17, we see twenty-two circles (twenty-six if we include Daat) on the surface of a sphere that contains a cube formed from the intersection of the three planes generated by the dragon axes. On each plane is a Tree of Life, joined at the center of the sphere. This breaks the sphered cube into eight cells, each of which has three faces reflecting outward from the central Tiferet point. From this arrangement we can see that the astronomical "Stone of the Wise" is also a depiction of a *tesseract* (see fig. 11.18), a four-dimensional or hypercube with 8 cells, 16 vertices, 24 faces, and 32 edges. Note within this the geometric progression (8, 16, 32) of the star and the sun on the Hendaye cross.

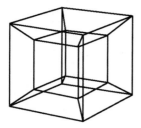

Figure 11.18. A four-dimensional hypercube, or tesseract.

As noted before, the cross at Hendaye is an exploded or schematic view of this philosopher's stone in the heavens. This is easy to see by simply collapsing the cross into the space of the pedestal, as in figure 11.19. The pillar folds in along the northwest–southeast axis, with the two arms of the upper cross forming the other two axes. Think of these as plane surfaces with Tree of Life patterns on them and we have the Precious Stone of the Wise from the *Bahir*.

The images on the three-dimensional surface of our pedestal-cube act as informational markers telling us how to align our hypercube to predict the quality of time in our age. As we saw above, this alignment involves the precessional equinox cross of Leo on the fall equinox combined with solstice markers that include the heliacal rising of the hidden God of the galactic center with the winter solstice sunrise. Our Bahiric philosopher's stone suggests that this season in time is one of great transformation, perhaps even the Day of Judgment alignment prefigured by Abraham's sacrifices.

Our Precious Stone of the Wise becomes even more curious when we consider that there are stars in each of the twenty-two or twenty-six circles on the surface of the celestial sphere. By using the most prominent star closest to the center of each circle, we can create a unique intergalactic distance/density zip code for our local solar system. If we had set out to design a system that tells us the specific quality of time in a specific locality of space, it is hard to imagine anything more simple and efficient than this apparently ancient perspective.

This information survived purges and persecutions until someone

Cross of Hendaye

Showing Cusps

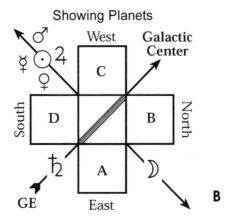

Figure 11.19. The Hendaye cross as a schematic for the hypercube "Stone of the Wise."
A. The Cube of Space aligned to the cusps of the great cross; SW/NE diagonal tells of the major energy gradient of the local galactic neighborhood; SE/NW is the galactic axis from center to edge.
B. The planetary alignments on September 22, 2002. Note that the planetary grouping around the Leo/Virgo cusp falls on the local galactic hot spot, indicating the fiery nature of the event.
C. Collapsed Hendaye cross showing, in 3D, the structures of the "Stone of the Wise."

Showing Planets

Folded into Cube

coded it in stone in the late seventeenth century at Hendaye. Even then the information wasn't lost; it was merely rediscovered in the nineteenth century and revealed to the public in the twentieth by Fulcanelli. When the Hendaye chapter was published in 1957, however, less than fifty years remained until the first precessional marker. Perhaps this was part of the plan, because only in the last fifty years or so has science caught up with Abraham the patriarch's level of understanding.

Now, with our chiliast season identified, we turn our attention to science. Is there any evidence connecting a cyclic, precessional-based catastrophe with the center of the galaxy? Could an asteroid swarm or a comet also be somehow involved, as Mevryl suggests? And most important of all, does the Hendaye cross truly point to a "place of refuge"?

TWELVE

CATASTROPHE AND REFUGE

COSMIC SUPERIMPOSITION: WILHELM REICH, ORGONE, AND THE CENTER OF THE GALAXY

Even though the center of the galaxy wasn't officially discovered until 1917, any primitive culture watching the skies would quickly discern that there was something special in that direction. The Milky Way, the heavenly Nile, bulges just where the sun's ecliptic crosses it (fig. 12.1).

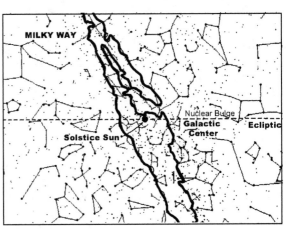

Figure 12.1. The Milky Way crosses the sun's ecliptic at its widest and narrowest points, the center and edge of the galaxy, which suggests some kind of radial flow, from center to edge, that causes this precise alignment.

At the other ecliptic crossing, the Milky Way looks thin and wispy, as if it is fading away. From this observation, we can see why this axis is described as a dragon or a snake, complete with the Pleiades as the snake's rattle. The sun crosses these points twice a year, but the precessional axis, marked by the sun's equinoxes or solstices, crosses these points only twice in a precessional Great Year.

One question for which the modern astronomer or cosmologist has no answer is why the ecliptic crosses the Milky Way at just those specific points (fig. 12.2). There seems to be no astrophysical reason why the ecliptic should intersect the plane of the Galaxy, the Milky Way, along its radial axis. It could as likely be at a right angle to that axis, or even more likely parallel to it so that the Milky Way matches the solar ecliptic. Yet, there it is, a cosmic synchronicity that suggests that some energy or magnetic "force" flowing from the center of the Galaxy, so womblike to the ancients, shapes our Cube of Space-time so that its long-term temporal quality, and perhaps even the evolution of life itself, is somehow related to its alignment along the radial axis of the Galaxy.

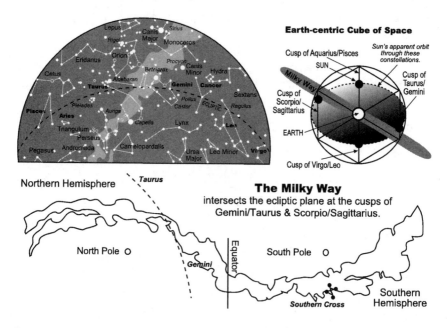

Figure 12.2. The alignment of the ecliptic, the solar cube of space and the galactic meridian. Note that the ecliptic crosses the galactic meridian at the edge, as shown, and at the center. The Southern Cross points to the galactic center crossing point.

But looking for subtle forces emanating from the center of the Galaxy that are capable of aligning the solar ecliptic takes us far away from mainstream astrophysics. One of the only thinkers who seemed to entertain anything close to our hypothesis was the radical psychoanalyst and biophysicist Wilhelm Reich. In *Cosmic Superimposition,* published in 1951, Reich developed his theory of sexual tension and release into a cosmological hypothesis based on the interaction of spinning systems. This superimposition of spin, in Reich's view, creates matter and gravity, implying a steady-state or constant-creation model of the universe.

Reich postulates that this constant superimposition of orgonic creation going on in the galactic core generates a radially flowing orgone stream that organizes the location and coherence of the solar systems of the galaxy. He suggests that the image of a spiral galaxy, such as ours, is the "most impressive picture of cosmic superimposition." After coming very close to uncovering the Abrahamic astronomy of ecliptic alignments we described in chapter 4, Reich concluded: "The ecliptic, accordingly, would be the result of a pull exerted upon the planetary system by the galactic Orgone energy stream, making its course deviate from the equatorial plane by 23.5 degrees."[1] He even goes so far as to declare that this cosmic orgone energy stream causes all gravitational effects.

Reich defines *orgone* as the "primordial cosmic energy; universally present and demonstrable visually, thermally, electroscopically, and by means of Geiger-Müller counters." In living bodies orgone is the "biological energy." This suggests that Reich was close to the alchemical secret on an energetic level. Alchemy lurks just around the edges of his words in *Cosmic Superimposition,* but never quite emerges as a subject.

But he was close, on several levels. "Orgone" sounds a little like the "Force" of the *Star Wars* films, but the description has the virtue of explaining an astronomical fact that modern astrodynamics seems reluctant to face. But as support for our hypothesis, and in providing an origin for the catastrophe, Reich's work, brilliant as it is, fell far short of our needs.

MESSAGES FROM MANY SOURCES

As we worked on this book, answers and suggestions about certain portions of the mystery kept emerging spontaneously from other researchers. The importance of the center of the Galaxy, and our alignment to it, is one of the best examples of this synchronicity. We knew of the significance of the galactic center through our connection with Moira Timms's work on the Djed pillar, through Santillana and von Dechend's book *Hamlet's Mill,* and through Terence and Dennis

McKenna's *The Invisible Landscape*. But in the summer of 1996, several people published articles or presented papers on the upcoming Great Cross of the equinoxes and galactic center in the years from 1998 to 2002. While none of these perspectives fit our Hendaye framework, or explained its importance, the idea was part of the cultural zeitgeist.

Around this same time, John Major Jenkins, one of the foremost scholars of the Mayan calendrical system, began to suggest in various articles that the end date of the Mayan calendar, the winter solstice of 2012, was chosen because of its precise alignment of the galactic center with the rising sun. The Mayan astronomers, as Jenkins has demonstrated, have much to tell us about our ancient philosopher's stone cosmology. While Jenkins's work supports our thematic interpretation of the ancient astronomical vision, he had no better suggestion than Reich about the catastrophe itself.

In "The Message of the Maya End Date," the last chapter in his *Maya Cosmogenesis 2012,* Jenkins asks the question: "What does the 2012 alignment mean for human beings on earth?" He tries to answer this by pointing to another factor involved in this rare precessional conjunction.

The Galaxy's equator is the center of the Milky Way itself, and by 2012 the solstice meridian will have crossed over this galactic equator. Jenkins postulates that the earth's equator delineates distinct field-effect properties common to all spinning bodies. Water in a drain, the spin of tornadoes, and hurricanes flow in opposite directions in each hemisphere. So too does the Galaxy. That would make the period from 1998, when the solstice meridian hits the exact center of the galaxy, and 2012, its heliacal rising, a sort of field-effect null zone, "much like the calm eye of a hurricane," Jenkins tell us, which "balances the surrounding chaos." Jenkins calls the shift a field-effect energy reversal.[2]

He doesn't predict any catastrophes from this energy reversal, but instead focuses on the psychological aspect. Jenkins sees the "2012 field-reversal as a moment in which the human spirit can emerge from unconscious patterns and blossom." He mentions the idea of a literal pole shift, so beloved of New Age doomsayers, but weighs in as leaning toward a pole shift in our collective psyche. He ends the chapter with a reference to ancient cultures such as the Magdalenian in eastern Europe 19,000 years ago, but refuses to speculate on what happened to end that Golden Age.

Ultimately we are convinced by his work that the Maya believed that this point marked a change significant enough to be called the zero point of time, but we are left wondering about the mechanism involved. If the Maya were simply extrapolating myth onto a celestial background, then it is possible that the astronomical indications alone were enough to define an end point. This approach ignores, however, the subtlety and sophistication of the cosmology itself. It is not just describing the flow of events in the sky; it is trying to interpret those events down here on earth. As Jenkins points out, the 260-day Mayan short count, based on the human gestation period, is also a factor of the precessional 26,000-year cycle. As above, so below, even in human evolution. But, as always, the question is the mechanism.

By the time Jenkins's *Maya Cosmogenesis 2012* appeared in the summer of 1998, our research was approaching critical mass. His conclusions, coupled with Terence McKenna's Time Wave Zero research (based on the trigrams of the I Ching and which also pointed to an end date of 2012), suggested that our interpretation of the Hendaye cross was closer to the truth than we had imagined. There seemed to be some connection, at the level of cosmology, between all of these idea streams. The astro-alchemical meme began to look more and more like a survivor from some prehistoric global civilization.

And if that was the case, then we were looking for a catastrophe, one so large that there must be some evidence of it left. Graham Hancock, in his groundbreaking work *Fingerprints of the Gods,* presented a catalog of cataclysmic events, and concluded that some sort of upheaval and flood occurred around 13,000 years ago. While he doesn't speculate on the cause of the cataclysm—which in his view resulted in a massive shift of the earth's crust—he does suggest that it is somehow related to the precessional cycle and its cosmic clock.[3] Hancock's perspective on this cosmic clockwork, however, is lacking a few key elements.

He focuses on precession as the movement of the celestial pole while ignoring the ecliptic pole. He emphasizes the celestial mill and its grinding without ever identifying the point around which it circles. Having missed the importance of the ecliptic pole in defining an unmoving axis, he is also unclear about the significance of the ecliptic crossing points on the Milky Way and thus misses the importance of the galactic alignments.

He does, however, confirm our notion that the catastrophe, whatever its cause, destroyed an advanced global civilization. He even speculates on secret societies: "If the circumstances were right it seems possible that the essence of the cult (the secret of the catastrophe's timing) might survive, carried forward by a nucleus of determined men and women."[4] Their objective would have been to preserve this knowledge for a future civilization facing the same event. We have seen how the *Bahir's* philosopher's stone and the cross at Hendaye function as just such devices for preserving the secret.

Still, a few pieces were missing. What caused the catastrophe? And could that disaster be related to the core transmutational process of alchemy? We had found that historically they were interconnected, but just how it worked was still elusive. The secret of alchemy and the secret of the double catastrophe, as we would learn from Paul LaViolette, are based on the same physics of creation.

EARTH UNDER FIRE:
THE DOUBLE CATASTROPHE REVEALED

We met Paul LaViolette at a conference in Boulder, Colorado. He was scheduled to talk about his big bang theories, which, because of their suggestion of a possible scientific model for the alchemical process, were of interest to us. We also knew that LaViolette had determined the importance of the galactic center and had speculated on the nature of the catastrophe that ended the ancient global culture. We were shocked to find, however, that in the course of a ninety-minute presentation, LaViolette apparently solved the problem presented by Fulcanelli's prediction of a double cataclysm.

Riveted to our seats, we listened as LaViolette ticked off possible solutions to one after another of our remaining problems. Why was the galactic-cross alignment of Leo/Aquarius and Scorpio/Taurus so important to the builders of the Hendaye cross and the Gothic cathedrals? LaViolette shows how this alignment pinpoints galactic microwave hotspots and how the ancients used this information to assign planetary qualities to the signs of zodiac, thus giving us the first coherent explanation for a very esoteric system of attributions.

How did the ancient scientists know the location of the exact center of the galaxy? LaViolette suggested that perhaps it was much brighter because it was actively erupting. By the end of the lecture, we were somewhat in shock. LaViolette's new book, *Earth Under Fire,* suddenly became the book of answers, and the question of Fulcanelli's warning attained a new level of significance. What had up to then been speculation on our part about an esoteric eschatology became a specific cataclysmic scenario with none of the vagueness of notions about disruptions in the orgone flow or galactic-equator field reversal. LaViolette, it seemed, had penetrated the alchemical meme to its core and seen the double cataclysm pointed out by Fulcanelli and the cross at Hendaye.

LaViolette's *Earth Under Fire* opens where his previous book, *Beyond the Big Bang,* left off, with an examination of the zodiacal cipher in the sky and a warning of a galactic core explosion. LaViolette points out the importance of the four fixed signs, Taurus, Leo, Scorpio, and Aquarius, and how, in the rearranged creation pattern, these are the only signs that retain their location on the ecliptic. He notes that Leo and Aquarius, which are opposite each other in the zodiac, "appear to be indicating a temperature polarity in space." He points to the traditional attribution of the Sun to Leo and Saturn to Aquarius as indications of this temperature gradient, the Sun of course being very hot and Saturn very cold.

He goes on to discover that the attributions of the planets to the signs and to parts of the body also follow this temperature pattern (see fig. 12.3). LaViolette speculates that "since the lore of astrology redundantly encodes essentially the same Leo-Aquarius temperature bias using entirely unrelated sets of symbols (planets and body parts), we are led to conclude that these symbol systems are being used to call attention to the temperature gradient features that both share."[5]

This is truly amazing when we consider that the microwave background radiation coming from deep space has precisely this kind of temperature gradient running across the heavens from the hot pole near Leo to the cold pole near Aquarius. It is almost as if there were a microwave "sun" in the direction of Leo.

The University of California at Berkeley team that discovered this temperature gradient in 1977 concluded, however, that it was produced by the solar system's motion toward the region of Leo. Because of our system's orbital motion around the galactic center, and the galaxy's bulk motion through space, we are moving toward Leo at a speed that is

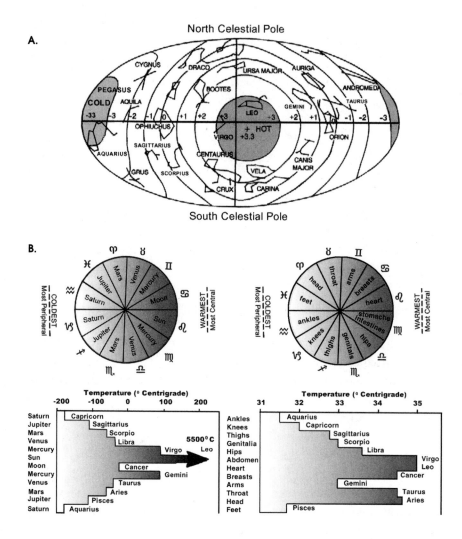

Figure 12.3. *A.* A sky map showing the temperature gradient of the universe; the hottest spots are near the constellation Leo. *B.* The relationships among the zodiacal signs, the temperature gradient, and the parts of the body. From Paul LaViolette, *Earth Under Fire* (New York: Starburst Publications, 1997)

twelve times that of our orbital motion. The precessional rising of Leo on the equinox, then, becomes a measure of alignment with the motion of the galactic spin.

But what of the Scorpio/Taurus alignment? LaViolette argues that the symbolism of Scorpio and Sagittarius not only locates the galactic center but also pinpoints it as the place of continuous matter/energy creation, and therefore the possible source of a catastrophic energy outburst, the sting, as it were, of the Scorpion (fig. 12.4). Such galactic outbursts have been the subject of speculation since Edwin Hubbell demonstrated that spiral nebulae were actually distant galaxies. In the 1960s, evidence emerged suggesting that the core of a galaxy could shine brighter than all the stars in the galaxy itself. Called Seyfert galaxies after their discoverer Carl Seyfert, some have been known to shine more than 100,000 times brighter than the center of our own galaxy. On average, one in five to seven galaxies is observed to be a Seyfert type.[6]

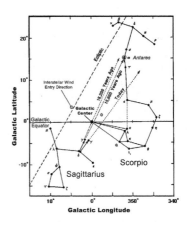

Figure 12.4. LaViolette's map showing the constellations of Scorpio and Sagittarius as they appeared in the distant past. The trajectory of the archer's arrow shows that it would have intersected the galactic center 15,000 years ago. (From LaViolette, *Earth Under Fire*)

"Astronomers have come to realize," LaViolette tells us, "that galactic core explosions occur in all spiral galaxies, even in our own, and that the majority of galaxies that have a normal appearance with no sign of core activity are simply galaxies whose cores happen to be in their quiescent phase. The statistics suggest that a galaxy core resides in this quiescent phase about 80 to 85 percent of the time. It spends the other 15 to 20 percent of the time in an active state, with eruptive episodes lasting from hundreds to several thousands of years."[7] In this sense, galaxies go on and off like the blinking lights of a Christmas tree.

The current black-hole model of the galactic core has difficulty accounting for these explosive episodes. Black holes consume matter and rarely eject it in explosive bursts as seen in Seyfert galaxies. Even a naked singularity, a rare black hole capable of emitting radiation, would be hard-pressed to match the energy output of Seyfert galaxies or quasars. LaViolette points out that modern radio-astronomy observations of the galactic core region reveal an object that acts more like a massive "mother star" than a black hole. The collapsing gravitational force, which causes a black hole, seems to be balanced by the outpouring of newly created matter and energy from within the supermassive star body, as predicted in subquantum kinetics. This model also predicts that the balance could at times become unstable, resulting in an explosive discharge of energy from the super massive core.[8]

Something as basic as a galactic core explosion in the relatively recent past should be easy to confirm with our modern astronomical instruments. And indeed, we find plenty of evidence for recent galactic core eruptions. Astronomers have found that gas clouds are moving radially outward from the galactic core like smoke rings from a central explosion.[9] A lumpy cloud of molecular gas five light-years out from the galactic center shows signs of massive disruption in the last 10,000 to 100,000 years, as if the central five light-years had been swept clean of interstellar dirt by an explosion. Farther out, around ten to twenty light-years, astronomers have found a literal smoke ring of oxygen-enriched gas propelled outward by a galactic core explosion less than 50,000 years ago. Even farther out is a cloud of molecular gas expanding outward at the rate of 150 kilometers per second. Astronomer Jan Oort estimated that it takes the force of 100,000 supernovas to propel this cloud out from the central core of the galaxy.

These pieces of evidence suggest that the microwave background radiation through which the sun is traveling in the direction of Leo was caused by the explosive waves of cosmic rays and gas clouds from the galactic center. Suddenly, the ancient cross of the fixed signs makes perfect sense. The first "beam" on the cross, Scorpio/Taurus, indicates the flow of the radial superwaves from the core explosions, and the other, Leo/Aquarius, indicates our solar system and planet's angular momentum to that flow. Our Bahiric philosopher's stone and the cross at Hendaye demonstrate these principles on a symbolic level.

LaViolette's galactic explosion hypothesis can be summarized in four broad points:

1. Periodically, the core of our galaxy enters an explosive phase during which it generates an intense outburst of cosmic-ray particles equivalent to several million supernovas.

2. These outbursts recur roughly every 10,000 years or so, and last for several hundred to several thousand years.
3. Some types of cosmic-ray particles generated in a core explosion, the electrons and positrons, travel radially outward at close to the speed of light. Others, the protons, lag behind the electron front and are mostly absorbed by the magnetic fields in the magnetic nucleus.
4. A superwave of cosmic-ray particles passed through the solar system toward the end of the Ice Age, injecting large amounts of cosmic dust into the system. This dust affected the sun and substantially affected the climate on earth, bringing on the sudden end of the Ice Age.

The galactic superwave, composed of superhot cosmic-ray particles traveling at close to the speed of light, would appear from Earth as a brilliant blue-white spot of light—about the size of Mars—in Sagittarius, surrounded by a slightly larger and less bright halo. This source, perhaps as much as a thousand times brighter than any other star, would be visible even in daylight.

LaViolette equates this new "sun" with the Hopi legends of Saquasohuh, the blue star spirit, and the Egyptian legends of Sekhmet, the all-destroying Eye of Re. It would remain in the sky as a second sun, or the sun behind the sun, for as long as a millennium, as a herald of catastrophe. Although the energy of this outburst is enough to affect electromagnetic systems on earth and produce weather changes, the real danger is the effect on the cloud of cosmic dust surrounding our solar system. According to LaViolette, the superwave will push massive amounts of dust into our solar system, with disastrous consequences (see fig. 12.5).[10]

This cosmic dust storm would begin to cause problems as it entered the solar system. At first the cloud of dust would block the sunlight and make the earth's surface very cold. Soon, however, a new problem would begin as the earth cooled rapidly.

Astronomers have noted that there are stars affected by large amounts of cosmic dust falling onto their surfaces, called T-Tauri stars. As the dust falls onto the surfaces of these stars it becomes heated and causes the skin of the star to brighten. This dust eventually forms around the star a cocoon that holds in the heat and causes the temperature of the star's corona to rise rapidly. This heating causes huge solar flares to appear on the surface of these T-Tauri stars. LaViolette postulates that

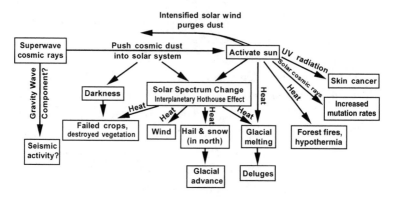

Figure 12.5. Superwave-induced cosmic-dust invasion can produce varying catastrophic results. (From LaViolette, *Earth Under Fire*)

this same event occurred with our own sun when the cosmic dust storm arrived soon after the blue star. As this dust gathered and finally settled on the surface of our own sun, it would also cause the sun to heat up, producing massive solar flares into the surrounding space.[11]

This solar activity and these flares would begin to have an effect on the weather here on earth. After the initial cooling period—brought on by the influx of dust—the sun would suddenly become very hot. A cocoon of cosmic dust and hot gases would gather around the sun, causing huge solar flares. It is possible that the superheated corona could increase in size until it overwhelmed our planet. This solar bubble would heat up the earth, causing tropical latitudes to become unbearably warm and the ice floes in the north and south polar regions to quickly melt. Lakes of fresh water that had been trapped in the polar glaciers would unleash their contents. These glacier waves would race down from the north and south polar ice sheets and drown and destroy all life in their deadly path.

This is LaViolette's explanation for the end of the Ice Age. Thousands of animal corpses have been found frozen in the wilderness of Alaska and Siberia. They seem to have been deposited there about 13,000 years ago at the end of the Pleistocene era. Hundreds of thousands of these animals died suddenly and inexplicably, including woolly mammoths, giant tree sloths, Arctic foxes, and many others. Their bodies are distributed in such a way as to indicate that they died from a violent influx of water. The bodies were then flushed down the rivers, collecting in gullies and ravines, until they were frozen in the cold that would return quickly after the bubble of hot gases from the sun disappeared. Hundreds of species did go extinct at the end of the Ice Age, about that there is no argument.

With astronomers openly admitting that galactic core explosions are highly probable, it is difficult to argue against LaViolette's explanation. LaViolette is saying that he has found proof of a catastrophe in the past that nearly destroyed all life on our planet. He is also saying that this catastrophe was of a "double" nature. The initial outburst from the galactic core caused electromagnetic shifts on earth, which may have caused crustal torque, pole shifts, tidal waves, and high winds. This first catastrophe was followed—sometime later—by an explosion of the sun's corona, caused by the influx of cosmic dust pushed by the galactic superwave. It was, in fact, just what Fulcanelli had said it would be, a double catastrophe.

In one fell swoop LaViolette had answered many of the questions that had haunted us as researchers. Amazingly, LaViolette had never heard of Fulcanelli, and knew even less about alchemy. He was a true modern scientist who wanted empirical proof for any thesis. And he had spent thirty years proving the very same information that had been engraved on the cross of Hendaye.

Perhaps the most convincing of all of LaViolette's evidence is the information provided by a radio contour map of a supernova remnant in Cassiopeia A (see fig. 12.6). This map, compiled from information published by astronomers Dickel and Greisen, clearly shows the expanded wave front of the supernova impacting the galactic superwave.[12] This distortion shows clearly in X-ray images, indicating a tremendous output of energy from the superwave's shock front. This also suggests that the galactic superwave might even be a factor in making a star into a nova.

It is indeed hard to argue with evidence such as this. LaViolette backs up his hypothesis with ice-core samples and cosmic-dust counts—including the 1993 Ulysses spacecraft results that conclusively demonstrated that cosmic dust is currently entering our system from the direction of the galactic center—and reaches the same conclusion as we have in decoding the cross at Hendaye. A double catastrophe happened 13,000 years ago, caused by an eruption of cosmic-ray energy from the center of the galaxy. Fulcanelli and the cross at Hendaye suggest that

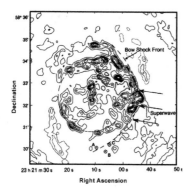

Figure 12.6. Radio contour map of Cassiopeia A. The small central cross represents the position of the supernova explosion center.

this catastrophe is about to happen once again. Ice-core samples show that galactic superwaves pass through our region of space once in about 26,000 years, or one complete precessional cycle. The galactic core explosion may in fact be the mechanism, through a type of gravity wave, that produces the precessional effect, the tilt of the planet on its axis, as Wihelm Reich predicted.

Although LaViolette steers clear of an exact prediction for the next superwave from galactic central, he does suggest that there might be a connection with the coming precessional alignments with the galactic center. He points to the many prophecies that indicate our immediate future as one of change and upheaval. The reality of the double catastrophe that he depicts, however, is firmly grounded in hard science, from ice-core samples to radio-telescope observations. Whenever it arrives, it will be the end of life as we know it.

Understanding this, our attention was drawn back to Fulcanelli's promise that the inscription on the cross at Hendaye pointed to a place of refuge during the time of the double cataclysm. We found that Hendaye did indeed point to a place of refuge, perhaps one from the last catastrophe. We would also find that Hendaye identified the only reasonable location for Atlantis, the center of the last global civilization. These discoveries would lead us to the final truth about alchemy, Fulcanelli, and the Great Cross, both of Hendaye and of the galaxy.

THE INSCRIPTION'S MESSAGE AND THE PLACE OF REFUGE

In the end, the mystery encoded in the cross at Hendaye boils down to the message contained in the oddly divided Latin inscription. Fulcanelli instructs the reader that its message concerns a place of refuge from the double cataclysm described by the monument. But how exactly does it tell us this? And does it give us any clue to where this place of refuge might be located?

Everything that Fulcanelli had alleged, regardless of how bizarre it sounded on first reading, we found to be based on truth. There seemed no reason to doubt Fulcanelli's word on the inner meaning of the inscription's message. But in the Hendaye chapter, Fulcanelli gives us no clue as to what or where this place of refuge might be.

He simply informs us that from the inscription "we can learn that a country exists where death cannot reach man at the terrible time of the double cataclysm." It is up to us to find it, implying that the inscription does indeed tell us the "geographical location of this promised land." Those who find it, Fulcanelli promises, will take up the mission of renewing mankind after the disaster. Fulcanelli assumes that this elite will be "the children of Elias"—that is, the followers of the astro-alchemical path of transformation. As we shall see, this hope may or may not have become reality.

With this in mind, let's take another, closer look at Fulcanelli's method of reading the inscription and see what other clues turn up. We are left with the seventeen letters of the inscription—OCRUXAVES / PESUNICA—and Fulcanelli's peculiar comments on it. As mentioned in chapter 11, he tells us that it is easy to recognize the inscription as the familiar mortuary phrase O *Crux Ave Spes Unica,* "Hail, O Cross, the Only Hope," but he notes that this one is different because of the misplaced S. He does not, however, tell us much more about the peculiar rendering of the word *spes* other than to call attention to the incorrect grammar of the second line, even though he knows that including the S on the second line would correct the grammar. As we have seen, *pes,* "foot" or "measure," can also be related to *unica,* the word "only," by transposing the *I* and the *C* to form *uncia,* "the twelfth part." This "measure of the twelfth part" can be connected to the cycles of the catastrophe measured by the galactic cross. Fulcanelli is calling attention to this interpretation with his fudging about grammar. But he doesn't say that this is the reason for the split *S;* he merely speculates that it was done on purpose.

"No doubt," Fulcanelli elaborates, "our workman traced them first in chalk or charcoal, and this rough draft must rule out any idea that a mistake occurred during the actual cutting of the letters. However, since this *apparent* mistake exists, it follows that it must really have been intended. The only reason that I can think of is that it is a *sign put in on purpose,* concealed under the appearance of an inexplicable blunder, and intended to arouse the curiosity of the observer. I will, therefore, state that, in my opinion, it was with knowledge and intent that the author arranged the inscription of his puzzling work in this way."[13]

Next, Fulcanelli explains something of his method: "I had already been enlightened by studying the pedestal and knew in what way and by means of what key the Christian inscription should be read; but I was anxious to show investigators what help may be obtained in solving hidden matters from plain common sense, logic and reasoning."[14] In this enigmatic paragraph, Fulcanelli is posing us a riddle, an intellectual test. And just in case we missed it, the reference to the key or cross in the sky made by the X of the snakes or dragons is, Fulcanelli informs us, "the helicoidal track of the sun, having arrived at the zenith of its curve across space, at the time of the cyclic catastrophe."

"The helicoidal track of the sun" is an archaic term for the sun's precessional motion against the ecliptic.[15] *Helicoidal,* literally "shaped like a spiral," is a description of the ecliptic and the slow "suspended" movement of the earth's wobble against it. The zenith of its curve across space is the moment when the solstices cross the galactic axis—the time, according to Fulcanelli, of the cyclic catastrophe.

When Leo coincided with the spring equinox 13,000 years ago, aligning the rising sun with the local energy gradient of the solar system's movement through the cosmic-ray field coming from the center of the galaxy, the summer solstice was slowly coming into alignment with the opposite end of the galactic axis, ninety degrees away, in the region of Taurus and the Pleiades. Now, half a precessional cycle later, Leo rises on the fall equinox as the winter solstice begins its alignment with the galactic center in Scorpio. As Fulcanelli insists, the crossing of these dragons creates "the image of the *Beast of the Apocalypse,* the dragon, which, on the days of Judgment, spews out fire and brimstone on macrocosmic creation."[16]

This knowledge, however, brings us no closer to finding our place of refuge. Fulcanelli simply says that the symbolic value of the *S,* displaced on purpose, gives us to understand that the phrase must be translated in the secret language. His explanation, though, of how this phrase can be translated in the phonetic language of the birds seems to lack any emphasis on the displaced *S*. He tells us to read in French "the Latin just as it is written. Then by making use of the permutation of vowels, we shall be able to read off the new words, forming another sentence, and re-establish the spelling, the word order and the literary sense."[17]

When we do this, Fulcanelli assures us we shall find the sentence *"Il est écrit que la vie se réfugie en un seul espace,"* which can be translated as "It is written that life takes refuge in a single space." Yet we have missed something if we take Fulcanelli's word for it and do not attempt to solve the puzzle ourselves.

He implies that we are to read the Latin letters as if they were French words. When we do this, certain words pop out at us. *"La vie,"* or "life," is easy to derive phonetically from AV, or *ah vee,* and *"espace"* is also obviously derived from ESPE, *ess pay ee.* We can find *"écrit"* in CRX, *eh cree teh,* by seeing the *X* as a *T,* and *"en un seul"* can be found in UNCA, *en un say ahh.* The *I* and the *S* form the *"il est"* that begins the sentence. Therefore, we have I S CRX, AV, ESPE, UNCA, or *"Il est écrit (que) la vie (se réfugie) en un seul espace."* There are two letters left, the *O* and the *U.*

Curiously, there is no way to make the French word *réfugie* from this Latin phrase. There is no consonant for the *jay* sound of *réfu-gie.* Even if we reuse the *R* and assign the *U* to the *oo* sound, we are left with only part of the word. Fulcanelli emphasizes the displaced *S,* which falls in the middle of the word *espace,* telling us that this is the key to the code. Since *refuge* is not directly attainable from the Latin inscription as it is, we are directed to the displaced *S* and its assignment in this specific case to the Greek letter chi, which is *X* or *K.* We can find the place of "refuge," and restore "the literary sense," only if we can solve the puzzle of the *S* that changes into an *X* and the *X* that changes into an *S.*

From this, we can see that Jules Boucher in his 1936 article appears to misunderstand the directions for translating the inscription. He clearly knows that it is a phonetic key, but doesn't follow through on this awareness. He gives us the French translation of the sound of the Latin words, *"O Croix Have Espace Unique,"* or "O Cross, the single pale space." From the above, the missing *jay* sound in *refuge,* it is easy to see how he arrived at this version, but it also shows that he was, perhaps intentionally, far from the mark. Fulcanelli uses similar methods and arrives at a conclusion that leads us deeper into the inscription itself. Boucher thinks the inscription points to the disaster—he changes *croix* to *mort,* or "death," to make the point—but seems unaware of its promise of refuge. Or, perhaps, he is unwilling to completely reveal the secret.

Our puzzle, then, is to find the place of refuge by changing the *S* into *K,* or a hard *C* sound. This suggests a cryptogramic or anagrammatic process, such as that proposed by Mevryl in his epilogue to *The Fulcanelli Phenomenon.* Mevryl's complex anagrams, however, are apparently designed to deceive the reader, to make sure that this sort of wordplay is discredited before anyone actually applies the riddle of changing the *S* to a *K* to the inscription itself. First and most curiously, Mevryl switches the attribution. In his version, *X* becomes *S,* not *S* becomes *X* or *K.* This is clearly not what Fulcanelli meant. He tells us that *S* corresponds to *K,* takes over its meaning, in fact, not the other way around. At this point, we cannot escape the conclusion that all of our commentators, Boucher, Fulcanelli, and Mevyrl, are in on the joke and doing their best to both reveal and obscure the message. Fulcanelli is oddly insistent on the *K* of khi and key, with khi or chi being the Greek letter *X.* As we shall see, Fulcanelli is pointing to an even deeper meaning to the idea of "khi/key."

Mevryl's interpretation of the inscription doesn't suggest any place of refuge, and his comments on Fulcanelli's translation indicate that he might not understand as much as Boucher, but given the amount Mevryl does know, we can feel sure this is another dodge. Mevryl tells us that Fulcanelli translated the inscription into French, Boucher's *O Croix Have Espace Unique,* and "then transposed it into the *langue diplomatique* by means of the rules of diplomacy." This parroting of Fulcanelli shows that Mevryl either did not understand it or chose to make it incomprehensible. A third option might be that a deeper meaning is implied, and this leads, inevitably, to Mevryl's use of anagrams.

He does suggest that the front paws of the Sphinx mark our observation point, which echoes Champagne's curious frontispiece to *Le Mystère.* He notes that Ha'il, in Saudi Arabia, is in the line of sight along the rising sun to the east from the Sphinx and that far beyond it are the Himalayas and the valley of Kathmandu. This, he suggests, is the place of refuge, drawing attention to the *cat, man,* and *hu,* or breath, combination found in the name Kathmandu. The valleys of Nepal are thought to be places of refuge in the Tibetan tradition, associated with both Padmasambhava and the Kalachakra Tantra, so Mevryl is pointing to a possible connection. His attribution, however, of Cat-Man, or Sphinx, and Hu, or breath, as the place of refuge has nothing to do with the message on the inscription. Once again, as we shall see, Mevryl is toying with us; he is directing the gullible toward a spot that is actually half the world away from the place of refuge discernible on the cross.

A SIGN POINTING TOWARD PERU

Let's go back to the inscription on the cross:

> OCRUXAVES
> PESUNICA

and let's take the middle *X* in the words OCRUXAVES as a symbol for the cross itself. Then—if we are to follow the symbolic motif of the pedestal—we should circle this central *X*, or cross. Dividing PESUNICA between the *U* and the *N* then leaves us four words each with four letters surrounding the central *X*. Just like the pedestal, this *X* then has four sides, and each side has a word with four letters. There are four letters in the inscription (INRI) on the other side of the cross, as well as four stars around the sun in panel three on the pedestal, and four groups of two bursting rays each in the great star of panel one. There are sixteen rays, a multiple of four, bursting out from the sun in panel three. There are also four *A*'s in panel four, and so we are not surprised to find that without the *X*, there are four words in the Latin inscription.

Split in this pattern, the inscription looks like this:

> OCRU X AVES
> PESU   NICA

No matter how one jumbles the letters, there are no interpretations that make sense of all four words in this layout, although the words *save* and *Inca* jump out at us from the right side. There is no certain answer to the inscription's riddle to be found in this first move.[18]

From Mevryl's clue, we know that the next step involves exchanging *K*'s, or a hard *C* sound, for *S*. The new phrase now possesses four *C*'s. This is interesting because the word *foresee* is mimicked by the clue. The major purpose of the cross at Hendaye is to "foresee" the future. To solve the puzzle, it is necessary to make sure that it has "four C's." Our inscription now looks like this:

OCRU   X   AVEC
PECU   NICA

This is not much better, but we are making progress. The next step is to reciprocate the transformation and turn the X into an *S:*

OCRU   S   AVEC
PECU   NICA

Now we have a simple anagram. Exchange the *R* and the *C* on the left side of the *S* and rearrange the right side with a few simple transpositions and we have:

OCCU   S   CAVE
PERU   INCA

Then, finally, do the same transposition of the top word on the left side, including the extra *S,* and the meaning becomes clear:

CUSCO CAVE
PERU   INCA

which can be transposed and written as:

INCA CAVE, CUSCO, PERU

While this is clear and simple in several languages, we still haven't found the importance of the displaced *S.* Merely changing it to a *C* in an anagram doesn't tell us why it is important. But there is more. There is another message encrypted within the inscription. This additional message is another interpretation of the Latin inscription's place of refuge and uses the displaced *S* to point to a specific place, the "single space." It uses only the top line of the inscription as originally written:

OCRU   X   AVES

Taking the *S* off the end of the phrase and placing it at the beginning is the only major shift in the letters. It then reads:

SOCRU   X   AVE

Now we have three words, read outward from the central cross. The first word is AVE; the second word is the *X*, or cross; the third word must be read backward. So instead of SOCRU the word now reads as URCOS. The line now looks like this:

AVE   X   URCOS

or

HAIL (TO THE CROSS AT) URCOS

which seemed rather obscure. Consulting a world atlas provided the answer. Looking closely at a map of Peru, we found a town called Urcos, in the Peruvian province of Cusco, only about twenty miles from Cusco city itself. The inscription's message is pointing to the city or the province of Cusco, Peru. It is also pointing to a cross that is in, or near, the town of Urcos. The conclusion must be that this is our place of refuge.

Fulcanelli mentions the Inca briefly in his discussion of the green language, but gives us no other obvious pointers. Mevryl mentions the Andes, but avoids any other suggestion of South America or its cultures. Van Buren, in her *Refuge of the Apocalypse*, thinks, on very slim evidence, that the place of refuge is Rennes-le-Château, not Peru.

The *Chronicle of Felipe Huaman Poma de Ayala*, written by one of Pizarro's conquistadors, presented us with an incredible coincidence concerning the images on the cross at Hendaye. As shown in figure 12.7, one of the very first drawings in de Ayala's chronicle of Peru is called "The Symbols of the Incas: The Sun; the Moon; Lightning; the hill of Guanacaure and the caves at Pacarictambo." These four symbols are astonishingly close to the four symbols found on the pedestal at Hendaye.

Mevryl implies that the *A*'s represent mountains with caves in them in either the South American Andes or the Himalayas, which suggests

Figure 12.7. Title page from the sixteenth-century *Chronicle of Felipe Huaman Poma de Ayala*, showing the close link to the symbols on the Hendaye cross.

"the caves at Pacarictambo" in de Ayala's sketch. The other three panels correspond directly to the sun, moon, and star images at Hendaye. The juxtaposition of the images in de Ayala's sketch and the cross at Hendaye is astonishing.

A few months after deciphering the message of the inscription, we met with Dr. Juan del Prado, professor of anthropology at Cusco University. He was touring the United States with William Sullivan, who had recently published the groundbreaking book *The Secret of the Incas*. We asked about the town of Urcos, and the possibility of a cross of some kind being there. Del Prado looked surprised and told us, "There is a strange cross in Urcos. No one knows where it came from or who built it."

Right then and there, we realized that a trip to Peru was the next step in our investigation.

ATLANTIS IN THE ANDES

It is hard to determine exactly when the Old World "discovered" the New. Columbus's voyages mark a watershed only of publicity and royal exploitation. Given that he seemed to know exactly where he was going and had fairly accurate sailing directions on how to get there, *discovery* is hardly the correct term. In fact, the farther back we go, the less of a distinction we find between the Old World and the New. One of the prime mysteries of the Bronze Age, roughly 3000 B.C.E. to around 800 B.C.E., is where did the enormous amounts of copper needed to plate whole buildings in bronze, such as we find in Minoan Crete, come from? As shown in figure 12.8B, the tin came from England and the coast of Cornwall, but there are no significant copper deposits in Europe or the Mediterranean basin. So where did all this copper come from?

In the five hundred years before Columbus, we find evidence of Vikings, Scottish and Welsh princes, and Irish monks all traveling to the New World. Indeed, the Vikings created a colony in North America. A twelfth-century pope even appointed a bishop to Vinland, and the remains of his church can still be seen today in Newport, Rhode Island. The Viking sagas show that they penetrated into the upper Midwest and the Great Lakes. The sagas also refer to the inhabitants of what is now New England as being Irish, labeling the region White Man's Land.[19]

In fact, New England has many Celtic and even megalithic-type stone structures whose closest analogs are found in Ireland and the west

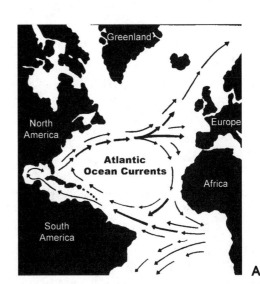

Figure 12.8. *A.* the prevailing Atlantic Ocean currents; *B.* map of ancient trade routes.

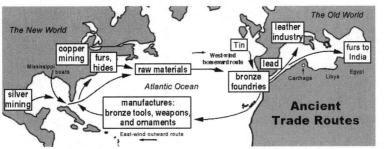

368 Hendaye's Message: The Season of Catastrophe and the Place of Refuge

coast of Britain. Such structures are found in odd places up and down the East Coast, and differ greatly from the clearly indigenous Hopewell and Adena cultures in the Ohio and Mississippi valleys.[20] In the Grave Creek burial mound in West Virginia, a clay tablet was found with an inscription in ancient Celto-Iberian exchanging greetings from the queen of a Celtic culture to the east and the king of the local Hopewell nation. This tablet has been dated to around 1000 B.C.E. One must assume that the copper trade was still viable at that point, since the Hopewell federation contained many sources of easily accessible copper.[21]

A megalithic or Celtic presence in North America seems indisputable given the evidence of the structures and inscriptions on the ground. But the Celts were not the only visitors to the New World. The Egyptians may have traveled in the middle of the third millennium B.C.E. as far as Australia, where the cartouche of Rajedef, the son of Khufu of Great Pyramid fame, has been found carved in stone in the desert outback.[22] By the time of Hatshepsut, a millennium later, regular trade voyages were under way to places that remain unknown to this day. One of these was the "land of the copper mountain," as the inscription reads on the porch of her mortuary tomb on the west bank at Luxor. The fact that cocaine and nicotine residue has been found in New Kingdom mummies suggests that this trade was in fact with South America.

Soon after Hatshepsut's reign, New Kingdom Egypt lost its overseas trade to the up-and-coming Sea Peoples, the Phoenicians and the Minoans. By the time the queen of the Celtic east in America was conducting her negotiations with the Hopewell magnate, a Phoenician was sure to be the middleman in the exchange. The Phoenician trading culture began to fade with the arrival of iron-equipped Aryans, such as the Doric Greeks, a century or so after the turn of the first millennium B.C.E. These are the Greeks of our history books, brash barbarians eager to acquire the knowledge of the ancient world.

The Greek connection brings us to Plato and his story of Atlantis. In his dialogues, Plato introduces the idea of an ancient civilization that died out in a great catastrophe roughly nine thousand years before the Golden Age of ancient Greece. In most of these dialogues it is hard to tell which are Socrates' ideas and which are Plato's, but the Atlantis story is solidly attributed. In the *Critias,* it is Plato's friend of the same name who relates the tale. He claims to have heard it from his grand-father, who learned it from the great Solon, one of Greece's Seven Sages, who heard it from an Egyptian priest of Sais named Sonchis. Thus, in the dialogue the story has a clear and prominent lineage.

Plato insisted four times that the story was true. He was quite definite about it. "The fact that it is not invented fable but a genuine history is all important," he tells us in the *Timaeus*. The most reasonable explanation is that Solon gave an accurate account of what his Egyptian source told him. From this, we would be wise to consider Atlantis a genuine Egyptian tradition, rather than a philosophical fable. Chances are, Atlantis really existed and it wasn't Minoan Crete, although they may have had "Atlantean" connections.

But where was Atlantis? Plato tells us "in those days the Atlantic was navigable; and there was an island situated in front of the straits which are by you called the Pillars of Hercules [the Straits of Gilbraltar]." This seems clear enough, but modern knowledge of sea-floor spreading and continental drift suggests that no extra island of any size is possible in the mid-Atlantic. The sunken continent idea seems improbable, even though Plato insists that Atlantis disappeared in a single day and night of catastrophe.

Modern consensus among archaeologists and scholars is that if there is any truth to Plato's tale, then it must be referring to the explosion of Thera, an island in the Aegean Sea, around 1500 B.C.E.[23] Along with ignoring Plato's precise location and dating, this theory has massive problems on its own terms. Dramatic as the destruction of Thera was, its loss hardly affected life in the Mediterranean. The Minoans did not fade out over night; their main cities were not abandoned or destroyed for another hundred years. The Phoenicians were untouched, and their expansion of trade routes increased in the centuries after Thera's explosion. Thera was a disaster, and its destruction was sudden, but it was hardly the fall of Atlantis.

Other theorists have located Atlantis in places as fanciful as Ceylon and as Heligoland in the Baltic Sea. Ignatius Donnelly, a nineteenth-century American politician and lecturer, wrote two massive books on Atlantis and the various catastrophes of prehistory. *Atlantis: The Antediluvian World,* while postulating a mid-Atlantic island and other outdated ideas, comes closest to being the textbook on Atlantis. Some of Donnelly's other suggestions are intriguing, however, as when he speculates that the end of the Ice Age coincides perfectly with Plato's dates for the destruction of Atlantis.

While Donnelly and the other mid-Atlantic theorists are right to take Plato literally—"in front of the pillars of Hercules" is clear and simple enough—their maps mislead them. If we look at a standard wall map of the world, we see only open ocean in front of the Pillars of Hercules. There is certainly room in the mid-Atlantic for a very large island or continent. But if we look at a polar projection map or a globe, such as the one shown in figure 12.9, we notice something right away. There already is a large island continent in front of the Pillars. It's called South America.

Figure 12.9. Polar projection of a world map showing Atlantis/South America opposite the Strait of Gibraltar.

Plato tells us "in a single day of misfortune, the island of Atlantis disappeared in the depths of the sea." Given the evidence of modern geology, it is hard to conceive of how an entire continent, or even a very large island, could become completely submerged beneath the ocean. Even extreme theories, such as crustal displacement, can't account for a complete disappearance. We would do better to interpret Plato's statement as being a description of a vast tidal wave that brought the depths of the sea to Atlantis than to insist on a literal sunken continent.

With that in mind, we turned to South America with new interest. Did it, in any significant way, fit Plato's description? Plato says that Atlantis was larger than Libya and Asia Minor combined, suggesting an accessible coastline of over a thousand miles. South America is the only candidate, including mythical mid-Atlantic islands, that fits these criteria. He goes on to say that Atlantis "was the way to other islands, and from these you might pass to the whole of the opposite continent, which surrounds the true Ocean."[24] However one reads Plato's account, it is quite startling and reveals that whoever told Solon originally knew much more of the true geography of the planet than he should have. Let us merely note that this description clearly could apply to South America. Evidence has also been found of ancient visits to the Andean coast from Japan and China.

In addition, South America has both advanced civilizations and evidence of their catastrophic destruction. On the shore of Lake Titicaca, high in the Peruvian Andes, stands the mysterious ancient city of Tiahuanaco, built, according to tradition, by the Andean culture hero Viracocha. Viracocha first appeared in Tiahuanaco after a great disaster had destroyed everything. This is from Father Molina in his chronicle *Relacion de las fabulas ritos de los Yngas:* "They say that in it [the catastrophe] perished all races of men and created things insomuch that the waters rose above the highest mountain peaks in the world. No living thing survived except a man and a woman who remained in a box, and, when the weather subsided, the wind carried them . . . to Tiahuanaco [where] the creator began to raise up the people and the nations that are in that region."[25]

Even today, the ruins of Tiahuanaco are impressive. To the early Spanish visitors after the conquest they were truly awe-inspiring. Garcilasco de la Vega, who visited in the mid-sixteenth century, described it this way:

> We must now say something about the large and almost incredible buildings of Tiahuanaco. There is an artificial hill, of great height, built on stone foundations so that the earth will not slide. There are gigantic figures carved in stone . . . these are much worn which shows great antiquity. There are walls, the stones of which are so

enormous it is difficult to imagine what human force could have put them into place. And there are the remains of strange buildings, the most remarkable being stone portals, hewn out of solid rock; these stand on bases up to 30 feet long, 15 feet wide and 6 feet thick. How, and with the use of what tools or implements, massive works of such size could be achieved are questions which we are unable to answer.[26]

One of the stone portals de la Vega describes stands at the northwest corner of a vast enclosure known as the Place of Upright Stones. This portal, while an amazing work of art, is also a complex and accurate calendar in stone. The whole complex has been found to be an intricate astronomical observatory, designed perhaps to calculate alignments of solstices and equinoxes with the galactic core and edge. Whatever it was designed to do, its astronomical nature allows us to date its construction with precision.

In the 1920s, Arthur Posnansky, a German-Bolivian scholar who had been investigating Tiahuanaco for almost fifty years, published his monumental, four-volume work, *Tiahuanaco: The Cradle of American Man*. By using the small differences in the earth's tilt against the ecliptic and its effect on the sunrise azimuth from century to century, Posnansky calculated a date for the construction of Tiahuanaco.[27]

The earth's tilt changes slightly over time, with a length of one and a half precessional cycles between maximum and minimum. As we saw above, Reich postulated that the tilt's angle is caused by the earth's spin in the midst of an orgone flow from the center of the galaxy. On the basis of this bobbing or rolling motion, which resembles that of a ship on an ocean, Reich predicted the reason for the narrow, three-degree band of the tilt.[28] LaViolette also speculates that the periodic eruptions from the galactic core could create the tilt, and therefore its relationship to precessional motion, Fulcanelli's "helicoidal track of the sun."[29]

Posnansky found that by establishing the solar alignments of key structures that now looked out of true, he could determine the angle of the ecliptic tilt at the time when the structure was built. He found a tilt of 23°8'48". Comparing this angle to the graph developed in 1911 by the International Conference of Ephemerids, we find a corresponding date of around 15,000 B.C.E. Naturally, most orthodox archaeologists found this hard to take.

But Posnansky's work was checked by a high-powered group of specialists, and at the end of a three-year study it concluded that Posnansky's observation were correct.[30] The sites at Tiahuanaco were indeed laid out to match a tilt-angle-derived date of circa 15,000 B.C.E. This confirmation did little, however, to change the prevailing archaeological paradigm, and even today glossy picture books of the Andes tell us that Tiahuanaco was built by the pre-Inca civilization around 500 B.C.E. No one has an answer for why anyone would build an observatory with its instruments fourteen and a half millennia out of alignment.

Tiahuanaco was originally built as a port on the shores of Lake Titicaca when the lake was at least one hundred feet deeper and far wider. In that case, Tiahuanaco would have been an island, and the visitor can see the changes in the lake level and shoreline for over 5,000 years of inhabitance. The geological record shows that sometime in the eleventh millennium B.C.E., a sudden natural disaster struck the city. The evidence of this disaster is still visible in the vast chunks of rocks littering the site like so many discarded matchsticks.

Posnansky argued that "this catastrophe was caused by seismic movements which resulted in an overflow of the waters of Lake Titicaca" in a vast flood. He cites the evidence of jumbles of human, animal, and fish bones covered by an alluvial deposit, suggesting that the water descended on Lake Titicaca and Tiahuanaco "in onrushing and unrestrainable torrents."[31]

This certainly sounds similar to Plato's description of the destruction of Atlantis. Curiously enough, it also matches LaViolette's predictions of the effects of the double catastrophe that would result from a galactic core explosion. And while the initial destruction was sudden, the disasters continued for almost two millennia before the people of Tiahuanaco gave up and departed. This also fits LaViolette' galactic-core explosion scenario and prediction, both in terms of dating and in terms of the long-felt effects of the core explosion.

Does that mean that Tiahuanaco is the lost city of Atlantis? Possibly, for there is one curious connection with Plato's tale that is hard to account for any other way. Plato tells us that Atlantis contained a great number of elephants, a fact that argues against Crete or Thera. Present-day South America has no elephants, of course, but during the Ice Age it apparently did. Remains have been found of a species called *Cuvieronius,* which was an elephant-like proboscidean complete with trunk and tusks. We find these animals carved on the great stone portal of the Gateway of the Sun (fig. 12.10), suggesting they were common in the Tiahuanaco area. These "elephants," however, became extinct around 10,000 B.C.E.

Figure 12.10. This tablet, found near Cuena, Ecuador, reads, "The elephant that supports the earth upon the waters and causes it to quake."

Suggestive as this is, Tiahuanaco, even as an island, fails to match Plato's description of the city of Atlantis. His account of the city may in fact be purely symbolic or allegorical. Paul LaViolette points out that the description of Atlantis matches a subquantum kinetic model of the primordial atom.[32] At the very least, this would suggest that the Atlanteans had a mythic understanding of continuous-creation ether physics.

While we can't definitely say that the ancient cultures of South America are the lost Atlanteans, we can say that the likelihood is strong. No other alternative matches Plato so closely, and an advanced civilization in 15,000 B.C.E., whatever its resemblance to Plato, must be considered a candidate for Atlantis.

The cross at Hendaye's inscription encodes a place of refuge, a place where the survivors of the last catastrophe gathered. One of our solutions of the inscription says "Inca Cave, Cusco, Peru," directing us to the cultural descendants of the mysterious builders of Tiahuanaco, the Incas. Whether or not Atlantis can be found in the Andes, Fulcanelli and the cross are telling us that the secret of the place of refuge from the last catastrophe can be found there.

During the writing of this book, long after the above section was finished, cartographer J. M. Allen published his *Atlantis: The Andes Solution,* which not only supported our ideas on Atlantis in the Andes, but also disclosed the actual location of the city itself.

Starting with the same commonsense deductions as ours, Allen focuses on South America as the most logical choice for Atlantis. He notes that the pre-Columbian Indian name for the continent was Atlanta, a name Allen feels is related to the Quechua word for copper, *antis,* and the Nahuatl word for water, *atl.*[33] Since *antis* is the origin of the word Andes, we might suspect that the phrase on Hatshepsut's mortuary temple is the Egyptian name for Atlantis.

Allen turned to Plato and, taking literally his description of a rectangular plain crisscrossed by a grid of canals in the middle of the island, settled on the Altiplano of southern Peru and northern Bolivia as the best match for the location of Atlantis. He built a three-dimensional model of the region and discovered Plato's "rectangular plain surrounded by mountains."

This, Allen believed, was the key to the mystery. Plato describes a plain in the center of the long side of the continent, next to a body of water. The plain was very smooth and level, surrounded by mountains, high above sea level with the form of "a quadrangle, rectilinear for the most part and elongated."[34] This is, in fact, a close description of the Altiplano, the largest level plain in the world, and which also contains the two inland seas of Lake Titicaca and Lake Poopo (see fig. 12.11).

With this in mind, Allen went looking for Plato's regular grid pattern. It was described as a 600-foot-wide canal running around the perimeter of the plain with regular intersections and transverse canals forming a vast grid work. "It only remains then to discover on site evidence of a channel 600 ft. wide to say without any more doubts that here indeed is the proof that the city and the civilization of Atlantis existed in these parts,"[35] Allen informs us. Satellite and aerial photos suggest that such canals do exist, and in the summer of 1995, Allen traveled to Bolivia in search of them.

"I found," he tells us, "the remains of a channel of enormous dimensions, the base of the canal was around 120 ft. wide and the gently sloping sides were each of some 230 ft., making it just under 600 ft. from crest to crest of the parallel embankments."[36] Atlantis, it seemed, had been located.

Allen buttresses his argument with examples of mineral wealth and early mining that match Plato's description. Atlantean use of gold to plate their sacred precincts has echoes in the Inca temples discovered by the Spanish, and a natural alloy of gold and copper, mentioned by Plato, oriculum, can be found as a mineral only in the region of the

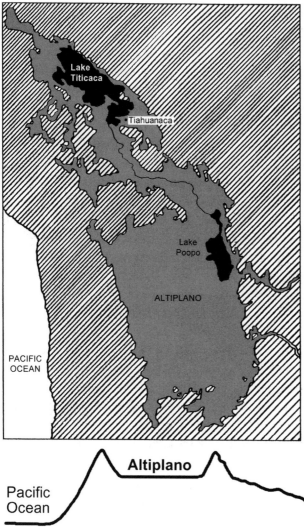

Figure 12.11. The region around the Altiplano, the irrigated plain mentioned by Plato, showing Lake Titicaca and Lake Poopo, probably the location of various Atlantean cities.

Altiplano. As the matches mounted up, we became convinced that Allen had discovered the source of Plato's tale.

For most interpreters and Atlantis seekers, the description of the city itself is the most problematic. Why concentric circles of water and land? It seems odd and unnecessary. But the Altiplano hypothesis addresses this very issue. Being an ancient volcanic region, there are many eroded volcanic cones near the Altiplano, including one on the northeast side of Lake Poopo, which match in size Plato's dimensions.

These cones form natural concentric circles out from the central flue of the volcano and can be easily shaped and filled with water to produce the specific Atlantis configuration, which Allen calls the Cross of Atlantis, as shown in figure 12.12. It is just possible that this ancient civilization built its greatest city as a model of the primordial atom of continuous creation and the Great Cross of the galactic alignment. Certainly these concepts remained in play down to the time of the Incas, and even today a Christianized version of the cosmic model survives in the remote village of Misminay, as we shall see a little later.

Figure 12.12. An overhead view of the plan of Atlantis reveals Allen's Cross of Atlantis. Three circular walls surround the island city with canals traversing them. The shaft of the cross is the large entrance canal.

There are a few problems, from the perspective of our inquiry, with Allen's work. He seems hesitant to let go of the Sea Peoples and the Bronze Age date of Thera, circa 1300 B.C.E., even though he tells us that Lake Poopo flooded the region around 12,000 B.C.E. It is hard to account for his reluctance to embrace the older dates. He is apparently unaware of Posnansky's work, and barely mentions archaeo-astronomy in any meaningful way. Even with these gaps, however, it is clear that Allen is presenting significant evidence for the location and date of Atlantis.

Here we have more proof that Fulcanelli's possible place of refuge was the ancient home of the advanced global civilization of prehistory. Carrying this scenario further, we can speculate that the Atlantean culture survived one thousand years or more of intermittent catastrophe before finally emigrating to colonies around the planet, which would include the ancient Nile Valley. The Incan Viracocha was the godlike survivor from the Atlantean civilization who brought back to cataclysm-ravaged regions the skills and graces of civilization, including perhaps the knowledge of how to calculate the time of the next cosmic disaster.

THE NAVEL OF THE WORLD

Lima, Peru, is one of the driest places on earth. It sits on the west coast of South America, at the north end of the Peru/Chile coastal desert. Ten to twenty years will sometimes pass without a single drop of rainfall. Although the ocean is just a stone's throw away, there is no moisture and very little life in this desert. Outside of the sprawling, poverty-ridden city there is nothing but miles and miles of dried yellow sand with not a weed, plant, or any other living thing in sight.

When the Spanish asked the Incas where the best place to put a city was, they were told to settle where Lima stands today. The Incas considered Lima to be the worst place on earth to live, so recommending it as a place of settlement was their way of getting back at the Spanish. Lima today is a sprawling metropolis that stretches for mile upon dusty mile in all directions. Only the Pacific Ocean mercifully stops it from going any farther. But the coastline doesn't stop everything; the beaches are filled with mountains of trash washed out by the tidal flow, every day, into the blue waters of the world's biggest ocean.

Lima is the only major city in Peru. Outside the city limits lies a country that is wild, unpopulated, and forbidding. There is no shortage of mysteries in this land. There are lost cities, hidden tunnel systems, gigantic ruins, and remnants of ancient societies. Peru also has four ecological zones that run the gamut from the hottest desert to the wettest rain forest on earth. Needless to say, there are countless places to get lost and remain hidden forever.

The one-hour flight from sweltering Lima to the cool mountains of Cusco brings welcome relief. Cusco is an Inca word for "navel of the world," possibly even an analog for the center of the galaxy. If we think of the curving, snakelike shape of the Andes Mountains as the Milky Way, then Cusco is indeed at the center.

The high Andes Mountains rise out of the earth to climb in places to altitudes over 20,000 feet. Their ragged cliffs, proof of their young age, attract the clouds and moisture out of the Amazon jungle far below and to the east. These clouds bring the necessary rainfall that keeps the high Andes fertile and verdant. In Cusco, as opposed to Lima, there is always a cool wind that blows through the green trees and fertile valleys. The people seem happier, too. The Quechua are a proud and handsome people with high cheekbones and honest eyes, reminding us of the Basque people on the border of Spain and France.

The Incas ruled their empire for less than 150 years before the Spanish conquistadors appeared. Around 1400 C.E., a group of Quechua nobles from Cusco managed to unite the warring factions left from the dissolution of the ancient empire of the Wari-Tiawanku, which had ruled the Andean highlands for a thousand years.[37] They accomplished this by returning to the way of Viracocha, producing a brilliant synthesis of Andean civilization going all the way back to the culture of Tiahuanaco and the prehistoric Atlanteans. The physical remains of the Incan empire, its roads and bridges, temples, towns, fortresses, and irrigation canals, can today be seen everywhere in Peru and Bolivia. The modern visitor is left with the impression that something very important happened in the Andean highlands long ago, and that nothing much has happened since.

It's hard to account for the sudden brilliance of the Incan civilization. The empire itself was an idea whose time had come. Several centuries of constant warfare had prepared the highlands to accept a political solution, but it is the cultural effervescence that catches our attention. The way of Viracocha taught that civilization must be in the image of the origin of all things. The word *inca* in Quechua means "archetype" or "original pattern." The world was "inca," or correctly aligned with the original model when it was formed as a cross with a unifying center point. As with most Native American cultures, this arrangement was visualized as the essential order of space.

In the high Andes, the Milky Way is the most striking feature of the night sky. It arches overhead like a great river of stars encircling the terrestrial sphere. To the Quechua, descendants of the Incas, it was simply Mayu, "the river," which brought water from the cosmic ocean upon which the terrestrial sphere floats and gave it back to the land as rain. However, the motions in the sky of the river of the Milky Way over the course of twenty-four hours create two lines, which cross at the zenith and divide the sky into four quarters. At one zenith, the galaxy stretches out in a northwest–southeast diagonal; twelve hours later, at the other zenith, the galaxy stretches northeast–southwest.

The zenith crossing point is called Cruz Calvario, the Cross of Calvary, by a group of Quechua in the small community of Misminay. This group of Incan descendants were studied in the 1970s by anthropologist Gary Urton, who discovered that the ancient cosmology of the Incas, and perhaps all the way back to Viracocha, had survived in the now largely Christianized worldview of the local community. This combination of ancient cosmology and Christian symbolism makes Urton's descriptions of the landscape organization of Misminay read like a living commentary on the Hendaye cross.

The great galactic cross, the Calvario, is mirrored on the ground by the two major roads of the region, which run northeast–southwest and southeast–northwest and cross at the center of the village (fig. 12.13).

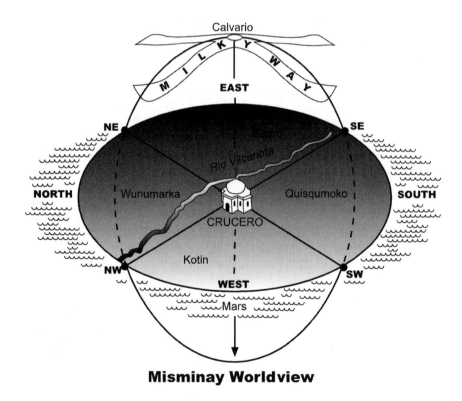

Misminay Worldview

Figure 12.13. The Misminay worldview: living inside sacred space. The cross below the chapel, or Crucero, mirrors the cross of the galaxy in the sky, the Calvario. (Redrawn from Geoffrey Cornelius and Paul Devereux, *The Secret Language of the Stars and Planets* (San Francisco: Chronicle Books, 1996))

Marking this spot is a small chapel, the Crucero, or cross, in the form of a cross, mirroring the galactic Calvario and linked by an invisible axis. The local river, the Vilcanota, runs beside the "middle way," the northwest–southeast axis that is the "day" diagonal of the Galaxy at the local zenith. The other road, which mirrors the "night" diagonal of the local zenith, is considered the ascending or vertical path and is called the "path of the great division." Canals and other water channels in the region also follow this cross pattern paralleling the roads.

The ancient Andean people based this ordering of the landscape on their observation of the behavior of the Milky Way, which appears to divide the sky and the horizon intercardinally. More than any other point, this basic arrangement of space and time into an intercardinal, northeast–southwest/northwest–southeast cross suggests the supreme importance of the galaxy, the great Mayu, in Andean mythology.

The Incas called their empire Tawantinsuyu, the United Four Quarters, to echo this primal alignment in the sky. The center of the cross was Cusco, the navel of the world (fig. 12.14).

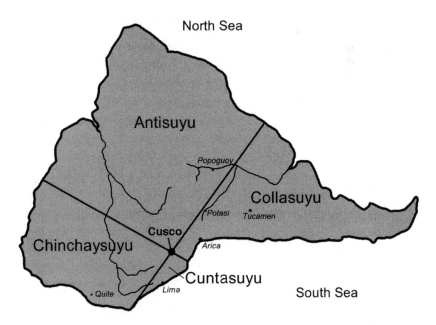

Figure 12.14. Tawantinsuyu, the Incan "United Four Quarters," divided at Cusco, navel of the world.

And if Cusco was the navel of the world, then the Corincancha, the great Temple of the Sun, was the navel of Cusco. Built at the confluence of Cusco's two rivers, the Corincancha was the center of an enormous ceremonial calendar alignment based on the sidereal lunar year of 328 days ($12 \times 27.33 = 327.96$). The key alignment was based on the winter solstice sunrise. The Sapa Inca, the archetypal man, or the king, would have been seated in a niche lined with gold and precious stones. As the rising solstice sun struck the niche, the Inca would have been bathed in a shimmering golden aura, making him truly the "Son of the Sun."[38]

Through Cusco, these alignments, shown in figure 12.15, with the heavens nourished the earth in the person of The Inca, the archetypal man, or the king. He was the center of the hub around which the crossed circle of time and space revolved. In Western terms, he is most like the pharaoh of Egypt as son of the Sun, and beyond that a composite of Adam, Christ, and the Grail King.

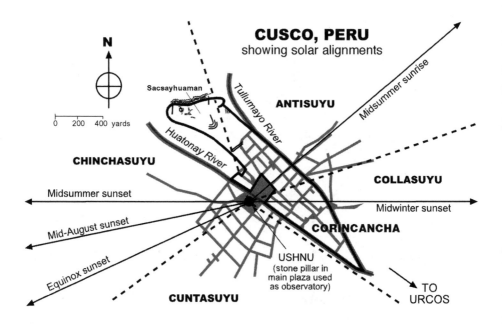

Figure 12.15. Map of ancient Cusco showing the Corincancha and the major alignments of the city. Also shown are the traditional names of the four quarters.

All of these correspondences become even more intriguing when we think of the Andes as a naturally suggestive pattern for the Milky Way, with Cusco at the galactic center. The cross of the four quarters then echoes the four projected Trees of Life on the celestial sphere. The Sapa Inca, the unique man in the form of the king, begins to look a lot like the Adam Kadmon, the cosmic man of the kabbalists, formed from the intersection of these Trees. The Adam Kadmon, a series of meditative and magical exercises, developed from the idea of the Tree of Life as it extends through the worlds, and was seen as a model for universal consciousness. The way of Viracocha could be the secret of astro-alchemy itself in a form lost to the West after Egypt's decline, a way to tap into this current of sentience that, theoretically at least, embraces Mind everywhere in the universe. The star religion of the early dynasties of Egypt, as recorded in the Pyramid Texts, can dimly be perceived as a practical application of this cosmological philosophy, and as we shall see, the arrangement of the Pyramids at Giza also reflects this quartering of the sky by the galactic river.

INCAN CAVES AND THE CROSS AT URCOS

When Pizarro learned of the Incas in 1526, by intercepting a strange craft far out on the western ocean loaded with golden and silver trade objects, the throne of Tawantinsuyu was occupied by the eleventh Inca since the unification of the four quarters, Wayna Qhapaq.[39] The Inca had been crowned in 1493, the year a corrupt pope, Alexander VI, divided the New World between the Spanish and the Portuguese, and lived out his long and illustrious reign in blissful ignorance of history's ticking clock. When word reached him of the strangers probing the borders of his empire, The Inca was in Quito consolidating his conquest of what is now Ecuador and thinking of pushing on into what is now Colombia. And then the Spaniards' secret weapon struck.

The pandemic that devastated Mexico and Central America arrived, either with Pizarro or overland through Colombia, and burst upon the twenty million inhabitants of the Incan empire with lethal effect. Half the population died, including The Inca. Pachakuti Yamki, an Inca noble writing a century later, described The Inca's vision: "And when he turned to the sea with his entourage, there were seen at midnight, as if surrounding him, a million people . . . living souls . . . [of those] . . . about to die in the pestilence."[40] Soon after this, word of the Spaniards' arrival reached Quito and the court began to die. Wayna Qhapaq and his son and heir died within a few days.

Had it not been for this plague, Pizarro would have faced a united and powerful foe with a wily and battle-hardened king at the helm. It is unlikely that he would have made much of a showing with only two hundred men, even armed with muskets, against such might as the Incan empire had just fielded in Ecuador. But The Inca was far from the center, and disaster occurred. After the plague, to compound the problem, fighting broke out between The Inca's two surviving sons as Waskhar, in control of Cusco, and Atawallpa, in control of the north, fought it out for the succession while the Spaniards moved into the valley of Peru and built settlements.

Atawallpa, after he had established himself on the throne, investigated the Spaniards' settlement and concluded that they posed little problem. In the old days of The Inca, this might have been true. But Atawallpa chose to negotiate with the barbarians and so was captured and held for ransom. When the Spaniards saw the amount of gold available to The Inca, they killed him, launched a palace revolt, and marched on Cusco in the name of Atawallpa's son Manku. The Spaniards played on the divisions caused by the civil war, which along with disease had decimated the army. By 1533, they were in control of Cusco. Their puppet ruler Manku revolted in 1536, but by then it was too late. Too many Spaniards and too many guns faced a declining population and a disorganized army, and the result was disastrous to The Inca.

Manku retreated to Machu Picchu, far into the Andes, and formed his own neo-Inca state, which survived for another two centuries. Interestingly enough, the Torreon, a now roofless temple structure at Machu Picchu, retains the traditional northwest–southeast alignment so that when the Pleiades rise in one window, Scorpio sets in the opposite. Even in the midst of disaster, the Incas clung to their belief in the importance of the galactic axis.

The Incas had mined the gold that Pizarro so coveted, and they used it in ceremonial ornaments and, hammered into large plates, to line the walls of their palaces and their great religious centers. The most famous of these was the above-mentioned Corincancha in Cusco. The original temple has disappeared and a cathedral has been built over the old Incan foundation. In fact, most of the city of Cusco is built on Incan foundations that are hundreds of years old. With no mortar or concrete, these people were able to build stone edifices that have stood the test of time.

The cathedral of Santa Domingo in Cusco is a decrepit and dark place. The magnificent building, the Corinancha that this cathedral replaced, can only be imagined now. In addition to the gold plates on its walls, stories say that a huge circular object of pure gold called "the Disk of the Sun" sat in its center. This disk was said to represent the central sun of the cosmos and was many inches thick, covered with precious jewels. It is said that when it reflected the light of the sun, it transformed it. The Incas believed that the light became so pure that the people in the temple, particularly The Inca himself, seated in his golden niche, were physically transformed.

The original Incan temple was much bigger than the cathedral that occupies the present spot. The Temple of the Sun was connected to the Temple of the Moon and the complex of Sacsayhuaman by a series of underground tunnels. After the conquest, Pizarro heard rumors from the remaining Incas that there was a vast subterranean tunnel system under the Andes. He had heard from the Indians that these tunnels were filled with gold and jewels hidden by Atawallpa's queen. The Incan queen had successfully hidden all of the tunnel openings from the Spanish.

Cieza de Leon states in his *Chronicle of Peru,* written in 1555: "If, when the Spaniards entered Cusco they had not committed other tricks, and had not so soon executed their cruelty in putting Atahualpha to death, I do not know how many great ships would have been required to bring such treasures to old Spain, as is now lost in the bowels of the earth and will remain so because those who buried it are now dead."[41] Perhaps the most aggravating part about any examination of the history of Peru is that the Spanish wrote it all. Pizarro and his band of men were brilliant at the goals of genocide, murder, and treachery. The voices of the Incas have been stilled and their secrets forgotten in the sudden strike of Spanish sword, gun, and horse. But the rumors of vast tunnels persist, inflamed by the legends of lost Incan gold, and perhaps even the Disk of the Sun itself, which lies waiting to be found in some cave in the Andes.

The ancient city of Cusco was laid out in the shape of a puma, a South American mountain lion (see fig. 12.15); this shape was made more pronounced by Incan emperor Pachacuti's rebuilding around 1440 C.E. The main part of the old city lies within the animal's torso, but the face of the puma and the nose are both part of the Sacsayhuaman complex, which towers high above the city. What is left today of the giant stonework of Sacsayhuaman tells only a tiny part of the story of these magnificent monuments and the unknown people who built them. At its height, the complex at Sacsayhuaman was enormous, with three tall towers and room for over five thousand defenders in its labyrinth of rooms. But it is only in the mind's eye that one can reconstruct the magnificence of this center, built to mark the origin of the sacred river, channeled through stone conduits and tunnels into the city. There are several tunnel openings still to be seen in the complex. But they appear to have been sealed to depths of twenty to thirty feet.

In his book *Jungle Paths and Inca Ruins,* William Montgomery McGovern writes about Sacsayhuaman: "Near this fortress [Sacsayhuaman] are several strange caverns reaching far into the earth. Here altars to the Gods of the Deep were carved out of the living rock, and the many bones scattered about tell of the sacrifices which were offered up here."[42]

There are caves—just as the inscription on the cross at Hendaye suggests—in the cliffs above Sacsayhuaman, at one of the highest places above Cusco. Although they are natural, it is obvious that humans have carved out major parts of the interior of the caves. Not much is known about these caves except that the Quechua have used them for ancient ceremonies for centuries. No one knows who carved these caves, and as far as we can tell, no one has done any archaeological study of them. They could very likely be places of refuge from an ancient catastrophe.

The area around the caves is as interesting as the caves themselves. Nearby are the ancient remains of a small city. This extremely old site is sculpted and carved in such a way as to reveal that it was once a ceremonial or spiritual center. Avenues and the foundations of buildings are laid out on the ground. Water pipes made of clay, for plumbing, are still visible.

Less obvious are the number of sculpted animal effigies that have been carved into the rocks. The figures of snakes, pumas, and monkeys are still discernible despite erosion. These carvings and statues are so old that many of the features have disappeared under the forces of wind and rain. Only faint traces of this once magnificent site remain.

The cross at Hendaye, which is over three thousand miles and an ocean away, points to a cave in Cusco, Peru. Once the trek is made and enough questions are asked of the local Quechua population, this fabulous and forgotten site becomes more interesting. One has to wonder if the caves are not an homage, or tribute, to the people who used them to survive the great catastrophe. Are they the ones who built the gigantic tunnel system that allegedly runs under the Andes?

One thing is for sure: The caves of Cusco referred to in the inscription on the Hendaye cross do exist. And it is also true that these same caves are held sacred by the local remnants of the Incas by virtue of the large piles of melted ceremonial candle wax that are found everywhere inside the caves. Our guide, a local Quechuan, told us that there are many ceremonies in these caves at night. He also said that the caves, although unknown to foreign tourists, are quite well known to the Quechua people. Many of the local Indians make pilgrimages to these caves at least once a year.

The Inti Raymi, or Festival of the Sun, is still celebrated every year at Sacsayhuaman on the eve of June 23, the winter solstice. What until the 1940s had been a small affair has now grown into a three-day festival based around a mock "Inca" and a procession from the square in front of the cathedral, the site of the Corincancha, the Sun Temple, to Sacsayhuaman, with its caves and underground water source.

When he was asked why these caves are so important, our Quechua guide shrugged his shoulders and said: "White people do not care for the earth in the same way that we do. When we grow our food, we always ask mother earth for help. These caves are inside our mother. They are closer to her soul. So we go there to talk to her and to ask for her help."[43]

Several of our questions are answered by the discovery of these caves. They are very old, and they still hold a deep significance to the local people. They are in old Cusco, the head of Cusco's puma. In fact, the caves, the sacred river's origin, and the ceremonial complex are near the tip of the nose of the puma, as if the animal were pointing his entire body at them. This site suggests Mevryl's cat-man's-breath image that he attributes to Kathmandu in Nepal. It actually fits the pattern on the ground in Cusco much more closely.

But we still had one clue from the Hendaye cross left to check. The inscription, and Dr. del Prado, had told us of a strange cross at Urcos, about twenty miles southeast of Cusco. The last piece of the mystery was the secret of this second cross.

Urcos is a small and poverty-stricken town sixteen miles southeast of Cusco, remembered by history only for its role in Manku's Incan rebellion. Every Sunday the local farmers make their way down the steep mountain paths with sacks of freshly picked fruits, vegetables, and coca leaves to sell at the outdoor market. There is a beautiful mountain lake next to the town. The cross at Urcos sits at the mouth of this body of water, appropriately called Lake Urcos.

No one knows who built the cross at Urcos. It is prominently displayed, sitting on top of a fifteen-foot-high stone pile (see fig. 12.16). One must walk up the sides of the steep pile to reach the cross that sits on top. The cross that is now on this promontory, however, is not the original one.

In perhaps the most heartbreaking part of our investigation, we found that the original cross at Urcos was missing. The only thing left was its base, to which a newer cross had been affixed. The base of the original cross is badly eroded and must be centuries old. The new cross is recent, perhaps less than fifty years old, and unadorned. No one knows how the old cross was broken or who took it away.

The locals say that there has always been a cross there. They say that the symbol of the cross was extremely important to their culture. Indeed crosses, as we saw in the imagery of the Four United Quarters, were a key concept in Incan tradition. In addition, Urcos falls on the southeast–northwest, galactic-center–galactic-edge alignment along the sight line from the ancient stone pillar in the main square of Cusco toward the bright star Alpha Crucis of the Southern Cross.

Beyond these tantalizing hints, however, the information—if there ever was any—on the cross at Urcos has been destroyed. Nonetheless, its location and alignment do provide us with a valuable clue. The *ushnu*, the stone pillar in the main square of Cusco, defines the solar sight lines of the solstices and equinoxes along the reconstructed line of the Huatanay River toward Alpha Crucis. This alignment leads to the valley gate at Rumicola and beyond to the cross at Urcos, suggesting that the cross was somehow associated with the Southern Cross of stars in the sky, a grouping that the Incas obviously found as fascinating as the movements of the sun.

Figure 12.16. The cross at Urcos, Peru, sits upon an ancient base. (Photo by Jay Weidner)

The message of the Hendaye cross comes down to "Hail, X (cross) Urcos." Fulcanelli alerted us, through green-language wordplay and anagrams, to the importance of this point. Assuming that Urcos is indeed the location and that its alignment is significant, rather than any lost inscription that may have clarified the matter, we are left with another mystery. How could a constellation all but ignored by the Greeks and not even observable from northern Europe provide the key to the place of refuge?

Interestingly enough, the Greeks thought of the four stars of the Southern Cross as part of the Centaur, the constellation just above it.

The constellation of four bright stars that is recognizably a cross strad-dles the Milky Way, a full four degrees wide at that point, and its ver-tical axis through Alpha Crucis points to the southern celestial pole. The horizontal axis points toward the galactic center at the cusp of Scorpio/Sagittarius, making it a perfect astral marker of the cosmic Great Cross and the Cube of Space.

The ability to observe the Southern Cross, and to successfully make calculations based on it, would inevitably lead to an understanding of both precession and the galactic alignments resulting from it. Owing to the motion of precession on the celestial poles, the constellations appear to rise and fall in the sky over vast periods of time. This can be seen best by observing Orion, located on the celestial equator, which therefore makes it an excellent marker for precessional motion as well. Like Orion, precessional motion causes the Southern Cross to rise and fall in the sky, as shown in figure 12.17. For roughly one-eighth of a preces-sional cycle, approximately three thousand years, the Southern Cross is visible above thirty degrees north latitude. In ancient Egypt during the New Kingdom, the Southern Cross was clearly visible as far north as Jerusalem.

At the latitude of Luxor, the source of the curious rose-cross ankhs

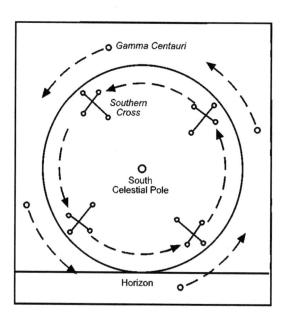

Figure 12.17. The Southern Cross never dips below the horizon in the southern hemisphere although its neighbor Gamma Centauri does, showing how the Southern Cross is circumpolar for that hemisphere.

of the Coptic Museum, the Southern Cross would have been high in the southern sky at the winter solstice. As the first rays of the rising sun flooded the inner sanctum of Karnak Temple, the Southern Cross would still have been faintly visible to the south, as the Milky Way in the sky matched almost exactly the course of the Nile. Just as the alignments at the Corincancha united the sight line to the Southern Cross and the midwinter sunrise, so too does the great temple of Amun at Karnak (see fig. 12.18). Unlike the Corincancha in the southern hemisphere, Karnak over time saw the celestial ankh slide down the sky until, soon after Egypt itself ceased to exist, the Southern Cross slipped below the horizon.

From Jerusalem, this celestial event occurred over the winter of 2 C.E. It is possible that event was the source of the "Jesus" myths, with their blend of alchemy and eschatology. The "earthing" of the cross, the place where the Southern Cross touched the horizon, could easily be seen as the "birthplace" of a messianic figure. In the first century C.E., the Southern Cross could still be seen from Luxor and Cairo, so its appearance with a bright star on top of it could easily became a "rose" ankh, connecting the ancient mystery tradition and the new messiah figure in one powerful symbol.

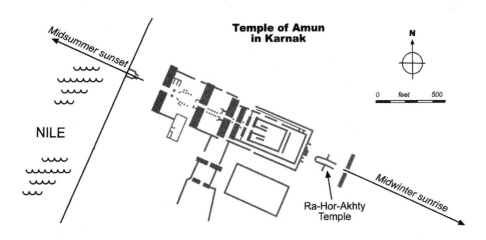

Figure 12.18. The solstice alignment of the temple of Amun at Karnak, showing the unification of the solstice axis and the axis to the setting of the Southern Cross, circa 1600 B.C.E.

Indeed, the key piece of information hidden in the ancient star charts preserved by the Arab scholars of Cairo and studied with such interest by Pope Sylvester II may in fact be the existence of the Southern Cross, with its rose-ankh appearance and the ability to use this constellation to precisely define the Great Cross of the galactic alignment. The medieval Italian poet Dante, in his *Purgatory*, refers to the Southern Cross, now lost to northern eyes, leaving the northern hemisphere "famished and widowed." The reappearance of this information in observations by fifteenth- and sixteenth-century explorers, and perhaps some information from Incan sources, seemed to have provoked a flurry of esoteric activity in Europe; the prophecies of Nostradamus and the Rosicrucians are two that come to mind.

Ultimately, the meaning of both crosses, Hendaye and Urcos, points to a metaphysical place of refuge, although it is just possible that the caves of Cusco did help survivors of a previous catastrophe. Even the surviving Quechua shamans agree that something more profound is involved this time around.

Alberto Villoldo has been a student of Quechua shamanism for over twenty years. He discovered that the traditions of the shamans of Peru contained astonishing information. The goal of this shamanic wisdom seems to be the attainment of a luminous body of light. These same shamans told Villoldo, and the rest of the planet on their 1996 tour of the Americas, that the world was truly coming to an end.[44] They also told Villoldo that the planet would be transformed over the next few years in ways beyond our current ability to comprehend. These shamans referred to the time period from 2002 to 2012 as "Pachacuti," the time when everything is turned upside down and reality is restructured.

Villoldo also speaks of a possible break between *Homo sapiens* and what he refers to as an emerging new species, *Homo luminous*. Perhaps the path toward the apocalypse and the path toward spiritual liberation are the same. The shamans in Peru possess the same nuggets of information as are encoded in the cross at Hendaye, the cathedrals in Europe, and the temple at Karnak, and that constitute the secret of alchemy.

The path toward extinction is very likely also the path toward a more enlightened state. As a species begins to collectively realize that it is dying out, an inner mechanism, possibly built into the blueprint of the DNA, begins to create the next level of being, a new species.[45]

Alchemy and the secret of esoteric philosophy are the pathways to *Homo luminous*.

Alchemy is nothing less than the science of how our species evolves. We can see traces of this fact in the ancient Andean civilizations from Tiahuanaco to the Cusco of the Incas, but unfortunately we have no written records, no literature, to allow us to flesh out these celestial beliefs within a cultural framework. For that we must turn to ancient Egypt and its sacred science of immortality.

PART SIX

The Great Mystery: Illuminated Masters, Apocalyptic Refuges, and Mythic Time

I know, myself, that the goddess Isis is the mother of all things . . . and that she alone can bestow Revelation *and* Initiation.

—LE MYSTÈRE DES CATHÉDRALES

THIRTEEN
FROM ATLANTIS TO SHAMBHALA

THE CROSS AND THE MYTH OF TIME

When we began our quest that chilly spring morning standing in front of the cross in the midst of Hendaye's market day, we had no idea of the strange pathways down which it would lead us. We started with a series of mysteries—the mystery of Fulcanelli, the mystery of the cathedrals, the mystery of alchemy and its connection with chiliasm and eschatology, the mystery of the Hendaye cross and its message of an approaching catastrophe—and the closer we came to solving these mysteries, the greater the overall mystery became.

The cornerstone of the greater mystery is the cross at Hendaye, a true monument to the end of time. From this simple, inelegant, and obscure monument, Fulcanelli derives his warning that our hemisphere will be tried by fire as well as his message of hope that there is a place of refuge. Our detailed decoding revealed that the monument does indeed suggest the mechanism of the double catastrophe, and it demonstrates that the ancient illuminated science of astro-alchemy creates an astronomically correct Cube of Space within the projected Tree of Life. This illuminated astronomy makes use of sophisticated alignments between the galactic core and the solar system's angular momentum to its radial energy flow. It also supplies us with a pattern that can be used to locate precisely our solar system in intergalactic space. Contemplating the source of this advanced cosmological knowledge gives us a glimpse of the greater mystery.

The cross at Hendaye uses this ancient illuminated astronomy to predict the timing of the double catastrophe. Its symbolism reveals a season

396

of destruction from summer solstice to winter solstice over a twenty-year period by pointing to its midpoint, the fall equinox of 2002, when the planetary and solar alignments formed a right-angled cross between our system's angular momentum and the galactic center. As we have seen, the equinox midpoint is bracketed by celestial events on the solstice, the most prominent of which is the heliacal rising of the sun and the galactic center on the winter solstice of 2012. As this is the end date of the Mayan calendar and a significant date in the Tibetan Kalachakra, its importance takes on added significance. Yet it is the cross as a symbol and a metaphor that has universally held man's attention.

The INRI above the starburst on the eastern face of the cross demonstrates how closely Christianity is related to the mystery of the Last Judgment. Maybe, however, given the reading of INRI of *"Isis Naturae Regina Ineffabilis,"* or "Isis, the Ineffable Queen of Nature," we ought to adjust our understanding of Christianity to reflect a more Egyptian perspective.

Perhaps the stories of the birth of a savior are symbolic references to a transformative time. Horus is born to avenge his father Osiris's death at the hands of his uncle Seth. This strange familial motif is carried through in literature and legends such as Shakespeare's *Hamlet,* the Greek Oedipus tragedies, the myths of Jason, and dozens more. What if these myths reflect the conditions in the sky thousands of years ago, at the time of the last catastrophe? And what if these myths are about to reappear in the skies of our time?

We can see this most clearly when we contemplate chiliasm's source, the New Jerusalem of Revelation. In chapter 21, verse 10, John tells us that the angel "showed me the Holy City, Jerusalem, coming down out of heaven from God." This suggests that the Holy City is a pattern in the heavens first, before it becomes a reality on earth. Since the Holy City, as the angel reveals in 21:16, is a vast cube, we can easily see this as the Cube of Space. The millennial moment, the climax and end of time, is the moment when the Cube of Space becomes the Holy City of the New Jerusalem.

This happens, of course, when the celestial markers—sun, moon, planets, edge, and center of the galaxy—assume their appropriate mythological positions, which occurs once every 13,000 years. At that moment, the Cube of Space becomes animated and the heavenly city descends. The cross at Hendaye tells us that we are in the moment now.

Only at this point in time, a twenty-year season marked by the midpoint that occurred at the fall equinox of 2002, do the alignments of the Cube of Space and the Tree of Life match the reality in the sky.

John Michell, in his seminal work *City of Revelation*, demonstrates that the sacred geometry of the New Jerusalem provides a link between various sacred structures, such as Stonehenge and the Great Pyramid, and the basic ratio of the moon's orbit around the earth.[1] Taking this as a clue, we can imagine that the cube of the New Jerusalem forms within the sphere defined by the moon's orbit. It would, of course, be aligned to the larger Cube of Space defined by the celestial events. This cube-within-a-cube image is a three-dimensional representation of a hypercube, the four-dimensional structure formed from the Cube of Space by projecting the Tree of Life onto its surface.

The phases of the mythological drama, the death of Osiris, the birth of Horus, and his triumph, like the phases of the alchemical transformation, represent the manifestations of the different celestial events forming the New Jerusalem cube and their spiritual consequences for the human psyche. If we assume that the Holy City is complete between 1992 and 2012, then it does indeed look like Revelation is specifically describing the twentieth and twenty-first centuries. Perhaps all the horrors of our times are the result of a cosmological alchemy in which the transfiguration of time triggers other transformations. It is possible that we are being pushed by cosmological events toward extinction or enlightenment as a species.

Paul LaViolette's work suggests that the mechanism of the double cataclysm could be the arrival of a galactic-core superwave, which would push dust into the sun, causing a massive coronal discharge. This double catastrophe is loosely tied to the precessional cycles, which the ancient illuminated astronomy measured by galactic-core alignments. Perhaps the alignments, such as depicted on Hendaye, occur before the arrival of the superwave and its destructive effects, as a kind of warning, the signs and portents Revelation promises in the sky. It could also be a window of opportunity for profound change, perhaps even the moment of ascension or the mass attainment of the Diamond Body, an immortal light body described in Tibetan Buddhism.

However we interpret the cosmic mythology, it is the oddly divided Latin inscription on the Hendaye cross that provides us with important clues; it confirms the timing of the catastrophe and then, most significantly, points to the location of a possible place of refuge. If we pass Fulcanelli's test and learn to search for the missing refuge within the "space" of the misplaced *S*, we find a precise location, Cusco, Peru, the Incas' analog to the center of the galaxy, their "navel of the world." Following this clear message, we stumbled upon the original location of Atlantis, our lost pre-catastrophe global civilization, and, from the inherited wisdom of its descendants, including the Incas, we discovered the importance of the celestial cross in the southern sky.

Andean traditions tell of a culture hero, Viracocha, who emerged from the center of the world and gathered the remnants of civilization together at Tiahuanaco, one of the ruined cities of Atlantis. Perhaps this is a memory of the survivors of the last catastrophe and their determination to rebuild their culture. The mysterious Raimondi stela found in the Peruvian highlands and dating to at least 1000 B.C.E. depicts a Viracocha-type shaman. In this image (fig. 13.1), the Viracocha shaman is shown with his internal centers aligned with their planetary equivalents

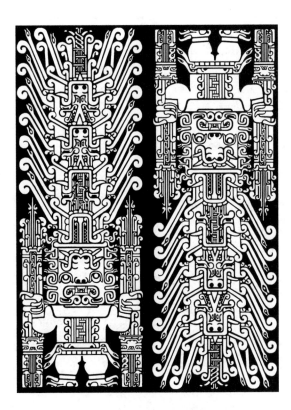

Figure 13.1. The Raimondi stela, *left,* viewed right side up, is a human figure in an elaborate headdress; *right,* viewed upside down, the figure appears as a dragon with a large gaping mouth.

while engaged in surveying stellar alignments with a pair of serpent-entwined staffs.

When we stand back and look at this vast panorama of connections and correspondences, the conclusions, strange as they may seem, are obvious. A high civilization existed in the Andes around 15,000 B.C.E. It was perhaps even far beyond our current level. A catastrophe destroyed that culture, except for isolated pockets of survivors. It is possible that some of these "survivors" were actually immortal beings who had attained a "light body" before the wave of destruction arrived. Whatever their exact nature, these beings worked for thousands of years to restart civilization from the ground up, perhaps literally.

The Viracocha shaman and his surveying staffs suggest that part of the revival had to do with reestablishing a kind of geomantic structure, aligned to the stars, the planets, and other galactic locations, that encouraged life and consciousness. Given that the geometry of both Stonehenge and the Great Pyramid is related to the New Jerusalem cube that is now forming in the sky, we might expect that the idea of an earth grid, Plato's spherical icosadodecahedron of triangles, would provide more confirmation of this structure.

And indeed it does. A mirror image of the structure of Notre-Dame-de-Paris's choir/apse (fig. 13.2) forms a perfect icosadodecahedron-grid pattern, indicating a connection between the cathedral's building and

Figure 13.2. Mirror symmetry of the apse of Notre-Dame-de-Paris produces the icosadodecahedron pattern of the earth's grid.

the earth grid. Even more intriguing, the long ley line through central England, which passes through Stonehenge and Avebury—two ancient sky temples, complete in Avebury's case with serpents—also passes through Tiahuanaco. Most curious of all, however, is the occurrence of an essentially interactive phenomenon along this ley line across England—the crop circles.

For thousands of years, "spirits" had been making simple circles in the grain of southern England. Children played in the fairy circles, and the farmers left them alone, figuring the little folk had claimed their share of the crop.[2] All that changed in the 1970s, when the phenomenon was discovered by "anomaly hunters" and the media. As more people became interested, and began tramping over the fields and camping out waiting for a glimpse of the circle makers, the designs grew more complex and involved. By the early 1990s, it was obvious that something very unusual was going on.

The 1999 vintage of crop circles included images that were startlingly close to the core of the astro-alchemical secret (see fig. 13.3). One was a perfect four-circle overlapping geometric structure of the Tree of Life. The Tree itself had appeared in 1996, but 1999 also saw several complex designs based on the Cube of Space. Most startling of all was the design that depicted an approaching object engulfing the sun, causing an eruption.[3] Perhaps the Viracocha cult programmed these interactive localities to teach us our cosmic geometry and warn us of the danger. Perhaps the Viracocha cult survived in other forms as well. If they were truly immortal, even if only in the form of the circle makers, then they might still be out there, trying to help us make the transition and survive the catastrophe.

As suggestive as the crop circles, their makers, and their message might be of the greater mystery, however, they have yet to provide us with more than tantalizing possibilities, and, as usual with the paranormal, more questions than answers. They do at least present us with a new spin on "green language," a geometric language written in the "green" of the grain fields. But without a broader perspective, this *"langue vert"* remains incomprehensible and elusive. The circle makers have provided a text, but what is missing is the suitable mythological host, a framework of myth and experience, some of it psychic, that "explains" the interaction between reality and the numinous.

At the primal level, there are two realities, earth and sky, and they

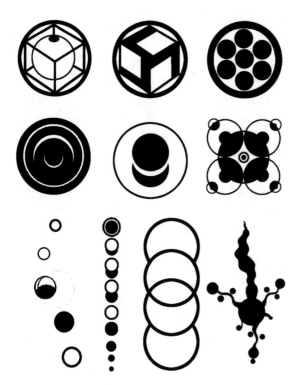

Figure 13.3. A selection of crop-circle designs from 1999, the geometry of which is suggestive of the Cube of Space and the aligning of celestial bodies.

form the foundation of our understanding of space and, as a result of that spatial understanding, time. As soon as a culture or a civilization attains a certain level of awareness, it recapitulates for itself a cosmogony, a description of the origins of the cosmos. One of the earliest of which we have any record, and in many ways one of the most complex, is the ancient creation myth of Heliopolis, the Egyptian city of On.[4]

In the virtual cosmic ocean of Nun, the Atum, whose name means "not to be" as well as "complete (unto itself)," slumbered in a lotus bud. By an act of will, Atum emerged from the virtual "not to be" into the completeness of manifestation, becoming in the process "Re," or the portal of existence, symbolized by the sun. The hieroglyph for *re* is a *vesica piscis,* the vibrating string of a standing wave function out of which, by the process of transformation, all things are created. This image became the "sun" in the sense of the primal source of light and energy (see fig. 13.4).

Atum-Re, the complete portal of existence, generated the first two polar qualities or attributes: heat, Tefnut, and moisture, Shu. They in turn created Geb, the earth, and Nut, the sky. Atum-Re learned that the sky and the earth had been indulging in a sexual dalliance and dispatched Shu to separate them. Nut was thrust upward, arching overhead as the starry sky, her arms and legs becoming the four pillars of the heavens. Geb, in longing for her, thrusts upward mountains in an effort to reach her. To prevent any more such shenanigans, Atum-Re decreed that Nut, the sky goddess, could not conceive during any month of the solar year.

Figure 13.4. Egyptian hieroglyphics of the name Re with simplified meanings.

Mouth: great vibration   **Arm: to give**   **Sun: the source of Light**   **Space**

However, the god of time, Tehuti, or Thoth (see fig. 13.5), had a different idea. While Atum-Re represents a solar view of space ordering time, Thoth represents a more lunar or biological view of time inhabiting space. Realizing that a primeval universe of quintessential ordering was also static and unchanging, Thoth played a strange game of proto-chess or checkers—Thoth was said to have invented the use of eight-by-eight, the magic square of Mercury, game boards—with the Moon, an aspect of himself, and won a seventy-second part of its light. From this "artificial light," Thoth created five days that did not belong to any of the months in the 360 days of Atum-Re's solar year. On these days, Geb and Nut had their romantic encounters, producing a new quintessence, that of the metaphorical "Neters," or forces: Osiris, Isis, Horus (the elder), Seth, and Nephthys.

In this tale we can also see another pair of opposites, the static solar time and the dynamic precessional time, measured by the Egyptians in terms of four lunar-eclipse cycles of roughly seventy-two years. These are the games of chess Thoth played with the Moon and "won," perhaps by landing on, and thereby predicting, the eclipses. From this very early cosmogony, we can determine that time and timekeeping went beyond merely tracking the local solar and lunar changes; indeed, they were derived from the larger celestial motion of precession. These changes in the larger mystery of the mythic sky had practical and ritual

Figure 13.5. Thoth, keeper of time.

significance for the ancient societies that incorporated them into their mythic structures.

This is the somewhat sweeping claim made by the most comprehensive look at the subject of stellar myths since Hewitt's *History and Chronology*. In 1969, Giorgio de Santillana and Hertha von Dechend published *Hamlet's Mill: An Essay on Myth and the Frame of Time,*[5] in which they argued that the geography of myth is actually that of the heavens and that the world of the mythic imagination is the whole of the cosmos. In this view, precession is the cause of a series of successive catastrophes as each group of constellations marking an Age falls away from its solstice or equinox marker point, and these catastrophes are assimilated within a framework of mythic events that give them meaning within the culture.

Santillana and von Dechend identified the mythic geography, its roads, oceans and rivers, and, most significant, its trees and poles, as components of the sky, the Milky Way, and the celestial axis. We saw how the Christianized Incas of Misminay still use the metaphors of roads and rivers to mirror the alignments in the sky, and in chapter 8 we examined the concept of the World Tree at some length. *Hamlet's Mill* adds another component, the recurring cosmological motif of a mysterious place where earth and sky connect and the lights of the sky, the stars, are born. In most myths, this connection is created by means of the World Tree, the unmoving axis around which creation revolves. Associated with this axis are two "gates," or alignments, whose intersection forms the Great Cross. Most often, this mythic point of contact falls on the intersection, or crossing point, of the galactic and ecliptic plane.[6]

A river or a road has almost universally been the symbol of the Milky Way, the largest and most spectacular object in the night sky. Sometimes, as at Misminay, an actual river mirrors the river in the sky. In ancient Egypt, it was the Nile that became the terrestrial counterpart of the celestial river; in India, the Ganges fulfilled the same function. As a road, it was thought to be the path of souls, entering and leaving this plane of existence through the "gates" at the galactic-ecliptic crossing points. This belief survived in Europe in the traditional association of the pilgrim route with the Milky Way: from various places in France, the arms and edges of the galaxy, through the center of the galaxy, symbolized by the mountain passes east of Hendaye, and on to the opposite arm of the galaxy at Santiago de Compostela in northwestern Spain.[7]

The World Tree stands at the center, where the roads meet, connecting the cross in the sky, the zenith alignment of the galactic-ecliptic crossing, with the cross on the ground, in the form of a crossroads, a chapel, a temple, or a cathedral. As the self-fertilizing Atum point, it is both a womb and a phallus, and to the Greeks it was known as *omphalos,* literally "mother's penis" or "navel." The stone in the center of Cusco, another "omphalos" point, served the same function by demarcating the quarters of heaven and earth and the major alignments of celestial events. This locator stone is very similar in concept to Hewitt's carved linga stone, the cross at Hendaye, and to the intellectual idealization of the philosopher's stone and the Stone, the *"lapsit exillis,"* of the Grail. It also suggests the cubic Cybele stone, whose removal from the ancient highlands of Anatolia made Rome the center of the world.

To the Finno-Ugaric tribes that once stretched from Finland and Lapland to western Siberia, this talismanic tree-stone-star was called the *sampo,* a mysterious model of the universe created by Ilmarenin, the Finnish version of Vulcan or Wayland the Smith. The root of this word, *sm,* is very similar to the Egyptian word *sma,* which denotes the concept of the two powers or forces that balance the axis pole of creation. In Sanskrit, the word for pole or pillar is *skhamba.* These linguistic similarities among widely differing cultures suggest that there is a connection between them, at least at the level of their symbolic function as metaphors for the unmoving axis of creation.[8]

To embody these metaphors was, as we saw among the Incas, to become the Sapa Inca, the divine god-man, Horus the pharaoh, the Sun King, or the Christlike redeemer Viracocha. These metaphors point to a successful completion of the quest by the hero/warrior/saint. These are beings that have become the Adam Kadmon, the universal man in tune with the sentience of all Mind in the universe, and the road or path to that attainment is the hero's journey, an inner and outer quest for the Holy Grail.

Alberto Villoldo, in his studies with the Quechua shamans of Peru, came to the conclusion that the current "Pachacuti," the time when everything is turned upside down and reality is restructured, is also the point where a new humanity, a *Homo luminous,* begins to emerge.[9] Villoldo's *Homo luminous* sounds much like the Tibetan concept of the Diamond Imperishable Body, as mentioned in chapter 12. Could this also be an expression of the Sapa Inca, Atum-Re, or Universal Man? Indeed, when we look at India and Tibet's foremost example of the attainment of the Diamond Body, Padmasambhava, we find not only linguistic echoes of our primal myths—*padma* is "lotus" in Sanskrit, echoing the lotus bud of Atum, and *sambhava* is "self-created one," from the same root as *skhamba,* which is the pole or pillar of the unmoving axis—but also a mythic framework that is still psychically active and contains all the motifs presented to us by Fulcanelli and the Hendaye cross, from a place of refuge at the time of the catastrophe to alchemy and immortality.

And so, having found Atlantis and the last catastrophe in the Andes, we must now turn to the East, toward Shambhala and the coming apocalypse.

LOOKING EAST: A REFUGE IN THE HIMALAYAS

Paul Mevryl, in his "Epilogue in Stone," directs us to Jean-Julien Champagne's frontispiece to *Le Mystère,* where "the alchemist stands elevated and protected between the front paws of the Sphinx," looking east to the rising sun.[10] As we saw in chapter 11, this is the place to stand to decode the astronomical riddle of the Great Cross at Hendaye. Mevryl is quite aware of this solution; he suggests that man and Sphinx "wait together for the return of *Horus-in-the-horizon*," which is a direct reference to the rising of Leo on the fall equinox of 2002, a return, after 13,000 years, of the equinox Horus-in-the-horizon. But could this image also point to another place of refuge, as Mevryl implies?

He [the alchemist] and Hu [the Sphinx] his protector, stare silently at the eastern horizon towards ancient Petra. In their narrow cone of vision is little Judea to the north and Ha'il to the south. Between them, very far away, is the Ande of Asia—the mighty Himalaya. *Man* and *Hu-man* wait together for the return of *Horus-in-the-horizon*. For now, in this Age, he will appear before them rather than behind their backs. . . . But Man and Human alike regard the future, not the past.

Hu's protection is twofold. Firstly, He symbolizes the protection of the *illuminated state*. Secondly, His gaze directs our attention towards one of the great *refuges* that man undoubtedly used during the Atlantean catastrophe. A refuge which, with others, may serve again? With these thoughts in mind, we note the similarity between the sound-forms of *Cat Man Hu* and *Katmandhu*, and the persistent legends of concealed entrances into the bowels of the mountains that are associated with that place.[11]

To Mevryl, the place of refuge is clearly in the Himalayas, even though the inscription on the Hendaye cross points, by means of the anagram we examined in chapter 11, to Peru. Mevryl, in his somewhat tortured anagram of the inscription, draws attention to Ha'il in Saudi Arabia, but, with the exception of the odd use of Ande in reference to the Himalayas, Mevryl ignores any connection to South America. At first, we were inclined to see this as an example of Mevryl's finely honed sense of misdirection, but after following our Peru interpretation and finding Atlantis in the Andes, we returned to Mevryl with new appreciation.

His insistence that we should look east from the Sphinx, along the 30-degree latitude line, does in fact bring us to the "Ande of Asia—the mighty Himalaya" (note the singular) in the form of Mount Kailas, which sits just north of the 30-degree-east line. This stand-alone, A-shaped mountain, sacred to both Hindus and Buddhists, rises like a great planetary omphalos from the highest plateau on earth to almost 26,000 feet. It is also the origin point for the four great rivers of Asia, the Indus, the Sutlej, the Brahmaputra, and the Ganges, which spin out from its base in the rough form of a sun wheel or swastika. Beyond that, just below the line, is the Tibetan capital of Lhasa at 90 degrees east longitude, exactly 60 degrees east of the Sphinx at Giza.

And, without struggling for any green-language combination of Cat, Man, and Hu, Katmandu is simply the ancient Nepalese word for "place of refuge."[12] Mevryl then is forcing us to look in the direction of Nepal and Tibet. When we do, we find a semi-historical illuminated master, Padmasambhava, who hid teachings, texts, and treasures in statues, cliff faces, and sacred lakes and arranged secret places of refuge from one end of the Himalayas to the other. Behind these legends looms a lost civilization that rivals Atlantis for antiquity. Unlike Atlantis, this civilization supposedly still exists in, to quote Fulcanelli, a place "where death cannot reach man at the time of the double catastrophe."[13]

Once, a long time ago, according to the ancient Newarri chronicles of Nepal, the valley was a vast lake called the Nag Hrad, or Tank of Serpents. The *nagas* were dragon-serpents who guarded a treasure deep in the lake. A Buddha from a past age tossed a lotus seed into its placid waters, and from this grew an amazing thousand-petaled lotus that shone with the blue light of transcendental wisdom.

Aeons went by. And then, one day, the bodhisattva Manjusri, a central Asian version of Apollo, who, having heard tales of the lotus and its light, arrived at the lotus lake to contemplate its splendor. He stopped at the edge and, being thwarted by the *nagas,* found that he could not approach the lotus. However, after consulting with Vajra Yogini, a manifestation of Dolma/Tara the mother goddess, he decided on a radical plan. He would drain the lake, bind the *nagas,* and thereby share the lotus light with everyone.

Seizing the great Sword of Discriminating Wisdom, Manjusri sliced the mountainous rim of the valley in a single stroke, creating a gorge through which the waters of the lake, and its *nagas,* poured. As the water rushed out, the *nagas* were caught in a bottomless pit, where, along with their treasure, they remain to this day. The lotus settled to a small mound in the center of the emerging valley, eventually to become the stupa of Swayambunath.[14]

Now, the curious point here is that geology agrees with and supports the myth. Roughly 15,000 years ago, an earthquake did in fact drain the vast lake that was Nepal valley, slicing open the rim as neatly as if it had been done with a sword. The lake formed as much as a million years earlier when the Himalayas lurched upward. Therefore, for many thousands of years, there was indeed a large, deep lake of placid blue water surrounded by high, white-topped mountains just as the traditions say. All we are missing is the giant lotus, radiating blue light.

The Newarri chronicles continue in a similar vein, telling tales of gods in human form and of kings with the power of gods and of their interaction. In this magical era, a single king could rule for a thousand years and temples were endowed with images of the gods who sweated, bled, and spoke as they communicated their desires. This sense of a magical reality within a mythological landscape remains strong even today in Nepal.

Buddhism arrived in the valley very early, so early, in fact, that it became woven into the fabric of its mythological past. During the reign of the semilegendary Kiratis—whose founder, Yalambar, fought and died in the epic struggle depicted in the Mahabharata—the Buddha and his disciple Ananda visited the valley. They founded a school in Patan, where the Buddha elevated a family of blacksmiths to goldsmith status and gave them his own clan name, Sakya.

A few centuries later, the great Indian emperor Ashoka, a convert to Buddhism, made a pilgrimage to the Buddha's birthplace at Lumbini, in the *terai,* or plain, to the south, and then continued on to Kathmandu valley. He built and enlarged stupas at Patan and Swayambunath, and his daughter married the local prince, Devapala. This link to the original Indian traditions ensured that Buddhism would survive in Nepal long after it had died out in India.

At the turn of the fourth century C.E., the last Kirati king, Gastee, was overwhelmed by an invasion of Rajaput princes from the areas of Bihar and Uttar Pradesh in India. The Licchavi princes spread a veneer of Hinduism over the local Buddhism, creating a unique mixture of practical shamanism and sophisticated philosophy. This Nepalese Buddhism owed as much to Rajaput Tantra as it did to the teachings of Siddhartha.

Later branches of the Licchavis, the Thakuris, were instrumental in bringing Buddhism to Tibet. Princess Bhrikuti brought some of the Buddha's relics with her when she married the king of Tibet, Tsrong-tsong Gompo, and eventually converted him. For her devotion, she was identified with Tara, the Tibetan mother goddess.

After this high point, the Thakuri dynasties settled into a kind of semi-mythological Dark Age. An example is the story of King Gunakamadeva. It seems that the god Indra, whose interest in the valley went back to the primordial blue lotus era, assumed human form to observe the Indrajatra festival in his honor. A group of tantric magicians spotted him and bound him with spells until he granted them a boon. Indra's boon was the wood from a celestial tree, used by the king to construct a large seven-tiered pagoda called the Kasthamandap, or the Wooden House of Refuge. From this came Kathmandu as time chipped away at the extra syllables.[15]

In these legends, we can see echoes of our primal theme. The blue-light lotus is the ancient primal center, dislodged by a catastrophe caused by the Tibetan sun god Manjusri. This center is then represented, in the same spot, by a stupa, an arrangement of the elemental shapes into an omphalos-like locator stone/tree. This same stupa/pagoda design, seen in the architecture of the original Kasthamandap, can be found throughout Buddhist Asia, from China to Burma. In the original hidden valley of Nepal, the place of refuge was clearly a magically constructed model of the World Tree.

However, long before the Kasthamandap was built, Nepal was a place of sacred pilgrimage. The caves in the south rim of the valley had an ancient history of use by traveling saints and yogis as meditation sites, going back, according to legend, to the time before the lake was drained. Indra himself was thought to have spent a few aeons contemplating the blue light from a cave high on the south wall of the valley. At some point after the lotus disappeared, a demon, one of the *asuras,* occupied the cave. He was still in residence, according to the local tradition, until the arrival of Guru Padmasambhava, who converted him to Buddhism and then occupied his cave for the attainment of his Diamond Imperishable Body.

Exactly when this occurred is obscure. The dating in the Newarri chronicles suggests that Padmasambhava's retreat occurred during the reign of the last Kirati king, Gastee, in the late third century C.E., but Tibetan sources, such as Yeshe Tsogyal's biography of Padmasambhava, point to an even earlier date, apparently in the era immediately before Ashoka in the second century B.C.E. Indications in some of Padmasambhava's teachings, given to Yeshe and others in Tibet, suggest that he was influenced by Rajaput Tantrism, and therefore Buddhist scholars have surmised that he learned his tantric Buddhism in Nepal between the fifth and seventh centuries C.E.[16] This is much closer in time to his historical appearance in the eighth century in Tibet, and therefore relieves the scholars of the burden of an individual almost a thousand years old when he first appears in the historical record.

Whatever the date when Padmasambhava settled in the Asura Cave, there can be little doubt that something spectacular occurred there as a result of his practices. On the floor of the cave can still be seen the melted-rock handprint that was left as a symbol of the attainment of the Diamond Body (see fig. 13.6). The entire hillside—from the riverside temple, to Kali and Durga in the tiny village of Pharping, up the ancient steps past the Vajra-Yogini shrine, and farther up the mountain, past the Ganesh shrine where a miraculous image of Tara is slowly growing outward from the rock, and on past the crossroads village and the Tibetan monastery—is imbued with a sense of light and transformation that is as palpable as the smell of incense and yak-butter lamps.

In front of the cave is a large flat space where one can sit and meditate on the entire range of the White Himalayas, with the peak of Chomolungma, the Mother of the Gods, Mount Everest, directly opposite to the north. Just to the east of Chomolungma is the White Mountain, Macherma Ri, and just beyond it can be seen the peak of Kangtega. Somewhere in between these two mountains is a real place of refuge on Mevryl's sight line from the sphinx—the hidden valley of Khembalung.

PADMASAMBHAVA AND THE TEMPLE OF THE COSMOS

Sometime after 760 C.E., the king of Tibet, Tsrong-tsong Gompo's son Tri-Tsrong De-tsen, summoned the most famous Buddhist tantrist of the era, Guru Padmasambhava, to help overcome the magical resistance of

Figure 13.6. Handprint of Padmasambhava melted into the rock at the entrance to the Asura Cave. (Photo by Vincent Bridges)

the older shamanistic Bön-pos. Buddhism had been brought to Tibet by his mother, Princess Bhrikuti of Nepal, and the king was determined to make it stick. However, the power of the Bön-pos had proved so far irresistible, and the new faith made little headway. Santaraksita, the king's Buddhist adviser, suggested bringing in the help of a real magician, the legendary Lotus-Born One, and so the call went out.

The king's envoys found Guru Padmasambhava in retreat near the great cities of the Ganges plain, and intrigued by the king's entreaties, he agreed to come to Tibet. "In the earth-male-tiger year, on the fifteenth day of the winter midmoon, under the sign of the Pleiades, he set out on his way," Yeshe Tsogyal's biography informs us.[17] The guru lingered for three months in Nepal, visiting old meditation retreats and hiding *termas* for future use in caves and temples, until on the first day of the first summer moon he had a dream in which all the trees of India and Nepal pointed their crest toward Tibet, and all the flowers opened their blossoms. In that moment, we are told, all the wise men of Asia had a vision: the union of the sun and the moon rising over Tibet, the new dharma refuge in the darkness of the Kali Yuga.

Guru Padmasambhava and his retinue of students and disciples set out over the high mountain passes for Tibet. Just inside Tibet, at Tengboche Monastery in the shadow of Chomolungma, he was met by the head of the Bön-pos and challenged to a magical contest.[18] The first one to reach the summit of Chomolungma would be acclaimed the greatest of all. Padmasambhava accepted, and then retired to his tent for a good night's sleep. The Bön-po lama, however, had a magic flying drum with which he planned to fly to the summit during the hours of darkness and so reach the top early in the morning, just as Padmasambhava had begun.

His students spotted the Bön-po lama flying on his drum in the moonlight and went to awaken the guru. He responded that there was no cause for alarm, even though the Bön-po was already halfway up the mountain, and that they should sleep while they could. Just before dawn, the guru arose, positioned himself for meditation on the rising sun, and waited, deep in trance. As the Bön-po lama, exhausted by his all-night drumming flight, slowly circled toward the peak, the first ray of the rising sun pierced the gloom. Guru Padmasambhava mounted the sunray and flew instantly to the topmost peaks, seating himself on the Throne of Gold and Garnet. Abashed, the Bön-po lama fled, his magic drum tumbling down the mountain.

While seated on the throne, Guru Padmasambhava looked out to the northeast toward the snowfields of Khumbu. Looking closer, he saw a perfect hidden valley, tucked away deep within the surrounding peaks and snowfields. Having the gift of seeing into time, Padmasambhava called upon the gods of the five directions, the Dhyani Buddhas, to hide the valley from the world and to provide for it all the needs of life. He declared that the hidden valley, Khembalung, would be a refuge for a time in the future when the barbarians of "Hor" would invade the central Asian plateau. He also predicted the names, in Tibetan, of its discoverers and the times in which its existence would be revealed, and hid as a *terma* a guidebook to its location.[19]

In the fifteenth century, a lama, Padma Lingba, found such a *terma* guide to the hidden valley and produced another prophecy of its use as a place of refuge. In 1976, Edwin Bernbaum, an American climber and Tibetan scholar, followed the directions in Padma Lingba's guide and, with the help of several local lamas and his Sherpa guides, actually found and entered the outer valley of Khembalung.

"The next morning, when we went exploring, we found an invisible palace in the beautiful forest of pine and rhododendron that filled the valley," Bernbaum explains, waxing poetic. "We heard the clear voices of birds singing to one another and saw the golden mist rising like smoke off the treetops. In the woods around us, drops of bluish water gleamed like diamonds on necklaces of hanging moss. Passing through corridors of trees, we came to sunlit clearings hung with tapestries of rich brown shadows and emerald leaves, And as we went deeper into the forest, through gaps in the foliage, we glimpsed and felt the presence of a majestic snow peak that seemed to rule over the valley, like the King of Khembalung."[20]

Guru Padmasambhava came down from Chomolungma after sealing the place of refuge and proceeded toward central Tibet. Along the way, he was met by a delegation from the king, which he awed by first throwing their offered gold to the four winds. Then, scooping up a handful of dirt as his *prima materia,* Guru Padmasambhava transmuted it into gold. These triumphs made even the Bön-po into converts, and Padmasambhava continued on to Samye, where a mandala-shaped monastery was under construction. Using his command of the spirit world, Padmasambhava caused Samye *chokor,* the Dharmachakra, to be built in the grand pattern of the Indian *vihara,* or plan of the cosmos.[21]

From the spiny ridge to the east of Samye, where a Bön-po temple once stood and Padmasambhava sat in meditation while Samye was built, the complex of temples and chapels surrounded by a flattened ellipse can be seen in all its grandeur, despite over twelve hundred years of use and misuse. At night, as in the Andean highlands of Peru, the river of the galaxy dominates the night sky, stretching at its summer zenith from northwest to southeast, with its bulging center high overhead. As at Misminay, the pattern of Samye *chokor* matches the path of the galaxy in the sky with its satellite chapels or *lings,* while the main structures, including the central Utse Rigsum, form the cardinal cross of the directions. The Utse Rigsum acts as the central omphalos and World Tree, and on the outside walls can still be seen vast cosmological murals and depictions of Samye in its glory.[22]

Along that northwest line, the celestial road of the galaxy from Samye, is the holy city of Lhasa. If we think of this axis as the galactic axis, then Samye lies on the edge of the galaxy, with Lhasa at its center. The palace of the king was there, atop the jagged ridge of Marpo Ri, and the most ancient center of Tibetan civilization, the Jokang Temple, stood nearby. Eventually, the Marpo Ri would become the Potala Palace, and Lhasa itself would become the absolute center of Tibetan life, both political and spiritual.

Standing on the roof of the Jokang Temple and looking west, back toward Mount Kailas and beyond to Mevryl's Sphinx, 60 degrees of latitude away in Egypt, we note immediately the alignment of two large hills, Chakpo Ri and Bompo Ri, on the due west line (fig. 13.7). Even the modern work of the Communist Chinese, when they rebuilt this avenue, follows the ancient path of the alignment straight to the Jokang. In the Serpent's Cave, on the northeastern side of Chakpo Ri, is a model of Samye, complete with supposedly self-generated stone statutes of the five Buddhas. This repeating pattern of how the cosmos aligns to create time and the meaning of time forms the center of the center, the point from which the dharma radiates throughout the land.

When his work was finished, Padmasambhava departed Tibet for the Copper Mountains of the southwest. Before he left, he gave a series of predictions and prophecies to his main followers. These included instructions on how to find the *termas* he left behind, as well as predictions and pointers to the time of the coming destruction: "When the iron bird flies, and houses run on wheels, the Dharma will come to the

Figure 13.7. Looking west from Jokang Temple, Lhasa, along Mevyrl's Sphinx line. The two hills between the modern office blocks are Chakpo Ri and behind it Bompo-Ri. (Photo by Vincent Bridges)

land of the Red Man. Know, by these signs, that the age of darkness is ending."[23] He also left instructions for the opening of the hidden valleys, such as Khembalung, and predicted that they would be needed at a time when the demons had been released by the barbarians and Tibet had fallen to unbelievers in the dharma.[24]

Such a moment has perhaps arrived. The dharma is fading in Tibet, even as it is taking root in strange ways in the West. Many Tibetan refugees have indeed fled to protected valleys, such as Nepal, in the fringes of the Himalayas. But Padmasambhava left us no further clues to the opening of the hidden valleys, no exact timing on which to hang a date or a time period. While Padmasambhava clearly saw the need for a place of refuge, a science of timing and transformation didn't arrive in Tibet for another two hundred and fifty years. The Kalachakra, or Wheel of Time, Tantra, introduced in 1027 C.E., brought it with a message from the hidden kingdom of Shambhala.

SHAMBHALA AND THE WHEEL OF TIME

The legends of a hidden civilization somewhere in central Asia have a long history, and as recently as the last century, this history could still influence world politics. The invasion of Tibet by British troops in 1904 was caused by a mistaken opinion on the part of some Tibetans that the czar of Russia was the king of Shambhala.[25] In the 1930s, the idea of a lost valley in the Himalayas exploded on the mass consciousness with James Hilton's best seller, *The Lost Horizon,* based in part on the experiences of a real Christian monk who converted to Buddhism in the seventeenth century. Shangri-la, the name of the hidden monastery in Hilton's book, became a kind of synonym for all hidden valleys and places of refuge. FDR, when asked where the planes came from that bombed Tokyo in the spring of 1942, replied simply, "Shangri-la." Roosevelt had his own "Shangri-la," a hideaway in the Maryland Hills now called Camp David.[26]

While most Westerners think of Tibet itself as the hidden kingdom, the Tibetans look to another, even more hidden land as the source of wisdom and inspiration. There, a line of enlightened dharma kings guard the most secret teachings of the Buddha, the Kalachakra Tantra. At the end of time, when the dharma is in danger of being totally destroyed by the barbarians of the age of darkness, the Kali Yuga, the king of Shambhala will emerge from the hidden land, defeat the forces of evil, and usher in a millennium of peace and prosperity.

The legends and ancient texts also say that it is possible, though very difficult and dangerous, to travel to the hidden kingdom and there learn the Kalachakra firsthand. Curiously, all versions of the route to the hidden kingdom begin with the planetary omphalos on Mevryl's Sphinx line, Mount Kailas.[27]

Our earliest glimpse of a hidden paradise to the north populated by sages comes from the *Mahabharata,* the vast epic of Vedic India. The main character, Arjuna, a cousin of the king of Nepal, Yalambar, who founded the Kirati dynasty, travels to border of the mysterious land of Uttarakuru but fails to enter. His route takes him to Mount Kailas, and then northwest, along the galactic axis, to the hidden paradise. To the Bön-po, Uttarakuru was known as Olmolungring, and it also lay to the northwest of Mount Kailas. One of the many Tibetan guides to Shambhala also suggests that the route is northwest from Mount Kailas to the region of Kashmir, and then farther north.

It is possible that this hidden kingdom was once a real country, somewhere in the region of the Tarim basin, north of Kashmir. Certainly, many ancient kingdoms, some of them Buddhist, flourished and died along the ancient Silk Route from China to the West, and the legend of Shambhala may have such a kingdom as its inner kernel of truth. But the idea of the hidden kingdom of enlightened sages goes deeper than just an ancient city-state, no matter how well organized and progressive it may have been. Like Atlantis, the myth of Shambhala points to an ancient cosmic unity of earth and sky.

This becomes apparent when we examine the principal symbolic feature of Shambhala, its eight-petaled, lotus-shaped design. The lotus as a symbol of completeness and attainment goes all the way back to Atum and the cosmic ocean. Shambhala is a version of the *vihara,* or cosmic pattern, the Dharmachakra displayed at Samya *chokor,* and the union of the Saint Andrew's solstice cross and the Saint George equinox cross, which represents the complete alignment of the Cube of Space, as does the Hendaye cross, as we saw in chapter 11. As shown in figure 13.8, the eight-petaled lotus, according to some Tibetan teachers, symbolizes the eight nerve channels that radiate from the heart center.[28]

In physical terms, Shambhala is depicted as a ring of 108 snow-capped mountains. Within it are ninety-six principalities or local regions divided into eight countries (see fig. 13.9) of twelve principalities each. The center region consists of a central five-tiered mountain, or stupa, surrounded by four smaller hills marking the intercardinal directions. Each of these locations is said to have seventy-two *devas*, or god-like sages, within them. At the very center is the throne of the king of Shambhala. All of these numbers are related to precession: $96 \times 270 = 108 \times 240 = (5 \times 72) \times 72 = 25{,}920$. As we saw with Atlantis, this mandala design echoes both internal and external systems and unites them with a sense of cosmology that is little short of remarkable for any era.[29]

Also, as with Atlantis, Shambhala is connected with the last catastrophe. The older, non-Buddhist versions of the legend point to the founding of Shambhala around 13,000 years ago. The Bön-po claim that Olmolungring was founded after the last catastrophe and that once every 13,000 years, another Bön-po exemplar enters the world to renew and revitalize the ancient teachings. The remaining Bön-po sects eagerly await such an exemplar. The Mahabharata also places the founding of

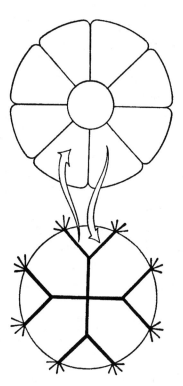

Figure 13.8. Correspondence between the lotus shape and the nerves of the heart center in the Tibetan tradition. Redrawn from Bernbaum. Compare this correspondence to the plan of Shambhala in fig. 13.9.

Figure 13.9. A drawing of the kingdom of Shambhala, surrounded by 108 snowcapped mountains and divided into eight countries. (Stylized representation from Bernbaum)

Uttarakuru at the turn of the last golden age, roughly 13,000 years ago, as we saw in chapter 10.

To the Buddhists, the history of Shambhala began when King Sucandra learned the Kalachakra from the last great teaching of the Buddha in the late sixth century B.C.E. He took this ultimate wisdom back to Shambhala, where it flourished and grew until the middle of the tenth century. A young Indian yogi named Tsilupa traveled, like Arjuna, to the edges of the northern paradise, where he met Manjusri, who taught him the Kalachakra and sent him back to India.

Whether or not Tsilupa actually met Manjusri on the road to Shambhala, scholars have determined that the Kalachakra was practiced and taught in Kashmir by 960 C.E. This brings us to an interesting point. Both Kashmir and points farther north on the Silk Road had prominent Jewish communities in the ninth and tenth centuries. Could the legend of Shambhala have been grafted on to an early form of the kabbalistic *Bahir*? And would the result have been the unusual complexity and astronomical involvement found in the outer teachings of the Kalachakra? Could the Kalachakra be a Buddhist version of the ancient Hebrew illuminated astronomy?

In the 1020s, another Indian yogi, Somanatha, brought the Kalachakra to Tibet and created the official chronology of Tibetan history. The astronomical calendar of the Kalachakra would spread across China, becoming eventually the elemental animals of Chinese restaurant menus. In Tibet it would have many applications, including the prophecy that 960 (10 for each principality in Shambhala) years after the introduction of the Kalachakra, the keys to Shambhala, or the clues to its reappearance, would be found. A teaching of the first Karmapa, one of the founders of the Karma Kagyu school, relates that after the 960 years have past comes a period of 25 years, five times through the five elements, in which the cycle of time comes to an end and the wisdom king of Shambhala will return to this world in the form of the female water dragon. By this measure, 960 + 1027 = 1987 + 25 = 2012; we are in the period of turmoil at the moment. Note also how closely this matches Fulcanelli's season of destruction.

Even the orthodox Tibetan sects, such as the Gelugpa, whose leader is the Dalai Lama, consider that twenty-five hundred years after the Dharma reached Shambhala, around the sixth century B.C.E., the twenty-fifth king, Rudra Kalkin, would emerge and defeat the barbarians, ushering in the new golden age. Even with some looseness, it is very close to twenty-five hundred years since the time of the Buddha. And even though this is not openly expressed, it may be considered the driving force behind the Dalai Lama's campaign to initiate as many people as possible, in the time remaining, into the Kalachakra Tantra.[30]

FOURTEEN
ALCHEMY AND
TRANSCENDENCE

Our quests led us from Egypt, to Europe, then on to Peru and Atlantis, beyond that to Tibet, India, and Nepal, and finally back to where we started, Egypt. In that long journey, we discovered early on that "alchemy," in the sense of turning base metal into gold, was merely a by-product of a much greater attainment. That the transmutation of metals was possible, and had in fact been part of the historical record from the fourteenth century on— right up to the twentieth century if we are to believe the legends surrounding Fulcanelli—seemed less important than what such a transmutation said about the nature of reality and the significance of enlightenment.

In the end, we discovered that alchemy actually is transcendence, the goal and the method united in one "process" that is ultimately never ending. The nature of that transcendence seems to be a gnosis about the nature of the cosmos, an alignment of inner centers—chakras or sefirot—with the outer alignments of the Cube of Space-Time. The inner "golden age" aligns the internal structure of one's cosmos with the Golden Age in the sky, bringing on a personal apokalypsis, or unveiling of the mysteries. When this happens, consciousness and the physical body are transformed. If the person has available to him the "skillful means" developed by other initiates who have had the same experience, then he evolves toward what Alberto Villoldo called the Homo luminous, the Diamond Imperishable Body. If not, then the results are incomplete, and sometimes disastrous.

In the story of the Djedi and King Khufu and in that of

Padmasambhava and King Tri-Tsrong De-tsen of Tibet told in chapter 13, we can see a basic pattern. Both "magicians" are immortal, or virtually so, and have command of the life force in unusual ways. Their names or titles are similar, the "Stable One" of the Djed has the same implications as the "Lotus-Born One" of the *skhamba* or cosmic axis, and they both possess the secret to a model of space-time. In the case of the Djedi, these were the monuments on Giza and the mysterious text hidden in Heliopolis; in the case of Padmasambhava, it was the plan of the Dharmachakra of Samye *chokor* and eventually, the text of the Kalachakra. In both cultures, we find legends of a lost, or hidden, advanced civilization: Atlantis from Egypt, by way of the Greeks, and Shambhala in Tibet.

These similarities ultimately help us understand Fulcanelli and *Le Mystère de cathédrales*. When we follow all the clues, run down all the threads and hints, we arrive at a few basic conclusions.

Fulcanelli is directing us to a time period, the twelfth and thirteenth centuries, when a coalition of initiates managed to have the text of the mystery carved onto the architectural structures designed to facilitate the personal alignment and gnosis of those who could read the mystery from the books of stone and then use the practical implications within the cathedral itself. In this way, Notre-Dame-de-Paris and Samye *chokor* are the same concept, modified only by the culture in which they were created. But the function, the connection of the inner and outer alignments of space-time, is virtually the same.

Our second conclusion concerns the Hendaye cross. It is also a model of the proper golden-age alignment of inner and outer realities, and a marker of the exact time period, now and for the next decade or so, in which these cosmological myths, these intrusions of mythic time, will be played out in the sky. In this way, the Hendaye cross truly is the philosopher's stone, because unless one understands the alignments in the sky depicted on the cross—that is, unless one has the key to the mystery—then even the greatest of these monuments to the end of time, from Notre Dame to Giza and Samye, are but mute wonders built for obscure reasons by people in the distant past.

Our third conclusion is a little more complex. It concerns the role of light in enlightenment. The Pyramid Texts suggest that after death, the pharaoh was reborn with Osiris in the star fields of Orion, which are a mere seventy light-years away and the closest area of stellar creation to our solar system. The pharaoh attained immortality in these star fields as he passed in death along the path of Nun, which in Egyptian is the word for the primeval ether soup out of which all creation arose, through the area of stellar formation in the body of Orion. Thus, by being reborn as a star in Osiris's company, the pharaoh reenacted on a local level the original creation of the universe.

But to attain this star birth in the *bardo,* or transition state, of Orion required first of all that the pharaoh understand the "number of the shrines of the secret chamber of the enclosure of Tehuti." As we saw above, this numbering of shrines creates the throne of Osiris, the Pyramid complex, from which, as the soul star place, the pharaoh made the jump to a light body in Orion, becoming thereby a new Osiris. We can see this same function in the grand design of Samye *chokor,* with the exception that becoming a star body, and thereby leaving this plane entirely, is not part of its plan. Unlike the pharaoh, when Padmasmbhava became a "new Osiris" in a light-body state comparable perhaps to a living star, he did not leave for Orion. He stayed on to help the rest of us make the transition.

And this brings us to the point of our conclusion. Alchemy may in fact be as simple as: Changes in the nature of Light create changes in the Mind of nature. And the shift of the age in the sky signals a profound change in the nature of both Mind and Light. It was this sense of impending change, even catastrophic change, that drove the cathedral-building frenzy in the thirteenth century and eventually led to Fulcanelli's message in a bottle, *Le Mystère des cathédrales,* in the twentieth century.

In the end, we can do no better than agree with Fulcanelli when he says: "I ask for neither remembrance nor gratitude, but only that you should take the same trouble for others as I have taken for you." It is our hope that in this book, we have followed his instructions, becoming, along with Fulcanelli, "a beacon on the great highway of the esoteric Tradition."

EPILOGUE
FULCANELLI REVEALED

In the end, one final mystery remains. The question of Fulcanelli's identity haunts all the other mysteries like the shadow of a high-flying bird on a sunny day. We can see his absence, the shadow, but when we look for the bird itself, we are blinded by the sun's brilliance. In Fulcanelli's case, the brilliance is that of the gnosis and intelligence of his works, and, just as with the sun, this intense light makes it hard to find the bird, the personality, casting the shadow.

When all the pieces of evidence and innuendo are sifted and sorted, we end up with less than what we had at the beginning. "Fulcanelli" vanishes, leaving apparently only a long series of jokers, pranksters, plagiarists, and sensationalists. The work remains, isolated in context and hermetic in meaning, a true message in a bottle from the last adept. Revealing the levels of complexity in that message, as we have done in this book, leaves us finally with a core of truth, both about ourselves and about the cosmos in which we live. That truth is the secret of alchemy, which perhaps can be revealed, fully, only at the end of time.

So who was "Fulcanelli"?

In chapter 1 we looked at the Fulcanelli legend as put forth by its main proponent, Eugène Canseliet. This legend, the myth of the missing alchemist, was cultivated by Canseliet and by others in the Brotherhood of Heliopolis for reasons of their own, and was meant both to reveal a truth and to conceal an even more important one, Fulcanelli's true identity. The truth it reveals is that the current of the underground stream actually survived into the twentieth century; what it conceals is the origin of that current's survival.

In her book *Fulcanelli dévoilé,*[1] Geneviève Dubois assembled all the circumstantial evidence relating to the initial group of conspirators, the Brotherhood of Heliopolis. Her conclusion, that "Fulcanelli" was the result of the combined work of Pierre Dujols, Champagne, and Canseliet, is the only plausible explanation that fits a majority of the demonstrated facts. We may suppose that Canseliet clung to the legend because it sold books; a mysterious alchemist, as immortal as Saint Germain, sounds much better as a selling point than a collective work from a group of occultists. But is that really all there is to it?

As we worked on the mystery of *Le Mystère* itself, we eventually re-created Pierre Dujols's "Library of Marvels" card file. This allowed us to identify an underlying structure organizing the somewhat over-whelming profusion of images and symbols in the text. This structure, simply put, is the four projected Trees of the "Tree of Life on the celestial sphere," the Cube of Space arrangement from the *Bahir*. As this structure emerged, two things became apparent: The Hendaye chapter, and its images, had in fact originally been intended for *Le Mystère,* and Pierre Dujols was the author of the text of *Le Mystère.*

In chapter 1, we speculated that the Hendaye chapter was meant for inclusion in *Dwellings of the Philosophers,* where the last two chapters touch on many themes, including catastrophes and Atlantis, inherent in the message of Hendaye's cross. It could also, we felt, be a fragment of Fulcanelli's lost last book, *Finis Gloria Mundi.* Intriguing as these speculations were, we couldn't seem to make the Hendaye piece of the puzzle fit comfortably in either. And then, rather late in our investigations, it occurred to us that we had been looking at the entire problem presented by the Hendaye chapter in the wrong way.

The chapter supports the developing pattern of four projected Trees by completing the fourth and final Tree, supplying the essential top three *sefirot*. At the very least, this meant that whoever arranged the second edition knew the basic structure and reinforced it by adding images correctly. But it is also just as likely that Canseliet, in preparing a new edition, simply followed the original pattern, the one intended but not implemented in the 1926 edition. The question of why this was done, why the Hendaye chapter was suppressed, led us indirectly to our second conclusion, that the author of *Le Mystère* was in fact Pierre Dujols.

The first chapter of *Le Mystère* is a broad overview in nine sections that, as we saw in chapters 8 and 9, outlines the first of the four Tree of

Life patterns in the work as a whole. The eighth section deals with the centrally important idea of the Black Virgins and their connection with Isis and ultimately with Cybele and the stone that fell from Heaven, the core idea of Wolfram's Grail romance. At the beginning of this discussion, Fulcanelli quotes a passage from "the learned Pierre Dujols," where Isis and the Virgin are identified as part of an "astronomical *theogany.*" In this somewhat unusual word (see chapter 9), we find a hint of divine genealogy as well as the sacred union of earth and sky.

A few pages later, after listing the ten most significant Black Virgins in France, Fulcanelli shifts back to the Dujols comment on a Cybele stone at Die in northern Provence, and does so with a first-person citation: "I have already mentioned that a stone at Die, representing Isis, referred to her as mother of the Gods."[2] Since it is Dujols himself who is quoted regarding the Die stone, we might infer that Fulcanelli is tipping his Phrygian alchemist cap to his real identity with this first-person nod. While this is not conclusive in and of itself, combined with all the other evidence presented by Dubois in *Fulcanelli dévoilé,* it is a very convincing, and revealing, slip of the pen.

So let us accept that the Hendaye chapter was originally part of *Le Mystère,* and that Pierre Dujols wrote the whole of that work. In chapter 10, we speculated that the chapter on the cross was not included because it pointed too directly to "Fulcanelli's" true identity and that of the group around him. If Dujols is the author of *Le Mystère* and the Hendaye chapter, does this still hold true?

Indeed it does, but with a twist. The joker, as always in this convoluted story, is Jean-Julien Champagne, the illustrator of both *Le Mystère* and *Dwellings.* Some, such as the publisher Jean Schémit, believed that Champagne was "Fulcanelli," while others, such as René Schwaller de Lubicz, claimed that the character he called Fulcanelli, by implication Champagne, had stolen the manuscript of *Le Mystère* from him.[3] Only one thing seemed certain: Champagne was the focal point around which the Fulcanelli legend originally swirled. And from this seemingly solid fact would come much future mystification.

But, in fact, neither the author of the text, Dujols, nor its illustrator, Champagne, was "Fulcanelli." In *Le Mystère,* the author takes the clear tone of a student elucidating the work of the master, or masters, from whom he learned his subject. In the preface to the second edition, Canseliet confirms this by including a letter whose "recipient was undoubtedly Fulcanelli's master," which letter was found among Fulcanelli's papers.[4] It is this individual, it seems, who has attained the great work, not his student, the author of *Le Mystère*. If this is not even more mystification—and that is always a possibility—then this mysterious master alchemist from the preceding generation can be thought of as the real "Fulcanelli," the source of the current, as it were.

It was this train of thought that led us to look at the cross in a completely different light. What if the Hendaye cross and its predecessors, including perhaps Hewitt's mysterious carved linga stone, were actually the starting point of Fulcanelli's story? Fulcanelli suggests that the base was carved in the 1680s, a date that is supported by the degree of weathering on the images. Who, in the 1680s, knew enough to code the complex astronomical and alchemical information into a series of oddly interconnected images on the base of an obscure monument in an obscure corner of the Basque Pyrenees? And why?

Just asking these questions sheds new light on the problem of Fulcanelli's identity. In chapter 2, we speculated that Fulcanelli's purpose, at least in part, was to stand witness to the flowering of an esoteric tradition in the West that was as profound and transcendent as that of the East. Fulcanelli traces this lineage, as it would be termed in the East, down to the era in which the Hendaye cross was carved, the mid- to late seventeenth century. As we saw in chapter 2, this period falls in the gap between the Rosicrucian movement and the emergence of Freemasonry. Apparently, the lineage was broken at that point, or at least portions of it died out or went underground. By the mid-nineteenth century, the West was so lacking in spiritual exemplars that Theosophy found its masters and mahatmas in the East.

Yet both Fulcanelli and the Hendaye cross are evidence that the lineage did not in fact completely disappear. The late seventeenth century was the high-water mark of "scientific" alchemy and the origins of chemistry, as well as the beginning of astronomy as a science. Louis XIV built the Royal Observatory in Paris about the same time the Hendaye cross was carved, and, as Fulcanelli reminds us, placed a Black Virgin in its vaults.[5] What seems to have happened is that the lineage shifted from its traditional chivalric and aristocratic base toward a community of the intellect that included scientists, artists, and writers. This shift started with the Rosicrucian movement and gained steam with the early Freemasons.

Following the French Revolution and its Napoleonic aftermath, the lineage was again in danger of vanishing completely. A few "initiates" remained from the ancien régime, and by the 1830s the tradition had begun to revive. The publication in 1832 of *Hermes dévoilé* by the mysterious Cyliani, rumored by Canseliet to be Antoine Dujols, older brother of Pierre, marks the turning point in the lineage's revival. The same year also saw the incredible popularity of Victor Hugo's *Notre-Dame de Paris* and the beginning of an upsurge of interest in all things Gothic. Thirteen years later, a young Eugène Viollet-le-Duc would begin the restoration of Notre-Dame-de-Paris itself, his drawings and reconstructions serving eventually as a model for Champagne's illustrations in *Le Mystère*.

In 1842, the d'Abbadie family in Hendaye moved the cross, with its Meso-American sun face and coded riddle about Peru, from its original location, possibly in the church's graveyard, to its current location on the south side of the church, just a few feet from the village square. That same year, another mysterious alchemist, one Tiffereau, announced that he had discovered the secret of transmutation in Mexico. The next year, one of the initiates from the ancien régime, Louis-Paul-François Cambriel, published the results of twenty years of research. In his *Cours de philosophie hermétique,* Cambriel, drawing upon the seventeenth-century work of Esprit Gobineau Montluisant, points directly to the cathedrals as hermetic monuments. By 1854, when Louis Figuier published his massive *Alchemy and Alchemists,* the idea of a secret alchemical wisdom had been revived and the groundwork laid for Fulcanelli/Dujols's brilliant explication in *Le Mystère*.[6]

Yet somehow, as we sorted through these connections, the Hendaye cross remained problematic. The dates that Fulcanelli/Dujols points out for us do seem to have a direct connection to the current and its survival. The mid-seventeenth century, when the base of the cross was carved, marked the shift from the chivalric to the artistic as alchemy became chemistry, as well as the first direct explanation, in Gobineau's *Explication très curieuse des enigmes et figures hiéroglyphiques,* of the hermetic meaning of the images on Notre-Dame-de-Paris. The 1840s, when the cross was moved to the churchyard, saw a serious alchemical revival, including again the connection to the hermetic figures on the Gothic cathedrals. These are undoubtedly important time periods, from Fulcanelli's perspective, but just why the Hendaye cross should be used to mark them remained unclear, particularly in light of the chapter's suppression in the first edition.

No matter how we shifted the puzzle pieces, the Hendaye chapter remained an oddity. Was it an afterthought, a mere exclamation point to the broader pattern of *Le Mystère* and *Dwellings*? Or was it the key to the secret of alchemy, the magic thread that unravels the veil and reveals the ultimate mysteries, and therefore the most important chapter of all in understanding Fulcanelli's message? The more convinced we were that the latter was the case, the more significant the whole issue of Hendaye became.

Working backward from Pierre Dujols brought us to a dead end. There was no evidence that he had ever visited Hendaye, or had any other connection to the region. Working forward from the nineteenth-century alchemical tradition brought us to the same impasse: no connection to Hendaye. Pierre Dujols could certainly have interpreted the cross in much the same way as we have done in chapter 11. He had connections to the esoteric currents of his era, including that of the Paris branch of the Hermetic Order of the Golden Dawn, and so had the symbolism available to him. Indeed, Jules Boucher's explanation, a decade after the first edition of *Le Mystère,* also shows a connection between the cross and the Tarot symbolism of groups such as the Ahathoor Temple of the Golden Dawn. And yet, the direct connection to Hendaye is missing or obscured.

If, as the Hendaye chapter suggests, the Hendaye cross in some way parallels the survival of the alchemical lineage, then its importance must have been obscured purposefully. We may never know who carved the cross, but we do know who recognized its importance and moved it to its present location. When we turn to the d'Abbadie family, and its most prominent member in the mid-nineteenth century, Antoine d'Abbadie, the puzzle starts to make more sense.

As we noted in chapter 10, in 1926 members of the d'Abbadie family were still prominent in society. A reference to Hendaye and the 1840s would have led directly to the family. Even today, that fact can be obtained with little effort, as the d'Abbadie family crest can still be seen on the church wall, just below the sundial, while standing at the cross. All of which raises the question of why it was so important to obscure this connection. Could it be hiding the source, as it were, of what later became *Le Mystère* and *Dwellings*?

Antoine d'Abbadie, although almost completely unknown outside of France, was a major figure in the nineteenth-century scientific community and the president of the French Royal Academy of Science in the 1890s. An explorer, linguist, astronomer, collector of folktales and esoteric manuscripts, and a supporter of the Gothic revival, Antoine d'Abbadie comes across as a very French predecessor of Indiana Jones. His expeditions included a search for the source of the Nile in Ethiopia, and even in the 1880s, when he was in his seventies, Antoine d'Abbadie continued to travel on a series of expeditions based on making astronomical calculations, including the 1883–84 transit of Venus across the Sun. His career parallels the emergence of the almost lost alchemical lineage, and his circle of friends and correspondents included everyone from Victor Hugo, Prosper Mérimée, and Viollet-le-Duc, who designed the Château d'Abbadie at Hendaye, to the above-mentioned Louis Figuier, Camille Flammarion, an astronomer sometimes considered to be Fulcanelli on the basis of a cipher on the name "Fulcanelli," Ferdinand de Lesseps, and, most interesting of all, Grasset d'Orcet, the scholar of the green language, the "language of the birds," quoted by Fulcanelli in the Hendaye chapter.[7]

In d'Abbadie's notes, letters, and published work we come across odd previsions of concepts that turn up later in *Le Mystère* and, most of all, *Dwellings*. Antoine d'Abbadie's notes from his 1835 tour of England, Ireland, and Scotland reveal a deep interest in Gothic architecture, including a look at the enigmatic icosahedron at Holyrood Castle in Scotland, discussed at length in *Dwellings*. His speculations on the connection between the Basques and Atlantis also find their way into *Dwellings,* as do his views on the age of the Sphinx and the antiquity of Egyptian civilization.[8]

Could Antoine d'Abbadie be the real, or original, Fulcanelli? And if so, how did this information come to be in hands of the Dujols brothers and the other members of the Brotherhood of Heliopolis? The d'Abbadies were also connected to the de Lesseps, and through them to Jean-Julien Champagne and R. A. Schwaller de Lubicz, and this is a possible avenue of transmission for at least part of the information. This also explains Champagne's attitude and position in the group. He, at the very least, considered himself the link to the "real" Fulcanelli. Could Pierre Dujols also have had a connection to the d'Abbadie family, one that was not as direct as Champagne's?

Such a connection seems likely, but to date the solid evidence is lacking. Whether the connection came from Champagne or from Dujols, or both, the connection was obscured, covered up, and finally confused beyond any resemblance to reality by the Fulcanelli myth advanced by Canseliet and the others. Antoine d'Abbadie was a public figure, a respected scientist and member of the establishment. Even after his death in 1897, his family remained prominent, and so the need for secrecy concerning a topic as far from the orthodox mainstream of Victorian science as alchemy is plausible. It is also likely that even the main conspirators of the Brotherhood didn't know the truth that their mythmaking was concealing.

In a way, this is very satisfying. It forces on us the most important conclusion of all.

Fulcanelli is not a person; he is a personification of the tradition, the lineage, as it emerged in the early twentieth century. Pierre Dujols wrote *Le Mystère* to sum up and preserve the teachings of the master, or masters, from whom he learned the tradition. He called himself Fulcanelli, which can be translated as "Vulcan's children," or Hephaistoi, or even Kabiroi, the divine blacksmiths who guard the secret of the stone that fell from heaven, to point to the current's antiquity as well as, by various permutations and codes, some of the prominent members of the group around the original nineteenth-century "Fulcanelli," Antoine d'Abbadie. *Dwellings* was pieced together from fragments of several works, some by Dujols based on d'Abbadie's work and some by Canseliet and Champagne, but all written as part of that voice, that spokesman, for the tradition itself.

In the end, it is the voice of Fulcanelli's message that proves more important than his identity. In that sense, the legend serves its purpose if, after we undertake the quest, we find the mysterious immortal adept inside ourselves.

APPENDIX A

FULCANELLI ON
THE GREEN LANGUAGE

Chapter 1, section 3, of Le Mystère des cathédrales

First of all it is necessary for me to say a word about the term gothic as applied to French art, which imposed its rules on all the productions of the Middle Ages and whose influence extends from the twelfth to the fifteenth century.

Some have claimed—wrongly—that it came from the *Goths,* the ancient Germanic people. Others alleged that the word, suggesting something barbarous, was bestowed in derision on a form of art, whose originality and extreme peculiarity were shocking to the people of the seventeenth and eighteenth centuries. Such is the opinion of the classical school, imbued with the decadent principles of the Renaissance. But truth, preserved in the speech of the common people, has ensured the continued used of the expression *gothic art,* in spite of the efforts of the Academy to substitute the term *ogival art.* There was an obscure reason for this, which should have made our linguists ponder, since they are always on the look-out for the derivation of words. How does it come about that so few compilers of dictionaries have lighted upon the right one? The simple fact is that the explanation must be sought in the *cabalistic origin* of the word and not in its *literal root.*

Some discerning and less superficial authors, struck by the similarity between *gothic* (gothique) and *goetic* (goetique) have thought that

From Fulcanelli, *Le Mystère des cathédrales,* trans. Mary Sworder (London: Neville Spearman, 1971), pp. 41–44.

there must be a close connection between gothic art and goetic art i.e., magic.

For me, gothic art *(art gothique)* is simply a corruption of the word *argotique* (cant), which sounds exactly the same. This is in conformity with the *phonetic law,* which governs the traditional cabala in every language and does not pay any attention to spelling. The cathedral is a work of *art goth* (gothic art) or of *argot, i.e.* cant or slang. Moreover, dictionaries define *argot* as a "language peculiar to all individuals who wish to communicate their thoughts without being understood by out-siders." Thus it certainly is a *spoken cabala.* The *argotiers,* those who use this language, are the hermetic descendants of the *argonauts,* who manned the ship Argo. They spoke the *langue argotique*—our *langue verte* ("green language" or slang)—while they were sailing towards the felicitous shores of Colchos to win the famous *Golden Fleece.* People still say about a very intelligent, but rather sly, man: *"he knows every-thing, he understands cant."* All the Initiates expressed themselves in cant; the vagrants of the *Court of Miracles*—headed by the poet Villon—as well as the Freemasons of the Middle Ages, "members of the lodge of God," who built the *argotique* masterpieces, which we still admire today. Those constructional sailors (nautes) also knew the route to the Garden of the Hesperides. . . .

In our day, cant is spoken by the humble people, the poor, the despised, the rebels, calling for liberty and independence, the outlaws, the tramps and the wanderers. Cant is the cursed dialect, banned by high society, by the nobility (who are really so little noble), the well-fed and self-satisfied middle class, luxuriating in the ermine of their igno-rance and fatuity. It remains the language of a minority of individuals living outside accepted laws, conventions, customs and etiquette. The term *voyous* (street-arabs) that is to say *voyants* (seers) is applied to them and the even more expressive term sons or children of the sun. Gothic art is in fact the *art got* or χοτ—*the art of light* or *of spirit.*

People think that such things are merely a play on words. I agree. The important thing is that such word-play should guide our faith towards certainty, towards positive and scientific truth, which is the key to the religious mystery, and should not leave us wandering in the capricious maze of our imagination. The fact is that there is neither chance nor coincidence nor accidental correspondence here below. All is foreseen, preordained, regulated; and it is not for us to bend to our pleasure the inscrutable will of Destiny. If the usual sense of words does not allow us any discovery capable of elevating and instructing us, of bringing us nearer to our Creator, then words become useless. The spoken word, which gives man his indisputable superiority, his dominion over every living thing, loses its nobility, its greatness, its beauty. It becomes no more than a distressing vanity. Besides, language, the instrument of the spirit, has a life of its own—even though it is only a reflection of the universal Idea. We do not invent anything, we do not create anything. All is in everything. Our microcosm is only an infinitesimal, animated, thinking and more or less imperfect particle of the macrocosm. What we believe we have ourselves discovered by an effort of our intelligence exists already elsewhere. Faith gives us a presentiment of what this is. Revelation gives us absolute proof. Often we pass by a phenomenon—or a miracle even—without noticing it, like men blind and deaf. What unsuspected marvels we should find, if we knew how to dissect words, to strip them of their bark and liberate the spirit, the divine light which is within! Jesus expressed himself only in parables; can we deny the truth which the parables teach? In present-day conversation is it not the ambiguities, the approximations, the puns or the assonances which characterize spirited people, who are glad to escape from the tyranny of the letter and thereby—unwittingly—show themselves cabalists in their own right.

Finally I would add that *argot* (cant) is one of the forms derived from the *Language of the Birds,* parent and doyen of all other languages—the one spoken by philosophers and *diplomats.* It was knowledge of this language which Jesus revealed to his Apostles, by sending them his spirit, the Holy Ghost. This is the language which teaches the mystery of things and unveils the most hidden truths. The ancient Incas called it the *Court Language,* because it was used by diplomats. To them it was the key to the *double science,* sacred and profane. In the Middle Ages it was called the *Gay Science* and the *Gay Knowledge,* the *Language of the Gods,* the *Dive-Bouteille.*[8] Tradition assures us that men spoke it before the building of the *Tower of Babel,* which event caused this sacred language to be perverted and to be totally forgotten

---

8. *The Life of Gargantua and Pantagruel* by François Rabelais is an esoteric work, a five-volume novel in cant. The good curé of Meudon reveals himself in it as a great initiate, as well as a first-class cabalist.

by the greater part of humanity. Today, apart from cant, we find its character in a few local dialects, such as Picard, Provençal, etc. and in the language of the gypsies.

Mythology would have it that the famous soothsayer, Tiresias[9] had perfect knowledge of the *Language of the Birds,* which Minerva, goddess of *Wisdom,* revealed to him. He shared it, they say, with Thales of Miletus, Melampus and Appolonius of Tyana,[10] legendary personages, whose names, in the science we are considering, ring eloquently enough to require no analysis from me.

9. It is said that Tiresias was deprived of his sight for revealing to mortals the secrets of Olympus. However, he lived "for seven, eight or nine ages of man" and is supposed to have been successively man and woman.

10. Philosopher, whose life, crammed full of legends, miracles and prodigious deeds, seems to be extremely hypothetical. The name of this semi-fabulous personage seems to me to be just a mytho-hermetic image of the compost or *philosophic rebis,* realized by the union of brother and sister, of Gabritius and Beya, of *Apollo and Diana.* In that case, the marvels recounted by Philostratus, being chemical in character, should not surprise us.

THE EMERALD TABLET

The most famous of all early alchemical texts, the Emerald Tablet of Hermes Trismegistos, became through the centuries the very credo of the alchemical adept. Tradition claimed that the tablet had been found clutched in the mummified hands of Hermes himself "in an obscure pit, where his interred body lay," as Jabir tells us, somewhere within the great pyramid of Gizeh. The text, as Jabir gives it, is very short and obscure. It is so important, in both a historic and a symbolic sense, that the full text is required for our examination. Comparing the three earliest known Latin translations with the Arabic original and its subsequent English translations, the goal was to give as clear and simple a version as possible of such an obscure text.

In truth, without falsehood and most real: That which is above is like that which is below, to generate the miracles of the one thing. And as all things have been derived from that one, by the thought of that one, so all things are born from that one thing by adoption. The sun is its father, the moon its mother. Wind has carried it in its belly and the earth is its nurse. Here is the origin point of every perfection in the world. Its strength and power are absolute when changed into earth; separate the earth from the fire, the subtle from the gross, gently and with great care. It ascends from the earth to the heavens, and descends again to the earth to receive the power of the superior and the inferior things. By this means, you will attain the glory of the world. And because of this, all darkness will flee from you. Within this is the power, the force of all forces. For it will overcome all subtle things and penetrate every solid thing. Thus was the universe created. From this will be, and will emerge, admirable adaptations. For this reason I am called Hermes Trismegistos, having three parts of the wisdom of the world. What I have said of the sun's operation is accomplished.

Whatever the origin of this text (we find a version of it in the divinatory invocation to Amon-Re given in column 29, lines 5–20 of the Leyden Papyrus, a second-century Greco-Egyptian magical text buried with its anonymous owner in the noble necropolis on the west bank of Thebes), its value as an alchemical blueprint is obvious in light of our examination of the "Isis the Prophetess" fragment. In fact, "light" is the operative point.

In line 6 of the Amon-Re invocation we read: "Lotus-of-the Stars, heaven, in its height and breadth, is open; I am become the pure light . . . in truth, without falsehood." In the Arabic version of Jabir, this has become: "Because of this event, obscurity [darkness] will flee from you." The "glory of the world" is the animated glow of the living gold, the generative radiation, the "pure light" seen by the alchemists as the Great Work was completed and gold appeared in their athanors. Once they had grasped this truth, the Emerald Tablet seems to tell us, the alchemists radiated light and the darkness fled from them, figuratively and literally.

NOTES ON MOUNT ZION

The word Zion first appears in the Bible in 2 Samuel 5:7 where David conquers the city of the Jebusites, and their fortress/temple of Zion. The word has no known meaning or origin. (A search of possible roots in Canaanite, Coptic, hieratic Egyptian, and Hebrew turns up nothing helpful.) Over time, Zion and Mount Zion became synonyms for Jerusalem itself.

Jerusalem was first occupied in the third millennium B.C.E. and was a royal city in the time of Abraham. Melchizedek introduces Abraham to the God Most High, and Abraham does his famous sacrifice where the "blazing torch" passed through the middle, on Mount Moriah, which is identified with Mount Zion in Davidic times (2 Chron. 3:1). Mount Zion is therefore the place where covenants with God are made.

David treated it as such, building his new capital around it. Mount Zion was also the location of the original resting place of the Ark of the Covenant when David brought it from Mount Tabor to his new capital. It was on the "threshing floor of Oruan" on Mount Zion that David danced before the Ark of God and received the assurance of divine kingship. In this kingly Davidic covenant, God tells David that his son will be the one to build a great temple.

In Nehemiah's description of the rebuilding after the Babylonian exile (Neh. 3:16), we find that David's Tomb was located on Mount Zion. In Psalms, particularly number 2 which is probably by David himself and may even be the song he sang as he danced in front of the Ark/Throne, Mount Zion is God's "holy hill" where he will judge the righteous and smite the wicked. Even more interesting is Psalm 48, which is a priestly invocation sung as a kind of circle casting before ritually opening the temple, where we find the words "in the city of our God, his holy mountain." Also included is the only known cognate of Zion, *Zaphon,* which unfortunately tells us little more than that it was an older form of Zion.

Isaiah cemented Mount Zion's eschatological importance with verses such as 2:2–4, where the "mountain of the Lord's temple" becomes the center of "the last days" and "all nations will stream to it." He also tells us that "the law will go out from Zion," which will bring about the peace of nations. Ezekiel also went in trance to the spiritual Mount Zion, where he witnessed the architecture of the Heavenly Temple in the New Jerusalem.

Obadiah 13:17–21 repeats this eschatological meaning by declaring that "Mount Zion will be deliverance" in the last days, the place where enemies are judged and the faithful rewarded. Zechariah 6:1 also mentions apocalyptic events on Mount Zion. After this, a strange silence falls on the subject of Mount Zion.

Jesus never refers, in the texts we have left, to Mount Zion. Given its eschatological and Davidic importance, this is truly odd. The closest he comes is a backhanded reference to Isaiah 14:12–15 in Luke that seems to imply that he has committed the impropriety of making himself like God and therefore must be punished. In Isaiah, it is the "morning star," or Lucifer, who ascends to Mount Zaphon, or Zion, and claims God's Throne. In Luke 10:18, Jesus identifies himself with these verses.

Mount Zion does appear in two places in the New Testament, the Letter to the Hebrews and the Revelation of Saint John. Hebrews is a strange letter once attributed to Paul but long recognized as not by him. The best candidate is the Alexandrian Jew Apollos, known to both Paul and Luke. He uses his letter, written before the fall of the Temple, to remind the Christians of Jerusalem of the original eschatological significance of Melchizedek's covenant with Abraham and David's kingly covenant. The author claims that Jesus reestablished this covenant, and all believers would share in it when the Temple on Mount Zion has been made new again (Heb. 12:22).

The Book of Revelation mentions Mount Zion as the place where the Lamb and the 144,000 faithful will gather for the judgment (Rev. 14:1). And it also marks the location of the New Jerusalem, the spot where the two Trees will stand in the remade heaven and earth.

So, Mount Zion is *(a)* the place where Abraham sacrificed to the

God Most High; *(b)* the original resting place of the Ark in Jerusalem and the place where God made David king; *(c)* the location of David's Tomb; *(d)* the holy eschatological mountain; and *(e)* not mentioned by Jesus, even in John's Gospel.

However, the Last Supper was held on Mount Zion, in the upper room of a house in the Essene quarter, which is just south of the old tower or fortress on the top of Mount Zion known as David's Tomb. This had to be chosen for a reason, probably to match the clues in the ritual invocation of Psalm 48:2. The Last Supper is the Melchizedekian covenant restored, and it is also the basic Osirian ritual of ancient Egypt. That it occurred on Mount Zion has apocalyptic significance.

Even more confused is the identity of Our Lady of Mount Zion. As the orthodox Christian church evolved, it found itself having to deemphasize the role of Mary Magdalene. This led to a strange multiplicity of Marys. We have Mary, sister of Martha of Bethany, Mary Magdalene, and Mary, Jesus' mother, as well as several other, peripheral Marys. Tradition holds that Mary, Jesus' mother, had a family home on Mount Zion, but this is somewhat odd. Mary's family, in the Gospels, is mentioned mainly by way of genealogy. Luke assumes her to be a descendant of David, as was Joseph, her husband, and so it makes sense that the family dwelling would be near David's Tomb on Mount Zion. However, Luke is the only evangelist to make that assumption. Matthew follows the Davidic descent through Joseph's line, but is silent on Mary's genealogy. Her background is not mentioned in either Mark or John. Indeed, in Mark, she appears individually only to question Jesus' sanity (3:21), and she doesn't show up in John until the Crucifixion. In both of these Gospels she is one of a crowd of Marys who multiply around the cross and the tomb. Jesus' references to his mother are also oddly cold, as if they didn't get along.

If we assume, with good reason, that the first-person portions of John's Gospel are the earliest of the Gospels, then Luke's Gospel becomes the last and latest. This lateness, around 90 C.E., accounts for its pagan, mythological flavor. Since the same author also wrote the Acts of the Apostles, in which the missionary journeys of Paul are described, we can assume that Luke was one of the syncretic Christians attempting to create a new religion from Hebrew sources. His insistence on the importance of Mary suggests influences from contemporary mystery religions, such as the Cult of Isis. The confusion over the Marys arises in part from this divine mother-and-child motif. The question becomes, Which child are we talking about? Luke relates John the Baptist with the family of Mary, and the genealogical implications arising from this are fascinating.

And, of course, there is Mary Magdalene. Her story also appears in Luke. In the other Gospels, she is mentioned only as one of the crowd of Marys at the Crucifixion and Resurrection. At first we are tempted to see her as another creation of Luke's, since he is the only evangelist to mention her directly. However, a close reading of John's Gospel reveals that there is another Mary, carefully edited out and obscured, who seemed to play an important role in Jesus' ministry. Our suspicions are aroused by the marriage at Cana, at which Jesus appears to be the groom. But who was the bride? Later in John we see a moment between Jesus, a woman named Mary, and her sister Martha, in which Mary and Jesus appear as man and wife. Later, John tells us, this same Mary had the power to anoint Jesus as the Messiah. John even has Mary Magdalene meeting Jesus shortly after his resurrection, which makes her the most favored of apostles. If we assume that Mary, Martha and Lazarus' sister, and Mary Magdalene are the same person, then an interesting pattern emerges.

The house at Bethany, where Jesus relaxed during his visits to Jerusalem, was his sister-in-law's house. So where did Mary live? The intriguing supposition is that she lived on Mount Zion, in the house where the Last Supper was held. Luke tells us how Mary Magdalene supported Jesus' ministry, and if she was his wife and related as well to the Davidic royal line, then she was perhaps the most powerful force in early Christianity. Since the orthodox apostolic church is a creation of Peter and Paul, both of whom were outside the main family circle, then it is easy to see how distortions and misdirection occurred over time. The Chroniclers of Pope Sylvester II may have discovered this Magdalenic connection to the roots of Christianity and chose their location on Mount Zion on purpose. We can say that from this source flowed a revived Marianist Christianity, which grew into the Gothic renaissance in the West.

TREE OF LIFE SYMBOLOGY IN *LE MYSTÈRE DES CATHÉDRALES*

The Etz Chaim, the Tree of Life from the *Bahir* and the *Sefer Yetzirah,* can be seen as the prototypical kabbalistic pattern, a sort of symbolic geometry. In *Le Mystère,* Fulcanelli shows us this by the arrangement of chapters and sections and by the images and plates referred to within those chapters. There are four chapters in the first edition: "The Mystery of the Cathedrals," "Paris," "Amiens," and "Bourges." These represent the four worlds, or levels of abstraction, and a Tree of Life, or a part of one, is formed in each world.

The first chapter, "The Mystery of the Cathedrals," contains nine sections, each of which can be attributed to one of the sefirot from Kether to Yesod. This tree represents the Divine World, where the theory of creation is displayed. Interestingly enough, Fulcanelli's thematic breaks in this chapter, while evolving the *sefirot* in the basic lightning-path order, divides naturally into a sword-in-the-stone pattern. The first three sections form the grip, the next five compose the stone, and the continuation of thought from section 1 straight through to section 9 creates the blade of the sword.

The next chapter, "Paris," creates an entire Tree of Life, with the addition of an image of the Black Madonna from the first chapter in the position of Binah. This arrangement, as we shall see, is a clue to the astronomical nature of this archetypal Tree of Life. On a projected or celestial Tree of Life, the earth's pole is tilted toward Binah—the Dark

442

Mother of the Cosmic Sea, in kabbalistic symbology—hence, its importance in Fulcanelli's design. He continues the pattern with the Kether image of "Alchemy" from the main porch at Notre Dame and the Chokmah image of the alchemist from the south tower. These three images form the top three *sefirot*, the Supernatural Triad, and then, quite appropriately, Fulcanelli creates a break to represent the abyss of Daat, or gnosis.

He starts over mapping the tree at the bottom, at the foot of the path of return, the Serpent's Path back up the Tree. Plates 4 through 25 in the second edition of *Le Mystère* represent the paths on the Tree, attributed to the letters of the Hebrew alphabet and the trumps of the Tarot. With plate 26, the *sefirot* pattern picks up again with Daat, the gnosis of the abyss, and proceeds down the Tree to plate 32, an image of the Massacre of the Innocents from Saint-Chapelle, appropriate for Malkuth, considering what happened to the gnostic current in the West. Fulcanelli has here provided us with a very clear and direct image of the entire thirty-two components of the classical Etz Chaim symbology. In terms of worlds, this second level is the archetypal realm, the world of ideas. Fulcanelli demonstrates this by including an almost complete idea Tree, a memory map or mnemonic pattern, at this level. Our inspiration, of course, Binah, or the Black Isis Madonna, comes across from the realm of the Divine.

The next level or world is that of the formational or the etheric. This is the level of the astral or spiritual world so beloved of shamans and mystics of all sorts. Fulcanelli shows great restraint by describing only part of the etheric Tree, not wanting to impart the information from the higher levels of the Tree because his readers were not initiated to that level. He focuses on the seven planetary intelligences and their influence on alchemy. In these seven images, six shown and one only mentioned in the text, Fulcanelli gives us clues to the operational nature of the work. The unshown image is the hidden sun, the mythical sun behind the sun, and the formative images all seem to show how this hidden or dark sun affects the planetary intelligences. Since these intelligences are also attributed to the seven metals, there does indeed seem to be a vast operational secret contained in these images.

Once this multiple Tree of Life pattern is built up from the sections of the first chapter and the plates from Notre-Dame-de-Paris and Amiens, with a few extra plates from Saint-Chapelle, Saint Victor, and elsewhere, an understanding of the basic process of astro-alchemy can be gleaned. This is the real secret, and from Fulcanelli's point of view there is no mystery about it. But once this secret is revealed, Fulcanelli goes on to propose a fourth Tree of Life that neatly ties the historical, mythological, and cosmological elements into one coherent framework.

This fourth Tree of Life pattern represents the world of action, our world of stars and suns and planets. This Tree of Life grows out of Bourges, in Berry. Fulcanelli ignores the town's Gothic cathedral, with its stunning apocalyptic stained glass, and concentrates on two mid-fifteenth-century contemporaries of Good King René, Jacques Coeur and Jean Lallemant, and their houses. This is a significant departure; up to this point Fulcanelli has focused exclusively on cathedrals. This departure signals the shift from the theoretical and mystical to the operational. Here we are firmly in the world of action.

Fulcanelli is pointing us toward a moment in the fifteenth century when the underground stream broke the surface of history. He suggests that the mystery of Bourges is the mystery of the esoteric current in the ancient past, the present of the fifteenth century, and the future down to and beyond the twentieth century. The mystery of initiation encompasses a vast reach of time, Fulcanelli insists, but the strands of the tapestry emerged into a pattern at Bourges in the mid-1400s.

Fulcanelli directs our attention toward eight images in the two houses. Two are from Jacques Coeur's house, plates 39 and 40, and six are from Lallemant, plates 41 to 46. They can be analyzed as two images that establish both individuals as alchemists, the scallop shell and the vessel of the Great Work; three historical and mythological themes, Tristan and Isolde, the Golden Fleece, and Saint Christopher; and three initiatory images from the inner sanctum of Lallemant mansion, the pillars, the ceiling, and the credence of the chapel.

Even this simple pattern reveals groups of threes within threes. The first of the three groups of symbols shows us that Jacques Coeur was a pilgrim, a fellow traveler, but Jean Lallemant was the operating agent with the vessel of the Great Work. The role of grand master, however, is undefined. We are left with the impression that a third personality exists, made conspicuous by his absence. Who was he?

The next of the three groupings reinforces this impression. Here we are met with three narrative images, symbolic stories balanced on that fine line between history and mythology. There is a core of reality to these tales, even when we are aware of their mythological elements. But, on the surface, there is nothing to connect the love story of Tristan and Isolde with the ancient Greek legend of the Golden Fleece, and both seemingly have nothing in common with the Christian legend of Saint Christopher and the very heavy Christ child. And yet, Fulcanelli presents the simple but overwhelming evidence from their own houses that these masters of the subtle art, the green language itself, placed the utmost importance on these three myths. What do these three stories have in common?

Of course, the third mystery grows out of the first two: Just what were these initiations designed to reveal?

The answer to that is the ultimate secret, the secret of time itself. In the second edition of *Le Mystère,* Fulcanelli provides the solution by adding the chapter called "The Cyclic Cross of Hendaye." The three plates from that chapter, numbers 47 to 49, added to the eight of Bourges, numbers 39 through 46, complete the *sefirot* of the fourth Tree of Life, including Daat, gnosis or knowledge. This Tree, as appropriate to the world of action, reveals the cosmological underpinnings of the entire hermetic philosophy of astro-alchemy. The final image in the group, plate 49, the tympanum of Saint Trophime at Arles, completes the circle, both symbolically and on the ground, returning us once again to the ancient city of the Argonauts.

There is also a threefold pattern reflected in the design of the whole book. The first secret, the Tree of Life itself, is formed from the sword-in-the-stone pattern of the nine sections in the first chapter. They form a framework for the *sefirot,* which is then amplified and deepened by the images from Notre-Dame-de-Paris. To this is added the third level, the planetary seals from Amiens cathedral. The next threefold pattern is the mystery of Bourges outlined above. The last grouping of three is the three interlocking cycles of the Hendaye cross, their symbolic reflection on the cathedral at Arles, and finally the three dragon axes in the sky that form the triple alignment of the galactic Great Cross.

This compounding of threes, $3 \times 3 \times 3$, or 3^3, = 27, presents us with the key number in the precessional cycle, the core of the secret hidden behind the Christianized INRI, whose letters in Hebrew add up to 270. From this brief explication of the mystery at the heart of *The Mystery of the Cathedrals,* it is possible to glimpse the genius and coherence of this very guarded and hermetic masterpiece. The message is the medium, language contains its own gnosis, and initiation truly is, as the Grail legends declare, the ability to ask the correct questions.

As we unravel the triple weave of this hermetic tapestry, we shall discover the answer to all of our questions, and in doing so experience a glimpse of a very different reality. Fulcanelli, whoever he was, wrote as the last initiate: not as the one who puts out the light as he leaves, but as the one who makes sure that the eternal flame is burning brightly in some lost corner of Plato's cave. What we have discovered in the course of this book about our own past, our spiritual heritage, and the hope for human evolution is due to his guidance and insight. Without the help of someone who knew, and could prove it, the mystery might never have been unveiled.

THE *SEFIROT* IMAGES OF THE FOUR TREES OF LIFE IN *LE MYSTÈRE DES CATHÉDRALES*

1) Kether, Crown
Tree 1: Section 1 of first chapter, cathedrals as books in stone
Tree 2: Plate 2, Alchemy, from the Great Porch, Notre-Dame-de-Paris
Tree 4: Plate 49, tympanum of porch, Saint Trophime at Arles

2) Chokmah, Wisdom
Tree 1: Section 2 of first chapter, the Philosophers' Church
Tree 2: Plate 3, the alchemist, Notre-Dame-de-Paris
Tree 4: Plate 48, the four sides of the base of the Hendaye cross

3) Binah, Understanding
Tree 1: Section 3 of first chapter, Gothic/*argotique* discussion
Tree 2: Plate 1, Black Virgin of the Crypts
Tree 4: Plate 47, the Cyclic Cross of Hendaye

11) Daat, Knowledge/Gnosis
Tree 1: (no corresponding section in first chapter)
Tree 2: Plate 26, the planetary metals, Notre-Dame-de-Paris, Saturn, lead
Tree 3: Plate 33, the wheel of fire, Amiens
Tree 4: Plate 46, the enigma of the credence

4) Chesed, Mercy

Tree 1: Section 4 of first chapter, the cross

Tree 2: Plate 27, the dog and the doves, Jupiter, tin

Tree 3: Plate 35, the cock and the fox, Amiens

Tree 4: Plate 45, chapel ceiling, Lallemant mansion at Bourges

5) Gevurah, Strength

Tree 1: Section 5 of first chapter, labyrinths

Tree 2: Plate 28, *solve et coagula,* Mars, iron

Tree 3: Plate 34, philosophic coction, Amiens

Tree 4: Plate 44, capital of pillar, Lallemant mansion at Bourges

6) Tiferet, Beauty

Tree 1: Section 6 of first chapter, the wheel of the year

Tree 2: Hidden sun image (unshown), Sun, gold

Tree 3: Fortress image (unshown), Amiens

Tree 4: Plate 43, the Golden Fleece, Lallemant mansion at Bourges

7) Netzach, Victory

Tree 1: Section 7 of first chapter, star themes

Tree 2: Plate 29, the bath of the stars, Venus, copper

Tree 3: Plate 38, the seven-rayed star

Tree 4: Plate 42, Saint Christopher, Lallemant mansion at Bourges

8) Hod, Splendor

Tree 1: Section 8 of first chapter, Black Virgin

Tree 2: Plate 30, Philosophical Mercury, Notre-Dame-de-Paris, Mercury

Tree 3: Plate 36, the first matter, Amiens

Tree 4: Plate 41, the vessel of the Great Work

9) Yesod, Foundation

Tree 1: Section 9 of first chapter, Notre-Dame-de-Paris

Tree 2: Plate 31, symbolic coat of arms, Moon, silver

Tree 3: Plate 37, the Philosophers' Dew, Amiens

Tree 4: Plate 40, Tristan and Isolde, Jacques Coeur's house at Bourges

10) Malkuth, Kingdom

Tree 1: (no corresponding section in first chapter)

Tree 2: Plate 32, Massacre of the Innocents

Tree 4: Plate 39, the scallop shell, Jacques Coeur's house at Bourges

FULCANELLI'S SEPHIROTHIC IMAGES

Figure App. D.1. Fulcanelli's sephirothic images from *Le Mystère des cathédrales*.

The plates numbered 4 through 25, inclusive, in the Paris chapter of *Le Mystère* are attributed to the twenty-two individual letter paths, which connect the eleven *sefirot* listed above. Their pattern is the classical Path of Return, pictured as a snake winding its way up the Tree. For example, plate 4, the foundation and the oak, is attributed to the

Hebrew letter *taw* and the Tarot image The World, linking the pilgrimage and persecution of the Kingdom, Malkuth, with the foundational symbology of Notre-Dame-de-Paris, heraldry, the Grail legends, and the Philosophical Dew in the *sefirah* of Yesod. Filling in the rest of the Tree with these symbols reveals the ongoing alchemical process of creation.

Fulcanelli's use of three numbered images to represent the *sefirah* of gnosis, Daat, reveals a deep and profound understanding of the numerical Kabbalah. This understanding can be traced with many subtleties throughout Fulcanelli's explication of the four Trees. An exhaustive examination of this underlying numerical Kabbalah belongs in an annotated version of *Le Mystère des cathédrales,* but for now it is enough to look at the obvious and significant connections between Fulcanelli's gnosis numbers.

Plate 26, our first Daat image, comes after Fulcanelli's explication of the Path of Return. This is appropriate since 26 is the number of the Unutterable Name of God, YHVH (Y [10] + H [5] + V [6] + H [5] = 26), and in the image, from the Porch of the Virgin at Notre-Dame-de-Paris, the Ark of the Tabernacle, YHVH's dwelling place, is clearly shown below the seals of the planetary metals. Other Hebrew words with the same numerical value include those for "vision" and "seeing," implying the light nature of the divine. The mystical kabbalists liked to see 26 as composed of pairs of words with the value of 13, such as *love* and *unity, emptiness* and *thunder.* It is also the sum of the numbers of the *sefirot* on the Middle Pillar of the Tree of Life, 1 + 6 + 9 + 10 = 26.

Plate 33, the wheel of fire from Amiens cathedral, begins a new Tree with an experience of the internal process of alchemy. In esoteric Freemasonry, a 33rd-degree initiate is one who has internalized the entire 32 paths of the Tree of Life. This master level indicates one who is ready to move from theory to practice, from speculative to practical alchemy. We can also think of 33 as the Trinity, 3, multiplied by the number of gnosis, 11, or as the experience of the nature of the Trinity. In Hebrew, the word for "spring" or "fountain" has the value of 33, indicating the Gnostic origin of the idea of an underground stream, 33, which reveals the sacred 7 of good fortune that flows from the divine source, YHVH, 26 (33 − 26 = 7).

In the same way, the underground stream, 33, supplies Elhi, 46, the God Most High, with the thunder, love, unity, or emptiness, all 13s (33 + 13 = 46).

Plate 46, the enigmatic credence from Lallemant mansion in Bourges, completes our gnostic trinity. Forty-six is an auspicious number. In esoteric Freemasonry, a 33rd-degree master has the opportunity to advance further by taking 13 extra grades, or degrees. Therefore, a 46th-degree initiate is supposedly a master of space and time, a bodhisattva-like enlightened adept. In the King James Version of the Bible there is the curious incident of Psalm 46. When one counts 46 words down from the first word in Psalm 46, one comes to the word *shake*. If one counts 46 words from the bottom of Psalm 46, one comes to the word *speare*. This would indicate that the author, or authors, of the works of William Shakespeare, called by Victor Hugo "a cathedral of words," are 46th-degree initiates. A hint of this can also be gleaned from the fact that 3 × 46 = 138, the number of the phrase *Ben Elohim,* or "Son of the Gods." It is interesting to note that Francis Bacon was chosen by King James to head the translation team for the Bible. Other interesting ramifications of the number 46 include the number of the name of Adam, the first man. It is also said that it took 46 years to build King Solomon's Temple. Each human being has 46 chromosomes. As we said above, 46 equals the name of God, Elhi, an ancient name for the El in the Sky, the High God of Draco. It is also the number of the Levite priests who ministered to that God. If we think of what the Lallemant credence has to tell us about the process of transformation, then 46 represents a level of personal attainment. By adding the extra three images of the Hendaye chapter, the personal connection of Elhi, 46, becomes the transpersonal connection of the Living God, El Chai, 49, depicted on the tympanum of Saint Trophime in Arles, plate 49.

APPENDIX E

THE CYCLIC CROSS OF HENDAYE

Hendaye, a small frontier town in the Basque country, has its little houses huddled at the foot of the first spurs of the Pyrenees. It is framed by the green ocean, the broad, swift and shining Bidassoa and the grassy hills. One's first impression, on seeing this rough and rugged landscape, is a rather painful and almost hostile one. On the horizon, over the sea, the natural austerity of the wild scene is scarcely relieved by the headland of Fuenterrabia, showing ochre in the crude light, thrusting into the dark greyish-green mirror-calm waters of the gulf. Apart from the Spanish character of its houses, the type of dialect of the inhabitants, and the very special attention of a new beach, bristling with proud villas, Hendaye has nothing to hold the attention of the tourist, the archaeologist or the artist.

Leaving the station, a country road, skirting the railway line, leads to the parish church, situated in the middle of the village. This church, with its bare walls and its massive, squat rectangular tower, stands in a square a few steps above ground level and bordered by leafy trees. It is an ordinary, dull building, which has been renovated and is of no particular interest. However, near the south transept there is a humble stone cross, as simple as it is strange, hiding amidst the greenery of the square. It was formerly in the parish cemetery and it was only in 1842 that it was brought to its present site near the church. At least, that is

[Text of this appendix is from Fulcanelli, *Le Mystère des cathédrales,* trans. Mary Sworder (London: Neville Spearman, 1971), pp. 165–71.]

what was told me by an old Basque man, who had for many years acted as sexton. As for the origin of this cross, it is unknown and I was not able to obtain any information at all about the date of its erection. However, judging by the shape of the base and the column, I would not think that it could be before the end of the seventeenth or beginning of the eighteenth century. Whatever its age, the Hendaye cross shows by the decoration of its pedestal that it is the strangest monument of primitive millenarism, the rarest symbolical translation of chiliasm,[1] which I have ever met. It is known that this doctrine, first accepted and then refuted by Origen, St. Denis of Alexandria and St. Jerome although it had not been condemned by the Church, was part of the esoteric tradition of the ancient hermetic philosophy.

The naivety of the bas-reliefs and their unskilful execution lead one to suppose that these stone emblems were not the work of a professional sculptor; but, aesthetic considerations apart, we must recognize that the unknown workman, who made these images, possessed real and profound knowledge of the universe.

On the transverse arm of the cross—a Greek cross—is found the following inscription, consisting of two strange parallel lines of raised letters, forming words almost running into each other, in the same order as I give here:

OCRUXAVES
PESUNICA

Certainly it is easy to recognize the well-known phrase: *O crux ave spes unica* (Hail o cross, the only hope). However, if we were to translate it like a schoolboy, we should not know the purpose either of the base or of the cross and we might be surprised by such an invocation. In reality, we should carry carelessness and ignorance to the pitch of disregarding the elementary rules of grammar. The masculine word *pes* in the nominative requires the adjective *unicus,* agreeing in gender, and not the feminine form *unica.* It would, therefore, appear that the corruption of the word *spes,* hope, into *pes,* foot, by dropping the initial consonant, must be the unintentional result of a complete lack of

---

[1] *Translator's note:* millenarism, chiliasm, doctrine of belief in the millennium.

knowledge on the part of out stone-cutter. But does inexperience really justify such uncouthness? I cannot think so. Indeed, a comparison of the other motifs, carried out by the same hand and in the same manner, shows evident care to reproduce the normal positioning, a care shown both in the placing and in the balance of the motifs. Why should the inscription have been treated less scrupulously? A careful examination of the latter shows that the letters are clear, if not elegant, and do not overlap (pl. XLVII). No doubt our workman traced them first in chalk or charcoal, and this rough draft must rule out any idea that a mistake occurred during the actual cutting of the letters. However, since this *apparent* mistake exists, it follows that it must really have been intended. The only reason that I can think of is that it is a *sign put in on purpose*, concealed under the appearance of an inexplicable blunder, and intended to arouse the curiosity of the observer. I will, therefore, state that, in my opinion, it was with knowledge and intent that the author arranged the inscription of his puzzling work in this way.

I had already been enlightened by studying the pedestal and knew in what way and by what means of what key the Christian inscription of the monument should be read; but I was anxious to show investigators what help may be obtained in solving hidden matters from plain common sense, logic and reasoning.

The letter S, which takes on the curving shape of a snake, corresponds to the Greek *khi* (X) and takes over its esoteric meaning. It is the helicoidal track of the sun, having arrived at the zenith of its curve across space, at the time of the cyclic catastrophe. It is a theoretical image of the *Beast of the Apocalypse*, of the dragon, which, on the days of Judgment, spews out fire and brimstone on macrocosmic creation. Thanks to the symbolic value of the letter S, displaced on purpose, we understand that the inscription must be translated in secret language, that is to say in the *language of the gods* or the *language of the birds,* and that the meaning must be found with the help of the rules of *Diplomacy.* Several authors, and particularly Grasset d'Orcet in his analysis of the *Songe de Polyphile* published by the *Revue Britannique,* have given these sufficiently clearly to make it unnecessary for me to repeat them. We shall, then, read in *French,* the language of the diplomats, the Latin just as it is written. Then, by making use of the permutation of vowels, we shall be able to read off the new words, forming another sentence, and re-establish the spelling, the word order and the literary sense. In this way, we obtain the following strange announcement: *Il est écrit que la vie se réfugie en un seul espace* (It is written that life takes refuge in a single space)[2] and we learn that a country exists, where death cannot reach man at the terrible time of the double cataclysm. As for the geographical location of this promised land, from which the élite will take part in the return of the golden age, it is up to us to find it. For the élite, the children of Elias, will be saved according to the word of Scripture, because their profound faith, their untiring perseverance in effort, will have earned for them the right to be promoted to the rank of the disciples of the Christ-Light. They will bear his sign and will receive from him the mission of renewing for regenerated humanity the chain of tradition of the humanity which has disappeared.

The front of the cross, the part which received the three terrible nails fixing the agonized body of the Redeemer to the accursed wood, is indicated by the inscription INRI, carved on its transverse arm. It corresponds to the schematic image of the cycle, shown on the base (pl. XLVIII). Thus we have two symbolic crosses, both instruments of the same torture. Above is the divine cross, exemplifying the chosen means of expiation; below is the global cross, fixing the pole of the *northern hemisphere* and locating in time the fatal period of this expiation. God the Father holds in his hand this globe, surmounted by the fiery sign. The four great ages—historical representations of the four ages of the world—have their sovereigns shown holding this same attribute. They are Alexander, Augustus, Charlemagne and Louis XIV.[3] It is this which explains the inscription INRI, exoterically translated as *Iesus Nazarenus Rex Iudeorum* (Jesus of Nazareth, King of the Jews), but which gives to the cross its secret meaning: *Igne Natura Renovatur Integra* (By fire nature is renewed whole). For it is by fire and in fire that our hemisphere will soon be tried. And just as, by means of fire, gold is separated from impure metals, so, Scripture says, the good will be separated from the wicked on the great Day of Judgment.

On each of the four sides of the pedestal, a different symbol is to be

---

[2]Latin *spatium,* with the meaning of *place, situation,* given to it by Tacitus. It corresponds to the Greek Χωρίον, root Χωρα, *country, territory.*

[3]The first three are emperors, the fourth is only a king, the Sun King, thus indicating the decline of the star and its last radiation. This is dusk, the forerunner of the long cyclic night, full of horror and terror, "the abomination of desolation."

seen. One has the image of the sun, another of the moon; the third shows a great star and the last a geometric figure, which, as I have just said, is none other than the diagram used by the initiates to indicate the solar cycle. It is a simple circle, divided into four sectors by two diameters cutting each other at right angles. The sectors each bear an A, which shows that they stand for the four ages of the world. This is a complete hieroglyph of the universe, composed of the conventional signs for heaven and earth, the spiritual and the temporal, the macrocosm and the microcosm, in which major emblems of the redemption (cross) and the world (circle) are found in association.

In medieval times, these four phases of the great cyclic period, whose continuous rotation was expressed in antiquity by means of a circle divided by two perpendicular diameters, were generally represented by the four evangelists or by their symbolic letter, which was the Greek *alpha,* or, more often still, by the four evangelical beasts surrounding Christ, the living human representation of the cross. This is the traditional formula, which one meets frequently on the tympana of Roman porches. Jesus is shown there seated, his left hand resting on a book, his right raised in the gesture of benediction, and separated from the four beasts, which attend him, by an ellipse, called the *mystic almond.* These groups, which are generally isolated from other scenes by a garland of clouds, always have their figures placed in the same order, as may be seen in the cathedrals of Chartres (royal portal) and Le Mans (west porch), in the Church of the Templars at Luz (Hautes Pyrénées) and the Church of Civray (Vienne), on the porch of St. Trophime at Arles, etc. (pl. XLIX).

"And before the throne," writes St. John, "there was a sea of glass, like unto crystal: and in the midst of the throne, and round about the throne, were four beasts full of eyes before and behind. And the first beast was like a lion, and the second beast like a calf, and the third beast had a face as a man, and the fourth beast was like a flying eagle."[4]

This agrees with Ezekiel's version: "And I looked, and behold . . . a great cloud, and a fire infolding itself and a brightness was about it, and out of the midst thereof as the colour of amber, out of the midst of the fire. Also out of the midst thereof came the likeness of four living creatures. . . . As for the likeness of their faces, they four had the face of a

---

[4]Revelation, ch.l v, v. 6 and 7.

man, and the face of a lion on the right side; and they four had the face of an ox on the left side; they four also had the face of an eagle."[5]

In Hindu mythology, the four equal sectors of the circle, formed by the cross, were the basis of a rather strange mystical conception. The entire cycle of human evolution is figured there in the form of a cow, symbolizing Virtue, each of whose four feet rests on one of the sectors representing the four ages of the world. In the first age, corresponding to the Greek age of gold and called *Creda Yuga* or *age of innocence,* Virtue is firmly established on earth: the cow stands squarely on four legs. In the *Treda Yuga* or second age, corresponding to the age of silver, it is weakened and stands only on three legs. During the *Touvabara Yuga,* or third age, which is the age of bronze, it is reduced to two legs. Finally, in the age of iron, our own age, the cyclic cow or human virtue reaches the utmost degree of feebleness and senility: it is scarcely able to stand, balancing on one leg. It is the fourth and last age, the *Kali Yuga,* the age of misery, misfortune and decrepitude.

The *age of iron* has no other seal than that of *Death.* Its hieroglyph is the skeleton, bearing the attributes of Saturn: the empty hourglass, symbol of time run out, and the scythe, reproduced in the figure seven, which is the number of transformation, of destruction, of annihilation. The Gospel of this fatal age is the one written under the inspiration of St. Matthew. *Matthaeus,* Greek Ματθαῖος, comes from Μάθημα, Μάθηματος, which means science. This word has given Μάθησις, μάθησεως, study, knowledge, from μανθάνειν, to learn. It is the Gospel according to Science, the last of all but for us the first, because it teaches us that, save for a small number of the élite, we must all perish. For this reason the angel was made the attribute of St. Matthew, because science, which alone is capable of penetrating the mystery of things, of beings and their destiny, can give man wings to raise him to knowledge of the highest truths and finally to God.

---

[5]Ezekiel, ch. I, v. 4, 5, 10 and 11.

NOTES

CHAPTER 1

1. Ernest Hemingway, *A Moveable Feast* (New York: Simon & Schuster, 1965).
2. For the world before the Great War, see Barbara Tuchman's *The Proud Tower* (New York: Macmillan and Company, 1966). John Keegan's *The First World War* (London: Random House, 1998) is the best single-volume work on the actual course of the war, while Robert H. Ziegler's *America's Great War* (London: Rowan and Littlefield, 2000) describes America's role in winning the war and losing the peace. Paul Fussell's *The Great War and Modern Memory* (Oxford: Oxford University Press, 1975) charts the importance of the war as metaphor for the modern world. Modris Ekstein's *Rites of Spring: The Great War and the Birth of the Modern Age* (New York: Doubleday, 1989) describes in absorbing detail the postwar intellectual ferment; see in particular chapter 7, "Night Dancer," pp. 241–74.
3. Other transformative firsts for 1926 include the first television broadcast, the first solid-fuel rocket launch, publication of *The Theory of the Gene,* the beginning of modern genetic research, the first motion picture with sound, and the founding of the first science fiction magazine, *Astounding Stories.* The year also saw the rise of two of the century's most prominent dictators, Josef Stalin and Benito Mussolini, while Adolf Hitler worked on *Mein Kampf* in prison and Father Coughlin begin his radio career as a racist and right-wing propagandist.
4. *Le Mystère des cathédrales* (Paris: Éditions des Champs-Elysées, Omnium littéraire, 1957). Strangely enough, the English edition translated by Mary Sworder (London: Neville Spearman, 1971) is also entitled *Le Mystère des cathédrales.* In this work, we shall use both the French and English titles interchangeably, and the citations in the notes will refer to the English edition of *Le Mystère.*
5. André Breton, *Manifestos of Surrealism,* trans. Richard Seaver and Helen R. Lane (Ann Arbor: Univ. of Michigan Press, 1969). For an excellent overview of surrealism's esoteric roots, see Nadia Choucha, *Surrealism and the Occult: Shamanism, Magic, Alchemy, and the Birth of an Artistic Movement* (Rochester, Vt.: Destiny Books, 1992).
6. Fulcanelli, *Le Mystère des cathédrales* (London: Neville Spearman, 1971), pp. 41–44. There is also an American edition (Albuquerque: Brotherhood of Life, 1984).
7. Victor Hugo, *The Hunchback of Notre Dame* (Herefordshire: Wordsworth Classics Edition, 1993), p. 138.

8. André Breton, "Manifesto of Surrealism 1924," in *Manifestos of Surrealism.*

9. Octavio Paz, *Marcel Duchamp,* trans. Rachel Phillips and Donald Gardner (New York: Seaver Books, 1978). See also Maurice Tuchman et al., *The Spiritual in Art: Abstract Painting 1890–1985* (New York: Abbeville Press, 1986), pp. 261–67 for a discussion of Duchamp's alchemical symbolism.

10. Arpad Merzei, "Liberty of Language," in *Surréalisme en 1947,* exhibition catalogue (Paris: Galerie Maeght, 1947).

11. André Breton, *Arcana 17* (New York: Brentano, 1944) and *L'Art magique* (Paris: Club Français du Livre, 1957).

12. One might not consider Joyce to be a metaphysical or esoteric writer until one looks at his original and personal creation of a "green language" in *Ulysses* and in *Finnegan's Wake.*

13. Preface, *Le Mystère des cathédrales,* pp. 5–6.

14. Guy Bechtel, "Entretien avec Eugène Canseliet sur Fulcanelli suivi du Mystère Fulcanelli" (Conversation with Eugène Canseliet on Fulcanelli Concerning the Fulcanelli Mystery), privately printed; two copies are on deposit at the Library of Hermetic Philosophy, Amsterdam, dated January 4, 1974.

15. Fulcanelli, *Les Demeures philosophales,* 2 vols. (Paris: Jean-Jacques Pauvert, 1959, 1964); first American edition (Colorado: Archive Press, 1999).

16. Colin Wilson and Christopher Evans, eds., *The Book of Great Mysteries* (New York: Dorset Books, 1990), pp. 358–61.

17. Geneviève Dubois, *Fulcanelli dévoilé* (Paris: Dervy, 1993).

18. "La Croix d'Hendaye," in *Consolation 26* (February 13, 1936) and *Consolation 27* (April 30, 1936).

19. *Consolation 26.*

20. *Le Mystère des Cathédrales,* p. 168.

21. Kenneth R. Johnson, *The Fulcanelli Phenomenon* (London: Neville Spearman, 1980), pp. 246–48.

22. Ibid.; and Robert Amadou, "L'Affaire Fulcanelli," in *L'Autre Monde* 74, 75, 76, (Sept.–Nov. 1983).

23. Johnson, *The Fulcanelli Phenomenon,* pp. 161–65.

24. Ibid., p. 163.

25. Ibid.

26. Ibid., p. 165; also Pauwels and Bergier, *The Morning of the Magicians* (London: Neville Spearman, 1963).

27. Ibid., p. 248.

28. Walter Lang, introduction to *Le Mystère des cathédrales* (London: Neville Spearman, 1971), p. 29.

29. Johnson, *The Fulcanelli Phenomenon,* pp. 246–48.

30. Eugène Canseliet, *Alchimie* (Paris: Jean-Jacques Pauvert, 1964), p. xiv.

31. Eugène Canseliet, "Alchimiques mémoires," serialized in the catalogue *La Tourbe des Philosophes,* in *La Table Emeraude,* n.d.

32. Eugène Canseliet, preface to *Les Demeures philosophales,* p. xxii.

33. Pauwels and Bergier, *Le Matin des magiciens* (Paris: Gallimard, 1960); English edition, *The Morning of the Magicians* (London: Neville Spearman, 1963).

34. Johnson, *The Fulcanelli Phenomenon,* pp. 277–99.
35. Elizabeth Van Buren, *Refuge of the Apocalypse* (Essex, England: C. W. Daniel Co. Ltd, 1986).
36. André VandenBroeck, *Al-Kemi: A Memoir—Hermetic, Occult, Political and Private Aspects of R. A. Schwaller de Lubicz* (Rochester, Vt.: Inner Traditions, 1987).
37. For more on the region and its history, see Mark Kurlansky's *The Basque History of the World* (New York: Penguin Books, 1999).
38. See also *South-West France,* The Lonely Planet Guide (London: Lonely Planet Press, 2000).
39. *Abbadie: Une rébus géant* (Cape Science, Bordeaux: Cape Science Foundation, 1998) is the only work available on the d'Abbadie family. See also the *French Catholic Encyclopedia* entry under Antoine d'Abbadie.
40. *Le Mystère des cathédrales,* pp. 165–71.

CHAPTER 2

1. James N. Powell, *The Tao of Symbols* (New York: Quill Books, 1982).
2. Walter Scott, ed. and trans., *Hermetica,* 4 vols. (Boulder, Colo.: Shambhala, 1985), vol. 2, pp. 386–91.
3. Ibid.
4. Ibid.
5. Ibid.
6. *Le Mystère des cathédrales,* p. 46.
7. Ibid., p. 158.
8. "Flying Roll VII" by S. A. [W. W. Westcott], in S. L. MacGregor Mathers, et al., *Astral Projection, Ritual Magic and Alchemy,* ed. Francis King (Rochester, Vt.: Destiny Books, 1987), pp. 179–91.
9. See Ellic Howe, *The Magicians of the Golden Dawn* (London: Neville Spearman, 1972), for more details on what the Golden Dawn hoped to accomplish.
10. See also Sapere Aude [W. W. Westcott], *The Science of Alchymy* (London: Theosophical Publications Society, 1983).
11. "Flying Roll VII," pp. 179–91.
12. Norman Davies, *Europe: A History* (Oxford: Oxford Univ. Press, 1996), pp. 409–13.
13. Frances A. Yates, *The Rosicrucian Enlightenment* (London: Routledge and Kegan Paul, 1972), and *The Occult Philosophy in the Elizabethan Age* (London: Ark Paperbacks, 1979).
14. "The Fame and Confession of the Fraternity of the Rosie Cross," trans. Thomas Vaughn (1652), in Paul Allen, ed., *A Christian Rosenkreutz Anthology* (Blauvelt, N.Y.: Rudolf Steiner Press, 1981), pp. 163–90.
15. Ibid.
16. *Hermetica,* vol. 2, pp. 386–91.
17. R. A. Schwaller du Lubicz, *Sacred Science: The King of Pharaonic Theocracy* (Rochester, Vt.: Inner Traditions, 1982), p. 214.
18. Mae-Wan Ho and Fritz-Albert Popp, "Biological Organization, Coherence and Light Emission from Living Organisms," in W. D. Stein and F. J. Varela, eds., *Thinking about Biology* (Reading, Mass.: Addison-Wesley, 1993).

19. M. Rattenmayer, "Evidence of Photon Emission from DNA in Living Systems," *Naturwissenschaften* 68 (1981): 572–73; and Fritz-Albert Popp et al., eds., *Recent Advances in Biophoton Research and Its Application* (Singapore: World Scientific, 1992).

CHAPTER 3

1. Kurt Seligmann, *The History of Magic and the Occult* (New York: Harmony Books, 1975), pp. 79–83.
2. *Cahiers de l'hermétisme: Sophia ou l'âme du monde* (Paris: Albin Michel, 1983).
3. *Le Mystère des cathédrales*, p. 58. See also Jonathon Cott, *Isis and Osiris* (New York: Doubleday, 1994), pp. 90–91.
4. Jeremy Narby, *The Cosmic Serpent* (New York: Tarcher/Putnam, 1998).
5. Seligmann, *The History of Magic and the Occult*, p. 102.
6. Ibid., p. 79.
7. Thomas L. Thompson, *The Mythic Past* (New York: Basic Books, 1999), pp. 191–96; also, Norman Cohn, *Cosmos, Chaos and the World to Come* (New Haven: Yale Univ. Press, 1993), chapter 8, pp. 141–62.
8. Karen Armstrong, *A History of God* (New York: Ballantine Books, 1984), pp. 55–61.
9. Jeremiah 31:31–39.
10. While fundamentalists, who believe the Bible is the direct and whole inspiration of God, hold that all of the book of Isaiah was written by the same person, modern biblical scholarship suggests that the great part of chapters 40–55 was written later, after the exile in Babylon. See Cohn, *Cosmos, Chaos and the World to Come*, pp. 151–57.
11. Morton Smith, *Jesus the Magician* (New York: Harper & Row, 1981).
12. Matthew 24:29–35.
13. Ibid.
14. "The Greek Alchemical Papyri," *Ciba Symposia* 3, no. 5 (1941).
15. Brackets indicate additions in the text.
16. Matthew 28.
17. Ibid., verse 20.
18. Elaine Pagels, *The Gnostic Gospels* (New York: Vintage Books, 1981).
19. Ibid.
20. Robin Lane Fox, *Pagans and Christians* (New York: Knopf, 1986).
21. Ibid.
22. Revelation 4:1.
23. Cohn, *Cosmos, Chaos and the World to Come*, p. 212.
24. Y. Rubinsky and I. Wiseman, *A History of the End of the World* (New York: Quill Books, 1982), p. 57.
25. Seligmann, *The History of Magic and the Occult*, p. 88.
26. Ibid.
27. Ibid.
28. Fox, *Pagans and Christians*.

29. *The Middle Ages: A Concise Encyclopaedia* (London: Thames & Hudson, 1989), s.v. "Francis I."
30. Rubinsky and Wiseman, *A History of the End of the World*, p. 56.
31. Jacob Burckhardt, *The Age of Constantine the Great* (Berkeley: Univ. of California Press, 1983).
32. Ibid.
33. Ibid.
34. Robert Payne, *The Making of the Christian World* (New York: Dorset Press, 1990).
35. Ibid.
36. Ibid.
37. Ibid.
38. Burckhardt, *The Age of Constantine the Great.*

CHAPTER 4

1. Louis Bouyer, *The Spirituality of the New Testament and the Fathers,* trans. Mary P. Ryan (Minneapolis, Minn.: Winston Press, 1963).
2. Pagels, *The Gnostic Gospels.*
3. Jeffrey Burton Russell, *The Devil: Perceptions of Evil from Antiquity to Primitive Christianity* (New York: New American Library, 1979).
4. Nehunya Ben ha-Kanah, *The Bahir,* translation, introduction, and commentary by Aryeh Kaplan (York Beach, Maine: Samuel Weiser, 1979).
5. Ibid., p. xix.
6. Ibid., verse 179, p. 69.
7. Ibid.
8. Psalm 78:2.
9. Neil Asher Silberman, *Heavenly Powers: Unraveling the Secret History of the Kabbalah* (Edison, N.J.: Castle Books, 2000).
10. *Bahir,* pp. 34, 40.
11. *Sefer Yetzirah: The Book of Creation,* 6:1, trans., Aryeh Kaplan (York Beach, Maine: Samuel Weiser, 1990), pp. 231–56.
12. Ibid., p. 232.
13. Ibid., p. 244.
14. John Major Jenkins, *Galactic Alignment* (Rochester, Vt.: Bear and Co., 2002).
15. *Sefer Yetzirah,* p. 238.
16. *Bahir,* p. 40.
17. Ibid., p. 35.
18. *Sefer Yetzirah,* p. 240.
19. Ibid., p. 242.
20. Max I. Dimont, *Jews, God and History* (New York: New American Library, 1962).
21. Gershom Scholem, *Jewish Gnosis, Merkabah Mysticism and Talmudic Tradition* (New York: Jewish Theological Seminary, 1965), quoting the Talmud on Genesis 15:5.

22. Caesar E. Farah, *Islam* (New York: Barron's, 1987).
23. Karen Armstrong, *Muhammad: A Biography of the Prophet* (San Francisco: HarperSanFrancisco, 1992), p. 249.
24. Farah, *Islam*.
25. A. J. Arberry, *Sufism: An Account of the Mystics of Islam* (New York: Harper & Row, 1970).
26. Personal communication from the Sheik of the Al Haggagi Sufis of Luxor, Egypt.
27. Arberry, *Sufism*.
28. Ibid.
29. Idries Shah, *The Sufis* (Garden City, N.Y.: Doubleday, 1964).
30. Peter Partner, *The Knights Templar and Their Myth* (Rochester, Vt.: Destiny Books, 1990).

CHAPTER 5

1. Raphael Patai, *The Jewish Alchemists* (Princeton, N.J.: Princeton Univ. Press, 1994), pp. 51–56.
2. For a good overview of the mystical developments, see Armstrong, *A History of God,* chapter 7, "The God of the Mystics." For a look at the decline of the West, see J. M. Wallace-Hadrill, *The Barbarian West* (New York: Barnes & Nobles Books, 1998), and Michael Wood, *In Search of the Dark Ages* (London: Facts on File, 1987). For the relationship between Europe's Dark Ages and the Islamic world, see R. Hodges and D. Whitehouse, *Mohammed, Charlemagne & the Origins of Europe* (Ithaca, N.Y.: Cornell Univ. Press, 1983).
3. W. P. Ker, *The Dark Ages* (New York: New American Library, 1958), p. 25.
4. Vivian B. Mann, Thomas F. Glick, and Jerrilynn D. Dodds, eds., *Convivencia: Jews, Muslims and Christians in Medieval Spain* (New York: George Braziller, 1992).
5. Robert Payne, *The Dream and the Tomb* (Ann Arbor, Mich.: Scarborough House, 1984).
6. Karen Armstrong, *Holy War: The Crusades and Their Impact on Today's World* (New York: Anchor/Doubleday, 1992).
7. James Reston Jr., *The Last Apocalypse* (New York: Doubleday, 1998), chapter 12, "Otto the Dreamer."
8. Taqi ad-Din al-Maqrizi, *The Book of the History of the Kings,* M. Ziyade's English/Arabic edition (Cairo, 1934).
9. Ker, *The Dark Ages,* p. 128.
10. See Saint Gregory of Tours, *The History of the Franks,* trans. and intro. Lewis Thorpe (London: Penguin Books, 1974).
11. Stanislas Guyard, "Un grand Maître des assassins au temps de Saladin," in *Journal Asiatique,* 7th series, 9 (1877): 324–489.
12. Taqi ad-Din al-Maqrizi, *The Book of the History of the Kings.*
13. Malcolm Billings, *The Cross & the Crescent: A History of the Crusades* (New York: Sterling Publishing, 1990).

14. Sir Stephen Runciman, *The First Crusade* (London: Cambridge Univ. Press, 1992), pp. 42–43.

15. Ibid.

16. Ibid., p. 48.

17. Sir Stephen Runciman, *A History of the Crusades,* 3 vols. (Cambridge: Cambridge Univ. Press, 1952).

18. René Grousset, *Historie des croisades et du royaume franc de Jerusalem* (Paris: Perrin, 1935).

19. Reston, *The Last Apocalypse.*

20. Peter Partner, *The Knights Templar and Their Myth.*

21. Will and Ariel Durant, *The Age of Faith* (New York: Simon & Schuster, 1950), p. 788.

22. The idea of the *prima materia* is a central one in alchemy. Later authors speculate that it is everywhere and in everything, as common as dirt, in one sense. But this was not the understanding current in the tenth and eleventh centuries. The eleventh-century manuscript of the pseudo-Khalid ibn Yazid, the major work of Hebrew and Arabic alchemy between Zosimos and the provençal kabbalists, comments that alchemy, "this magisterium of ours about the secret stone," was kept hidden among the descendants of Abraham, "His people." Khalid also comments that the stone "is not a stone, that is, neither a stone nor of the nature of a stone," implying that it is a "stone" not from this earth. (See Patai, *The Jewish Alchemists,* chapter 9.) As we shall see in later chapters, this idea of a "stone" not of this earth recurs in the Grail legends, and even has some scientific foundation as a *prima materia* according to the research of Dr. Paul LaViolette and modern pseudo-alchemists such as David Hudson.

23. Graham Hancock, *The Sign and the Seal* (New York: Simon & Schuster, 1992).

24. Ibid., pp. 409–24.

25. W. Montgomery Watt, *Muhammad's Mecca: History and the Qur'an* (Edinburgh: Edinburgh University Press, 1988).

26. Taqi ad-Din al-Maqrizi, *The Book of the History of the Kings.*

27. Michael Baigent, Richard Leigh, and Henry Lincoln, *Holy Blood, Holy Grail* (New York: Delacorte Press, 1982).

28. Seligmann, *The History of Magic and the Occult.*

29. Ibid.

30. Titus Burckhardt, *Alchemy* (London: Penguin Books, 1967).

31. Seligmann, *The History of Magic and the Occult.*

32. Partner, *The Knights Templar and Their Myth.*

CHAPTER 6

1. R. S. Loomis and L. A. Loomis, eds., *Medieval Romances* (New York: Random House, 1957), foreword to Chrétien's *Perceval* pp. 5–7. Also D. D. R. Owen, trans. *Arthurian Romances of Chrétien de Troyes* (London, Everyman, 1993), pp. xi–xxii.

2. Julius Evola, *The Mystery of the Grail,* trans. Guido Stucco (Rochester, Vt.: Inner Traditions, 1997), argues that Robert de Boron's work represents an earlier and parallel tradition not directly derived from Chrétien's sources.

3. Baigent, Leigh, and Lincoln, *Holy Blood, Holy Grail.*

4. Nigel Bryant, trans., *The High Book of the Grail (Perlesvaus)* (Ipswich, England: D. S. Brewer, 1978).

5. P. M. Matarasso, trans., *The Quest of the Holy Grail* (London: Penguin Classics, 1969).

6. Wolfram von Eschenbach, *Parzival,* trans. A. T. Hatto (London: Penguin Books, 1980).

7. See Evola, *The Mystery of the Grail,* pp. 70–71, for a discussion of the "stone" and its connection to both the Black Stone of Mecca and the "stone" of exile of the Hebrew alchemical tradition.

8. See Malcolm Godwin, *The Holy Grail* (New York: Viking Books, 1994), for a discussion of the importance to the alchemical tradition of Wolfram's *Parzival.*

9. Lord Byron, "The Prisoner of Chillon," from *Lord Byron: The Major Works* (Oxford: Oxford Press, 2000).

10. David Ovason [Fred Gettings], *The Nostradamus Code* (London: Arrow Books Limited, 1998).

11. Archibald Lyall, *The South of France* (Englewood Cliffs, N.J.: Prentice-Hall, 1983).

12. Ibid.

13. Michael Grant, *The Jews in the Roman World* (New York: Barnes & Noble Books, 1995).

14. Ibid.

15. Roselyne Moreaux, *Les-Saintes-Maries-de-la-Mer* (Marseilles: Éditions PEC, 2000).

16. Ibid.

17. Pindar, *Fourth Pythian Ode,* mentioned in Robert Graves, *The Greek Myths* (London: Penguin Books, 1960), p. 219.

18. Lyall, *The South of France,* pp. 141–42.

19. *Catholic Encyclopaedia,* Internet edition (2002), s.v. "St. Trophime" and "Alyschamps."

20. The Anglo-Norman Pseudo-Turpin Chronicle of William de Briane (London: Blackwell and Sons for Anglo-Norman Text Society, undated copy).

21. *Le Mystère des cathédrales,* pp. 46, 170.

22. Lyall, *The South of France.*

23. Jacobus de Voragine, *The Golden Legend,* trans. William Caxton (Cambridge: Cambridge Univ. Press, 1914).

24. Owen, *Arthurian Romances of Chrétien de Troyes.*

25. Adolf Kroeger, *The Minnesinger of Germany* (New York: Hurd and Houghton, 1873), and J. Rowbotham, *The Troubadours and the Court of Love* (London, 1895).

26. Ernst Richard, *History of Germany Civilization* (New York: Macmillan, 1991), p. 186.

27. Ibid.; see also Runciman, *A History of the Crusades,* vol. 2.

28. Stephen Howarth, *The Knights Templar* (New York: Atheneum, 1982).

29. Ibid.

30. Zoe Oldenborg, *Massacre at Montségur,* trans. Peter Green (New York: Random House, 1961).

31. Runciman, *A History of the Crusades,* vol. 2.

32. Ibid.

33. E. Vacandard, *The Inquisition,* trans. Bertrand Conway (New York: Longmans, Green, 1908).

34. Oldenborg, *Massacre at Montségur.*

35. Ibid.

36. E. Vacandard, *The Inquisition.*

37. Quoted in Paul Johnson, *A History of Christianity* (New York: Atheneum, 1979), p. 117.

38. Oldenborg, *Massacre at Montségur.*

39. Ibid., p. 376.

40. Ibid., p. 378.

41. Jean Guiraud, "Le Consolamentum ou l'initiation cathare; le repression de l'heresie au moyen age," in *Questions d'historie et d'archeologie chrétiennes* (Paris: V. Lecoffre, 1906). Also discussed in Oldenborg, *Massacre at Montségur.*

42. Quoted in Roger J. Woolger, "The Holy Grail: Healing the Sexual Wound in the Western Psyche," privately printed pamphlet article in *Pilgrimage* 2, no. 2 (Summer 1983).

43. Ibid.

44. Durant, *The Age of Faith,* p. 1037.

45. Ibid., p. 1038.

46. *Le Mystère des cathédrales,* pp. 42, 44.

47. Quercob Historical Society, pamphlet about Château Puivert, n.d.

48. Durant, *The Age of Faith,* p. 1036.

49. Ibid.

50. Owen, *Arthurian Romances of Chrétien de Troyes,* pp. xi–xxii.

51. Friedrich Heer, *The Medieval World* (London: Wiedenfield, 1993), p. 181.

52. Kaplan, *The Bahir.*

53. Ibid., p. xiii.

54. Gershom Scholem, *Jewish Gnosis, Merkabah Mysticism and Talmudic Tradition.*

55. Silberman, *Heavenly Powers: Unraveling the Secret History of the Kabbalah.*

56. Pierre Dujols, "An Explicative Hypotose of Magaphon on the Mutus Liber," in *Les nobles écrits de Pierre Dujols* (1914; reprint, Grenoble: Mercure Dauphinois, 2000).

57. Kaplan, *The Bahir.*

58. Silberman, *Heavenly Powers.*

59. Patai, *The Jewish Alchemists.*

60. Ibid.

61. Silberman, *Heavenly Powers.*

62. Oldenborg, *Massacre at Montségur.*
63. Shulamit Shachar, "Catharism and the Origins of the Kabbalah in Languedoc," in *Tabriz* 40 (1970–71), 483–507.
64. Kaplan, *The Bahir.*
65. Ibid.
66. Silberman, *Heavenly Powers.*
67. Kaplan, *The Bahir.*
68. Rubinsky and Wiseman, *A History of the End of the World.*
69. John Hogue, *The Last Pope* (London: Element Books, 1998).
70. James Trager, *People's Chronology* (New York: Henry Holt, 1992).
71. Arthur Upham Pope, "Persia and the Holy Grail," in John Matthews, ed., *Sources of the Grail* (New York: Lindisfarne Press, 1997), pp. 332–46.
72. Oldenborg, *Massacre at Montségur.*

CHAPTER 7

1. Durant, *The Age of Faith,* p. 863.
2. Robert Cole, *A Traveller's History of Paris* (New York: Interlink Books, 1994).
3. Ibid.
4. Ibid.
5. Allen Temko, *Notre-Dame of Paris* (New York: Viking Press, 1955), p. 22.
6. Erwin Panofsky, trans., *Abbot Suger on the Abbey Church of St. Denis and Its Art Treasures* (Princeton, N.J.: Princeton Univ. Press, 1946).
7. Ibid.
8. Peg Streep, *Mary, Queen of Heaven* (New York: Book-of-the-Month Club, 1997).
9. M. R. James, *Excluded Books of the New Testament* (London: Nash & Grayson, 1927), translations in text from Peg Streep, *Mary, Queen of Heaven.*
10. *Le Mystère des cathédrales,* p. 57.
11. Ibid., p. 61.
12. Malcolm Billings, *The Cross & the Crescent.*
13. Ian Robertson, *Blue Guide: France* (New York: Norton, 1997), p. 713.
14. Graves, *The Greek Myths.*
15. O. R. Gurney, "The Hittites," in *The Penguin Encyclopedia of Ancient Civilizations* (London: Penguin Books, 1988), p. 115.
16. Sir James Frazer, *Adonis, Attis, Osiris* (London: Macmillan, 1907).
17. Arthur Weigall, *The Paganism in Our Christianity* (New York, London: G.P. Putnam's Sons, 1928).
18. Frazer, *Adonis, Attis, Osiris.*
19. Franz Cumont, *Oriental Religions in Roman Paganism* (New York: Dover Books, 1956), p. 47.
20. Ibid.
21. Quoted in Weigall, *The Paganism in Our Christianity,* p. 181.
22. Streep, *Mary, Queen of Heaven.*
23. Ibid.
24. Ean Begg, *The Cult of the Black Virgin* (London; New York: Arkana, 1996).

25. *Le Mystère des cathédrales,* p. 57.
26. Begg, *The Cult of the Black Virgin.*
27. Durant, *The Age of Faith.*
28. *Le Mystère des cathédrales,* p. 71.
29. Leo Schaya, *The Universal Meaning of the Kabbalah* (London: Allen & Unwin, 1971).
30. Panofsky, *Abbot Suger on the Abbey Church of St. Denis and Its Art Treasures.*
31. Temko, *Notre-Dame of Paris.*
32. Ibid.
33. Ibid.
34. Ibid.
35. Ibid.
36. Richard and Clara Winston, *Notre-Dame de Paris* (New York: Newsweek, 1971), p. 93.
37. Ibid., pp. 28–29.
38. Ibid.
39. André Trintignac and Marie-Jeanne Coloni, *Decouvrir Notre-Dame-de-Paris: Guide complet de la cathédrale* (Paris: Cerf, 1984).

CHAPTER 8

1. *Le Mystère des cathédrales,* all quotes in this section, pp. 35–39.
2. Ibid.
3. Wolfram von Eschenbach, *Parzival.*
4. Hugo, *The Hunchback of Notre Dame.*
5. Fox, *Pagans and Christians.*
6. *Catholic Encyclopaedia,* Internet edition (2002), s.v. "Feast of Fools," "Feast of the Donkey," and "Feast of the Epiphany."
7. Patai, *The Jewish Alchemists.*
8. Moshe Idel, *Golem: Jewish Magical and Mystical Traditions on the Artificial Anthropoid* (Albany: State Univ. of New York Press, 1990), pp. 86–91.
9. *Le Mystère des cathédrales,* p. 110.
10. Ibid., p. 109. (The next four notes from pages 109–118 of *Le Mystère.*)
11. Ibid.
12. Ibid.
13. Ibid.
14. Kaplan, *Sefer Yetzirah,* pp. 38, 44.
15. Rigveda 1.164.10, trans. James Powell and reprinted in *The Tao of Symbols.*
16. Jonathon Shear, "Maharishi, Plato, and the TM-Sidhi Program on Innate Structures of Consciousness," in *Metaphilosophy* 12, no. 1 (1981): p. 73. See also Shear's "Plato, Piaget and Maharishi on Cognitive Development," in *Scientific Research on the Transcendental Meditation Program: Collected Papers,* vol. 2 (Rapid City, Iowa: TM Press, 1983).
17. Ibid.
18. Ibid.

19. Raimundo Panikkar, *The Vedic Experience: Mantramanjari* (Berkeley: Univ. of California Press, 1977).

20. William Stirling, *The Canon: An Exposition of the Pagan Mystery Perpetuated in the Cabala as the Rule of All the Arts* (1897; reprint, York Beach, Maine: Samuel Weiser, 1999), intro. Keith Critchlow.

21. Ibid.

22. Ibid.

23. Ibid.

24. *Le Mystère des cathédrales,* all quotes in this section from p. 17.

25. Ibid., pp. 153–54.

CHAPTER 9

1. *Le Mystère des cathédrales,* p. 36.

2. Ibid., p. 41.

3. Ibid., p. 45.

4. Giorgio de Santillana and Hertha von Dechend, *Hamlet's Mill: An Essay on Myth and the Frame of Time* (Boston: Gambit, 1969).

5. Sig Lonegren, *Labyrinths: Ancient Myths and Modern Uses* (New York: Sterling, 2001).

6. *Le Mystère des cathédrales,* all Fulcanelli quotes in this section from pages 45–66 of *Le Mystère.*

7. Ibid.

8. Ibid.

9. Ibid.

10. Ibid.

11. Ibid.

12. *Le Mystère des cathédrales,* p. 158.

13. Ibid., p. 159.

14. Ibid.

15. Ibid., p. 161.

16. Ibid., pp. 160–61.

17. Ibid., pp. 159–61.

18. Ibid., p.162.

CHAPTER 10

1. *Le Mystère des cathédrales,* p. 165.

2. Mark Kurlansky, *The Basque History of the World* (New York: Penguin, 1999).

3. *Le Mystère des cathédrales,* p. 166.

4. Ibid.

5. Colin Renfrew, *Archeology and Language* (London: Cape, 1987).

6. James F. Hewitt, *History and Chronology of the Myth-making Age* (London: James Parker and Company, 1901), p. xiv.

7. Ibid., p. xvi.

8. Ibid., pp. xxiv–xxv.
9. Ibid., p. 269.
10. Swami Sri Yukteswar, *The Holy Science* (1949; reprint, Los Angeles: Self-Realization Fellowship, 1990), p. 7.
11. David Frawley, *The Astrology of the Seers* (Salt Lake City: Passage Press, 1990), p. 48.
12. John Major Jenkins, *Galactic Alignment,* p. 130.
13. Ibid., p. 133.
14. Ibid., p. 134.
15. Hewitt, *History and Chronology of the Myth-making Age,* p. 272.
16. See J. Godwin et al., *The Hermetic Brotherhood of Luxor* (York Beach, Maine: Samuel Weiser, 1995), p. 438.
17. Ibid., p. 19.
18. *Le Mystère des cathédrales,* p. 166.
19. Personal communication with M. Arnoud, curator of the museum at the Château d'Abbadie.

CHAPTER 11

1. See Matila Ghyka's *The Geometry of Art and Life* (1946; reprint, New York: Dover, 1977), p. 123, where the cross formed by this zigzag pattern is one of several examples of Gothic Masons' marks.
2. *Consolation* 37 (April 30, 1936).
3. *Le Mystère des cathédrales,* p. 167.
4. Matthew 28.
5. Ibid., verse 20.
6. All quotes from Mevryl in this section from pages 277–299 of *The Fulcanelli Phenomenon.*
7. Frances Israel Regardie, *The Golden Dawn* (St. Paul, Minn.: Llewellyn Publications, 1978).
8. Scholem, *Jewish Gnosis, Merkabah Mysticism and Talmudic Tradition.*
9. Moira Timms, "Raising the Djed," in 1995, 1998; http://vincentbridges.com/Egypt/djed.html.
10. Ibid.
11. See John Major Jenkins, *Tzolkin: Visionary Perspectives and Calendar Studies* (Garberville, Calif.: Borderland Sciences, 1994), for the precessional aspects of the planet Venus.
12. Johnson, *The Fulcanelli Phenomenon,* p. 291.
13. Regardie, *The Golden Dawn.*
14. *Le Mystère des cathédrales,* p. 167.
15. Most notably Aleister Crowley's *Thoth Tarot* (New York: U.S. Games, 1997).
16. *Le Mystère des cathédrales,* p. 168.
17. Peter Lemesurier, *The Great Pyramid Decoded* (1977; reprint, New York: Barnes and Noble Books, 1995).

18. Hermann Kees, *Ancient Egypt: A Cultural Topography* (Chicago: Univ. of Chicago Press, 1961).
19. Edwin Bernbaum, *The Way to Shambalah* (New York: Jeremy P. Tarcher, 1980).
20. Scholem, *Jewish Gnosis, Merkabah Mysticism and Talmudic Tradition.*

CHAPTER 12

1. Wilhelm Reich, *Ether, God, and Devil* and *Cosmic Superimposition,* trans. Therese Pol (1951; reprint, New York: Farrar, Straus and Giroux, 1973), p. 257.
2. John Major Jenkins, *Maya Cosmogenesis 2012* (Santa Fe: Bear & Co., 1998).
3. Graham Hancock, *Fingerprints of the Gods* (New York: Crown, 1995).
4. Ibid., p. 495.
5. Paul LaViolette, *Earth Under Fire* (New York: Starlane Publications, 1997), p. 25.
6. Ibid.
7. Ibid., p. 54.
8. Ibid.
9. Ibid.
10. Ibid.
11. Ibid.
12. Ibid.
13. *Le Mystère des cathédrales,* p. 164.
14. Ibid.
15. See John L. Casti, *Paradigms Lost* (New York: Wm. Morrow & Co., 1989), for a discussion of "helicoidal," and "heliocoidal."
16. *Le Mystère des cathédrales,* p. 165.
17. Ibid.
18. Although in a very antique and archaic medieval dialect of Sardinia, a combination of Italian, Greek, and Catalan, this version the inscription can be read. It says: "The Evil One's Cross (or *perhaps X* mark) salutes the crushing victory." One of Fulcanelli's antiquarian jests, no doubt, that at least suggests we are following the correct path.
19. Barry Fell, *Saga America* (New York: Times Books, 1983).
20. Robert Silverberg, *The Mound Builders* (New York: Ballantine Books, 1970).
21. Barry Fell, *America B.C.* (New York: Pocket Books, 1976).
22. Paul White, "The Oz-Egyptian Enigma," in *Exposure* 2, no. 6 (1996).
23. Robert Ferro and Michael Gumley, *Atlantis* (New York: Bell Publishing, 1970).
24. *Timaeus and Critias,* trans. Desmond Lee (London: Penguin Classics, 1977).
25. D. Felipe Huaman Poma de Ayala, *Some Account of the Illustrated Chronicle by the Peruvian Indian,* trans. Richard Pietschmann (London: Harrison and Sons, 1912).
26. Garcilaso de la Vega, *Royal Commentaries of the Incas and General History of Peru,* 2 vols. (1609; Austin: Univ. of Texas Press, 1966).
27. Arthur Posnansky, *Tihuanacu: The Cradle of American Man* (New York: J. J. Augustin, 1945–58).
28. Reich, *Cosmic Superimposition,* p. 257.

29. LaViolette, *Earth Under Fire*, p. 25.
30. Hans Schindler Bellamy, *The Calendar of Tiahuanaco: A Disquisition on the Time Measuring System of the Oldest Civilization in the World* (London: Faber & Faber, 1956).
31. Posnansky, *Tihuanacu: The Cradle of American Man*.
32. LaViolette, *Earth Under Fire*.
33. J. M. Allen, *Atlantis: The Andes Solution* (New York: St. Martin's Press, 1998).
34. Ibid.
35. Ibid., p. 25.
36. Ibid.
37. W. Wiesenthal, *Peru and the Inca Civilization* (New York: Crescent Books, 1979).
38. Geoffrey Cornelius and Paul Devereux, *The Secret Language of the Stars and Planets* (San Francisco: Chronicle Books, 1996).
39. Ronald Wright, *Stolen Continents* (Boston: Houghton Mifflin, 1992).
40. Ibid., p. 136.
41. Ibid.
42. William Montgomery McGovern, *Jungle Paths and Inca Ruins* (New York and London: The Century Co., 1927).
43. Personal communication from Juan, the authors' guide in Cuzco.
44. Personal communication from Dr. Villoldo.
45. Robert Pollack, *Signs of Life: The Language and Meanings of DNA* (Boston: Houghton Mifflin, 1994).

CHAPTER 13

1. John Michell, *City of Revelation* (New York: Ballantine Books, 1972).
2. W. Y. Evans-Wentz, *Fairy Faith in Celtic Countries* (1911; reprint, New York: Citadel Press, 1990).
3. See the crop circle connector Web site at http://www.cropcircleconnector.com/index2.html for a complete archive of all known crop circles from 1978 to 2003.
4. George Hart, *Egyptian Myths* (Austin: Univ. of Texas Press, 1990).
5. Giorgio de Santillana and Hertha von Dechend, *Hamlet's Mill: An Essay on Myth and the Frame of Time* (Boston: Gambit, 1969).
6. Ibid.
7. Joan Evans, ed., *The Flowering of the Middle Ages* (London: Thames and Hudson, 1985).
8. Cornelius and Devereux, *The Secret Language of the Stars and Planets*.
9. From the video *Healing the Luminous Body: The Way of the Shaman* with Dr. Alberto Villoldo, copyright 2002, Santa Barbara, Calif.: Sacred Mysteries Productions.
10. Paul Mevryl, "Epilogue in Stone," in *The Fulcanelli Phenomenon*, pp. 277–95.
11. Ibid., pp. 295–96.
12. Dominic Sansoni and Jim Goodman, *Kathmandu* (New Jersey: Hunter Publishing, 1988).
13. *Le Mystère des cathédrales*, p. 167.

14. Kerry Moran and Helka Ahokas, *Nepal: The Mountain Kingdom* (Lincolnwood, Ill.: Passport Books, 1995).

15. Sansoni and Goodman, *Kathmandu.*

16. Rajendralala Mitra, *The Sanskrit Buddhist Literature of Nepal* (1882; reprint, Calcutta: Sanskrit Pustak Bhandar, 1971), see in particular the preface discussion on Buddhism in Nepal, pp. xix–xlx.

17. Yeshe Tsogyal, "The Life and Liberation of Padmasambhava," trans. Tarthang Tulku, in *Crystal Mirror* 4 (1975): 14.

18. Sybille Noel, *The Magic Bird of Chomolungma* (New York: Doubleday, Doran & Company, 1931), pp. 1–3.

19. A *terma* is a hidden treasure, either physical, such as a statue, ritual implement, or text, or nonphysical, such as a teaching, an empowerment, or a prophecy. See Tulku Thondop Rinpoche, *Hidden Teachings of Tibet* (London: Wisdom Publications, 1986), for a complete examination of *termas.* See also Edwin Bernbaum, *The Way to Shambalah* (New York: Jeremy P. Tarcher, 1980) for an overview of Shambhala and the *terma* guides.

20. Bernbaum, *The Way to Shambalah,* p. 60.

21. Keith Dowman, *The Power Places of Central Tibet* (London and New York: Routledge and Kegan Paul, 1988).

22. Ibid.

23. Tsogyal, "The Life and Liberation of Padmasambhava."

24. Ibid.; see also Bernbaum, *The Way to Shambalah.*

25. Peter Fleming, *Bayonets to Lhasa* (New York: Oxford University Press, 1986).

26. Bernbaum, *The Way to Shambalah.*

27. Ibid.

28. Ibid.

29. Ibid.

30. The 2,500 years is counting 100 years for each of the twenty-five kings of Shambhala. See Geshe Ngawang Dhargyey, *Kalachakra Tantra* (Dharamsala: Library of Tibetan Works and Archives, 1985), for the Dalai Lama's position on the Kalachakra.

EPILOGUE

1. Dubois, *Fulcanelli dévoilé.*

2. *Le Mystère des cathédrales,* pp. 57–61.

3. VandenBroeck, *Al-Kemi: A Memoir—Hermetic, Occult, Political and Private Aspects of R. A. Schwaller de Lubicz.*

4. *Le Mystère des cathédrales,* p. 10.

5. Ibid., p. 60

6. Dubois, *Fulcanelli dévoilé.*

7. *Antoine d'Abbadie International Congress on the Centenary of His Death,* 3 vols. (Hendaye, Sare: Édition de Patri Urkizu, 1997); see vol. 2 for collection of articles and letters.

8. Papiers d'Antoine Th. d'Abbadie, MS XII (2081), Bibliothèque de l'Institut de Paris.

BIBLIOGRAPHY

Abbadie, Antoine d', *Antoine d'Abbadie International Congress on the Centenary of his Death*. 3 vols. Hendaye, Sare: Édition de Patri Urkizu, 1997.

Abécassis, Armand. *Sophia et l'âme du monde*. Cahiers de l'Hermétisme. Paris: Albin Michel, 1983.

Abraham, Pol. *Viollet-le-Duc et le rationalisme medieval*. Paris: Vincent, Fréal & Cie, 1934.

Albertus, Frater [Albert Riedel]. *The Alchemist of the Rocky Mountains*. Salt Lake City, Utah: Paracelsus Research Society, 1976.

Allen, Carol and David. *Eclipse*. Melbourne, Australia: Allen & Unwin, 1987.

Allen, J. M. *Atlantis: The Andes Solution*. New York: St. Martin's, 1999.

Allen, Paul M., comp. and ed., in collaboration with Carlo Pietzner. *A Christian Rosenkreutz Anthology*. Blauvelt, N.Y.: Rudolf Steiner Publications, 1981.

Allieu, B., and B. Lonzième. *Index général de l'œuvre de Fulcanelli*. Le Mesnil-Saint-Denis: B. Allieu, 1992.

Amadou, Robert. "L'Affaire Fulcanelli." In *L'Autre Monde* 74, 75, 76 (September–November, 1983).

———. *Le Feu du Soleil: Entretien sur l'alchimie avec Eugène Canseliet*. Paris: J. J. Pauvert, 1978.

Amargier, Paul A. *Les Saintes-Maries-de-la-Mer au moyen-age*. Aix-en-Provence: Centre d'études des sociétés méditerranéennes, 1985.

Ambelain, Robert. "Dossier Fulcanelli," *Les Cahiers de la Tour-St.-Jacques* 9 (1962).

Arberry, A. J. *Sufism: An Account of the Mystics of Islam*. New York: Harper & Row, 1970.

Armstrong, Karen. *A History of God: The 4,000-Year Quest of Judaism, Christianity and Islam*. New York: Ballantine Books, 1984.

———. *Holy War: The Crusades and Their Impact on Today's World*. New York: Anchor/Doubleday, 1992.

———. *Muhammad: A Biography of the Prophet*. San Francisco: HarperSanFrancisco, 1992.

Arnold, Paul. *Historie des Rose-Croix et les origines de la Franc-Maçonneries.* Paris, 1955.

————. *La Rose-Croix et ses rapports avec la Franc-Maçonneries.* Paris: 1970.

Ayala, D. Felipe Huaman Poma de. *Some Account of the Illustrated Chronicle by the Peruvian Indian.* Trans. Richard Pietschmann. London: Harrison and Sons, 1912.

Baigent, Michael, and Richard Leigh. *The Temple and the Lodge.* New York: Arcade Publishing, 1989.

Baigent, Michael, Richard Leigh, and Henry Lincoln. *Holy Blood, Holy Grail.* New York: Delacorte Press, 1982.

Bailey, James. *The God-Kings and the Titans.* New York: St. Martin's, 1973.

Bauval, Robert and Adrian Gilbert. *The Orion Mystery.* New York: Crown, 1994.

Bayley, Harold. *The Lost Language of Symbolism.* 2 vols. New York: Citadel Press, 1988.

Bechtel, Guy. "Entretien avec Eugène Canseliet sur Fulcanelli suivi du mystère Fulcanelli" (conversation with Eugène Canseliet on Fulcanelli concerning the Fulcanelli mystery). Privately printed, two copies are on deposit at the Library of Hermetic Philosophy, Amsterdam, dated January 4, 1974.

Begg, Ean. *The Cult of the Black Virgin.* London; New York: Arkana, 1996.

Bellamy, Hans Schindler. *The Calendar of Tiahuanaco: A Disquisition on the Time Measuring System of the Oldest Civilization in the World.* London: Faber & Faber, 1956.

Ben ha-Kanah, Nehunya. *The Bahir.* Trans., intro., and comm. by Aryeh Kaplan. York Beach, Maine: Samuel Weiser, 1979.

Benoist, Luc. *The Esoteric Path: An Introduction to the Hermetic Tradition.* England: Crucible, 1988.

Bernbaum, Edwin. *The Way to Shambalah.* New York: Jeremy P. Tarcher, 1980.

Billings, Malcolm. *The Cross & the Crescent: A History of the Crusades.* New York: Sterling Publishing, 1990.

Bishop, Morris. *The Middle Ages.* New York: Houghton Mifflin, 1987.

Bleakly, Alan. *Fruits of the Moon Tree.* London: Gateway Books, 1984.

Boucher, Jules. "La Croix d'Hendaye." In *Consolation* 26 (February 13, 1936).

————. "La Croix d'Hendaye." In *Consolation* 27 (April 30, 1936).

Bouyer, Louis. *The Spirituality of the New Testament and the Fathers.* Trans. Mary P. Ryan. Minneapolis, Minn.: Winston Press, 1960, 1963.

Breton, André. *Arcana 17.* New York and Paris: *L'Art magique,* Club Français du Livre, 1957.

————. *Manifestos of Surrealism.* Trans. Richard Seaver and Helen R. Lane. Ann Arbor: University of Michigan Press, 1969.

Bruce, F. F. *New Testament History.* New York: Doubleday, 1971.

Bryant, Nigel, trans. *The High Book of the Grail: A Translation of the Thirteenth-Century Romance of Perlesvaus.* Ipswich, England: D. S. Brewer, 1978.

Burckhardt, Jacob. *The Age of Constantine the Great.* Berkeley: University of California Press, 1983.

Burckhardt, Titus. *Alchemy.* London: Penguin Books, 1967.

Burman, Edward. *The Templars: Knights of God.* Rochester, Vt.: Destiny Books, 1986.

Cable, Carol. *Viollet-le-Duc, 1814–1879: A Bibliography of Recent Scholarship.* Monticello, Ill.: Vance Bibliographies, 1990.

Cahiers de l'hermétisme: Kabbalistes chrétiens. Paris: Albin Michel, 1979.

Cahiers de l'hermétisme: Sophia ou l'âme du monde. Paris: Albin Michel, 1983.

Calder, Nigel. *Timescale: An Atlas of the 4th Dimension.* New York: Viking Press, 1983.

Campbell, Joseph. *The Mythic Image.* Bollingen Series. Princeton, N.J.: Princeton University Press, 1981.

Canseliet, Eugène. *Alchimie: Etudes diverses de symbolisme hermétique et de pratique philosophale.* Paris: J.-J. Pauvert, 1964.

———. *L'Alchimie et son livre muet "Mutus Liber."* Paris: J.-J. Pauvert, 1967.

———. "Alchimiques memoires." Serialized in the catalogue *La Tourbe des philosophes,* from *La Table d' Emeraude.* N.p., n.d.

———. *L'alchimie expliquée sur ses textes classiques.* Paris: J.-J. Pauvert, 1972.

———. "Les Argonauts et la Toison d'or." *Atlantis* 6 (July 21, 1935).

———. *Deux logis alchimiques.* Paris: J.-J. Pauvert, 1979.

———. "*Lueurs sur* Le Mystère des cathédrales." *Initiation et Science* 46 (December 1958).

———. *Trois anciens traités d'alchimie.* Paris: J.-J. Pauvert, 1975.

Cape Sciences Foundation. *Abbadie: Une Rébus géant.* Bordeaux: Cape Science Foundation, 1997.

Carny, Lucien. *Notre-Dame de Paris: Symbolisme hermétique et alchimique.* With texts by Eugène Canseliet. Le Groupe des 3, 1969.

Casti, John L. *Paradigms Lost: Images of Man in the Mirror of Science.* New York: Wm. Morrow & Co., 1989.

Chaillan, M. *Les Saintes-Maries-de-la-Mer: Récherches archéologiques et historiques avec documents des fouilles du XVe siècle.* Marseille: A. Dragon and Tacussel, 1926.

Cheetham, Nicolas. *The Keeper of the Keys: A History of Popes from St. Peter to John-Paul II.* New York: Scribner's, 1982.

Choucha, Nadia. *Surrealism and the Occult: Shamanism, Magic, Alchemy, and the Birth of an Artistic Movement.* Rochester, Vt.: Destiny Books, 1992.

Chrétien de Troyes. *Arthurian Romances.* Trans., intro., and notes by D. D. R. Owen. London: Everyman, 1993.

Chrétien de Troyes. *Perceval.* In *Medieval Romances,* ed. Roger Sherman Loomis and Laura Alandis Loomis. New York: Random House, 1957.

Cirlot, J. E. *A Dictionary of Symbols.* London: Routledge & Kegan Paul, 1978.

Cohn, Norman. *Cosmos, Chaos and the World to Come*. New Haven & London: Yale University Press, 1993.

Cole, Robert. *A Traveller's History of Paris*. New York: Interlink Books, 1994.

Cooper, J. C. *An Illustrated Encyclopedia of Traditional Symbols*. London: Thames & Hudson, 1978.

Cornelius, Geoffrey, and Paul Devereux. *The Secret Language of the Stars and Planets*. San Francisco: Chronicle Books, 1996.

Cott, Jonathan. *Isis and Osiris*. New York: Doubleday, 1994.

Coudert, Allison. *Alchemy: The Philosopher's Stone*. Boulder, Colo.: Shambhala, 1980.

Couliano, Ioan P. *The Tree of Gnosis*. San Francisco: HarperSanFrancisco, 1992.

Courjeaud, Frédéric. *Fulcanelli: Une Identité révélée*. Paris: C. Vigne, 1996.

Crowley, Aleister. *777 & Other Qabalistic Writings*. York Beach, Maine: Weiser, 1973.

Crowley, Aleister, and Frieda Harris. *Aleister Crowley Thoth Tarot*. New York: U.S. Games Systems, 1997.

Cumont, Franz. *Oriental Religions in Roman Paganism*. 1911. Reprint, New York: Dover Publications 1956.

Dalai Lama. *Concerning the Kalachakra Initiation in America*. Madison, Wis.: Deer Park, 1981.

Dalai Lama, Jeffrey Hopkins, and Mkhas-grub Dge-legs-dpal-bzan-po. *The Kalachakra Tantra: Rite of Initiation for the Stage of Generation. A Commentary on the Text of Kay-drup-ge-lek-bel-sang-bo*. London: Wisdom Publications, 1985.

Daraul, Arkon. *A History of Secret Societies*. New York: Carol Publishing Group, 1990.

Davidson, Gustav, *A Dictionary of Angels*. New York: The Free Press, 1967.

Davies, Norman. *Europe: A History*. Oxford: Oxford University Press, 1996.

Davis, Joel. *Journey to the Center of Our Galaxy*. Garden City, Illinois: Contemporary Books, 1991.

De Camp, L. Sprague. *Lost Continents: The Atlantis Theme*. New York: Ballantine Books, 1970.

De la Vega, Garcilaso. *Royal Commentaries of the Incas and General History of Peru*. 2 vols. Trans. and intro. H. V. Livermore, with a foreword by Arnold J. Toynbee. Austin: University of Texas Press, 1966.

Dhargyey, Geshe Ngawang, trans. *Kalachakra Tantra*. Dharamsala: Library of Tibetan Works and Archives, 1985.

Dimont, Max I. *Jews, God and History*. New York: New American Library, 1962.

The Divine Pymander of Hermes Mercurius Trismegistus. Trans. Dr. Everard. San Diego, Calif.: Wizard's Bookshelf, 1978.

Dowman, Keith. *The Power Places of Central Tibet*. London and New York: Routledge & Kegan Paul, 1988.

Dubois, Geneviève. *Fulcanelli dévoilé.* Paris: Dervy, 1993.

Dujols, Pierre. *Bibliothèque des sciences ésotériques: Bibliographie générale de l'occulte.* Ancienne Séries 19. Paris, 1912.

———. *La Chevalerie amoureuse troubadours, félibres et rose-croix.* Unedited manuscript with commentary by J. F. Gibert. Paris: La Table d'Emeraude, 1991.

———. "An Explicative Hypotose of Magaphon on the Mutus Liber." *Les Nobles écrits de Pierre Dujols.* 1914. Reprint, Grenoble: Mercure Dauphinois, 2000.

Durant, Will and Ariel. *The Age of Faith: A History of Medieval Civilization— Christian, Islamic, and Judaic—from Constantine to Dante: A.D. 325–1300.* New York: Simon & Schuster, 1950.

Eban, Abba. *Heritage: Civilization and the Jews.* New York: Summit Books, 1984.

Eccu, O. O. R. *Tajemství kamene Mudrcu: Fulcanelli—Osho—Minarík.* Olomouc, Czech Republic: Votobia, 1998.

Edwards, I. E. *The Pyramids of Egypt.* London: Penguin Books, 1982.

Ekstein, Modris. *Rites of Spring: The Great War and the Birth of the Modern Age.* New York: Doubleday, 1989.

Ellerbe, Helen. *The Dark Side of Christian History.* San Rafael, Calif.: Morningstar Books, 1995.

Engels, Dagmar. "The Politics of Childbirth: British and Bengali Women in Contest, 1890–1930." In *Society and Ideology: Essays in South Asian History Presented to Professor K. A. Ballhatchet,* ed. Peter Robb. Delhi: Oxford University Press, 1993.

Epstein, Perle. *Kabbalah: The Way of the Jewish Mystic.* London: Shambhala, 1988.

Erdoes, Richard. *A.D. 1000: Living on the Brink of Apocalypse.* San Francisco: Harper & Row, 1988.

Eschenbach, Wolfram von. *Parzival.* Trans. A. T. Hatto. London: Penguin Books, 1980.

Evans, Joan, ed. *The Flowering of the Middle Ages.* London: Thames and Hudson, 1985.

Evans-Wentz, W. Y. *Fairy Faith in Celtic Countries.* 1911. Reprint, New York: Citadel Press, 1990.

Evola, Julius. *The Mystery of the Grail: Initiation and Magic in the Quest for the Spirit.* Trans. Guido Stucco. Rochester, Vt.: Inner Traditions, 1997.

Farah, Caesar E. *Islam.* New York: Barron's, 1987.

Farr, Florence. *Egyptian Magic.* London: Theosophical Publishing Society, 1896.

Faulkner, R. O. *The Ancient Egyptian Pyramid Texts.* England: Aris & Phillips, 1993.

———. "The King and the Star Religion in the Pyramid Texts." In *Journal of Near Eastern Studies* 25 (1966).

Fell, Barry. *America B.C.: Ancient Settlers in the New World.* New York: Pocket Books, 1976.

————. *Saga America*. New York: Times Books, 1983.

Ferris, Timothy. *Coming of Age in the Milky Way*. New York: Wm. Morrow & Co., 1988.

————, ed. *The World Treasury of Physics, Astronomy and Mathematics*. New York: Little, Brown & Co., 1991.

Ferro, Robert, and Michael Grumley. *Atlantis: The Autobiography of a Search*. New York: Bell Publishing, 1970.

Fleming, Peter. *Bayonets to Lhasa: The First Full Account of the British Invasion of Tibet in 1904*. New York: Oxford University Press, 1986.

Fortune, Dion. *The Mystical Qabalah*. York Beach, Maine: Samuel Weiser Company, 1984.

Fox, Robin Lane. *Pagans and Christians*. New York: Knopf, 1986.

————. *The Unauthorized Version: Truth and Fiction in the Bible*. New York: Knopf, 1992.

Franz, Marie-Louise von. *Alchemy: An Introduction to the Symbolism and Psychology*. Toronto: Inner City Books, 1980.

Frawley, David. *The Astrology of the Seers: A Comprehensive Guide to Vedic Astrology*. Salt Lake City: Passage Press, 1990.

Frazer, Sir James George. *Adonis, Attis, Osiris: Studies in the History of Oriental Religion*. London: Macmillan, 1907.

Fulcanelli. *Les Demeures Philosophales et le symbolisme hermétique dans ses rapports avec l'art sacré et l'ésotérisme du Grand Oeuvre*. 2 vols. Preface by Eugène Canseliet. Paris: Schémit, 1930.

————. *Les Demeures Philosophales et le symbolisme hermétique dans ses rapports avec l'art sacré et l'ésotérisme du grand oeuvre*. 2 vols. 2nd edition. Preface by Eugène Canseliet, illustrated by Jean-Julien Champagne. Paris: Les Éditions des Champs-Élysées, Omnium littéraire, 1960.

————. *Les Demeures Philosophales et le symbolisme hermétique dans ses rapports avec l'art sacré et l'ésotérisme du grand oeuvre*. 2 vols. 3rd edition. Expanded with three prefaces by Eugène Canseliet, illustrated by Jean-Julien Champagne. Paris : J.-J. Pauvert, 1977.

————. *The Dwellings of the Philosophers*. Trans. Brigitte Donvez and Lionel Perrin, illustrations by Jean-Julien Champagne. Boulder, Colo.: Archive Press and Communications, 1999.

————. *Le Mystère des cathédrales et l'interprétation ésotérique des symboles hermétiques du Grand-Oeuvre*. Paris: J. Schémit, 1926.

————. *Le Mystère des cathédrales et l'interprétation ésotérique des symboles hermétiques du grand-oeuvre*. 2nd edition. Collection Alchimie et Alchimistes. Paris: Éditions des Champs-Elysées, Omnium littéraire, 1957.

————. *Le Mystère des cathédrales et l'interprétation ésotérique des symboles hermétiques du grand-oeuvre*. 3rd edition. Prefaces by Eugène Canseliet, with 49 new photographic illustrations, mainly by Pierre Jahan, frontispiece by Jean-Julien Champagne. Paris: J.-J. Pauvert, 1964.

————. *Le Mystère des Cathédrales: Esoteric Interpretation of the Hermetic Symbols of the Great Work*. 2nd edition. Trans. Mary Sworder, prefaces by Eugène Canseliet, introduction by Walter Lang. London: Neville Spearman, 1971.

————. *Le Mystère des Cathédrales: Esoteric Interpretation of the Hermetic Symbols of the Great Work*. Trans. Mary Sworder, prefaces by Eugene Canseliet, introduction by Walter Lang, preface to American edition by Roy E. Thompson Jr., Albuquerque: Brotherhood of Life, 1984.

Fussell, M. J., and Stuart Dike. *The Crop Circle Connector*. http://www.cropcircle-connector.com/index2.html

Fussell, Paul. *The Great War and Modern Memory*. Oxford: Oxford University Press, 1975.

Geshe Ngawang Dhargyey. *The Bodhicitta Vows and Lam-rim puja*. Dharamsala: Library of Tibetan Works & Archives, 1974.

————. *Tibetan Tradition of Mental Development: Oral Teachings of a Tibetan Lama*. Dharamsala: Library of Tibetan Works & Archives, 1974.

Geyraud, Pierre. *Les Sociétés secrètes de Paris*. Paris: Éditions Émile-Paul-Frères, 1939.

————. *L'Occultisme à Paris*. Paris: Éditions Émile-Paul-Frères, 1953.

Ghyka, Matila C. *The Geometry of Art and Life*. 1946. Reprint, New York: Dover Publications, 1977.

Gilbert, R. A. *The Golden Dawn*. Northamptonshire, England: Aquarian Press, 1983.

Gilbert, Adrian, and Maurice Cotterell. *The Mayan Prophecies*. London: Element Books, 1995.

Godwin, Jocelyn, Christian Chanel, and John P. Deveney. *The Hermetic Brotherhood of Luxor: Initiatic and Historical Documents of an Order of Practical Occultism*. York Beach, Maine: Samuel Weiser, 1995.

Godwin, Malcolm. *The Holy Grail*. New York: Viking Books, 1994.

Grant, Michael. *From Alexander to Cleopatra*. New York: Scribner's, 1982.

————. *The Jews in the Roman World*. New York: Barnes & Noble Books, 1995.

Graves, Robert. *The Greek Myths*. London: Penguin Books, 1960.

"The Greek Alchemical Papyri." *Ciba Symposia* 3, no. 5 (1941).

Greer, Mary K. *The Women of the Golden Dawn*. Rochester, Vt.: Park Street Press, 1995.

Gregory, Saint. *The History of the Franks*. Trans. and intro. Lewis Thorpe. London: Penguin Books, 1974.

Grotjahn, Martin. *The Voice of the Symbol*. New York: Delta Books, 1971.

Grousset, René. *Histoire des croisades et du royaume franc de Jérusalem*. Paris: Perrin, 1935.

Guiraud, Jean. "Le Consolamentum ou l'initiation cathare; le repression de l'heresie au moyen age." *Questions d'historie et d'archeologie chrétiennes*. Paris: V. Lecoffre, 1906.

————. *Histoire de l'Inquisition au moyen age.* Paris: A. Picard, 1935.

Gurney, O. R. "The Hittites." *The Penguin Encyclopedia of Ancient Civilizations.* London: Penguin Books, 1988.

Gutwirth, Israel. *The Kabbalah and Jewish Mysticism.* New York: Philosophical Library, 1987.

Guyard, Stanislas. "Un grand Maitre des Assassins au temps de Saladin." In *Journal Asiatique* series 7, 9. Paris, 1977.

Hadingham, Evan. *Early Man and the Cosmos.* New York: Walker & Co., 1984.

Hall, Manly P. *Freemasonry of the Ancient Egyptians.* Los Angeles: Philosophical Research Society, 1937.

————. *The Secret Teachings of All Ages.* Los Angeles: Philosophical Research Society, 1988.

Hancock, Graham, *Fingerprints of the Gods.* New York: Crown, 1995.

————. *The Sign and the Seal: The Quest for the Lost Ark of the Covenant.* New York: Simon & Schuster, 1992.

Hancock, Graham, and Robert Bauval. *The Message of the Sphinx.* New York: Crown, 1996.

Hart, George. *Egyptian Myths.* Austin: University of Texas Press, 1990.

Heer, Friedrich. *The Medieval World: Europe, 1100–1350.* 1962. Reprint, London: Weidenfeld, 1993.

Hemingway, Ernest. *A Moveable Feast.* New York: Simon & Schuster, 1965.

Henry, William. *One Foot in Atlantis.* Juneau, Alaska: Earthpulse Press, 1998.

Hewitt, J. F. *History and Chronology of the Myth-Making Age.* London: James Parker and Company, 1901.

Hitchcock, Ethan Allen. *Alchemy & the Alchemists.* Los Angeles: Philosophical Research Society, c. 1976.

Ho, Mae-Wan, and Fritz-Albert Popp. "Biological Organization, Coherence and Light Emission from Living Organisms." In *Thinking about Biology: An Introduction to Current Theoretical Biology,* ed. W. D. Stein and F. J. Varela. Reading, Mass.: Addison-Wesley, 1993.

Hodges, R. and D. Whitehouse. *Mohammed, Charlemagne & the Origins of Europe.* Ithica, N.Y.: Cornell University Press, 1983.

Hogue, John. *The Last Pope: The Decline and Fall of the Church of Rome: The Prophecies of Saint Malachy for the New Millennium.* London: Element Books, 1998.

————. *Nostradamus: The Complete Prophecies.* Rockport, Mass.: Element Books, 1997.

Hollister, C. Warren. *Medieval Europe: A Short History.* New York: McGraw-Hill, 1994.

Hopkins, John Arthur. *Alchemy, Child of Greek Philosophy.* New York: Columbia University Press, 1934.

Howard, Michael. *The Occult Conspiracy: Secret Societies—Their Influence and Power in World History.* Rochester, Vt.: Destiny Books, 1989.

Howarth, Stephen. *The Knights Templar.* New York: Atheneum, 1982.

Howe, Ellic. *The Magicians of the Golden Dawn.* London: Neville Spearman, 1972.

Hugo, Victor. *The Hunchback of Notre-Dame.* Wordsworth Classics Series. Ware, England: Wordsworth, 1993.

Idel, Moshe. *Golem: Jewish Magical and Mystical Traditions on the Artificial Anthropoid.* Albany: State University of New York Press, 1990.

Jacobus de Voragine. *The Golden Legend: Lives of the Saints.* Trans. William Caxton, ed. George V. O'Neill. Cambridge: Cambridge University Press, 1914.

James, Jamie. *The Music of the Spheres.* London: Abacus, 1993.

James, T. G. H. *An Introduction to Ancient Egypt.* New York: Farrar, Straus and Giroux, 1979.

Jenkins, John Major. *Galactic Alignment.* Rochester, Vt.: Bear and Company, 2002.

———. *Maya Cosmogenesis 2012.* Santa Fe: Bear & Co., 1998.

———. *Tzolkin.* Garberville, Calif.: Borderland Sciences, 1994.

Jochman, Joseph R. *Nostradamus Now.* Albuquerque: Sun Books, 1993.

Johnson, Kenneth Rayner. *The Fulcanelli Phenomenon: The Story of a Twentieth-Century Alchemist in the Light of New Examination of the Hermetic Tradition.* London: Neville Spearman, 1980.

Johnson, Paul. *A History of Christianity.* New York: Atheneum, 1979.

Joyce, James. *Finnegan's Wake.* New York: The Viking Press, 1939.

———. *Ulysses.* New York: Modern Library Edition, 1961.

Kals, W. S. *Stars and Planets.* Santa Barbara, Calif.: Sierra Club Books, 1990.

Kaplan, Aryeh. *Sefer Yetzirah: The Book of Creation.* York Beach, Maine: Samuel Weiser, 1990.

Keegan, John. *The First World War.* London: Random House, 1998.

Kees, Hermann. *Ancient Egypt: A Cultural Topography.* Chicago: University of Chicago Press, 1961.

Ker, W. P. *The Dark Ages.* New York: New American Library, 1958.

Khaitzine, Richard. *Fulcanelli et le Cabaret du Chat Noir: Histoire artistique, politique et secrète de Montmartre.* Villeselve, France: Ramuel, 1997.

King, Francis. *Modern Ritual Magic.* Dorset, England: Prism Press, 1989.

Klingaman, William K. *The First Century: Emperors, Gods and Everyman.* New York: HarperPerennial, 1991.

Knight, Christopher, and Robert Lomas. *The Hiram Key.* London: Element Books, 1996.

Kroeger, Adolf Ernst. *The Minnesinger of Germany.* New York: Hurd and Houghton, 1873.

Krupp, E. C. *Beyond the Blue Horizon: Myths & Legends of the Sun, Moon, Stars and Planets.* Oxford, England: Oxford University Press, 1991.

———. *In Search of Ancient Astronomies.* New York: Doubleday, 1978.

Kuntz, Darcy. *The Complete Golden Dawn Cipher Manuscript.* Chicago: Holmes, 1996.

Kurlansky, Mark. *The Basque History of the World.* New York: Penguin Books, 1999.

Lamy, Lucie. *Egyptian Mysteries: New Light on Ancient Knowledge.* London: Thames and Hudson, 1981.

LaViolette, Paul. *Beyond the Big Bang.* Rochester, Vt.: Park Street Press, 1995.

———. *Earth Under Fire.* New York: Starburst Publications, 1997.

Lemesurier, Peter. *The Great Pyramid: Your Personal Guide.* London: Element Books, 1987.

———. *The Great Pyramid Decoded.* 1977. Reprint, New York: Barnes and Noble Books, 1995.

Le Plongeon, Augustus. *Maya/Atlantis: Queen Móo and the Egyptian Sphinx.* 1896. Reprint, with a new introduction by Paul Allen. Blauvelt, N.Y.: R. Steiner Publications, 1896, 1973.

———. *The Origin of the Egyptians.* Intro. Manly P. Hall. 1914. Reprint, Los Angeles: Philosophical Research Society, 1983.

———. *Sacred Mysteries among the Mayas and the Quiches—11,500 Years Ago: Their Relation to the Sacred Mysteries of Egypt, Greece, Chaldea and India.* 1886. Reprint, Minneapolis: Wizards Bookshelf, 1973.

Lings, Martin. *Muhammad: His Life Based on Earliest Sources.* London: Islamic Texts Society, Allen & Unwin, 1983.

Lonely Planet Publications. *South-West France.* Oakland, Calif.: Lonely Planet Publications, 2000.

Lonegren, Sig. *Labyrinths: Ancient Myths and Modern Uses.* New York: Sterling, 2001.

Loomis, Roger Sherman, and Laura Alandis Loomis, eds. *Medieval Romances.* New York: Random House, 1957.

Loyn, H. R., ed. *The Middle Ages: A Concise Encyclopedia.* London: Thames & Hudson, 1989.

Lyall, Archibald. *Companion Guide to the South of France.* Englewood Cliffs, N.J.: Prentice-Hall, 1983.

Mack, Burton L. *The Lost Gospel: The Book of Q and Christian Origins.* San Francisco: HarperSanFrancisco, 1993.

Manchester, William. *A World Lit Only by Fire.* Boston: Little, Brown & Co., 1993.

Mann, Vivian B., Thomas F. Glick, and Jerrilyn D. Dodds, eds. *Convivencia: Jews, Muslims and Christians in Medieval Spain.* New York: George Braziller, 1992.

Al-Maqrizi, Taqi ad-Din. *The Book of the History of the Kings.* English/Arabic edition. Trans. M. Ziyade. Cairo, 1934.

Marcard, René. *Petite Histoire de la chimie et de l'alchimie.* Bordeaux: Éditions Delmas, 1938.

Markham, Sir Clements, trans. and ed. *The Travels of Pedro de Cieza de Léon, A.D. 1532–50, Contained in the First Part of His Chronicle of Peru.* 1864. Reprint, New York: B. Franklin, 1964.

Marly, Claude. "Le langage secret des Cathedrales." In *Tout Savoir* 74 (July 1959).

Martínez Otero, Luis Miguel. *Fulcanelli: Una Biografia Imposible*. Barcelona: Ediciones Obelisco, 1986.

Masters, Robert. *The Goddess Sekhmet*. New York: Amity House, 1986.

Matarasso, Pauline Maud, trans. *The Quest of the Holy Grail*. London: Penguin Classics, 1969.

Mathers, S., L. MacGregor, et al. *Astral Projection, Ritual Magic and Alchemy*. Rochester, Vt.: Destiny Books, 1987.

———. *The Kabbalah Unveiled*. London: Arkana, 1991.

McGarry, Daniel D. *Medieval History and Civilization*. New York: Macmillan & Co., 1975.

McGovern, William Montgomery. *Jungle Paths and Inca Ruins*. New York and London: The Century Co., 1927.

McIntosh, Christopher. *The Rosicrucians: The History and Mythology of an Occult Order*. London: Crucible, 1987.

McKenzie, A. E. E. *The Major Achievements of Science*. New York: Touchstone Books, 1983.

McLean, Adam. *The Alchemical Mandala: A Survey of the Mandala in the Western Esoteric Traditions*. Grand Rapids, Mich.: Phanes Press, 1989.

Merzei, Arpad. "Liberty of Language." In *Surréalisme en 1947*. Exhibition catalogue. Paris: Galerie Maeght, 1947.

Mevryl, Paul. "Epilogue in Stone." Afterword to *The Fulcanelli Phenomenon* by Kenneth Rayner Johnson. London: Neville Spearman, 1980.

Meyer, Marvin W. *The Secret Teachings of Jesus: Four Gnostic Gospels*. New York: Vintage Books, 1986.

Michell, John F. *City of Revelation: On the Proportions and Symbolic Numbers of the Cosmic Temple*. New York: Ballantine Books, 1972.

Mitra, Rajendralala. *The Sanskrit Buddhist Literature of Nepal*. Intro. Alok Ray. 1882. Reprint, Calcutta: Sanskrit Pustak Bhandar, 1971.

Moran, Kerry, and Helka Ahokas. *Nepal: The Mountain Kingdom*. Lincolnwood, Ill.: Passport Books, 1995.

Moreaux, Roselyne. *Les Saintes-Maries-de-la-Mer*. Marseilles: Éditions PEC, 2000.

Much, Otto. *The Secret of Atlantis*. New York: Pocket Books, 1979.

Narby, Jeremy. *The Cosmic Serpent: DNA and the Origins of Knowledge*. New York: Jeremy Tarcher/Putnam, 1998.

Naydler, Jeremy. *Temple of the Cosmos*. Rochester, Vt.: Inner Traditions, 1996.

Neumann, Erich. *The Origins and History of Consciousness*. New York: Pantheon Books, 1954.

Neusner, Jacob. *Self-Fulfilling Prophecy: Exile and Return in the History of Judaism*. Boston: Beacon Press, 1987.

New Advent, Inc. "d'Abbadie, Antoine." Article transcribed from *The Catholic Encyclopedia: An International Work of Reference on the Constitution, Doctrine, Discipline and History of the Catholic Church*. Appleton, 1907–12. Internet edition, 2002. http://www.knight.org/advent/cathen/.

———. "Alyschamps." Article transcribed from *The Catholic Encyclopedia: An International Work of Reference on the Constitution, Doctrine, Discipline and History of the Catholic Church*. Appleton, 1907–12. Internet edition, 2002. http://www.knight.org/advent/cathen/.

———. "Feast of the Donkey." Article transcribed from *The Catholic Encyclopedia: An International Work of Reference on the Constitution, Doctrine, Discipline and History of the Catholic Church*. Appleton, 1907–12. Internet edition, 2002. http://www.knight.org/advent/cathen/.

———. "Feast of Fools." Article transcribed from *The Catholic Encyclopedia: An International Work of Reference on the Constitution, Doctrine, Discipline and History of the Catholic Church*. Appleton, 1907-1912. Internet edition, 2002. http://www.knight.org/advent/cathen/.

———. "Feast of the Epiphany." Article transcribed from *The Catholic Encyclopedia: An International Work of Reference on the Constitution, Doctrine, Discipline and History of the Catholic Church*. Appleton, 1907–12. Internet edition, 2002. http://www.knight.org/advent/cathen/.

———. "St. Trophime." Article transcribed from *The Catholic Encyclopedia: An International Work of Reference on the Constitution, Doctrine, Discipline and History of the Catholic Church*. Appleton, 1907–12. Internet edition, 2002. http://www.knight.org/advent/cathen/.

Noel, Sybille. *The Magic Bird of Chomolungma*. New York: Doubleday, Doran & Company, 1931.

Norelli-Bachelet, Patrizia. *The Gnostic Circle*. London: Aeon Books, 1994.

———. *The New Way: A Study in the Rise and Establishment of a Gnostic Society*. London: Aeon Books, 1981.

Oldenborg, Zoe. *Massacre at Montségur*. Trans. Peter Green. New York: Random House, 1961.

Ovason, David. *The Nostradamus Code*. London: Arrow Books Limited, 1998.

Pagels, Elaine. *The Gnostic Gospels*. New York: Vintage Books, 1981.

Panikkar, Raimundo. *The Vedic Experience: Mantramanjari: An Anthology of the Vedas for Modern Man and Contemporary Celebration*. Berkeley: University of California Press, 1977.

Panofsky, Erwin, trans. and ed. *Abbot Suger on the Abbey Church of St. Denis and Its Art Treasures*. Princeton, N.J.: Princeton University Press, 1946.

Partner, Peter. *The Knights Templar and Their Myth*. Rochester, Vt.: Destiny Books, 1990.

Patai, Raphael. *The Jewish Alchemists: A History and Sourcebook*. Princeton, N.J.: Princeton University Press, 1994.

Pauwels, Louis, and Jacques Bergier. *The Morning of the Magicians*. Trans. Rollo Myers. London: Neville Spearman, 1963.

Payne, Robert. *The Making of the Christian World*. New York: Dorset Press, 1990.

———. *The Dream and the Tomb*. Ann Arbor, Mich.: Scarborough House, 1984.

Paz, Octavio. *Marcel Duchamp*. Trans. Rachel Phillips and Donald Gardner. New York: Seaver Books, 1978.

Picknett, Lynn, and Clive Prince. *The Templar Revelation*. New York: Simon & Schuster, 1997.

Plato. *Timaeus and Critias*. Trans., intro., and appendix Sir Henry Desmond Lee. New York: Penguin Books, 1977.

Pollack, Robert. *Signs of Life: The Language and Meanings of DNA*. Boston: Houghton Mifflin, 1994.

Pope, Arthur Upham. "Persia and the Holy Grail." In *Sources of the Grail: An Anthology*, ed. John Matthews. Hudson, N.Y. : Lindisfarne Press, 1997.

Popp, Fritz-Albert, et al., eds. *Recent Advances in Biophoton Research and Its Application*. Singapore World Scientific, 1992.

Posnansky, Arthur. *Tihuanacu: The Cradle of American Man*. 4 vols. New York: J. J. Augustin, 1945–58.

Potok, Chaim. *Wanderings: A History of the Jews*. New York: Fawcett Crest Books, 1978.

Potter, Rev. Dr. Charles Francis. *The Lost Years of Jesus Revealed*. New York: Fawcett Gold Medal, 1988.

Powell, James N. *The Tao of Symbols*. New York: Quill Books, 1982.

Quercob Historical Society. "Château Puivert." Untitled, undated pamphlet.

Rattenmayer, M. "Evidence of Photon Emission from DNA in Living Systems." In *Naturwissenschaften* 68 (1981): 572–73.

Regardie, Frances Israel. *Garden of Pomegranates*. St. Paul, Minn.: Llewellyn Publishing, 1978.

———. *The Golden Dawn*. St. Paul, Minn.: Llewellyn Publications, 1978.

———. *The Philosopher's Stone: A Modern Comparative Approach to Alchemy from the Psychological and Magical Points of View*. 2nd ed. St. Paul, Minn.: Llewellyn Publications, 1970.

Reich, Wilhelm. *Ether, God, and Devil* and *Cosmic Superimposition*. Trans. Therese Pol. New York: Farrar, Straus and Giroux, 1973.

Renfrew, Colin. *Archeology and Language: The Puzzle of Indo-European Origins*. London: Cape, 1987.

Reston, James, Jr. *The Last Apocalypse: Europe at the Year 1000 A.D.* New York: Doubleday, 1998.

Richard, Ernst. *History of German Civilization*. New York: The Macmillan Company, 1911.

Ricoeur, Paul. *The Symbolism of Evil*. Boston: Beacon Press, 1967.

Robertson, Ian. *Blue Guide: France*. New York: Norton, 1997.

Robinson, James M., ed. *The Nag Hammadi Library*. New York: Harper & Row, 1978.

Romer, John. *Testament: The Bible and History*. New York: Henry Holt, 1988.

Rossi, Aldo. *The Architecture of the City*. Trans. Diane Ghirardo and Joan Ockman. Cambridge, Mass.: MIT Press, 1982.

Rougemont, Denis de. *Love in the Western World.* Trans. Montgomery Belgion. New York: Pantheon, 1956.

Rowbotham, J. *The Troubadours and the Court of Love.* London: 1895.

Rubinsky, Yuri, and Ian Wiseman. *A History of the End of the World.* New York: Quill Books, 1982.

Runciman, Sir Stephen. *The First Crusade.* Canto Edition. London: Cambridge University Press, 1992.

———. *A History of the Crusades.* 3 vols. Cambridge, England: Cambridge University Press, 1952.

Rundle Clark, R. T. *Myth and Symbol in Ancient Egypt.* London: Thames and Hudson, 1959.

Russell, Jeffrey Burton. *The Devil: Perceptions of Evil from Antiquity to Primitive Christianity.* New York: New American Library, 1979.

Russell, Peter. *The White Hole in Time.* New York: HarperCollins, 1992.

Sadoul, Jacques. *Alchemists and Gold.* Trans. Olga Sieveking. London: Neville Spearman, 1972.

Sanders, E. P. *The Historical Figure of Jesus.* London: Allen Lane/Penguin Press, 1993.

Sansoni, Dominic, and Jim Goodman. *Kathmandu.* New Jersey: Hunter Publishing, 1988.

Santillana, Giorgio de, and Hertha von Dechend. *Hamlet's Mill: An Essay on Myth and the Frame of Time.* Boston: Gambit, 1969.

Sapere Aude [Dr. William Wynne Westcott]. "Flying Roll VII." In *Astral Projection, Ritual Magic and Alchemy,* ed. Francis King, with additional material by R. A. Gilbert. Rochester, Vt.: Destiny Books, 1987.

———. *The Science of Alchymy, Spiritual and Material: An Essay.* London: Theosophical Publications Society, 1983.

Sauneron, Serge. *The Priests of Ancient Egypt.* New York: Grove Press, 1980.

Schaya, Leo. *The Universal Meaning of the Kabbalah.* London: Allen & Unwin, 1971.

Schimmel, Annemarie. *Mystical Dimensions of Islam.* Chapel Hill: University of North Carolina Press, 1975.

———. *The Mystery of Numbers.* Oxford: Oxford University Press, 1993.

Schock, Robert M., and Robert Aquinas McNally. *Voyages of the Pyramid Builders: The True Origins of the Pyramids.* New York: Jeremy Tarcher/Putnam, 2003.

Scholem, Gershom. *Jewish Gnosis, Merkabah Mysticism and Talmudic Tradition.* New York: Jewish Theological Seminary of America, 1965.

Schonfield, Hugh J. *The Jew of Tarsus.* London: MacDonald & Co., 1946.

———. *The Passover Plot.* New York: Bantam Books, 1971.

———. *Those Incredible Christians.* New York: Bantam Books, 1969.

Schwaller de Lubicz, R. A. *The Egyptian Miracle: An Introduction to the Wisdom of the Temple.* Rochester, Vt.: Inner Traditions, 1985.

———. *Sacred Science.* Rochester, Vt.: Inner Traditions, 1982.

———. *The Temple of Man.* Rochester, Vt.: Inner Traditions, 1999.

Schwartz, Hillel. *Century's End: A Cultural History of the Fin-de-Siècle from the 990s Through the 1990s.* New York: Doubleday, 1990.

Schweitzer, Albert. *The Quest of the Historical Jesus.* New York: Macmillan Co., 1968.

Scott, Walter, ed. and trans. *Hermetica: The Ancient Greek and Latin Writings Which Contain Religious or Philosophic Teachings Ascribed to Hermes Trismegistus.* 4 vols. 1924. Reprint, Boston: Shambhala, 1982.

Segal, Charles. *Pindar's Mythmaking: The Fourth Pythian Ode.* Princeton, N.J.: Princeton University Press, 1986.

Seligmann, Kurt. *The History of Magic and the Occult.* New York: Harmony Books, 1975.

Shachar, Shulamit. "Catharism and the Origins of the Kabbalah in Languedoc." In *Tabriz* 40 (1970–71).

Shah, Idries. *The Sufis.* With an introduction by Robert Graves. Garden City, N.Y.: Doubleday, 1964.

Shear, Jonathon. "Maharishi, Plato, and the TM-Sidhi Program on Innate Structures of Consciousness." In *Metaphilosophy* 12, no. 1 (1981).

———. "Plato, Piaget and Maharishi on Cognitive Development." In *Scientific Research on the Transcendental Meditation Program: Collected Papers*, vol. 2. Grand Rapids, Iowa: TM Press, 1983.

Sheehan, Thomas. *The First Coming: How the Kingdom of God Became Christianity.* New York: Dorset Press, 1986.

Shick, Hans. *Das altere Rosenkreuzertum: Ein Beitrag zur Entstehungsgeschichte der Freimaurerei.* Berlin: Nordland Verlag, 1942.

Sidgewick, J. B. *Observational Astronomy for Amateurs.* Elizabeth City, N.J.: Enslow Publishers, 1982.

Silberman, Neil Asher. *Heavenly Powers: Unraveling the Secret History of the Kabbalah.* Edison, N.J.: Castle Books, 2000.

Silverberg, Robert. *The Mound Builders.* New York: Ballantine Books, 1970.

Smith, Morton. *Jesus the Magician.* New York: Harper & Row, 1981.

Sociedad de Estudios Vascos, Congreso Extraordinario. *Antoine d'Abbadie, 1897–1997: Congrès International.* Donostia and Bilbao: Eusko Ikaskuntza, Euskaltzandia, 1998.

Stirling, William. *The Canon: An Exposition of the Pagan Mystery Perpetuated in the Cabala as the Rule of All the Arts.* 1897; reprint, with an introduction by Keith Critchlow, York Beach, Maine: Samuel Weiser, 1999.

Streep, Peg. *Mary, Queen of Heaven: Miracles, Manifestations, and Meditations on Mary.* New York: Book-of-the-Month Club, 1997.

Sullivan, William. *The Secret of the Incas: Myth, Astronomy, and the War Against Time.* New York: Crown Publishing Group, 1996.

Temko, Allen. *Notre-Dame of Paris.* New York: Viking Press, 1955.

Thompson, Thomas L. *The Mythic Past: Biblical Archaeology and the Myth of Israel*. New York: Basic Books, 1999.

Timms, Moira. "Raising the Djed." Unpublished manuscript.

Trager, James. *People's Chronology*. New York: Henry Holt, 1992.

Trefil, James S. *The Moment of Creation: Big Bang Physics*. New York: Scribner's, 1983.

Trintignac, André, and Marie-Jeanne Coloni. *Découvrir Notre-Dame-de-Paris: Guide complet de la cathédrale*. Paris: Cerf, 1984.

Tsogyal, Yeshe. "The Life and Liberation of Padmasambhava." Trans. Tarthang Tulku. In *Crystal Mirror: The Journal of the Tibetan Nyingma Meditation Center*, vol. 4. Emeryville, Calif.: Dharma Publishing, 1975.

Tuchman, Barbara. *The Proud Tower*. New York: McMillian and Company, 1966.

Tuchman, Maurice, et al. *The Spiritual in Art: Abstract Painting 1890–1985*. New York: Abbeville Press, 1986.

Tulku Thondop Rinpoche. *Hidden Teachings of Tibet: An Explanation of the Terma Tradition of Tibetan Buddhism*. Ed. Harold Talbott. Boston: Wisdom Publications, 1997.

Vacandard, Elphège. *The Inquisition: A Critical and Historical Study of the Coercive Power of the Church*. Trans. Bertrand L. Conway. New York: Longmans, Green, 1908.

Van Buren, Elizabeth, *Refuge of the Apocalypse*. Essex, England: C. W. Daniel Co. Ltd, 1986.

VandenBroeck, André. *Al-Kemi: A Memoir—Hermetic, Occult, Political and Private Aspects of R. A. Schwaller de Lubicz*. Rochester, Vt.: Inner Traditions, 1987.

Vaughn, Thomas, trans. "The Fame and Confession of the Fraternity of the Rosie Cross." In *A Christian Rosenkreutz Anthology*, ed. Paul Allen. Blauvelt, N.Y.: Rudolf Steiner Press, 1981.

Villoldo, Dr. Alberto. *Healing the Luminous Body: The Way of the Shaman*. Video, Santa Barbara, Calif.: Sacred Mysteries Productions, 2002.

Viollet-le-Duc, Eugène Emmanuel. *Eugène Emmanuel Viollet-le-Duc, 1814–1879*. London: Academy Editions, 1980.

The Virgin of the World. Trans. Anna Kingsford and Edward Maitland. St. Paul, Minn.: Wizard's Bookshelf, 1977.

Waite, Arthur Edward. *The Brotherhood of the Rosy Cross*. London: Rider, 1924.

Wallace-Hadrill, J. M. *The Barbarian West A.D. 400–1000*. New York: Harper & Row, 1962.

Watt, W. Montgomery. *Muhammad's Mecca: History and the Qur'an*. Edinburgh: Edinburgh University Press, 1988.

Webb, James. *The Occult Establishment*. Chicago, Ill.: Library Press Books, 1976.

———. *The Occult Underground*. Illinois: Library Press Books, 1975.

Weigall, Arthur. *The Paganism in Our Christianity*. New York, London: G. P. Putnam's Sons, 1928.

West, Edward N. *Outward Signs: The Language of Christian Symbolism.* London: Walker & Co., 1989.

West, John Anthony. *Serpent in the Sky.* New York: Julian Press, 1987.

White, Paul. "The Oz-Egyptian Enigma." In *Exposure* 2, no. 6 (1996).

Wiesenthal, W. *Peru and the Inca Civilization.* New York: Crescent Books, 1979.

Wilson, Colin. *From Atlantis to the Sphinx.* New York: Fromm International Pub., 1999.

Wilson, Colin, and Christopher Evans, eds. *The Book of Great Mysteries.* New York: Dorset Books, 1990.

Winston, Richard and Clara. *Notre-Dame de Paris.* New York: Newsweek, 1971.

Wood, John Edwin. *Sun, Moon and Standing Stones.* Oxford: Merrivale Books Ltd, 1978.

Wood, Michael. *In Search of the Dark Ages.* New York: Facts on File, 1987.

Woolger, Roger J. "The Holy Grail: Healing the Sexual Wound in the Western Psyche." In *Pilgrimage* 2, no. 2 (Summer 1983).

Wright, Ronald. *Stolen Continents: The Americas through Indian Eyes since 1492.* Boston: Houghton Mifflin, 1992.

Yates, Frances A. *The Occult Philosophy in the Elizabethan Age.* London: Routledge and Keegan Paul, 1979.

———. *The Rosicrucian Enlightenment.* London: Routledge and Kegan Paul, 1972.

Ye-ses-mtsho-rgyal, O-rgyan-glin-pa, and Tarthang Tulku. *The Life and Liberation of Padmasambhava.* 2 vols. Berkeley: Dharma Publishing, 1978, 1992.

Yukteswar, Swami Sri. *The Holy Science: Kaivalya Darsanam.* 1949. Reprint, Los Angeles: Self-Realization Fellowship, 1990.

Zalewski, Pat and Chris. *The Equinox and Solstice Rituals of the Golden Dawn.* St. Paul, Minn.: Llewellyn Publications, 1992.

Ziegler, Robert H. *America's Great War.* London: Rowan and Littlefield, 2000.

Zink, David. *The Stones of Atlantis.* New York: Prentice Hall, 1978.

ACKNOWLEDGMENTS

With a project of this size, there are many people to thank. Thanks are due first of all to our artist, Darlene, who provided all the line drawings and diagrams. Without her skill, patience, and commitment this book would not have been possible. We would also like to thank The Tate Gallery, London, for permission to use Max Ernst's painting on page 18.

Thanks to Richard Buehler of the Brotherhood of Life for permission to use illustrations and quotes from the English version of *Le Mystère* and to Kevin Townley of Archive Press, who let us read the translation of *Dwellings* as it was finished and confirmed the importance of the Cube of Space. Thanks to Robert Lawlor for correcting some misperceptions early on and to Dr. Paul LaViolette, who kindly let us use illustrations from his work *Earth Under Fire* and encouraged us to see alchemy through an even larger lens. Dr. Alberto Villoldo, Dr. Juan del Prado, and William Sullivan deserve thanks for pointing us so directly to Peru as does J. M. Allen for guiding us to Atlantis in the Andes. Thanks are also due to our many local guides and friends in the far corners of the earth where our research led us: Mlle. Marie Yavanna de Rokay in Paris, Juan-Jesus de la Vega in Cusco, Mohammed ibn Ali in Luxor, Su Ling in Lhasa, and the mayor of Pharping, and his rice brandy, in Nepal.

As this book grew over time, many people had the opportunity to read parts of it and supply some helpful comments. Foremost of these long-suffering test readers are the e-group Priory of Sion (http://groups.yahoo.com/group/priory-of-sion). Thanks to Stella, Nick, Tim, Andrea, Steven, Alice, and all the rest for their unflappable scholarship in time of need. Also thanks to Moira Timms, John Major Jenkins, and Steve Crockett for sharing their research and thereby contributing to our own. And thanks to elfsbeth for just being a fan.

Finally, major thanks are due the team that helped produce this new edition. Dr. Terri Burns lent her invaluable research skills to the job of locating sources and references in libraries on three continents. Our copyeditor Cannon Labrie performed wonders; being edited by someone of his skill and erudition was a pure pleasure. Cannon forced us to deal with the hard questions, and the book is far better for his input. Also at Inner Traditions, thanks are due to Jon Graham for remembering a two-year-old manuscript, Jeanie Levitan for her diplomatic skills and grace under pressure, and the entire production staff for solving riddles of style involving names in many languages and from different centuries. A sweeping tip of the Phrygian cap to you all . . .

On a personal note, I would like to especially thank my coauthor, Jay Weidner, for graciously allowing me to take the lead role in reworking this new edition. Any errors in the text are mine, therefore, not Mr. Weidner's.

VINCENT BRIDGES

INDEX